"Think you know everything there is to know about the legend that is MJ? Think again." — ESPN

MICHAEL JORDAN

ROLAND LAZENBY

Aiden

Praise for Roland Lazenby's
MICHAEL JORDAN

"An utterly definitive biography....The most comprehensive attempt yet made to explain the factors that have gone into producing the most famous basketball player and marketing phenom in the history of world sports....I don't know how it would be possible to write a more complete biography of him."

—Allen Barra, *Chicago Tribune*

"In his thoughtful, extraordinarily well researched biography *Michael Jordan: The Life*, Roland Lazenby...gives us the life and much more....The exhaustive narrative of Jordan's basketball career is written with appropriate awe. But what makes this portrayal especially worthwhile is everything else."

—Mike Greenberg, *New York Times Book Review*

"Right from its early pages it's clear that Roland Lazenby's biography of Michael Jordan is in full-press mode to be the best volume ever written on perhaps basketball's greatest player....Lazenby's a born researcher and some serious legwork went into gathering all of the quotes and facts here, which add up to a kind of Jordan-centric encyclopedia."   —Colin Fleming, *Boston Globe*

"It's not every day that I'm blown away by a book about a sports figure. But *Michael Jordan: The Life* by Roland Lazenby ranks up there with the very best: *The Boys of Summer* by Roger Kahn, *Friday Night Lights* by Buzz Bissinger, and *Joe DiMaggio* by Richard Ben Cramer. The depth of reporting, his frequent ascent into poetry, and his intelligent analysis of the life of this complicated, fascinating American icon deserve Pulitzer Prize consideration. For the first time I understand what makes Michael Jordan tick. I was captivated, fascinated, and beguiled from beginning to end."

—Peter Golenbock, author of *George* and
In the Country of Brooklyn

"A lot has been written about arguably the greatest basketball player of all time, Michael Jordan, but Roland Lazenby's *Michael Jordan: The Life* is easily the definitive version. The journalist has covered Jordan's career for nearly thirty years, and his knowledge of the game and of this miraculous player shows in what is one of the best sports biographies in years." —Scott Neumyer, *Parade*

"When a world-class biographer writes about a world-class athlete, you have a biography for the ages. This is the ultimate study of Michael Jordan, and I know you will be as captivated as I was."
—Pat Williams, senior vice president of the Orlando Magic and author of *Coach Wooden's Greatest Secret*

"Think you know everything there is to know about the legend that is MJ? Think again. In *Michael Jordan: The Life*, Roland Lazenby looks beyond the on-court exploits of a sports and cultural icon to find the complicated, and often contradictory, man behind the myth." —ESPN.com

"Roland Lazenby's new biography of Michael Jordan is as breathtaking as a dunk by 'His Airness.' . . . A richly detailed, thoroughly researched book. . . . Lazenby expertly sifts through the myths to produce a definitive portrait of Michael Jordan."
—Bob D'Angelo, *Tampa Tribune*

"Lazenby's thoroughly enjoyable biography is an impressive portrait of a man consumed by his competitive ambitions. It is also by far the most complete book on Michael Jordan to date. . . . Essential reading for all sports fans and particularly for those interested in American cultural history and popular culture."
—Derek Sanderson, *Library Journal*

"Revelatory. . . . A fascinating examination into the lonely, prideful man behind the glimmering icon." —*Publishers Weekly*

"Lazenby's book is impressive in its research. There are details bound to surprise even the most die-hard Bulls fan."
—Mike McGraw, *Chicago Daily Herald*

"What could have been just another sports hagiography unfolds as a complex portrait of a gifted athlete who was also a deeply flawed human being, a man whose extreme competitiveness (on and off the basketball court), personal history, and often-troubled family life make him one of the most compelling figures in American sports." —Kevin Nance, *Chicago Tribune Printers Row*

"The definitive portrait.... The dream of the nonfiction writer is to condemn future books on the same subject to irrelevance. It's possible Lazenby has achieved this lofty goal: nothing more needs to be written about Jordan." —Adrian Lee, *Maclean's*

"A comprehensive look at the life and times of the man and the legend.... A great work for any sports enthusiast and b-ball fan to read about one of the best that ever came to the game." —Brook Stephenson, *Ebony*

"Lazenby is one of the best, most thoughtful, and thorough people writing books on the NBA today, which makes all his books fascinating reads and great looks at the psychology of teams and great players. His stuff is must-read." —Kurt Helin, NBC Sports's *ProBasketballTalk*

"MJ's life is a movie worth watching again, and Lazenby adds enough deleted scenes to add some oomph to the familiar story." —*Booklist*

Also by Roland Lazenby

Jerry West: The Life and Legend of a Basketball Icon

The Show: The Inside Story of the Spectacular Los Angeles Lakers in the Words of Those Who Lived It

Mindgames: Phil Jackson's Long Strange Journey

Mad Game: The NBA Education of Kobe Bryant

Blood on the Horns: The Long Strange Ride of Michael Jordan's Chicago Bulls

Bull Run! The Story of the 1995–96 Chicago Bulls

Air Balls! Notes from the NBA's Far Side

The Lakers: A Basketball Journey

The Golden Game (with Billy Packer)

The NBA Finals

Fifty Years of the Final Four: Golden Moments of the NCAA Basketball Tournament (with Billy Packer)

MICHAEL JORDAN
THE LIFE

ROLAND LAZENBY

BACK BAY BOOKS

LITTLE, BROWN AND COMPANY

New York • Boston • London

Back Bay Books / Little, Brown and Company
Hachette Book Group
1290 Avenue of the America, New York, NY 10104
littlebrown.com

Originally published in hardcover by Little, Brown and Company, May 2014
First Back Bay paperback edition, May 2015

Back Bay Books is an imprint of Little, Brown and Company. The Back Bay Books name and logo are trademarks of Hachette Book Group, Inc.

The publisher is not responsible for websites (or their content) that are not owned by the publisher.

The Hachette Speakers Bureau provides a wide range of authors for speaking events. To find out more, go to hachettespeakersbureau.com or call (866) 376-6591.

ISBN 978-0-316-19477-8 (hc) / 978-0-316-19476-1 (pb)
LCCN 2014932746

10 9 8 7 6 5 4

RRD-C

Printed in the United States of America

Dedicated to the memory of
Tony Travis, Roy Stanley Miller, Lacy Banks,
L. J. Beaty, and Ed McPherson, brothers one and all

CONTENTS

MICHAEL JORDAN

Prologue

THE DEFENDER'S EYES grow wide, as they well should. He's about to face the kind of kinesthetic brilliance that first motivated humans to invent slow-motion technology—something, anything, that would allow them to review exactly what happens when movement plays tricks on the mind.

The setting is painfully familiar. Something in the offensive structure has broken down at the other end of the floor, igniting a fast break. The entire defense is retreating. The defender has sprinted back down the floor and, as he turns, he sees the blur. The dark form in red has the ball, dribbling and winding his way through the chaos at great speed. He crosses the ball over from right to left and draws it up in two hands just off his left hip in midstride.

At this exact moment, the tongue falls out of his face. Sometimes, it shows just slightly between the teeth, but at this moment, the full tongue drops grotesquely, like some comic doll silently mocking the defender. There's a leering, obscene quality to the expression, as if the coming dunk itself won't be insult enough. For ages, warriors have instinctively made such faces to frighten one another. Perhaps there's some of that going on here, or perhaps it's just what he has said it is—a unique expression of concentration picked up from his father.

Whatever, the twenty-two-year-old Michael Jordan gains full clarity now, flashing his tongue at the defender like he is Shiva himself, the ancient god of death and destruction, driving the lane. Just as quickly, the tongue disappears and, as he strides, Jordan brings the ball up to his left shoulder, then rotates it in front of his face with his two hands as he leaves the floor just inside the foul line. The defense has collapsed to the lane, but the spindly form is already airborne, floating through them, switching the ball to his mammoth right hand as he approaches the goal. For an instant, his arm is cocked, cobra-like, ready to strike as he glides toward the rim, hanging alone, time seemingly suspended, as he calmly measures the finish. For spectators, the singular thunk of the throwdown is deeply stirring. It elicits a Pavlovian response, perhaps almost carnivorous, like watching a lion devour an antelope on the Nature channel.

The arc of the attack has formed a seemingly perfect parabola from takeoff to landing. In time, physics professors and even an Air Force colonel will take up an intense study of the phenomenon, trying to answer the question that obsessed a global audience: "Is Michael Jordan flying?" They will all measure his "hang time" and declare that his flight is an illusion made possible by the momentum delivered by his speed at liftoff. The more they talk of extraordinary thigh and calf muscles and fast-twitch fibers, of his "center of balance," the more they sound like men grasping at air.

Jordan's entire journey from the foul line to the rim lasts barely one second.

Yes, Elgin Baylor and Julius Erving, too, were capable of extraordinary hang time—but they performed mostly before video technology allowed the audience to savor their feats. Air Jordan was something altogether different, a phenomenon of the age, a departure from the past that surely seemed immune to the future.

Of the millions who had played the game, he was the one who could fly.

Jordan himself considered the question in those early months of his pro career, after viewing videotape of himself. "Was I flying?" he asked. "It sure seemed like it, at least for a short time."

The rarest talent is like a comet streaking briefly across the sky, captured only by the trailing flash of its brilliance. Michael Jordan's entire mesmerizing playing career left fans, the media, his former coaches and teammates, even Jordan himself, still struggling to comprehend what had happened years after he last played.

"Sometimes I wonder what it will be like to look back on all of this," he once observed, "whether it will even seem real."

Was it real? The time would come in his later years when a plumper Jordan with a drawn face would find himself the target of great ridicule and Internet invective over his missteps as an executive or his personal shortcomings, yet even that couldn't dim the light he had cast as a player, when he was nothing short of otherworldly.

In the beginning he was simply Mike Jordan, just another adolescent from North Carolina with an uncertain future, contemplating a stint in the Air Force after high school. The early 1980s marked his startling transformation into Michael, the archangel of the rims. In the process, his persona propelled the rise of Nike's business empire, which soon made him its young emperor, a role that both freed and imprisoned him. He became the very picture of competence. Nobody, it seemed, could do anything quite as well as Michael Jordan played basketball. "His competence was exceeded only by his confidence," noted longtime Chicago sportswriter Lacy Banks.

The professional game had always struggled against its gritty image: grown men running around in what amounted to underwear. But Jordan elevated all of that with his "flight." It was subtle at first, the element of "cool" he brought to the sport. He soon enough infatuated a worldwide audience just as American television programming was reaching the apex of its influence. For a generation, his impossibly fetching 1991 Gatorade commercial quickly came to serve as a soundtrack, a mantra: "Sometimes I dream that he is me. You've got to see that's how I dream to be.... If I could be like Mike...."

The convergence of culture and technology had thrust him into this unparalleled role as the soaring godhead of a global sports and merchandizing empire who left just about everyone agog at his spectacle. Art Chansky, the basketball writer who had covered Jordan as something of a regular Joe at the University of North Carolina, recalled his surprise later upon visiting him in Chicago. "I was just amazed in old Chicago Stadium, when he had to walk down the aisle between the baseline seats behind the basket to get to the floor, just the effect he would have on people as he walked by. Grown men and women. You know how much they had to make just to afford those seats to begin with? Just the fact that Michael was within a couple of feet of them. I watched their faces, the contortions. It was like the Messiah walking by. Then, in the locker room afterward, the press would be like ten deep around him."

Messiah, indeed. The worship grew so fearsome over the seasons that longtime Bulls PR man Tim Hallam began referring to Jordan as Jesus. Hallam would turn to a publicity assistant and ask, "Have you seen Jesus today?"

This evolution had been propelled by a seemingly unshakable good fortune. Ralph Sampson competed memorably against Jordan in college when both were vying to be named the national college player of the year, and he watched with fascination his opponent's rise over the ensuing decades. Yes, Jordan had all of the physical gifts and an unparalleled work ethic, Sampson acknowledged, but Jordan's abundance of luck could not be overlooked. He was blessed with the best coaches and joined by great teammates.

"I mean, he worked at the game, and if he wasn't good at something, he had the motivation to be the best at it," Sampson observed in a 2012 interview on the eve of his own selection for the Hall of Fame. "But he also got put in the right situation with the right team, the right coaches that saw his talent and ability, and they put a team around him that worked. So I think it's the combination of all that that has made him."

No one was more aware of the extraordinary chain of events that drove his life than Jordan himself. "Timing is everything," he offered, looking back as he neared age fifty.

Yet timing and luck were merely the foundation of the mystery. Sports psychologist George Mumford was transfixed the first time he observed Jordan's animated approach to practice at age thirty-two. Having heard about his great appetites and how little he slept, the psychologist, who had just begun working for the Bulls, immediately suspected that the star was manic depressive or bipolar, or perhaps even both. "He was frenetic, all over the place with this hyper energy," Mumford recalled of that practice. "I thought, He can't sustain that."

Surely, Jordan was in the manic stage of some condition, Mumford thought. Manic depressives display periods of extreme highs, followed by profound lows. Over the coming weeks, the psychologist looked closely for signs of depression in the wake of Jordan's highs. But after studying him, Mumford came to realize that the animation and hypercompetitiveness were simply Jordan's normal state. Having played basketball himself at the University of Massachusetts and roomed with Julius Erving, Mumford had plenty of experience around elite talent. But Jordan was clearly something else, Mumford soon decided. The "zone" of high performance that other athletes struggled to achieve was something that Jordan accessed on a regular basis. "Michael did have to find something to motivate himself into that state," Mumford explained. "The more you have those moments in the zone, the more you want to have them. Most people can't sustain it. His ability to find that state, his ability to concentrate, his ability to lock in were almost superhuman. He was coming from a different place, man."

And in games? "He was the eye of the hurricane," Mumford offered. "The more frenetic things got, the calmer he was."

Jordan would spend much of his early career figuring out how to harness these gifts and to use them in a team format, because above everything else, he badly needed to win. While his "flight" had first gained the audience's attention, it was his overwhelming competitiveness that allowed him to keep it. Soon enough, the public's fascination turned to his relentless drive, which led him to test almost everyone and everything throughout his career. He tested his friends and sweethearts for loyalty, tested his coaches, tested his teammates to see if their hearts and minds were strong enough to share the floor with him. The more he accumulated, the more he tested. He established a record for being quite harsh in this testing. James Worthy, his friend and teammate from North Carolina, described him as a bully.

Jordan would admit as much. "I can be hard," he acknowledged in 1998.

Mostly he tested himself.

It seemed that he discovered the secret quite early in his competitive life: the more pressure he heaped on himself, the greater his ability to rise to the occasion.

It all added up to immense complexity.

Tex Winter, the Chicago Bulls' longtime assistant coach who worked with Jordan longer than any other coach, said that in six decades of basketball he'd never encountered a more complicated figure. "Personality-wise, he's a study. He really is," Winter said of Jordan as their run together was nearing its end. "I guess I don't have the intelligence to grasp a lot of things that make Michael tick, that make him what he is. I think I analyze him pretty good, but he is a mystery man in an awful lot of ways, and I think he always will be, maybe even to himself."

That realization was hammered home for many fans in 2009 by Jordan's jarring acceptance speech during his Basketball Hall of Fame induction when he offered a harsh assessment of so many major figures in his career, including UNC coach Dean Smith. Former colleagues, media commentators, fans—all expressed surprise and dismay in the wake of Jordan's induction. He was not what they had assumed he was in those early years when his image seemed so perfect.

They thought they knew him. They did not.

PART I

CAPE FEAR

Chapter 1

HOLLY SHELTER

THE "GOD OF BASKETBALL," as he would be called by fans worldwide, was born with a bloody nose, in Brooklyn of all places, on the kind of chill February Sunday in 1963 that sent steam rising from the sidewalk sewer grates outside the ten-story Cumberland Hospital. Basketball guru Howard Garfinkel would later enjoy pointing out that the hospital also served as the birthplace for brothers Albert and Bernard King, making it something of a fabled location in a city that treasures its sports figures.

Despite the aura of this Brooklyn beginning, it was elsewhere and much earlier that the full force of Jordan's extraordinary life gained its first traction, just before the turn of the twentieth century, with the birth of his great-grandfather down on North Carolina's Coastal Plain.

In those days, death seemed to be everywhere. It had a nose to it that crept upstream each morning and curdled with the brackish air. The gulls screamed like banshees in those little shantytowns, where nobody dared take simple survival for granted. That's really where the story of Michael Jordan's life begins, in a shotgun shack on the banks of a blackwater river that winds among the pine forests and swamps, where the moonshine drips oh so quietly and the mystery hangs like clumps of gray moss sagging from the trees.

The year was 1891, just twenty-six summers removed from the great violence and confusion of the American Civil War. The place was a little riverside hamlet called Holly Shelter, in Pender County, about thirty miles northwest of Wilmington, forty miles if you rafted down the winding Northeast Cape Fear River as Jordan's ancestors often did. The place supposedly earned its name after Revolutionary War soldiers took refuge under the holly trees there on cold winter nights. The savannah is bordered by swamplands that during slavery's days also provided shelter of another sort, for runaways. One of the region's vast plantations was supposedly owned by a white preacher from Georgia named Jordan. With emancipation, many freed slaves gravitated to Holly Shelter. "They settled the swamp," explained Walter Bannerman, a distant Jordan relative. "Holly Shelter was nothing but swamp."

Soon enough, though, the hard times of the era would render the name devoid of meaning, for there was little shelter to be had.

Which was the first remarkable thing about the baby boy.

He arrived on a typically sweltering day in late June 1891, following yet another run of the coastal storms that so often menaced the people living on the river. Coroners recorded staggering numbers of stillbirths and infant deaths in those shotgun shacks, so many in fact that families often waited days, even weeks, to name their newborns. This baby, however, was very much alive, evidenced by a squalling that would jolt his mother awake — just as many years later his rich basso profundo would make his fidgety six-year-old great-grandson Michael snap into focus and behave.

The dawn of the Jim Crow era and the politics of white supremacy were breaking across North Carolina with such vengeance that the impact would be felt long after those laws had passed into history. In that world of routine cruelty, Michael Jordan's great-grandfather would live a life of grinding poverty, amid relentless racism. Worse yet was the grim death that would take his loved ones and friends and cousins, just about anybody really, infants and little girls and strapping young men, take them all, mostly right in the bloom of life in those coastal communities.

But all of these things lay ahead in life for the baby boy. On the day of his birth in June 1891, his twenty-one-year-old mother, Charlotte Hand, was in a bit of a pinch, as she was not married to his father, a man named Dick Jordan. The very concept of marriage was somewhat alien in this shantytown world, as North Carolina law had long forbidden the marrying of slaves, along with most other rights and privileges. The state's laws had been particularly brutish, once allowing, for example, slaveholders to punish any unruly young buck with castration.

In the immensely uncertain 1890s, the one thing young Dawson Hand could rely on was his mother's love. He would be her only child, and they would share an abiding affection for many years. After the birth, Charlotte took refuge with her family and raised the boy among the Hands, as they lived first with one brother's family and then another's. For most of the first two decades of his life, he would be listed in official documents as Dawson Hand. Yet as welcome as mother and son were among her siblings, it wasn't long before he grew old enough to notice the glaring contrast.

The Hands were light-skinned, so much so that numerous members of the family could "pass" for white or Indian, while the Jordans were a people of rich chocolate complexion. Of an entire generation of Hand siblings and cousins, only one was dark, family members would recall years later. The white Hands in Pender County were a prominent slaveholding family, and their black offspring long talked of the time that a white Hand man had finally acknowledged the unspoken truth—that one of the dark Hand men was his brother. This perhaps helps explain why sometime in his teen years, the boy would assume the name of his father and become Dawson Jordan in official records.

Dawson Jordan grew into a young man who at first glance would seem to have little in common with his statuesque great-grandson. Dawson was short—just five feet five by some accounts—and stocky. And he was crippled, consigned to dragging a bad leg along with him wherever he went over the course of his long life.

But like his great-grandson, Dawson Jordan possessed tremendous physical strength. And he proved equally fearless, with an uncommon toughness, accomplishing feats as a young man that would become the subject of lore in his community for decades after. More importantly, against foes that those in later generations couldn't begin to understand, Dawson Jordan somehow remained unbowed, undefeated.

In such an exceptional life, it's easy to overlook the one factor that arguably shaped Michael Jordan's character more than any other: through most of his formative years, he lived with four generations of Jordan men, a substantial accomplishment considering the societal factors that had long threatened the lives of African American males.

His great-grandfather "Dasson," as he was often called, loomed as a figure of authority in the young life of Michael Jordan. The entire family lived together for almost a decade in the farming community of Teachey, North Carolina. Even well into the age of automobiles and four-lane highways, Dawson Jordan insisted that his mode of transportation remain the mule he proudly hitched to his oxcart. Even as an old man, he would wrap the feet of his mule in pads and keep the axle of his cart extremely well greased so that he could move silently on late-night moonshine runs. In the daytime, his great-grandchildren loved jumping on that little wagon for a ride into town, and Michael and his older brothers sometimes amused themselves by teasing the hogs that the old man raised until he passed away in 1977, just days after Michael turned fourteen.

Little did the Jordan boys realize that the mule and the hogs—indeed, all the memories of their great-grandfather—were the trophies of a life well lived. As Michael explained years later, Dawson Jordan was not one to talk about the past or the significance of the animals. But even the casual mention many years later of Dawson Jordan could cause a tear to mist up in the eye of his famous great-grandson.

"He was tough," Jordan would say of the old man. "He was that. Yes, he was."

The River

You begin to gain the slightest sense of Dawson Jordan's world if you stand in the morning air along the Northeast Cape Fear River in Holly Shelter. Today the place is mostly a rural game and wildlife preserve, but the light there was then as it is now, harsh and blinding most days, dancing as it glints off the water, diffused only by patches of morning fog. To find relief, you have to push inland, among the swamp forests and creeks, to the solitude in the shadows once cast by the majestic virgin stands of longleaf pines.

Dawson Jordan spent his youth there, working amidst the tar pits on the forest floors, taking down the last of the magnificent trees, bundling the logs into huge rafts and floating them down the Northeast Cape Fear River to the shipyards of Wilmington.

It was no job for cowards.

Dawson Jordan grew into manhood just after the turn of the twentieth century, just as this old way of life on the river was fading, along with the last of the great longleaf pines and the arrival of the trucking industry. The ancient river and the dependable forests and woods had been the defining element in his young life. He knew how to hunt for wild game, knew how to clean what he killed and cook it up just right. Years later, as an old man, he would be employed by the region's hunting lodges to cook tasty wild game delights for its members.

His working life began at age nine, when he convinced census workers he was eleven and old enough to head into the fields. He could already read and write, having attended the local one-room "common school for coloreds," where the four-month academic year was frequently interrupted so the children could work in the fields or at the nearby sawmills. "My parents used to tell me how hard it was making them shingles at that mill," recalled Maurice Eugene Jordan, a distant relative who lived and farmed in Pender County. The students cut their own firewood and tended their own stove in the little schoolhouse, which was the standard even for the white children in their better-appointed schools.

In those first decades of the twentieth century, there was no electricity, little running water or plumbing, and few paved roads. And, not surprisingly, there was almost no middle class, which meant that just about every male, black or white, spent his days in the desperate business of subsistence farming as sharecroppers and tenants and laborers providing service to a select few landholders.

An in-depth study of one thousand farming families by North

Carolina's Board of Agriculture in 1922 found that the state's share-croppers earned less than thirty cents a day, sometimes as little as ten cents, despite working long hours; the report added that most sharecroppers had no means of growing their own food and often needed to borrow money just to eat and pay the bills. Some forty-five thousand landless farm families lived in cramped, one- and two-room shacks with no indoor plumbing and nothing but sheets of newspaper to cover cracks and holes in the walls and ceilings. Only a third of the sharecropper homes even had an outhouse.

The unsanitary conditions explained to a large degree the high rate of disease and infant mortality among landless farm families, the report said, adding that the death rates for blacks more than doubled that for whites.

Charlotte Hand and her son, Dawson, somehow managed to get by in these bleak circumstances with the help of the Hands, who worked logging the river and likely taught Dawson how to steer a raft; family and community lore has it that he became very skilled at a young age. It wasn't easy building those huge log rafts and moving them down the treacherous river, with its snakes, storm surges, and shifting tides. It took tremendous physical strength to steer a chain of three log rafts through the river's many bends and turns. But, as perilous as it was, Dawson apparently relished the river, which was the main road of commerce for that era.

Young Dawson worked with his cousin Galloway Jordan, who was also crippled. Maurice Eugene Jordan, a relative who lived and farmed in Pender County, recalled hearing his own father, Delmar Jordan, recount tales of Dawson Jordan. "They say he was real good with rafting those logs," Maurice Eugene Jordan remembered. "Galloway Jordan, he had a bad leg just like Dawson. They was real close."

The Northeast Cape Fear was a tidal river, which presented an extra challenge, Maurice explained. "They had to watch out for them tides. They ran in and out, in and out, on a cycle with the moon. If the tide was high enough, they could make a move. But when the tide would get so weak, they'd have to tie their rafts off on a tree and wait for it to come back." The wait would take hours. "They'd have pots and food, and when the tide was out, they'd tie off the rafts and get off on a hill and cook 'em up a little something to eat."

It was cold, dangerous work that had been performed since Colonial times by a mix of freed slaves, rafters, and roughnecks equal to the challenge. Those doing the work on the rivers inhabited the lowest rank in social class and were poorly paid, often making just a few cents a day, about the same as the lowliest sharecroppers. Still, Dawson Jordan seemed to enjoy the independence of working on the river. Census records list him as working on his "own account" rather than in the employ of someone else. In addition, the work offered the regular opportunity to ride down to the exotic port city of Wilmington, with its busy harbor full of ships and sailors from all over the world, and its many bars and bordellos.

One can imagine Dawson Jordan sitting on his raft in a calm spot in the river on a cold, clear night a century ago, gazing up at the brilliant stars. It is likely that those nights on the river underneath the firmament offered young Dawson his only true moments of escape from a world that was often overwhelming. This was, perhaps, about as good as it got for Michael Jordan's great-grandfather.

Decades later, his great-grandson would remark that his moments on the basketball court were his only haven, his only times of true peace, his singular escape from a world that was deeply troubling and far more frustrating than any of his millions of fans and followers could imagine. In very different ways, these two Jordans shared much across the span of a century, although their stations in the world were so vastly different. On many of his brutally difficult days Dawson Jordan would certainly have loved just a taste of the sweet gravy of his great-grandson's lifestyle.

Clementine

Unlike Michael, who would have his choice among legions of the planet's most sophisticated and attractive women, short, crippled Dawson lived in a small, isolated community with his mother while working long, dangerous days in the woods and on the river. He got a hint of what romance might be like when his mother found love at last with an older sharecropper in Holly. Isac Keilon was twenty years her senior and well into his sixties when they married in May 1913, and their happiness must have served to spur on Dawson's thoughts about his own prospects.

In time, despite the odds stacked against him, Dawson began to find favor with a girl named Clementine Burns. The song "Oh My Darling, Clementine," which had first gained wild popularity in 1884, probably factored into her naming at birth. She was a year older than Dawson and lived with her parents and seven younger siblings right there in Holly Shelter. In some regards, her prospects may have been as limited as his. Their courtship began like all others in that day, with shy talk that grew bolder over time. Dawson was soon in love, never a casual thing for the deeply emotional Jordans.

They exchanged vows in late January 1914 and began their lives together. About eight months later Clemmer, as she was known, told Dawson she was pregnant, and in April 1915, she delivered a strong, healthy boy in their tiny shack. They named him William Edward Jordan. There's every indication that the event brought immense happiness for the new father.

If only that happiness could have lasted.

The first signs of trouble came hard on the heels of the birth, the night sweats and the urinary discomfort. Then Clemmer began coughing blood. The most telling symptom was the development of the tubercles themselves, the small rounded masses or nodules that attached themselves to bone and tendon.

"That was the black people's disease, tuberculosis," recalled Maurice Eugene Jordan. "Back then there wasn't too much they could do about it."

The airborne disease was highly contagious, and though North Carolina was one of the first Southern states to open a sanitarium for blacks, in 1899, the privately financed facility had a mere dozen beds, and the cost was exorbitant. The only other option for the families was to set up a white screened tent or temporary building in the yard outside their homes, which allowed loved ones to spend their last days close to family with a hope of not spreading the tuberculosis. The demise of loved ones could drag on over agonizing months or years. Clemmer Jordan saw a doctor in the early stages of the disease but died on an April morning in 1916, not long after her son's first birthday.

It was not uncommon for a young widower to abandon his children in that era. It would have been simple enough for Dawson to allow Clemmer's family to raise the boy. Certainly Dawson Jordan had his options. As a seaport, Wilmington was alive with opportunity to sign on as a cook with one of the many vessels coming and going. But the simple truth that emerges from the public records of his life was that he loved his mother very much, just as he loved his toddling son. That's what his actions said. And his determination to build a family provided the first great fiber of strength in the story that would become Michael Jordan.

A few months later, Dawson suffered another great blow when he learned that his mother, only in her late forties, was dying of kidney disease. Death visited early and often on the Coastal Plain, but mortality rates doubled, then tripled and quadrupled, in Pender County in 1917 and 1918 with the notorious Spanish flu epidemic. Dawson saw members of the Hand family, as well as his coworkers and their loved ones, pass in record numbers. In ninety days, between September and November of 1917, the influenza epidemic killed more than thirteen thousand North Carolinians.

Dawson's mother's worsening disease necessitated her moving from Isac Keilon's home back in with her son. As her end neared and she could no longer help Dawson care for his young son, he took on a boarder, a young woman named Ethel Lane who had a small daughter, and who was able to care for the children as well as for Charlotte. A short time later, Isac Keilon died unexpectedly. They buried him, and three months later, Dawson's mother succumbed to her kidney disease.

Dawson buried Charlotte Hand Keilon down by the river on Bannerman's Bridge Road in Holly. The boy who always wanted a family was now quite alone, except for the busy little child under his feet. Father and son would spend the rest of their lives together, living and working in one small shack after another in the same small coastal communities, pooling their resources to make their way in the face of poverty.

The public record would eventually show that neither man acquired much of anything in life, yet time would reveal that they still bequeathed a great deal to the next generation. They did so despite another legacy lurking in the haze of Cape Fear, something insidious and even surreal.

Chapter 2

BLOODY WILMINGTON

THE PATH BACK through yesteryear is one that Michael Jordan himself has taken often enough, back down through the country roads and simple memories of the Cape Fear coast. If you roll east down Interstate 40 out of Chapel Hill, the Piedmont gives way to the Coastal Plain, its rich, open fields bordered by a drab mix of scrub pines and decaying tobacco barns. Soon enough come signs for Teachey, then Wallace, and later Burgaw and Holly, the farming communities where the Jordan Brand first took root many years ago.

These days the interstate highway system cloaks much of Cape Fear's disquieting legacy with miles of even pavement and clusters of gas stations and chain restaurants relieved only by the faintest connection to Carolina's cultural past, an occasional barbecue stand. Nowhere, it seems, can you find mention now of the Democratic party's white supremacy movement, but it was much in the air during Dawson Jordan's early years, and these ancient injuries—tied to events long ago in old Wilmington—would surface in odd, ironic fashion in Michael Jordan's life.

By the 1890s, Dixie Democrats had been able to reestablish white political control over much of the rest of North Carolina in the years following Reconstruction, but Wilmington and the Coastal Plain stood apart, largely on the strength of more than 120,000 black male registered voters. The place was on its way to becoming a peer of Atlanta with an emerging black upper class, two black newspapers, a black mayor, an integrated police force, and an array of black-owned businesses. The answer for Democrats was to foment rebellion in Wilmington with a race riot on November 11, 1898, in which whites, stirred by Democratic political rhetoric, took to the streets to burn the offices of a black newspaper that had dared to challenge the Democrats.

Later that day, gunfire broke out, with armed whites, called Red Shirts, taking to the streets. The local morgue reported fourteen bodies, thirteen of them black, the next day, but others claimed the death toll ran as high as ninety. As the violence spread, terrified blacks took their families and fled into the nearby swamps, where the Red Shirts were said to have followed to execute many more whose remains were allegedly never recovered.

The second phase of the well-planned rebellion began the next day as whites escorted prominent blacks—clergymen, business leaders, politicians—to the local train station and packed them out of town for good.

The resounding victory for white supremacy would secure the doctrine for decades to come. Charles Aycock, elected governor in 1900, set a legislative agenda that followed through on the riot's violent message. "There shall be no progress in the South for either race until the Negro is removed permanently from the political process," Aycock had declared. The backbone of the plan was to limit voter registration with a literacy test, and the number of black males on North Carolina voting rosters quickly plummeted to fewer than 6,000 from better than 120,000 before the riot.

Such inequity and violence had the tacit backing of state and local law enforcement, with strong intimidation by other forces as well. By the 1940s and '50s, there were only two black voters registered in all of Duplin County, where Jordan's family lived, according to Raphael Carlton, one of those two registered voters.

The son of a sharecropper, Raphael Carlton worked as a contemporary of the Jordans in Duplin as a young man, even as his father insisted he allow time for school. Carlton eventually went to nearby Shaw University, earned his teaching degree in the 1940s, and returned home as part of a generation of dedicated black educators. He recalled attending a black faculty meeting at the height of segregation; the local school system's white superintendent stood up and told his black teachers, "You niggers better get your act together."

"People in modern times don't understand how we could be so intimidated back then," Carlton said. "But the intimidation was complete. You didn't dare challenge them."

Changing the Mind-Set

In 1937, John McLendon was hired to coach basketball at the North Carolina College for Negroes (later to become North Carolina Central University) in Durham. He was astounded by the beaten-down mind-set of his young players. "My biggest challenge as coach," McLendon recounted, "was to convince my players that they were not inferior athletes. Even the black population didn't know it and didn't believe. They had succumbed to the one-sided propaganda."

The coach's mere presence in North Carolina served to highlight yet another major influence in Michael Jordan's life, one that also had come to being in 1891. Just five months after the birth of Jordan's great-grandfather, James Naismith nailed up a peach basket in a gymnasium in Springfield, Massachusetts, thus beginning the age of basketball. Decades later Naismith would move to the University of Kansas as a member of the education faculty, where he coached the university team for a while before turning it over to Phog Allen, who would come to be considered the "father" of basketball coaching.

John McLendon had come to Kansas in the early 1930s as one of the university's first black students, but he was barred by Allen from competing on the basketball team and from swimming in the university pool. The situation would have been far worse for the black student if Naismith himself had not sought him out and arranged for McLendon to coach a local high school team while he earned his undergraduate degree at Kansas. After McLendon graduated in 1936, Naismith helped him obtain a scholarship to earn a master's degree at the University of Iowa. Finishing his graduate studies in a year, McLendon took the coaching job at little North

Carolina College, where he founded the first physical education program that began training generations of black teachers and coaches in North Carolina. That program would produce Clifton "Pop" Herring, Jordan's high school coach.

The early black college teams operated on shoestring budgets in the dangerous climate of segregation. They achieved success despite a culture that made travel nearly impossible, with no public restrooms, drinking fountains, restaurants, or hotels available to them. "A simple trip from one school to another was like plotting your way through a minefield," McLendon said.

Over the next few years, McLendon put together such impressive teams that officials at nearby Duke University were inspired to issue an invitation for the young coach to sit on the Blue Devils' bench during an upcoming game. The only stipulation, they said, was that McLendon would have to wear a white jacket so that he would appear to the crowd to be a steward.

McLendon politely declined.

The coach vowed never to put himself or his players in any circumstance where they might be disrespected or humiliated. "You did not want to get into a situation where your dignity would be destroyed right in front of your team," he explained. Maintaining his players' respect was critical in convincing them that they were every bit as good as whites.

A breakthrough came during World War II, when the military used Duke University's medical school to train wartime physicians, several of whom were top-notch basketball players. The all-white med school team's wins were trumpeted daily in the Durham papers. Meanwhile, McLendon's undefeated team received no publicity. Upset over the disparity, Alex Rivera, McLendon's team manager, arranged for the two teams to play a game. With the Klan vigilant to bar such a mixing of the races, the Duke coach agreed to a "secret game" on a Sunday morning with no fans or media allowed. By halftime, McLendon's pressing, full-court team had doubled the score on its high-profile opponents. That's when the white players approached McLendon's bench and suggested that they evenly divide the roster among blacks and whites to compete in the second half.

It was the first great victory for McLendon against racism, one that opened his players' eyes. Long after he had departed, McLendon's influence was felt in North Carolina, first in the prominence of basketball in black communities across the state, and then more significantly at the college level. A highly innovative coach, McLendon was invited by the Converse shoe company to teach at its coaching clinics. It was at one of McLendon's clinic presentations that a young assistant coach at the Air Force Academy named Dean Smith got his first blueprint for the famed four corners spread offense, which Smith confirmed in a 1991 interview.

McLendon and his friend Big House Gaines of Winston-Salem State came to be viewed as lions of the coaching business, but at the time neither coach could have fathomed that their sport would also help to break down the state's racial barriers. Never could the coaches have imagined that in their lifetimes, black and white North Carolinians would embrace a black player the way they would embrace Michael Jordan.

Nor could the coaches have dreamed that they themselves would one day become members of the Basketball Hall of Fame named for James Naismith.

The Corn

Over his long lifetime, Dawson Jordan encountered none of the good timing that would mark his great-grandson's experience. By the time Dawson turned twenty-eight, he had not only suffered great personal loss, but had been forced to change careers, with the disappearance of log rafting and the birth of the trucking industry. While he continued working at the local lumber mills, Dawson Jordan also became a sharecropper, like the majority of the southern population, the lowest on society's totem pole for that era.

The critical element to survival on rented land was the mule. As such, the animal carried a status, as explained by a cousin, William Henry Jordan. "When I was a child, a mule cost more than a car, because you had to make a living with a mule."

As farmers in later generations would purchase farm equipment, the sharecroppers and tenant farmers bought and rented mules from local dealers. Maurice Eugene Jordan recalled, "You could get a mule from [the mule dealer], but if you had a bad year, he'd come and get that mule. The seed and fertilizer man you borrowed from would do the same. You catch a bad season and get in a hole, it could take a year or two to get out."

"You didn't have a choice," explained William Henry Jordan. "You didn't have anything else."

For men like Dawson Jordan and his son, there was no escape from the circumstances, but they somehow managed to keep themselves fed. Sometimes they worked early mornings, milking at a nearby dairy farm, then taking the cows out to graze. In the leanest times, a farmer might slip from tenant farming—where he leased land and handled everything himself—back into sharecropping. "That's where you would furnish the labor," William Henry Jordan explained, "and the people who owned the farm would furnish the mule, the seed, and the fertilizer. At the end of the season, you'd get a third to half of what was left over. Lots of times there was nothing left over."

That's why many farmers looked to other sources of income— and why moonshining became so important to so many of them. Farmers, both black and white, of the Coastal Plain had been making their own corn liquor as far back as the Colonial era. Most of them certainly didn't have the money to buy it, so they made their own. "Since way back, that's about all it was, was corn liquor," explained Maurice Eugene Jordan. "So there was a lot of moonshine. They'd have them stills everywhere, on the river, in the woods, in the swamps, wherever the water was good."

It's unlikely that Dawson Jordan ever intentionally set out to be a moonshiner, but he soon gained a reputation as a prominent figure in Pender County's illegal trade. Perhaps he first got into the business when he was working logs on the river. "Those rafts might have been full of whiskey," Maurice Jordan said with a knowing laugh. "Nobody could tell what they were hauling."

Corn liquor perhaps relieved the hardship a little. It certainly loosened up the atmosphere on long nights, making the conservative farmers amenable to a little gaming. The hardworking men of

Pender County would roll the bones for a few pennies, nothing like the huge sums that Michael would wager decades later.

"Nobody had nothing to gamble with," Maurice Eugene Jordan said. "Wasn't no gambling but to shoot a little dice."

That was the Jordan character. Work hard, and pick your spots for recreation. In that regard, too, Dawson Jordan was first in a line of Jordan men. He knew how to turn to the devil's playground for a little fun. He liked a little drink, a little smoke, and perhaps a wee bit of action on a slow Carolina night.

The New Generation

As he gained adulthood in the 1930s, Dawson's son, William Edward, came to be known as Medward. He found work driving a truck for a landscaping company. While he still helped his father farm, his modest salary meant they were no longer dependent solely on the ups and downs of a cropper's life. Driving the small dump truck around the area to deliver landscaping materials also brought Medward a newfound status and the opportunity to meet people, a fairly dramatic change from the isolated life of a farmer. He became known as something of a ladies' man in the community, according to family members.

In his late teens he took up with a pretty young woman named Rosabell Hand, a distant relative on his mother's side of the family. She became his wife in 1935, and two summers later a son was born—Michael's father. They named him James Raymond Jordan.

The couple would live for decades with Dawson Jordan yet never seemed to rebel against his commanding presence in their cramped household, the same one in which Michael Jordan and his siblings would grow up. Rosabell was as sweet and soft-spoken as her father-in-law was sonorous. As he neared fifty, Dawson took more and more to walking with a cane, but his word ruled the Jordan household.

As with most farming families, financial difficulty remained a steady companion for the Jordans, but they never seemed to allow that to affect their lives too deeply, family members recalled. Perhaps it was because Dawson had learned early in life that there were far worse things than coming up a little short on cash to pay the bills. When financial trouble struck hard enough, he finally did what other poor sharecroppers and tenant farmers had done. He packed up the wagon, hitched the mule, and moved on.

He didn't have to go far for a fresh start. Dawson, his son, his pregnant daughter-in-law, and their small son settled in the farming community of Teachey, a mere twenty-five miles from Holly Shelter. Not long after they moved in, Rosabell gave birth to a second son, Gene.

In all, Rosabell Hand Jordan bore four children for Medward, and they in turn would produce a dozen grandchildren who regularly populated the modest household. In time, the Jordans saved enough through Medward's work to purchase a tiny, inexpensive house on Calico Bay Road just outside of Teachey. It had three small bedrooms and an outhouse, but it was a castle for Dawson Jordan and his family. It would also serve as the center of a young Michael Jordan's world.

Before long, the Jordans purchased additional lots along Calico Bay Road, as they continued to prosper with Medward's work and Dawson's moonshining, and the area blossomed into a small residential community. The emotional significance the property held for the family can be gauged by the fact that decades later the Jordans, despite all of Michael's wealth, maintained ownership of the house and leased it out as rental property.

Along with their new prosperity, the most important shift in the lives of Dawson and his son was the presence of the deeply spiritual Rosabell Jordan. She shared an abundance of love with all her children and grandchildren—and even the children her husband fathered in his dalliances around the community. "Ms. Bell," as she was often called, seemed to be especially proud of her oldest son. There was just something different about James Raymond Jordan. He had a special light and energy. For starters, he was plenty smart. By age ten, he was driving a tractor to help his father in the field and showing him how to fix it when it broke down. By the time he was a young man, he had impressed the entire community with his mechanical abilities and dexterity. Medward was said to be openly negative toward James, but the boy idolized his grandfather Dawson. One of James's traits was the intense concentration he'd reveal by sticking out his tongue as he focused on a task. According to some in the family, sticking out the tongue was something James picked up from Dawson.

As he grew from a child into a teen, working alongside his father and grandfather, James moved easily in both Holly, where he was born, and in Teachey, where he grew up. "He was kind of quiet," recalled Maurice Eugene Jordan, who attended Charity High School in Rose Hill with James. "If he didn't know you, he didn't do a whole lot of woofing." However, if James knew you, he could be charming, especially with the ladies, just like his father, Medward. Like a lot of teens, he loved engines and baseball and automobiles, except that James was really good with all of them. Which meant that he usually had working transportation, conferring a special status on the teenaged James Jordan in the 1950s. He also had a taste for fun and knew where to find it on those nights when the full moon rose up and spilled its light across the Coastal Plain. While many blacks in the region sought to avoid white people wherever possible, that was not the way of Dawson or his grandson James.

Times remained hard for blacks in the 1950s. Many had served their country well in World War II, which in turn had encouraged the slightest loosening of the country's negative mind-set. Yet the old attitudes still held a grip on North Carolina's society, as the coming struggle for civil rights would soon demonstrate. Dick Neher, a young white Marine from Indiana, married a local girl and settled in Wilmington in 1954. Neher loved baseball, as did the nearby town of Wallace, so sometimes Neher would pick up some black guys he knew to ride up there to play. It's likely that Neher played against James Jordan in the 1950s in Wallace. He didn't play there long, however. Neher returned home one evening to find a pickup truck parked in his yard. Klan members were there to warn him about riding around with blacks and playing in mixed baseball games. Neher ignored the warning, but Klan members returned to his house. That second time, they told him they wouldn't warn him again. Neher stopped going to Wallace to play baseball. He stayed in Wilmington, though, and much later became Michael Jordan's youth baseball coach.

In such an atmosphere, Dawson Jordan and his family remained far too challenged by day-to-day living to place any sort of real trust in the future. Even so, family members and neighbors saw that James Jordan represented a generation that just might be able to move beyond the old world to something newer and better.

Little did anyone understand, in the early 1950s, what that newness might look like, or the strange ways it would blend hope and hurt. The easy assumption is that if the Jordans had only known the unimaginable things that the future held, they might have run toward it. Just as likely, some family members would later say, they might have fled.

PART II

EARLY TIMES

Chapter 3

THE INFLUENCE

IF HIS GREAT-GRANDFATHER Dawson Jordan first stoked the furnace of Michael's life, it was Michael's mother, Deloris Peoples, who brought fiery propulsion to the mix. She was born in September 1941 into a relatively prosperous family in Rocky Point, North Carolina. Her father, Edward Peoples, was a distant, some would say humorless man, known for his ambition and hard work. Among the many frustrated and penniless black farmers, a generation of men who spent their lives in overalls, confounded by an economic system that almost guaranteed their failure, Edward Peoples found rare success.

"I knew her father," recalled Maurice Eugene Jordan. "Old man Edward Peoples, he didn't sharecrop. He had his own farm."

Denied any sort of access to the politics of that era, Edward Peoples was one of a number of North Carolina's blacks who had focused instead on economic advancement. A "Black Wall Street" flourished in nearby Durham under the leadership of John Merrick, who founded several insurance companies and banks. Edward Peoples's modest success was nothing on that scale, but the record indicates that he was tireless in his focus on making money. In addition to his farming, Deloris's father also worked for Casey Lumber Company in Rocky Point, and his wife, Inez, labored as a domestic. While they were not wealthy, the Peoples were far from poor. Theirs had been a determined progress through the hazards and pitfalls that claimed so many farmers, white or black, in the early decades of the twentieth century. Like the Jordans, the Peoples had found their share of heartache in that era of disease and death. Still, they became landowners free to farm for their own interests. Although the Peoples are little known and seldom mentioned in the Jordan story, there's no question that the family's drive and work ethic factored into Michael's mother's approach to her own life and then to that of her famous son.

The Jordan family fable has been told again and again, but it is a false narrative in many key aspects, which is understandable. Whenever families have found immense fame and fortune in the spotlight, they've quickly constructed such mythologies. They've often done this out of self-preservation, to protect family members from the all-consuming media-driven pop culture.

Deloris Jordan had to shield her family from many situations as her son became famous in the 1980s. So it's not surprising that she began the creation of such a narrative, one that omitted or glossed over many hard facts. She did this first in interviews and later in her book, *Family First,* which offered child-rearing advice, by implication, on how families could raise their children to "be like Mike." The bestselling book would enable Mrs. Jordan to travel the world, making public appearances in support of family issues.

The reality of Deloris Jordan is so much more powerful than the made-up story because it reveals her character and, later in her life, her ability to move her own family through brutal circumstances. There's little question that the obstacles Deloris Jordan faced fired her efforts in raising her family. As a result, they also provided the very fuel of Air Jordan.

Rocky Point

Appropriately, the families that would become Michael Jordan's gene pool first met on the hardwood in a cramped gym filled with cheering students. According to vague community and family memories, James and his younger brother Gene Jordan played for

Charity High. Deloris's brothers, Edward and Eugene Peoples, played for the Rocky Point Training School of Pender County. The two schools enjoyed a rivalry back in those days, and folks in the community recall that the Peoples boys were good players.

They also recall the love students and faculty had for Rocky Point. Opened in 1917, it was one of five thousand schools, shops, and teachers' homes built for African Americans in communities across the country with money provided by the Rosenwald Fund, a trust set up by Sears, Roebuck and Company president Julius Rosenwald. The equipment wasn't always the best; used furniture and books, often with pages torn out, were passed down from the county's white schools. "We got what they had worn out," recalled William Henry Jordan, a relative of the family. But in an age when black education was at best an afterthought for local school boards, the school's dedicated teachers prepared students for every sort of challenge, which made Rocky Point important to the African American population of Pender County right up until integration in the late 1960s.

Basketball games were played after school, in a space cleared in the school's auditorium, and usually lasted until the early evening. Deloris originally told reporters that the contest that brought her and James together occurred in 1956, when she was fifteen. However, she corrected that miscalculation in *Family First*, explaining that, in fact, she first met her husband after a 1954 game.

She was barely thirteen years old at the time and was truly excited to be a part of the school spirit at Rocky Point. She was pert and spunky, but a good girl, too. She prayed often, and went to church regularly with her family.

"She was a good student when I taught her," recalled Mary Faison, a former faculty member at Rocky Point.

It's not clear whether James played on Charity's team that night. He was seventeen and a senior, and he was there with a car, which was indicative of the Jordans' improving financial situation as well as his strong mechanical bent.

As in many teen love stories, she noticed him before he was aware of her. He had doe-like eyes and high cheekbones, but that wasn't what captured her fancy. "What attracted me was his personality," she explained. "As far as looks, it was no more than some of the other guys. He was outgoing, had a good sense of humor, and was a caring, kind person."

Deloris and several of her cousins jumped in the backseat of his car to get a ride home after the game. When it appeared that he was going to drive right past her house, she called out for him to stop.

"Oh, I didn't realize I had somebody else in here," he said. "You're pretty cute."

"You're pretty fresh," she supposedly retorted.

"Could be. But someday I'll marry you," he replied, according to her recollection.

"I knew he was going out with somebody else," she said. "I stayed away from him."

Deloris ran into her house and slammed the door behind her as thirteen-year-old girls are wont to do.

In that small community, James Jordan was likely already aware that Edward Peoples farmed his own land, and he had to have noticed the girl's house, which was larger than most. It was a two-story frame house that sat back from the road. "There was a lot of big ol' shade trees in the yard," recalled Maurice Eugene Jordan.

"A lot of colored peoples were just farm labor back then," he added, explaining that the industrious Edward Peoples kept his own land busy year-round, all the while working at Casey Lumber Company. Beyond his farming, he invested time and money in another cash crop, just as so many of his neighbors did: Edward Peoples was a moonshiner. In fact, Peoples was said to be close with David Jordan, one of Dawson Jordan's many moonshining cousins. As Maurice Eugene Jordan explained, "They had quite a few stills. The revenooers would find them, tear 'em up, but they'd go right back at it. The key was not to get caught."

It wasn't long before James approached Edward Peoples about dating "Lois," as he called her. A hardworking, no-nonsense man, Peoples didn't think much of the idea. She wasn't old enough, he said. Young love—not to mention ambition—has long had a mind of its own, however. The two were soon seeing each other despite her parents' wishes. "We quickly fell in love and dated for the next three years," Deloris remembered.

The relationship lost little steam, even when James finished school in 1955 and joined the Air Force, making his father and grandfather quite proud. James underwent training in Texas, while Deloris's family sent her off to Alabama to live with an uncle and take classes in a two-year cosmetology program. She has said that the move was made as an attempt to slow things down with the young airman, but the relationship had already hit its own warp speed. By early 1957, she was fifteen and pregnant—a fact she didn't acknowledge in her own memoir—and dealing with the fallout of her family's anger. The sudden enrollment in Alabama seemed a typical solution at a time when a pregnant teen was often sent away to have her child.

That April both James and Deloris were back in Pender County and went to a movie together, ostensibly to sort out their situation. The resolution came when he proposed in his car after the show. Once James did the right thing, she informed her parents that she would not be returning to Alabama, another decision that apparently didn't sit well. Years later, she would remark that her mother should have insisted she go back to school. "My mother should have put me right back on the train," Deloris once told a reporter.

Instead, she moved into her fiancé's crowded family home in Teachey, where Dawson Jordan, now sixty-six, still very much ruled the roost. There, the pregnant teenager soon formed a lasting friendship with Rosabell Jordan, who had just turned forty. A devout and worldly woman, James's mother loved children, loved filling the little house with relatives and friends on holidays and weekends. Deloris took to calling her "Ms. Bell," and in a time when things were so strained with her own parents, Deloris found a wise and nurturing older soul. The friendship between the two women would grow into one of the tight family bonds that helped shape Michael Jordan's later success.

James and Deloris soon celebrated the birth of their first child, James Ronald, that September. The mother, who had just turned sixteen, held her baby close and wondered what the world would hold for him. In time, the infant would grow into the sort of industrious young man that her own father had been. Ronnie, as they would call him, held down two jobs in high school—driving a school bus and managing a local restaurant in the evenings—all while excelling in junior ROTC and making his parents proud. This first son, it seems, had drawn on Dawson Jordan's commanding presence. He would go on to a distinguished career as a master sergeant in the U.S. Army with multiple tours of combat duty.

Deloris brought the new baby into the already crowded Jordan household. James had been assigned to a base in Tidewater Virginia, a little better than two hours away, and came home on weekend leave to see his young son. Deloris would later admit that this was when she entertained the first doubt and self-recrimination about the turn of events in her life. She longed to see her own family more, but they were almost a half hour away, in Rocky Point. She kept faith, and her new mother-in-law helped her remain positive. James did his part as well, determined that his service experience would start him on a path to becoming the sort of breadwinner who could provide a middle-class upbringing for his own children.

Brooklyn, Then Teachey

James Jordan's young family welcomed their second child, Deloris, in 1959. Early in her life, the child would go by Delores as a given name before settling on Deloris as an adult. For clarity's sake in the early years, the family called her Sis. That same year, James left the Air Force and returned to Teachey, where he took a job at a local textile plant. For the time being, the young family crowded in with his parents until they could build a small home right across Calico Bay Road from Dawson, Medward, and Rosabell.

It was handy to have grandparents close by, as Deloris Jordan would give birth to five children by the time she reached twenty-three. In the early years, much of the burden of child-rearing fell to Rosabell Jordan, who wanted nothing more than to shower love on each new grandbaby that came along. As strong as the bonds of the extended Jordan family were, Deloris's time away in Alabama and James's stint in the Air Force had opened their eyes to the world beyond North Carolina. And so it happened that even as they were building their house across Calico Bay Road from his parents, they began to realize that deep down, they wanted something more beyond the offerings of the little farming communities of Teachey and Wallace.

In that regard, they were no different from millions of others of their generation. African Americans, in particular, were drawing the first breaths of a new air after suffocating for so long. The serf systems of sharecropping and tenant farming had begun to die off in the wake of the Great Depression and World War II, which hastened the movement of millions of rural blacks to cities, particularly in the North, in search of new economic survival.

The march to freedom picked up its pace on February 1, 1960, when four black students from North Carolina Agricultural and Technical State University went to a Woolworth's store in Greensboro, bought a few things, then sat at the lunch counter and ordered coffee. Their simple act rang across North Carolina. The store's management ignored the students, so they sat there in silence until closing time. The next morning the A&T students returned with five friends and again sought service at the lunch counter. Met again with management's silence, the students began what they described as a "sit-in," a quiet, nonviolent demonstration. White youths soon showed up to taunt them and flick cigarette butts at them, but similar protests appeared in Winston-Salem, Durham, Charlotte, Raleigh, and High Point. And then it spread to fifteen cities and many more Woolworth's stores across the country, all in a matter of about two weeks. Woolworth's, a national chain, soon relented and began serving black customers at its lunch counters. The company was clearly unwilling to perpetuate racism in the public spotlight, before network TV cameras.

The unfolding civil rights movement was but one part of the tremendous cultural upheaval affecting the country. With that change came new promise for life itself, and James and Deloris couldn't help but share in that expectation. It was an exciting time, yet confusing, and still quite dangerous.

Deloris delivered the couple's second son, Larry, in early 1962; two months later she learned that yet another child was on the way. Shortly thereafter, the twenty-one-year-old Deloris and her husband scooped up baby Larry and headed to Brooklyn, New York, where they would live for almost two years as James went to trade school on the GI Bill to learn to build, repair, and maintain hydraulic equipment, a logical extension of his Air Force training. The move required their leaving their two oldest children, both under age five and still in their formative years, in the care of the Jordan grandparents for almost two years. Later, Deloris Jordan would remark that in essence she and James had two families: the older children, who remained behind, and the younger children. This would come to create no small gulf in their family.

As joyful as the new additions would be, they were tempered by heartbreak. The Jordans hadn't been in New York more than a few weeks when Deloris received the news that her mother, Inez, had died suddenly. The shock of the loss and the instant torrent of grief staggered Deloris and imperiled her unborn baby. Her doctor ordered bed rest for a week.

"The near miscarriage was very bad," James Jordan recalled years later.

Relations had improved between Deloris and her mother since the difficult period of her early pregnancy and marriage, but unresolved issues remained, as is so often the case with the sudden, premature death of a loved one. Deloris's grief was compounded by her precarious pregnancy and her situation, far away from home in a crowded, alien city. Michael Jordan's delivery was a particularly hectic scene that Sunday, February 17, 1963. Deloris had gone into labor a bit early, which was how she wound up at Cumberland Hospital in Brooklyn, even though her doctor was in Manhattan. Even before the hospital attendants could get Deloris onto an emergency room gurney, the large, strapping male child made his startling appearance, clogged with mucus and struggling to breathe.

"When Michael was born, we thought there might be something wrong with him," James Jordan revealed years later in an interview with the *Chicago Tribune*. "He was born with a nosebleed. The hospital kept him three days after Deloris was discharged. He'd have nosebleeds for no reason until he was five, and then they just stopped."

"After Michael's birth the doctors did keep him a couple of days to be sure that his lungs were clear of some mucus," his mother recalled.

In many ways, the arrival helped punctuate her months of grief. "I always said that Michael's birth was like a sign," she later explained. "I lost my mother unexpectedly while carrying Michael, and he was my godsend. Michael was the happiness He sent me after a very sad time in my life."

Michael himself would learn some details of his birth years later from Chicago newspaper reporters, who had gathered them from his family. "My nose still bleeds easily," he told Bob Sakamoto of the *Tribune*. "That's one story my mom never told me. The only thing my mom told me was the time when I fell behind the bed as a baby and almost suffocated. There have been some very close calls in terms of my life."

The near suffocation, which happened after the family returned to North Carolina, only served to raise his mother's anxiety levels over her special gift. "He was such a jolly baby," she remembered. "He never cried. Just feed him and give him something to play with, and he was fine."

By the time Michael was five months old, the family had retreated from Brooklyn back to their home on Calico Bay Road in Teachey. They made the move with Deloris pregnant one final time (daughter Roslyn was on the way), and back home, James put his education to use as a maintenance employee for the General Electric plant in Castle Hayne, near Wilmington.

Soon the young mother found herself in the small house with five children, four of them under the age of five. Her husband called her Lois, as did the rest of the family. And her term of endearment for him was Ray. He cut an impressive figure in the small farming community with his Air Force experience and his job at GE. Although generally warm and friendly, he began to show a harsher side as well. He proved to be a stern taskmaster with children, whether they were his own or somebody else's. Word soon enough got out among the neighborhood children: Ray didn't play. He'd whip your butt in a minute.

Young Michael would spend his formative years on sleepy little Calico Bay Road. By all accounts, he was easy to laugh, eager to please, and hungry to entertain, which also earned him his share of spankings.

"You had to discipline him," Deloris Jordan once remembered. "He would test you to the limit. Michael was always getting into things."

As a two-year-old he wandered outside one late afternoon while his father worked on an auto in the family's backyard and used a lamp powered by two extension cords stretched across the damp ground from the kitchen. Before his father could stop him, the toddler grabbed the two cords at their juncture. The ensuing shock knocked young Michael back three feet, leaving him stunned but otherwise unhurt.

Already strict with their children, the Jordans were prompted by the incident to tighten their control. No one was to leave the house under any circumstances without permission. And each night the children had to be in bed by eight o'clock, no matter if others in the neighborhood were still outside playing. But it soon became evident that Michael's bountiful nature could not be contained as he grew into childhood.

One time he found trouble under his granddaddy Dawson's wagon, with a wasps' nest that he attempted to douse with gasoline. That was followed by his adventure with a stack of lawn chairs he piled amazingly high to demonstrate his flying prowess. He suffered a long cut on his arm from that one.

James Jordan couldn't wait for his boys to be big enough to hold a bat. He was always eager to get them into the backyard so he could toss a baseball their way and teach them how to swing. One day Michael was swinging away with a bat at a block of wood with a nail in it, only to discover that the missile had struck his older sister in the head and stuck there.

Perhaps the biggest trouble came at age four when he slipped away from the house and crossed the road to his grandparents' place, where he found an older cousin chopping wood. Little Mike hoisted the axe a time or two, and the cousin said he'd give him a dollar to chop off his own toe. Eager to impress, he raised the axe and let it fall, just on the tip, then immediately howled in pain and took off back across the road, hopping and screaming and bleeding the whole way home to his mother.

"He was a mischievous child," James Jordan would later remember—with a smile.

Sis, the older girl in the family, recalled that her parents had their favorites. She and Larry were her father's pets, while Ronnie and little Mike—born nearly five months apart—could do no wrong in their mother's eyes. Roz, the baby of the family, had everyone's undivided affection. Young Michael Jordan faced much competition for attention in that busy household, and a lifelong dynamic was set in place. He was always eager to please—first his parents and family, and later his coaches and an adoring public.

"He mastered the art of entertaining and spent hours amusing us," remembered Sis of those early years. "Dancing, singing, teasing or whatever it took to bring a smile, grin, or laugh, he did. And never content to play by himself, he always needed an audience and would not let us ignore him no matter how hard we tried."

Moving Again

Michael's idyllic early childhood in Teachey was not easy to come by in 1960s America. But circumstances changed dramatically before he started kindergarten in the fall of 1968. In January that year, James and Deloris Jordan sold their house in Teachey, packed up the family, and moved to Wilmington, about sixty miles away on the coast. One reason for the move was that James had tired of his forty-minute commute to the GE plant in Castle Hayne each day. But more importantly, as Deloris Jordan would explain later, the family longed for something beyond the rural life. They wanted more for their children, too. They remained quite close to the grandparents, and planned to make frequent visits to Wallace and Teachey. In particular, they promised to return at least one weekend a month to attend services at Rockfish African Methodist Episcopal Church, the Jordan family's place of worship for decades.

They hardly had time to unpack their things in Wilmington when Martin Luther King Jr. was assassinated, which threw the entire nation into turmoil. Even in Wallace and Teachey, blacks and whites began brawling in the wake of the murder, and Wilmington was no better. The community had made some progress in race relations since the 1950s, when local leaders saw that attracting businesses to the area hinged on changing old ways. The city had long been a railroad town until the Atlantic Coast Line Railroad moved its central office to Jacksonville in 1955, causing Wilmington to look around for new industry to replace the lost jobs. Companies like General Electric had asserted that they would locate their plants in Wilmington only if the city made opportunity equal.

Even so, the racial atmosphere in Wilmington remained tense. The Jordans had arrived there just as the schools launched into a court-ordered desegregation plan that sparked controversy and bitterness. Headlines and emotions were dominated by the city's evolving plans for bringing blacks and whites together in schools. Because the elementary schools were the last to be integrated under the plan, Michael and others his age began school that fall in classrooms that were still divided by race.

This atmosphere sizzled until it finally exploded in February 1971, when a white-owned grocery store in a predominantly black neighborhood was fire-bombed. Ten people, nine black males and a white female, were later arrested in connection with the incident and received heavy prison sentences upon their conviction. Dubbed the Wilmington Ten by the news media, the group made appeals that would play in the headlines for years until the convictions were overturned by the federal courts.

This climate of conflict heightened Deloris Jordan's concern as her children adjusted to new schools in the community.

The family had lived in one location briefly before moving into the Weaver Acres neighborhood on Gordon Road. They lived in one home there for a time, until they moved again, within the same neighborhood, to a large, split-level brick and clapboard house that James Jordan built in a stand of pines on a twelve-acre tract of land. It was convenient to the suburban schools of New Hanover County and to downtown. The ocean was just a few miles away, and James and Deloris sometimes escaped there on quiet summer evenings. Young Michael, however, soon developed an aversion to the water. At about age seven, he was swimming with a friend in the ocean when the friend panicked and grabbed onto Michael. Michael pushed away to keep the boy from dragging him under, and the child drowned. A few years later Michael himself got in trouble in a pool during a baseball trip and had to be pulled from the water. Years later, one of his college girlfriends drowned while she was home on break.

"I don't mess with water," Jordan was known to say thereafter.

Weaver Acres was a relatively new neighborhood, mostly black, but families of various races lived there in relative harmony. Both James and Deloris had always taught their children to be respectful of all people, instructing them that stereotypes were of little use. You had to treat people as people, regardless of their skin color, they explained. Indeed, a white family had lived near the Jordans back on Calico Bay Road, and the kids enjoyed the company of their play-mates without incident. The family's open-mindedness suggested that the Jordans were taking great pains to prepare their children for a brand-new world.

This attitude of tolerance proved to be a hallmark of Jordan's early years in Wilmington. By the time he reached third grade, Michael had become fast friends with David Bridgers, a white schoolmate and neighbor. The two would remain close long after one of them became world-famous. They played baseball and rode bicycles together and explored the wooded areas and creek beds in and around Weaver Acres. Bridgers was the son of a taxi driver in a family that had recently moved from South Dakota. When his parents' marriage broke up, Bridgers's bond with Jordan grew even closer. They shared a love of baseball with Michael's father, who welcomed David into the household. Bridgers and Jordan took turns pitching for a strong Little League team. The one who wasn't pitching took up residence in center field.

"Before every pitch, I'd look at Mike in center, and he'd give me thumbs-up," Bridgers once recalled. "With him on the mound, I'd do the same."

One sizzling afternoon before Michael's fear of swimming took hold, they snuck into a neighbor's backyard to steal a dip in the pool while they thought the neighbors were away. The people caught the boys in the water and ordered them out, but in such a way that both kids could tell there was a racial motivation involved.

"They saw Mike and threw us out," Bridgers said. "The rest of the bike ride he was very quiet. I asked him if he knew why they threw us out. He said yes. I asked if it bothered him. He said no. Then he just smiled. I'll never forget it. He said, 'I got cooled off enough. How about you?'"

Chapter 4

THE COMPETITOR

It took the fewest of words to set him off, sometimes nothing more than the faintest trace of a smirk. He was also capable of making things up, conjuring up an affront out of thin air. That's what they would all realize afterward. He would seize on apparently meaningless cracks or gestures and plunge them deep in his heart, until they glowed radioactively, the nuclear fuel rods of his great fire.

Only much later would the public come to understand just how incapable he was of letting go of even the tiniest details. Many observers mistakenly thought that these "affronts" were laughable things of Michael's own manufacture, little devices to spur his competitive juices, and that he could jokingly toss them aside when he was done with them, after he had wrung another sweaty victory from the evening. But he could not let them go any more than he could shed his right arm. They were as organic to his being as his famous tongue. Many of the things that deeply offended Michael Jordan were hardly the stuff of stinging rebuke, except perhaps the very first one, which, as it later turned out, was the most important of all.

"Just go on in the house with the women."

Of the millions of sentences that James Jordan uttered to his youngest son, this was the one that glowed neon-bright across the decades.

"My father is a mechanical person," Jordan would recall later. "He always tried to save money by working on everybody's cars. And my older brothers would go out and work with him. He would tell them to hand him a nine-sixteenths wrench and they'd do it. I'd get out there and he'd say give me a nine-sixteenths wrench and I didn't know what the hell he was talking about. He used to get irritated with me and say, 'You don't know what the hell you're doing. Go on in there with the women.'"

His father's words rang as a challenge to his adolescent masculinity. Even then, as the first hormonal surges were starting to thicken his features, he remained a cherubic figure, one that his siblings adored and his mother delighted in pulling into her embrace. But it was a disguise.

His father's mean words had activated deep within him some errant strain of DNA, a mutation of competitive nature so strong as to almost seem titanium. They represented a contempt articulated almost daily in manner and attitude in the Jordan household throughout Michael's tender years.

"Years later," his sister Deloris recalled, "during the early days of his NBA career, he confessed that it was my father's early treatment of him and Daddy's declaration of his worthlessness that became the driving force that motivated him.... Each accomplishment that he achieved was his battle cry for defeating my father's negative opinions of him."

Michael himself would later reveal that as a child he was keenly aware of his father's preference for brother Larry.

James Jordan had endured a similar treatment by his own father. Medward's contempt for him would become a fixture in family lore. James himself confirmed it, and that contempt is what drove him to leave Teachey to prove himself in the Air Force. Medward was proud of his son, family members said, but he never seemed to find the means to express it to him face to face.

James paid him back again and again, by achieving so much in a life that his father could never hope to grasp.

This is what offspring of disapproving fathers often do. Without even realizing it, they lock in on an answer and deliver it over and over, confirming that they do not need to just go in the house. And they continue to confirm it even after the father has gone to dust, as if they are unconsciously yelling across time in an argument with the old man.

Around the time that he was telling Michael to take up life among the women, James Jordan put up a basketball hoop for his sons in the backyard of the family home. Up to that point, the family's athletic focus had been on James in the backyard throwing pitches to his young sons, teaching them to hit and to love baseball. They had started at ages five and six playing T-ball. At seven and eight, the boys moved to a machine-pitch league. They faced their first live pitching at nine and ten, which was when the dichotomy emerged. Larry was all about hitting singles, while Michael would swing for the fences.

It was Larry, as the older brother, who first became infatuated with basketball. Michael was already on his way to success as a Little League player when the basketball court was laid out. Suddenly, things took off in another direction.

Instinct had perhaps guided James, telling him that with Michael set to star in baseball, he should build the basketball hoop for Larry. The younger brother, however, was already quite taken with basketball himself. At age nine, Michael had watched intently on TV as the United States, led by a frenetic young guard named Doug Collins, battled its way to a showdown with the Russians in the 1972 Summer Olympics. When the Americans lost amidst great controversy, Michael retreated to the kitchen to tell his mother. "He said, 'I'm going to be in the Olympics one day and I'm going to make sure we win,'" Deloris recalled later. "I smiled to myself and said, 'Honey, that takes a lot to win the gold medal.'"

The plot, however, had been set in motion. From there, it was a matter of taking in all the basketball that broadcast TV had to offer, which wasn't much. In those days, before cable and the constant presence of pro basketball on television, the once and future king of hoops wasn't able to view NBA games. But the local affiliates brought him a weekly diet of Atlantic Coast Conference (ACC) contests, which allowed Michael to follow the high-flying antics of David Thompson and the North Carolina State Wolfpack against the enemy, the University of North Carolina. NBC aired national games, featuring another of his favorite teams, the UCLA Bruins. Years later, former UCLA great Marques Johnson would be puzzled to see his poster on Jordan's wall at the University of North Carolina, but it was because he had been a TV star in Jordan's adolescence.

By the time Michael was eleven, James Jordan had purchased the family's first basketball, and soon after he put the finishing touches on the court. The Jordans' backyard soon attracted players from around the neighborhood, but the Jordan family rules applied. Homework had to be completed before anyone took to the court, and the eight o'clock bedtime remained strictly enforced. Still, the main event every day became Michael versus Larry in titanic games of one-on-one.

Though Jordan was nearly a year younger, he already stood above his stronger, older brother. Michael was mouthier, but they both talked trash, anything to get under the other's skin. The contests quickly turned physical, then heated. When the yelling and arguing grew to a pitch, Deloris Jordan would step to the back door to enforce the peace. Some days she had to order them into the house. Day after day after day, they went at each other, with Larry able to use his strength to dominate his younger brother despite the height disadvantage.

The constant thumpings from his shorter brother hammered at Jordan's young psyche. The pattern of defeat would stretch out for more than a year and a half.

"I think Michael got so good because Larry used to beat him all the time," James Jordan would explain later. "He took it hard."

"We grew up one-on-one," Larry remembered.

"I always played hard," Jordan said. "My brother and I would play every day until my mother had to call us in.... We never thought of brotherhood at all. Sometimes it would end in fighting."

Michael was reed-thin and lacked strength, but he gradually learned how to take advantage of his height. For the longest time they became so evenly matched as to almost present mirror images of each other. "When you see me play, you see Larry play," Jordan would later explain.

"I won most of them until he started to outgrow me," said Larry, "and then that was the end of that."

By the time Dick Neher, Jordan's youth baseball coach, visited the Jordans' backyard when Michael was a young teen, the rim was already beat up and tilted to one side, damage likely wrought by Larry's dunks, a testament to the beating that Michael's own psyche had suffered at the hands of his older brother.

These backyard battles would determine the nature of the two brothers' adult relationship, a closeness tempered by sibling rivalry. They also established the manner in which Michael would relate to teammates throughout his playing career. James Worthy recalled Jordan as a new freshman on the University of North Carolina basketball team pestering him to play one-on-one: "His mission was to seek out the best player on the team and I was that guy my junior year. He was a bully and he bullied me."

Even before that, it had become his modus operandi at Wilmington's Empie Park, and at the Martin Luther King Community Center in the city. "It got to the point that I had to ask him not to come over and play," recalled William Murphy, the center's director.

"I didn't want him to get hurt," Murphy said. "I was afraid he would get cut off his feet. He used to be a challenge for everybody." His attacking inspired that kind of visceral response.

It was the same everywhere he went, explained George Mumford, the psychologist who worked with Jordan as a pro player. Each opponent loomed as a Larry to be conquered. Much later, the mythology of the one-on-one games would bring his brother a certain status among Michael's coterie, first in college and later in Chicago.

"Michael and Larry had obviously competed wildly as boys, and Larry loomed very large in his life," explained David Hart, Michael's roommate and the team manager at the University of North Carolina. "Michael really loved Larry and talked about him all the time—really revered him. But if Michael had gone far beyond Larry as an athlete, he never let it affect his feeling for his brother—his emotional connection and his respect for his brother were very strong. When his brother was around, he dropped all his mounting fame and his accomplishments and became nothing more than a loving, adoring younger brother."

Later, in Chicago, Larry Jordan would join a pro basketball league that allowed no players taller than six feet four, but he soon injured his shoulder and dropped out, concerned that his family name was being exploited. "I never really felt overshadowed, because I was able to see his work ethic close up," Larry said in a 2012 interview. "I played sports all my life, but I wasn't as passionate about basketball as Michael was. I was more of a handyman, mechanical like my dad."

"He was a stud athlete," Doug Collins, who coached Michael in Chicago, once said of Larry. "I remember the first time I saw him—this rather short, incredibly muscled young man with a terrific body, about five seven, more a football body than a basketball body. The moment I saw him I understood where Michael's drive came from."

Pop Herring coached the brothers at Laney High School in Wilmington, where Michael became a star and Larry found limited playing time. "Larry," Herring once said, "was so driven and so competitive an athlete that if he had been six two instead of five seven, I'm sure Michael would have been known as Larry's brother instead of Larry always being known as Michael's brother."

Perhaps some of this praise is overstated, due in part to the warmth that family and friends felt for Larry Jordan. They often described him as genuine, low-key, gentlemanly, but something of a painful lesson in fate. He was so close to his brother in ability as an adolescent but lived eternally in Michael's shadow. It was a circumstance that would trouble Deloris Jordan over the years. It would intrude on even the fun moments between the brothers as adults. After Michael became a star in the NBA, they reprised their old one-on-one matchup one day, during which Michael paused, looked down at Larry's feet, and said, "Just remember whose name is on your shoes."

Bill Billingsley recalls the two brothers taking their first steps together in organized basketball. It was in early 1975 in the ancient gym at Wilmington's old Chestnut Street School, where the city held a youth basketball league. Billingsley, twenty-four at the time, was coaching against the team the Jordans played on. "If you saw them, you'd think Larry was the younger one," he said. "Michael was so much taller. Even then Larry was not the player Michael was, and by a long shot."

Larry recalled that it was actually their youth baseball coach who had gotten them involved in basketball. Dick Neher was helping to form a youth hoops team and phoned Ned Parrish, who had coached Michael in youth baseball. Parrish had immediately suggested the Jordan boys.

In a 2012 interview, Neher laughed at the memory of the younger Jordan on that basketball team. "He was a big-time gunner," the coach recalled. "He had never played organized ball. His Little League baseball coach had put him on the team. He was a good dribbler. He could handle the ball. He was quick. But if you gave him the ball you'd never see it again. It was going up to the hoop. We laughed about it."

Billingsley's team played three games against those first basketball Jordanaires and won two of them mostly because Billingsley's team played man-to-man while the rest of the teams in the league played the stiff and lazy zone defenses typical of youth basketball.

Billingsley assigned his star player, Reggie Williams—who later played some college ball—to guard Jordan. "Michael was their best player. To show you how smart he was even at that age, he posted up Reggie and hit a short jump shot in the lane," the coach recalled. "Even at twelve years old he already had real basketball skills and smarts." Billingsley believed that such a move was instinctive, that no youth coach could have had the time or inclination to teach something like that.

"When I was twelve years old, my brother Larry and I were the starting backcourt in Pee Wee League," Jordan remembered of the experience. "He was the defensive guy, and I was the scorer. So I hit the winning basket, and as we were riding home, my father said, 'Larry, that was great defense you played.' I'm saying, 'Damn, I stole the ball and scored the winning layup.' In my mind I'm thinking that evidently my father didn't see what I did, so I had to show him. It's funny how you look at those situations and all the steps that led to your competitive attitude."

In baseball, it had been the same, he recalled. He would go for a home run, Larry would aim for a base hit, and his father would always say, "Larry, that's a great attitude to have, going for the base hit."

This first recreation league basketball experience came in an era before AAU (Amateur Athletic Union) basketball brought in players at a younger age. At the same time, baseball, a game played predominantly by whites, had more sophisticated support in Wilmington, Billingsley explained. The resources for youth basketball were scarce by comparison.

At the end of the season, Michael was named to the all-star team, even though he was one of the youngest players in the league. Because Billingsley's team had won the league, he was named the all-star coach. He began preparing the group for a statewide tournament, and encountered James and Deloris Jordan for the first time.

"His parents saw every game he played," the coach recalled. "You talk about devoted parents, their children were everything to them. Mr. Jordan, he was a quiet man. Mrs. Jordan, she was the dynamic personality in that relationship. Anybody who spent time around them had to be impressed by the strong will of Deloris Jordan. She was protective of her children. Some parents just dropped the kids off. Not them. They were there, but they were not meddlesome or trying to influence my decisions." In fact, they never said a word to him about how he coached the team.

The Wilmington all-stars drove to Shelby, near Charlotte, for the state recreation tournament that spring of 1975. James Jordan was among a small group of parents who made the trip. Billingsley recalled that the team played in four games over two days, making it all the way to the tournament semifinals, where Wilmington lost to a team from Chapel Hill that had large, overpowering players in the frontcourt.

"The last night we were staying in our hotel," the coach recalled. "The kids were in their rooms playing. A few of the dads and the coaches dealt up some cards. It was nothing serious, just fun. Somebody said, 'Let's get some beer.'"

Billingsley was impressed that James Jordan immediately pointed out that they were in a dry county, no alcohol.

"Mr. Jordan, he knew exactly where to get some beer. He drove over the state line and came back with two or three six-packs," Billingsley remembered. "We stayed up late, just having a good time, not really gambling. Mr. Jordan was a really good guy."

It was the first of so many basketball trips that father and son would take over the coming years. Whoever they met had the same overwhelming opinion of James Jordan. What a nice man, people would say time and again, a person with hands-on friendliness, who had a smile and a pat on the back, generous with his affection, extending warmth even to a man like Bulls executive Jerry Krause, who would have more than his share of conflict with Michael.

"He was just such a friendly guy," Billingsley said.

Most importantly, people saw something else. Michael Jordan had thoroughly and completely secured his father's affection. Clearly, on some level Jordan himself had gained that knowledge. But on another level, the one that mattered most, such information never registered on the impenetrable core of a competitor's psyche. Michael Jordan's immutable agenda had been set, and on the slightest trigger it could let loose a tide of passion that would stir others to wide-eyed wonder.

No one, of course, would become more surprised by these moments than Jordan himself. As they came to him time and again over the years, that same blinking surprise was always there. And always the same question, too: What will I do next?

The Darkness

Despite appearances, the union of James and Deloris Jordan teetered on the brink of self-destruction in the mid-1970s. They projected an image of happiness, but their marriage was plagued by a discord that lurched at times into violent arguments. In the worst of these conflicts, beginning on Calico Bay Road, James and Deloris would go at each other in front of the children, who would run across the street hoping to find a grandparent to break up the melee. The move to Wilmington had done nothing to break this pattern. They didn't fight every day, but when they did, things got out of hand in a hurry. Daughter Sis recalled one set-to where her mother went after her father and he responded by knocking her out cold. The children feared she might be dead, but the next morning she appeared from the bedroom, ready to face another day. Another incident brought a frightening car chase down a road near their house, with the children in one of the cars. Such incidents fitfully interrupted a general peace that kept the family moving forward, but always with a lurking element of fear.

James's job at General Electric allowed the family to live a comfortable life and provided opportunities for their children. All the kids were involved in activities outside of school, and the older ones even had part-time jobs. But even with James's salary, they faced financial pressures. Once Roslyn, the youngest child, entered school, Deloris took a job on the assembly line at the local Corning plant. It was shift work with a rotating schedule that threw the family routine into turmoil until one day Deloris finally could take no more and abruptly quit. She hadn't discussed it with James, but he took it in stride. Months later, she found work as a teller at a branch of United Carolina Bank.

As if managing all of this wasn't enough, the couple decided to open a nightclub, Club Eleganza, which somehow seemed like a good idea at the time. They were both in their midthirties and had spent a good portion of their teen years and all of their adult lives raising children. Neither of them ever mentioned the club in any of their later interviews with reporters about Michael's upbringing. It seems likely, however, that Club Eleganza played a role in their marital issues. Such ventures often drain time and money, and James and Deloris were already challenged by busy schedules with their children.

Sis implied that the unhappy home life may have prompted Ronnie's shipping out for Army basic training just two days after he graduated from high school in 1975. Others suggested that he had dreamed of a life in the service for years, evidenced by his involvement in high school ROTC. Whatever the reason, Ronnie's departure added to the family's emotional strain. Deloris wept as the family saw him off at the bus station.

"It was like somebody in the house had died," Deloris said of

Ronnie's departure. "I couldn't go into his room for many, many years. He was the first to leave."

Like many women facing the stresses and challenge of motherhood, she had also gained substantial weight. Although she would later lose the weight, the period proved to be a deeply emotional time for the mother of five. And, mindful of her own troubles as a teen, she had grown quite anxious over signs that daughter Sis was becoming sexually active. Never close, mother and daughter soon found themselves in what seemed like an almost daily series of ugly arguments. The two were engaged in just such a bout one summer morning in 1975 as Deloris was driving her daughter to her job. The exchange grew especially heated as they pulled up to Sis's place of work, Gibson's Discount Store. Deloris supposedly called her daughter a slut. "If I'm such a slut, why don't you keep your husband out of my bed?" Sis retorted, as she would later detail in a book she independently published, *In My Family's Shadow.*

Deloris's jaw dropped. She was staggered by the comment, but before she could gather her thoughts to reply, her daughter jumped out of the car and ran into work. Deloris responded by leaning on the car horn in an attempt to bring her daughter back outside. Inside the store, Sis tried to ignore the blaring horn, but finally the store manager told her to go back outside and see what her mother wanted.

When Sis got back in the car, Deloris told her daughter to explain what she had just said. The mother listened silently as Sis told of a pattern of persistent abuse over eight years in which James Jordan would visit her late at night in the bed she shared with Roslyn, who was a preschooler when the alleged abuse began. Sis recounted how her father first explained that he was teaching her to kiss like an adult, how confused she was, how the abuse escalated over time.

What followed next was a harrowing scene, according to Sis's account. They drove to Club Eleganza, where James was doing some maintenance work. His wife ordered him into the car, and they drove to a little-used road and pulled over, where Deloris told her daughter to repeat the allegations. As Sis delivered her account, Deloris told her husband that now certain things about the marriage made sense. James flew into a fury and began choking his daughter while screaming, "Are you going to believe this tramp over me?" Sis recalled being stunned at her father calling her a tramp. With Sis gasping, Deloris told him to stop or she would kill him.

Finally, then, the angry moment broke, Sis recalled in her book. They all calmed down and rode home, where the daughter retreated immediately to her bedroom. After about an hour, her mother came and told her that the circumstances made it impossible for the three of them to live together. Because Sis still had two years of high school left, she would have to leave the family to live in a girls' home. She told her daughter that James had explained that he was "only trying to help her" and that she had terribly misunderstood his affection.

Under no circumstances, Deloris said, was Sis ever to mention her allegations to anyone else, inside or outside of the family. The daughter did not tell her mother that it was already too late; at age twelve she had confided to a cousin her same age. In turn, that cousin supposedly told her brother, but if word of the situation spread in the larger Jordan family, it was only in whispers. No one else, it seemed, was about to confront James Jordan, who was both admired and feared in the family.

The Jordans never acted on their threat of sending their daughter to a home for girls. The parents somehow managed to absorb the incident and move forward, all the while keeping a cheerful outward demeanor. James Jordan, in particular, would continue to earn praise and affection as the amiable father of a very special athlete.

Evaluating Sis's allegations, once they became public decades later, in 2001, would prove nearly impossible because they had never been reported to authorities or investigated by social services or police at the time. Deloris Jordan had apparently considered her daughter's claims and concluded that taking the matter to authorities would destroy the family and endanger the other children as well. Criminal charges against James would have likely resulted in the loss of his employment and the family's primary means of support.

A decade after the disclosure to her mother, Sis contacted a Charlotte lawyer about the possibility of filing a lawsuit against her parents. She recalled in her book that the lawyer referred her to criminal authorities in Wilmington, who in turn told her that the statute of limitations had expired.

Michael was twelve at the time and unaware of the situation; he didn't learn of his sister's claims for many years. Sis left the family in 1977 to marry and begin a family of her own, although her life would be marked by depression and questionable behavior, which would later be used by some in the family to discount her allegations. Advocates for the victims of sexual abuse assert that such traits are often the symptoms experienced afterward by victims.

The allegations of abuse would prove to be an unarticulated seed of division in the family, twisting it in many difficult directions over time, no matter the efforts to push them beyond memory. Michael Jordan drew his competitive spirit from the same deep feelings of love and loyalty he felt toward his parents. His emotions regarding his family existed on a far deeper level than his public could ever fathom. For so many years his upbringing would be seen as the perfect story, a public view aided by his mother's persistent message that her family was a normal middle-class unit.

As with the story of her teen pregnancy, there was an attempt to cover up a reality that was far from normal. Her defenders would say that her decision that day in 1975 reflected what she thought best to protect her family.

The real story may help explain why late in life, well into her seventies, Deloris continued to travel the world, speaking in dozens of countries about family issues. She was never forthcoming on the deepest conflicts that threatened her own family, yet she often talked about the thing she clearly knew best: survival.

Chapter 5

THE DIAMOND

In the midst of this family turmoil in 1975, Michael Jordan had an extraordinary year as a twelve-year-old Little Leaguer. He was named the state's most valuable player while throwing two no-hitters in leading his team to a state championship. Later, in regional play in Georgia, Michael would show his hitting prowess by driving a ball out of the park in a key moment, a feat that kept his father smiling for years afterward.

"He used to talk about the time my Little League team was going for the World Series," Jordan would remember, "and we were playing in Georgia, and there was an offer that if anyone hit a homer they'd get a free steak. I hadn't had a steak in quite a while, and my father said, 'If you hit a homer, I'll buy you another steak.' It was a big ball field, and in the fourth inning I hit that sucker over the center field fence with two on to tie the game, 3–3. We lost it anyway, 4–3, but I've never experienced anything in sports like hitting one out of the park."

At the time, James Jordan began to entertain the thought that his son was headed toward the big leagues. William Henry Jordan, a cousin, saw it, too. "Michael pitched in an all-star game against my son when he was twelve years old," he remembered. "You could only pitch four innings under the rules at that time. He struck out all twelve batters he faced, if I remember correctly. He was throwing so hard. He pitched for New Hanover and my son played for

Pender County. We were sure that day when we watched him that MJ would be a pro player."

Jordan wasn't just a pitcher. "When he was twelve years old, he was an outstanding Little League player," recalled Dick Neher, who later coached Jordan in Babe Ruth League. "He was lanky. He played shortstop, too. He'd go over behind third base to dig out a grounder, he'd backhand the ball. You've seen Derek Jeter do this. He'd jump up in the air and throw it over to first. He was named Mr. Baseball in North Carolina."

With the award, Jordan was given a scholarship for two weeks that summer to Mickey Owen Baseball Camp in Missouri. It was a huge honor. The family proudly displayed his Little League trophies for years. "Michael hit a 265-foot home run in the elimination game in Georgia," James would tell visitors. "From the very start in Little League he loved it and excelled in it."

However, young Michael plummeted almost as swiftly as he had peaked. Neher had taken Jordan and four other thirteen-year-olds in the Babe Ruth League draft that spring. The Babe Ruth League included players thirteen to fifteen years old. "He was a superstar coming out of Little League, but I'd always tell the parents of my thirteen-year-olds, 'Your son's probably not going to get to play much this year,'" Neher recalled.

There was another reason that young Michael didn't get to play at age thirteen. The diamond was larger in this league, with longer base paths and a greater distance from the mound to home plate. Jordan no longer had the arm to dominate. "When I got him, I couldn't play him at shortstop," Neher recalled of Jordan's first year, 1976, in Babe Ruth League. "He couldn't make the throws. Mike didn't get into but about four games for me when he was thirteen. I don't think he got to bat but four times that season."

If the Jordans were infuriated by the circumstances, they never allowed Neher to see it. James Jordan even helped the coach build a baseball field during his time as a team parent. "Mike's dad and mom, they had no problem with it," the coach recalled in a 2012 interview. "They were good-natured people anyway.... James was not an interfering dad with me for three years, not at all. He was nothing but helpful."

The thirteen-year-old Jordan never complained either, Neher said. "My experience with Mike for three years, he was a joy to coach, very cooperative. All the time I knew him, he just wanted to play."

Bill Billingsley, who watched the team play, was struck that the thirteen-year-old Jordan often wound up standing on the sideline in a windbreaker, coaching first base. The opportunities were clearly limited for Jordan. Youth sports can be cruel like that, heaping glory on a young player at one stage of the game, then snatching it away at another.

Because he wasn't playing much, Jordan turned to amusing himself and others. "He was a loosey-goosey guy," Neher said. "He kept all the guys loose." Always a joker, the young Jordan stepped up the pace of his antics, putting shaving cream in his teammates' batting helmets, tapping people on the shoulder and hiding, or any other prank he could dream up. Jordan's old friend David Bridgers was on the team as well. "He was Mike's number one fan," Neher recalled. "They called him the white Michael Jordan. He and Mike were the best of friends, but they'd get in a physical fight nearly every practice. They were both so competitive; they'd pick on each other. And Bridgers was a good athlete."

Neher looked up one day at batting practice to find Bridgers on top of Jordan, whaling away. Jordan, who had been catching, began talking trash as Bridgers whiffed on some pitches. He told Bridgers that if he tried swinging at the ball with his big ears he might actually have a chance of getting a hit. "Mike was lying on the ground, with all his equipment on, and David was on top of him just pounding away on the mask," Neher recalled. "Like hockey players. They used to get into it all the time."

Neher separated the two. He recalled the tears rolling down Bridgers's face. When the coach heard what had caused the brouhaha, he laughed and asked Jordan if he'd looked in a mirror lately. Jordan's own unusual ears had been the subject of Larry's taunts during their backyard battles. Neher had nicknames for all his players. So he nicknamed Jordan "Rabbit" in honor of the jug handles on the side of his head, and the anger was apparently diffused.

"The kids liked that," the coach said. "We were messing around with Mike. Mike's ears lay real close to his head, just like a rabbit. So we all were standing around one day trying to decide, 'Why don't we call him Rabbit?' Those ears lay real close. Everybody laughed. Mike was fine with it. When they were in Chicago, James told the reporters that Mike was nicknamed Rabbit because he was so fast. That didn't have nothing to do with it."

Jordan did get into the lineup in a big game that first year. Two of the team's catchers couldn't play when Neher's undefeated team was facing another undefeated club sponsored by Mutual of Omaha. Jordan talked the coach into letting him catch, despite the fact that his throws from behind the plate could only reach second base on the hop. "Mike said, 'Coach, I'll catch.' He was so little and skinny, but he had huge hands," Neher recalled. "I said, 'Come on, Rabbit, there ain't no way. You can't get the ball to second base. That's 128 feet down to that bag.' He said, 'Coach, I'll do it.' That's the kind of kid he was."

One of Neher's assistant coaches suggested they teach Jordan how to "skip hop" the ball accurately to second base on the bounce. The assistant coach told Jordan to throw the ball tight, just over the pitcher's head. Jordan picked up the technique right away. He delivered the ball low on the bounce, right where the second baseman could put a tag on a sliding runner.

Neher recalled warm-ups before the big game that day: "We were taking infield, and the Mutual players were all standing by the fence watching. When they saw Jordan throw on the bounce, they started laughing. They went crazy and started razzing him, 'Oh, look at that spaghetti arm. We're gonna run on you tonight, Mr. Spaghetti Arm.' Mike flipped up his catcher's mask and looked at them. He grinned and said, 'You run and I will gun.' We all laughed. That was funny. In the second inning, they sent a man and Mike threw him out. They sent three or four. Mike threw 'em out, and they quit running. We laughed about that. After the game, Mike said, 'I told you I could do it.'"

Many years later, in Chicago, Jordan would confide to Bulls assistant coach Johnny Bach that the circumstances were difficult, that he felt a sense of isolation and pain as one of two black players on his youth baseball teams. In all of Neher's thirty-seven years of coaching he had only three black players on his teams, including Jordan. "That'll give you a feeling for how it was," the coach said. "I got the NAACP on me because I didn't have any blacks on my team. Generally, you'd go out there and see a twelve-man squad, and only one would be black. I told the NAACP it was hard if you got 250 kids trying out for the league and there are only three black kids among them."

For his first two years in the Babe Ruth League, Jordan had Terry Allen as his only black teammate. His last year in the league, his only black teammate was Clyde Simmons, who would go on to a career as an All-Pro defensive end for the Philadelphia Eagles. If anything, perhaps the numbers emphasized the Jordan family's great pains to include their son in a game that was overwhelmingly white. When his teams traveled about the region playing games that required overnight stays, Jordan would be placed with local black families. The situation allowed him to meet people and make friends, but the circumstances were clearly awkward. The Jordans never expressed any negative feeling about the racial makeup of the teams. "There was never any resentment from Mike that I ever saw," Neher said.

The coach recalled the team practicing one evening on a field in a rough neighborhood. During the practice two men went into the dugout and started rummaging through the team's cooler. Neher asked the men to stop, and they responded with threats and curses. Someone from the team went to phone the police, and while the players waited, Jordan used the "N" word in referring to the two men, Neher recalled. The moment reflected the difficulty of the situation. Youth baseball, the largely white game, found itself in awkward circumstances, practicing on the only available fields in predominantly black neighborhoods in an era when racial animosity still ran high. It's only logical that an adolescent Jordan might have trouble negotiating identity issues in that context.

That winter, over several days in late January 1977, ABC aired the award-winning miniseries *Roots*, author Alex Haley's saga about the African American experience and the inhumanity of slavery. Jordan was transfixed and profoundly moved by the story. "It was hundreds of years of pain that they put us through, and for the first time, I saw it from watching *Roots*," he explained years later. "I was very ignorant about it initially, but I really opened my eyes about my ancestors and the things that they had to deal with."

He hadn't had any overwhelming personal experience with racism, he would explain later. But the knowledge of America's ugly past was so infuriating, it occupied his mind. Everywhere he turned there were things he hadn't noticed before, things that only raised more questions about racism and injustice and how it affected his own family.

The Hunt Club

The boys from the whites-only Wallace Hunting Club would remember the face decades later, even those who had no idea he was the great-grandfather of a legend. Dawson Jordan, the hunt club cook, made that kind of impression. He was the old man with the crutch who walked with startling quickness, always teetering on the brink of disaster that never materialized, the master who somehow turned out sumptuous meals. And who could forget those biscuits? He wore overalls and an apron and always sported a gray stubble of beard on his deeply wrinkled face. But mostly it was the sadness in his tired, bloodshot eyes that struck them. The countenance suggested a hard life.

"It was a rough-looking face," remembered Mike Taylor, who came to the hunt club with his father each week. "Dawson Jordan was indeed a colorful man and beloved for his crusty character as well as his food by the members of the Wallace Hunting Club."

Ken Roberts, who also spent his boyhood there, was first struck by Dawson's kindness. One of the first times they met, Roberts asked how he should address the older gentleman. "He told me just to call him Dawson," Roberts recalled.

The club was little more than a rundown barracks that sat on a vast parcel of rented land above the Northeast Cape Fear River in Pender County. Later it would be torn down and replaced with another structure and then abandoned altogether. "The clubhouse would be considered a ramshackle, filthy place by today's standards," explained Mike Taylor. "I remember a long, one-story clapboard structure, rather low-slung and hardly off the ground, in need of painting, with a porch that ran the length on the front. Inside were common sleeping areas filled with bunks and metal single beds, with a dining room featuring a long table. I think Dawson cooked on a woodstove."

It was the kind of place where even the screen doors needed repair. That fact sticks out because one of the hunting dogs that always seemed to be lying about the yard went through the torn screen one Saturday and stole a hog's head from the kitchen that Dawson was planning on cooking and turning into one of his mysterious delights.

The primary figure in the operation of the hunt club was Robert Carr, known as "Mr. Robert" to all those who dealt with him. He was a presence in Pender County, where he owned an oil distributorship and served as chairman of the North Carolina Game and Wildlife Commission. Carr could be overbearing, but he held a fierce affection for Dawson Jordan. Their relationship was just one of those paradoxes left over from an earlier time.

"Mr. Dawson was real good to Mr. Robert, and Mr. Robert was real good to Mr. Dawson," explained Ken Roberts, adding that Carr's respect for Jordan set the tone for the rest of the members of the club. "Everybody respected Mr. Dawson. Didn't nobody mess with him because Robert Carr would have had their ass."

Roberts recalled, "Mr. Robert would pick him up and carry him down to the hunt club every Wednesday. Even when it wasn't deer season they'd go down each Wednesday. They just enjoyed getting away."

The two men would ride out North Carolina Highway 50 to the club, where they'd prepare for the usual gathering, a good ol' boy funfest of eating, drinking, telling tales, and even doing a little hunting and fishing every now and then.

Jordan's legendary meals were highlights of the experience. "The breakfast was traditional Southern fare with country ham, biscuits, gravy, eggs, grits, and other dishes full of salt, butter, and fatback for seasoning," Mike Taylor recalled. "I'm sure the lunch was equally as delicious and unhealthy. There was coffee, but men also brought their own liquor, which was freely consumed as well."

The boys at the hunt club, much like Dawson's own family, wondered at all the work he did while hobbling around the club's kitchen and dining room. "I recall being concerned how he could possibly prepare that meal, clean the dishes, and do all that work," Taylor remembered. "I think I asked my dad if he had any help, and he replied they pitched in to get the food to the table. It was served family style, with big bowls and platters passed around the long table."

Ken Roberts, who was about ten at the time, also recalled being concerned about how much work the crippled old man had to do to cook for the gathering, so he made every attempt to help him with the chores, getting the jars of molasses on the table each morning and helping with the dishes.

"I'd get up in the morning, it would be cold as hell," Roberts remembered. "Mr. Dawson would be lighting the stove. He was a quiet man, but he kind of took to me because I was one of the youngest down there."

Roberts recalled one unforgettable day that brought "the first cusswords I ever heard." Robert Carr was entertaining the other members of the state Game and Wildlife Commission at the hunt club. These were men of success and community standing from all across North Carolina, all seated at the long table waiting for Jordan to bring out one of his famous meals.

"Every meal was biscuits," Roberts said. "No matter what he was serving, there were biscuits."

Jordan was coming out of the kitchen with a steaming plate of biscuits fresh from the oven when he suddenly stumbled and spilled them all across the club's well-trafficked hardwood floor. For a moment, the group sat in silence. "Then Mr. Robert said, 'Dawson, put them biscuits on the table.' This was a gathering of distinguished city guys," Roberts explained. "Mr. Robert looked around the table and said, 'These are Dawson's biscuits. Anybody who doesn't eat one is a son of a bitch.' Those biscuits disappeared. They ate 'em all."

When he wasn't cooking, Dawson Jordan retreated to an adjacent small building, what appeared to be a former tobacco pack house, where he slept. Roberts, who would sometimes visit with him there, said, "I can remember in that little room he had an old-style feather bed. There was a small oil lamp and a little stove. He was always sitting on his bed reading. He didn't socialize with those folks at the hunt club a lot. He was just a nice fellow, but he probably wasn't too keen on spending a lot of time with the white people there."

That late winter of 1977, three short weeks after Michael had watched the TV series *Roots,* his great-grandfather died in Teachey, just months short of his eighty-sixth birthday. From resting in his sweet mother's arms as a baby in Holly Shelter to rafting logs on the great river, to struggling behind the plow and moving silently on a still Carolina night to deliver moonshine, to feeding the hungry folks at the Wallace Hunting Club, Dawson Jordan had survived much. In the process, he'd managed to build a family that would somehow find a way to endure the harshest blows that the dark recesses of human behavior could deliver, even in the context of great wealth and fame. His grandchildren and great-grandchildren would long treasure their time spent in his commanding presence, and Dawson Jordan had affected the people at the Wallace Hunting Club as well. Ken Roberts recalled his family being struck in 1977 by the news of Dawson's passing. "I remember my granddaddy telling me that Dawson had died," he said. "It was a big thing to him."

The Jordan family wept freely that day. His great-grandfather had been well aware of Michael's exploits on the baseball field, but his fame in basketball had yet to unfold. That, in itself, would prove a thing of wonder for the members of the hunt club and the people of Pender County. "I remember when MJ made it big," Ken Roberts said with a laugh. "My father-in-law said, 'Ol' Dawson would have loved to see that.'"

The deep sadness the whole family felt at Dawson's passing perhaps reinforced Michael's newly discovered racial anger. He didn't know every detail of his grandfather's life, but he had only to look at the pain deep in the old man's face to get an idea of how troubled his restless journey had been and of the many senseless barriers he had been forced to endure.

Later that year, a girl at school called Michael a "nigger."

"I threw a soda at her," he recalled. "It was a very tough year. I was really rebelling. I considered myself a racist at that time. Basically, I was against all white people."

Jordan was suspended for the incident. But rather than let him spend his days at home, his mother required that he sit in her car in the parking lot of the bank where she worked, so that she could keep an eye on him from the teller's window. That way she could make sure he was doing his schoolwork and staying out of trouble. Michael was furious, and years later he would joke with her that the situation presented an obvious case of child abuse. Yet Deloris got her message across. Over the course of the following months, she talked time and again about the wasted energy of bitterness and racial anger, how destructive they could be to a young boy. It wasn't about forgetting but about forgiving, she said.

It would take more than a year for the message to sink in and the feelings to subside. "The education came from my parents," Jordan recalled. "You have to be able to say, OK, that happened back then. Now let's take it from here and see what happens. It would be very easy to hate people for the rest of your life, and some people have done that. You've got to deal with what's happening now and try to make things better."

In shaping her son's attitude, Deloris Jordan was drawing on her own experience coming of age on the Coastal Plain. But it was much more than that. She was so focused on the future, on the positive, on achieving, that she would let neither infuriating social injustice nor her daughter's heartbreaking allegations of abuse stand in the way. She had no time for a single issue, no matter how grave, that didn't involve betterment. Stopping for anything meant certain defeat to Deloris Jordan. Having tasted such disappointment early in her own life, she was not about to be defeated again.

Here It Comes

In March 1977, Jordan watched the University of North Carolina's twisting run through the NCAA basketball tournament on TV but wouldn't allow himself to be impressed. He would admit later that, as an NC State fan, he absolutely despised the Tar Heels.

Still, it was a spellbinding moment for college basketball fans as network television discovered the potent chemistry of what would come to be known as March Madness. The attention certainly had something to do with the fact that the dunk returned to college ball that season after being outlawed for nine years, dating back to the Lew Alcindor era at UCLA. There was likely another instinctive reason young Michael disliked the Tar Heels. Just as dunking was set to electrify crowds again, Dean Smith and North Carolina made the four corners slowdown offense famous — or infamous.

That tournament had the state of North Carolina smeared all over it, thicker than barbecue sauce. Upstart UNC–Charlotte, led by Cedric "Cornbread" Maxwell, upset Michigan in the Mideast Regionals, putting two teams from the same state in the Final Four. North Carolina eventually met Marquette for the national championship. The Tar Heels were led by point guard Phil Ford, who competed despite an injured elbow, but he couldn't shoot and was no help against Marquette's zone. Dean Smith was denied a championship yet again, having made it to the Final Four five times without winning the title. Jordan gleefully watched the game on TV with his family. "My mom liked Phil Ford, but I couldn't stand him or any of them Carolina guys," he recalled. "I rooted for Marquette in the '77 championship game. My mom got mad."

That spring and summer, a fourteen-year-old Jordan started every game for Dick Neher's Babe Ruth League baseball team, but the magic he had known as a twelve-year-old never returned. "I couldn't play him at shortstop," Neher recalled. "He couldn't make the throws. Occasionally I'd put him at third base. I played him at first base. I'd play him left field. He would pitch. When he was fourteen, he was in the rotation to pitch. He'd pitch every couple or three games."

However, his pitching was no longer dominant. And at the plate, his bat speed wasn't quite there. "He hit .270, .275 that year," Neher said. "That was the highest he ever had for me. Usually in a youth league, you'd see kids hit .380, .400, that kind of stuff. Mike could hit. He was dependable. He'd be probably one of your better .230

hitters. He was an integral part of what we did. But he was never the star in Babe Ruth that he was at Little League. He played for me for three years and he never made an all-star team."

In the fall of 1977, Jordan entered D. C. Virgo Middle School, where he quickly became an early morning fixture in the gymnasium. Staff member Dave Allen would open up the facility each day and soon noticed Jordan's leaping ability and his tongue sticking out as he went to the basket. "Son, I'm afraid that you're going to bite it off," Allen told him. Sure enough, about a week later, a bloodied Jordan appeared in the principal's office. Allen asked if it was the tongue. Jordan could only nod.

One of his partners in these preseason sessions was Harvest Leroy Smith. At almost six feet seven, it was his height against Jordan's quickness in their one-on-one battles. "He and I practiced every day together and he always had to win. If it was a game of Horse and you beat him, you would have to play another game until he won," Smith recalled. "You didn't go home until he had won."

Jordan, then just over five feet seven, found many ways to get to the basket. "You'd see him get a shot off, and you'd wonder how he did it, because he wasn't that big," Smith said, "but it was the quickness. The only question was how big he was going to be—and how far up he would take his skill level."

Jordan answered that with an eye-opening ninth-grade basketball season for a team coached by Fred Lynch. Jordan soon piqued the interest of varsity coaches around the area. "I watched him at Virgo, right after he made his debut," remembered Dick Neher, whose son Steve played basketball with Jordan. "Their team went down to Burgaw to play a junior high team. Mike dropped 44 points, and they didn't play but six-minute quarters in junior high."

Jordan scored 44 of his team's 54 points that game, Neher recalled. "He got to where he started hitting shots, then he started going to the bucket."

Jim Hebron, the varsity coach at nearby New Hanover High School, began watching Jordan closely. "I remember Jim Hebron told me when he was a ninth grader that he was going to be something special," recalled Marshall Hamilton, then the coach at nearby Southern Wayne High School.

The buzz wasn't loud, but without a doubt it began there in the ninth grade at D. C. Virgo. Jordan emerged at a time before basketball exploded in popularity. AAU competition would soon blanket the sport with an elaborate process that commodified young talent. "Now kids twelve and under playing AAU basketball think they've made it," Tom Konchalski, a veteran basketball scout, observed in a 2011 interview.

In 1977–78, Jordan had only the short basketball schedule of the public school league to develop. The AAU competition that came later gave young players many hours of game experience, but the grind and the coddling of that talent machine likely would have robbed Jordan of his essence, Konchalski added. "I don't think he would have had this all-consuming competitiveness. The thing that really set him apart is he had tremendous competitiveness, that XYY chromosome in terms of competitiveness. That's maybe been his downfall in other areas of his life, but in basketball that defined him. That transcended his athleticism. He wouldn't have had that because what happens with AAU is there's always another game. You will play three games in a day. You can lose a game in disgrace and two hours later, there's always the next game. So you're not as focused on winning. Winning's not a critical obsession, and that's what set Michael Jordan apart from other players, that he was an obsessively competitive player. Had he grown up in an AAU culture, he would have lost his winning edge. He would have lost what his real thing is, and that's his competitiveness."

As fate would have it, Bill Billingsley, who had coached Jordan on the twelve-year-old all-star basketball team, was hired that spring as a substitute teacher at D. C. Virgo, and was assigned to coach the ninth-grade baseball team. He was well aware of Jordan's frustration with the game.

"He was losing interest," Billingsley said of Jordan's relationship with baseball. "His body was changing, growing, and he had already had some success in basketball."

In fact, many of the best memories of Billingsley's ninth-grade baseball team at D. C. Virgo school involved basketball. Bud Blanton, a white kid, and Jordan were clearly the two best athletes on the baseball team. Billingsley would find them each afternoon engaged in heated battles of one-on-one in the school gym. "They'd go in there and they'd play basketball and you'd think it was World War III," the coach remembered with a laugh. "They would really go at it."

One day Jordan even coaxed Billingsley, who was in his twenties, into a game. "He wasn't as hard on me as when he played Blanton," the coach explained. "He'd stand all the way out at the top of the key and say, 'Hey, coach, you gonna let me have this?'" Billingsley had sagged back into the lane to protect against Jordan's quickness to the hoop, only to watch him drain three straight shots from outside in those days before the three-pointer was legal. He's adding a little range, the coach thought.

The young Jordan was already spicing such moments with a taste of trash talk, Billingsley said. "When he was fourteen, he wasn't exactly modest. He was a chatterbox. He loved the verbal gamesmanship." Some didn't take so well to the commentary. "He did have a scrap with one of the boys. Michael whacked him around a bit," Billingsley said. "I think he got in some trouble for it and was taken to the principal's office. Michael was a very respectful, well-behaved kid. But he wasn't shy about defending his interests."

Jordan did some pitching for Virgo that season, but mostly he caught. Bud Blanton was already displaying the talent that would earn him a scholarship to pitch in the Southeastern Conference at the University of Kentucky. Jordan's act behind the plate mixed a little Mick Jagger with some Richard Pryor.

"He'd catch the ball and laugh and dance out from behind the plate. The whole place would be rocking," Billingsley said of Virgo's home games.

Blanton, the son of a local deputy who had passed away, was blessed with a mix of good stuff, speed as well as a doozy of a knuckleball, which gave Jordan a lot to work with. There was one game in particular against nearby Jacksonville, Billingsley remembered. "Blanton could throw hard, then change to that knuckleball. The hitters were baffled and seemed a little scared. What really baffled them was the guy behind the plate. 'You can't hit this ball,' Michael would be telling them. Blanton would be winding up to deliver, and Jordan was there telling them, 'Here it comes! Here it comes!'"

Billingsley sat behind the backstop, chuckling. "I can see it and hear it. With the knuckleball, those guys wouldn't even swing. The hitters were so confused, and Jordan was back there just basting them. Instead of looking at the pitch, they were peeking back at Jordan. I was laughing so hard I almost fell out of the chair. Every time Bud Blanton threw, Jordan would be telling them, 'Look out now. Here it comes.'"

That summer, Jordan played his final season of Babe Ruth ball. "At fifteen, he was supposed to be one of my main pitchers," Dick Neher said. "That didn't happen. I was able to put him in the outfield, and a little at first base." Jordan didn't hit as well as the previous year either. But he was still effective. "We played small ball, a lot of bunting, hitting, and running," Neher explained. "Mike loved that. He could run. He didn't run fast. He just had a long stride."

Which was just enough to help his team win a championship. The telling moment came in a makeup game that went into extra innings, scoreless. "Mike walked, and he stole second," Neher said. "I think we bunted him to third. So I put on a suicide squeeze. We had a thirteen-year-old who could really bunt. I put him in the lineup and told him to bunt and to protect Mike on third. But Mike was already halfway down the line when the pitcher let it go." Neher looked over at the plate, and the batter had stepped out of the batter's box.

His team looked to be headed for disaster, the coach recalled. "There was the catcher with the ball, sitting there looking at Mike about forty feet away. So he jumped up. And the third baseman was standing beside the bag with his legs crossed, chewing his fingernails. Mike just turned around and faked like he was going back to third. And the catcher threw the ball into left field, so Mike came charging on down the line with the catcher sitting three feet in front of home plate. Mike hurdled him and landed on the plate, jumped completely over him. Everybody was like, 'Wow, did you see that?' We won the ball game 1–0 on Mike's play."

But, Neher emphasized, it wasn't just that he had the athleticism to make the play, he also knew the rules. "There was a rule that if you made contact and the catcher didn't have the ball, they could throw you out. So Mike avoided the contact. He jumped clean over the catcher."

That next fall, Jordan went out for the junior varsity football team at Laney High School. He was already taller than the rest of the men in his family, nearing five nine. But his mother tried to talk him out of it, pointing out his skinny arms and legs. He pleaded, she finally relented, and he found a spot in the defensive backfield, where he was soon leading the team in interceptions. Well into the schedule, Laney faced Brunswick County, a team that featured a big, bruising running back who broke through the line early in the contest. Skinny Mike Jordan gamely stepped in to fill the gap. Suddenly, he was on the ground writhing in pain and complaining about his shoulder.

"It's broke, coach. It's broke," he yelled as coach Fred Lynch walked out to see what was wrong. Lynch, quite used to Jordan's constant joking around, told him, "Get up, you're holding up the game." Then he realized it was no joke.

Deloris Jordan had arrived late and was just taking her seat when she saw that the action had stopped. A friend informed her that Michael was injured and that they were bringing an ambulance around to take him to the hospital. She recalled that her first instinct was to run down to see if he was all right, but she remembered that she had made a promise not to embarrass him. So she went back to her car and drove to the hospital to wait for him there.

The shoulder was separated, but by the time the team had its banquet several weeks later, it had mended. Before the banquet, Michael and Bud Blanton threw around a football for a time, then went to the backyard basketball goal for some one-on-one. After that, Jordan took a running start and tried to dunk. He couldn't get it down, but it was close enough to encourage him to try again. Then again. And again. And again. Sweating and frowning, he spent much of the next hour taking the ball to the rim, tongue out. Finally, after about thirty tries, he got it over the cup and flushed. His smile said everything.

"He was excited," Blanton remembered years later. "He was glad he had done it, but it was only a matter of time."

PART III

EMERGENCE

Chapter 6

THE CUT

THE FIFTEEN-YEAR-OLD BOY who pinned his hopes on trying out for the Laney High School varsity basketball team in the fall of 1978 was a far cry from the supremely confident Michael Jordan the world would come to know. That young man was stalked by self-doubt. He wasn't a bad student, mostly Bs and Cs, but there was no indication that he was headed for stardom in academics. And he hated working, making no effort to do anything to earn extra money. He was oblivious to the example of his brother Ronnie's two jobs during high school, and it was clear to his father that Michael would do anything to avoid anything that resembled effort.

That's the laziest boy I've ever seen, James Jordan would say time and again. "If he had to get a job in a factory punching a clock, he'd starve to death. He would give every last dime of his allowance to his brothers and sisters and even kids in the neighborhood to do his chores. He was always broke."

Yet that laziness magically disintegrated when it came to sports. If it involved a ball in the air, a contest to be settled, the switch came on. In his adolescent mind, Michael figured maybe he could be a professional athlete. That was really about the only thing that interested him, which made him no different from millions of other daydreaming boys his age. He couldn't see how to make that happen, but rarely is there a clear or even a sane path to a life in professional sports.

Time had narrowed his options. He had watched his advantages in baseball mostly disappear. And his mother was determined that he drop football entirely. His choices seemed so bleak that Deloris even suggested he begin taking home economics courses so that he could learn to sew and cook for himself. Chipping away at his self-esteem, she implied it might be wise to do so because he didn't seem to be the kind of guy who could easily attract a mate. It was her way of saying, "Just go on in the house with the women."

Rather than getting bent out of shape, Jordan took her suggestion and signed up for the courses—and found he liked them. "I remember he baked a cake in school that was so good we couldn't believe it," his mother said. "We had to call his teacher to verify it."

Nonetheless, at age fifteen, Jordan was verging on the melancholy common to so many teens. Truth be known, he didn't have a lot of friends. The single beacon, the one bright spot in his life, was basketball.

After that ninth grade year at Virgo, Jordan and his lanky friend Leroy Smith attended a basketball camp run by Pop Herring, Laney High School's varsity coach. The school was just three years old, with a shiny new gym. Laney was a symbol of Wilmington's hard-won victories in integration, with a student population that was about 40 percent black. The city still ached racially, in so many ways reflecting the Wilmington that had been rocked by the 1898 riot when blacks were ushered to the railroad station and told to leave. "For a lot of African Americans, the only way to get ahead still was to get out," offered Bill Billingsley, who would go on to earn a PhD in history and write about the city's racial struggles.

Laney High School, though, enjoyed relative tranquility during Jordan's years there, due in part to black and white students joining forces on the playing fields. Beyond the important gains brought by integrated classrooms, athletic competition became the primary place where the races learned to coexist, on a footing of newly developing mutual respect. But only in retrospect would such things be important. In 1978, Jordan was just another kid trying to make the varsity.

Jordan clearly had been the best player on the ninth-grade team, and was just as impressive at Herring's camp that summer. Afterward, he began visualizing the kinds of things he would do on the floor that winter for the Laney Buccaneers. He was pretty confident that he would make the varsity for the upcoming season. After all, even Leroy Smith and his other ninth-grade teammates readily agreed that Jordan was the team's best player.

This, of course, is the moment at which the Jordan mythology intersects with the tragedy that became coach Pop Herring's life, resulting in a misunderstanding that would multiply fitfully over the ensuing decades. The story has been told in an endless wash of magazine pieces, newspaper stories, TV segments, videos, and radio broadcasts, just about every way that someone could recount how superstar Michael Jordan had been cut from his high school team.

Buried under the avalanche of mythmaking was his coach, Pop Herring. He was a proud son of Wilmington who had attended New Hanover High School, where he played for a legend, coach Leon Brogden, who guided eight different teams to state championships. Herring had played for Brogden's final team to win a title and then went off to play quarterback at North Carolina Central, where John McLendon had set up the coaching program in the 1930s. Herring probably could have played basketball, but in college he turned to football as the ticket to a degree. He returned to Wilmington afterward and went to work for a time as Brogden's assistant. When Laney High opened in the mid seventies, Herring had the pedigree to be named the basketball coach. It was significant that he was an African American head coach, which was rare at the time. Herring was a smart and personable young educator with a bright future when Michael Jordan came into the Laney High School program in 1978. In fact, Herring lived near the Jordans and was soon in the habit of stopping by in the mornings to pick up Michael to take him to the school gym for early workouts. He went the extra mile for his players, to the point of helping them write letters to colleges about the possibility of playing after high school. As his handling of Jordan would later prove, winning wasn't the most important thing in Pop Herring's world. His players were.

Dick Neher, who made a practice of closely observing coaches, had a son on Herring's team. "He was a great guy," Neher recalled. "He had a mental breakdown. He was funny. He was good to the kids. He was a good coach. He was personable. But he really bottomed out."

Sadly, within three years of Jordan's graduation from Laney, Herring's struggle with schizophrenia would end his career. When the mental disease surfaced, it brought about a sudden and swift disintegration of his personality. The once thoughtful, energetic young coach could be seen walking the city's streets, transformed almost overnight into a disheveled zombie in pursuit of unseen demons, often talking to himself or to no one in particular. This proved terribly distressing to old friends. "How could this happen?" they asked time and again. "How could this bright, special human being be reduced to this?" Medication helped ease his condition somewhat, but his life descended into an increasingly familiar pattern of vicious mood and behavior swings, all accompanied by a plunging social status.

His coaching friends tried to protect him the best they could, but even as his life came apart, the Jordan narrative was gaining a momentum of its own. In time, it would produce a storm of interest in one of the strangest mysteries in Jordan's background. He was cut from his high school team? The logical question followed: What dummy did that?

The community in Wilmington over the years held tightly to the hard truth of Herring's situation, coming to grips with it, even as the media returned to the story time and again in their accounts of Jordan. The first reporter to make a major breakthrough on the truth was Kevin Sherrington from Dallas. Much later, *Sports Illustrated* would delve into the situation with a beautifully written piece about Herring. These and other stories came to imply that Jordan's claim itself had the trappings of a false narrative, that it was somehow a creation of the superstar's intensely competitive nature.

But that doesn't seem to be the exact truth either, although the perception, shaped by the *Sports Illustrated* story, came to be another talking point of Jordan's mythology. The basic facts of the story stand out amidst all of the misunderstanding and well-intentioned revisionism. It's the age-old truth of public school competition: Young athletes try out for a team. Some make it. Some don't.

After years of answering questions about the Jordan story, the coaches began to imply that there weren't really any serious tryouts that fall for the Laney varsity. That revision, of course, opens up its own questions. If there were no tryouts, then they certainly would not have posted a list with the names of the players who made the varsity. But late that fall, Herring posted the list, in alphabetical order, of those who had been selected. Jordan had anticipated the news for days and hours and then seconds. And when it was posted, he was there almost immediately to read it. Then to reread it. Certainly there must be a mistake, he first thought. Even a fifteen-year-old Jordan knew that he was the best player on the ninth-grade team, and it wasn't even close. But the only sophomore on the list was his long, tall friend, Leroy Smith.

The realization of his defeat fell on him like a boulder that day. He walked home alone, avoiding anyone along the way. "I went to my room and I closed the door and I cried," Jordan later recalled. "For a while I couldn't stop. Even though there was no one else home at the time, I kept the door shut. It was important to me that no one hear me or see me."

The extenuating circumstance for Herring was the mix of his veteran team that fall. Eleven seniors and three juniors were returning to the varsity. Eight of them were guards. Leroy Smith gave the team much-needed size, although he played sparingly. Given time to absorb the decision, Jordan came to an inescapable conclusion — size mattered. "I was pissed," he would tell writer John Edgar Wideman in 1990. "Because my best friend, he was about six six, he made the team. He wasn't good, but he was six six, and that's tall in high school. He made the team and I felt I was better." Years later, Smith himself would emphasize his own surprise at his selection "because it certainly wasn't based on talent."

"The debate," recalled Ron Coley, Herring's assistant coach, "was what do we do with Leroy Smith." Coley, who later became a head coach in Pender County, claimed that he didn't even remember Jordan trying out, but he also described the young Jordan as a "shy ballplayer."

The coaches admitted later that the situation could have been handled better. Herring may well have talked to the sophomore about his future, but if he did, Jordan didn't comprehend it. And no one else recalled it. More likely, nothing was said because the situation was common and involved a long-valued principle of public-school athletics: Coaches coached and made their decisions. There was not a lot of discussion involved in the process. The searing element was the list itself, which apparently remained posted for much of that season. "It was there for a long, long time without my name on it," Jordan recalled.

Years later, reporters would travel to Wilmington to solve the mystery of the cut. Former coaches and teammates alike would tell them that it was for the best, that Jordan wasn't ready, that he was too short, too thin, that he couldn't possibly have beaten the older, stronger players on the varsity even in games of one-on-one. "I always felt he was confident," recalled longtime Wilmington sportswriter Chuck Carree. "He just was short and could not do the things he eventually could until he had a growth spurt."

Perhaps that was true, although certainly it would be hard to argue against the results of the coming years. Those answers rang with clarity for just about all of the witnesses to the events of 1978—except, of course, for the most important one.

Jordan's heart was broken. He wanted to quit the sport and would later credit his mother with challenging him to fight through the immense disappointment. Fortunately, his spirit remained intact that winter.

"We thought he'd be better off playing on the JV team," said Fred Lynch, the coach of the younger team and an assistant on the varsity. "He didn't sulk, he worked. We knew Michael was good, but we wanted him to play more."

Being on the varsity would have meant a substitute's role, with little playing time, little development, Lynch explained. On the JV, he had room to rule. Still, the status of a junior varsity player came with the usual teen indignities. The players in the Laney program took note of the shape of his head and began calling him "Peanut" or "Shagnut." From baseball, he had had enough of other people selecting his nicknames.

"He never answered to it, though," noted Michael Bragg, a junior on the Laney varsity at the time. "Michael judged his game by how he played against the upperclassmen, but he couldn't beat any of them one-on-one until the end of his sophomore year."

Jordan's response to the situation became clear on the floor each night the junior varsity played, and soon the members of the varsity made sure to gather to watch the spectacle, hanging on each detail of his performances until it came time for them to get ready for their own game. He scored points in furious bunches, twice even racking up more than 40, an absurd number in contests with six-minute quarters. He averaged 28 points on the season as a play-making guard.

Jordan was only about five foot ten at the time, but one day Kevin Edwards, a senior reserve guard on the varsity, noticed Jordan's hands and held his own up next to them. "His was twice as big as mine," he recalled. Large hands make for players who can easily control the ball off the dribble, and that in turn allows for stupendous finishes, as Julius Erving was then demonstrating in professional basketball. Young Michael had begun taking note of the pro game on TV. Later, thanks to the rise of ESPN, the televising of NBA games became omnipresent, and Jordan's own play would spawn a generation of young players attempting to imitate his game. He explained that he had done the same, finding rare and special instructors through television. First there was David Thompson, followed by the acrobatic Dr. J.

"Final game of our sophomore year, we were playing down at Goldsboro. Mike stole the ball and had a breakaway, and he went in and dunked it—I mean he threw one down," teammate Todd Parker once recalled. "I believe that was the first competitive dunk of his life. We were like, 'Wow, where did that come from?'"

Jordan would recall that his first in-game dunk had actually occurred at Virgo. "It was a baby dunk, just basic," he remembered. "I didn't even know I did it until after the fact. I surprised myself. Other kids had done it, but still it was spectacular for a junior-high kid to be dunking. I felt proud that I could do it." Whether or not it was the first, Jordan's late-season dunk as a sophomore came with the authority of a slam, at a time when the college sport had just made the emotional, spectacular play legal again.

As baseball was fading for him, Jordan was finding the game that suited his startling athletic skills. At each step along his path, others would express amazement at how hard he competed. At every level, he was driven as if he were pursuing something that others couldn't see. On the basketball court it was as if everything that he was had been wound into a fury. Combined with his evolving physical gifts, this fury became a spectacle that the many witnesses along the way would never forget.

"The first time I ever saw him, I had no idea who Michael Jordan was. I was helping to coach the Laney varsity," recalled Ron Coley in a 1999 newspaper interview. "We went over to Goldsboro, which was our big rival, and I entered the gym when the JV game was just ending up. There were nine players on the court just coasting, but there was one kid playing his heart out. The way he was playing I thought his team was down one point with two minutes to play. So I looked up at the clock and his team was down 20 points and there was only one minute to play. It was Michael, and I quickly learned he was always like that."

Salted Shoes

Jordan was proving prone to the same vagaries of joy and confusion and sorrow that visited so many other adolescents. Despite their own profound troubles, the most important thing his mother and father did was to look beyond themselves. They may have been unwilling to deal with the family's issues of abuse, but James and Deloris Jordan somehow managed to keep a focus on their children. Deloris, in particular, maintained her vigilance and steered her children clear of any possible pitfalls. And James, despite the pressures of work and owning a nightclub, made it to every single event even if he and his wife kept a distance between them.

On a superficial level this parenting had long been apparent in the time and material gifts they had showered on their children. After the three youngest started school, the Jordans bought them small ponies. Once they reached adolescence, James gave Michael and Larry a small motorbike, an experiment that ended when the boys attempted a daredevil jump over a ramp together and crashed. Then there was the full effort made to support both Larry and Michael in Little League baseball as the parents traveled back and forth to practices and games, while still holding down demanding jobs.

Beyond the gifts and involvement, the greatest impact of their parenting came in the constant shaping of the children's attitudes. They preached a constant refrain: Work hard. Achieve. Set goals. Think ahead. Don't be denied. Be considerate. Don't dwell on race.

"To grow, you have to work hard," Deloris Jordan told them. "Discipline yourself and set goals."

Her words were perhaps never more important than when her youngest son failed to make the varsity roster as a sophomore. As he said of his career and development, "Timing was everything." This comment was perhaps the closest he would ever come to acknowledging that what happened to him in the fall of 1978 was a mere stagger step that aided his progress. Perhaps the cut itself might not have wounded him so deeply if not for what happened next. It had been customary for high school coaches at the end of a season to bring the best JV players up to varsity for the district play-offs. Jordan expected that would happen for him. He knew from feedback that people had noticed his play. But Herring and his staff mysteriously said nothing to the sophomore. Apparently the thought occurred to none of the coaches.

"Never even discussed it," recalled Coley, Herring's assistant.

Jordan took deep offense. As fortune would have it, the team manager took ill as the playoffs were set to begin, which allowed Jordan to devise a plan to accompany the team to its games as a quasi manager and statistician. He would recall having to carry another player's uniform into the building to avoid having to pay admission. He was so angry he would rather have spit than cheer for the Laney Buccaneers.

"They went into the playoffs and I was sitting at the end of the bench, and I couldn't cheer them on because I felt I should have been on that team," he would recall.

He had found it hard to cheer for the varsity during his JV season, but he had done it. By the district playoffs, it wasn't possible. "This is the only time that I didn't actually cheer for them," he explained. "I wanted them to lose. Ironically, I wanted them to lose to prove to them that I could help them. This is what I was thinking at the time: You made a mistake by not putting me on the team and you're going to see it because you're going to lose." The Buccaneers finished with fifteen wins and seven losses that spring. They did not make the state playoffs after losing three of their last four games.

The experience brought Jordan face to face with his own selfishness for the first time. It would be one of the dominant themes of his career, learning to channel the tremendous drive and ego of his competitive nature into a team game.

The other immediate effect of this sophomore setback was that he became obsessed with growing. If coaches could pick a taller player over a talented player for a team, well, then he was just going to have to get taller. He spent hours hanging from a bar in the backyard, hanging anywhere on anything that afforded a good grip, trying to make himself taller.

His mother had witnessed everything that had unfolded and talked with him about his anxiety. They prayed together about it, and Jordan prayed alone at the end of each day, and when he woke up in the morning, and all during the day as well. Please, Lord, make me taller. Let me grow.

The prospects for that seemed slight. At five ten, he already towered over the males in the family. His parents counseled him to think about growing in his heart and in his mind. But I want to be taller, he insisted, in almost the same discussion night after night. Finally, his mother told him, "Go put salt in your shoes and pray."

"He would tell me I was being silly, but I had to pacify him so I could finish dinner," Mrs. Jordan remembered. "Then his dad would walk in and he'd tell him he wanted to be tall. We'd say, 'You have it in your heart. The tallness is within you. You can be as tall as you want to be in your thinking.'"

So, in addition to hanging from the bar, Jordan would put salt in his shoes before going to bed and praying again. Many nights his mother would bring the salt into his room before bedtime. She didn't have the heart to tell him she had made it all up, that salt was, well, salt.

Not long after, an older cousin came to stay with the Jordans, and he was six seven. Six seven! Suddenly hope was very much alive. The only concern was the constant pain in Michael's knees. It hurt so much that he could hardly sleep some nights. His mother took him to the doctor about the pain and his desire to grow. The doctor took one look at the X-rays and saw the growth plates and told mother and son not to worry. Young Michael still had plenty of growing to do.

Indeed. By summer he had shot to six three and was far from done. In fact, he would continue growing right into college and even a bit in the NBA until he was six six and towered a foot above everyone else in his family.

"Mike was about five ten at the end of tenth grade, no more than five eleven. He always had talent," Fred Lynch remembered. "He was our best ninth grader and our best tenth grader. He played with a lot of heart, he had guard skills, and he always had big, strong hands. By his junior year he shot up to six three, almost six four. All of a sudden you had size to go with that talent and drive.... He just blossomed."

Chapter 7

NUMBER 23

IN THE SPRING of 1979, Earvin "Magic" Johnson, a sophomore at Michigan State, had just led his Spartans to the NCAA championship over senior Larry Bird and the Indiana State Sycamores. Their meeting, featuring an emerging black star from the Big Ten Conference against an emerging white one from a little-known university in Indiana, had triggered the nation's curiosity, measured by the largest television audience ever to watch an NCAA title game.

Among that infatuated mass was young Mike Jordan of Wilmington, North Carolina. And he kept watching the next season as Bird joined the Boston Celtics and Johnson took his talents to the Los Angeles Lakers, two of pro basketball's "storied" franchises. The following spring, when Johnson carried the Lakers to an NBA title with a magical display of talent, his spell over young Mike was complete. The teen in Wilmington was in love with the Lakers. They were his team, and Magic Johnson was his guy.

That same year Jordan's parents gave him his first automobile. Knowing just the way to his heart, Jordan's girlfriend, Laquetta Robinson, bought him a vanity plate that he displayed proudly on the front bumper of his new ride: MAGIC MIKE.

Certain basketball people, many of them coaches, would later smile ruefully at such a revelation. Bird and Johnson were both big men, six nine each, who handled the basketball beautifully and played in the open court with a verve that inspired millions of new

NBA fans. Both were brilliant passers, particularly Johnson, but both could deliver the ball to teammates in ways that brought a rush of blood to the hearts of all who saw it. The sport had never seen someone like Johnson running the fast break.

Over the summer and fall of 1979, as Magic Johnson was still basking in the joy of his NCCA tournament win and his selection by the Lakers, Michael Jordan was in Wilmington and about to ignite his own roiling legend. That fall Jordan would begin play for the Laney High School Buccaneers. While his skills were far from perfect, his effort in those first varsity games was something to behold. His prayers for more height had been answered. He had grown to six three and was already headed to six four. His hands were larger, his arms longer, his stride greater. He had new tools with which to expand his game. While he had been aggressive offensively as a sophomore point guard on the junior varsity squad, he was also mindful of distributing the ball to his teammates. As they watched his considerable talents unfold on the varsity, Laney coach Pop Herring and his assistants soon saw that Jordan was far too unselfish. He was so talented he needed to do more scoring to help the relatively inexperienced team rather than deferring to someone else, Herring concluded. Jordan listened closely to his coaches but was hesitant to change. He still believed that basketball was a team game, and he was going to look for his teammates.

Finally, Pop Herring turned to James Jordan and asked for his help. The father was at first reluctant, explaining that he never cared much for the kind of father who didn't leave the coaching to the coach. Getting involved would violate that principle. Ultimately, though, he relented and urged his son to do what his coaches asked.

At this urging, Michael began to take on more individually, which in turn revealed even more of his gift. It was then that the pattern was established: the more he did, the more his coaches and his audience wanted him to do. And the more it began to please him to discover just what he was capable of doing. His game and his image then began to feed on themselves, still only subtly in those early days of his career. But it would soon enough become clear that everything about him was beginning to multiply. To those around him, including his parents, this development wasn't troubling at first. But later it would grow obvious that his success was accompanied by a burden. The greater his success, the greater the weight, and it would never go away, no matter how leveraged the lifting.

The Varsity

Bobby Cremins, the thirty-one-year-old head coach at Appalachian State, was both happy and tired in 1979 as he went about the business of running his summer camps. A former point guard for Frank McGuire at the University of South Carolina, Cremins had spent four difficult years building the program at Appalachian, a gem of a public university in the Carolina mountains. That effort had just been rewarded in 1979 by his team's first trip to the NCAA tournament, where his appropriately named Mountaineers promptly lost to LSU. The excitement had just begun to settle that June as Cremins opened his camp for high school teams. The camp allowed teams to get away to North Carolina's cool upper elevations for some summer hoops, and at the same time it afforded a young coach like Cremins the opportunity to look at a range of players he might not otherwise get to scout.

Cremins was watching the Laney High team from Wilmington when he noticed the player with the spindly legs, whose energy and athleticism sent a charge through the camp's games and drills. The more Cremins watched, the more his amazement grew. Finally, Cremins dialed up Bob Gibbons, the editor of a local basketball talent "poop sheet," and said excitedly in his thick New York accent, "Bob, there's a kid up here you're not going to believe."

In a few short years, Gibbons would become known as one of the high priests of high school basketball talent, but at the time his publication had a small readership. Cremins's raving about an unknown player, one who hadn't even played a varsity game, piqued Gibbons's interest, so he drove over to Appalachian State to take a look for himself.

"I saw a six-three player with explosive athletic ability," Gibbons told writer Al Featherston. "But what impressed me was what

Michael said when Bobby introduced him to me—'Mr. Gibbons, what do I need to do better to be a better player?'"

Cremins and Gibbons weren't the only surprised observers. Jordan's own teammates would later recall witnessing a startling transformation. "He comes back for junior year, he's a different guy, no longer skinny little Mike," remembered Todd Parker, a Laney teammate. "He's jumping out of the gym. I'm like, 'What?'"

"I could see a real big difference," agreed Mike Bragg, a senior on the Laney varsity at the time. "He was much more determined, and he had more ability."

Gibbons didn't know any background about this transformation, but he made note of Jordan's potential in his next report, the scout recalled. "I wrote about what a good prospect he was, but I only had a couple of hundred readers and a small regional audience."

"I certainly wasn't the one people were talking about," Jordan said of his time that summer at Appalachian State. "No one knew me that much."

Pop Herring, though, took note of the interest in Jordan and was pleased. It confirmed his belief that he was about to coach someone very special. Herring was not given to braggadocio, but the record speaks remarkably well of his actions despite Jordan's obsession with "the cut." There is nothing to indicate that Herring thought about how he might exploit this singular talent, as coaches were often known to do. The record does show that Herring took every opportunity to expand the youthful Jordan's options. In fact, the coach would deftly manage his player's recruitment by colleges, which got off to a very slow start, then blew up almost overnight.

In the fall of 1979, before the storm, Herring sat down and composed a letter seeking interest in Jordan from the University of North Carolina coaching staff. Not every high school coach took an interest in the future of his players, and it was extremely rare for a coach to write such a letter before a player had even participated in a varsity game. But that's what Herring did, along with rising early each weekday morning to pick up Jordan at six thirty to work on his game.

"He had a weakness with his left hand," Herring once recalled. "I told him to improve with the left hand and work on shooting off the dribble."

The early-morning sessions focused on those things and on getting up as many shots as possible. So much of Jordan's later success was seeded in the extraordinary efforts of the young coach. From several accounts, Herring and Jordan would become quite close, but never close enough to allow Jordan to forget his rejection as a sophomore. Thinking back on all those early mornings in the Laney gym, Jordan would recall, "Whenever I was working out and got tired and figured I ought to stop, I'd close my eyes and see that list in the locker room without my name on it, and that usually got me going again."

That fall, Herring called Jordan into his office to consult about a jersey number for the upcoming season. He gave the junior a choice of two numbers: James Beatty's 23 or Dave McGhee's 33, the team's two all-district seniors who had graduated.

Apparently something of a numerologist, Jordan decided he'd like to wear Beatty's 23. Years later he explained that he made the selection because 23 was close to half of 45, a number that his brother Larry had worn. Before he would be done, coaches across basketball would come to understand the number as a sign. Whether in AAU play or public school leagues or even a recreation contest for ten-year-olds, coaches began to figure that anyone bold enough to wear 23 must deserve extra defensive attention.

Likewise, future generations of the best young players would vie to wear the number 23 and take on the pressure and expectation that came with it. For Jordan, the number would soon enough become a signature that would brand everything from his line of boutiques to the sky-blue personal jet that he used to hop about the planet from one exclusive resort to another in search of the perfect golf round.

The first sizzling moment in his emergence that varsity season happened to come in a road game in Pender County, of all places. There, before a collection of family, friends, and distant cousins, he scored 35 points to carry Laney to an 81–79 overtime win in the first game of the season. His family, his teammates, his coaches, even Jordan himself—all were taken aback by the display.

From there, his pent-up emotion and frustration erupted game after game as he took off on a high-octane spin through everything he had dreamed about. The early ferocity just leapt at anyone watching. Time and again, as he attacked the basket, his mouth would fly open like the intake valve on a dragster, sucking in air along the way with enough g-force to pin his lips high on his gums, his exposed teeth flared vampire-like as if he were about to devour the rim itself. The tongue popped out for no other reason than to get out of the way of it all. He did this over and over while charging the basket. His visage alone was enough to give defenders pause. And when he took rebounds, he rose up and snatched the ball with the same ferocity. His quickness off the floor left teammates and opponents alike agape. He presented a physical challenge that quickly separated him from the boys around him. A select few took on the challenge of rising up with him, but many simply resorted to principle-of-verticality poses, throwing their arms straight up and hoping for the best.

Among the many who took notice was Mike Brown, the athletic director of New Hanover County schools. He had been wowed by Jordan's opening salvos as a varsity player, so much so that he contacted Bill Guthridge, Dean Smith's top assistant at the University of North Carolina, and told him there was an exceptional young guard in Wilmington that he needed to see. Like that, the seed was planted.

The Laney lineup also included Leroy Smith in the post and senior Mike Bragg at guard. Another guard/forward was senior Adolph Shiver, whom Jordan had gotten to know a few years earlier on the courts at Wilmington's Empie Park. Shiver was a chippy sort, always talking trash with a toothpick hanging out of his mouth, Jordan recalled. While Shiver's behavior frequently annoyed others, he seemed mostly to amuse Jordan with the constant chatter and trash talking, much as the court jester might entertain the king. One time, Jordan threw Shiver up against a wall after Shiver insulted David Bridgers's sweetheart, but there was something in Shiver's edginess that endeared him to Jordan. It also seems likely that Shiver's presence and attitude brought Jordan some street cred in high school. In turn, Shiver fed off of Jordan's vast energy, as did everyone on the Laney varsity, even the coaches.

The two began a friendship that carried far into adult life. The bond between them began with Jordan finding Shiver reliable as a teammate. Time would reveal Jordan to be steadfastly loyal to the tight circle of friends he accumulated in his life. Shiver was merely the first to pass the audition. Jordan would come to accept some questionable behavior from his friends, but not disloyalty. Trust was a precious commodity for Jordan, and he would establish a bond of trust with Shiver that first varsity season. By Jordan's Chicago days, Shiver would be in the hotel suites on the nights before big games, dealing hands of tonk to help relax his old pal.

The Buccaneers got another win in their second game, with Jordan exploding for 29 points, this time at home, but then came the inevitable wake-up call. Southern Wayne had a team that featured two of Jordan's future college teammates—big man Cecil Exum and point guard Lynwood Robinson—both considered blue-chip players at the time. Against Laney, Robinson scored 27 and Exum 24. Jordan's 28 points raised yet more eyebrows, but his dazzling performance didn't prevent the loss. Southern Wayne embarrassed the Buccaneers, 83–58.

Herring could only whistle afterward. "It'll help us playing somebody this good," he said, trying to put a positive spin on the drubbing. "Jordan is just a junior, and we'll all get better as the season goes on. We have to regroup. We got spanked tonight."

Laney looked better three nights later, with Jordan and Leroy Smith ripping down rebounds and powering out on the fast break. Michael's 24 points led Laney past crosstown rival Hoggard, with help from brother Larry, who came off the bench to score 6. The older Jordan would have his moments during the season, but he also spent a lot of time sitting and simply admiring the player his kid brother was becoming. "We played one year of varsity basketball together when I was a senior and Michael was a junior, and that's when his play just went to another level," Larry would recall later. "Even though there were five guys on the floor, he pretty much played all five positions. His level of play was just so much higher than the rest of us. People ask me all the time if it bothered me, but I can honestly say no, because I had the opportunity to see him grow. I knew how hard he worked."

Despite the intensity of their earlier sibling rivalry, Larry proved to be another remarkable element in Michael's good fortune. His fundamental decency and patience evidenced itself in the absence of drama on the Laney varsity. Not many high school seniors could tolerate sitting on the bench night after night watching a younger sibling rival grab the public's attention.

In fact, all of the family would be caught off guard by Michael's suddenly elevated status, even James and Deloris. "I remember going to Laney High on a Friday night, Michael's junior year, and now he'd grown," James's younger brother, Gene Jordan, would later recall. "Before the game he's telling me, 'Watch me, I'm going to slam dunk three balls tonight. You'll see. I'm going to slam three.' And I'm there saying, 'Boy, who you kiddin'? You can't slam no ball.' Well, he didn't slam three, but he sure as hell slammed two. And I told my brother that night, 'Hey, that boy is devastating.'"

A few other keen observers agreed. "Laney's top player has been Mike Jordan," Chuck Carree noted in the Wilmington paper on December 18. A night later Jordan scored 31 in a win over Kinston and earned his first headline: JORDAN PACES BUCS PAST KINSTON. With the early wins, Laney's record stood at 4–1, and Herring grew even more optimistic.

"This is the best defensive team in my tenure here at Laney," Herring declared. The defensive success depended partly on Jordan's ability to get into the passing lanes and his attention to rebounding. He played wing on offense but played a mix of guard and forward on defense, thanks to his quickness and recovery speed. Like his idol Magic Johnson, he spent much time around the basket defensively, with the idea of collecting rebounds and quickly getting the ball back up the court.

Years later, he would look back with amusement on the explosion of his raw power in high school. The unbridled nature of the experience showed him the kinds of things he could do athletically, things about which even the best coaches had no earthly concept.

As basketball evolved, another theme began to emerge: The sport, more than any other, furthered the process of whites understanding and coming to terms with the rise of black athletes. This process had begun during the first years of integration, well before Jordan appeared on the scene. But in those first decades of racial collaboration in basketball, many white coaches had a limited understanding of the athletic style of play that had developed in black communities. The only way coaches could learn it was to witness it in action.

In high school and, later, at the University of San Francisco in the 1950s, coaches had cautioned Bill Russell not to leave his feet to block opponents' shots. Russell tried it their way briefly, then followed what his instincts told him — to rise up and block shots like no one ever had.

"We were born to play like we do," Jordan would later observe in a conversation with writer John Edgar Wideman. "Can't teach it."

Of all the coaches Jordan played for, only the first two were African American. Fred Lynch and Pop Herring were able to sit and watch Jordan explore the range of his special athleticism in those high school years. They did so without sounding excessive alarms about his violation of one or another of the game's fundamentals. Lynch and Herring worked with him on basketball's basics and helped him channel his unique athleticism. Herring would show him how to maximize his quickness in his first step, with a move that would later prompt college officials to call traveling violations on him at North Carolina, until Dean Smith was able to demonstrate that Jordan was not using an extra step.

The record shows that Herring spent much time talking to Jordan and his teammates about shot selection and the tempo at which they would play, just as he focused on their defensive unity. Jordan made such talks easy, assistant coach Ron Coley remembered. "Nobody ever had that kid's drive, even in high school. He took pride in his defense. Mike was furious if his teammates didn't play good defense in practice."

As much as he praised his team, Herring was pointedly limited in his public commentary about Jordan in those early months. Nor did the coach talk about the letters he wrote or his work with the young player those early mornings in the gym. So many coaches viewed their teams and players in terms of their own professional resumes, but Herring kept his efforts to himself. They would become known only much later, mostly from Jordan's recollections. Little did Herring know it at the time, but Jordan's moment would be his own brief moment. The coach's actions were not perfect, but in retrospect, they were clearly extraordinary. Herring was enthusiastic but restrained in most of his efforts with his inexperienced team that season.

Considering Jordan's height and leaping ability, most coaches would have kept him inside, near the basket or working along the baseline. While Jordan worked all over the floor, Herring played him mostly at guard. "Pop gave him the opportunity to play the position he was going to play in college and the pros," New Hanover coach Jim Hebron observed. "If Pop had played him inside or on the baseline, he might have won the state title."

The Spreading Word

Two days after Christmas, Laney opened play in the Star-News–New Hanover Invitational, which Herring's team had won the previous season. The event pitted local schools against talent from as far away as New York. Up first for Laney was Wadesboro-Bowman, a team that had traveled from south-central North Carolina. "We had heard about him," Wadesboro coach Bill Thacker recalled in 2011. "Some of our kids thought they could play like Michael Jordan, but they weren't up to the task."

In particular, his team featured an athletic player named Tim Sterling, Thacker recalled. "He thought he could match MJ dunk for dunk. It was really a neat game, going up and down."

The teams traded blows at a furious pace, driven by Laney's pressing and trapping. With six minutes left and Laney leading 46–44, Herring called a time-out to give his players a breather and to remind them to focus on good shots down the stretch. The one thing that had worried him in their early wins was his team's tendency to get out of control. The game tightened a bit and stood at 48 all with 3:47 to go. Having gained their poise, Jordan and his teammates once again turned up their defensive energy and shot off on an 18–2 run that closed it out, 66–50. "Our kids turned in a good defensive effort all night, and it was really good down the stretch," Herring said afterward. Particularly Jordan.

"He had a lot of energy, a lot of energy," Thacker recalled.

Those late-game expectations failed to pay off in the semifinals the next day against Holy Cross, a team that had driven fifteen hours from Flushing, New York. Laney was up by 6 midway through the fourth period and led 51–47 with two minutes to go. But Jordan missed two free throws with 45 seconds on the clock, which allowed Holy Cross to tie it. Jordan got an open look at the buzzer but again missed, and from there Holy Cross got control in overtime and won, 65–61.

Afterward, Herring was quite angry. "They're supposed to do a job," he complained to a reporter. "We had a meeting about it."

What he did next perhaps foreshadowed the mental instability to come. It's possible that he just didn't want to give rival New Hanover a look at his starters, or maybe he was simply angry. Herring benched his starters the next day for the entire third-place game against New Hanover. Perplexed and steamed, Jordan watched as his teammates played well but lost 53–50.

Whatever his purpose, the move backfired on Herring. His team plummeted through five straight losses over the next three weeks, although the setbacks weren't without highlights. Jordan scored 40 against powerful Goldsboro and Anthony Teachey, who would later star for Wake Forest. Teachey blocked 17 Laney shots that night, which left Herring shaking his head after the 72–64 loss.

"Teachey was just unbelievable," he said. "Blocking 17 shots is unbelievable."

Perhaps the backstory helps to explain Jordan's 40-point outburst that night. At sixteen, he was dating a girl from Goldsboro, about two hours northwest of Wilmington, which meant overnight trips to visit her. The girlfriend, Laquetta Robinson, lived in Teachey's neighborhood, so the Goldsboro star had encountered Jordan from time to time. "He was seeing a girl, a classmate of mine, so he knew people here in Goldsboro," Teachey recalled in a 2012 interview. "He would come to Goldsboro a lot."

Even then, Jordan had a certain air about him, Teachey remembered. "He kept things close. He carried that aura about him. He carried that with him on the court, too. If he didn't know you, he was not going to hang out with you off the court. If he didn't know you, he wasn't going to hold a conversation with you."

It wasn't that Jordan was rude. He was friendly enough, Teachey recalled. "He just didn't trust a lot of people."

Jordan obviously wanted to make an impression against his girlfriend's school. The best measure of an extra spark? The star of one team scored 40 points and the star of the other blocked 17 shots. Teachey couldn't recall how many of the shots he swatted that night were Jordan's but acknowledged, "He was attacking the goal quite a bit."

Goldsboro's veteran coach, Norvell Lee, had already heard a lot from his contacts about Jordan that first varsity season, Teachey recalled with a laugh. "My high school coach said we needed to start checking him as soon as he got off the bus.... The offense that they had, he was pretty much it."

Teachey recalled Jordan talking trash that night but not directing any of it at him. "He already had the advantage as far as his talent," Teachey explained. "I think he knew that. But then the talking game, to add that in? There wasn't too much you could do because whatever he said, he did."

Jordan showed surprising polish for a first-year varsity player. "At that time I didn't see any real weakness in his game," Teachey remembered. "Somehow he had been able to open up his game at an early age. He wasn't really doing a lot of dunking. He was showing his midrange. And he had range, too. It wasn't one side or the other. It was all over the court. He could pull up or drive. He had the green light, too."

That would become more obvious with each succeeding game. Jordan rang up 26 two nights later in another loss, their second to rival New Hanover. Again, he was the only Laney player in double figures. Next, lowly Jacksonville beat them on a made free throw after time expired. Jordan scored 17 but made only 7 of 14 free throws on a night that the entire team shot 36 percent from the line.

Bill Guthridge, whose keen eye for talent Dean Smith prized, went down to Wilmington in early 1980 to see what all the fuss was about, but by the time he could scout Jordan, the Laney Buccaneers had slipped into their losing streak and Jordan himself had gone a bit adrift. Guthridge watched him clang a number of long jumpers and reported back to Smith that this particular prospect had ample athleticism and superior quickness and had played very hard throughout the game, but that he had spent much of the time jacking up shots that reduced his efficiency. Guthridge told Smith that Jordan was "unmilked." Still, it was decided that Jordan was obviously an ACC-level talent and that Carolina would need to see more of him. Smith never liked for his recruiting targets to become public knowledge, and that was true with Jordan as well, although the excitement of their apparent discovery did leak out.

Art Chansky, who was covering Carolina for a local newspaper, was a close friend of assistant coach Eddie Fogler. "Even though I was a newspaper guy I kept things confidential that they told me," Chansky recalled. "I knew that he was on their radar and that they thought he was a lot better than he thought he was. Michael was just hoping to get a scholarship somewhere. He was thinking about going into the Air Force. That's what kind of late bloomer he was. He was just flying under the radar at Laney. When Carolina started to recruit guys, not only did everybody else start paying attention, but the kid's ratings would start going up in all the recruiting ratings. Sometimes it would backfire on a kid because everybody thought he was great and he didn't turn out to be that good."

Roy Williams, a Carolina graduate assistant, had first been assigned to scout Jordan but couldn't do it due to a conflict. Apparently Williams tipped one source that the Tar Heels had some interest in Jordan. He phoned Brick Oettinger, a friend who covered recruiting for an ACC tip sheet.

"Roy told me I had to keep the tip secret because Coach Smith didn't want the media people talking about him," Oettinger recalled many years later. "He told me 'There's this guy named Mike Jordan at Laney. Coach Guthridge has been to see him three times. He does 360-degree dunks like it's nothing.'"

Jordan wasn't aware of the small buzz that had been generated among the recruiting writers. In fact, he hadn't learned that North Carolina was scouting him until after Guthridge's visit. Herring didn't tell Jordan, most likely because he didn't want to make his star player nervous. When Jordan did learn of the visit, he was both surprised and excited, and got a boost to his confidence, which had sagged a bit with his midseason shooting struggles.

"I never thought I'd be able to play Division I ball," he said of that period in his development. "I was really happy and enthusiastic that they were even interested. I was happy someone was interested."

Part of his difficulties on the court had come from the fact that opposing coaches had begun devising plans to contain him. As word spread, Jordan encountered far more defensive attention from opponents than he had earlier in the season. Jordan found himself facing ever-bigger challenges as opponents adjusted to his play. The answer to the question of his ability would lie in how well he adjusted to the adjustment, so to speak. As January became February in 1980, Jordan showed that he was adjusting quite well, that he could still produce big efforts in the face of additional defenders.

He had just crossed the first big hurdle of his career. The use of videotape for scouting had yet to become prominent in basketball at any level, so the opposing coaches in the Coastal Plain's Division II conference could work only from memory and play charts that first varsity season. Still, Jordan had given them and North Carolina's coaches plenty to see. Later, as he advanced into college and professional basketball, his performances would send opponents more and more into the film room to study his game, to look for a means of containing him.

The accounts vary between Dean Smith and Roy Williams as to exactly how the Carolina staff felt about Jordan after watching him that first time. "Bill Guthridge is an outstanding judge of talent," Dean Smith later recalled. "And after seeing Michael the first time, he said he was an ACC player, but we weren't sure we would go after him." On one thing the various accounts agree—the Carolina coaches wanted to get him into Smith's camp that summer to see just how good he might be.

Jordan's performance over the final weeks of the 1980 season gave them no reason for pause. With their seventh victory against five losses, Laney High headed out to visit Southern Wayne with Robinson and Exum. Jordan was ill and lay quietly in the back of the bus, which assistant coach Ron Coley would recall seventeen years later after Jordan fought off illness to lead the Bulls to a win over the Utah Jazz in an NBA Finals game. In 1980, he was just gaining the first sense of his tremendous ability to focus, and how certain setbacks, such as illness or some particular slight, could send that focus to even higher intensity.

Herring went to a slow-down offense that night, which almost allowed the Buccaneers to pull off the upset before falling 36–34. Jordan scored just 7 points (including two at the end of the game on a meaningless heave) as most of the points came inside from Shiver and Smith.

From there, Laney added a win over Hoggard, and then took on Kinston in a back-and-forth affair. With a minute to go and the score tied at 51, Herring called a time-out and put his team in the four corners offense to spread the floor. This time, however, there was something different. Larry Jordan was off the bench with the ball in his hands, and when he saw his opening he drove down the middle of the lane and scored on a layup. JORDAN BROTHERS DUMP KINSTON, read the headline the next morning in the *Wilmington Star-News*.

"Larry Jordan came off the bench and did well," Herring told sportswriter Chuck Carree. "Game experience has been his only problem."

Larry's younger brother helped the cause with 29 points.

Next, they lost at New Bern, then faced Goldsboro and Anthony Teachey again, this time in Wilmington. It didn't matter. Jordan still struggled against his girlfriend's hometown. He scored just 2 points in the first half. He recovered with 15 in the final two quarters, which drove their comeback from 15 down. The Buccaneers caught up but couldn't close it out, which left Herring complaining afterward that he was tired of getting overwhelmed by Goldsboro. The loss dropped Laney's record to 9–9 on the season and put in peril their hopes for a first-round home game in the playoffs.

After that was their final showdown with rival New Hanover in Wilmington. New Hanover coach Jim Hebron had studied Jordan and set up his defense accordingly. Laney's last four games of the season, though, would reveal just how much Herring's team had grown. The coach rebalanced Laney's attack. Jordan scored 21 as

New Hanover's lineup collapsed on him, but he had far more help, with Shiver adding 17 and Mike Bragg 16.

"Pop deserves a lot of credit," Hebron said after Laney got the win.

Two nights later, Shiver scored 24 to go with Jordan's 18, as Laney defeated Jacksonville in Wilmington. That was followed by a Valentine's Day victory over Eastern Wayne in which Jordan discovered a rhythm that would become familiar to him over the years, what he would come to call "the math" of big games. He scored 15 of his team's 22 points in the second period, then added 7 more in the third and 11 in the fourth to finish with a school-record 42 points. The performance had a little bit of everything—jumpers, transition baskets, a couple of dunks. Best of all, it hadn't turned his teammates into spectators. Shiver, who was learning to find his scoring opportunities alongside his "horse," finished with 14.

Acting on Roy Williams's tip, basketball writer Brick Oettinger went to see Laney's big win over Eastern Wayne in February 1980. "Jordan was just fabulous," Oettinger recalled. "He was out of sight. When you saw him play, it was like, 'How could this guy not have even made the team the year before?" In fact, Oettinger turned to his friends that night and said, "The coach had to have been an idiot." Oettinger was clearly excited: "I wrote in our next issue—February of 1980—that 'You probably haven't heard the name Mike Jordan, but he has the best combination of athleticism, basketball skills, and intangibles of any high school wing guard that I've ever seen.'"

The victory allowed Laney to secure third place in the 4A Division II conference, the state's highest classification. "Goldsboro and Southern Wayne are two of the best teams in the state, and there's no disgrace finishing behind them," Herring told the *Star*. For Laney, the finish meant a home game to open the district tournament. Jordan came out aggressively and quickly found foul trouble, so he watched as his teammates again demonstrated their balance. Shiver scored 17, Jordan 20, Leroy Smith 13, and Mike Bragg 9 to beat Hoggard.

Laney then traveled to Dudley, to take on Southern Wayne, one of North Carolina's top-ranked teams with a 21–2 record, in the

District II semifinal. Southern Wayne would go on to win the state championship that year, and Lynwood Robinson would be named MVP of the tournament. The Buccaneers almost derailed Southern Wayne's championship run that night by playing a tight 1-2-2 zone that allowed them to push the issue to overtime. Southern Wayne coach Marshall Hamilton threw a furious mix of defenses into the effort of stopping Jordan, using triangle and two, diamond and one, man-to-man, even a full-court press, anything to keep pressure on him. Jordan shook it all off in the first half to score 12 points, but the changing defenses began to take their toll over the second half and the overtime, when Jordan managed just 6 points. Hamilton's strategy worked and his team survived the tense affair, 40–35. Laney's season ended at 13–11. The final game, however, documented Jordan's growing maturity.

"We have so much trouble matching up with Jordan, but everybody does," Hamilton observed afterward. "The thing that makes him so good is that he's so patient. We could hurt someone like that if all he did was shoot because we could force him into bad shots. Jordan just doesn't take any."

He had averaged 24.6 points and 11.9 rebounds on the season. "What more can I say about Michael?" Herring told the *Star-News* after the season. "He's as good a player as I've seen through here since the New Hanover state championship year in 1968. I think he's going to be great. He's already a great shooter and scorer, and he doesn't think the world revolves around Michael Jordan."

Better yet, the coach had started to gain a sense that he was helping Jordan build a future. "Coach Guthridge has watched him," Herring pointed out, "so the big schools know he's around."

Chapter 8

THE TRANSFORMATION

MICHAEL JORDAN HAD felt isolated his sophomore year, worried that he hadn't made many real friends in the much larger school. He was an outgoing jokester, but inside he struggled with the uncertainty that so many fifteen-year-olds feel. His self-doubt had been compounded by his inability to make the varsity basketball team that first year at Laney. "You know how kids worry and think," he said later, looking back on the fact that his sudden height also played a role in his self-image. Already thin, he had become almost bladelike with the growth. "I was really lanky, really tall, so I stood out. That can present problems when you're a kid."

There was a sense then that even when people smiled or joked with him they were somehow laughing at him. Others saw it differently, however. "Laney seemed like a family back then," Leroy Smith recalled. "It had about a 60-40 white-to-black ratio, but it was really cool. No tension or anything. It was a new school. For there to be no real 'sides'—that was unusual. Mike being Mike, he was unusual, too. We all were searching for an identity. But Mike... it was like he'd already found his."

Nonetheless, Jordan seemed to think that he was hopeless socially. "I always thought I would be a bachelor," he remembered. "I couldn't get a date.... I kidded around too much. I always used to play around with women. I was a clown. I picked at people a lot. That was my way of breaking the ice with people who were very serious. I was good in school. I'd get As and Bs in my classes but I'd get Ns and Us in conduct because I was kidding around, talking all the time."

His older sister recalled a loving, upbeat Michael during this period. She was now married and somewhat distanced from the family. In those days, he was often the one who reached out to her. He looked up to her husband and enjoyed spending time with her family. She had two children, whom Michael adored. He had long had an easy way with children. Where other boys his age might have been indifferent to these delicate little creatures, he delighted in them almost from the very start, sweeping them up in his arms as they grew into toddlers. "He likes kids," his father would explain later. "I guess because kids theoretically are active people. And Michael is pretty active. He has completely spoiled my daughter's two kids to death." Even the younger children in the neighborhood were attracted to him and would drop by just because Michael was a ready playmate, his father explained.

In some ways, it wasn't just that he loved children. He was eager to please and just wanted attention from anyone who would give it. It quickly became clear to him during and after that junior season that basketball could deliver attention like nothing else he had attempted. His rapid elevation as a varsity star meant that everywhere he went in Laney's hallways he was now met with smiling faces and comments about his play. It transformed his status — from a life on the margins to big man on campus — in a way that most teens can only dream about. He would attribute it all to the strength of the group dynamics on the team.

"Before I started playing basketball in high school, I didn't have a lot of friends," Jordan said that April, looking back on his first electric season. "It helped me to get to know people. I love my teammates. They have helped me and I have helped them.... Teamwork. That's what counts. I've found that as you get better and better in athletics, you make friends or meet people that are better and better people. You make better friends." He couldn't have gotten better without the people around him, he said. "I would like to give my coaches and teammates credit for it."

Although he was only seventeen at the time, his off-the-cuff comments reflected a significant understanding of the impact of the things that were happening to him. Thirty years later, there would be many people who, upon hearing his harsh comments during his induction to the Hall of Fame, surely wished that he had remembered those words of wisdom as a teen. But so many challenges lay ahead, and to meet them, he would turn time and again to his talisman, the diamond-hard disappointment that he seemed to wear around his neck.

His favorite subject in school was math, and it was in math class that this youthful change was most dramatic, according to Janice Hardy, who taught him first algebra and later trigonometry. "The first year I had him, he was scared to death. I liked that. The next year he wound up in the front row. He'd laugh at my jokes and muss my hair."

He had longed for popularity, and when it came, it seemed he couldn't get enough of it, hurrying to fill the part of his life that wasn't consumed by sports. "He could never be in his room by himself," his mother remembered. "He always had to go out, spend the night with a friend, go camping."

Deloris Jordan greeted Michael's success with quiet enthusiasm, although it wasn't entirely clear whether her dominant emotion was relief or joy. Whatever the root, the product was a blossoming pride. Her youngest child, Roslyn, had turned to academics to earn parental approval. The younger daughter, who was close with her mother, had a secret plan to finish high school a year early so that she could graduate with Michael and head off to college at the same time. Not surprisingly, her efforts stirred Michael's competitiveness, and while he couldn't match Roslyn's showing, the circumstances helped him register solid grades, which made him all the more appealing to the colleges that would soon vie to recruit him.

Easily the biggest difference between Michael and his younger sister was that no newspaper reporters showed up to interview the family when Roslyn made the honor roll. Michael's growing prowess would stir the media's inquisitiveness about his upbringing over the coming years, and Deloris Jordan was ready to answer their questions. She would talk proudly about the record of her younger children. "They knew that they had to come straight home after school," she told a Wilmington writer. "They could have no visitors in the house until their parents got home. They got off the bus, came in and got a sandwich, and did their homework....Academics were always very important. But you've also got to be involved with your children. You can't just bundle them up and send them off. You have to support them, go to the PTO meetings, and learn as much about them and what they're doing as you can. All they're searching for is love and attention. We kept together a lot. We knew where they were all the time and who they were associating with."

She was clearly proud of the effort with her brood. But Deloris Jordan's sense that she and her husband had raised two families gained clarity in this period. Often at odds with her older daughter, Deloris had watched Sis's life blow up in family conflict. And oldest son Ronnie had faced his own conflicts with James, which may well have played a role in his hurrying off to the Army. Maturing children have always sought escape from the watchful eye of their parents, but given the divisions in the Jordan household it seems no surprise that their children were looking to be elsewhere. The Jordans had brought abundance to the lives of their offspring, yet it was hard to avoid the fact that escape had become a theme in their lives.

If there was any mystery in all of this, it was Deloris Jordan's relationship with her own parents. She rarely mentioned her upbringing in her many interviews over the years, or even in her book, but her children readily acknowledged their mother's awkwardness with her widowed father. James and Deloris usually drove right past his house in Pender County on their way to the many visits with Ms. Bell and Medward. When they did stop to visit with Edward Peoples, Sis remembered a cold and intimidating atmosphere in the house.

Medward Jordan had his own brand of intimidation, but it was nothing like the apparent gulf between Deloris and Edward Peoples. It seems likely that she was dealing with her own history of fatherly disapproval. At the very least, the circumstances in the Peoples household had been difficult with her pregnancy and subsequent departure.

However, there was no question that her discipline and high expectations for her younger children were drawn from her family background. The Peoples had employed this same singleness of purpose in grinding out their hard-won success in the unforgiving business of farming. Edward Peoples's accomplishments perhaps seem trivial compared with the wealth his grandson would amass, but when considered in terms of degree of difficulty, his rise through the harsh challenges of sharecropping to own and manage his own land was an immense feat.

Something in that process had led to a mysterious estrangement, and not just from her father. Over the coming years, as the Jordans were drawn into the magical world of their youngest son's success, Sis observed that they seemed to harbor a growing embarrassment about the homespun nature of James's parents as well, of all the older generation that had come up on the land. It was almost as if James and Deloris were trying to put the world of Teachey and Rocky Point behind them.

James and Deloris Jordan were also being tugged in another direction, drawn into their son's shared sports dream. This was a family that would go anywhere and do anything to pursue a sports opportunity for their children. Such behavior would become a prominent feature of family life at the end of the century, but the Jordans were well ahead of the curve. The games themselves would become a powerful drug, riveting the family's attention with the anticipation, the thrill of competition, and the afterglow. They'd immediately be eager for the next game, for the whole thing to start all over again.

They were perhaps the original helicopter parents.

It became a happy addiction in those first months of the uptick. They'd been obsessively following their kids in sports for years, and now here was the sign of a big payoff. They'd been through the highs of Michael's Little League baseball only to fall to reality with the Babe Ruth competition. But basketball seemed to be the real thing. Coaches from the University of North Carolina had come calling. Feedback like that allowed them to imagine the future. The Carolina coaches had invited Michael to their summer camp. It all smelled very good, except for one little matter.

James Jordan's priority as a parent that spring was to get his youngest son to accept the idea of work. He had badgered Michael about it relentlessly. It was an embarrassment for the entire family. Deloris fretted and worried about it, too, until she came up with the notion of asking H. L. "Whitey" Prevatte for some help. He was a nice man, a customer at the bank where she worked. He owned a hotel and restaurant. So she asked about a job for her son.

"I can't say enough about his mother," Prevatte recalled. "She was a bank teller and we used to do business there. She called and asked if there was anything Michael could do here."

"I was a hotel maintenance man," Jordan remembered. "I was cleaning out pools, painting rails, changing air-conditioner filters, and sweeping out the back room." The job paid Michael minimum wage, $3.10 an hour. Who could have imagined that the one and only paycheck stub of his entire working career, a slip from Whitey's for $119.76, would one day wind up in a display case at the Cape Fear Museum in Wilmington as part of its Jordan collection?

"That thing has sent me a lot of business," Prevatte would confide to a reporter years later. "I had people from Germany come in here one time asking about him because they saw the stub at the museum."

Prevatte remembered Jordan as a nice kid who carried himself well, but for several reasons, the job didn't work, perhaps most importantly because it involved pool maintenance. Jordan simply didn't do water, never having forgotten the drowning of his young friend as a child.

"We were out wading and riding the waves coming in," he would recall years later. "The current was so strong it took him under and he locked up on me. It's called the death lock, when they know they're in trouble and about to die. I almost had to break his hand. He was gonna take me with him.... He died.

"I don't go into the water anymore.... Everybody's got a phobia for something. I do not mess with water."

It was also the sweeping and cleaning. Jordan admitted later to the shallowest of excuses, that he feared friends would see him and tease him.

He wanted no part of it, making his parents, particularly James, furious. That didn't matter. "He tried to change me," Jordan recalled, "but it never worked....I quit after a week...

"I said, never again. I may be a wino first, but I will not have a nine-to-five job."

Here's to You, Miss Robinson

What Michael did have that spring was that jewel of teen expectation, the junior-senior prom. Laquetta Robinson did not attend Laney but lived in Goldsboro. Although she suffered from childhood arthritis and wore leg braces, she was a cheerleader for rival Southern Wayne High. She first thought he was making fun of her. In those days before texting they corresponded by the US Postal Service. Jordan wrote her many letters, each of them dashed off on notebook paper, as he sat bored in one class or another. She kept them all, as teenage girls are known to do, and years later two of the letters would appear on the collectors' market after allegedly being purloined by one of her relatives. One of them surfaced in 2011 and sold for five thousand dollars, but when Laquetta complained, it was returned by the auction house, although not before the content made swift rounds across the Internet.

It revealed Jordan's awkward, somewhat careless attempts at the emotional expression common to so many teenaged males. "I was really happy when you gave me my honest coin money that I won off the bet," he wrote one day from his advanced chemistry class. "I want to thank you for letting me hold your annual. I show it to everyone at school. Everyone think you are a very pretty young lady and I had to agree because it is very true. Please don't let this go to your head. (smile) I sorry to say that I can't go to the game on my birthday because my father is taking the whole basketball team out to eat on my birthday. Please don't be mad because I am trying get down there a week from Feb. 14. If I do get the chance to come, please have some activity for us to do together."

The young Jordan seemed quite ardent in expressing his love, yet like any young suitor he made sure to leave himself escape routes should it turn out that his feelings were unrequited. As soon as the letter appeared in 2011, Laquetta Robinson was interviewed by a variety of television crews. She was guarded in her comments, making it clear that she was appalled by the violation of her privacy. Police reports of the incident confirmed that it was not she who sought to profit from the letters. She did reveal that young Mike would often compliment her, only to take it back moments later, telling her in the process, "Don't let it go to your head." And the revelation about their undisclosed bet and his excitement at extracting "coin money" from her afterward suggests that his gaming instincts evolved early in his life, right along with his competitiveness.

Their prom photo is a highlight of their months together. They attended in all white, she in a proper dress that rose high and tight around her delicate neck, with three-quarter sleeves that allowed her to display proudly the white wrist corsage he had bought her. Most telling was the hair. She parted it simply, right down the middle, no frills, no stacks, no bouffant, revealing her bright eyes, splendidly high cheekbones, and the open, honest smile of a gentle soul. She looked completely relaxed, seated with her hands folded contentedly across her lap. She gave the appearance of someone utterly lacking in pretension, and this at an age when young people—including Jordan himself—tended to assume poses. He stood tall beside her in white tails, one hand resting on her shoulder, the other thrust in his pocket, his youthful attempt at sophistication. The evening tie, even the carnation in his lapel, were white, and the tux, the collar of his shirt, were both too big for him. His smile, meanwhile, if it was that, was restrained, as if to say the moment was okay, but he had much bigger plans for himself. This memory ultimately would be like so many others for Jordan, not a recollection of how much fun they'd had, but more a sense of marking time, that he was on his way to somewhere else. He didn't know where just yet, but he very much wanted to know. He already had begun to acquire that sense of purpose where a lot of the common business of life was really just filling in gaps. Unless he was playing basketball. Or baseball.

Michael played for Laney that spring and earned all-city honors as a right fielder on a team that was coached by Pop Herring. He had gained strength and confidence, but he was being evaluated differently, too, by a coach who understood his athleticism. He also pitched for Laney, although David Bridgers seemed to be the ace of the staff. Jordan would struggle some afternoons on the mound, but he had good stuff and triumphant moments to go with the losses. Beyond that, he had a bat, which he put to work right from the start.

He went four for four and drove in three runs as Laney pounded Southern Wayne 9–2 to open the season. He pitched against Hoggard in the second game and got shelled as he struggled with control and gave up a number of walks. He suffered a similar fate two games later on the mound against New Hanover.

"He didn't have a lot of velocity and can throw harder than this," Herring remarked after Jordan gave up six runs in a sixth inning that sank the Buccaneers. Laney then lost the next game to Jacksonville despite Jordan's two-run double in the seventh inning.

Against Southern Wayne he gave up seven hits before being pulled in the seventh inning of another loss. Laney finally got a win against Kinston as Jordan delivered an RBI single. Three days later at home against Kinston, Jordan scored the winning run and turned in a three-hit pitching performance that rewarded Herring's patience. He moved to center field and earned another RBI in a narrow loss against New Bern, then returned to the mound against Goldsboro to deliver another three-hit victory, his second against four losses.

That was followed by his third win, 6–1, against Jacksonville, as Jordan allowed no hits over five innings and struck out seven. Early in the game, he lost focus after disagreeing with the umpire's calls. Herring removed him, let him sit a couple of innings to calm down, then put him back on the mound (allowed under high school rules) and watched him close out the win.

He had two hits, including a solo homer, but he took a loss for the final game of the season in Goldsboro when he came on in relief and gave up the winning run. Laney finished 8–8 in Division II and 9–11 overall.

The baseball season only confirmed what had become clear during varsity basketball that year. Herring, the coach who would harvest so much contempt for "the cut" over the coming years, was absolutely focused on his young star's development.

In late April, Chuck Carree had written a column in the *Star-News* Sunday sports section with a headline that read LANEY'S JORDAN: VERSATILE PREP STANDOUT. Herring talked extensively about Jordan: "I think he's just an outstanding athlete, period. As a sophomore, he led the JV football team in interceptions. He chose not to play varsity football. It was a strictly family decision that he not play. Mike's a great basketball player. He's got to be one of the top five players in the state. In my book, Jordan's a high school All-American. There aren't enough words to describe him on the floor. I don't think anybody can guard him one-on-one. When he's had low-scoring games, it's because it was a slow-tempo game."

Jordan had even found time to do a little jumping for the Laney track team that spring. "I love to jump," he told Carree. "That's what I do in track. I love baseball. It's my number one sport. I want to play both baseball and basketball in college. I believe basketball would be my number one priority, though, in college. I'd go basketball first and then try to walk on in baseball if I didn't get a scholarship in both. I plan to get advice from my parents and coaches."

At seventeen, he had a clear notion of what he wanted—and he wasn't reluctant about expressing it publicly. "If I have an opportunity, I'd go pro as long as I get my education in college," he offered. "My goal is to be a pro athlete. My other goal is to just make it in college."

Jordan would continue his relationship with Laquetta Robinson through his freshman year of college. "He was all macho in front of other people," she recalled in a 2014 interview. "But around me he was sensitive. He wrote poems."

That was not information that hard-nosed Michael Jordan would have wanted his opponents to know.

Chapter 9

THE FIVE-STAR

DEAN SMITH AND his coaching staff got a better look at Michael Jordan early that summer of 1980 at their camp. They took a good look at his parents, too. James and Deloris visited the camp and met Smith and his assistants, allowing both parties to bask in an early mutual admiration. Even so, the recruiting of Wilmington's undiscovered star left both parties unsure of what to make of each other.

The room assignments at Dean Smith's camp suggest that the coaches had a growing interest in Jordan, although the signals were mixed. Jordan and Leroy Smith, young black men from the Coastal Plain, were housed with Buzz Peterson and Randy Shepherd, white teammates from Asheville, in the mountains at the western end of the state. Peterson, who would be named North Carolina's Mr. Basketball in his senior year, was already a prime recruiting target for the Tar Heels, as was Lynwood Robinson. Peterson was a veteran of Smith's camps from previous years. He and Jordan began a friendship that first week that would grow over the coming months. But it was Shepherd who was placed in a group with Jordan for drills and competition. He was soon reporting to Peterson each evening about the Wilmington guard's astounding feats. This was a type of player he'd never seen, Shepherd told Peterson. Each day his amazement grew, until by the fourth day he commented that surely Jordan had the kind of talent that would take him to the NBA.

The Carolina coaches were seeing the same things. What Brick Oettinger saw only confirmed his impression of Jordan from the Laney game in February. "Lynwood Robinson was at that session," Oettinger recalled. "Buzz Peterson was there, but Michael Jordan was clearly the best player there. He was out of sight." Roy Williams reported to the coaching staff that Jordan was the best six-foot-four player he had ever seen. "Very few people knew about him at that time," Williams later recalled. "Michael came and he just destroyed everybody in the camp."

Williams's job at the camp was managing the ebb and flow of the various age groups during the brutal heat that week, so that each group was able to move off the outdoor courts and get some time on the big floor in air-conditioned Carmichael Auditorium, where the Heels played their games.

After watching Jordan perform in some drills, Williams invited him back to play with the next group of older players coming through the gym. The coach would later recall that Jordan kept sneaking back into succeeding groups for more work that evening. The coaches saw that as proof that he loved to compete just as much as he liked the air conditioning.

When the sessions ended each day, the four roommates found an easy time hanging out with each other. Jordan and Peterson, in particular, formed a friendship based on the fact that both players now realized they were being recruited by the Tar Heels. While Shepherd and Smith had come to the camp with some hope that Carolina might be interested in them, the week confirmed that their games were better suited for smaller schools. Indeed, Leroy Smith would end up playing college basketball at UNC–Charlotte and Shepherd at UNC–Asheville.

Although Robinson and Peterson were high priorities for Dean Smith's program, by the end of the camp it seemed that Jordan was moving much closer to the top of the coaching staff's list. Dean Smith had taken the time to eat two separate meals with him at the camp, which, combined with Smith's visit with Jordan's parents, had given the coach more confidence that this kid from Wilmington was the kind of person who would fit in well in the structured basketball program.

As excited as he was by the response, Jordan was not completely sold on North Carolina. An NC State fan, he had disliked UNC for so many years, and while he would eventually come to revere Dean Smith, there was something in the coach's controlling approach that left both Jordan and Herring a bit wary.

"He tried to keep me hidden," Jordan recalled of Smith.

At this critical juncture in the recruiting process, Herring stepped forward with a subtle move that would open up Jordan's options. One evening at the Carolina camp, Herring mentioned to Roy Williams that he would like to get Jordan more exposure and was thinking of trying to get him into Howard Garfinkel's Five-Star in Pittsburgh or Bill Cronauer's B-C camp in Georgia, the two main destinations for top-flight talent in the days before the grading of high school talent became big business.

Williams understood that Smith didn't want word to get out about Jordan, but even as a young assistant he was aware of the need to establish trust with a high school player's family. Williams agreed to help Herring, apparently without Smith's approval, although others would later question that.

"He asked me what I thought," Williams said of Herring. "I said, 'I think he should go. I think it would be a great test of him. If I had my choice, I would go to the Five-Star camp.' I thought that would be better for him because it was such a good teaching camp. It wasn't just about playing games. It was teaching the fundamentals of the game of basketball."

A few days later Williams mentioned Jordan to Tom Konchalski, who helped run the Five-Star camp. Konchalski, an erudite man with excellent recall who liked to quip that the most athletic thing he had ever done was jump to a conclusion, was establishing a reputation as one of the most thorough evaluators of high school basketball talent. Years later he was quite clear about his ride with Williams that day: "Roy said, 'You know, there's a kid from North Carolina who may be a great player. We're not sure. He came to our team camp this summer, but we don't have a lot of great players there and he didn't play against a lot of great competition.'"

The two men discussed the fact that the first session of Five-Star camp, known as Pittsburgh 1, offered the stiffest collection of talent among Five-Star's weeks. "Roy said, 'I don't know if he's good enough for Pittsburgh 1,'" Konchalski recalled. Both Konchalski and Garfinkel clearly remembered that the Carolina coaches were not yet sold on Jordan. It was almost as if this kid from Wilmington was too good to be true. So Williams and Konchalski decided that Jordan would work best in Pittsburgh 2 and possibly Pittsburgh 3, the second and third sessions of the summer.

"I called Howard Garfinkel," Williams would recall, "and told him that Michael was coming and he would really be pleased with him as a player. I told Garf, 'He's going to be good enough to be a waiter.' You see, if you could wait tables, you could go two weeks for the price of one. So I did call Garf and talked about the opportunity."

Garfinkel recalled slightly different circumstances. He remembered getting a highly unusual call from Williams asking him to make room at the last minute in one of his camps for a recruit that Carolina was considering. "He introduces himself," Garfinkel said of his conversation with Williams. "We talk for a bit, and he says, 'We have a player that we think is very good. He was at our camp; he won the MVP, killed everybody, but the competition wasn't that good. So, we're not one hundred percent sure. We're like ninety-five percent sure. We want to be one hundred. Can you get him into your camp so he can play against the best players in the country?'"

Never in all his decades of running camps had Garfinkel ever gotten such an unusual request. After all, Williams was merely a graduate assistant at Carolina. At first, Garfinkel didn't think he could fit Jordan in at the last minute, but Williams almost insisted that he get it done. This was Dean Smith's program calling, so Garfinkel relented and moved things around to create a spot for Jordan in the second week of his Pittsburgh camp. He even worked it out so that Jordan could attend the camp at a reduced cost by working on the camp's wait staff. Garfinkel later heard that Smith was upset about Jordan going to the camp, but the camp owner said he never bought that story. "I mean why would Roy Williams call me and push this so strong if Dean Smith didn't want him to go?" While there was nothing wrong or illegal about it, apparently the Carolina coach didn't want to be identified as the person making it happen.

If anything, the circumstances revealed the tortured thinking of college coaches when it came to recruiting. Dean Smith brought dozens of highly coveted players to his programs over the years, and did so with an unparalleled integrity. He had a reputation for never promising playing time to young athletes in order to get them to sign with the Tar Heels. In addition, Smith was very good at keeping at bay recruiting's shadow game, in which rich university alumni provided recruits and their families with cash, cars, and other illegal inducements. Other coaches and other programs may have relied on such activity, but Smith had managed to succeed in the sport with few questions about his methods.

That didn't mean, however, that Smith didn't have his quirks, one of which was an obsession with the image of his program. In a later era, Carolina's actions regarding Jordan might well have raised eyebrows at the NCAA, but they were clearly within the rules. Smith was, in fact, perturbed, according to Williams's memory. Williams recalled that he had some explaining to do: "I said, 'Coach, in my opinion, he was going to go and I was just trying to give him some guidance about what I thought would be best for him. And Michael's family really appreciated it.'"

The result was that the unknown player from Wilmington, still something of a mystery to the Carolina coaches, was headed to Five-Star's Pittsburgh 2 camp to see how he stacked up against other players from across the country, players who had actually made their varsity teams as freshmen and sophomores and distinguished themselves. The conventional wisdom was that the best young players had already been identified.

Jordan had been nervous heading into Carolina's camp, but that was nothing compared to the tension he felt over the Five-Star camp, where he would be measured against elite talent. The players in the Pittsburgh 1 session were supposedly the best, but session 2 in Pittsburgh also included seventeen high school All-Americans. On that list was Wichita's Aubrey Sherrod, whom many scouts considered the best wing guard in that class of rising high school seniors.

Jordan worried about competing against top players, but Pop Herring told him to relax, that he would be fine. Still, Jordan found it hard to relax when he first surveyed the busy scene at Pittsburgh's

Robert Morris College, where the Five-Star opened in late July. The place was packed with a throng of 150 coaches and scouts who were there with clipboards taking note of each player's flaws and assets. From eight o'clock till eleven o'clock on Five-Star's first night, the players were thrown into pickup teams to play informal games so that the coaches of the camp's twelve teams could select players.

The camp's top-level league was known as the NBA. As a newcomer, Jordan was far from guaranteed an NBA slot. It would all depend on how he played that night, on outdoor courts, his least favorite way to play the game.

"I was so nervous my hands were sweating," he recalled. "I saw all these All-Americans, and I was just the lowest thing on the totem pole. Here I was, a country boy from Wilmington."

Under the NCAA rules of the day, college coaches were allowed to participate in the All-Star camps as coaches and counselors. Brendan Malone, a smart, tough assistant at Syracuse University, had been working the Five-Star camp for several years. The previous summer, his team had included Aubrey Sherrod and a highly ranked center, Greg Dreiling, and they had won the camp championship.

Coaching the team to the camp title was an honor for the aggressive Malone, just the kind of distinction that an assistant coach needed to boost his career. For the 1980 camp, Malone again planned on drafting Dreiling and Sherrod, with his eye on another title. In particular, Malone held the first pick of wing players in the draft and knew Sherrod could provide his team the scoring it needed to win another title. But the day before the camp's opening, Malone had to return home for a brief family emergency. So he asked Tom Konchalski, his good friend, to watch the opening-night tryouts and draft the team for him. Malone left strict instructions for Konchalski to select Dreiling and Sherrod.

Konchalski was prepared to follow Malone's instructions that night—until he saw an unknown player from Wilmington. "What I remember is he had a great jump stop," Konchalski recalled. "He could stop on a dime, could really elevate, go straight up, and get really great elevation on his jump shot. There was no three-point shot in the game then, so he didn't have extended range. But he had a great midgame and a great jump stop. He would explode into his jump shot to the point that players were defending his belly button. He just was so explosive athletically."

Over the decades of Garfinkel's Five-Star camp, there had come into being a phrase for the very best of the best, the sort of extremely rare talent that just leaps out at observers. "It was what we called 'one-possession player,'" Garfinkel explained. "A one-possession player means that all you have to do is see them once."

Garfinkel was sitting in his office watching the first games through a window when he first noticed Jordan. "He goes up for the jump shot, there's three players guarding him. He goes up for a jump shot and there's nobody in the air but him. He's all alone. He's up in the air. And like that, he's spectacular." My gosh, Garfinkel thought immediately, this is a one-possession player.

Jordan, too, could sense immediately that he had something the others didn't. "The more I played, the more confident I became," he remembered. "I thought to myself, 'Maybe I *can* play with these guys.'"

Suddenly, Konchalski had a decision to make. Should he draft as Malone directed or should he take a player who was unlike any player he'd ever seen? Malone showed up early the next morning and went directly to Konchalski, who was having breakfast in the camp cafeteria. "He said, 'Show me my team,'" Konchalski recalled. "I said, 'I got number one.' And he said, 'You got Dreiling?' And I said, 'Yes.' He said, 'You got Aubrey Sherrod?' And I said, 'No.' And he said, 'What do you mean?' Aubrey Sherrod was considered the number one shooting guard in the rising senior class at that time. I said, 'I took a kid from North Carolina.'"

Garfinkel laughed as he recalled the exchange. "Brendan says, 'Who the hell is Mike Jordan?' And he goes ballistic, only he didn't say hell. He goes berserk. 'What did you do to me? Who's Mike Jordan?' Tom told him, 'Relax, relax, he's a great player.' Brendan's all steamy. He walks away. He's all pissed off."

Malone didn't remember the sequence just that way, but he did recall that it only took one look at Jordan to calm him down. "I remember the first time I saw Michael," Malone said. "We were at an afternoon game that day. Michael was on an open court, asphalt, and he was moving, and the way he moved was like a thoroughbred, his stride, just the graceful way he ran and cut. He was a standout right away. You could look at him, look at how he moved and ran. It was apparent to even a person who didn't have a sophisticated eye. It was apparent to you right away that Michael was superior to the other players in the camp or that were playing high school ball at that time."

Legend has it that a few days into the camp, Jordan scored 40 points in one half of play, all of twenty minutes.

"What really got me is that he couldn't be defended," Konchalski recalled. "Because he jumped over people, and had a nice touch.... I mean he could get his shot anytime he wanted."

Anthony Teachey from Goldsboro was also at the camp and recalled that it was Jordan's competitive nature that pushed him so far above the others. "You got the top seventy-two players in the country at the time," Teachey explained. "So everybody had their moments during that week.... He just happened to shoot up the charts that one summer."

Garfinkel realized he should phone Dave Kreider, a friend who edited Street & Smith's *Yearbook*, the major preseason publication in college basketball in that era. The magazine listed 650 high school seniors as top prospects. "Dave," Garfinkel asked, "where do you have Mike Jordan on your list?"

Kreider supposedly checked the list and reported there was no Mike Jordan, only a Jim Jordan. Garfinkel then advised Kreider to add an extra Jordan somewhere high on the list. "I called Street & Smith's to get him first or second team preseason All-American," Garfinkel said.

Kreider replied that it was too late, the magazine had already gone to press. Garfinkel told Kreider he should do something because it would be embarrassing not to have a major player like this Jordan kid listed.

"In those days they'd print it weeks ahead of time," Garfinkel recalled. "Dave told me, 'You will not see Mike Jordan's name in the top 650 players of the Street & Smith's preseason magazine.'" Kreider later revealed that his North Carolina writer for the 1980–81 edition didn't even include Jordan among the top twenty juniors in the state.

Everywhere Jordan went in the camp, Roy Williams was there, following him with a mix of anxiety and elation. "Every time we went to stations Roy Williams was at the stations watching," Malone remembered. "It was apparent North Carolina had identified him as an outstanding player even though he only played one year of varsity ball in Wilmington, North Carolina. What I truly remembered about Michael is that during that week everybody was kind of awed at his driving the ball because that's what he did best back then."

He would scissor-kick on the way to the basket, hitting an extra stride to accelerate past defenders, Malone recalled. "He was going to the basket hard. Everybody was in the lane and packing it in, trying to stop him."

Jordan led Malone's team to the NBA title that first week. "The last seconds of the championship game, I called a time-out and told them the game was on the line. I said, 'Michael, you have to take this game over.' He was very receptive to coaching. And the next defensive sequence he put his hands on the ground like he was determined to stop the guy he was guarding." That's when Malone realized that Jordan's competitiveness might be even greater than his abundant athleticism.

"He was the co-outstanding player of the week with a player named Mike Flowers from Indiana and he won the MVP of the All-Star Game, and he got several other awards," Garfinkel remembered.

Jordan was injured for part of the second week in Pittsburgh and had to sit out a number of games. "What happened was he hurt his ankle and he only played half the games," Konchalski recalled. "He ended up being the MVP of the All-Star Game for the second week in a row. He didn't get the most outstanding player. That was Lester Rowe, a kid from Buffalo who later played for West Virginia. He was about six four, six five. He won because he played the entire week."

"I got nine trophies," Jordan proudly told the *Wilmington Journal* upon his return home.

Jerry Wainwright, who was then a high school coach, had witnessed the breakout performances. At the end of the second week, when the campers had just about all cleared out, Wainwright heard a bouncing ball in the gym and found Jordan there pushing himself through full-court shooting drills. Wainwright, who would later coach at UNC–Wilmington, asked Jordan what he was doing. Wainwright recalled his reply: "Coach, I'm only six four, and I'm probably going to play guard in college. I've got to get a better jump shot."

The Five-Star camp had quickly opened a new chapter in the Jordan legend. "It was the turning point of my life," Jordan reflected.

The experience served as another reminder of how rapidly fortunes change in athletics, a truth Jordan had first learned with Babe Ruth baseball. Early success was no guarantee of anything. "Coming into Pittsburgh 1," said Tom Konchalski, "Lynwood Robinson was the guard that was North Carolina's prime target, more so even than Michael Jordan. They thought he was going to be the next Phil Ford. But he would get injured in high school. He had surgery on his knee and he was never the same player. He never had the force he once had." Dean Smith stuck by his scholarship offer for Robinson although the player never found success at that higher level. Robinson eventually transferred to Appalachian State where he played well, but never fulfilled the Phil Ford comparisons.

Jordan's biggest trophy coming out of Five-Star was a newly hatched reputation. Even his own family now saw him differently. Up until the camps, James Jordan still imagined his son's future as a baseball player. After the camps, those thoughts began to recede, Michael acknowledged to the *Wilmington Journal*. "My father really wanted me to play baseball, but now he wants me to pursue basketball." Indeed, basketball was now pursuing him, something that baseball never did, no matter how tightly his father clung to that dream.

Garfinkel began spreading the word that Jordan was one of the top ten national prospects in the high school class of 1981, which was led by a young center from Massachusetts named Patrick Ewing. Brick Oettinger ranked Jordan as the second-best rising senior behind Ewing. But analyst Bob Gibbons took it one step farther and rated Jordan the top player nationwide, even ahead of Ewing. "I had gone to several of his games during his junior year and I was there at Five-Star," Gibbons recalled. "You can't believe how I was ripped for ranking Jordan ahead of Ewing—everybody said I was taking care of a hometown boy."

The dramatically upgraded rankings brought recruiting interest from hundreds of schools. And North Carolina just as suddenly found itself competing with a variety of programs for the affection of the Chosen One. Over the years Dean Smith had learned to be cautious with recruits, but now it seemed he was going to pay a price for that.

"To me, when you see something like Jordan's talent, it stands out," Brendan Malone observed. "I'm surprised that they had to make up their minds, was he worth a scholarship? I would have pounced on him right away the first time I saw him play."

Malone later made a phone call to Wilmington in an effort to recruit Jordan for Syracuse. Despite his high regard for Malone and the experience at Five-Star, Jordan politely declined, saying his interest was elsewhere. Like many, Malone assumed that Jordan meant he was a lock for North Carolina. But Jordan's thoughts had turned away from Carolina. Part of his hesitation was driven by doubt. Everywhere he went, he encountered people in Wilmington suggesting that his eyes were bigger than his talent, especially in regard to the Tar Heels program. "The people back home, stardom was the last thing they saw for me. People said I'd go there, sit on the bench, and never get to play. I kind of believed 'em myself."

The circumstances left him musing about his options. If North Carolina was this hot after him, why not look at other schools that really interested him? Larry Brown had just coached UCLA into the national championship game. Jordan loved what he saw in the Bruins that spring. "I always wanted to go to UCLA," he explained later. "That was my dream school. When I was growing up, they were a great team. Kareem Abdul-Jabbar, Bill Walton, John Wooden. But I never got recruited by UCLA."

Known as a coaching gypsy, Brown was already looking for his next job and on his way out after just two years at UCLA; he would leave the school at the end of the 1981 season. Plus, Brown had played for and coached with Dean Smith. Jordan didn't realize it at the time, but it was unlikely that Brown would have stepped in to take away a prized local recruit from Smith.

Another option, one that wasn't disclosed publicly at the time, was the University of Virginia, where freshman sensation Ralph Sampson had just taken the Wahoos to the championship of the National Invitation Tournament in New York. Jordan could see himself fitting in well there. So he contacted the Virginia coaches. "I also wanted to go to Virginia because I wanted to play with Ralph Sampson for his last two years there.... I wrote to Virginia, but they just sent me back an admission form. No one came and watched me."

In a 2012 interview, Terry Holland, then the coach at Virginia, acknowledged Jordan's interest, adding that his coaching friend Dave Odom had been among the talent evaluators looking at Jordan during Garfinkel's camp. "I know that Dave Odom was impressed by Michael at the Five-Star camp the summer prior to his senior year," Holland recalled. "Up until then, Michael was pretty much a late bloomer. We had already committed scholarships to Tim Mullen and to Chris Mullin at that position and were in pretty big battles for both with Notre Dame, Duke, and St. John's. But it looked good for getting both so we elected to focus on them to protect the recruiting investment we had already made in them. We got Tim but lost Chris to his hometown team after a huge battle. Michael has told me that he liked our team and was hoping that we would come after him hard, but he has never indicated that he would have chosen UVA over UNC." The Virginia coach couldn't have known how unwise it would be to dismiss the Wilmington player's interest. Michael clearly kept the snub in mind for his future meetings with the Cavaliers.

Virginia's decision not to recruit Jordan would loom over the coming seasons as North Carolina and Virginia battled for supremacy in the Atlantic Coast Conference. In 1981, Virginia beat Carolina twice, and both teams met again in the semifinals at the Final Four in Philadelphia, where the Tar Heels finally prevailed.

Years later, Jordan would reveal to Sampson that he had been eager to play alongside him. The seven-four center had spent four years in college trying to win a national championship for Virginia. "It is what it is," Sampson said stoically when asked about the missed opportunity to have Jordan in a Virginia uniform. "I appreciated the teammates that I had."

Many years later, Howard Garfinkel would produce a book about his memories of running the Five-Star camp, of which the greatest was the discovery of Michael Jordan. Garfinkel had not visited with Jordan often since those summer days in 1980, but he took the book to an NBA arena one night where Jordan was playing with the plan of giving a copy to the star after the game. Garfinkel had waited a half hour in the crowd outside the locker room and was about to give up, he recalled. "All of a sudden a little kid comes running down the hall and says, 'Here he comes! Here he comes!' Sure enough down the hallway comes Michael Jordan. So I step out. I make my Jack Ruby move and I step in front of his entourage. But two of the largest cops I've ever seen are in front of him. Jordan's in the middle, and two cops are escorting him down the hallway. I step in front and the cop shoos me away. And he says, 'Don't touch him please, no autographs, no autographs.' So I step aside, and Jordan goes by. But out of his peripheral vision he sees me and yells, 'Stop! That's Howard Garfinkel! He's the reason I'm here.' That's not true, of course. I'm not the reason. But that's what he said. Swear to God."

Chapter 10

THE MICHAEL

So MANY COLLEGE campuses across the land offered the same basic mix of musty old brick buildings with the fluted columns and tree-lined sidewalks, filled with the graceful forms of coeds moving back and forth to classes. But he saw that if you lingered in Chapel Hill, there were things to be treasured—the way the fall sunlight dappled the yellow leaves of the oak trees in the quad, the sight of students lazily stretched out on the library steps with books in their laps, the thump of rubber basketballs filled with too much air beating rhythmically on the asphalt of an outdoor court. It would be the small things that he treasured as he clicked along on his bicycle at an unfettered pace in the hazy dream that was undergraduate life.

Yes, other schools offered similar allure, but there was no place that seemed to put these elements together quite like the University of North Carolina at Chapel Hill. He didn't realize it at the time of his visits in the fall of 1980, but he was selecting the place where he would spend the last days of his true freedom, before success took possession of his life.

UNC would suit him well. At least that's what he concluded after he visited there in a loud, trash-talking appearance that brought chuckles to those who remembered his skinny figure bouncing down the hallways of the athletic dorm. Patrick Ewing, a seven-foot Jamaican from Boston, the most heralded recruit in that year's senior class, met Jordan for the first time that weekend in October when they made their official visit to the Carolina campus. Years later, Ewing smiled at the memory. "He was talking a lot of junk," he recalled. "He was talking how he was gonna dunk on me. He talked smack from that moment on. He's always had that swagger."

"I remember Michael's recruiting trip well," agreed James Worthy, a Tar Heel sophomore at the time. "You heard him before you saw him." At least part of that was his youthful fear, Jordan would admit. After all, he supposedly didn't belong at Chapel Hill, according to people back in Wilmington. He had conquered Five-Star, but the fear still welled up in him as he walked into the place.

His doubts about the Tar Heels had started to fade once they showed interest in him. The bonding began with the care and concern shown by the coaches, and deepened as he experienced the place itself during his visits. He inhaled that elite air, and soaked in the great tide of soothing light blue UNC regalia that swirled everywhere and infused the place with a certain joie de vivre. It all helped him come to the conclusion that so many other top-flight athletes had reached over the years: "I could get used to this."

Patrick Ewing had thought the same thing after meeting Jordan on that first visit to Chapel Hill. Years later, the center would reveal that he was seriously considering playing for Dean Smith until he returned to his hotel that weekend and saw a Klan demonstration nearby. That chilled any thought he had of going to UNC. If not for that Klan moment, Ewing might have joined Jordan to create an all-powerful Tar Heels team, one capable of claiming multiple national championships.

Jordan may have seen the same demonstration that weekend, but if he did it never registered. The wishes of his parents carried the true weight. "His family loved North Carolina," Bob Gibbons pointed out. Just a dozen years after watching their son enter a segregated first-grade classroom in Wilmington, they now saw the state's prestigious university seeking his services. The grant-in-aid offered to attend Chapel Hill resonated with meaning for James and Deloris.

"I told Deloris, if he were my son, I'd send him to Carolina," Whitey Prevatte remembered. "That Dean Smith always impressed me as a fine man and a fine coach."

As if the Jordans needed encouragement. Already bursting with pride, they thought of their son in Carolina blue and became inflated like dirigibles for the Macy's parade. And when Dean Smith and his entourage came to their home for a visit that fall, it was, as Tom Konchalski observed with a chuckle, "like Zeus had come down from Mount Olympus." Smith had a certain way of connecting with families and parents. He was as sincere as any coach could be about academics and priorities. The Jordans sat in their living room, with Michael cross-legged on the floor, twirling a basketball. As they took in the message, he spun the ball slowly. There would be no promises made, Smith said. Jordan would have to earn it. "It was all about the education spiel at that point," explained the writer Art Chansky. "Dean knew James and Deloris were very interested in that."

From the very first moments, the Jordan family saw the hallmark of Dean Smith's style as a coach, a thorough and uncommon involvement with his players as people, even as he maintained the distance and objectivity that coaching demanded.

"Developing a relationship with Coach Smith was probably the easiest thing," James Worthy observed, "because he was just that kind of brutally honest kind of a guy, very conscious of everything. He really understood where you came from. He spent a long time getting to know your parents and what they would want for their son. And that's how he related to players.... Honesty is the best, and that's why a lot of players are attracted to that in lieu of all the recruitment and visits to college and stuff like that," Worthy added. "It's something special about someone who kind of understands you."

Despite the lack of interest from Virginia and UCLA, Jordan had entertained the advances of several schools in the region. When he visited the University of South Carolina, he accompanied coach Bill Foster to meet the governor's family and spent time shooting hoops with the governor's young son. "They weren't worried," Art Chansky said of the Carolina coaching staff, "but they kind of laughed when Bill Foster, who was at South Carolina at the time, took him to the governor's mansion for dinner. So that was the kind of shit that was going on in terms of the competition. I don't think they ever really thought he was going somewhere else."

At the University of Maryland, Lefty Driesell badly wanted to steal Jordan away from Dean Smith and tried to sell the Jordans on the idea that the new Chesapeake Bay Bridge had shortened the drive to Maryland into just about the same time from Wilmington as going to Chapel Hill. Jordan's parents merely rolled their eyes. Jim Valvano, the new coach at NC State, also made a pitch for Jordan and even played the David Thompson card. Valvano encouraged Jordan to think about channeling the high-flying days of his childhood hero.

Well before Jordan took his official visit to Chapel Hill, he had gone there on his own to look over the place thoroughly. "The Jordans came to Carolina a lot, a lot of unofficial visits," Art Chansky recalled, adding that while graduate assistant Roy Williams couldn't go on the road recruiting he was free to entertain the Jordans on campus. James Jordan and Williams became so close that the father later built Williams a wood stove for his home in Chapel Hill. But it was the official visit that finally settled things in Michael's mind. Herring was encouraging him to get the recruiting decision made before the season started, so that he could concentrate on winning a state high school championship. Jordan's recruitment also had the potential to distract his teammates, if not the entire Laney student body. "Valvano, Lefty Driesell...Roy Williams spent so much time down here, we thought he was working at Laney," teammate Todd Parker remembered. "Then Dean Smith showed up, in this powder-blue suit, and it was over. If Dean Smith shows up, Carolina really wants you."

Jordan agreed with Herring. He wanted to get the decision out of the way. "Carolina was the fourth school I visited," he recalled, "and afterwards there was no question in my mind. I committed within a week and canceled my visits to Clemson and Duke."

He made the official announcement at his home on November 1, 1980, before just two microphones supplied by local TV stations. Lynwood Robinson chose that same day to announce his own plans to attend UNC, so a lot of the attention was diverted to him. Durham sportswriter Keith Drum said at the time that Jordan would be much more important to the Tar Heels program, but the assignment editors for the various media outlets must not have gotten the memo.

The Jordans sat on the couch in the living room with the two microphones set on the coffee table in front of them, right there with the glass turtle and potted plant. With his mother on his right and his father on his left, Jordan folded his arms across his knees and leaned forward to confirm that, yes, it was Carolina after all.

His mother, who had just turned thirty-nine a few weeks earlier, sat back, her manicured hands folded where her stylish dark skirt crested her knee. She had slimmed considerably in recent years and showed the first signs of maturing into a person quite comfortable with the spotlight her son would bring. She took in his announcement with a smile expressing absolute rapture and hinting at all the effort that she had expended to get her laziest child to this moment. Seventeen-year-old Michael, meanwhile, appeared almost sleepy-eyed, looking into the klieg lights of the TV crews with a calm that would become his trademark in thousands of future interviews. The slightest trace of smile, suggesting a repressed sense of glee, fell across his face as he processed the questions and formulated his answers.

His father likewise sat back on the sofa, as if to take care not to invade his son's spotlight. His immense pride was tinged with a solemnity that day. He was obviously filled with an emotion that he made every effort to mask.

Pop Herring was there, too, standing well out of the way during the announcement but equally full of pride. The young coach and Jordan mugged for the cameras, leaning forward in tandem to measure their hands. And later, as Jordan held a white and blue Carolina ball, the coach made as if to defend him, a playfulness born of their morning workouts together in the Laney gym.

"He is like a father to us," Jordan would say of Herring in an interview with the *Wilmington Journal*. "We can go to him anytime and talk to him about anything, things that you wouldn't tell your own parents, because he's so understanding. I think that he can lead us into a championship."

Mike Krzyzewski, Duke's enterprising young coach, had hinged his hopes on Deloris Jordan's respect for the school's academics and her infatuation with former Duke star Gene Banks. Once Jordan's intentions became clear, Krzyzewski wrote Michael a letter, lamenting that he would not be joining the Blue Devils and wishing him well. The letter would resurface some years later in the Jordan room of Wilmington's Cape Fear Museum, where it was said to be a favorite display of Tar Heel fans.

Empie Park

With recruiting done, Jordan could turn his attention to his goal of winning a state championship. Laney would first have to defeat a large and physical New Hanover County team in District 1 of Southeast North Carolina's 4A classification. "He played in a league, the Mideastern Conference, that was loaded with talent," longtime Wilmington sportswriter Chuck Carree recalled.

New Hanover had long been Wilmington's main white high school, with a tradition of athletic success led by Hall of Fame coach Leon Brogden. It had a particularly strong football legacy, having produced NFL quarterbacks Sonny Jurgensen and Roman Gabriel. With the coming of integration, Williston, the city's longtime black high school, had been made into a junior high, a move so resented by the black community that it supposedly helped spark the Wilmington Ten incident.

Racial tensions had begun to ease by the time Laney was opened in 1976 and Pop Herring was hired as the city's first black head coach. No one made public comment about Herring's new status, but all eyes were watching his progress, especially when it came to the meetings between Laney and New Hanover, coached by Jim Hebron. Michael Jordan's status as a star North Carolina recruit only served to heighten the public awareness and increase the focus on Herring.

The two coaches, both in their early thirties, provided an interesting contrast of styles. The New Hanover roster for 1980–81 featured Clyde Simmons, who would later become an All-Pro defensive end for the Philadelphia Eagles of the NFL, and big man Kenny Gattison, who would star at Old Dominion University, then enjoy a solid career playing and coaching in the NBA. Gattison was a junior in the fall of 1980 and approaching six eight and 240 pounds.

Clyde Simmons was almost six six, well muscled, and quick. New Hanover's team included two other exceptional athletes who never gained fame, although they should have, Gattison recalled. "Rondro Boney was six three, 215 pounds, and ran the forty-yard dash in 4.25 seconds. When he turned the corner as a running back in football, he was gone. He had the same silhouette as Herschel Walker. Ronald Jones was a six-four wide receiver, also with great speed. He was like Jerry Rice. Those two guys should have played in the NBA or NFL."

New Hanover enjoyed a ten-win football season in 1980 with those players, who became even more intimidating when they donned basketball uniforms. By contrast, Hebron was a compact man who incessantly worked a jump rope. He loved Wilmington's beach and surfing scene second only to his coaching duties at New Hanover. His physical education classes at the school were known for their laid-back atmosphere, but Hebron was in complete command of the team he coached.

"He really was physically unimposing," remembered Gattison. "He reminded you of Dustin Hoffman. He had the most unassuming personality. He never yelled, he never screamed. But you knew the guy had your back, so whatever he asked we just did it."

While the community found Hebron interesting enough, it was Herring, the African American, who drew the quietly intense notice. "Like anything else, it was a test to see if it could work," Gattison remembered. New racial stereotypes were being hastily drawn in those first decades of integration. For example, black athletes were almost never chosen to play quarterback, a perception that only began to change in 1986–87 when Doug Williams led the Washington Redskins to a Super Bowl title. Head coaching jobs were also often reserved largely for whites. But Herring had earned his position, and had shown plenty of early promise as a head coach. His style on the sideline was animated, to say the least. "If Jim Hebron was Dustin Hoffman, Pop Herring was Fred Sanford," Gattison recalled with a laugh. "Pop was a little more fiery than Jim Hebron, I can tell you that. Those were two totally different coaching personalities. They'd put those leisure suits on and go to work during games. Those were the good ol' days, really."

Despite their size and power, Gattison and Clyde Simmons were headed into their first varsity season as juniors that fall. "In New Hanover County, you didn't play varsity sports in the tenth grade," Gattison explained. "It didn't matter who you were. When your JV season ended, if you were good enough, they allowed you to sit on the end of the varsity bench and watch."

Thus this powerful New Hanover lineup would be getting its first experience playing against Jordan in his blue and gold Laney uniform. They already knew him well, due to their many battles against him in pickup ball on the city's courts, particularly at Wilmington's Empie Park.

"It was such a close-knit community that everybody knew everybody," Gattison explained. "We always played. We played at the Boys Club. We played at Empie Park. Some of the classic games that we had were outside on asphalt at Empie Park. There was nobody there. He'd bring his guys. I'd bring my guys."

Jordan's "guys" were his regular crew of brother Larry, Adolph Shiver, Leroy Smith, and Mike Bragg. Gattison usually showed up with his New Hanover teammates — Boney, Jones, and Simmons — who had grown up together playing sports in the city's various leagues.

"We had a good mix," Gattison said of his teammates. "When it came down to sheer athleticism, Michael had the advantage at only one spot. We had the advantage at the other four. We had our battles. We'd play all day Saturday. You'd play each game to 11. Somehow at the end of those games, it seemed a lot of times that we'd be up 8–3, and then Michael would block every shot and score every point, and my team would end up losing 11–8. Whether we were playing outside at Empie Park or inside Brogden Hall with five thousand people watching, we both wanted to win."

Hebron frowned on trash talking during high school ball. Even if the coach hadn't taken that position, the New Hanover lineup was so imposing that it tended to quiet opposing teams by its mere presence. But during and after those pickup games at Empie Park the tenor could turn a bit chippy.

"Adolph talked more than Mike," Gattison recalled. "A toothpick or a straw, he always had something in his mouth. Adolph was a guy who could talk but couldn't play. When we played school ball, he's the guy who did all the talking and woofing in the layup line, but when the game started he'd pass the ball to Michael and get out of the way."

After the Five-Star camp in 1980, Jordan had returned to Empie Park with a new sense of confidence. "I'd never heard of Five-Star," Gattison recalled. "Mike goes to Five-Star and he wins every trophy up there. As usual we meet up at the gym after he comes back, and Mike tells us, 'Man, you gotta go to Five-Star.' And he said, 'We have no idea how good we are down here in Wilmington.' He said it was because we were used to playing against each other. It was true. We really didn't understand the level of talent we had on our high school teams. We could have combined those two teams and a whole lot of college teams would have had trouble matching up."

At the time, Gattison was being recruited by dozens of major colleges as a football tight end. He might well have accepted a scholarship had he and his New Hanover teammates not taken Jordan's advice the next summer. They attended a Five-Star session where Gattison attracted the attention that led to a basketball scholarship with Old Dominion and then a long NBA career.

"In that sense, I owe my career to Mike. He was right," Gattison said. "We didn't know how good we were."

One thing that both he and Jordan did know was that they were headed to a major showdown that winter of 1980–81. In fact, since the close of the Five-Star camp Jordan had eagerly awaited the opening of basketball season. He would attend Laney football games and watch his friends under the Friday night lights, but he badly wanted basketball practice to start so that he could get going and show off the things he had learned over the summer.

Still, Ruby Sutton, who taught physical education at Laney, observed that the Jordan who returned that fall didn't appear much affected by his sudden acclaim. He remained the same happy-go-lucky guy, always ready with a smile, she remembered. As the season neared, Jordan did acknowledge in an interview with the *Wilmington Journal* that he looked forward to getting a thrill from the crowd's response to his slams, especially his theatrical sorties to the basket in the open court after a steal. "It inspires me to really play," he said. His energy fed from their energy, he realized early on.

"I enjoyed it to the point that I started to do things other people couldn't do," he recalled some years later in a conversation with John Edgar Wideman. "And that intrigued me more... because of the excitement I get from the fans, from the people, and still having the ability to do things that other people can't do but want to do and they can do only through you.... That drives me. I'm able to do something that no one else can do."

His signing with Carolina drew fans from across the region to Laney games that winter, Chuck Carree recalled. "When word spread how good Jordan was, Laney had to turn fans away because the gymnasium was so small and it would have violated fire-marshal laws." Many of them wanted to be able to say they saw Mike Jordan play in high school. There were long lines to get into the Laney gym on opening night November 26, 1980. Those who got in saw Jordan score 33 points and seize 14 rebounds in a win over Pender County. It was the first of six straight wins to open the season, propelling the Buccaneers to the top ranking in the state. In the midst of this streak, Dean Smith consecrated the Buccaneers with an appearance at a game in early December. The crowd broke the Laney gym record for rubbernecking that night, according to those in attendance. The sighting convinced some of the naysayers about Jordan's suitability for North Carolina. More doubters were converted when he stacked up 9 assists to go with 26 points and 12 rebounds in a win over Kinston that same week. He also rejected 3 shots. "Jordan just hypnotized us," Kinston coach Paul Jones allowed, pointing out that his players were so focused on Jordan that they left his teammates wide open.

The true highlight of the season came in late December when Laney won the Christmas tournament at New Hanover's Brogden Hall. It proved to be a physical rematch with his playground foes, now dressed in New Hanover's black and orange uniforms. Jordan was quickly snared in foul trouble that night and watched his teammates fall behind. With less than five minutes left, Herring sent him back into the game and watched as Jordan scored 15 points in a whirlwind. "All I remember is Mike taking every shot," Gattison said. "I mean we were grabbing him, holding him, pulling his jersey, knocking him down. And he still made every shot." The game came down to a final possession that found Jordan working the ball while looking to attack the basket. Then he took off.

"I remember that shot he made in the Christmas tournament to beat us at the buzzer," Gattison said. "I had grabbed his shorts to pull him down and then his jersey and he still went up and made the shot."

For the final season, Herring had cast aside all pretension and acknowledged that his main strategy was to get the ball to Jordan and encourage him to attack the rim. That approach mostly worked, because many nights Jordan was good enough to win games by himself. But by mid-January the Buccaneers had two losses and were tied for third place in the District II standings, hardly the circumstances to build confidence for a state title.

"Laney often appears not so much a team as a group of players waiting for Jordan to happen," observed *Wilmington Morning Star* sportswriter Greg Stoda.

The theme would surface again and again over Jordan's career. His displays of athleticism were so extraordinary, teammates and opponents alike would find themselves pausing just to watch him work. "We're getting better about that, though," Herring told Stoda, adding that the team seemed to play better at times when Jordan was on the bench. "But of course I want to get the ball to him whenever possible. He's super."

Jordan himself had initiated an effort to take things in another direction, one inspired by his hero. His vanity plates now read MAGIC on the back of his car and MAGIC MIKE on the front, evidence of his wanting to perfect Magic Johnson's ability with the no-look pass. "It started one day in practice," he told Chuck Carree, "when I started doing some freaky things like Johnson does. I made some passes looking away and one of my teammates started calling me 'Magic Mike.' He bought me the license tag on the back, and my girlfriend got me a T-shirt and front license tag with 'Magic Mike' on it."

He routinely gave up the ball to teammates, an unselfishness documented by the 6 assists he averaged that senior season, yet it too often seemed that the ball was a hot potato for Laney, that his teammates were too eager to get it right back to him. "If they're open, I'm going to pass them the ball," Jordan explained to Greg Stoda. "Coach tells them to shoot and I tell them that. But I know they depend on me a lot."

New Hanover's Hebron understood the other players' reaction. "Kids are awed by him," the coach acknowledged. "They're intimidated. Several coaches have told me that he's the best high school player on the East Coast. I've seen him walk into a gym for a pickup game and everyone else stopped playing. This might sound weird, and a lot of people won't understand, but some kids are just happy to be on the floor with him. He'll go to Carolina and then maybe to the pros. Kids will be able to say that they played against him or on the same team as he did."

"He was evolving right in front of our face," Gattison explained. "It wasn't about studying him, because he did something new and different every game. He found a new way to beat you every game. Athletically, he was doing things that nobody had seen. He'd jump and the rest of us would jump with him, but we'd come back down to earth. It didn't take long to realize he was cut from a different piece of cloth than the rest of us."

Jordan buttressed those observations by averaging 27.8 points and 12 rebounds in carrying Laney to a 19–4 record that season. The total included three different wins over New Hanover during the regular schedule. Each defeat had left Gattison and his teammates vowing not to lose again to Mike Jordan. They would have one last chance in their fourth meeting that season, in the district semifinals, the game that would determine which team went on to the state tournament. Played in Laney's gym, this deciding game seemed well in hand for Jordan and his teammates, who were up 6 points with under a minute to go.

"We had been down as many as 10 or 11 points with a minute and forty seconds to go," Gattison remembered. "There was no shot clock. All they had to do was dribble out the clock to close it out. Somehow we came back to win that game. To this day, I don't remember what happened in the last two minutes. They could have dribbled the whole clock out. Somehow we created turnover after turnover. It involved trapping Mike in some kind of way."

Gattison would later wonder how they could have pulled off all of the pressing and trapping without fouling more.

"On their home court?" he asked.

With seven seconds to go, the score was tied at 52 when Jordan made a move and launched a jumper. He was called for an offensive foul on the play, his fifth, which sent him to the bench, fouled out. The home crowd sat stunned. Gattison himself recalled being surprised at such a foul being called in the final seconds on Jordan's home court.

New Hanover made the free throws to advance. The sudden turn of events left the crowd in a surly mood, not uncommon in high school basketball on the Coastal Plain. Just that season, New Hanover had won in Goldsboro, Gattison said. "I remember playing a game over in Goldsboro, where Anthony Teachey went to high school. You beat those guys on their court, we had to stay in the locker room until the police physically could come and get us out."

The game at Laney involved far more familiarity and shouldn't have been as threatening. "People knew each other," Gattison explained. But Hebron was bumped by Laney fans walking off the floor. "When we won that game, we went in the locker room, and coach said, 'Forget your showers. Get your stuff and let's get out of here,'" Gattison said. "The referees were really who they were after, but there were no showers that night."

As for Jordan, the unexpected end to his high school career was a profound disappointment. He had badly wanted to win a state championship. "He was really obviously dejected," Gattison said. Equally disappointed, Herring likewise had little to say that night, except for this: "We reached for the moon and landed on the stars."

In an interview almost thirty years later, Gattison's memory of the final game was still laced with regret. Although they would encounter each other many times throughout their careers, Gattison explained in 2012 that he had never once mentioned that final game in Wilmington to Jordan, no matter how relaxed or informal the occasion. Even after Jordan had won many pro championships and it would seem that the pain had long eased, Gattison still considered the subject far too sensitive to broach. Likewise, Jordan would never mention it again either.

And the players from the two teams would never again gather at Empie Park to go at each other. It was as if the moment had poisoned the innocent competition of their youth. They all knew how much it mattered to Jordan.

"You got to understand what fuels that guy, what makes him great," Gattison said. "He took the pain of that loss ... for most people the pain of loss is temporary. He took that loss and held on to it. It's a part of what made him. And it made me. He beat me three times, two of those were in my own gym. Then we win the fourth game and to this day I still feel bad about it."

A few days after the loss to New Hanover, Herring boldly projected that North Carolina would win a national championship with Jordan in the lineup. But not many months afterward, the coach would begin his dark descent into mental illness.

"Pop went years with people trying to help him," Gattison said of the bizarre reversal. "Everybody tried to do what they could. He just went years without the proper diagnosis, so he went years without the proper treatment. He just really spiraled down so fast. It was so debilitating mentally. The guy who was standing on the sidelines with all this fire in him, he became a ghost. Some years later, if you ran into Pop on the street, you didn't know which Pop you were going to be talking to. It was very sad. Mental disease is such a traumatic thing."

Even so, Gattison said that Herring's legacy as a coach was Jordan's career, not because he kept Jordan off the varsity as a sophomore, but because of the many thoughtful decisions he made on Jordan's behalf. "Back then in high school ball it was almost an automatic. If you were six four, you were considered a big man," Gattison said. "You were considered a center or a power forward and played close to the basket. But Pop had the wherewithal to really understand what Michael's talents were and to put him out on top of the floor at the guard position."

So many tall players in high school are never allowed to develop as guards, and they often become "tweeners" in basketball jargon. "A lot of tweeners at age seventeen are six five or six six, but they don't grow any more," he added. "Then going to college they try to play power forward. They might even have good college careers and average something like 20 points and 8 rebounds. But when they get to NBA camps, they're expected to be off guards. And they've never played the position before so they can't make the adjustment. They're done." Herring, however, had allowed Jordan to prepare for success at the next levels.

"Pop, he saw where Michael's future was in basketball," Gattison explained, "and he made it possible for him to get there."

Big Mac

Jordan's consolation that senior year was that he had been selected as one of *Parade* magazine's top prep players in America, but he was stung after the season when Buzz Peterson edged him out in an Associated Press poll selecting North Carolina's top high school player.

"We just played New Hanover too many times," he told the *Star-News* three weeks after the season, when asked to sum up his disappointment. "When you play a good team that many times, it's bound to catch up with you. It's just hard to beat a good team four times. It was just their turn to win."

Next on his agenda was his senior baseball season, but that was complicated by an invitation to play in the prestigious McDonald's All-American Game. A new rule required North Carolina high school players to forfeit their eligibility if they participated in such games, which set up an immediate choice for Jordan between baseball and McDonald's. He took the team photo with the baseball team and appeared in the season opener, but it was a miserable, error-filled outing, which settled the issue. To his father's great anguish, Jordan dropped baseball.

"I knew my mind wasn't into it," he told the Wilmington papers.

The first of the McDonald's high school tournaments in 1981, in Landover, Maryland, pitted local stars against players from around the country. Ed Pinckney, a senior from New York, was one of the All-Americans who traveled down to Washington for the event. He hadn't attended the Five-Star session with Jordan the previous summer, but other players from New York had been there, and had returned home with stories about a really good player from North Carolina. Pinckney couldn't recall his name that March, but he didn't have to go to more than one McDonald's practice to figure out just whom they were talking about.

"He wasn't talking a lot," Pinckney recalled of seeing Jordan in that first practice. "He was just playing. It was like, 'Holy Cow.' When you're from New York, the mind-set is that the best basketball is played in New York City. Well, the two practices we had completely changed my mind about who the best players were."

Jordan may not have been talking smack to Pinckney, but he was once again to Patrick Ewing. "He was talking he was gonna dunk on me," the center recalled years later with a laugh. "He was dunking on me. He was just talking trash. We were going back and forth."

Surprisingly, Jordan was not in the starting lineup for that first McDonald's game. And Pinckney couldn't even recall who was coaching (it was Mike Jarvis, then Ewing's high school coach at Cambridge Rindge & Latin). But it was clear by the second half that the coach was determined to win.

"What happened, in the first half of the game, everybody gets a chance to play," he recalled. But in the second half, particularly down the stretch, the game was turned over to the skinny kid from Carolina. "He got the ball and scored literally every time we came down the court," Pinckney said with a laugh. "So it wasn't an issue as to when or if we were going to win. It was just a matter of where he was gonna get the ball and how many he was gonna score."

For the record, Jordan scored 14 in that first game, and Buzz Peterson scored 10, a good enough performance to assure that the pair of North Carolina recruits started together in the backcourt of the national McDonald's game, played in Wichita two weeks later.

It was the first big basketball trip for James and Deloris Jordan as well. Among the activities was an address from John Wooden, the legendary UCLA coach. Billy Packer, the former All-ACC guard at Wake Forest who had become a broadcaster for CBS, also made the trip. Packer had been busy broadcasting the Final Four in

Philadelphia during the first McDonald's game. Now that the big event was over, he had come to Wichita, in particular to get a look at Jordan.

Packer also lived in North Carolina and was a broadcaster for ACC games, so he was curious about any freshmen coming into the conference. He was surprised at the strong level of talent in the game. The East roster included Milt Wagner, Bill Wennington, Adrian Branch, Chris Mullin, and Jeff Adkins. Aubrey Sherrod, who had been named MVP at the first McDonald's game in Washington, was a hometown hero in Wichita and a big drawing card for the event.

"But Michael stole the show," Packer said. Jordan scored 30 points, a McDonald's game record. Best of all, he delivered victory when he went to the line facing a one-and-one with eleven seconds on the clock and his team down, 95–94. Jordan calmly canned both. He put up extraordinary stats, hitting 13 of his 19 field goal attempts, making all 4 of his free throws, and adding 6 steals and 4 assists.

Yet at game's end, the three judges who had been selected to choose the MVP—John Wooden, Philadelphia hoops legend Sonny Hill, and Morgan Wootten, the great high school coach from Maryland—selected Branch and Sherrod as the game's MVPs, despite Jordan's record-setting performance. According to some reports, Wootten did not vote because he was Branch's high school coach. Branch was headed to the University of Maryland.

"We broadcast the game," Billy Packer recalled, "and of course when they announced that the most valuable player wasn't Michael it was astonishing. It turned out to be Sherrod and Adrian Branch, who had played high school for Morgan Wootten. I know Morgan's integrity and Coach Wooden's as well. They obviously saw something I didn't particularly see in the game. But I don't think either one of them would have stooped to 'I'm going to pick my player no matter what.' Adrian played fairly well, too, but not as well as Michael did."

No one was more furious than Deloris Jordan. She dropped her normal composure and let anyone within earshot know that her son had been robbed. Bill Guthridge looked up after the announcement and saw an obviously angry Mrs. Jordan headed for the floor with Buzz Peterson's mother in tow. The Carolina assistant headed them off and defused the situation.

"His mother was furious," remembered Tom Konchalski.

"She was very upset," Howard Garfinkel recalled. "I just explained to her there's only one list that counts, and that's the night of the first pick of the NBA draft."

Later that evening, Packer encountered the Jordans outside the arena. "His mom was still upset about it," the broadcaster said. "I was kidding with her and said to her, 'Don't be so upset about this game. Michael's going to be an outstanding player and he's going to play for a great coach at North Carolina. Some day you'll forget this night he didn't get the MVP."

Soon Packer would realize that while Mrs. Jordan might forget the snub, her son wasn't about to. "Michael might have been playing tiddlywinks against Adrian Branch, and Adrian might not even realize it," Packer said with a laugh, "but Michael would still have that image of that game in Wichita in his mind. Nobody in the ACC would realize just how motivated he was by things like that. But he never forgot anything."

Michael and sister Roslyn graduated from Laney that spring of 1981 and began preparations for their next round of challenges in Chapel Hill.

Laney's yearbook, *The Spinnaker,* detailed Jordan's curriculum vitae: "Homeroom Rep 10, Spanish Club 11…New Hanover Hearing Board 12…Pep Club 10." *The Spinnaker* also included a passage acknowledging Jordan and Leroy Smith: "Laney only hopes that you…expand your talents to make others as proud of you as Laney has been. Always remember Laney as your world."

Jordan's world, of course, was about to expand exponentially. And every single soul, especially Jordan himself, would be stunned at how swiftly that happened.

PART IV

TRUE BLUE

Chapter 11

THE FRESHMAN

Fᴀɴs ᴀᴛ ᴏᴘᴘᴏsɪɴɢ schools around the ACC always seemed to fixate on what they saw as Dean Smith's large nose and beady eyes. To them, he was a caricature, one that embodied an air of snarky superiority. This public image proved a radical departure from how he was seen inside the Carolina program itself, where he was held in uncommon esteem. In his players' eyes, his self-deprecation underscored his relentless emphasis on team play.

"One thing I'll always remember is his honesty," NBA great Bobby Jones once told *Sports Illustrated*. "We all knew he had problems, just like everyone else, but most coaches would never admit to them. He also admitted he didn't have all the answers."

That honesty provided the foundation for the deep respect and love his players so often expressed for Smith, particularly after they stopped playing for him, when he ceased being their coach and worked hard at being their friend. Michael Jordan would come to call Smith his second father, the sort of sentiment echoed by just about everyone who ever played for him.

Sometimes, Smith's efforts involved a major issue, such as James Worthy's arrest for solicitation of a prostitute during his days with the Los Angeles Lakers. "Coach Smith was the second person to call me," Worthy acknowledged, "and he said, 'We're all human. I know you're a great man. Just deal with it as a man.'"

Smith got involved on less dramatic issues as well, such as

problems in a former player's family or career. He had a prodigious memory, often recalling the names of his players' friends and relatives, people he had seen only once or twice. Lakers general manager Mitch Kupchak, who played at Carolina, was amazed once by a phone conversation in which Smith mentioned that Kupchak's sister Sandy had given birth to a boy. "He met my sister in the summer of 1972," Kupchak said. "How could he even remember her name?"

Pete Chilcutt, another of Smith's players, observed that he frequently ran into NBA players who spoke bitterly about their college coaches or programs. That wasn't the case with North Carolina, Chilcutt once explained. "One thing all Tar Heels have in common is pride." Which meant that Smith's players frequently returned to Chapel Hill during the summer, to play pick-up basketball or to gather for the program's annual golf outing. That family atmosphere paid off for Smith in terms of connections and recruiting. His program set the standard in the days when the ACC was viewed as the nation's best college basketball conference.

Outsiders, however, did not share that reverence. Smith was often reviled by students and fans from other teams in the hotly contested conference. Part of what drew this contempt was his use of the four corners, the spread offense that became a signature of the North Carolina program. Ric Moore, a former high school player and basketball fan in Virginia, recalled the extreme disgust he felt as a teen watching Smith's teams play on television. "There was no end to my hatred of Dean Smith," Moore said. "You have some of the greatest players in the game on the floor, and he would have his team stalling out the clock. It was a curse on the game." Smith generally responded that the four corners gave his team its best chance to win, but few basketball fans seemed to buy it. And neither did the Atlantic Coast Conference, which pioneered the use of the shot clock in college basketball largely in response to the four corners.

For his detractors, it went beyond team strategy. Opponents complained that he was smug and self-righteous, a charge also leveled at UCLA's John Wooden. And like Wooden, Smith was viewed as excessively manipulative, working every angle of the competitive environment. NC State's Jim Valvano once joked that if Dean was complimentary of an ACC referee, the rest of the league's coaches would quickly blackball the guy. Irked once by what he perceived as Smith's manipulation, Duke coach Bill Foster seethed, "I thought Naismith invented the game, not Dean Smith."

"There is a gap between the man and the image he tries to project," Virginia coach Terry Holland once explained. A common joke around Charlottesville back in the 1980s was that Holland had a dog, a bitch, that he named Dean.

It sometimes came across as though Smith felt he was above the rules. Holland recalled an incident: "He thought one of my players, Marc Iavaroni, was roughing up Phil Ford, and at halftime when the teams came off the court at the ACC tournament in 1977, he confronted Marc—physically touched him and said things. That's one area where I think Dean always had a problem. He felt he had a right, in order to protect his players in his own mind, to confront other people's players. That's extremely dangerous and way over the line."

"We've all probably done things we're not proud of, backing up one of our players," said Smith's rival, Duke coach Mike Krzyzewski. "But I can't think of a time I've ever heard him blame or degrade one of his own players, and in return, his kids are fiercely loyal to him. That kind of loyalty doesn't just happen. Things done on a day-to-day basis develop that kind of relationship."

Billy Packer spent his share of afternoons observing Smith's practices, which were often eerily quiet as players hustled through the structured agenda. Every drill and scrimmage was precisely timed and measured and observed, all with the aim of sublimating individual prowess to the strength of the team.

"Even in scrimmages we've tried to apply that standard," Smith once explained. "If a player took a bad fadeaway jump shot and made it, I'd tell the manager, 'Score that a zero.' If he got a layup, it would be plus three. We'd only have to score it that way a few times before the guys would realize what we were after."

Detailed practice schedules were posted each day. As players ran through drills, managers stood on the sideline holding up fingers to indicate how many minutes were left in each period. The structure of Smith's program made possible all of the team success that Jordan later experienced in pro basketball, explained Tex Winter, Phil Jackson's longtime assistant coach with the Chicago Bulls.

"If Michael hadn't played for Dean Smith, he wouldn't have been as good of a team player as he was," Winter said in a 2008 interview.

An overlooked factor in the Jordan legend is that Bill Guthridge, who worked for decades as Smith's top assistant, had played for Winter at Kansas State, then served as Winter's assistant. Winter, of course, had developed the complex triangle offense, used by his Kansas State teams and later in the NBA by Jordan's Bulls. While the Tar Heels did not use Winter's triangle offense, they did employ what Winter liked to call "system basketball," an approach based on a core philosophy and fundamental principles. Winter explained that many coaches used no such system, choosing instead to employ a freewheeling amalgam of various plays and isolated, often disconnected, strategies.

In Smith's program, "the system" was more important than individual talent. Chemistry also superseded talent. "I think a very underrated part is the chemistry of a team and their confidence in one another," Smith once explained to Packer. "And unselfishness in our game is huge. And, of course, they have to play hard. We've always said, 'Play hard, play smart, play together.' And playing smart means you have to work real hard in practice to repeat things so you'll react even when the circumstances are disorienting, when fans are yelling at you, yet you still know what to do."

"With Dean, there was no stone unturned on or off the floor," Packer said. "And when you take into consideration his total involvement as a coach, whether you were the lowly manager or a player like Michael Jordan, that to me was the greatest asset that he had." Smith was controlling in game situations as well, pointedly instructing his players not to engage in flashy plays that might show up an opponent. When Jimmy Black once threw an alley-oop to James Worthy for a resounding dunk late in a blowout win over Georgia Tech, Smith was furious and punished the transgression in the next practice. Carolina players simply did not contemplate such behavior.

Yet, he could just as easily offend others with his obsessiveness. "I'm doing a game between NC State and Carolina, a big game," Packer remembered. "I'm talking about two teams in the top five and I'm ready to go out on the floor to announce the starting line-ups. The teams are at their respective benches and Dean walks by me and says, 'I don't appreciate your tie.' And I look down and I have on a red tie. And it was the first time I realized I was wearing a red tie. I thought, 'That guy never stops. Here the teams are getting ready to go out and play the game. How the hell could he be worried about what tie I had on?'"

Packer admitted to often becoming annoyed that Smith would craftily use his postgame news conferences not for a frank discussion of the competitive proceedings but to send messages to his players, even to the officials, and sometimes to opposing coaches and their players. "I would always try to judge what he would say about the game when it was over," Packer recalled. "He used to say things and I would say, 'Gosh, that's damn stupid. That wasn't the key to the game.' It used to annoy me because it would be something that I hadn't even talked about on air during the game." He would make statements that would have underlying meanings. "You eventually realized how smart he was and how dumb you were not to understand it."

Thus Michael Jordan arrived on the North Carolina campus in the fall of 1981 to find that he was about to play for a very different kind of coach. Where Pop Herring had been a blessing for his early development, the next stage of Jordan's journey brought a total immersion into the discipline of the sport. "When you come out of high school, you have natural, raw ability," Jordan once explained. "No one coaches it. When I was coming out of high school, it was all natural ability. The jumping, the quickness. When I went to North Carolina, it was a different phase of my life. Knowledge of basketball from Naismith on...rebounds, defense, free-throw shooting, techniques."

Even as he was recruiting Jordan, Smith had put together one of his best teams for 1981, featuring Worthy, guard Al Wood, and center Sam Perkins. Virginia had beaten North Carolina twice that season, and the two teams met again in the national semifinals in

Philadelphia. Holland coached his team to go against Carolina's system. But Smith tricked the Cavaliers coach by uncharacteristically turning the offensive spotlight over to the athletic Wood, whose dynamic play helped win the day.

It was Smith's sixth trip to the Final Four. From 1962 to 1981, his teams had stacked up better than 460 wins, with nine ACC championships. The only validation he lacked was a national championship. His 1981 team lost yet another title game that first Monday night in April and had to watch Indiana coach Bobby Knight and point guard Isiah Thomas take home the trophy, extending North Carolina's frustration another season. Afterward, his players gathered and vowed that the next season would bring an end to the drought. Michael Jordan watched the event on television, and for the first time in his life felt a deep allegiance to Smith and the Tar Heels. He also felt a frustration that he wasn't able to help them against Indiana.

"I guess we can be like Penn State football," Smith mused after the Indiana loss. "Number 2 all the time."

Comparing his program to that of Penn State's legendary Joe Paterno was Smith's way of asking for more patience from North Carolina's fans. Both Paterno and Smith had well-established reputations for doing things the right way, with an admirable balance between championship ambition and academic achievement for the athletes.

"He expected you to go to class," Worthy explained, "and if you were a freshman you had to go to church unless you had permission from your parents not to. He promised you that in your four years you would graduate. It was simple, and his family philosophy was good."

Yet it was hard to ignore the gnawing dissatisfaction among North Carolina's fans and the media covering the team. There was a sense that the balance that Smith brought to the cynical business of college athletics was not enough, that his insistence on doing everything the right way was preventing him from winning "the big one." Neither Smith nor his assistant coaches—not even the players—talked about the growing derision aimed at North Carolina, but they felt it more than ever after that sixth trip to the Final Four.

In truth, Smith had built the nation's best, most consistent basketball program. It produced the best players, who also finished school with a much clearer understanding of themselves as people. No one understood this better than the players themselves.

"Coach Smith taught us to be able to get along with people," Worthy explained. "It helps you socially when there is a certain set of rules, when you have to communicate with people, when you have to learn to agree to disagree, when you have to submit to authority without losing your integrity. So it teaches you to learn how to deal with people and then how to rely on and trust people." Smith's structured "system" focused on the players doing all the little things correctly for one another, sharing shots and setting picks for one another, Worthy said, adding that you couldn't overestimate the value of Smith's elevated treatment of team managers and practice players.

"All of those things playing the game, they transfer over to life," he said. In turn, the players' allegiance to Smith and his mentorship made the winning of a championship vitally important to them all, Worthy explained.

Some longtime observers actually took hope from the loss in Philadelphia. Smith had shown a willingness to open his system a bit to accommodate the special talents of a player like Al Wood. It showed that the coach was willing to adjust to a shifting landscape in the college game. Huge amounts of money and much higher levels of public attention were ushering in great change. In another few years, it might well have been impossible for a player of Jordan's special abilities to find his way into a system run as tightly as Dean Smith ran the program at North Carolina.

Jordan, meanwhile, had liked much of what he had seen about the Carolina program on TV during the Final Four. He liked the camaraderie and the spirit and the talent. He figured that even though he was a freshman he would find a way to come off the bench. If he managed to get in the games, Jordan believed he'd find a way to help the Tar Heels.

Help, indeed. Thirty years later, on the eve of his own selection to the Basketball Hall of Fame, Ralph Sampson reflected on Michael Jordan, this force that had upset all of his best-laid plans and monumental expectations. No one had seen him coming. Sampson pointed out that Jordan's unprecedented rise all began with a piece of remarkable fortune: Jordan had been able to walk into a ready-made championship team at North Carolina, as if God himself had placed the reservation for him.

"He was very fortunate to be in that situation," Sampson pointed out.

As a freshman in Dean Smith's system, Jordan merely had to fall in line. In all the years of Smith's program, only three other players — Phil Ford, James Worthy, and Mike O'Koren — had made the starting lineup as freshmen. Like most programs in that day, Smith's system was heavily weighted toward seniority. He allowed his veteran players input into the rules of conduct off the court. He scheduled games in or near their hometowns during their senior seasons. He accorded them every conceivable honor and privilege, because it was their four-year involvement and dedication that sustained the program.

Freshmen, meanwhile, were lower, supposedly, than even team managers and training assistants. Freshmen carried team bags and equipment and performed other menial chores. It was the freshmen, not team managers, who chased down loose balls at practice each day. They had to earn a place in the program. Among Jordan's tasks that first year, for example, would be hauling the team's heavy film projection equipment around from venue to venue. Yet even that was part of the blessing: as a freshman, he faced no great pressure or expectations.

Sampson, a tall, silent observer at seven feet four, watched it all happen, and with no small dismay. Virginia's 1981 battles with North Carolina had been the prelude to what would become known as the Jordan Era in Chapel Hill. Sampson had signed with Virginia, an ACC school in his home state with little basketball tradition, in 1979, and had led the Cavaliers to the NIT title in 1980 as a freshman. He was projected as basketball's next great giant, compared often to Kareem Abdul-Jabbar, and as such labored under tremendous media pressure and fan expectations. The 1981 Final Four loss to the Tar Heels had been a huge setback, but many in the national media projected that Sampson would carry the Cavaliers to a national championship in 1982. The greatest single obstacle in his way was the University of North Carolina, despite having lost talented senior Al Wood.

The big question for Dean Smith that fall of 1981 was who would take Wood's place on the team. It was obvious that the six-nine Worthy was ready to step in as the team's top scorer, and Perkins, also six nine, made for quite a weapon himself. Smith needed a wing to play heady ball, energize the defense, and knock down open shots when zones collapsed around Worthy and Perkins.

Jim Braddock seemed the likely candidate early in the fall. He was a junior, a fine shooter, and a decent defender. The other two candidates were freshmen Peterson and Jordan. Peterson could run and jump and had speed. He wasn't a bad shooter either. Smith had been toying with certain thoughts since he watched Jordan's raw high school performances. But fans remembering the scenario would long roll their eyes. How could the Carolina coach waste time looking past the obvious? The answer was Jordan.

Smith, however, was very much a man of process, and he had much to consider that fall. He had received early reports of Jordan from the pickup games he was playing with his new teammates and others around campus. Jordan's internship in the games at Wilmington's Empie Park had served him well, as had his childhood battles with brother Larry. As Bulls team psychologist George Mumford later pointed out, those heated verbal and physical exchanges with Larry set the format for how Jordan would relate to just about all of his future teammates. His game was rooted in the combat between brothers. Jordan's new teammates had no idea about the brother thing, although they quickly got a sense of the combat. As Worthy explained, Jordan seemed eager to "bully" the older players at North Carolina, and part of his bully game was talking trash.

"I saw it then," Worthy said. "He had raw talent. And that was all he was. He came in very confident and seeking out the best and trying to target who he's going to dismantle."

The freshman began telling his new teammates he was going to dunk on them. That irritated Worthy the most, it seemed. Others mostly laughed off his talk, but the behavior triggered a concern among the team's veteran players. They had vowed to return to the Final Four in 1982 to win a title for their coach. It was immensely important for them. The last thing they needed was a loud-mouthed freshman hotshot to wreck the team's prized chemistry. It wasn't that Jordan was oblivious to the team's desire to win a national championship. He felt a part of the North Carolina program, and recalled his frustration and disappointment at watching the Tar Heels lose that spring. Still, he was a freshman that fall of 1981, and his aggressiveness was met with mixed reviews.

"I remember that people thought that he was really cocky, or that he just talked a lot," Art Chansky recalled. "And he wanted to have the nickname Magic. People in Wilmington had started calling him Magic. Dean said to him, 'Why do you want to become Magic? Somebody else already has that name.' If you look in the 1982 Carolina brochure, he was Mike Jordan. 'What would you like to be called?' 'They call me Michael.' Dean said, 'Well, we'll call you Michael Jordan from now on.' That was the smartest move they ever made because he became just Michael. Calling him Magic was bullshit. Dean was smart about that."

Whatever his name, it soon enough became clear to the older players that Jordan had a boiling spring deep inside him that fueled his need to dominate. They saw that Jordan possessed a complex personality; in one sense the trash talk seemed silly and innocent, but in another sense it showed that he really was intent on challenging them. But his teammates soon began to realize that he was using the trash to push himself. The more he talked, the more he had to back it up. Jordan was not the first young player to do this. The difference was that he had the ability to back up whatever he said. Thus Jordan immediately presented himself as a figure who could turn the world of Carolina basketball upside down. At least, that was how it seemed to Worthy.

The new guy targeted Worthy for a little one-on-one as a measuring-up exercise. Worthy sensed that Jordan was making an immediate play for his status and declined to be pulled into the freshman's mind game. In many ways, they were diametric opposites. Rather than mouthing off, Worthy tended to internalize things. It would take him years to learn to express his raw feelings the way that Jordan was already doing as an eighteen-year-old. So Jordan was a challenge to the older player on many levels.

"Physically, he was a scrawny kid but strong and confident mentally," Worthy remembered. "He had already surpassed a lot of people older than him. He had already reached that level of confidence."

And it wasn't just their personal confrontation that mattered. All basketball teams are a hierarchy, Smith's teams even more than most. Jordan's youthful challenge had the potential to mess with Carolina's established team dynamics before the varsity even played a single game.

"Oh come on, big fella," Jordan would say to Worthy, trying to goad him into playing.

It would take a while before he wore the junior down about the one-on-one. "After he started to get better, he would pick on Sam Perkins and me," Worthy, with a slight smile, recalled in an interview thirty years later. "He'd say, 'Let's play a little one-on-one.' Finally I did. We played three games and I won two that I know of." The victory would confirm the program's hierarchy, although it clearly left Jordan unsatisfied, which was probably a good thing. Worthy mused that it took Jordan almost thirty years to admit the losses, in an interview for an HBO special on the Duke/North Carolina rivalry.

At the time, though, there were at least some who wondered if the brash freshman wasn't out of place in Chapel Hill. "He had a personality that you wouldn't think would fit a Carolina player, because as a Carolina player you're slow to speak and eager to listen," Worthy explained. "And Michael came in and was eager to talk and slow to listen. But he knew who Coach Smith was. He knew about Phil Ford and Walter Davis, so he knew what he was getting into."

"He was the obnoxious younger brother more than anything," Art Chansky recalled of Jordan the freshman. "At that time, nobody thought that Michael Jordan was going to be the greatest anything....Nobody really thought that he was going to become king of the world. So he was like a pain in the ass to them as a freshman.... But they liked the confidence, the moxie that he had as a freshman. They liked that, and they wanted to make sure it was channeled in the right way. So they didn't discourage him. He talked a lot, but I think he talked less as his career went on because the spotlight got brighter."

Off the basketball court, Jordan seemed like any other freshman trying to find his way. ESPN's Stuart Scott, who was then in the Carolina football program, recalled Jordan at that time as just a regular guy tooling around Chapel Hill on his bike. One thing that kept Jordan grounded was the presence of his loving younger sister on campus. Reserved and cautious, Roslyn made an effort to ensure that her brother's domestic life remained smooth. She wasn't above cleaning his room before it reached a toxic level. James and Deloris also made numerous trips to Chapel Hill to check on their children. Roslyn was particularly close to her mother, and Jordan was something of a momma's boy himself. Once the season started, he couldn't seem to settle down to play unless he knew his parents had arrived safely and were in the stands.

Clarence Gaines Jr., the son of Winston-Salem State's Hall of Fame coach, was a graduate student at UNC that year (he would later become a Chicago Bulls scout) and lived in Granville Towers on campus, where a number of athletes were housed. Gaines knew just about all of the Carolina players.

"I remember veteran players, specifically Jimmy Black, talking about this cocky newcomer who was going to be a part of the program," Gaines remembered. "So I knew MJ before he was 'MJ.'"

He recalled Jordan playing pickup ball on the outdoor courts near Granville Towers. "MJ always had an aura about him," Gaines said. "Some people just have presence, and obviously he is in that category."

Still, many wondered what would happen when the fiercely competitive freshman collided with Smith's system in practice. As it turned out, things went surprisingly well. The unbridled athleticism on display in those fall pickup games seemed to disappear almost overnight. Much later, after Jordan had emerged as a pro star, the public began to realize just how deep his absorption into the Carolina program had been, how much of his game had been masked there. Yet it wasn't just Dean Smith's system reining him in. There were other moderating forces coming into his life.

The Early Posse

In each of the two summers before he entered college, Jordan had made time to attend the basketball camp at Campbell University in Buies Creek, North Carolina. The camp had become a well-worn stop on the southern basketball circuit, with top coaches and players often making appearances. Jordan played and worked as a counselor at Campbell, an affiliation he would continue through college. It was there that he met Fred Whitfield, who became a lifelong friend and major influence. Whitfield, who was from Greensboro, was one of the all-time leading scorers at Campbell. Upon graduation, he had gone to work at the school as an assistant coach while pursuing his master's in business administration.

As a counselor then in his early twenties, Whitfield took an interest in Jordan and Buzz Peterson, and their friendship grew. The counselor was bright and friendly, someone Jordan could look up to. He had been through the ups and downs of the college game, and was able to offer observations and opinions that often made sense to Jordan.

Whitfield was both a mentor and a friend. "Michael actually came down to our basketball school going into his senior year in high school," Whitfield recalled. "He happened to be in my group. We hit it off and became friends. I was either playing there or coaching there at the time, and I was working at the camp. When he went to North Carolina for college, I was an assistant coach at Campbell. When we didn't have games on the weekends I would go up to Chapel Hill and go to his games and kind of hang out with him and Buzz Peterson. Part of my job as an assistant coach was to bring in ACC players to make appearances at our summer camp. Michael was a guy, while he was at Carolina, that I'd get to come down for a day and speak to the kids. Our friendship just continued to grow.

"I think for whatever reason he and I just connected down in Buies Creek," Whitfield said of his early relationship with Jordan, "but more than that we formed a friendship and a trust and I think from that point it became as much about encouraging each other to be as successful as both of us could be."

Those weekend trips marked the early formation of Jordan's first tight circle of friends away from the team, what would later become his well-defined posse. "It was in college that he developed this entourage of people like Fred Whitfield, who was a really nice guy," Art Chansky explained. "Michael aligned himself only with people he could trust." Besides Whitfield, Adolph Shiver was in Chapel Hill. His friendship with Jordan helped Shiver land for a time on the Tar Heel JV basketball team, coached by Roy Williams. Shiver would long chair the entertainment division of MJ's inner circle, while Whitfield was far more grounded.

James and Deloris Jordan approved of Whitfield. He was a bright young man with much on the ball. Whitfield's influence certainly helped counter the foolishness of Shiver, as well as other less-mature influences on a college freshman. Shiver could "talk the lips off a chicken" but rarely said anything other than what appealed to Jordan's raw ego. Whitfield could talk as much junk as anyone, but he was developing his own sophistication and served as something of a bridge from Jordan's adolescence to the larger world.

The relationship with Whitfield was another of the exceptional but little-discussed factors in Jordan's good fortune. Between his parents and siblings and the Carolina coaching staff and roommate Buzz Peterson and Whitfield and, yes, even Adolph Shiver, an impressive support system had formed around him as he moved into big-time college athletics. It was almost as if this sizeable mass of influences was necessary to nudge Jordan, a hypercharged eighteen-year-old package of testosterone and ego, in the right direction.

The Listener

Easily the greatest reason Jordan was successful in those first months in Chapel Hill was his ability to listen, a trait that moderated his powerful life force, and that arose out of his relationship with his mother. From his earliest moments in the spotlight, Deloris Jordan had guided her son around the many pitfalls she saw, and he listened to her in a way that would prove critical to his success. It was a gift that they developed together, mother and son, mostly because at one of the pivotal moments in her youth, Deloris Jordan had failed to heed her parents' warnings and soon paid dearly for it. Even when it was difficult for Michael, even when his many appetites and friends tugged him in another direction, he mostly listened. It often took time for him to process what she said, especially if he didn't like what he heard. But he clearly understood from an early age that she was his guide star.

"My personality and my laughter come from my father," he once explained. "My business and serious side come from my mother."

Deloris was his greatest critic but could deliver harsh messages in a manner that allowed him to accept them. It was not easy for Jordan, as he matured, to set aside his own instincts to listen to her. But it was this relationship with her that made him receptive to coaching, which in turn set up so many of his great successes. Years later, he would describe his mother as his "coach."

This ability to listen was among his most precious gifts, James Worthy's allegations to the contrary. To his coaches his capacity to be coached was his single most impressive attribute, beyond even the eighteen-year-old's spectacular physical gifts. Dean Smith asserted, "I had never seen a player listen so closely to what the coaches said and then go and do it."

Even so, Jordan's approach was not perfect. At one point early in his tenure there, Jordan's occasionally casual effort had raised a red flag. When Roy Williams challenged him on it, Jordan replied that he was working as hard as the others, which prompted Williams to reply that if he wanted to accomplish great things, he had to work that much harder than the others. Williams was struck afterward by the fact that it took only one conversation with Jordan. No one would ever outwork him again.

This listening made Smith realize that the freshman, despite all the concern about his strong personality and the woofing, was the lead candidate to replace Al Wood. "My greatest skill was being teachable," Jordan later observed. "I was like a sponge. Even if I thought my coaches were wrong, I tried to listen and learn something."

This was something that the legion of imitators that would follow him in basketball would overlook. They believed their great skills and physical gifts elevated them above the game. That was never Jordan's assumption. That attitude would find its first great test that freshman year.

The Cover

Jordan was slowed by injuries as the season neared but remained the obvious leading candidate to start. North Carolina entered the season as the top-ranked team in the polls, and *Sports Illustrated* wanted to pose the starting five on the cover of its college basketball preview issue. Word had continued to grow about Jordan, driven by the reports of his playground feats. He had done things in practice that fall, particularly once when he challenged a double-team by Worthy and Perkins, that made coaches and teammates alike step back in awe. With the bubbly Roy Williams on the staff, those types of things were always going to leak out. Having heard the talk, the *Sports Illustrated* photo editors wanted Jordan included in the cover shot, but Smith refused. There was no way he was going to allow someone who had never played a minute for North Carolina to be on the cover of *Sports Illustrated*.

"He was not a factor in all the usual promotion and everything at the start of that season," Billy Packer recalled. "Probably a lot of it done at Dean's direction. Today freshmen have become very big in college basketball. But back then that wasn't the case."

Appearing on the *Sports Illustrated* cover and being touted in the preseason media blitz would excite any young athlete. Jordan was deeply offended that he couldn't join the others on the cover. It was his first real collision with the Smith approach.

Yet as infuriated as Jordan could get about such things, he never allowed himself even a nanosecond of petulance. It was as if the slights were absorbed into the great black hole of his soul, to rest there as a mass of pure energy. No one would be more astounded by this than roommate Buzz Peterson. Since meeting at the summer camp, the two had become quite close. Peterson had wavered during his senior year in his plans to go to North Carolina. He appeared bent on signing with the University of Kentucky. Jordan phoned him and seemed deeply hurt that Peterson had forgotten their pact to room together as Tar Heels. Ultimately, Peterson gave in and signed with Carolina.

As college roommates, the two continued to grow their friendship even though they were competing for the starting spot in Carolina's lineup. Only over time would Peterson come to realize that despite their friendship, Jordan burned to prove the fallacy of Peterson's selection as Mr. Basketball in North Carolina their senior year. Nor had Jordan forgotten what people in his hometown, even the teachers at Laney, had said about him sitting on the bench at Carolina. "A lot of my friends were putting me down for coming to Carolina," he recalled. "They were telling me freshmen can't play here. Even a couple of my teachers were on me about that, although they were State fans."

The entire fall had been about answering all those slights, real and imagined. In the process of proving that he belonged, Jordan soon won over the team's veterans. "When you come to Carolina there are vicious running programs," James Worthy explained. "There are three groups, A, B, and C. Usually A is for the quick guards, B is reserved for guys like Michael in that medium range, and then C is for the big guys. And you have certain times you have to make." The shorter guards began teasing Jordan that he had it easier because midrange players had three more seconds to finish the run. "He asked Coach Smith to put him in A group and he just tore these guys up," Worthy said. "So I saw it then."

Jordan didn't want to be considered "just a freshman," recalled Sam Perkins, a sophomore that year. "He caught on quickly. He was a freshman, and even though freshmen weren't supposed to really play, this man out of Wilmington had to play."

While he missed two weeks of practice that fall with blood vessel issues in his ankle, he continued to hope. Smith agonized over the decision and waited until the very last moment to make known the fifth starter. The coach knew that competition was always good for team growth and involvement, so why end it early? The Tar Heels opened their season against Kansas in Charlotte, a game televised on a fledgling cable network named ESPN. Due to the time lost with his injury, Jordan had assumed he wouldn't start. He counted on finding a role as a sixth or maybe even seventh man.

"I was shocked when Coach Smith put my name on the blackboard to start our first game of the year," he recalled.

"Ten minutes before the game, one of the coaches came up and told us that Michael was going to start," James Jordan said in an interview three years later. "We couldn't believe it."

Jordan scored the first Carolina basket of the season—and of his college career—that day, a short jumper along the left baseline. ESPN's Bucky Waters noted that the freshman starter for the Tar Heels had generated a buzz among fans, who compared him to both David Thompson and Walter Davis.

Jordan would score in double figures for the first six games. He showed a steady jump shot right away and an uncanny knack for slipping into the gaps of the various zones that Carolina faced. Smith's teams were known for moving the ball well, and the freshman showed he could hold his own in that regard. If there was any immediate criticism, it was that he seemed to pass up shots against the zones to try to push the ball inside. Yet that was the trademark of Smith's teams, that they persisted in trying to get better shots, rather than settling for jumpers.

As the nation's top-ranked team, the Tar Heels were literally all over the map early that season. After the game in Charlotte and another against Southern Cal in Greensboro, they played two quick tune-ups in Carmichael Auditorium. Then it was off to New York for the holidays, playing Rutgers in Madison Square Garden the week before Christmas. There Jordan treated the crowd to two breakaway dunks among his 15 points. Two days after Christmas, the Tar Heels faced highly rated Kentucky in the Meadowlands. Once again, he seemed almost oblivious to the big-game pressure of a highly ranked opponent under the TV lights, as North Carolina took a confidence-building win. Afterward, they jetted to the West Coast, to play in the Cable Car Classic in Santa Clara, California, where they beat Penn State in overtime and pounded host Santa Clara.

Determined to see every game, James and Deloris Jordan followed the dizzying whirlwind that was Carolina basketball. The travel expenses taxed their family finances severely, but they were transfixed by the unfolding fairy tale of their son's life. They made sure, as always, to keep an appropriate distance. "Dean Smith really ran that ship as far as keeping control of the parents," Art Chansky explained. "If any of the parents were getting out of line, Dean was great at controlling that. James Jordan was known as just a great guy, just real supportive of his son. He was always in the locker room after the games."

Some observers in and around the Carolina program did detect that James and Deloris weren't always on the same page, but nobody articulated it because it wasn't perceived as a problem. "Deloris, she was a rock," Art Chansky explained. "Everybody said that from the first moment." Just as everybody noted that James Jordan was no saint. Chansky observed, "Michael watched his father. He took that imprint. He took some of that edginess from James and for the most part he channeled it into becoming the most competitive player. You know, he was an assassin on the court."

The Jordans would see thirty-two of the thirty-four games he played that season, sometimes taking daughter Roslyn along. For home games, Larry would drive over from North Carolina A&T in Greensboro, where he was going to school.

Despite the growing excitement in the voices of broadcasters of these early games, it was a relatively low-key introduction. Jordan was obviously precocious, but fears about his abrasiveness had been laid to rest. His transition into the team proceeded smoothly as the trust of his coaches and teammates grew with each game. As Ralph Sampson would later contend, it had much to do with the context. "To come into a situation with veterans like James Worthy and Sam Perkins and Matt Doherty and Jimmy Black?" the Virginia center observed. "Those guys were very high-level players at that point. They were hungry to be really, really good. So you come in there as a freshman, and what are you going to do? You got to get on board and learn from those guys. You know I think he took a piece from everybody."

The team truly was ready-made, but the coaching staff had put together a roster that season that was surprisingly short of depth.

They made up for this with a surfeit of good fortune. The season somehow rolled along without major injuries. In years past, with more talent on his roster, Smith had often been accused of over-substituting during games and killing his team's momentum. This season, the depth would all but eliminate that question. The starters—Jordan, Perkins, Worthy, point guard Jimmy Black, and six-eight forward Matt Doherty—averaged between thirty-five and forty minutes per game. Perkins, another player destined to become an NBA first-round draft choice, was a willowy sophomore with an even temperament. Black was the efficient point guard, a low scorer but a glue man all the same. Doherty was the role player, good for defense and 9 points a game. All of them shot better than 50 percent from the floor.

Jim Braddock, Buzz Peterson, and Cecil Exum contributed off the bench, but none averaged even 2 points per game. There was the traditional heavy focus on New York players in Black, Doherty, and Perkins. Worthy and Jordan were the native Carolinians in the lineup, but they hailed from the very different cultures at the opposite ends of the state.

Worthy was an excellent team leader, steeped in all things Carolina. His respect for coaching and authority began with a devout mother and father from Gastonia, North Carolina, just past Charlotte. He had been coming to Smith's summer camp since his early teens and had no inner conflict about the team's purpose that season. At six feet nine, he offered rare quickness and open-court speed. No player his size in college basketball could stay with him. He was the kind of forward who could make a team dangerous in a half-court offense, or he could prove the perfect finisher in transition with his speed and hands. Smith's systematic approach left room for his team to attack in transition, and the Tar Heels had the speed to get back and defend against almost any break.

Most of all, basketball purists loved to watch Worthy work in the low post. There, it was usually over in a matter of seconds. "His first step is awesome," observed Maurice Lucas, who would later guard him often in professional basketball.

"He'll give a guy two or three fakes, step through, then throw up the turnaround," Lakers coach Pat Riley once explained. "It's not planned."

Worthy and Perkins, the other frontcourt presence, drew much of the defensive attention in terms of zones and double-teams. Perkins was also six nine but with arms that seemed to extend forever, which allowed him to function exceptionally well as a college center. He was laconic, with a sleepy countenance that would earn him the nickname "Big Smooth" as a pro. Even at Carolina, he was plenty of that.

Black and Doherty were role players. "For a team to be good you have to have people that aren't trying to get their points," Smith explained. "If Jimmy and Matt were thinking points we never would have been a great team. We would have been a good team, but wouldn't have been a championship team. They knew their roles, and played them well. Everybody did."

Doherty, from Hicksville, New York, had been a big scorer in high school. Black was from the Bronx, where he played Catholic school ball and was all set to go to Iona to play for Jim Valvano in 1979 when he caught Bill Guthridge's eye. The Carolina coaches could see that he couldn't shoot too well, but they loved his ball handling, steady free-throw shooting, smarts, quickness, decision making, and ball-pressure abilities. Smith couldn't hide his affection for Black. Time and again, the Carolina coaches offered the opinion that there would have been no magical 1982 season without their point guard.

"I don't know how integral I was," Black would say later. "We all played well together, we enjoyed each other, we communicated well. I still go back to the total team effort."

As a sophomore, Black had lost his thirty-nine-year-old mother to heart failure. Then, just months later, he was injured in an auto crash that almost left him paralyzed. He battled through rehab to return for his junior year and opened practice that fall running in a neck brace. It was Black's determination that carried them back to the brink of success as 1982 unfolded. It would be hard to imagine a Carolina player who enjoyed more respect.

As for Jordan, his play was not quite explosive that season, but he showed considerable promise. He averaged 13.5 points a game and shot 53.4 percent from the field. Even so, Art Chansky pointed out that on that veteran team Jordan "was a complete role player. Look at who he played with."

"Many people don't remember that even then Michael was inconsistent and had an up-and-down freshman year," Smith recalled. The coaches constantly nudged Jordan to improve his passing and ball handling. They also offered pointers on his defense and tried to teach him to play without the ball in his hands, something he really hadn't had to do very often in high school.

Billy Packer didn't see much of the expected pyrotechnics that first season. "In his freshman year, even up to the Final Four, you did not have any idea how good he was," Packer remembered. "He did good things, but he didn't control games. He didn't explode offensively. He did what he was told to do within the system. He basically was a system player and I never saw him do the breakout things that we would see out of him later as a pro. I never saw him where you would say, 'Holy mackerel.' Obviously we now know he was going to be a good player. But when you started talking about Michael Jordan then, you never thought about him in the terms, 'Yeah, he's going to be an all-time player.' Now that history's gone by you say, 'What? Are you nuts?' But he played within the system, and when they attacked the zone, he did what he was supposed to do. When they ran the fast break, he went where he was supposed to go."

Of course, there were those "moments," usually the result of a lesson learned. The Tar Heels returned from the West Coast after the holidays for a quick tune-up at home with William & Mary, then headed up to Maryland to open up the ACC schedule, which they did in savory fashion, beating Lefty Driesell's team by 16. They returned home to entertain Ralph Sampson and Virginia, the nation's second-ranked team. North Carolina came out aggressively that day, opening with a full-court press and hoping to push the pace. It backfired as Virginia's young guards, Othell Wilson and Ricky Stokes, helped them prosper. Stepping on the court against Sampson for the first time, Jordan was astounded at the center's size and performance that day, 30 points and 19 rebounds. Jordan missed his 3 shots from the field in the first half and grew timid, passing up open fifteen- and twenty-footers as Virginia sat back in zone. He managed to contribute 4 free throws in the first twenty minutes. However, Worthy took him aside as the teams were taking the floor after halftime and told him not to pass up the open shots he was getting against Virginia's zone.

"Early in the game, I kept looking for something better," he explained to reporters afterward. "We wanted to get the ball inside more and maybe get Ralph Sampson to pick up some fouls."

Despite a sore shoulder, he followed Worthy's advice in the second half and scored 12 points to give him 16 for the game. "I didn't want him to force anything," Worthy later told reporters. "But I noticed he passed up shots in the first half that he can make. We needed the offense."

Still, Virginia had seemed in command with an 8-point lead with a little over seven minutes left when Jimmy Black fouled out. Braddock came in and fired North Carolina's comeback to a 65–60 win. The turnabout would resonate in a big way at the end of the season. Sampson, meanwhile, made no effort to hide his annoyance afterward. "I still think we're the number one team in the country," he said. "They just got the breaks down the stretch. They still have to come to our place, you know."

The Tar Heels next beat NC State by 20, then took on the weaker Duke in Durham, struggling until five minutes into the second half when Jordan hit three straight jumpers, then added another bucket on a tip-in. He scored 13 of his 19 points in the second half. But the next game he scored just 6 as North Carolina took the first loss of the season, at home no less, to Wake Forest.

"We limited their touches," Wake's Anthony Teachey recalled in 2012. "I just tried to control the boards. We had to play Michael head up, because you had Worthy and Sam Perkins and those guys. We couldn't just concentrate on him because of the lineup they had." It was obviously a great, great team, Teachey offered.

North Carolina won the next three, but then, as Sampson had anticipated, the Tar Heels had to ride up to Charlottesville to visit the Cavaliers. This time around, Smith chose mostly to avoid using his press. Rather than seek to force turnovers, the Tar Heels sat back in a zone and hoped for missed shots. There weren't many. The Cavaliers shot 64 percent and whipped them soundly, 74–58. The scale of this second loss was unsettling. Upon their return to Chapel Hill, Jimmy Black called a team meeting, where he reminded them of their championship ambitions.

Duly refocused, the team won its final eight regular-season games to head into the ACC tournament at the Greensboro Coliseum. By tradition, the tournament somehow mixed southern charm with heated rivalry for three intense days. But for 1982, it was all about the Cavaliers and Tar Heels. North Carolina easily dismissed Georgia Tech and NC State to meet Virginia for the championship.

Terry Holland's team had faced one battle after another heading down the backstretch of the schedule, including tight victories against Clemson and Wake Forest in the tournament that sidelined starting guard Othell Wilson. Both coaches knew that the winner of the conference tournament would receive the top seed in the NCAA tournament's east regional. The loser would have to travel to another region, usually a losing proposition.

These were two splendid college teams, and well matched. Both had finished 12–2 in the ACC. Carolina surprisingly controlled the opening tip over Sampson, which resulted in a slam dunk for Worthy. From there, the Tar Heels vaulted to an 8–0 lead, then 24–12. In an early time-out, Smith told his players that Virginia would rebound from the deficit and to be ready for their run. On cue, the Cavaliers cut the lead and gained further advantage when Jordan picked up his third foul with less than three minutes left in the first half. North Carolina managed to hold a 3-point edge at the intermission, but Virginia scored the first six buckets of the second half and forced Smith to take an early time-out as he expected Holland to drop his players into a tight zone.

The Cavaliers had the lead and were surging. It was in that stretch, as the pressure soared, that Jordan stepped up to make four straight jump shots to seize back the momentum. His first shot out of the left corner cut the deficit to one. Holland took a time-out, but his team missed its first shot of the second half, which allowed Jordan to work from the right for another eighteen-footer. With a

1-point lead, Smith signaled for a spread floor in an effort to pull Virginia out of its zone. Holland, though, declined. Instead, he had his guards loosely defend the perimeter, just enough to avoid a ten-second call. The game then crawled through three minutes of Carolina's spread stall until finally Jordan came off two screens at the key and hit his third jumper.

Sampson then scored to trim Carolina's lead back to one, but Smith called for a repeat of the previous play, with Jordan popping off the screens to hit his fourth straight shot for a 44–41 lead. "Michael made some unbelievably clutch shots against Virginia in the ACC championship game," Art Chansky recalled. "If he hadn't made those shots, gutsy, ballsy shots from the elbow, where Sampson wouldn't come out...that's as close to the basket as you could get. If he didn't make those shots, they wouldn't have won that game. That was where you could see he was starting to get assertive."

"He had that penchant for making big shots even back then," agreed veteran basketball writer Dick Weiss.

There remained almost nine minutes on the clock. Carolina went into a tight zone, and Virginia's Jeff Lamp answered with a twenty-footer that cut the lead back to one.

Without hesitation, Smith put up his four fingers and sent his team into the four corners, a move that enraged quite a broad array of spectators, media, and even league officials. But it worked. Virginia would not take another shot in the half until the very end, after the Tar Heels had drained the clock. Holland declined to foul Carolina until twenty-eight seconds remained. Doherty made one of two free throws, but Virginia couldn't capitalize. Jimmy Black made two late free throws, and Sampson slammed a final bucket at the buzzer. It didn't matter. Carolina took the top seed in the East, 45–43.

Broadcast on NBC nationwide, the game stirred wide protest among media and fans. It is viewed as the contest that drove officials to adopt a shot clock, which the ACC added, along with a three-point shot, on an experimental basis the next season.

Lost in the ruckus was a coronation of sorts. James Worthy saw it, however. "Michael Jordan emerged from the ACC tournament that year," the forward recalled. "To watch him say, 'This is my ball, this is my court' was amazing." Jordan's confidence had grown over the close of the schedule. Secure in the context of the veteran team, he was now free to dream about bigger things.

The Tar Heels entered the NCAA tournament ranked number one and maintained that status despite a close call or two. It didn't hurt that every game of the regional would be played in their home state. The Heels struggled in their first game in Charlotte, against Virginia's little James Madison University, but Carolina fought to a 52–50 victory. In the regional semifinals in Raleigh, Alabama served Smith's team its next round of troubles before succumbing, 74–69. The regional final brought Rollie Massimino's Villanova with Ed Pinckney. Carolina again proved too strong that day, but a throwaway moment in the contest proved revealing. The Tar Heels forced a turnover, then threw the ball ahead to a streaking Jordan. Villanova's big center John Pinone had retreated to protect the basket.

"Our coach always taught us if you're in a bad way, wrap a guy up and don't let him get an easy layup," Pinckney explained. "I knew John was going to foul him. So he jumps, and John, whose nickname was 'The Bear'—he was a pretty strong guy—grabs him. In midair, Jordan like spins out of his arms and the ref calls the foul. It was like an impossible play to make but he did it anyway.... We were losing to them. And we all shook our heads like, 'You've got to be kidding me.' He couldn't dunk because Pinone grabbed him with two arms around his waist. He literally had to lift up a 240-pound guy and dunk. To us Pinone was like the strongest guy ever. But he spun out of his arms. Jordan should have fallen on the ground. He shouldn't have been able to maintain his balance and get free to complete a shot. It was like a freakish, freakish play."

Having cut his teeth against Kenny Gattison, Clyde Simmons, and Anthony Teachey back on the Coastal Plain, Jordan had no hesitation, no fear, in attacking the rim, regardless of who was guarding it.

After a 10-point win over Villanova in the regional finals, the Heels began to sense that they were about to give Smith his much-wanted prize. Held at the Superdome in New Orleans, the Final Four offered a fascinating field. North Carolina. Georgetown. Louisville (with four starters off its 1980 championship team). And

Houston. All dominant teams of the decade, with eleven Final Four appearances between them, and rosters studded with some of the modern game's best players: Michael Jordan. James Worthy. Hakeem Olajuwon. Patrick Ewing. Sam Perkins. Clyde Drexler.

The assembled media were ready with a big question for Smith: How did it feel to make six Final Fours and never win? "I've handled it well," he replied. "I don't feel the emptiness."

In the semifinals, North Carolina faced Houston. By 1983, the Cougars would become known as Phi Slama Jama, the dunking fraternity. For 1982, however, they were just another Cinderella.

Undaunted by the noise or the crowd of the cavernous Superdome, Jordan scored the first two baskets for his team against Houston. From there, Perkins took charge for the Heels with 25 points and 10 rebounds, while the Carolina defense held Houston's Rob Williams scoreless from the floor. North Carolina never trailed, and advanced to the championship round, 68–63. "I remember what a great game Sam Perkins had in the semifinals against Hakeem Olajuwon," Bill Guthridge recalled on the game's twentieth anniversary. "If Sam doesn't play that way against Houston, there's a chance we wouldn't have gotten to the championship game."

The Georgetown Hoyas, with freshman center Patrick Ewing and All-American guard Eric "Sleepy" Floyd, had defeated twentieth-ranked Louisville, 50–46, in the other semifinal, setting up a sportswriter's dream for the finals: Dean Smith versus John Thompson. Two friends and America's Olympic coaches from 1976 facing each other for the championship both wanted dearly. Both Smith and Thompson played down their involvement. They weren't playing, they said, their teams were. Regardless, North Carolina's contest with Georgetown in the 1982 NCAA finals is considered by many to be the most dramatic ever. Veteran broadcaster Curt Gowdy thought it was the game, more than any other, to lift the Final Four to the entertainment level of the World Series and Super Bowl. The Louisiana Superdome crowd shattered college basketball's attendance record with 61,612 spectators. Another 17 million watched on television.

"I had mixed emotions about playing against Dean because I

have a great deal of respect and affection for him," Thompson later said. Then he admitted, "Because it was Dean, it caused me to be even more fired up." As close friends, they were aware of each other's tricks. The media seized the drama and squeezed, though there were other plums in the story line. For instance, Worthy and Georgetown's Floyd were both All-Americans, both from little Gastonia, North Carolina, both the stalwarts of their teams. The pregame tension was thick despite the vast open space. "Choke, Dean, choke," the Georgetown student section chanted.

The nineteen-year-old Ewing opened the game by swatting away four Carolina shots, two of them by Worthy. All four were ruled goaltending, as was a fifth Ewing block later in the first half. The Heels scored their first 8 points without putting the ball through the hoop.

"Patrick was an excellent shot-blocker," Thompson told Packer in an interview five years later. "We wanted to establish ourselves inside as much as we possibly could. I still question some of the goaltending calls."

Some coaches might have worried that the blocked shots would flatten Worthy's confidence, but not Smith. "I knew that didn't bother James in the least," the Carolina coach said. "Some guys hate to see their shots blocked, but James was so sky-high."

From there, the game settled into the coaches' cat-and-mouse. The Hoyas grabbed a lead, then Carolina evened it at 18. Worthy came alive with 18 first-half points. The lead became a pendulum. Georgetown held it at the half, 32–31.

"Georgetown was relentless," Worthy recalled. "They were intent to make us crack with their defense, and they nearly did. There was a point they had gone up three or four, and back then that was a big number. So Jimmy Black misses a layup and Michael flies in and tips it back—an 'Ice' Gervin finger-roll tip-in over Ewing." The swinging momentum continued throughout the final twenty minutes. At the six-minute mark, Carolina eased ahead, 57–56, on a pair of Worthy free throws. The pace became agony after that.

Jordan, of course, would become best known for "the shot" at the end, but for the Carolina coaches, the key moment came on another Jordan left-handed basket with 3:26 left in the game. "One of the best shots of the game," Bill Guthridge recalled, "was a driving layup a few minutes earlier when he laid it almost off the top of the backboard to get it over Ewing."

"I thought it was a great drive," Smith said on the game's twentieth anniversary, "and then I saw Patrick come in and it flashed through my mind that it was going to be blocked. That was a sensational shot."

"I don't know why I threw a left-handed layup," Jordan told *Tar Heel Monthly* in 2002. "I hate using my left hand. My left hand is the weakest part of my game. But I used it that one particular time. Couldn't believe it. It turned it around. Threw a shot that was totally unbelievable, almost hit the top of the backboard and went in, over Ewing."

The basket gave North Carolina a 61–58 lead, but the Hoyas pushed back. With 2:37 left, Georgetown pulled to 61–60 when Ewing lofted a thirteen-foot shot. When Carolina missed a key free throw on its next possession, the young Georgetown center rebounded. Sleepy Floyd scored on a short jumper, and the Hoyas had the lead, 62–61, with less than a minute left.

With thirty-two seconds left, Smith called a time-out to set up a play to counter Georgetown's anticipated move back to a zone. "Usually, I don't like to take a time-out there," Smith said. "We should know what to do. But I expected Georgetown to come back to the zone and jam it in. I said, 'Doherty, take a look for James or Sam, and, Jimmy, the cross-court pass will be there to Michael.' As it turned out, Michael's whole side of the court was wide open because they were chasing James. If Michael had missed, Sam would've been the hero because he'd have had the rebound."

Smith was at his best in that huddle, so calming that assistant Roy Williams recalled glancing at the scoreboard, thinking surely he must have misread it. The way Smith was talking, Carolina must have the lead, Williams remembered thinking. As the team broke from the huddle, Smith gave Jordan a pat and said, "Knock it in, Michael."

Thirty years later, Packer, who called the game courtside for CBS, still expressed doubt about the circumstances as described by the Carolina contingent. "I always felt a shot like that couldn't have been designed by Dean Smith, although he says to this day that it was designed to go over there," the broadcaster offered. "You've got Worthy and Perkins and you've got them inside. What are we talking about? We're going to rotate the ball to Michael? Now everybody these days says, 'Sure you would.' But back then you wouldn't. You'd get the ball to Worthy first, Perkins second, and then maybe a penetration and then kick it over there. I'm not going to question Dean's basketball knowledge. Certainly when I was broadcasting that game, that wasn't an option I had in mind for one, two, or three."

Carolina worked for a good shot, and, with 15 seconds to go, Black passed to Jordan for a sixteen-foot jumper from near the left sideline.

"It was an open shot, relatively speaking," Packer said. "But the thing now that you look back, I don't care who was planning on getting the ball, Michael wanted the ball and Michael knew he would make the shot. That was the beginning of one of the great things in our lifetime. Certain guys get open shots, they can't make them. Certain guys get open shots, they don't want to take them. Michael wanted the shot, and that you saw. There was no hesitation, no extra faking. It was, 'Hey, give me the ball and I'm going to put this in the basket.' That's that level of competitive nature that he had."

Most players run from such moments, but a select few run toward them, Packer said. "He wasn't hiding in the corner. He was wanting that ball over there." Jordan would later reveal that he had visualized just such a moment on the team bus ride over to the event.

At the far end of the court, the figures on the Georgetown bench twisted in agony. Just feet away as Jordan elevated for the shot, the Carolina coaching staff all sat stoically. Smith merely pursed his lips and flinched his eyebrows into the slightest grimace. Such Final Four moments of the past had rendered no good for him.

Jordan rose up, his tongue instinctively sampling the Superdome air. At the apex, the ball graced his right fingertips as he pulled his left away and let fly.

The swish blew a heavenly light blue breeze across Tar Heel Land and stirred a thunderous roar in the building.

"There we were in the Superdome, and Michael hit that shot," Deloris Jordan recalled. She looked around for her husband and daughter Roslyn, but they had already bolted for the floor. "I could only think, 'No, not a freshman.'"

Dick Weiss recalled in a 2011 interview that he was stunned by the move, by the fact that Dean Smith would trust the last shot to a freshman. "That was the biggest game of Dean's career to that point," Weiss marveled.

"It was predestined," Jordan said in 2002. "It was destiny. Ever since I made that shot, everything has just fallen into place for me. If that shot hadn't gone in I don't think I would be where I am today."

Actually, one final, unforgettable sequence remained to seal that fate. Down 63–62 with adequate time, Georgetown attacked immediately with guard Fred Brown working the ball at the edge of the Carolina defense. He thought he saw Sleepy Floyd out of the corner of his eye, but the shadowy form in white was Carolina's Worthy. Worthy was stunned when Brown mistakenly passed him the ball. The Carolina forward grabbed it and streaked downcourt, where he was fouled.

Thompson drew criticism immediately for not having taken a time-out before the possession. But Smith agreed with Thompson's approach. "John was wise not to take the time-out," he said, pointing out that Jordan's defense had made Brown decide to reverse the ball. "Michael makes a heck of a play to cover Floyd, and James goes for a steal and doesn't get back in. To this day, I think that if Georgetown had been in their white uniforms that they had worn all during the tournament instead of wearing their dark uniforms, Brown would not have thrown the ball to James. James had gone for a steal on a fake moments earlier and was out of position. He shouldn't have been where he was on the court, and it fooled Brown."

Thompson saw the pass as a reflex action by Brown. Attempting to make a steal, Worthy had run out of the defense and was out of position. "We were playing five against four," Thompson said. "Worthy was coming from the direction an offensive player normally would come from, and I think Freddie reacted reflexively. It was like the old playground thing where the defensive player stands out where the offensive player should be and calls for the ball. But Worthy didn't call for it, he was just coming from the other side and by reflex Freddie threw him the ball."

Worthy missed both free throws with two seconds left, but it didn't matter. The Tar Heels had their blue nirvana, 63–62. There was much more to Carolina's victory than Jordan's shot, Thompson said. "We thought that Worthy hurt us more than anybody. You hear a lot about Michael Jordan's shot. That certainly broke our backs, but we were having a lot of difficulty with Worthy. He was quick enough to create problems for our big people and strong enough to create problems for our little people."

The usually impassive Worthy, named the tournament's outstanding player, dropped his stoic countenance to celebrate deliriously. Smith and Carolina had reached the top.

"I'm especially happy for coach," Jimmy Black said afterward. "Now I won't have to read any more articles from you sportswriters about how he chokes in the big games."

"I don't think I'm a better coach now that we've won the national championship," Smith told the reporters who crowded around him in the interview room. "I'm still the same coach."

Afterward, Jordan shed his shoes and sat quietly in front of his dressing space, answering questions from a single NBC reporter. James Jordan, in a three-piece suit, sat beside him and leaned slightly into the klieg lights as his son tightened his lips and waited for the reporter to form a question about the moment.

"I really didn't feel any pressure," he said calmly. "It was just another jumper over the weak side of a zone."

Chapter 12

SOMETHING NEW

BILL BILLINGSLEY HAD been invited by a group of friends to ride to New Orleans for the Final Four. After the game, he was out, part of the raucous, elated throng jammed into the French Quarter, when he ran into Michael Jordan and two teammates quietly taking in the scene.

Jordan recognized his old ninth-grade ball coach immediately. "Billingsley!" he said. "What are you doing here?" They exchanged small talk, and Billingsley happily offered up congratulations before moving on. Afterward, the coach was struck that Jordan could enjoy the moment without being instantly swarmed by celebrating fans. Neither perhaps realized it at the time, but they were experiencing the final moments of Jordan's anonymity, and even that would be tested later that evening of March 29. Back in Chapel Hill, thirty thousand fans gathered on Franklin Street as soon as they heard UNC radio broadcaster Woody Durham announce, "The Tar Heels are going to win the national championship."

"As soon as the game was over I ran screaming out there onto Franklin Street," recalled David Mann, a junior at Carolina at the time. "And of course everybody else did the same thing. There were thousands of people there just dazed. Dean Smith had never won, and it was just an unbelievable moment. Everybody was just crying and ecstatic."

"Pandemonium, hysteria, fireworks, and beer," the *Greensboro*

Daily News declared the next day. "This is the stuff national championships are made of." The celebration ran until four o'clock in the morning and got going again a couple of days later as twenty thousand fans gathered to welcome the team back into town.

It would take weeks for the celebration to calm, but the new parameters of his life would be revealed to Jordan over the coming months. "I was like a deer in the headlights," he would say, looking back much later. "I didn't realize the magnitude of what I'd done." The moment had delighted millions — many with no previous connection to the University of North Carolina — and converted lots of them instantly into lifelong Tar Heels fans. The national championship struck a note of pride for blacks and whites alike across the state. The victory they shared erased doubts about Dean Smith and his program, and marked the coronation of young Michael as the prince of hoops. "It was like a young kid coming out of his shell," Jordan observed. "My name was Mike. Everybody referred to me as Mike Jordan. After the shot, it was Michael Jordan."

If he had been a megawatt trashtalker before the shot, he became almost unbearable afterward. He and Ewing would remain lifelong friends from their shared experience. "I remember him hitting that shot," Ewing said ruefully in 2010. "I don't talk to him about that. He rubs it in enough, so I never bring it up."

Just months after enduring the taunts of local folks that he wouldn't make an impact at UNC, he returned home to discover the rising walls of his newfound notoriety, a fame that would soon enough box him into an insular world. He had planned to go to the local courts in Wilmington for a spin of pickup games, like in the days before college. But he arrived to find a mob awaiting him. He couldn't even get out of the car that day, according to a local official who witnessed the event. It was the first sign that his old way of living was soon to be gone forever.

The city hosted a Michael Jordan appreciation banquet a couple of weeks later. He signed autographs for dozens of fans, including thrilled young basketballers who showed up in their uniforms. Jordan ate at the right of Dean Smith at the banquet table that evening. His coach sported a contented smile and made light conversation while the usually ebullient young star sat quietly, still obviously very much an adolescent, almost childlike, awkward in the face of so much attention.

His parents were there, somehow managing to maintain decorum amid this wellspring of pride and excitement. "Wherever they went they always comported themselves nicely," said Billy Packer, who ran into the Jordans often. He had enjoyed a laugh with them the night of the championship, which had come exactly a year after Mrs. Jordan's angry disappointment at the McDonald's game in Kansas. "You see some parents who have to be front and center. The Jordans never were that way. They were always polite and carried themselves extremely well. I was always impressed by that." It had been a spring to remember for both of them. Deloris had returned home to find a display of Carolina Blue congratulations at the bank where she worked. One colleague greeted her with, "Hello, Mrs. Michael Jordan's Mother." She tried to sell the idea that they would have been just as proud of their son if he were a mere Carolina freshman who didn't play basketball. She did admit to an interviewer that her maternal instinct had her clutching her stomach as the Tar Heels passed the ball back and forth like a hot potato on that last possession. When it finally landed in her son's hands, her first thought was that she hoped he would pass it to someone else.

For James, the arrival home brought a special "Welcome Home, Michael Jordan" meeting at the GE plant where he worked. It wasn't just Michael's life that would be changed forever by his big shot. His parents had also been swept up by the tide.

Jordan's youthful discomfort at the banquet that evening didn't stop him from reveling in his newfound status. After all, most freshmen returned home after a year of independence at school only to find that their parents still viewed them as adolescents. His return home brought the first realization of the new status that would require huge adjustments in their family relationships. His personal stature would soon enough eclipse theirs and alter the nature of the family dynamic. Even now, at the end of his freshman year, they all sensed it. He wasn't a pro yet, but he was going to be one.

They tried not to focus on that vision of the future, especially Mrs. Jordan. If anything, she became more vigilant the more his dream gained texture in the wake of the championship. Be humble. Don't place too much emphasis on yourself. Be sure to mention your teammates. It was as if she and Dean Smith were reading from the same script. Every time she talked to a reporter, she made sure to stress how proud she was of all her children. Michael just happened to be the one who received all the public attention, she explained.

For Jordan, the immediate challenge that spring of 1982 was a search for a place where he could still enjoy the freedom of his former life. Somehow he scored a one-on-one contest with a local star in Pender County. That seemed at first as if it would be secluded enough, but even there a crowd of hundreds turned out to watch the combat, won by Jordan two games to one, according to local memory.

Ultimately, he found safe harbor in Chapel Hill. Thanks to the family atmosphere that Dean Smith had built, many of the coach's former players, including NBA stars like Walter Davis and Phil Ford, would show up in the summers for pickup games. That summer after the championship, they were all eager to size up against the young guy who had made "the shot." The alums were fascinated by Jordan's playground persona. Unlike Worthy, Al Wood had taken him on during those first months at Carolina and thought Jordan to be a bit timid. Wood had shot him an elbow in their first pickup meetings, but heading into his sophomore year, Jordan made a point of sending an elbow Wood's way, letting him know he was no longer going to be intimidated. Eventually, the bonding with Wood evolved as they worked on dunks in and around the pickup games that summer. It was Wood who gave him the idea for the one-handed, cradle-rocking dunk he would eventually trot out against Maryland. Of course, there had been those, like Worthy, who thought his confidence as a freshman had been too much. But this second year they all began to grasp that Jordan's belief in himself reflected a level of intensity no one had contemplated before.

Granville Again

Jordan and Buzz Peterson now lived on the first floor of Granville Towers on a short hallway that was locked off at both ends to protect the smattering of basketball players and regular students in residence there. Among the regular students living on the floor was David Mann, a senior who was majoring in radio, television, and motion pictures. Short, slightly built, and unassuming, Mann was afforded something of an inside view of Jordan's life at age nineteen, just as his status was soaring.

"He was very cocky even back in those days," Mann recalled. "He was Mr. Confident and he was sure of himself."

Mann would see girls hanging outside the locked hallway doors, hoping for a chance to get inside. Like most of the "regular" students on the hall, Mann took note of just about everything he saw Jordan doing. He was surprised to see little evidence of a party animal.

"He was a pretty serious guy," Mann recalled. "There were some party guys on the hall, players and students, and he never really got into that."

Buzz Peterson, for example, could be seen, drink in hand, dancing in the hallways with his girlfriend, still obviously enjoying the fact that the Tar Heels had just won the national title a few months earlier.

"Buzz was definitely not as dedicated to basketball as Michael was," Mann observed. "Buzz was more of a party guy. He didn't take things as seriously, near as seriously as Jordan did. He was kind of a goofball, to be honest."

Sports Illustrated published a photo that fall of Jordan, headphones on, dancing in his room under an umbrella, which angered Mann because it was so obviously staged. Peterson might dance around, but not Jordan, even though he had good reason to celebrate life a little.

"That's what was unique about him," Mann observed. "He could have become totally self-absorbed and gotten into partying and all that fun stuff and the women and all these other things, but the impression I got was that he was so committed he wouldn't allow himself to become sidetracked, even at that age. He knew he wanted to be the best and he knew the pitfall, and he wasn't going to fall into it. He seemed very sure of himself, sure of what he wanted to do, and nothing was going to stop him."

Mann noticed that although Jordan was just a nineteen-year-old sophomore, he seemed to command things merely with his presence, even among the other basketball players rooming on the floor. "He wasn't a loud guy. He didn't dominate everything as far as verbally, but when he talked you definitely listened. He didn't order the other players around or come across as a big shot or anything like that, but I sure think the other players respected him. I think they were intimidated by him a little bit. But he didn't go around barking orders or anything like that."

Jordan soon discovered that Mann was studying media with a plan of working in the film industry in Hollywood. "Michael thought that was nuts," Mann recalled, "and after that he would come up to me and say, 'You know you ought to go speak to Dean Smith's wife.' Dean Smith's wife was a psychiatrist and every time I would see Michael, he would say, 'Have you seen Dean Smith's wife yet? Have you talked to her?' He thought it was funny that somebody like me would want to move out to Los Angeles and have any sort of chance working in the movie business."

This teasing went on for a couple of weeks, with Jordan mocking Mann's Hollywood plans every time he saw him. It was then that Mann learned what every person who survived Jordan would have to learn—you had to stand up to him.

"Finally I told him, 'Michael, I mean this is my dream. I've always wanted to work in movies. Didn't you ever have a dream?' And he said, 'Yeah, I have a dream to play in the NBA.' After that he never really bugged me about it anymore."

Jordan soon discovered that, as a media student, Mann had a video recorder in his room, a rare development since video technology was still relatively new and quite expensive. Mann was also a huge basketball fan and would tape the Carolina games. Jordan began dropping by to watch himself on replay.

"This was so long ago that the remote was wired," Mann recalled. "You had to tilt this twelve-foot-long wired remote. He would sit there and watch himself and back it up to watch himself again. I think he learned a lot from doing that. I don't know how much the coaches did this kind of videotape work, but he definitely did it on my VCR a lot."

The player who would do so much to define the video age was getting the first opportunity to study himself.

One of the first things Mann and Jordan watched together was the championship game versus Georgetown. During the broadcast, commentator Billy Packer remarked that Worthy was the fastest player on Carolina's team.

"That's bullshit," Jordan fussed. "I'm the fastest guy on the team."

When they came to Jordan's big shot, Mann asked him about it. "He said when he hit that last shot he really wasn't sure if that was where Coach Smith wanted him. He was thinking he had screwed up. He told me he was a little confused about where he was supposed to be on that play. He happened to be open and he took the shot and made it."

As the season went on, Jordan would stop in Mann's room to study his game. "He was totally silent," Mann recalled. "He didn't say much of anything. He was totally concentrating on what he was thinking and what he was strategizing in his head. He didn't say much when he watched, and I just sort of left him alone."

One day Jordan encountered Mann putting into a cup in the hallway. "He wants to do it too, and he wants to bet on putting the ball into the cup," Mann recalled. "It was only like a quarter or a dime, but anyway we did this for like thirty minutes and I was beating him. I had to go to class, and he wouldn't let me stop. So he's making me stay there, but I didn't want to lose so I kept putting it into the cup."

Finally, in exasperation, Jordan threw down the putter and walked off. "He ended up owing me about seventy-five cents," Mann remembered, "and he never paid."

The Upgrade

After the summer rounds of camps and appearances, and his pickup battles and individual work, it was an upgraded Jordan who had arrived in practice that fall. "Preseason, sophomore year," Smith later recalled. "I couldn't believe the improvement since the end of his freshman season. Every time he did a drill with the Blue Team, the Blues would win. Every time he did one with the White Team, the Whites would win. The staff started saying to one another, 'What's going on here?' He hadn't been on any preseason All-America teams, but he'd grown two inches, had worked hard over the summer to improve his ball handling and shooting, and he had so much confidence."

"Dean always said the biggest improvement that guys make is between their freshman and sophomore years," Art Chansky offered. "He always told them after a year of basketball what they have to work on. If they go back and work on it, they get it because they've played a year of college basketball. They get bigger physically, and there's this quantum leap in their games, if they work on it. Michael came back, and it was like, 'Whoa. Holy shit.'"

He was bigger, stronger, faster. His time in the forty-yard dash had fallen to 4.39 seconds, almost two-tenths of a second faster than his freshman year. All the arrows, it seemed, were pointing up. In his unguarded moments, Jordan acknowledged that his goal was to win more national championships, which suggested that he didn't recognize how fortunate he'd been to win one. The odds on another title might have been better had Dean Smith been a bit more selfish and persuaded James Worthy to stay at North Carolina for his senior year.

However, the coach continued to prize the success of his players above his own, even perhaps above the team's. Another coach would have pointed out to Worthy that the Tar Heels were on the brink of winning back-to-back national championships. With Worthy, the school would be returning a team with four starters, a team that could make real history. Yet instead of exerting any sort of pressure to keep Worthy in school, Smith began researching Worthy's prospects for the upcoming NBA draft.

When he learned that Worthy was likely to be the top pick, he dutifully advised him to claim "hardship" status and enter the draft. The risk of injury and the loss of huge sums were too great for Worthy to continue to play amateur basketball. It was a remarkable display of integrity from Smith, another reason his players held him in such esteem. Five seasons earlier he had done the same for point guard Phil Ford, had all but insisted that he turn professional after his junior season, Art Chansky recalled. Ford, however, declined to leave, explaining to Smith, "Who's going to tell my mother?" He came back to Carolina and was player of the year that final season.

Worthy's family also prized education, but Smith emphasized that the prudent step was to enter the draft. Worthy was selected by the Los Angeles Lakers as the top overall pick. To replace him, Smith brought in the next round of high school All-Americans, including a sixteen-year-old seven-footer, Brad Daugherty, and an athletic six-five guard, Curtis Hunter, so there was a lot of reconfiguring in the lineup. Still, the Tar Heels entered the year as the top-ranked team in the polls, a status that changed almost immediately.

There were several reasons the 1982–83 campaign would fall short of expectations. Six weeks before the season started, Jordan broke his left wrist. He practiced anyway, with a cast on. Buzz Peterson injured a knee midway through the season, which prompted Jordan to begin wearing his trademark wristband midway up the left forearm as a tribute to his roommate. Mostly, though, the Tar Heels felt Worthy's absence. As Billy Packer had pointed out, he was a tremendous player who left an almost unfillable void.

Dick Weiss went to Chapel Hill to visit with Jordan as the season was set to open. Jordan talked pridefully about the fact that he and his father were NASCAR fans. Weiss noted that this was a young man with an inclination not to play to any sort of stereotypes. He was a nice kid, Weiss remembered in 2011, adding that he saw absolutely nothing in Jordan or in Jordan's game to give him the slightest clue that "this kid was the next savior of the NBA." The sportswriter did come away believing that Georgetown and Carolina would meet again for the title that next spring.

It never happened.

Despite the cast on his wrist, Jordan scored 25 points to go with Perkins's 22 in the season-opening overtime loss to Chris Mullin and a deep St. John's team, 78–74. A week later they traveled to St. Louis for a physical confrontation with Missouri. Again, they lost, 64–60, and it became clear there would be no absence of drama this season. Not surprisingly, each team they played came at them with maximum focus. Three days later, Tulane came to Chapel Hill with their impressive center John "Hot Rod" Williams. The contest wasn't too old before the idea settled on the crowd that Carolina might just do the unthinkable — lose three straight games to open the season. No North Carolina team had done that since 1928–29.

The real trouble started when Perkins got his fifth foul at the 4:33 mark, which allowed the six-nine Williams more freedom to work. Tulane took a 51–49 lead. Jordan tied it with an offensive rebound and putback with thirty-six seconds left. Carolina then sent Williams to the line with eight seconds left, and he made both to put the Green Wave up two. Once again, Jordan found himself with the ball in the closing seconds. He made his move to the basket but was whistled for an offensive foul.

James Jordan sat between his two daughters watching the proceedings. "I thought, 'We have lost this one,'" he recalled in a 1984 interview. Roslyn looked at him and said, "Daddy, you give up too fast." The clock showed four seconds when Jordan stole the inbounds pass and tossed in a thirty-five-foot shot to tie the game at the buzzer. Carmichael erupted, but the tension was far from over.

The contest was settled finally with just under two minutes to go in the third overtime period when Jordan motored along the baseline, banked in a shot, and drew the foul to extend Carolina's lead to five, enough to give the Tar Heels their first win of the year, 70–68.

"He started the season with a cast on his left wrist, and still he won a game for us against Tulane," Smith recalled.

The schedule afforded few breaks. Next they faced LSU in the New Jersey Meadowlands, a game they won by four. They got their third win over Santa Clara in Greensboro and a week later headed to Tulsa at the start of the Christmas break in the Oil City Classic.

The Golden Hurricane beat them by 10 in the first game. The Tar Heels were still adjusting to life without Worthy, who had given them not just a post game but lots of activity down low. Three days later they traveled to play UT–Chattanooga and found themselves down one with just under four minutes left. Jordan produced one of those "MJ moments," scoring 11 of the team's final 17 points to secure another win.

For the holidays, the Jordans packed up and followed the team to Honolulu for the Rainbow Classic, where in addition to luaus they feasted on three wins, including a 73–58 avenging of their earlier loss to Missouri. That sparked an eighteen-game winning streak. The Tar Heels arrived home and immediately took on Rutgers in Greensboro, then rode to Charlotte to measure their power against Syracuse before wading into the ACC schedule. Syracuse assistant Brendan Malone, Jordan's coach at the Five-Star camp, had an opportunity to assess his progress. The Orangemen figured they'd test him with a double-team. "We trapped in the backcourt," Malone recalled. "I was impressed by his poise under pressure. He took the double-team, dribbled away from it, got low, looked through the double-team, and made a perfect pass. He never panicked in that kind of situation."

As a reaction to Smith's stall in the 1982 ACC title bout, the conference had instituted a shot clock and a three-point shot on an experimental basis that season. No longer could Smith spread the floor and play cat and mouse to protect a thin lead. Nor could a team just sit mindlessly packed into a zone defense. Teams now had to have better plans for guarding the perimeter.

Jordan scored just 2 points in the first half at Maryland, then came alive with 15 in the second half. His big play, however, came at the end when he blocked a layup by Chuck Driesell, the son of Maryland coach Lefty Driesell, to save a 72–71 win.

The Tar Heels had yet to face Ralph Sampson and Virginia, but that didn't mean the upcoming game wasn't on their minds. Teammates Warren Martin, Curtis Hunter, and Brad Daugherty also roomed on the first floor of Granville Towers. "The day before the game the players were standing out in the hallway talking about the game, and they were scared to death," David Mann recalled. "I mean people don't realize how much Ralph Sampson was feared in those days. He was like Godzilla in the basketball world back then. Brad Daugherty was a freshman, and he didn't want to have to go up against Sampson. So the guys are standing in the hall talking about what they're going to do and how nervous they are. Michael's sitting there and he's not saying a word. And after a few minutes of this, all of a sudden he jumps up, about forty inches straight up, and slams his hand against the wall and screams out, 'Fuck Sampson!'"

Startled, his teammates went silent.

"Everybody just sort of scattered after that," Mann recalled with a laugh.

The teams' first meeting the next day was broadcast on NBC from University Hall. Virginia was ranked second and the Tar Heels held the eleventh spot in the polls. The Cavaliers were also guarding a forty-two-game win streak on their home floor during the Sampson era. It was the first Virginia home game in almost six weeks, and the Tar Heel presence was enough to incite the nine thousand fans to cheer each time Sampson approached the basket in warm-ups. And they hooted when Smith stood by his bench, his NCAA championship ring glittering in the television lights. They chanted, "Sit down, Dean. Sit down, Dean."

The Tar Heels immediately sandwiched Sampson in a zone and ran off a string of three-point goals for a 12-point lead. By halftime the air in the small arena was dead from disappointment. Smith put the seven-foot freshman Brad Daugherty at one of Sampson's shoulders and six-foot-nine Sam Perkins at the other, with a wing player from either side also ready to collapse. The Tar Heels effectively denied him the ball while keeping the other Virginia players from establishing any offensive flow. Sampson hit only 2 of 8 field goal attempts in the first twenty minutes. Meanwhile, Perkins gave one of the best offensive performances of his career, scoring 25 points, including three three-point goals, in the first half.

After intermission, the arena settled into near silence as Sampson was called for his third and fourth fouls and North Carolina widened its lead to 23 points, at 85–62, with 9:41 remaining. Then, two minutes later, Sampson hit his first three-pointer of the season, a nineteen-foot shot from the left baseline, and Virginia began a comeback. Virginia's Ricky Stokes, Jimmy Miller, Rick Carlisle, Tim Mullen, and Othell Wilson each scored. Then Sampson again. And Carlisle followed with a three-pointer. Within a five-minute span, the Wahoos had sliced the lead from 23 to 6 points. With two minutes remaining, and Carolina holding on, 96–90, Sampson rose up to the right of the lane for a short jumper. Jordan simultaneously leaped from the other side of the lane and ferociously smacked down the ball.

The play drew gasps along press row. Standing on the sideline, Virginia coach Terry Holland caught himself applauding. "Michael and David Thompson," Holland recalled, "are the only two players that have made plays against my own team that made me applaud in sheer amazement...before I realized that I was cheering against my own team.

"I was also hollering at the referee that it 'had to be goaltending' at the same time," Holland said. "I think the referees were as stunned and amazed as I was and could not figure out how he did it either. Technically, the block had to be goaltending—it had to be heading down since Ralph released it from above the rim. Looked like a Titan missile. Not sure why he would even think about going after it."

"That was back in my young days," Jordan said fifteen years later, admitting that he had no idea he could make the play. "I surprised myself. That was the beauty of my game, and it has propelled me to my career to some degree. No one could sit there and tell you what I could do. I couldn't tell you what I couldn't do and what I could. And that was the beauty of everything."

Playing in Smith's system, Jordan had yet to discover anything close to the full range of his abilities.

Fourteen seconds after the block, Othell Wilson hit a three-pointer, and Virginia pulled within two with fifty seconds to play. But the Cavaliers were forced to foul, and Jordan and Jimmy Braddock made their free throws for a 101–95 win. Sampson left University Hall that day without speaking to reporters.

With the victory, Carolina moved to first place in the ACC. The Tar Heels then beat NC State and Duke by large margins. With Worthy gone to the NBA, Jordan began slipping down to the box, where he showed the first flashes of the post-up game that would be a staple of his professional play. He ran the floor well and often benefited from being the open man in Smith's secondary break. Even when he wasn't open, Jordan could produce a shot with his quick first step and elevation. He still drew occasional traveling calls for the move, but Smith had sent a slow-motion videotape of the first step to the NCAA to confirm that Jordan was not traveling. The Carolina offense also produced bunches of back cuts and backdoor plays that helped an athletic player like Jordan fill out the stat sheet.

"Jordan worked as hard as any player I've seen, especially an excellent player," said Duke coach Mike Krzyzewski after that January game. "He set the tone for the game. He was as tough mentally as I've ever seen him play. He said, 'I want it, give it to me. I'm going to work.' He was just excellent. We wanted to play defense on him. We diagrammed and said, 'This is what he's going to do.' He still did it. I admire that. Even when he missed shots, he was working so hard to get them. He never gave us a chance to get back into it."

Jordan's run continued against Georgia Tech the next week when he made 11 of 16 shots on his way to his career high in college, 39 points. His totals included seven three-point attempts. He made six of them.

His efforts had impressed ESPN commentator and former coach Dick Vitale as Virginia came to Carmichael Auditorium. The winning streak had driven the Tar Heels to number one in the country, with Virginia number two in one poll. The Virginia sports information people were irritated by Vitale, whom they accused of conducting a one-man campaign against Sampson in the national Player of the Year balloting. Vitale had extolled the talents of Jordan, but Terry Holland and the Virginia PR staff felt that Vitale was not merely supporting Jordan, but had been snidely attacking Sampson.

Vitale used the word "superstar" with a tinge of derision regarding Sampson, they said. The broadcaster felt he was being misunderstood. He said that Sampson, unlike some other great centers, had played with inferior talent at Virginia. But Vitale remarked that at times during his final college season, Sampson had lacked enthusiasm while Jordan, on the other hand, oozed it.

Thirty years later, Holland observed, "There's no argument that Michael was a legitimate candidate and that Dick had every right to vote for as well as promote whomever he wished to promote. But our objection was to his comments about why Michael should be the Player of the Year instead of Ralph. That was just Dick being Dick as he tends to get carried away. But there seemed little reason to criticize Ralph in order to promote his candidate." Holland added that Sampson was already a two-time college Player of the Year who had stayed in school for four years.

The debate would be settled on Carmichael's floor. The pregame noise from the packed student section was so deafening, Virginia's players could barely hear their own names during the introductions. Nonetheless, they played brilliantly and had stacked up a 16-point lead with nine minutes left in the second half.

With 4:48 left, Virginia's Jimmy Miller finished a three-point play, opening a 63–53 lead. The Cavaliers never scored again, but stumbled through a rash of turnovers and steals. At 1:20, with his team still leading 63–60, Sampson missed a foul shot. Then came the signature play, with 51 seconds on the clock, as Jordan stripped the ball from Rick Carlisle at midcourt, sped to the rim, and jammed in a 64–63 Carolina lead. Decades later, the play would still stir testimonials from those who watched it happen. Virginia then whittled down the last fifty seconds until Carlisle missed a long jumper with 0:05 remaining on the clock.

Jordan outjumped Sampson to claim the key final rebound, which was telling, Billy Packer recalled. "That particular year his highlights were not offensive. His highlights showed me, number one, his incredible competitive nature, but also his defensive skills. I learned more about him in '83 in regard to how well he could guard somebody. Obviously he was a good scorer, too, but where he was phenomenal was defensively."

Holland agreed. "Michael was a terrific all-around college player, but he was most effective defensively," he recalled in 2012. "And that is a lot more difficult to prepare for than a great offensive player since you can't double-cover a defender or devise ways to keep the ball out of his hands."

The Carolina crowd stood and cheered long after the game was over. "We were back in the dorm later that night," David Mann recalled, "and my voice was totally gone. I screamed my voice out, and I was downstairs at the snack machine and Michael comes down there. It's just me and him, and I'm talking to him about how great the game was and how awesome he was. He was like matter-of-fact about it. 'Yeah. Okay.' And he started talking about class. He was totally nonchalant about the whole thing, like nothing had even happened. He wasn't even interested in talking about the game."

Three days later Villanova came to town for a rematch of the 1982 regional finals. Eddie Pinckney had remained in touch with Sam Perkins, fellow New Yorkers eager to get any inside info they could, it seems. Some of their talk focused on the growing competition between conferences. Villanova belonged to the Big East, which included Georgetown.

"We didn't want to fraternize too much because they had the potential to embarrass you if you let them," Pinckney recalled of the Tar Heels. "What Perkins would say is Jordan was the best player he'd ever seen. And, of course, I would say it was Ewing. For us, just going down there and getting a chance to play against Jordan and an ACC team that was ranked number one at the time is something you never forget, because the ACC ruled at the time. They were the premier conference and they had all the great players.

"They were ranked at the time as number one, and they had Jordan," Pinckney explained. "We didn't really think we could deal with him. You just knew this guy was a great player. You're saying to yourself as a player, 'I've seen this guy play before. When's it going to happen?' 'Cause you knew what's coming. 'When's he going to take over the game?'"

It didn't happen that day. Jordan didn't play particularly well, and Villanova defeated the number one team in the country, in their own building. "They were supposed to just squash us, and we put up a pretty good fight," Pinckney said. "We played out of our minds."

The loss sent the Tar Heels into a spiral. They traveled to Maryland three days later and lost by 12, then lost again three days after that at NC State by 7 points, foreshadowing their loss to the Wolf-pack later in the ACC tournament semifinals that year. Jim Valvano's players had fallen into a rhythm that would carry them all the way to an improbable national championship against Houston.

The Heels, meanwhile, made their way to the NCAA regional final in Syracuse, where they were snuffed by Georgia, 82–77. Jordan broke loose for several flashy dunks but couldn't deliver victory. Afterward, he told Roy Williams he was burned out and was going to take a break from basketball. The assistant understood the competitive burden that Jordan had assumed with Worthy's departure. Smith's system helped to ease the circumstances, but Jordan's very best had been required each game for the Carolina basketball machine to keep rolling forward. Williams told Jordan that taking a break made sense, so he was understandably surprised the next day to find him back in the gym, working on his game. Asked about his change in plans, Jordan just said that he had to get better.

The Tar Heels had suffered a blow with the season's end, but the Jordan reputation had climbed several levels. He was now seen as "easily the best defensive guard in the land," according to *Sports Illustrated*, this a mere year after striking the coaching staff as almost indifferent about defense as a freshman. "Jordan always seems to know where the ball is and where it's going," said Maryland forward Mark Fothergill. "He roams around like a madman, playing the whole court and causing all kinds of confusion."

With the ACC's three-point shot experiment, Jordan had raised his average to 20.0 points a game (good enough to lead the ACC), along with 5.5 rebounds. Still, he wasn't pleased. He had shot 53.5 percent from the floor, but the outside shot, critical with Carolina facing so many zones, wasn't as strong as it was during his freshman campaign. "I think the three-pointer altered my thinking," he decided. "I was pressing, trying to hit too many long ones." Actually, he had hit an impressive 44.7 percent on three-point shots, good enough to rank him fourth among Carolina's guards. "Plus, my arc got higher and higher," he said. "I think the winning shot in '82 went to my head or something. I must have watched it on film thirty times. That thing was a rainbow. Wow."

As a freshman, he had never won the defensive award selected by the Carolina coaches after each game, but he won it thirteen times as a sophomore. He had slipped into the passing lanes for deflections and used his long arms for back-tips, recording 78 steals on the season, just shy of Dudley Bradley's Carolina record. The defensive activity meant that he racked up 110 personal fouls, fouling out of four games, all of which the Tar Heels lost.

Beyond the stats, there had been several startling displays. He had, in one instance, jumped over the head of NC State guard Sidney Lowe. And *Sports Illustrated* had named one of his slams against Georgia Tech a "demoralizer dunk." He had left the ground at the foul line, displayed a disconcerting hang time, then redirected his slam to the side of the goal at the last moment. "I thought I was watching Superman," Georgia Tech's Tim Harvey exclaimed afterward.

The Jordan legend mushroomed again. He was named to the ACC's first team and to the AP All-America team, although he didn't take the national Player of the Year award away from Sampson. Jordan did finish second in the AP national Player of the Year award, and the *Sporting News* named him its College Player of the Year. "He soars through the air," the sports weekly noted. "He rebounds, he scores (more than 1,100 points in two years, a school record), he guards two men at once, he vacuums up loose balls, he blocks shots, he makes steals. Most important, he makes late plays that win games."

Regardless, Jordan plunged into a deep funk at the abrupt end of the season. "It left a bitter taste in my mouth," he said later that year. "Maybe I got spoiled, winning the NCAAs as a freshman." He was also upset with certain teammates who he felt lacked the necessary competitive drive. Such questioning of teammates came to be a common theme in his life, which he often acknowledged. "It was hard to deal with a guy who wasn't competitive," he later explained. "I was always testing that aspect of my teammates' character on and off the court. You pick on them to see if they will stand up. If they don't take it, you know you can trust them to come through when the pressure is on in the game." He explained that he became better at dealing with these issues as a professional, although many of his Bulls teammates would disagree.

David Mann remembered things turning quiet on the hallway in Granville Towers with the disappointing end to the season. "Nobody spoke about it." Finally, Mann mustered the courage to ask Jordan how he felt about NC State winning the national title. "He said, 'You know, I'm mixed. I kind of like State, but it should have been us.'"

It would later be reported that Jordan took up golf to soothe his raw emotions in the wake of the Georgia loss, that he was taught the game by Buzz Peterson and Davis Love III, who was then an All-American golfer for UNC. There was some truth in the story, although it happened more gradually.

Peterson had played high school golf and knew Love, whose father had given Dean Smith golf lessons. Peterson, Love, and Roy Williams spent many days on the links, and Jordan didn't like feeling left out. Love recalled that he began tagging along. "He ended up coming out riding in the cart and eventually wanted to play, so Buzz and I rounded up a set of clubs and some old balls and got him started.... We kind of created a monster," Love remembered. Brad Daugherty, Matt Doherty, and several other players also joined the group from time to time. Competitive as ever, Jordan and his teammates were drawn to the driving range to work on their swings.

"A lot of the players would come down and play," Love recalled. "One time Coach Smith said, 'All the players are down on the driving range. Could you send them back up to the gym?'"

"It was fun to get to know him and watch him grow," Love said years later. "The best thing about golf for him is that it gives him something to do away from the crowd, away from his celebrity status. I think that's why he likes it so much. It's hard to do and it's a challenge, but it's also a release for him to get away from basketball."

There were other outlets besides golf, Art Chansky recalled. "They had the campus championship softball team at Granville Towers with all the basketball players, and Michael was a big star. I think he was the shortstop. That drew big crowds to the campus intramural fields. But the guys were not like they are today, where they can live in apartments. Back then they all lived in Granville Towers and they all hung together. It was something. It was a different day. He was on his way to being a star, although no one had any idea about what kind of star he would become."

Pan Am

Jordan may have needed a break from basketball, but the Pan American Games in Caracas, Venezuela, soon called him back. He was more than eager to try out for the US team after the NCAA disappointment. It would be important international experience, but mostly, it was just basketball.

"I couldn't wait for the next game," he would remember.

The tryouts for the Pan Am squad brought together dozens of players from two US amateur teams. Jack Hartman of Kansas State coached the team under the watchful eye of Indiana coach Bobby Knight, who had been picked to lead the USA in the 1984 Olympic Games in Los Angeles.

Ed Pinckney remembers Jordan playing with a fury and talking trash like Pinckney had never heard it talked, even in New York. "There must have been a hundred guys trying out for this team," Pinckney recalled, "and they split us all up. I will never forget how he played during those tryouts. They split us up into groups of four. I was on his team. Bobby Knight was on this scaffold in the middle of the court and he would overlook all the courts. I think there were some other coaches up there with him. With Michael on our team, we did not lose a game. It was ridiculous. You played each game to seven. They had this clock and you played until seven or until the clock sounded off."

The process was designed to maximize competition, but Jordan actually minimized it, Pinckney said with a laugh. "We'd go to one court, and we'd beat a team seven to nothing. He'd score every basket. We'd go to the next court and win seven to three and he'd scored five in a row. Maybe somebody else got a layup or something.

It was a joke. That's when I said to myself, 'He's out of control, he's so good.' "

Pinckney and Jordan made the team with Chris Mullin, Leon Wood, Michael Cage, Sam Perkins, Mark Price, Wayman Tisdale, Anthony Teachey, and several others. Hartman took the team to Kansas to play two warm-up games against a collection of NBA players, including Larry Drew and Eddie Johnson from the Kansas City Kings.

"Certain guys were talking about the NBA," Pinckney recalled. "We all knew Michael was going. There wasn't any question if he was going. He knew he was going to the NBA. But we all kind of wanted to see how we would match up. He dominated those two games. He was stealing the ball. It was the first time I saw him do his rock-cradle dunk. He had no problem playing against those guys at all, at all. I mean he just stood out."

The hotel featured a small par-three golf course, which immediately attracted Jordan's attention. "The only thing he wanted to do when we weren't playing basketball was play golf," Pinckney remembered. "We practiced, and that guy would come back and he'd spend his time there. That's all he did. He'd go do that and then we'd go practice. It was the same deal when we went away. He just loved to play. I know he didn't sleep much. He hung out with Leon Wood all the time. Those guys went everywhere together."

The team played an exhibition game in Puerto Rico, en route to Venezuela. Teachey recalled that although the Puerto Rican players on the other team may not have been able to understand Jordan, that didn't stop him from trash talking. "He always believed in letting those guys know that we pretty much invented the game. He was very competitive when we traveled abroad. And he wasn't shy about it."

From there, Team USA made its way to Venezuela for the August games, and discovered that their dormitory was little more than a concrete shell. Lon Kruger, who would go on to a career coaching in college and the NBA, was the team manager for the event. "The village wasn't completed," Kruger recalled. "The windows weren't on. The doors weren't on. We looked at each other like, 'What's going on?' "

Jordan took one look at the bare concrete, then pitched his travel bag on the floor and said, "Let's get to work." Hartman was struck by the all-business approach, no whining or complaining about the accommodations.

"Michael Jordan stepped up and said, 'This is the Athletes' Village. We're okay,'" Kruger remembered. "And when Michael said it, everyone else was good with it."

Wood, who would later become an NBA referee, remembered Jordan's attitude as "there's nothing we can do about it now."

"We're here to get our medal," Jordan told his teammates. "Let's go about our business."

The Americans faced eight games over twelve days against international teams. In the first game, the Americans fell behind Mexico, 20–4, and Jordan aggravated the tendinitis in his right knee. He fought through it to help deliver a win. He played with pain in the second game, against Brazil, and scored 27 points, including a dunk that secured Team USA's come-from-behind victory. Afterward, he sat with his leg encased in ice. "It's a tendinitis injury from way back," he told a reporter. "It won't be a problem. Besides, I wouldn't miss playing now for anything."

Despite the injury, Jordan attacked each successive opponent, Pinckney remembered. "He's stealing the ball on defense, hitting post-up shots on offense. If something didn't go right he was pissed. He played with a fury. He was kind of like the leader of the team, so when you were out on the court, you had to bring it. Guys we were playing against were foreign pros and played ball overseas in Europe and in South America. You're talking about playing against older guys. He'd get out there and he didn't care. It was like, 'Bring it or get somebody else out on the court.'"

Jordan struggled at times with his outside shot during the event. It was actually point guard Mark Price who came through, Billy Packer pointed out. "Our guys didn't play well. We played a lot of zone. We didn't do a lot of running, and the other teams were not intimidated by our kids. Mark Price was probably the guy that pulled out more games than anybody. Michael was good but he wasn't great."

Jack Hartman was plenty impressed, however. "This kid takes it to the hole as hard as anybody ever has," the coach said afterward. "Sometimes I felt cheated coaching him. Michael created so many incredible moves I wanted to see them all again on instant replay. But I couldn't because I was there, live."

Jordan led the team in scoring, averaging 17.3 points over the eight games. He may have missed out on a second NCAA title, but he now had an international gold medal.

No sooner had he returned home than Deloris Jordan took one look at her exhausted son and told him to forget about going out in search of pickup games. "Enough," she said. "You're going to stay home."

To make sure of it, she took away his car keys and told him to do something he never seemed to have the time or inclination to do. She demanded he get some sleep.

Chapter 13

SYSTEM FAILURE

Once rested, Jordan headed back to Chapel Hill late that summer of 1983. "The freshmen were already talking trash. I had to see what they had," he said. Dean Smith had pulled in two forwards from the *Parade* All-American team, Joe Wolf and Dave Popson, but it was the point guard he had recruited from New York who piqued Jordan's interest. Kenny Smith had already earned a nickname, "The Jet," and he aced Jordan's test for competitiveness. He had both speed and quickness aplenty. He wasn't above scoring but, like Jimmy Black, he understood the game and the role of a true point guard. With Buzz Peterson back from injury and sophomore Steve Hale having shown that he was capable of playing big, Dean Smith had a good mix competing for the position.

"It's the toughest position to adjust to here," he explained to *Sports Illustrated*. "We throw so much at them."

The biggest thing the coach threw at them was Jordan himself, recently immortalized by "The Jordan" sandwich on the menu at Chapel Hill's Four Corners restaurant—crab salad on a pita.

Jordan's leadership relied on more than instilling the fear of a scolding in his teammates. No one on the team, including freshmen, wanted to let him down. It was not something Jordan articulated. As he often explained, he wasn't much of a rah-rah type. More, he played all out, and insisted on the same from his teammates, as Pinckney had described on the Pan Am team. Often he could motivate them with a mere frown. None of them wanted to be the target of his furrowed gaze. Mostly, he presented a picture of efficiency. "Coming from New York I've seen so many players with great talent waste it," Matt Doherty, then a senior, explained at the time. "Michael puts every ounce of talent to use."

The veteran roster seemed focused on matching Jordan's intensity. Brad Daugherty was now a year older and much stronger. Perkins was already a two-time All-American, and as Jordan had explained to a skeptical Jack Hartman, "He'll be there when you need him." Carolina had admirable depth in the post with junior Warren Martin. Doherty was the small forward, and Curtis Hunter was back from a foot injury to provide depth on the wing.

Jordan, too, was very much a different player now, polished and determined. Duke guard Johnny Dawkins had observed his growth. "Jordan goes all out," he said. "Not just physically, like he used to, but now he outthinks you. Back door here. Lob to me here. Good defensive play there. Of all the players he's the most impressive."

Which meant that North Carolina for 1983–84 was a very special college basketball team, one of the top teams of all time, according to Billy Packer. "It was amazing. That team was Dean Smith's best team. You've got to figure, it had the backcourt, the frontcourt, the explosive scoring, all the things, the size. They had the experience. We're talking about guys that could really play at the highest of levels. You've got three starters who were on the national championship team in terms of experience." Brad Daugherty and Kenny Smith would both enjoy excellent NBA careers with Jordan and Perkins, Packer pointed out.

It was, the broadcaster said, looking back in a 2012 interview, a team for the ages, better than Smith's two teams that won national titles.

Kenny Smith was a talkative sort who would slip down to Jordan and Peterson's room in Granville Towers for late-night bull sessions. Smith's excellent court vision and passing ability bonded him quickly with Jordan on the floor as well. Their alley-oop connection soon became a thrill button for delighted Carolina fans.

The Tar Heels reeled off twenty-one straight wins (the first seventeen victories were by an average margin of 17.4 points) to open the season before suffering their first loss February 12 at Arkansas. The ACC had moved on from its one-year experiment with the three-point shot, which meant that Jordan's shooting percentage rose to 55.1. His scoring dipped slightly to 19.6, but his focus and energy brought raves from the media.

He surprised sportswriters in the midst of the winning streak one day in January by showing up with his head nearly bald. "My dad's bald, so I figured I might be bald one day," he told them. "I wanted to get an advanced look at it and know how it feels." They began laughing at his explanation, so he quickly confessed, "Actually, it was just a matter of the barber cutting more than I told him."

His pate glistening, he produced highlights at almost every turn. But his close to Carolina's 74–62 victory at Maryland in January left Lefty Driesell stomping and fussing. Dean Smith would tell people that the phrase "tomahawk dunk" was coined that day. Others would call the shot a cradle-rocker. The ACC would later use the footage in a promo. The play subtly seeded the idea that Jordan could fly. And once again, it surprised Jordan himself.

"Before you know it," he later recalled, "I'm cranking the ball back, rocking it left to right, cuffing it before I put it down....The breakaway after that seemed like a chance to try something new."

For Billy Packer, the dunk was a revelation. "I never saw him do that spectacular thing until that dunk that the ACC used in a promotional tape where he cupped the ball up in Maryland and threw it down in a wide open break," the broadcaster said. "Because at Carolina you just didn't do that. If you had a fast break opportunity, you went in and took a proper layup. You didn't tomahawk the ball and dunk it when you're all alone. It was like, 'Holy mackerel!' That's the first time I ever saw the unbelievable athleticism and dexterity. That's the first time I saw it from him."

Indeed, Dean Smith called Jordan into his office the very next day. He first pointed out that Kenny Smith had been available for a throw-ahead on the play, and then reminded Jordan that such displays were not the Carolina way.

"He never wanted to show up an opponent," Jordan explained.

Art Chansky recalled that Smith refused to allow producers of his TV show to air the footage of the dunk. "He told Woody Durham and his TV show producers that he didn't want that play in there because he thought that showed up Maryland a little bit, on that breakaway. He was pissed at Michael about that."

Jordan accepted his coach's correction, although he did later point out that such displays were "part of who I was, a way of expressing myself."

Anthony Teachey asserted that if you paid close attention, you could see that Jordan wasn't entirely happy with the situation either. "I think there were times in college that it frustrated him, because he didn't have the freedom to really expose his talent like he wanted to," Teachey said in a 2012 interview. "The limitations frustrated him once he got in college because of the lack of freedom. I could see it, because in high school he didn't have Worthy or Perkins or those guys on his team. The frustration came with the lack of freedom. He controlled it very well."

Teachey thought Jordan had displayed remarkable maturity in restraining his considerable talent to play in Smith's system. "I don't think he could have played for him in high school," Teachey said. He observed that Jordan had dramatically adjusted his game to fit in at North Carolina, and had never gotten credit for having the character to make such an adjustment.

The good times rolled on for another month, until Jordan scored 29 in a win over LSU, a game marked by an ugly "frustration foul" from the Tigers' John Tudor as Kenny Smith was going in for a breakaway score. Tudor swung hard across Smith's face, and the freshman guard tumbled on his arm under the basket. Jordan rushed up and shoved Tudor before being pulled away by the officials. Smith missed eight games with a broken wrist, and while backup Steve Hale played very well in his absence, the injury was viewed as a factor in breaking Carolina's momentum. It always seemed there was one injury or another that altered the course of the best seasons for Dean Smith's teams.

Wearing a rubber cast, Kenny Smith returned not long after a loss at Arkansas, and Jordan resumed his reel of highlights. He scored 24 against Virginia on 11 of 15 shooting. He hammered down 32 in a 25-point win over NC State. And there was always something about Maryland (thought by media observers to be

Adrian Branch's MVP in the McDonald's game) that inspired Jordan's best dunking displays. He went for 25 in his final game against Lefty Driesell's team, finishing with another dunk, this one high over center Ben Coleman, who fouled him for a three-point play. He had an 18-point second half in a win over Georgia Tech, and then came his last appearance in Carmichael. Krzyzewski's young Duke team pushed the Tar Heels to double overtime before succumbing, 96–83. Jordan scored 25, but the game was a harbinger. A week later, the two teams met again in the ACC tournament semifinals, and the Blue Devils completed the upset, 77–75.

"What's amazing about the ACC tournament," Billy Packer observed of Jordan, "in all of his career, that is the one place where he doesn't stand out. He doesn't have a good ACC tournament record. Except, of course, for his brilliant work as a freshman against Virginia to win the league championship."

Once again, a loss in the ACC tourney would drain Carolina's momentum for the NCAA tournament. The Tar Heels took on Temple in Charlotte in the round of thirty-two and were bothered by the speed of Terence Stansbury, who scored 18 points in the first half. Fighting to stay ahead, Dean Smith called for so many alley-oops to Jordan that he grew exhausted and asked the unusual—to come out of the game to catch his breath. Carolina had trouble with coach John Chaney's persistent zone, but the alley-oop, combined with Carolina's size, proved too much. The Tar Heels advanced to the Sweet Sixteen at the Omni in Atlanta, an arena in which Jordan hadn't played well. They were to face Bobby Knight's unranked Indiana Hoosiers, led by freshman Steve Álford, with a 22-8 record.

The night before the game, Billy Packer talked privately with Knight about what the Hoosiers faced the next day. Knight asked if Packer thought the Hoosiers could somehow beat Jordan and the Tar Heels, the broadcaster recalled. "I said, 'No, you can't beat North Carolina.' He said, 'No, I don't think so either, but I'm going to do some things to them. They're probably going to beat us anyway, but they're not going to get any of those backdoor cuts. I'm going to let them take any kind of jump shot they want beyond eighteen feet.' He said, 'If they can make those jump shots, we're not going to be in the game. I don't think Michael can make those shots, and I don't think they've got anybody else who can either.'"

Knight also decided to defend Jordan with Dan Dakich, who had started only five games all season. Dakich was tall and had some quickness. Knight planned for Dakich to lay off Jordan to protect against the drive. If Jordan went up for the jumper, Dakich would lunge in a closeout and hope to distract the shot, which is exactly what he did. The Indiana coach waited until three hours before the game to inform his big reserve guard of the assignment. "I went back up to my room and threw up," Dakich said later.

It helped Knight's plan that the officials whistled Jordan for two early fouls that day. Any time he had gotten two fouls in the first half in earlier games that season, Smith had always brought him to the bench. He did the same in the regional semifinal and would be criticized for it later. Jordan scored just 4 first-half points.

"Everybody thought Coach Smith was at fault for keeping me on the sidelines," Jordan recalled for Mike Lopresti of *USA Today* years later. "But with me not on the floor, we were still a strong basketball team."

"Michael was on the bench during the time Indiana took control of the game," Packer recalled.

Packer questioned the decision to keep Jordan on the bench while the Hoosiers remained packed back in the lane on defense. The pace of the game was slow, the broadcaster pointed out. "Indiana's playing that pull-back man-to-man, almost like a zone. They're not running. It's going to be a shortened game because of the style of play, so your chances of getting five fouls is somewhat limited." With Jordan on the bench, Indiana took a 32–28 halftime lead. Knight didn't vary from his approach for the final twenty minutes. "When I got back in the second half, I felt like I was trying to cram forty minutes into twenty minutes," Jordan recalled. "I could never find any sync in my game."

"Michael didn't take the shots," Packer said, "and they were so packed in North Carolina never got any of those backdoor cuts. But it wasn't just that. Indiana decided to do two things and Carolina never countered."

Knight used the lightly regarded Dakich to keep Jordan in check, and it worked. Packer and other reporters couldn't believe what they were watching. "Just put Michael on the wing and say, 'OK, Michael, we're going to get you the ball. Take it every time.' Packer observed. "How does Dakich ever stop him from getting off a good shot?'"

"I am not diminishing what he did. I think he did exactly what Coach Knight wanted him to do," Jordan said of Dakich. "But [the media] made it a one-on-one proposition. Being the competitor that I am, and hearing the only one who could ever stop you was Dan Dakich...when I look back at the shots I had, I lick my chops. I just missed them."

Smith never adjusted his offense to free up Jordan to attack. The spread went to 12 points, but the Tar Heels had cut it to two at the end when they fouled freshman Steve Alford. He made both, good for the upset, 72–68. Indiana had to shoot almost 70 percent from the floor to make it happen. Alford finished with 27. Jordan fouled out, having scored 13 points on 6-for-14 shooting. In his three years at North Carolina, he had never taken more than 24 shots in any game.

The North Carolina locker room was deeply emotional afterward. Jordan and Perkins were especially downcast. "I felt like I let them down," Kenny Smith later recalled. Dean Smith never cared for talking a lot with his players after games. On that day, he called the group together for the usual postgame prayer and then went to the interview room, where he grew more emotional with each question and answer. Finally, Smith ended the session early and walked out.

"I think it was a game where the system and the program got in the way of winning," Packer said in 2012. "Of all the games he ever coached, I'm sure that's one game he'd like to have back, just the fact that the system got the best of him on that particular day. Indiana played good, but they didn't play great. They played great going down the stretch because they were able to protect the ball and Alford was such a great free throw shooter. But you knew that going in. You never want to be in a position where his free throw shooting and him holding the ball is going to beat you in that game."

"I thought we were the best team in the country," Jordan said, looking back. "But in one game, that can be swept away from you."

"There were games at North Carolina that were sacrificed for the good of the program," Packer said. "That Indiana game may be one of them. But if you just tell Michael to go out there and throw them up and attack and tell Sam Perkins to get all the rebounds, then the game's over. But Dean never would sacrifice the program for an individual game."

Art Chansky disagreed: "That's like saying that he would rather preserve the system and lose rather than break the system and win. I don't think that. Dean did believe that his way was the best way. He believed that Michael needed to sit out the last eight minutes of the first half with two fouls because that would allow him to play aggressively in the second half. Within the system, Bobby Knight knew how to guard him, and he had the guy to guard him. Michael was good, but he was terrible his last game. He got locked up by Dakich. Five white guys beat Sam Perkins, Michael Jordan, Brad Daugherty? Come on. Get serious. They couldn't beat them without the shot clock. It was pass and release, pass and release, and get them out of their rhythm. They shot 65 percent, too. It was the only way they could have won that game, but they did it."

Chansky acknowledged that Smith had to adjust his system later in the decade after Duke coach Mike Krzyzewski followed Knight's pattern and stymied Smith's passing-game system. Smith had to take chances with the kinds of players who could go one-on-one and beat the defense off the dribble. "Later on, in the late eighties, when Carolina lost the Jordan-caliber players, they couldn't get into their offense," Chansky recalled. "Dean recognized that. He realized they had to break down the first level of the defense."

Jordan later said he would have felt better if Indiana had gone on to win the national title, but in an immense irony, a Virginia team without Ralph Sampson (he had graduated and been selected by Houston with the top overall pick in the 1983 NBA draft) defeated the Hoosiers two days later to reach the Final Four. Virginia finished sixth in the ACC standings that year.

Jordan returned to Chapel Hill thoroughly depressed and

contemplating his future. He would win every major honor that college basketball had to offer that spring, every Player of the Year award.

"The publicity has been fun, I have to admit," Jordan said at the time. "It wasn't too hard to handle, and isn't now. I guess it used to be a little more fun at the beginning, though, because people are more and more after you now. All in all, it's better and more fun to be noticed."

He had averaged just 17.7 points over his three seasons at North Carolina. This, in turn, would spur a viral criticism, packaged in the form of a joke that spread across basketball in the late 1980s: Who was the only person to hold Michael Jordan under 20 points a game? The answer, of course, was Dean Smith, although statisticians duly pointed out that Jordan actually averaged 20.0 points per game as a sophomore at UNC. Regardless, there may have been an element of truth to the charge. But Jordan would always stand by the Carolina coach, explaining that Smith showed him how to use his gifts to greater efficiency. "I didn't know the game. Coach taught me the game, when to apply speed, how to use your quickness, when to use that first step, or how to apply certain skills in certain situations. I gained all that knowledge so that when I got to the pros, it was just a matter of applying the information. Dean Smith gave me the knowledge to score 37 points a game, and that's something that people just don't understand."

"When he went to North Carolina he had the heart, he had the competitiveness, he had the athletic ability," Brendan Malone observed. "But while at North Carolina he became a better shooter and more sound in fundamentals. When he came out of North Carolina he was ready to be a star in the NBA."

Indeed, that time had come. Smith had known for some time that the junior season would likely be Jordan's last in Chapel Hill, and that spring informed him it was time to discuss the future. The final decision to enter the 1984 NBA draft had to be made by Saturday, May 5. On April 26, Smith and Jordan held a preliminary news conference that only confused local reporters. Jordan informed them he still didn't know what he was going to do. "I'm planning on staying here and I'm looking forward to my next year here," he told them. "Coach has always looked out for his players and wants what's best for them."

Jordan said he would also listen to his parents: "My folks know a lot more than I do. And I'll take their advice into consideration, too. My mother, she's a teacher, and I think I already have an idea of what she thinks. But my father's a clown. I really don't know what he's thinking about. I don't know. I don't want to put any pressure on them."

Deloris Jordan was firmly opposed to her son leaving. But after the press conference that day, Dean Smith met with agent Donald Dell from the sports management firm ProServ, which local reporters took as a bad sign. It appeared to Jordan that if he left school, the worst he could do was go to the Philadelphia 76ers, who seemed likely to have between the fifth and the third pick in the draft. That was a decent option, but Jordan had hopes of playing for the Lakers. He didn't want to leave Chapel Hill to be a professional with just any team.

Jordan met with his coach that Friday, May 4, and later that evening with his parents and brother Larry. Then he went out to eat with Buzz Peterson and some friends. His roommate pushed him about his decision. Did he really want to leave behind the cinnamon biscuits at Hardee's and the grape soda and honey buns? What about all the good times in their room, talking late into the night, with Kenny Smith always showing up to run his mouth? Jordan admitted he still didn't know.

It was the same the next morning when he arose to get ready for the eleven o'clock news conference at Fetzer Gymnasium. "I knew what he was going through," Deloris Jordan recalled later that summer. "But I also knew it was something he had to decide for himself. We talked to him about it several times. Then Coach Smith called us on that Friday night before Michael was to make the announcement the next day. We left and went up there then. We talked with Michael and with Coach Smith. At ten thirty the next morning, he had a meeting with the coach. They came just a couple of minutes before the press conference was to start at eleven. Coach Smith squeezed my arm when they came out and I knew."

After the announcement, Jordan departed quickly and headed to the golf course, where he spent the entire afternoon.

Thirty years later, former Bulls executive Jerry Krause offered a harsher take on Jordan's exit, based on his many years working around college basketball as an NBA scout. "Dean told him to leave North Carolina," Krause said. "He told him to get out of there. He was getting bigger than the program. I don't know if Dean would ever admit that, but that's what happened." It wasn't that Jordan did anything wrong or openly challenged Smith in any way, Krause explained. "Dean was great. He was very gracious. Guys didn't leave his program. He told them to leave. When they started getting bigger than the program, he told them it was time to go."

Packer disagreed with Krause: "Let me tell you something, if Dean Smith wanted him out, no one would know it. Dean Smith never told you what he was doing. To say to Michael, 'It's time to go,' he did that for a lot of players."

Bob McAdoo was one of the first Carolina players to get the nod from Smith, back in 1972, after the coach had done his research on the player's draft prospects. "This was when it was actually illegal by NCAA standards to be getting that information, talking to agents and teams and so forth," Packer said. "But Dean was a master at that. He'd be able to sit down with a player and players would listen to him. He'd say, 'I've talked to this team that's got this draft choice. Michael, you're probably going number three.' The only way Dean would have wanted him out of the program was if it was the best thing for Michael, not if it was the best or worst thing for Dean. That's what made him a special person."

For Jordan to be bigger than the program, he would have had to be bigger than Smith himself, and in North Carolina, nobody was bigger than the coach. Kenny Smith offered the opinion that the coach, not Jordan, was the reason for the competitive atmosphere because of "how he psychologically guided us to go at each other."

Carolina assistant Eddie Fogler got married in the evening on the day that Jordan announced he was headed to the NBA. The ceremony was infused with a sort of gallows humor, Art Chansky recalled. "Eddie was like, 'Hey, I'm getting married, but, hey, we just lost the best player in the country.' There were a lot of Carolina fans at the wedding."

Among them was Jimmie Dempsey, an old friend of Dean

Smith's who was an important supporter of the Tar Heels program, close enough to use his private plane to ferry Smith on recruiting trips. "He and his wife were the godparents of the basketball players," Chansky recalled. "At the wedding that night, Jimmie said he was pissed at Dean. He said, 'His job is to put the best basketball team on the floor for the University of North Carolina. That's his job. His job is not to send guys out to pros while there's still eligibility.' I laughed and said, 'Go tell Coach Smith that.' He said, 'I will. I'll go over and tell him right now.' He went over there and told him and then came back. I said, 'What did he say?' He said, 'Dean laughed.'"

While James Jordan was delighted that the coach was putting Michael's interests first, Deloris Jordan had long held to the dream of having her two youngest children graduate from North Carolina on the same day. Jordan assured his mother that he would return to school promptly to earn his degree, which he did, making use of the summer school program in the next few years. Even as his future rested in the balance that spring, Jordan had insisted on studying for his exams and pressing ahead with academic issues. He was so earnest, in fact, that Kenny Smith assumed Jordan was returning for a senior year. Why, otherwise, would a guy headed for the NBA even bother taking a test?

"They made the announcement and it hit me," Mrs. Jordan said. "The press room was packed, and we had to answer all these questions. But then I finally had to be alone. When we got home, we had to leave the house because the phone wouldn't stop ringing. It was hard for a while." Reality would settle in for the Jordans over the coming months. They had attended almost every game that their son played. "Thank God for the General Electric credit union," James Jordan had said when people inquired about all the travel costs. But within months he would plead guilty to a charge of accepting a kickback from a private contractor. The matter was handled quietly, but it still made the newspapers in Wilmington and across the state.

"It was a shock at the GE plant," recalled Dick Neher in a 2012 interview. "Nobody could believe it. All the women loved him. He was charming. I worked with him about twenty-five years. We worked in different buildings, but I saw him about every day.... James was a pretty sharp guy. He was very personable. Everybody liked him."

According to statements made by authorities at the time, Mr. Jordan had held inventory control duties at the GE plant in Castle Hayne. During his son's sophomore season at North Carolina, James Jordan had written a phony purchase order to buy thirty tons of hydraulic equipment from a company called Hydratron, headed by a man named Dale Gierszewski. According to legal accounts of the charges, General Electric then paid Gierszewski $11,560 for the thirty-ton cylinders. James Jordan acknowledged in court that Gierszewski did not deliver the cylinders, and instead paid Jordan a $7,000 kickback.

In March 1985, Gierszewski pleaded guilty to embezzlement. He was fined $1,000 and given a suspended jail sentence. Three weeks later, James Jordan entered his own guilty plea and was handed a similar suspended sentence and fine.

"He shoulda went to prison for what he got involved in," Dick Neher said in 2012. "Because of Mike, he got out of it."

Each man could have gone to jail for ten years with the felony conviction. The case effectively ended James Jordan's employment at General Electric. Neher, also a supervisor at the plant, said the situation was much more involved than authorities revealed. "He was in charge of our company store," Neher explained. The company store served as a club for employees, where they could purchase refrigerators, TVs, toasters, tools, and various items at discount. As manager, James Jordan would reroute merchandise meant for the store, Neher said. "He'd check it in and it would never make it to the store. He was stealing it. I assume he was selling it. They charged him with stealing about $7,000. It was much more widespread. Other people were doing it, too."

Obviously the family's determination to attend each of Michael's games around the country, even internationally, had put pressure on the father to pay for it all. "Put all that aside, you'd never find a better guy," Neher said, recalling James Jordan's good deeds in the community and his willingness to volunteer his time in building a field for youth baseball.

It was around this time that their oldest daughter, Sis, began exploring her options for filing charges and a lawsuit against her parents regarding her sexual abuse claims. Her marriage had fallen apart, and for a time she had checked herself into the mental health ward of a local hospital. An older male relative had visited and informed her that her grandparents were deeply troubled by her circumstances. Sis wrote in her book that she checked herself out and went to visit with Medward and Rosabell Jordan.

"What is wrong with you, girl?" they asked.

Sis wrote that with Michael's sudden rise in basketball, her parents hardly found time for visiting with the elderly grandparents in Teachey. More and more, Medward had taken to quietly passing time on the front porch of his house on Calico Bay Road, and it was as if the Jordans were embarrassed by the "country ways" of James's parents, now that they were associating with the Carolina basketball crowd, their older daughter said. It was a common scenario for families to get caught up in the whirlwind surrounding prominent young athletes as they advanced through the levels of their sport, and the Jordans had found themselves in the brightest of spotlights. Everyone in basketball-crazy North Carolina followed the Tar Heels as if they were the reality television of the day.

The Jordans had endured three years of constant travel and competition, and relentless media exposure. On game days, they had left Wilmington usually at three in the afternoon to make a night game. They'd visit with their son briefly after the game, then make it home in time to watch a videotape of the game. They were usually too keyed up to sleep, Deloris Jordan explained. "We videotaped all the games so that Michael could see them when he got home. He'd sit there and say, 'Did I really do that?' See, when he's playing, he's so into the game and what's going on around him that he didn't remember some of those things."

They formed bonds with the parents of the other Carolina players, and they'd spend time together at the games and on the many road trips. One such night during the 1982 regional playoffs the Jordans described as magical. "Sam Perkins's folks, the Elacquas, were there, and the Braddocks, the Petersons, the Worthys, the Dohertys, and the coaches and their wives," Deloris Jordan recalled in 1984. "We had gone out and gotten a bunch of Chinese food and we ate that all night."

"About three or four a.m.," her husband chimed in, "I'll never forget it. We were all in the street singing the Carolina song, acting like a bunch of kids, but we really enjoyed every minute of it."

The shock for them all in May 1984 was that it had passed so quickly.

"We don't feel cheated one bit," James Jordan said. "We've been to every one of the games he's played in. It's not worth any amount of money anybody can give you. These have been good years for Michael, and they have been good years for the Jordan family.... I'm convinced that you couldn't have taken a kid and gone out and had a script written and gotten a producer and a director and told him to 'play this through your life,' that you couldn't have planned a more perfect life than the one Michael's had."

PART V

THE ROOKIE

Chapter 14

GOLD RUSH

JORDAN SELECTED DONALD Dell of ProServ out of Washington, DC, as an agent in July. Even before the official hiring, David Falk, who worked with Dell and ProServ, had begun exploring Jordan's options in the upcoming draft. Contrary to what Jordan had expected, Philadelphia's record improved a bit that spring, while the Chicago Bulls suffered two late losses to the New York Knicks that improved their draft status. Critics cracked that the Bulls were simply making their way through yet another disastrous season, only to follow it up with equally disastrous draft picks.

The architect of these failed draft selections was the team's general manager, Rod Thorn, a self-deprecating gentleman of the Southern Appalachians who admitted freely the team's longtime struggles in drafting and finding players. In 1979, the Bulls had a fifty-fifty chance of drafting Earvin "Magic" Johnson, who had just led Michigan State to the NCAA title. They again had a terrible record and had to flip a coin with the Los Angeles Lakers for the right to pick first. Rod Thorn called heads, following a suggestion based on fan polling. Tails it was.

Thorn lost Magic Johnson to the coin flip, then overlooked Sidney Moncrief in the draft itself to take David Greenwood out of UCLA. Although he was troubled by injuries, Greenwood played six solid seasons for the Bulls. He averaged about 14 points and 8 rebounds over his first five seasons with the team. Those were good numbers for a power forward, but he simply could not compare to Magic Johnson, who led the Lakers to five NBA championships, or even Moncrief, for that matter. Of course, if the Bulls had taken Moncrief, they might not have needed to draft another shooting guard in 1984. Regardless, Greenwood's selection by the Bulls would always be viewed as a failed draft pick. The value of the Lakers during Magic Johnson's dozen years with the team jumped from about $30 million to $200 million, according to *Forbes* magazine.

At the time, Jonathan Kovler, part owner of the Bulls, had joked that it was a "$25 million coin flip."

"It turned out to be a $200 million coin flip," he said later.

It got worse in 1982, when Thorn drafted guard Quintin Dailey out of the University of San Francisco, shortly before it was revealed that Dailey had attacked a student nurse in a dorm at the school. When he arrived in Chicago, Dailey declined to express remorse for his actions, and soon women were gathering to protest at Bulls games. He and another talented Bull, Orlando Woolridge, would also struggle very publicly with cocaine. Such disasters helped bring the team perilously close to insolvency by the spring of 1984.

That February, Thorn had traded crowd favorite Reggie Theus to Kansas City for Steve Johnson and a draft pick. Almost immediately, Chicago's team got worse and its luck got better. The Bulls finished the season at 27–55 and missed the playoffs for the third straight year, fueling speculation that the team would be sold and moved out of Chicago. With the miserable finish, Thorn again faced another high draft pick.

"We didn't win a lot of games that year," recalled Bill Blair, a Bulls assistant coach. "But Rod reminded us that there was a guy down at North Carolina who was a great, great player. He just kept on and on about Michael Jordan. Rod was always positive and sure that this guy was gonna be one of the great all-time players. But a lot of people said, 'Well, he can't play guard. He can't play small forward.' Even Bobby Knight had made a statement like that. But Rod said, 'This kid has got something special.'"

"Nobody, including me, knew Jordan was going to turn out to be what he became," Thorn recalled. "We didn't work him out before the draft, but we interviewed him. He was confident. He felt he was gonna be good. It was obvious that Michael believed in himself, but even he had no idea just how good he was going to be."

Once the regular season had concluded, Houston and Portland were tied for the top pick, followed by Chicago. The Rockets planned to take Hakeem Olajuwon, the athletic center from the University of Houston, while Portland was considering taking Kentucky center Sam Bowie, who had been plagued by injuries. "Houston had made it clear from the start that they were going to take Olajuwon," Thorn recalled. "About a month before the draft, I had a conversation with Stu Inman, Portland's general manager at the time. Stu told me they wanted Sam Bowie. Their doctors had said Bowie's health would be fine, and they needed a big man and weren't really considering anyone else."

The Bulls held the third pick in the draft, while Houston won the top pick in a coin flip with Portland. The Trail Blazers were left with the second pick. "We could tell that we were going to get Jordan when Houston won the coin flip over Portland," explained Irwin Mandel, a longtime Bulls vice president. "If Portland had won the flip, they would have taken Olajuwon, and Houston probably would have taken Jordan. I remember how excited Rod was. He was thrilled, because in his mind there was a major difference between Jordan and Bowie."

Sure enough, on the day of the draft, Jordan was there for the Bulls with the third pick. Heading into the draft, he had admitted that he'd like to play for the Lakers, where James Worthy was on his way to becoming a star. But Chicago would be fine, Jordan explained that fall, because the Lakers "are so stacked I probably couldn't have helped them anyway."

"Jordan was available, and they had to take him," recalled Jeff Davis, a TV sports producer in Chicago. "They had no choice. Sure the guy was two-time college Player of the Year and had led North Carolina to the title. But nobody knew how good he really was." Davis recalled that it was fortunate Portland had drafted Bowie, because it looked as if Thorn would have taken the Kentucky center if he got the chance.

"We wish Jordan were seven feet, but he isn't," Thorn told the

Chicago Tribune when asked about the selection. "There just wasn't a center available. What can you do? Jordan isn't going to turn this franchise around. I wouldn't ask him to. He's a very good offensive player, but not an overpowering offensive player."

It was an odd statement from the general manager of a team that was supposedly trying to sell tickets. Portland's mistake would go down as the greatest blunder in draft history. Stu Inman later pointed out that he was making a move supported by the opinions of his staff, including Hall of Fame coach Jack Ramsay. Inman would later suggest that Dean Smith's system at North Carolina had kept Jordan's talents hidden, a position echoed by Ramsay. However, the Portland coaches and staff had seen Jordan during Olympic tryouts that spring and still missed him. Rick Sund of the Dallas Mavericks had seen what Jordan could do. Sund offered the Mavs' hot young star Mark Aguirre in a deal for Jordan.

Thorn declined. "Rod didn't even waver," Sund recalled. "He knew."

The Knight Factor

With the draft settled, Jordan could now turn his full focus to the Olympic tryouts and practices, which would stretch from before the draft right up until the eve of the games in Los Angeles. Jordan was never in peril of not making the Olympic team, but he didn't have Knight's full confidence after their teams met in the Sweet Sixteen. "After that I think that Bob kind of thought that maybe Michael can't shoot the ball," Billy Packer recalled. "And in the Olympic trials he didn't shoot that great."

Knight was even more of a system coach than Dean Smith. "You go from a guy who played for Dean Smith and accepted roles and responsibilities and the system." The broadcaster laughed. "He goes and plays in the summer for Bob Knight, who is basically more rigid than Dean."

Smith certainly could be crafty and manipulative, but he always conducted himself with a degree of diplomacy. Knight had a raw, uneven temperament and an ego the size of the Hoosier Dome in

Indianapolis. Plus, he was beyond crass. To many, he was a profane bully. "Coach Smith is the master of the four corners offense and Coach Knight is the master of the four-letter word," Jordan quipped.

Knight let his Olympic charges know from the very first day that he was focused on perfection. "I have told them I have no interest in who we're playing or what the score is," Knight explained. "I'm interested in this team being the best team it can possibly be, and I'll push you any way I can to get to that end."

The player and coach were well matched. Jordan herded his teammates with his glowering countenance and determined clapping. Knight did the same with his moods and intimidating histrionics. His spotty behavior in international play made him a curious selection by the committee overseeing amateur basketball in the US. Authorities in Puerto Rico had issued an arrest warrant for him after his confrontation with a police officer there in 1979 at the Pan Am Games. He was later convicted in absentia of aggravated assault.

Now, Knight was on a mission. He wanted to bring the hammer of American basketball down on the international game. To that end, he compiled a staff of twenty-two assistant coaches and conducted thorough tryouts involving better than seventy players.

Charles Barkley, Sam Perkins, John Stockton, Karl Malone, Chris Mullin, Chuck Person, and dozens of other fine players labored as Knight watched the proceedings from a tower. Charging up and down the floor with brilliant displays of athleticism and ball handling, Barkley was clearly the second-best player in the trials behind Jordan, but he seemed more interested in impressing the pro scouts than making a hit with Knight, who could see only the Auburn forward's 280 pounds of girth.

Barkley, Stockton, and Malone were among the game's greats who were cut by Knight during the trials. An angry and confused Stockton told Barkley and Malone he'd love to team up with them to take on the dozen that Knight had picked.

The final twelve selected for Olympic play were Michael Jordan, Sam Perkins, Patrick Ewing, Chris Mullin, Wayman Tisdale, Leon Wood, Alvin Robertson, Joe Kleine, Jon Koncak, Jeff Turner, Vern Fleming, and Steve Alford.

Rather than wear his traditional number 23, Jordan was assigned jersey number 9 for Team USA.

The Indiana coach had the roster he felt he needed to embarrass the international field. He told his friend Packer that he didn't mind his Olympic team scoring 90 points in a game so long as they held the opponent to 30. "He had incredible focus," Packer recalled. "Bob, as is the case with Michael, is an incredible competitor. He was just so well prepared. People forget how he selected that Olympic team. All the constituents of intercollegiate basketball he pulled together from a coaching standpoint. He used the selection process to get everybody to buy in. Obviously his players had to understand, 'This is the way we're going to do it, how I expect you to play.' So in those games, they were dominant. He wasn't looking and hoping to win a gold medal. He was looking to dominate the world of basketball, and that they did."

Actually it was the exhibition games before the Olympics, played against NBA players, that afforded Packer an inside view of the emergence of Michael Jordan. His many years of broadcasting and his friendship with Knight provided Packer a courtside seat for the fascinating nine games before the Olympics in Los Angeles, arranged by Larry Fleisher, the general counsel to the NBA.

"What happens sometimes when you get an exhibition game with NBA guys," Packer said, "is that they just show up that afternoon. They put on a uniform and play a little bit. But this thing got to be a hell of a rivalry in a period of three or four weeks."

Driving the rising temper of the proceedings were Knight and Jordan. The exhibition tour began in Providence, Rhode Island, at the end of June and made stops in Minneapolis and Iowa City before coming to Indianapolis to play before a huge crowd on July 9. "By the time we got to Indianapolis the Olympians had won four games," Packer recalled. "So the pros were going to put a stop to that, that night. Larry Fleisher didn't want to see the NBA lose to a bunch of college kids."

Fleisher recruited Larry Bird, Magic Johnson, Isiah Thomas, and several other stars, making for an electric atmosphere in front of thousands of fans at the Hoosier Dome. Pete Newell, Knight's longtime mentor and one of the assistant coaches for Team USA, had visited the Olympians' locker room before the game, then sought out Packer. "Man, I've never seen anyone fired up like this in my life," Newell confided to Packer about Knight. Despite the NBA's loaded lineup, the Olympians won again in Indy.

The real test came in Milwaukee, Packer recalled. "I never saw Michael have one of those truly great offensive performances until that night in Milwaukee against the NBA players. That was the first time I ever saw Michael Jordan play at that level offensively. He got cut in the nose by Mike Dunleavy driving to the basket. The game was an unbelievably brutal game. Oscar Robertson was coaching the NBA guys. Bob Knight gets thrown out of the game on that play. Michael's bleeding from the nose. Meanwhile, the ball bounces over to Knight, and he puts it behind his back and refuses to give it to the referees. So they threw him out of the game. He and Oscar were really going at each other. There was a no-foul-out rule in the game. So the NBA guys were clubbing the Olympic kids."

A time-out was called while the Olympic assistant coaches tried to get organized in the wake of Knight's departure, Packer recalled. "They went back out on the floor, and Michael took over the game like the NBA guys were standing still. It was unbelievable. That was the first time I ever saw Michael Jordan, the truly great offensive player, even though I'd seen him play high school and three years of college ball. I never saw that side of him where he could just take over a game. Bobby's not even on the bench, but Michael just came out and he was saying, 'I don't care what the system is, I'm taking this game over.' And he did."

The Olympians went to Phoenix for a final exhibition with eight victories against no losses. "And this was against NBA teams," Packer said. "This was not ragtag NBA players. By the time the exhibition got to Phoenix, Bob and I had a conversation. Michael had made a believer of him. He told me, 'I'll tell you what about Michael Jordan. I had questions about him before, but he's going to be the greatest damn basketball player that ever lived.'"

Knight had said little publicly to reporters about any Olympic player, because he didn't want to upend the team's balance with inflated egos. Even so, he admitted to reporters after coaching the exhibition games, "Michael is a great, great basketball player."

The Olympians claimed the last exhibition game in Phoenix, 84–72, with Jordan's 27 points including an open-court slam in which he accelerated past a retreating Magic Johnson. On another sequence, he fed the ball to Ewing in the post on the left block, then somehow managed to bolt to the right block to score on a stick-back of the center's missed shot.

Play after play, Jordan proved quite a spectacle. "The NBA guys would stand around and watch him," USA teammate Jon Koncak told a reporter.

Lakers coach Pat Riley, who was on the bench for the NBA stars that day, said afterward, "He's as gifted a player as I've ever seen play ball."

Later, Jordan would observe that it was the physical challenge of the exhibition games that prepared him to charge out of the gate for his rookie NBA season. Packer pointed out that Knight's roster had no true point guard, rather a collection of versatile players, the most versatile of whom was Jordan, capable of playing three positions — both guard spots as well as small forward.

1984

Olympic basketball play opened July 29 at the Great Western Forum in Los Angeles, with the Soviet Union and Hungary both boycotting the games, ostensibly in protest of the United States boycott of the 1980 games in Russia. The US men's team encountered no stiff opposition and won eight games by an average of 32 points. Jordan led the team in scoring at 17.1 points per game. "It became obvious what Michael could do and how he could do it as an all-around player," Packer pointed out. "But it's not like Michael went out and scored 40 a game in the Olympics. That's not how that team played."

Although Knight's systematic offense gave him limited playing time and scoring opportunities, Jordan thrilled crowds and teammates alike during practices and games. "When Michael gets the ball on the break, only one thing's going to happen," said Steve Alford. "Some kind of dunk."

"Sometimes the players get into the habit of just watching Michael," Alford said, "because he's usually going to do something you don't want to miss."

As the Americans raced past their opponents, one international journalist showed Jordan a foreign magazine with his photo on the cover declaring him the greatest player in the world. The journalist asked Jordan what he thought of it. "So far," he said frankly, "I haven't come across anybody who can keep me from doing what I want to do."

From dominating the teams filled with NBA stars to humbling the best international teams, he had experienced quite a rise that summer. The only real drama came when the Americans blew a 22-point lead against West Germany as Jordan committed six turnovers and hit just four of fourteen shots from the field. Knight exploded in anger on the bench, but Team USA caught itself in the free fall and preserved a 78–67 win. The coach's nasty humor boiled over in the locker room afterward when he ordered Jordan to apologize to his teammates.

"You should be embarrassed by the way you played," he yelled at Jordan, whose eyes were tearing up as he stood speechless and shocked in the midst of his teammates.

Jordan was the team's leader, the one whose fire had stirred them all. They appreciated his talent and his drive, and were shocked to witness him being berated, Sam Perkins would later reveal. "We didn't think Michael played that bad, really. But that was us. Coach Knight knew what was in store. And it propelled Michael."

Later, in his pro career, Jordan would be accused often of bullying his teammates. Perhaps he had learned some of that in his short months with Bobby Knight. "It's not that I'm scared of him," Jordan told reporters covering the Olympic team. "But he's the coach, and he's been successful with this style of coaching. And I'm not going to challenge that at all. Playing for him for four years is something I don't want to think about. But he's straightforward. He says what he means. Whatever words he uses, you don't have any trouble understanding."

Having been humiliated by Knight, Jordan played with a fury down the stretch, including 20 points in the final as Team USA doused Spain, 96–65, for the gold. He embraced the smiling Knight in a long hug afterward and moments later waved a small American flag on the medal stand. He kissed the medal, sang the national anthem, and then bolted into the stands to present the gold medal to his mother.

He reminded her of the vow he made as a disappointed nine-year-old after the American loss to the Russians in 1972. He couldn't have known then that the price of a gold medal would be submitting to Knight's bullying. Jordan was not someone who took humiliation well. As sweet as the moment proved to be, it left a bitter aftertaste.

Anthony Teachey hadn't made the cut for the Olympic team, but had the opportunity to observe Jordan sacrifice his talent to meet the demands of yet another controlling coach. That struck Teachey as nothing short of remarkable. "A lot of people have never seen it," Teachey said in a 2012 interview. "If you look at his style, he adjusted from high school to college, from college to Olympics, from Olympics to pros, because he had the character to play for coaches like Dean Smith or Bobby Knight or Phil Jackson."

No one was more pleased and relieved by Jordan's Olympic performance than Rod Thorn. It confirmed that the Bulls general manager had gotten the draft right. "Playing in the Olympics really gave Michael an impetus," Thorn explained in looking back. "He became a household name, because the Olympics were in Los Angeles, because the games became a highlight film every night of his dunks and flashy moves, even though he didn't get to play that much."

Two weeks later, on September 12, 1984, the Bulls announced Jordan's signing to a seven-year, $6 million deal, the third highest in league history, behind those given to Houston big men Hakeem Olajuwon and Ralph Sampson. It was by far the greatest deal ever offered a guard. "It took some give and take," Bulls partner Jonathan Kovler quipped. "We gave, and they took."

Within days, other NBA agents would voice the opposite view. Why would an obvious star like Jordan sign a contract that could stretch out for seven years at inferior money? "It doesn't make sense," George Andrews, the agent for Magic Johnson and Isiah

Thomas, told the *Southtown Economist*. Agent Lee Fentress said such a deal would seemingly guarantee trouble down the road as the value of player contracts had already begun to increase dramatically.

"I don't want to play God," David Falk had said in announcing the deal. "Michael and his mom and dad made the decision themselves."

One key element was a "Love of the Game" clause that Jordan had insisted upon. The standard NBA contract called for the agreement to be voided if the player was injured in some activity other than a team-sanctioned one. Jordan wanted the freedom to compete wherever and whenever he wanted with impunity, as defined by his love of the game. The team made the concession in light of the favorable terms the Jordan family had approved.

"My attorneys had some problems with the contract, but I didn't," Jordan told reporters in Chicago. "I'm happy the negotiations are over, and I'm anxious to start fitting in with the Bulls. It won't be the Michael Jordan show. I'll just be part of the team."

Chapter 15

BLACK POWER

The first time officials from Nike met with Sonny Vaccaro, they wondered if he might be a mob figure. He certainly looked the part, with his name, his accent, and his mannerisms, and there was an air about him that suggested he knew secrets, things regular people didn't know. The same impression struck Michael Jordan when he initially sat down with the pudgy Italian with the droopy eyes. "I'm not sure I want to get mixed up with this shady kind of element," Jordan later admitted thinking.

Vaccaro privately chuckled at the awkwardness of it all. His close friends were fairly sure that there was nothing the least bit criminal about him. But Vaccaro never did much to dispute the impression that he was a mafioso. He sort of liked the idea that people thought he was connected. In the business world, any edge helped.

Besides, Vaccaro was indeed connected to any number of made men in gaudy suits. But they were basketball coaches, not gangsters. America's top college coaches couldn't really be sure about him either. They just knew that the fat checks Vaccaro wrote them cleared. In basketball in 1978, you could buy your way into a hell of a lot of good graces. Sonny Vaccaro would transform Nike into living proof of that axiom.

Just looking at Vaccaro in his rumpled warm-up suits with a day's shadow of fuzz on his face made Billy Packer laugh. "It would be another thing if he was a Wall Street executive or a Madison

Avenue hotshot," Packer said. "But that's not what he was. He was a guy from the streets. Basketball wasn't there to let him into its inner circle. So he operated outside the circle and became incredibly successful for himself and the company."

Vaccaro revolutionized the sport without ever really attempting to cover up what he was: that friendly guy from Pittsburgh. Well, at least for half of the year. The other half of the year he was from Vegas. If his goombah aura by itself didn't rattle people, then his Vegas connection did the trick. For half of each year you could find Vaccaro hanging out at the seedy sports books in establishments like the Aladdin or the Barbary Coast, where you could get odds on just about anything. There he made part of his living on "commissions" earned from placing football bets for "clients." Hearing Vaccaro explain it made it seem all the sketchier. He was also rumored to do a little gambling of his own. He was a Runyonesque figure who stood out even in Vegas, a place with an abundance of Runyonesque figures. It was said there that the closer it got to kickoff time, the more you heard his name being paged over the loudspeakers in the sports books.

That a character like Sonny Vaccaro could ever wind up working for a company like Nike is better explained by what Vaccaro did with the other half of each year, back in Pittsburgh. He was just twenty-four years old in 1964 when he and college roommate Pat DiCesare founded the Dapper Dan Roundball Classic, one of basketball's first high-profile tournaments for all-star high school players. They had developed it as a charitable event in Pittsburgh, but in a relatively short time, Vaccaro discovered that his tournament satisfied a huge need by providing a showcase for high school players to be seen by college coaches. The Dapper Dan was soon drawing top players each year and top coaches, everyone from John Wooden to Dean Smith.

That was the key to his influence, Vaccaro would tell anybody who would listen. It was all about relationships. "The Dapper Dan gave me entrée," he said, looking back in 2012.

The tournament itself never netted more than about $3,000 in any given year, but it was a gold mine in terms of connections. Vaccaro got friendly with all the top coaches. His power came to mirror that of Five-Star's Howard Garfinkel, except that Vaccaro's vision involved basketball marketing, whereas Garfinkel focused on evaluating talent.

Drawing the top basketball celebrities to an event also meant drawing the top media. By 1970, *Sports Illustrated* was reporting on Vaccaro's game. "It was impossible to turn around in the William Penn Hotel without bumping into one coach or another looking for high school players in lobbies, hallways, coffee shops, elevators, and occasionally under a potted palm," the magazine's Curry Kirkpatrick wrote of the scene. "The ubiquitous group had converged on Pittsburgh to watch the Dapper Dan Roundball Classic, an annual high school All-Star game that in the six years of its existence has emerged as the best event of its kind."

It was immensely entertaining just to watch Vaccaro work a hotel lobby, according to talent evaluator Tom Konchalski. "He had conversations going with about eight different people at the same time in different parts of the lobby. John Thompson had just been hired at Georgetown, and Jerry Tarkanian was still at Long Beach State. Sonny Vaccaro knew everyone there. It was like he was juggling coaches. There would be like thirty coaches in the lobby. He was showing respect toward them and keeping conversation afloat with all thirty."

By 1977, Vaccaro had grown bold enough to pay a call to Nike's offices in Portland, Oregon, to pitch his idea for a new shoe. Nike wasn't interested, but Rob Strasser, one of the company's top executives, was fascinated by Vaccaro's relationships with all those coaches. Other Nike bosses wanted to have the FBI run a background check on Vaccaro, but Strasser would have none of it.

He hired Vaccaro at $500 a month, put $30,000 more in his bank account, and told him to go sign coaches to Nike endorsement contracts. "You have to remember," Vaccaro said. "At the time, Nike was just a $25 million company."

It was an easy play for Vaccaro. He'd sign the coaches to a simple Nike contract, write them a check, and send them free shoes for their players to wear. He began signing coaches in bunches, including John Thompson at Georgetown, Jerry Tarkanian, who had just taken the job at UNLV, Jim Valvano at Iona, and George Raveling at Washington State.

"You got to remember back in those days $5,000 was a lot of money to a coach," Packer recalled. "I just got glimpses of that stuff. Only Sonny knows how much he paid coaches."

To the coaches, it seemed almost too good to be true. "Let me get this straight," Jim Valvano supposedly said. "You're going to give me free shoes and pay me money? Is this legal?"

It was essentially basketball's version of payola. It was legal, but the ethics of it raised eyebrows. The main idea was simple enough, to get coaches to outfit their amateur players in Nike shoes, sending a strong message to fans and consumers. When Indiana State's Larry Bird appeared on the cover of *Sports Illustrated* in 1978 in a pair of Nikes, it was a huge boost to Vaccaro's credibility. He had snared the ultimate payoff for his new "client."

The company's sales soared, and soon Strasser was depositing another $90,000 in Vaccaro's bank account with a directive to sign more coaches. When the *Washington Post* wrote an article questioning the ethics of Nike's approach, company executives braced for a blast of negative publicity. Instead, they mostly received inquiries from coaches wanting a piece of the action. Vaccaro had unleashed a tide of cash into American amateur basketball. Soon shoe companies were not only underwriting college coaches and their teams, but they also moved into youth basketball. "It has changed the game," Tom Konchalski said of the payola that Vaccaro pioneered. "Now kids twelve and under playing AAU basketball, they think they've made it."

The Vision

By 1982, Vaccaro was paying out millions in Nike money to college coaches. He was a guest of John Thompson that year at the Final Four in New Orleans when he was struck with his next great idea. He saw that while James Worthy had been named the Most Outstanding Player, it was Michael Jordan who had stolen the show.

"Something happened," Vaccaro said of Jordan's shot to beat Georgetown, "in front of the world." A star had been born.

Vaccaro didn't know Michael Jordan. Dean Smith was under contract to endorse Converse shoes, which his Tar Heels wore in games. Jordan himself loved all things Adidas. He especially liked the shoes because you could just pop them out of the box and they were ready to wear. You didn't have to break them in. He wore Adidas shoes in practice, then dutifully donned Converse for games. Vaccaro believed that Jordan's charisma was going to make him a great force in marketing. He wanted Nike to sign Jordan to a contract and build a product line around him. Vaccaro made that known to Rob Strasser and other Nike officials in a January 1984 meeting. At the time, Jordan was still a junior and had not yet decided to skip his senior season.

Company executives had a $2.5 million budget for pro basketball shoe endorsements and were thinking about spreading it among several young players, including Auburn's Charles Barkley, whose style of play and offbeat charisma had brought him recognition, and Sam Bowie, who would be drafted by Portland, so close that he was almost on Nike's "campus" in Oregon. It made sense to spread the Nike budget across the array of interesting young players in the very deep 1984 draft. "Don't do that," Vaccaro told Strasser. "Give it all to the kid. Give it all to Jordan."

He went into something of a rant about Jordan's appeal, how he was the figure to drive athletic shoe marketing to a new level. Most important of all, Vaccaro went on, Jordan was the best player he had ever seen.

Jordan could fly, Vaccaro told Strasser.

In that era, many pro basketball shoe endorsement contracts ran less than $10,000. Only one player, Kareem Abdul-Jabbar of the Los Angeles Lakers, was thought to be making even $100,000 a year from his shoe deal.

What made Vaccaro's appeal seem even stranger is that the public had yet to adopt Jordan as an icon. "Back then, Michael wasn't glorified, glamorized," Vaccaro pointed out. "He was very good, but he was seen as another guy on Dean's team." Vaccaro argued that Jordan was about to zoom off into an unimaginable stardom, unlike anything a mere basketball player had ever achieved. And Nike had to hitch its fortunes to that rising star. "My point was, whatever money we had, give it to him," Vaccaro recalled. "Rob listened to me. That's when Rob asked me, 'You gonna bet your job on it?'"

Vaccaro had gotten raises from Nike over the seven years he had been with the company, and was doling out hundreds of thousands of dollars to college coaches, but he was making just $24,000 a year in base pay for his efforts. So he smiled and said, "Sure."

Strasser had learned to trust Vaccaro's instincts, but he had misgivings about the gamble. To make one player work, Nike would have to tie together many things, including shoes and clothing, into a unique product line, complete with advertising and branding.

Rob Strasser approached David Falk and told him that Nike was thinking of signing Jordan. Falk and Strasser had worked deals with other athletes, and they agreed that Jordan should be marketed as they might market a tennis player, as an individual, more than as a basketball player, who had been traditionally marketed through team connections. Strasser suggested that Falk make a pitch to sign Jordan. Falk told him he would begin exploring that idea, although he cautioned Strasser that it was rare for players to leave Carolina early, which wasn't entirely true. The easy part of the deal would be getting Dean Smith's attention, since David Falk's partner Donald Dell already had a relationship with Smith.

Dean Smith would be seen several times that spring having private conversations with Falk and others at ProServ, so perhaps Smith was taking into account the shoe endorsement prospects when he nudged Jordan into turning pro later that spring. Smith never disclosed such a connection, but as Billy Packer observed, Smith never disclosed anything. For the most part, Smith was gauging Jordan's pro appeal based on his conversations with NBA teams, including the Philadelphia 76ers, who at the time were coached by Billy Cunningham, one of Smith's former stars.

The Sixers told Smith that if they were able to get the second or third pick in the draft, they would select Jordan. But while Cunningham loved Jordan, owner Harold Katz seemed intent on taking Charles Barkley, former Sixers coach Matt Guokas revealed in a 2012 interview.

Regardless, Jordan's "decision" to leave college early added momentum to Vaccaro's plan to build a product line around him. Rob Strasser and Peter Moore, Nike's creative designer, met with Falk in Washington, DC, in August 1984. By that time, Falk had put together a list of ideas for the name of Jordan's shoes and gear. On the list was the name "Air Jordan." Strasser and Moore fixed on it immediately.

"That's it," Moore said. "Air Jordan."

By the end of their meeting, Moore had already sketched out the logo, complete with a badge with wings around a basketball and the words "Air Jordan."

Meanwhile, Vaccaro still had to persuade reclusive Nike chairman Phil Knight that making such an extravagant offer to a young, relatively unknown and untested NBA rookie was a good idea. He set up a dinner meeting with Knight during the Olympics in Los Angeles, and invited Billy Packer to come along, ostensibly to help sell Knight on the idea.

Knight, a former miler, founded Nike along with Bill Bowerman, the legendary track coach at the University of Oregon. Knight allowed extroverts like Rob Strasser to conduct much of the day-to-day operations of Nike. The big decisions and strategies, however, still required his blessing. Knight was acutely aware that Vaccaro had built relationships that paid off in huge sales growth for Nike. In fact, the *Sporting News* would soon include Knight and Vaccaro on their list of the one hundred most powerful people in sports. Over dinner, Vaccaro talked at length about the young player named Jordan, Packer remembered. "Knight was very noncommittal. He asked a lot of questions but was noncommittal. There was no, 'Boy, Sonny, I hope you can get him.' I didn't know if that was just Phil Knight's demeanor or what. But it wasn't like he was gushing or saying, 'Jeez, is there any way we can help you? We've got to have this guy.' It wasn't that at all. It was very businesslike, very calm. And Sonny was going on as to why he thought Michael could be this great marketing item. Even at the Olympics it was obvious there was still a lot of selling to be done for Michael to be a commodity for Nike."

Meanwhile, Strasser and Vaccaro also still had to sell the Jordans on the idea of Nike. Michael would admit later that at age twenty-one he was still quite immature and really didn't know or care much about the business of shoes. But Vaccaro turned to his old friend George Raveling, an assistant coach on Bobby Knight's Olympic team, to help bridge the gap to Jordan. Raveling introduced Jordan to Vaccaro in Los Angeles during the games. "It was at Tony Roma's and George brought Michael over there and introduced me," Vaccaro recalled. "That's the first time in my life I'd ever met Michael. We sat down and talked about his going to Nike. He didn't even know about Nike. You have to understand that. And I told him, 'Michael, you don't know me, but we're going to build a shoe for you. No one has this shoe.'"

It was not a great first impression, from either perspective. Jordan thought Vaccaro seemed shady. Vaccaro considered Jordan something of a brat. That became obvious when Jordan seemed to ignore the talk about the product line to ask Vaccaro for a car. "If you take this deal you can buy any car you want," Vaccaro told him.

"I want a car," Jordan emphasized.

"Michael was a pain in the ass, he was," Vaccaro recalled. "First of all, he didn't compute the money. Second of all, he was still a kid, this guy coming out of North Carolina. Whatever. A shoe contract meant nothing back in the eighties. So he was totally indifferent. He didn't want to come with us. He wanted to go with Adidas. In the eighties, Adidas had the nicest sweat suits."

Jordan did ask about money, and Vaccaro told him not to sweat it. If the deal came together, Jordan would be a millionaire. Jordan's main interest continued to be a new car. Vaccaro came to understand that if the car was what snared Jordan, then he needed to produce a car.

"We'll get you a car," he promised.

Jordan smiled, but that did nothing to reassure Vaccaro. "You know Michael's got that smile," he said. "He looks at you. It's a very tricky smile. You never know what that smile means."

The Nike contingent knew that Falk was also talking to Adidas and Converse, but Strasser's relationship with Falk kept them confident. That September, the agent was wrapping up Jordan's contract with the Bulls. Plus, Nike knew its plan for Jordan went far beyond what Adidas or Converse contemplated. Vaccaro and Strasser felt sure that Jordan would realize what an incredible deal he was being offered.

The day after Team USA won the gold, Falk, Strasser, and Vaccaro sat down to negotiate the scope of the Jordan deal. Indeed, Nike threw its entire budget at Jordan, a $2.5 million package over five years, a combination of guarantees, a signing bonus, and annuities. Nike also agreed to a major commitment to advertise Air Jordan. In terms of pro basketball shoe deals, the agreement was unprecedented, due to the 25 percent royalty Jordan would get on each Air Jordan shoe sold. He would also get royalties on Nike Air shoes. Truth be told, Falk could have perhaps gotten as much as 50 percent on the royalty for Jordan, Vaccaro said in 2012. "David wanted more cash up front. In 1984, there was no guarantee any of these shoes were going to sell."

Nonetheless, the deal represented an enormous gamble. After all, Jordan was headed to a poorly managed team in a league that was still under the long shadow of its partying and cocaine-abusing culture of the 1970s. The Bulls team that had just signed Jordan featured several players who had deeply invested in the idea that things go better with coke. If Nike had done a formal risk assessment, it might well have been enough to kill the deal. However, this was not about business plans. It was about Sonny Vaccaro's hunch.

The night before Jordan and his parents were to fly to Oregon to hear Nike officials present their vision for the Air Jordan campaign, Jordan phoned his parents and told them he wasn't going. He was tired of all his recent travels and the last thing he wanted was a cross-country trip for a shoe he didn't even like. Deloris Jordan insisted that her son be at the airport in the morning. She would have it no other way. Sure enough, Jordan was at the Raleigh-Durham airport early the next day.

Strasser, Vaccaro, and all the Nike people were there at the meeting. Among them was Howard White, the former University of Maryland basketball player who would play a role in the company's long-term relationship with Jordan. Phil Knight even dropped in, a rare thing for the chairman. Vaccaro and the other Nike representatives were immediately struck by Deloris Jordan's focus and professionalism. "I can tell you she is one of the most impressive people I've met in my life," Vaccaro said, "because she was able to negotiate this life for her son."

Jordan sat expressionless during the presentation, as if he didn't care. He didn't want to be there and was determined not to be impressed. He looked at the red and black shoes and commented that red was "the devil's color." Too bad, he added, that he wasn't still at Carolina. That way the shoes could be swathed in "blue heaven." Despite Michael's attitude, Vaccaro couldn't take his eyes off Deloris Jordan. He watched her expression as it was explained that her son would receive royalties on each shoe sold. Vaccaro told the Jordans that Nike was "all in" for its commitment. "I said it, and I'm so glad I said it," he recalled. " 'We're all in.' I was betting my job. Nike was betting their future. It was unbelievable. That was our whole budget. For Michael's mother, it was like a family, if we were willing to bet it. It was like we were saying, 'We wanted you this much.' It was like, 'You're going to make my son the future of this company.' Like we said, 'Michael, we're going to go broke if you bust out.' That's basically what I was saying. That was the whole point of it."

What wasn't articulated was the key thought on the minds of everyone in the room. This was not just an unprecedented offering in terms of finance. It was that this pot of gold was being offered to a twenty-one-year-old African American who had never played a minute of professional basketball. America had witnessed the emergence of a progression of iconic black athletes, from Jackie Robinson to Willie Mays to Bill Russell to Wilt Chamberlain to Jim Brown to Muhammad Ali. They had made their way through the gauntlet of the nation's civil rights struggle. At no point had Madison Avenue perceived any one of these men as a suitable candidate to be the centerpiece of the kind of campaign that Nike envisioned for young Michael Jordan.

Timing was truly everything. Though the matter was far from settled, Vaccaro gained confidence from the look that crossed Mrs. Jordan's face. "It was Deloris's reaction," he recalled. "Someone was making them a partner instead of paying them a wage. And she loved that. This woman was everything. Michael loved his father, he did. But Deloris ran the show."

It would not immediately be recognized as such, but the meeting marked a black power moment, although it was not the black power born of protest against social injustice and racial prejudice. The black power represented by Deloris Jordan had come straight from the Coastal Plain of North Carolina, where blacks had been violently barred from politics and society. The black power she knew came from her father, and it was based in the economic realities of sharecropping and tenant farming. It was an economic black power, and it was arguably the greatest power that blacks possessed, marked by the black-owned banks and small businesses that had come to thrive during segregation in cities such as Atlanta and Durham. The often-anonymous economic gains of black professionals and entrepreneurs may not have been highly publicized, but that accumulated wealth sat at the heart of the African American experience.

Those first Nike negotiations would bring Michael Jordan the beginnings of a life-changing economic power. Before that could happen, however, the Nike executives and Deloris Jordan would have to persuade her somewhat petulant son that the deal was in his best interest. His immediate response had been the stone face. Then he looked at Vaccaro and asked again about a car. Vaccaro pulled two miniature toy cars out of his pocket and rolled them across the table at Jordan. Years later, Vaccaro was pretty sure one of them was a Lamborghini.

"There are your cars, Michael," Vaccaro replied. He then reiterated that the deal would enable Jordan to buy whatever cars he wanted. In fact, Jordan was set to be paid more by the shoe company than by the Bulls. Everyone in the room seemed to smile except Jordan himself. Phil Knight quipped that the company was buying Jordan cars even before he had agreed to the deal. Then the chairman excused himself from the room.

"Michael, at some point in time you have to trust people," Vaccaro recalled telling Jordan. "Now in those words what I said was, and he knew it for a fact, 'We're betting as much on you as you're betting on us.'"

As the meeting concluded, the Nike contingent had no idea how Jordan felt about the presentation. Afterward, he told Falk he was simply fed up with meetings. It wasn't until later that night at dinner with his parents, Strasser, and other Nike officials that Jordan began to relax. The young star was impressive that evening, gracious and charming, able to move among the clientele in the upscale restaurant with ease. His persona that night reassured the Nike executives that they were making a wise choice, that indeed this young man had that certain special something, an ability to connect with people of all backgrounds. The term "post-racial" hadn't entered the vocabulary yet, but it could have described what they sensed about Jordan. After dinner, they had prepared a highlight reel of Jordan's great moments at North Carolina for his viewing on the VCR in the limo on the way back to their hotel. It was the perfect touch. He also took a second look at the video of the Air Jordan line that could be his. The deal had not been closed, but bonds had been formed, impressions made.

"He listened to her," Vaccaro said of Jordan and his mother. "She was the deciding vote. She told him, 'They want us as a partner.' She convinced him. She did. I'll never forget that day."

Falk dutifully went to Converse and Adidas to see what they had to offer. Jordan even approached a Converse rep that he knew, telling the rep that his company "just had to get close" to the Nike offer. Neither Converse nor Adidas was prepared to offer anything near the treatment that Sonny Vaccaro had envisioned for Michael Jordan.

Phil Knight supposedly never officially sanctioned or gave his approval to the deal. But he didn't move to stop it either, as Rob Strasser seized on Vaccaro's idea and made it happen. As a result, Knight's silence became his tacit approval.

"Phil Knight listened to a guy like Sonny and bought into it," Packer said. "Whatever they paid Sonny, it was way below whatever he did for them. He had great vision, and one of his greatest visions obviously is that Michael would not only be this kind of a player but would be this magnetic personality that could sell sneakers and anything else." Nike officials didn't realize it at the time, but they had just taken the first irrevocable step in making Michael Jordan a full partner in the company.

"He's as much an image as he is a symbol," David Falk said that fall after revealing that Jordan had signed deals with Nike, Wilson Sporting Goods, and the Chicagoland Chevrolet Dealerships Association. The Nike deal in particular sent gasps of surprise—and resentment—across pro basketball. Jordan himself sensed it before he had encountered a single opponent. Yet, as young as he was, he had no idea of its proportions.

"I know everybody's eyes are on me," he said as he headed into his rookie season, "and some of the things I do even surprise myself. They aren't always planned. They just happen."

Meanwhile, Sonny Vaccaro rejoiced at the realization that his grandest idea was about to take flight. "We could have gone under if he had been a failure," Vaccaro said three decades later, looking back. "We put all the money we had into him. What if he'd been an average player? Nobody knew for sure at the time. We'd have been embarrassed. I mean, I don't know what would've happened. But I do know what didn't happen. He wasn't an average player. He was someone who crossed over and made millions of dollars."

Chapter 16

THE FIRST LOOK

JORDAN RETURNED HOME in late August for yet another ceremony honoring his achievements, this time at Wilmington's Thalian Hall, where he formally presented his mother with his Olympic gold medal. Laney High also used the occasion to retire Jordan's number 23 Buccaneers jersey. A month later he made the trip to Chicago for the opening of training camp.

He had assumed that his life as a Chicago Bull would be very different from his days as a North Carolina Tar Heel. Even so, he had no idea how dramatic the difference would be. It began with coaching. No longer was he bound by the dictates of Dean Smith or Bobby Knight. His new coach was forty-four-year-old Kevin Loughery, a flamboyant product of the madcap age of pro basketball in the sixties and seventies, when he had starred for the old Baltimore Bullets. Loughery had a thick Brooklyn accent and a lopsided grin that matched his mirthful approach to the game.

"Kevin was from the old school," recalled former Bulls trainer Mark Pfeil. "At that time, guys were still having fun in pro basketball. You come in, do your work, then get together afterwards and hit the bars and have some fun."

Loughery had an intuitive feel for basketball. He had played well in the pros, averaging 15.3 points per game over twelve NBA seasons. He appealed immediately to Jordan because he had coached Julius Erving and the New York Nets to two American Basketball

Association titles. As a player, Loughery had defended Jerry West in the 1965 Eastern Conference finals when West was tearing through records with a string of 40-point games. Between his experiences with West and Erving, Loughery was a man who understood that superior athletic talent dictates its own agenda. Under Loughery the team's young star was going to get the ball as often as possible.

Jordan would say many times that Loughery was by far the most fun of the coaches he played for. "He gave me the confidence to play on his level," Jordan later explained. "My first year, he threw me the ball and said, 'Hey, kid, I know you can play. Go play.' I don't think that would have been the case going through another coach's system."

Suddenly, the Jordan on the floor appeared a lot like the gums-bared, high-flying specter who had haunted Laney's gym in high school, albeit with a more developed physique and a much more polished game. There was no hiding the athleticism now.

Loughery made the year about Jordan finding his identity and his confidence as a player. The coach allowed Jordan to discover his game on his own, rather than trying to impose it on him. He recognized Jordan's great hunger and realized that it was his job to feed it. Where Dean Smith's system, and even Bobby Knight's system, had confined his development, Loughery wanted to give Jordan the freedom he needed to explore it. It helped that Loughery's base of power with the Bulls was GM Rod Thorn, who had been his assistant with the Nets and had full confidence in his coaching.

Just as important was Loughery's personal relationship with his young star. "I could relate with him as a friend," Jordan explained. Loughery had been in the same position himself and understood the challenges the rookie would face, including his new teammates. Unlike the motivated young All-Americans at UNC, Jordan would now be working with an array of cynical castoffs and casualties, some of them deeply troubled by cocaine and alcohol abuse. Talented guard Quintin Dailey was in the midst of a very public breakdown in Chicago, which had begun well before Jordan arrived. "Q was a good friend," recalled trainer Mark Pfeil. "I felt bad for him. We would try to threaten him, but how do you threaten somebody who came from nothing? He said, 'I'm gonna end up on the street? I've been on the street. I survive on the street. You can't threaten me with that.'"

Also beginning his descent into alcohol and cocaine abuse was the team's other immensely talented player, Orlando Woolridge, a second-year forward out of Notre Dame. Ultimately, both team-mates were following a sad trail to an early grave. The roster was full of troubled souls. As Bulls PR man Tim Hallam explained, Jordan was much too competitive to pay mind to either drugs or alcohol. That would have meant exposing a weakness to an opponent, something Jordan would never do.

Journeyman Rod Higgins, one of the few stable personalities on the team, was three years older than Jordan. Amidst the chaos that season, they formed a fast friendship, one that would last far beyond their playing days. Six years later, Jordan would look back and comment that of all his teammates, those on that first team were the most physically gifted and also the most clueless. "Looney Tunes," he called them.

The Bulls' practice facilities at Angel Guardian Gym appeared no more conducive to success than Jordan's troubling new team-mates. "It was kind of a dark, gloomy gym with a real hard floor," explained Tim Hallam. "There were no frills there. You parked your car in the grass in the back. They had one little sidewalk where the players were allowed to pull their car up on the sidewalk and then had to pull off in the grass. It had an antiquated locker room. There was no food. You know, there were no amenities at all, whatsoever."

And Angel Guardian was always filled with little ones, the Bulls' longtime ticket manager Joe O'Neil recalled. "The team had to wait in line for the third graders to get off the court, literally, so the Bulls could practice. The players would be lined up and there would be a line of kids across the hall, going to the pool or going to the gym."

The place was also just plain cold, offering little respite from Chicago's notorious weather, recalled former Bulls guard John Pax-son. As he had in Venezuela during the Pan Am Games, Jordan placed absolutely no importance on the circumstances. Angel Guardian was every bit as good as the outdoor court at Empie Park or the many other places he had played growing up. So he simply shrugged and went to work.

For those first weeks, the Bulls housed their new rookie at the Lincolnwood Hyatt House, not far from Angel Guardian. When Jordan had landed at O'Hare a few days before training camp, he was greeted by a twenty-nine-year-old limo driver named George Koehler, who had just missed one fare and was looking to pick up another. He had seen the skinny young rookie, mistakenly called him "Larry Jordan," and offered to take him anywhere in the city for twenty-five bucks. "Do you know my brother?" Jordan had asked, tilting a confused eye at the driver. Nonetheless, it would be the beginning of a beautiful relationship. Koehler would become Jordan's regular driver, then his personal assistant and lifelong friend.

He remembered a Jordan that first day who was green and unsure of himself in the big city. "I looked in the rearview mirror and I couldn't even see him because he was scrunched down like a little kid," Koehler recalled. "I don't know if he'd been in a stretch limo before; he didn't know anyone in Chicago. I was a stranger and he was obviously a bit nervous that I could drop him off in an alley somewhere."

Jordan soon found his bearings. "He came to practice every day like it was Game 7 of the NBA Finals," Joe O'Neil recalled with a laugh. "He would destroy you in practice. That's what set the tone for our team."

Loughery had watched Jordan from afar, but the impact up close was far more dramatic. "When we started doing one-on-one drills," the coach recalled, "we immediately seen that we had a star. I can't say that we knew we had the best player ever in basketball. But we always felt that Michael could shoot the ball. A lot of people had questioned that. But Michael had played in a passing game system in college under Dean Smith and in the Olympics under Bobby Knight. So people never got the opportunity to see him handle the ball individually the way he could handle it. Then when we found out how supremely competitive he was, we knew we had a player who had it all. "

Bill Blair, Loughery's assistant, recalled that the coaches decided to have a scrimmage on the second day of practice to check out Jordan's skills in the open court. "Michael took the ball off the rim at one end," Blair said, "and went to the other end. From the top of the key, he soared in and dunked it, and Kevin says, 'We don't have to scrimmage anymore.'"

"His anticipation was so great—he could see the floor—and his quickness, and then his strength," Loughery recalled. "That's another thing that was overlooked, how strong Michael was. He really had the whole package."

Yet from the start Jordan remained focused not on what he had, but on what he didn't have. "There's no doubt I'm playing a new, tougher level," he said after his first pro practice. "I've got a lot to learn."

"You knew you had somebody special because Michael was always there at practice forty-five minutes early," Blair recalled. "He wanted to work on his shooting. And after practice he'd make you help him. He'd keep working on his shooting. He didn't care how long he was out there. The thing that I always loved about him, when you'd take him out in practice to give him a rest during a scrimmage, he was constantly back on you to get him back in. Michael loved to play the game."

Secretariat

The media contingent covering Jordan's first day of training camp consisted of exactly one newspaper reporter, one magazine writer, four photographers, and a TV crew. Sure, the Cubs were bringing a storybook season to a close that weekend, and the Bears faced Dallas at Soldier Field that Sunday, but the cold truth was that no one in Chicago cared much about the Bulls in September 1984, Michael Jordan or no Michael Jordan. "The Bulls were the poorest child in the town," explained Jeff Davis, who in those days was a sports television producer in the Second City.

It wasn't just Chicago—the NBA didn't much care either. The league had a new television contract with CBS Sports that season and hadn't included a single Bulls appearance on the schedule.

Even the local stations weren't interested in shooting footage of the Bulls for their newscasts, Davis explained. "TV rarely came around in those days." If a camera crew did show up at Angel Guardian, Loughery paid it no mind. There were no media restrictions involving the team's practices. Jeff Davis would go just because he was a basketball fan, he recalled. "I'll never forget seeing those practices early that year. Good grief, there was an intensity in Jordan that was unlike any other player who'd come along, because he was so talented. You could see that he was such a hard worker and you knew he was going to do things. He'd take it to the rack with such ease, against everybody. He was demanding. He wanted defenders to stick to him. 'Tighter. Come on, defend me. Damn you!' He'd call out names. He was a trash-talking son of a gun, too."

"Michael would pick on somebody every day," trainer Mark Pfeil remembered. "You saw this early on. Every day. Somebody was gonna be his goat. It would be anybody on the team, guys like Ennis Whatley and Ronnie Lester and Quintin Dailey. Michael would shoot, stick it in their faces time and time again. He used to get their goats to make them play harder, mainly because he was so competitive. There were times during his rookie year when practice was unworkable. Loughery would just toss up his hands and let Michael do his thing."

"It's interesting when you have a rookie who comes in like Michael did," Rod Higgins recalled in 2012. "Instantaneously he got respect from the veterans because of his competitiveness. When we started out in that training camp I noticed that this kid would embarrass you if you didn't bring your level of play up. He didn't really care who the veteran was that was guarding him either."

"Michael is like Secretariat," assistant coach Fred Carter quipped early that year. "All the other horses know they have to run to keep up with him."

"In practice, Loughery used to put Michael with different teams, just to see what he could do," Rod Thorn said. "Whatever team Kevin put him on, that team would win. Kevin told me, 'I don't know if our other guys are that bad, or he's that good.'"

"Kevin always had a thing in practice," Pfeil recalled, "where he'd divide the roster into two teams, and the first team to 10 won.

The team that lost ran 10 laps. Kevin called it 10 points or 10 laps. Michael never ran a lap the whole year. One time Michael's team was up 8–0, and Kevin switched him to the other team. Michael was furious. He scored the first 9 points by himself, and his team won."

"Once I saw him in camp I changed my thinking about what we were going to do offensively," Loughery recalled. "He dictated what type of offense we were going to need. We weren't a very strong roster outside of Michael, so he was gonna have to do a lot of shooting. I immediately started thinking of ways to isolate him, of having him going one-on-one. It made sense to post him up because he was stronger than most guards. You had to gear your offense around him."

Jordan had hoped to play off guard with the idea that he could match up against smaller opponents. Loughery took this notion one step further, however, to the idea that this rookie could really create mismatches at the point. Actually, he could also play small forward. The versatility essentially meant that the Bulls had gotten an upgrade at three positions.

The team headed out to play a quick run of exhibition games before the season. The era opened in Peoria at the Civic Center in front of 2,500 fans with Jordan on the bench. He came on to score a game-high 18. The schedule also took the Bulls to Glens Falls, New York, where Jordan dunked freely during warm-ups to the delight of the crowd, which cheered him right up until the moment it became clear that Jordan was going to defeat their Knicks that night.

Tim Hallam first recognized something different about the fan connection to Jordan in an exhibition stop in upstate Indiana. He scored 40 points that night, and afterward a string of fans, many of them young boys, followed him down the hallway, like Jordan was their Pied Piper. This magnetism became more apparent with each passing day. In the future, it would become necessary to wall him off, to protect him from the unharnessed power of that affection. But constructing that wall would take months. In the early days of that season, his growing public was merely amusing.

From the reaction of his coaches and teammates in that first training camp to the fan interest he generated during exhibition season, Jordan had reinforced the idea that he could turn the franchise around. "We saw his skills," Loughery recalled, "but you've got to be around him every day to see the competitiveness of the guy. He was gonna try to take over every situation that was difficult. He was gonna put himself on the line. He enjoyed it."

The franchise needed all that their new rookie had to offer. The first time they attended a Bulls game in Chicago Stadium, James and Deloris Jordan were taken aback by the sparse attendance and the dead atmosphere. Compared to the intense basketball energy at the University of North Carolina, Bulls games seemed pathetic. The Jordans wondered how this team could afford to pay their son hundreds of thousands of dollars each year. This will get better, Deloris told her husband, but she was far from sure. The negativity began with the Stadium itself, the "Madhouse on Madison," which sat in the middle of one of Chicago's worst neighborhoods. The area had been hit hard during the Chicago riot of 1968 following the assassination of Dr. Martin Luther King Jr. In the decade and a half since, conditions on much of the West Side had grown utterly bleak. For any fans brave enough to attend a Bulls game, parking their cars and finding their way to the gate often produced a heart-in-throat experience. "You had kids that would say, 'Can I wash your car, mister?'" Jeff Davis recalled. "If you parked on the street and if you didn't give them a little folding cash, you'd get your tires slashed. That was not uncommon. If you were with the media, you were told, 'Do not park anywhere but in the team-sanctioned parking lots, and get out of there as fast as you can after the games.' So, you had a mass exodus within a half hour, forty-five minutes from that place. People did not linger around the arena afterwards."

"The Bulls were struggling at that time and the Stadium was on the West Side," explained Tim Hallam. "Back then it didn't look the way it does now, with all the economic development. It was the second-oldest building in the league, behind the Boston Garden. You know, it was a great place when it was packed. It was loud. The noise was contained, because it would bounce off the roof and come back. There weren't any acoustics, which was good for a loud crowd, but we weren't drawing huge crowds at the time. So it was mostly dead."

"We still had a very small season ticket base," Joe O'Neil admitted. "In the third quarter I could count the attendance. I'd just go out and count the fans."

Steve Schanwald, who would eventually become the Bulls' VP, had come to Chicago in 1981 as a marketing executive for the White Sox. A University of Maryland grad, he had loved the enthusiasm of ACC basketball, and made a point to take in a few Bulls games. He'd been shocked as well. "The Stadium was a dead building for basketball," Schanwald recalled. "I used to enjoy coming out because I could get a seat and stretch out. But it was really kind of an embarrassment to see. I couldn't believe this was NBA basketball. It seemed more like the CBA, or worse. The Stadium itself was always great when it was filled with people. When it was devoid of people, it was kind of a depressing setting, like a tomb. There was no glitzy scoreboard. I am told that in the early days Bulls fans used to watch basketball games through the hockey Plexiglas. That's how little respect the Bulls had."

That sparse atmosphere only multiplied Jordan's difficulty on opening night. He was trying to juggle two female guests without them finding out about each other. He had been in the city for just a month—his mother living with him for much of that time no less—and yet on his guest list for opening night, he had included comp tickets for two women, and was scrambling just before game time to make sure they were seated in different sections of the arena. Best to have them in opposite corners so he could keep things straight, he reasoned. Of course, typical of a rookie, he undercut his own furtive efforts at manipulating the seating arrangement that night by tipping off a reporter. In time, he would become more mindful of what he said within earshot of the media.

Still, he had obviously come a long way since the days in high school when he had struggled to find a date. After hitting the shot to beat Georgetown in 1982, he and roommate Buzz Peterson had soon discovered they had a skyrocketing popularity with the female population in Chapel Hill. Jordan had found an even larger and more active social life in Chicago, one that had been pioneered by former Bull Reggie Theus, who had cut such a dashing party figure downtown that he had come to be called "Rush Street Reggie." Theus's departure in 1983 had left an opening for the rookie Jordan to fill as Chicago's premier ladies' man. Jordan was serious about basketball but not so serious as to pass up opportunity. At Carolina his fame had been the big appeal. Now, in Chicago, he was discovering that fortune was even more alluring.

The Beginning

At age twenty-one, Jordan was bursting with anticipation to play that first game on Friday, October 26, 1984, against the Washington Bullets in the creaky old Stadium. There were none of the laser shows that marked his pregame introductions later. Instead, he came onto the court that first time accompanied only by the strains of Michael Jackson's "Thriller." The 13,913 fans, about six thousand more than the Bulls' opening night a year earlier, cheered loudly to greet him, and erupted each time he did something to change the flow of the game. It became clear that very first quarter that Bulls games would no longer be known as sleepy little affairs.

Twenty-one seconds into the action he missed his first shot, an eighteen-footer. A minute later he stole the ball from Washington guard Frank Johnson to register his first steal. The game was only minutes old when he drew the crowd's first gasp, after he took off from the left for a slam over the top of brawny Bullets center Jeff Ruland, who shrugged off the intrusion and knocked him to the floor. The Stadium grew quiet as Jordan lay motionless. Finally he got up and later complained of a sore neck and head. He and Ruland agreed afterward that the collision was inadvertent, but it would signal an early pattern—Jordan reaching through the trees to attack the rim and the trees having something to say about it.

At the 7:27 mark of the opening period, he scored his first NBA bucket, a twelve-foot bank shot from the right side of the lane. From there, his nervousness made for an uneven shooting night. He made just five of sixteen shots from the floor, scored 16 points, and had 7 assists and 6 rebounds. He also had 5 turnovers to go with the 9 missed shots. Yet there had been much for fans to delight in.

"This was a good start for my career," he said afterward. "My main concern was to get everybody going tonight. First, I figure you keep hustling. Then you get the big guys going. Then, everything falls in place." Certainly one thing would change. In that first game, the ball seemed to spend much of the night in the hands of his teammates.

The coaching staff got another eyeful at the second game, in Milwaukee, assistant Bill Blair recalled. "When he started abusing Sidney Moncrief, who we considered one of the top five defensive guards in the league, we knew that we had a special person."

In his third game, also against the Bucks, he scored 37 points, including 22 in the fourth quarter, as 9,356 fans in the Stadium saw the Bulls claim a come-from-behind win over Milwaukee.

As the games melted away, Jordan found the ball in his hands more and more. Eager not to disappoint, the rookie would race up and down the floor, tongue out tasting the air. He was blindingly quick to the ball, taking rebounds and breaking into the open court like a scatback heading to daylight. Because he could cross the ball over while going full speed upcourt, opponents learned to step up to cut off the crossover, only to find that he was ready with a buttery reverse pivot that he could likewise execute at full speed. Such moves were difficult even for "water bug" guards, but to have someone six-six doing them?

If opponents hesitated about getting back on defense, he was gone. And if they did get back to protect the rim, Jordan presented a new sort of challenge. Time and again, he left the tarmac early and flew toward the goal, taking time to decide just how he was going to finish. Elgin Baylor had first shown the league hang time in the late 1950s, and Julius Erving later added a certain poetry. But this Jordan glide to the stuff proved spellbinding. There seemed to be a calm that settled on him as he closed in, tongue out, surveying the defensive landscape. Now he could cradle the ball and contemplate his moves without worrying about what his coach was thinking. With all his spectacular dunking, observers hardly mentioned his stupendous ability to measure the reverse. If the defender had position and went for the principle of verticality, Jordan simply floated around that and flipped the ball in from the backside.

"Once Michael started playing, and playing well, the fans got interested," Rod Thorn remembered. "At the start of the season, we were selling in the six thousand range. Then, all of a sudden, we were up over ten thousand. He was a show." Consistent sellouts would take a while longer, but the business model for the Chicago Bulls had clearly gotten an upgrade.

Now that Jordan had turned his youthful fire on opponents, conflicts arose with a variety of earthbound defenders. "In his early games, this guy was going to the basket every time he had the ball," Thorn explained. "He was putting up dunks and whirligig shots. Players on other teams were knocking him down out of the air. We pretty soon realized he was going to get killed." In his first game against the Pistons, Jordan was floating up for a dunk when Detroit center Bill Laimbeer slammed him to the floor, creating an uproar in the Stadium. He needed a protector on his team, yet none emerged immediately.

Chicago's early victories did get Quintin Daily and others to crowing about how they couldn't wait for the early visit of the defending champion Boston Celtics. Jordan scored 27 against Larry Bird and company, but the Celtics won handily, having been fired up by reading aloud the Bulls' boasting. Still, Bird was impressed. "I've never seen one player turn a team around like that," he told *Trib* columnist Bob Verdi afterward. "All the Bulls have become better because of him.... Pretty soon this place will be packed every night....They'll pay just to watch Jordan. He's the best. Even at this stage in his career, he's doing more than I ever did. I couldn't do what he does as a rookie. Heck, there was one drive tonight. He had the ball up in his right hand, then he took it down. Then he brought it back up. I got a hand on it, fouled him, and he still scored. All the while, he's in the air.

"You have to play this game to know how difficult that is. You see that and say, 'Well, what the heck can you do?' I'd seen a little of him before and wasn't that impressed. I mean, I thought he'd be good, but not this good. Ain't nothing he can't do. That's good for this franchise, good for the league."

"The scouting report said play me for the drive, that I couldn't go left," Jordan recalled. "They didn't know about my first step or the moves or the jump. I knew I was taking everybody by surprise, including myself."

Having sensed this impending stardom, Loughery quickly set up an "all-Jordan, all the time" offense, Tim Hallam recalled. "Kevin was one of those coaches where, how do you describe it? It's kind of like, if you've got a horse, he's gonna ride it, you know. And that was certainly the case here with Michael."

That trust between the two built from game to game as Jordan grew comfortable with Loughery's style, Hallam said. "Kevin was a good coach, a great situational coach. He was a tactician back then. Michael respected that."

Jordan's presence, of course, seemed to answer just about all tactical questions. In just his ninth pro game, he scored 45 points against San Antonio. Six weeks later he burned Cleveland for another 45. Then came a 42-point performance against New York. And another 45 against Atlanta. The energy level was almost unnerving, recalled Doc Rivers, the Atlanta Hawks' veteran point guard at the time. "I remember the first year saying to the guys in the locker room, 'There's no way that guy will be able to play with that energy for an entire season.'" Indeed, NBA rookies traditionally "hit the wall." They would play twenty-five games or so, the length of a college season, and discover their legs gone, their bodies worn down. Not Jordan.

"Two years later he was still doing the same thing," Rivers marveled. "His intelligence always stood out, but with MJ his intensity always stood out even more. There are very few who have that. It's rare to see a superstar with that level of intensity who can still do it every night, who is a target every night. It was amazing."

His first triple-double (35 points, 15 assists, and 14 rebounds) came against Denver. Then, just before the All-Star break, he zipped in 41 against defending champion Boston. Every time he played Bird he thought of the disrespect the Boston star had shown him during the Olympics exhibition tour. During warm-ups, Jordan's ball had rolled down to the NBA players' end of the floor, where Bird scooped it up. Instead of throwing it to a waiting Jordan, the Celtics star tossed it over his head. "Bird was showing me it was all business, and I was beneath him," Jordan said of the incident. "I didn't forget."

Celtics boss Red Auerbach knew a showman when he saw one. "You can see it in his eyes," Auerbach told one interviewer. "He is happy when he sees a crowd out there and he can perform."

Boston's legendary center Bill Russell agreed, saying, "He's one of the few guys that I would pay to watch."

Banned

As the rookie caught fire in early 1985, Nike released its first Air Jordan shoe, a red and black model that drew an immediate ban from the NBA. The league's guidelines called for players to wear white shoes, and the NBA said Jordan would be fined five thousand dollars each time he wore the new shoe. Nike's Rob Strasser and Peter Moore immediately phoned Sonny Vaccaro. "Both Rob and Peter said, 'Fuck 'em.' That's exactly what they said," Vaccaro recalled. "I said, 'What do you mean? We're going to do it without him wearing the shoe on the court?'"

Strasser quickly decided that Nike was going to have Jordan wear the shoes anyway and that the company would pay his fines each night. Plus they were going to tell fans about the banned shoes through an ad campaign. The NBA couldn't have handed the shoe manufacturer a better marketing platform. "When you tell the public that something is banned, what does the public always do?" Vaccaro recalled with a laugh. "Tell them you're not allowed to do something and they'll do it."

Nike moved quickly to take advantage of this gift horse, building the shoe's popularity on the fact it was banned. "And then it happened," Vaccaro recalled. Jordan's early play, along with the ban and subsequent marketing, sent sales soaring. Nike would ring up an astounding $150 million in Air Jordan sales over the first three years, which in turn brought Jordan the first wave of profound personal wealth.

For that first season, Nike pushed hard to make Air Jordan products available for the All-Star Game in Indianapolis, Vaccaro recalled. "We made red and black everything. Wrist bands, T-shirts, everything in the Bulls' colors."

That All-Star Weekend of 1985 would long be remembered for the flashy rookie with the fancy new outfits—and for how some of the league's veteran stars engaged in a freeze-out of Jordan during the main event. The alleged collusion was so subtle that at first even Jordan failed to recognize it. The story broke afterward, when Dr. Charles Tucker, an advisor to Magic Johnson, Isiah Thomas, and George Gervin, talked about it at the airport. Tucker told reporters, "The guys weren't happy with his attitude up here. They decided to teach him a lesson. On defense, Magic and George gave him a hard time, and offensively, they just didn't give him the ball.

"That's what they're laughing about," Tucker explained to the media as he stood near the stars waiting to fly out of the Indianapolis airport. "George asked Isiah, 'You think we did a good enough job on him?'"

Their reaction had apparently been triggered by the rookie wearing his new Air Jordan jumpsuit at the Slam Dunk Contest. Jordan, bedecked with gold necklaces during the event, lost in the finals to Atlanta's Dominique Wilkins. Tucker revealed that the veterans also thought the rookie seemed arrogant and standoffish. Thomas had supposedly been offended when Jordan had little to say during an elevator ride to a player meeting the first night of the weekend. "I was very quiet when I went there," Jordan later explained. "I didn't want to go there like I was a big-shot rookie and you must respect me."

For the All-Star Game itself, Jordan had played only 22 minutes and taken just 9 of the team's 120 shots.

Agent David Falk explained that Jordan had been asked by Nike to wear the prototype of the Air Jordan clothing. "That makes me feel very small," Jordan said of the snub. "I want to crawl in a hole and not come out."

Asked about the incident by reporters, Isiah Thomas denied any freeze-out of Jordan. "How could someone do anything like that?" the Detroit guard said. "It's very childish."

Asked later for comment about the freeze-out, Bulls teammate

Wes Matthews said, "He's got gifts from God. He's God's kid; let him be God's kid."

In retrospect, Vaccaro saw the incident as a backlash against Nike by athletes who earned comparatively little from Converse. "Nike was the enemy," he explained. "It was Nike. We created this guy. It was Nike. It wasn't so much he appeared in the dunk contest and was a fan favorite. Dr. J was a fan favorite. Nobody got mad at Dr. J. It was what we did with him."

Doctor, Doctor

Few saw at the time the immense power that Jordan was acquiring as a result of his captivating play and his Nike contract. Jordan himself would acknowledge that the incident made him realize that the game's established stars were against him. It planted the seeds of his dislike for both Isiah Thomas and Magic Johnson. The feelings against Thomas intensified with their two teams competing in the league's Central Division. Jordan's dislike for Johnson grew after word reached him that the Lakers guard had apparently encouraged team owner Jerry Buss to trade his old friend James Worthy after Los Angeles lost to Boston in the 1984 championship series.

The incident was gasoline on the fire of Jordan's competitiveness, explained Vaccaro, who had begun spending substantial time behind the scenes with Jordan. "That became his personal crutch," Vaccaro recalled. "That's why we watched this person turn into the killer on the court that he is. He took them all to task. He never forgot that day. He's smiling today and he's kissing with everybody and all that stuff, but he never forgot that. That was the first public snubbing of Michael Jordan. Do any of those guys today remember that? Does anybody admit that? When he got the snub from Isiah, who was a great player obviously, Michael took it and made it a thing he put in the back of his mind."

The Pistons were scheduled to play in Chicago Stadium the first game after the break, and Thomas chafed when reporters asked about his involvement in the freeze-out. "That never happened," Thomas said. "I was very upset when I read that. That could affect a potential friendship between Michael and me." Before the game, the Detroit star sent a message to Jordan that he needed to talk. Granted a brief meeting, Thomas apologized in person, a display that Jordan later termed "mostly show." That night, Jordan scored 49 points with 15 rebounds to help the Bulls to a 139–126 overtime win. On one breakaway, Jordan clearly paused, giving Thomas just time enough to run into the picture before throwing down an emotional dunk, which the game's broadcasters immediately identified as taunting. Afterward, Thomas again grew angry with reporters. "It's over. It's over," he told them. Far from over, their personal confrontation would play out over the ensuing seasons as the Bulls battled to overtake the Pistons in the Eastern Conference.

The heightened competitiveness was just one of many changes afoot. During the All-Star Game in Indianapolis the men who had owned the Bulls for more than a decade revealed their plans to sell the controlling interest in the team to Jerry Reinsdorf. Reinsdorf told the press that the transaction would be consummated about March 1, 1985.

Jordan and his Bulls suffered through a twelve-game road losing streak down the stretch before closing out the season with thirty-five wins, an improvement of eight over the previous year and good enough to make the playoffs for the first time since 1981. But with their frontcourt thinned by injuries, the Bulls lost to Milwaukee, 3–1.

"As the year went on and we made the playoffs, Michael just got bigger and bigger with the fans," assistant coach Bill Blair recalled. "I remember the trip in Washington where we won to secure a playoff position. Two days later we played Philly, but Michael stayed in Washington and went with Senator Bill Bradley and made an appearance in Congress. Then he got on the plane and flew up to Philadelphia that night. He had the shootaround the next day and got 40 against Philly. So you knew Michael could handle all the other stuff outside of basketball and still get it done."

The loss in Philadelphia left Jordan winless in five attempts that first year against Julius Erving and the Sixers. Long known for his classy approach to the game, Erving had not been implicated in the All-Star freeze-out, even though he too endorsed Converse, but Sixers coach Matt Guokas wondered about the effect of the Jordan hoopla on the very proud Erving. First as a broadcaster, then as a Sixers assistant, and finally as head coach, Guokas had been able to observe Dr. J's career up close for more than a decade. "I saw Doc from all those different perspectives," Guokas, who had also played alongside Wilt Chamberlain on the Sixers' great 1967 team, recalled in a 2012 interview. "Julius was mesmerizing as an individual, and the stature he gave our organization, the way he was looked up to, the way he treated people was just magnificent. He always seemed to have time for everybody, no matter who they were. And it was genuine. Julius was coming to the end of his career when Michael was just starting to blossom. But you know I think there was a mutual respect there between the two, and Michael was always very—I don't want to say careful—but he always made sure that he recognized Julius for the star and the person he was, what he brought to the NBA before Michael, as somebody who brought the 'wow' factor to professional basketball. And I think Doc appreciated that. Michael, unfortunately, didn't get a chance to play against Doc at his peak. But I'll tell you what, there were a number of games I saw them play against each other. Doc more than held his own and on a number of occasions got the best of the situation. It was never a one-on-one matchup. It was always a team deal. But Doc would always stick his nose in there and have a little extra hop in his step every time we played Michael. Those great players, they didn't want to be embarrassed. They knew that if they went out there with just an ordinary effort, like it was just another of eighty-two games, Michael could make you look bad. Real bad. So they were always ready for the challenge."

Guokas admitted that he, too, had fallen under the sway of Jordan's aura in those early seasons. The Sixers coach recalled that he was obsessing about Jordan in the locker room one night before a game at Chicago Stadium. "The locker room in the Stadium was stark and dank and just awful," Guokas recalled, "but the arena was great. It was my favorite place to play and be in. I remember we were getting ready to play. It was in a back-to-back situation, and I was trying to make sure our guys were ready to go. I was going on and on about Michael. Doc kind of like had his head down and he was sort of fiddling with his sneakers or whatever. He finally looked up. He'd had enough of it. He said, 'Hey, wait a minute. We can play, too, you know.'

"I said, 'You're right.' It was a good lesson to learn. Enough said. I didn't need to be going on about how great he is," Guokas recalled with a laugh. "He and Andrew Toney went out and beat the bejeebers out of Michael that night. Julius would invariably end up matched up against Michael at some point during those games. Doc kind of gave me that look after the game. He still had a little gas in the tank."

PART VI

FLIGHT SCHOOL

Chapter 17

THE YOUNG PRISONER

DEAN SMITH HAD suggested that Jordan take a communication course at North Carolina to help prepare him for interviews and public appearances. He had some awkward, hesitant moments during his NBA debut, but that was to be expected. He could get by on poise alone and would enjoy excellent relations with the media over the course of his career, even when they annoyed him. Almost overnight, local TV and radio stations that once had little interest in the Bulls began showing up to cover the city's newest star. "He was so articulate," former Chicago sports TV producer Jeff Davis explained, "and he photographed like a charm." Jordan's fame exploded quickly from there, starting as a splash of Nike commercials and highlight footage, which in turn fed enough word-of-mouth momentum to drive a craze.

Bulls PR man Tim Hallam watched Jordan mature into a remarkably self-possessed public figure. Julius Erving had brought a grace to the role of pro basketball superstar that Jordan admired and emulated in his relations with the media. It also didn't hurt that Deloris Jordan watched her son's every move and was in his ear if something seemed amiss. Furthermore, his ability to listen meant that he understood reporters' questions and routinely formulated engaging answers.

"I think he grew in every way," Hallam observed. "If you look back to his early interviews, he wasn't as articulate as four years, or eight years, or twelve years down the road. You know, everything changed about him. Everything he wore changed about him, too. It's funny to go back in his first year and see what he was wearing and then go four years from there. He went from sweatpants to designer suits."

As positive and profitable as the public spotlight was, it also hastened Jordan's alienation, a process that Hallam began to notice by February of that rookie year. Some of it had to do with his mushrooming fame and some of it stemmed from the humiliation of the All-Star freeze-out. Sonny Vaccaro flew to Chicago to talk with him in the aftermath of the freeze-out to explain the reaction of the league's biggest stars. "After the All-Star Game, no one at Nike knew what to do," Vaccaro recalled. "Michael and I talked. I told him, 'This shows you the depth that they're going to go because you're better than all of them, Michael.'" The talk did little to alleviate the disappointment. Magic Johnson had been his hero. As Jordan told reporters, the incident made him want to crawl in a hole and hide. He was already rapidly on his way to becoming a prisoner in his hotel room, unwilling to venture out into public outside of games and scheduled appearances. Only occasionally would he emerge from this isolation, Tim Hallam recalled. "It was like, 'Wow, Michael's out!' You were happy for him. Meaning, it's kind of like a lion getting out of the cage and walking free within the boundaries of the zoo for a while."

Beyond the apparent rejection by the league's stars, the pressure of such sudden stardom was overwhelming and a large part of Jordan's new life that could not be avoided. Teams still flew commercially in those days, which meant that road life began early in the morning with five-o'clock wake-up calls and immediate exposure to a public that recognized him at every turn. People simply felt compelled to approach the sports world's newest magician, and it usually wouldn't take long before he was mobbed, Hallam explained. "I would say, 'You know what, he's got to just say, the hell with it, and go about what he wants to do.' But then you find out when you see him come out like that, that he can't. Because people would go so gaga over him, whether it be an adult or kid or whoever, they couldn't hold themselves back. They'd lose their fucking minds. That's how it was for him."

The situation sent him looking for refuge. "Michael used to talk about going to a movie theater," Joe O'Neil explained. "You go sit in a movie theater, you're just like a regular person. Aside from that, restaurants, malls, the gas station, anywhere you go, people are going to be all over you."

Nike and the NBA itself would ultimately bear some of the responsibility for the sacrificing of Jordan's private life, observed George Gervin, who became Jordan's teammate in 1985. "That's where it changed everything, man. They made him bigger than life. That made it tough on him. They made him the most famous guy to ever play. But that's a tough life where you have to have a guard with you everywhere you go. You can't eat, you can't sit down without somebody sitting around you. He had that Michael Jackson kind of life. That's a tough life, man. That can drive you to an early death. And the game was changing. How ESPN and cable TV came in. He really had to isolate himself because they promoted him so hard. And Nike and all them promoted him so hard. It made it hard for him to be just a regular guy. You get robbed of your life."

"Trying to deal with the public just got to be too much," Tim Hallam recalled. "I think it was just a change in that the demands were pretty incredible. And you've got to remember, the demands were incredible just from the Bulls side of it, let alone his own ventures and commercials and Nike, and life in general. All of it together was chaotic, especially at that time in the NBA."

Longtime Chicago radio reporter Bruce Levine perceived that Jordan came to feel objectified "much like a very beautiful woman who can't get by the fact that people focus only on her exterior. Because people are so taken by what she is on the outside and what she is physically. He knew that people didn't deal with him as a person but as an object."

"He had a lot going on," Hallam said. "I don't think it really changed his personality, but it made him a different person because he had to be different. You can't satisfy everybody. You may try for a while, but then you learn that, you know what, I can't do this and it's not worth my energy to try and do it. And so certain things are going to fall by the wayside and certain people are going to think that it's because, you know, I have a huge ego or I'm big-headed now, or I have money or fame now. That simply was not the case. There's only twenty-four hours in a day. I think that was the biggest thing that I saw that I felt bad for him, in that, no one could control that.

"And yet," Hallam added, "he still went out and did what he was supposed to do."

Caught in the Struggle

Strangely, Jordan found some relief around the regular reporters covering the team, people whom he had come to trust enough to chat with before games. He also continued to draw support from his family, with his mother and brothers making regular visits to Chicago to stay with him. His father visited, too, but that created its own problems, because of the growing conflict between his parents. Soon people involved with Jordan and the team in Chicago began to notice that they rarely saw his parents together. Sonny Vaccaro pointed out that after those initial meetings it seemed he almost never dealt with James and Deloris Jordan together. "At first it would be normal on the trips," Vaccaro recalled. "They'd be together. When it first happened we had a meeting together. But then, after a time or two, the lines were drawn in the sand. I can't honestly say that I remember more than a one-sentence conversation with them together after that."

And the Nike staff members felt some relief at that. They could always rely on Mrs. Jordan to be professional.

"You trusted Deloris Jordan," Vaccaro explained. "She was an impeccably dressed, very educated woman, whereas James was crude in a way." Still, they were in business with his son, and Nike officials soon found themselves dealing with the father, a task that Vaccaro disliked. James Jordan was known to drink, he said, and time would show that he was unreliable in business, as shaky as Deloris Jordan was solid.

Sis, Michael's older sister, pointed out that the parents had fallen into their own intense competition to influence their son. Her father was quiet and reserved while her mother moved into the spotlight, she explained. "Though his sudden popularity brought with it a resounding level of success, it also brought an avalanche of contention between my parents."

As with their marital conflicts a decade earlier, this new conflict could erupt with surprising intensity outside of the public's eye.

"Michael was split between his parents from day one," Sonny Vaccaro explained. "I mean not to the public, but there was this contemptuous relationship."

Mostly the parents had competing views of what Jordan should be and how he should conduct himself. The son loved both his parents, felt a loyalty to each, and somehow managed during his first few years to keep their conflict from reaching toxic levels. But as his career advanced, that became increasingly harder to do, Vaccaro said, an opinion shared by the family's older daughter.

James Jordan's own life was far from perfect during his son's first season in Chicago. The father was going through the humiliating process of dealing with his criminal charges in North Carolina. And Sis had made it known to her parents she was exploring legal action against both of them in connection with her sexual abuse allegations. She had checked herself in for psychiatric treatment at a Wilmington hospital. No wonder James found easy escape in the fantasy life his son was living, no matter how confining the circumstances.

Bulls employees and fans alike took notice of the closeness between father and son. James Jordan presented an amiable, low-key figure. The media and Bulls staff members enjoyed his constant good nature. And as he had done when Michael was in high school, James made it clear that he was not there to meddle with the team in any way, but only to help his son's adjustment off the court.

"Michael adored him," former Bulls assistant coach Johnny Bach recalled in 2012.

"They were like buds, you know," Tim Hallam said of Jordan and his father. "I thought that was kind of nice. He was always with him. He always hung with him. I think it was good for Michael."

Yet in many ways James's companionship only served to intensify the tension with Deloris as they both sought to influence their son. Not everyone saw or felt that conflict. Joe O'Neil recalled spending time with the Jordans when the Bulls went on the road. "I remember sitting in the hotel lobbies with James and Deloris Jordan. Their attitude was, 'We'll get there someday. You know we will.' They were always very, very positive and supportive. Mike's dad was a funny, funny guy, a jokester. Deloris, she was like everybody's mom. She looked over Michael like any mother would. She was as sweet and nice of a person as you could imagine. She never had any air about her that, 'My son's a superstar,' or whatever. Michael's parents were protective of him, very, very proud of him. Just like regular parents."

Posse Time

A number of other people took up residence in Jordan's young life, beginning with Nike executive Howard White, a former University of Maryland basketball player who also happened to be African American. "Howard was like his guy," Vaccaro explained. "He was a basketball player. Howard was a good person. He was his companion on the road, too."

The entourage expanded from there, Vaccaro explained. "That's when Michael got the North Carolina group back up. Rod Higgins remained close. Michael started forming his own posse. All of that was starting to happen." It was a revolving group, with an understood mission of keeping Jordan company on road trips, when his hotel room began to feel like a prison. The agenda included card games, golf, mixed drinks, pool, whatever it took to lighten the mood. This group soon came to include old friend and teammate Adolph Shiver and "the three Freds": Fred Whitfield, who soon had jobs working with Nike and David Falk; Fred Glover, an insurance adjuster who had met Whitfield and Jordan at the basketball camp back in Buies Creek; and Fred Kearns, a Charlotte mortician who had often golfed with Jordan.

That first season James Jordan was alarmed to get a large bill for the expenses the entourage had run up while they stayed with Michael for an extended road trip. "I first thought it was a waste of money until I thought about it a little longer," the father said at the time. "Then it occurred to me that it was in Michael's best interest to keep close friends around him instead of strangers. These guys were good for Michael."

Other regulars in the early days included Buzz Peterson and Gus Lett, a former security guard at Chicago Stadium who assumed some of those duties for Jordan. But it was George Koehler, Jordan's driver and impromptu valet, who proved especially constant and reliable over the years, Joe O'Neil explained. "George has been the perfect kind of buffer for Michael. With a guy like Michael, you almost always need somebody with you. Somebody to run a little interference. To have another set of eyes out there for you. George is a great guy. He's a Chicagoan. His and Michael's relationship is very, very special. Michael didn't have a big entourage. His closest friends were kind of regular guys—Rod Higgins, Adolph, the different Freds."

Those in the entourage soon took to calling Michael "Black Cat," perhaps because he could pounce as quickly in a social setting as he could in any game. Jordan seemed driven by an insistence on challenging those around him in even little ways. His verbal gamesmanship was conducted at a level that seemed worthy of anything he did on the court. "With his friends and people who are close to him, Jordan will see something and ride you and crack on you," Rod Higgins once explained. "To deal with him, you have to go right back to him just to make the night not so long."

He seemed to enjoy back and forth banter as much as he relished a good game of one-on-one, and he approached it with the same mentality. "He's the kind of guy," Tim Hallam explained, "if he comes at you, you've got to go right back at him.... You've got to be able to take his hits, his barbs, if you will, and come right back at him. Otherwise you're a dead man. The best way to get him is if you throw it back at him and people around him are laughing. Then he kind of backs down a little bit, 'cause you've let him know, 'I got some shit too, okay?'"

As Hallam explained, Jordan believed his team should go 82–0 each and every season. He carried a similar level of expectation into his social life, which didn't make it easy to be around him. "If you make a mistake, he'll let you know about it," Buzz Peterson once pointed out.

Hallam added, "It's kind of like you have to be competitive with him, too, at whatever, or one, you're either discarded, or two, you're no fun to compete against."

Sometimes his companions had to make sure they weren't too good at coming back at Jordan. "He hates to be embarrassed," Whitfield once explained with a laugh. "He can't take that. He can dish it out all the time, though."

"If he's gonna tease...you gotta volley," Hallam said. "He likes to volley. But you have to do it in the right way. You can't be bullshit and it's gotta be good. Would we yell at each other? No. But, he'd say something like, 'You know, I could get you fired.' And I'd say, 'Hey, don't do me any favors. You think I'm enjoying this shit right now?'"

This hard edge was also tempered by the childlike nature that George Koehler first observed. Jordan displayed a vulnerability at times that contrasted with the fierceness of his competitive persona. Early on in his new life in Chicago, he showed much of the complexity that would come to define his personality. For starters, he wrestled with intense, and complicated, emotions about his family.

He prized trust, and when he found it, Jordan was capable of almost staggering displays of loyalty. "Once you are friends with him he really works at keeping that friendship and nursing that friendship," Rod Higgins explained. Conversely, if that trust was violated, or he sensed some affront, his response could be just as intense, a factor that he had learned to channel into his competitiveness.

Perhaps the most important thing to all of his friends, the thing that kept them traveling back and forth at their own expense to hang out with him, was the uncommon loyalty. Jordan was able to communicate to all of them that he cared about them. "What people don't understand," said former teammate and longtime friend Charles Oakley, "is that he really is a good guy."

And without doubt, there was the sheer joy and fascination of being an insider in Michael Jordan's lofty world. The view from those heights was exhilarating for those around him. He was basketball's Elvis. "He created this mythology for all of us," Vaccaro explained. "Whether it was Nike, whether it was me personally, whether it was his friends, whoever it was with him, the small group of guys that he had with him that, the ones who have gone up and down with him, they were his friends. They were the only ones he could trust for eight or nine years."

So they made themselves useful as friends, and then something more. For example, Adolph Shiver, Jordan's oldest friend, filled a role as something of a mouthy social director and bartender for the gatherings. Mostly, Shiver brought the feel of home to the group, along with a sixth sense for the party atmosphere and a humor about Jordan's limitations. "That boy don't know how to make drinks," Shiver once said of Jordan. "He just be throwing shit together."

"The reality of it," said former Bulls psychologist George Mumford, "was that if he hadn't created that cocoon, he probably wouldn't have won those six championships."

Juanita

By far the most important addition to Jordan's private world was Juanita Vanoy, whom he met in December of his rookie season. They were introduced by a friend who set up a meeting at a Bennigan's in Chicago. A few weeks later, the friend had a small party to give them a second opportunity to spend time together. Vanoy was a beauty, said to be one of Reggie Theus's former flames. She was almost four years older than Jordan, and he immediately found that appealing. It challenged him to raise his own level of maturity. He found that he could talk to her, as he could with his mother.

This ability to talk led to something of a magical connection, and they began spending more time together. As Lacy Banks of the *Chicago Sun-Times* explained, Jordan's existence had quickly become that of a young prince, so it probably helped that Vanoy had already dealt with a Chicago player who was popular with the ladies. By all accounts, she was classy, intelligent, and patient. She was self-confident and low-maintenance, both critical to managing a relationship with Jordan. "Both my wife, Pam, and I found Juanita to be a lovely person," recalled Sonny Vaccaro, an assessment echoed by Jordan's golf partner Richard Esquinas.

"I knew Juanita from day one," Joe O'Neil offered. "Juanita was a great person. I grew up on the South Side of Chicago like she did. For whatever reason, it all never seemed to go to her head. She always seemed the same Juanita that I always knew."

Nonetheless, Jordan's parents did not approve of her and spent some effort at trying to counter her influence, according to Sonny Vaccaro, which might explain, in part, the on-again, off-again nature of the relationship over Jordan's first years in Chicago.

Truth be told, no one figure, no one factor, was likely to distract Jordan from feeding the competitive monster inside him. That ate up a substantial portion of each day. His main outlets were basketball and golf, although not always in that order. Fortunately, his fix required nothing elaborate. In the early days, when Jordan was still figuring out what to do with himself in Chicago, he would often drop by the Bulls offices, where he, Hallam, and O'Neil had set up their own miniature golf course.

"We'd play putt-putt," Joe O'Neil recalled. "We'd put together a little eighteen-hole golf course in the office and we'd bet. We'd walk around the office putting golf balls into waste cans, and that son of a gun, he was as competitive playing putt-putt in the office as he was on the court. He'd take twenty dollars from me, and that's when twenty dollars was like four hundred dollars. I still remember giving him twenty dollars in the office and my wife yelling at me for gambling with him."

When the weather was good they'd take it outside, O'Neil recalled. "We played public golf courses, we played at Medinah Country Club. He was about as good as I was at the time. Then he started playing about 150 rounds a year and he became a very good golfer. But when Tim and I first started golfing with him, Michael was just taking up the game. He could hit the hell out of the ball but you never knew where it was going."

Jordan often talked of how he prized the solitude of the course. However, his unrestrained joy didn't exactly make it peaceful. "He never shut up," O'Neil recalled with a laugh. "He talked when you're swinging, talked when you're putting. He could be a great commentator on TV someday if he wanted to. He could just mentally give it to you, whether you were putt-putting in the office or out playing on the golf course or shooting a game of pool. He would always ride you." For the few brief hours, he could be Mike Jordan, regular guy. "That's why golf became so important to him," O'Neil said. "It gave him some solitude away from people. He said the golf course and the movie theater were two places he could get away from people...where he could go like he was anybody else."

That spring of 1985, Jeff Davis was producing a regional golf show that featured celebrities playing a round with baseball broadcaster Ken "The Hawk" Harrelson. Once the season ended, Davis contacted Jordan about appearing on the show and he jumped at the chance.

"He came on and he couldn't have been happier than to do this," Davis recalled.

On the course, Jordan asked for three do-overs. "He wasn't satisfied with his showing," Davis said with a chuckle. "There was no money on the line. It was a matter of pride, and he wanted to beat Harrelson, who was a terrific golfer. He couldn't get closer, but he looked nice, he had a nice swing for a guy that size. Golf is not a sport made for the tall man anyway. But Jordan was bound and determined to succeed at everything."

The scenes were shot on a course in Chicago's north suburbs that day, and after the shooting was finished the crew packed up their van and headed back down into the city. "It was about an hour from downtown," Davis recalled. "And we were coming back down the Edens Expressway, driving along. All of a sudden, our cameraman, who was driving, said, 'Jeez, there's this Corvette that's flying behind us!' And here comes this car, it pulls right up beside, and it was him. He's grinning ear to ear, just laughing, and then he just gave a little wave of his fingers and bam, he was off again and gone."

Chapter 18

THE FOOT

J ERRY KRAUSE GOT the call during spring training 1985, when he was working as a scout for Jerry Reinsdorf's Chicago White Sox. Reinsdorf wanted him to come to Chicago to talk about running the Bulls. The conversation went well, considering that Krause had already been fired several years earlier as the Bulls' GM.

Krause had bounced around for years scouting in baseball and basketball until he found his way into working for Reinsdorf and the Sox. Reinsdorf had grown up in Brooklyn, "where being a Dodgers fan was almost a religion," he explained. He was a dutiful follower, along with every other kid on Flatbush Avenue. Reinsdorf also loved the New York Knicks, especially Red Holzman's teams of the early 1970s. Later, after he had finished law school and begun amassing a fortune in Chicago real estate, Reinsdorf seized the opportunity to own sports teams, first the White Sox, then the Bulls.

Learning of his boss's admiration for the Knicks, Krause was no fool. He soon took to regaling Reinsdorf with tales of his days competing as a scout against Holzman. It was the early sixties, Krause's first year in scouting for the old Baltimore Bullets. Other scouts in the business were already making fun of him. He was dumpy and short and looked nothing like a scout or like anybody who had anything to do with athletics. He was also secretive and wore a trench coat and a hat, like Inspector Clouseau. They called him "the Sleuth" and snickered behind his back.

Everywhere he turned, it seemed Krause was running into Holzman, who was scouting for the Knicks at the time. Early one morning they happened upon each other in an airport and Holzman asked Krause where he had been.

"Down the road," he replied.

Krause loved recounting what happened next: "He looks at me and he says, 'Son, I want to tell you something. I know where you've been, and if you've got any brains in your head you know where I've been, so let's cut the bullshit and let's be friends.' "

Friends they became, even as they competed fiercely to find hidden gems among the available college players. Krause thought he was about to make the steal of the 1967 draft with a rawboned young forward named Phil Jackson out of the University of North Dakota, but Holzman snuck in and stole him for the Knicks with the seventeenth pick.

"Fuckin' Holzman," Krause had muttered on the day of that very special draft. Scouting for the Baltimore Bullets, Krause had set the table for Baltimore to take Winston-Salem State's Earl "The Pearl" Monroe with the number 2 pick, and Holzman had picked Walt Frazier out of Southern Illinois with the number 5 pick. Both players would wind up in the Hall of Fame, as would Jackson, as a coach. Holzman went on to coach the Knicks to two NBA championships, with Frazier, Monroe, and Jackson all playing a role along with guys like Dave DeBusschere and Bill Bradley. And Krause made his way as a scout, all the while battling the snickerers and naysayers who seemed to question everything about him. In the process, Krause built the kind of knowledge that would impress a no-nonsense man like Reinsdorf.

When Reinsdorf bought the Bulls that spring of 1985, he had thought he might keep Rod Thorn as director of the team's basketball operations. But the Bulls went on a losing streak, which prompted the new owner to feel out what Krause would do to improve the team.

First, Krause said, he would get rid of the bad apples. "The way I figured it we had a whole bunch of Fords making Cadillac pay," Krause recalled. "It was selfish. Everyone was playing for themselves." Next, because he knew a thing or two about spotting college talent, he would use the draft to make the Bulls a team with a future. They would stop signing bad free agents.

Reinsdorf liked the draft philosophy and trusted Krause as a scout. Krause said the first player he would look for would be a tough power forward, a banger to protect the basket and the Bulls' shiny new star. Beyond that, he would attempt to draft athletic players with long arms. Finally, he said, he would find good jump shooters to make opponents pay when they double-teamed Jordan.

Just as important, he would look for solid citizens. Chicago had to clean up its history of bad eggs.

After the talk, Reinsdorf realized he had to fire Rod Thorn and bring in Krause.

"Krause was atop the scouting hierarchy at the White Sox, and I had gotten to know him," the owner explained later. "There had to be a cultural change in the Bulls' organization, and Krause believed the same things I did." In time, they would become known in Chicago as "the two Jerrys," the men who held sway over the Jordan era with the Bulls.

"I want a team that will play Red Holzman basketball," Reinsdorf said in announcing the changes. "An unselfish team, one that plays team defense, that knows its roles, that moves without the ball. Jerry Krause's job will be to find the DeBusschere of 1985 and the Bradley of 1985."

Krause had been named the Bulls' GM once before, about five years earlier, and lasted all of a few months before he got crossed up, offering to hire DePaul's Ray Meyer as the team's coach. Krause's mistake was that he didn't have the authority to make the offer to Meyer. Bulls ownership promptly fired him in the wake of that very public embarrassment, making him the laughingstock of the city.

The news of his return hit the sports desks at Chicago newspapers like a bomb. Jerry Krause is gonna be Michael's boss? "Jerry had this reputation for being a guy who went out in public with gravy stains on his tie," longtime Chicago sportswriter Bill Gleason once explained. "Personally, I never saw any gravy stains, but some of the other guys claim they did. Of course he was overweight. Jerry always had a problem with overeating."

He stood just under five six and weighed 260 pounds.

"Jerry's been around forever," said one longtime Bulls employee in 1998. "He knew all the coaches, the assistants, the scouts in the league. The previous Bulls administration despised Jerry. They had all these stories and tales and ripped him all the time. Lo and behold if he didn't come back here and get the job as general manager."

Krause was elated to return to the Bulls. "I'd left in disgrace, and I'd come back on top," he explained.

His first step was to fire coach Kevin Loughery. His second was to bring in his old friend Tex Winter, a retired college coach, to work with the coaching staff that Krause would hire. He picked journeyman Stan Albeck, most recently of the New Jersey Nets, to replace Loughery. "I knew it was a mistake almost as soon as I did it," Krause would say later.

Then he turned his attention to the roster. "I had a brutal start," Krause recalled. "I had nine players I didn't want and three I did. I wanted Dave Corzine, I wanted Rod Higgins, and I wanted Michael. The rest of them I couldn't have cared less about. And they were talented. All of them were very talented. But it wasn't a question of talent."

Krause recalled sitting down to discuss the team with Jordan. "I told him, 'I believe you have a chance to be a great player. I'm going to try to get players around you to work with you.' He said, 'No, don't get players who can work with me. Get players we can win with.'"

After two decades of upheaval in the team's front office, Bulls fans were openly leery of Krause's seemingly unorthodox approach. But Krause knew what he wanted and set about the business of making it happen. He had long told himself that if he ever got another chance as an NBA general manager, he had a certain vision of what he wanted to build. It began with Tex Winter's basketball system, the triangle offense. Second, he wanted to develop Phil Jackson as a head coach. Krause had known Jackson since the days he had scouted him in hopes of drafting him. The son of two Pentecostal preachers, Jackson had been raised in Montana and North Dakota. By the end of high school, he longed for relief from his strict upbringing and found escape with an athletic scholarship to the University of North Dakota, where he played basketball for an engaging young coach named Bill Fitch. The six-foot-eight Jackson developed into a two-time NCAA Division II All-American, a legitimate pro prospect. Krause and Holzman were probably the only two pro scouts that had made their way out to North Dakota to check out Jackson.

As a Knicks fan, Reinsdorf liked Krause's idea of developing Jackson into an NBA coach. After his thirteen-year playing career in New York and New Jersey ended, Jackson had worked as an assistant coach and broadcaster for the Nets before moving on to become head coach of the Albany Patroons in the Continental Basketball Association for five seasons. In 1984, Jackson's Patroons won the CBA title, and the next season he was named CBA Coach of the Year. He was coaching in Puerto Rico when Krause contacted him about an assistant coaching job with the Bulls in 1985.

"I kept up with Phil as a player through the years," Krause recalled. "We'd talk from time to time, and I followed his coaching career in the CBA. When I got the job in Chicago in 1985, I talked to him again. I told him I needed scouting reports on the CBA. Within a week, I had typewritten reports on the whole league, details on every player."

"I went to the CBA and had some success," Jackson recalled, "but still nothing came in my direction.... Jerry Krause was like the only person that really stayed in touch with me from the NBA world. And he had just gotten back in it. But that was my connection. Jerry had seen me play in college, and we had a relationship that spanned twenty years. Jerry's a remarkable guy. He's an enigma to the athletic world. He's not what you would consider an athlete. And even as a scout back there thirty years ago, he was a very unusual type of fellow to be out there scouting a basketball player."

Jackson had been known as a nonconformist during his playing days with the Knicks. In *Maverick*, his 1975 autobiography written with Charlie Rosen for Playboy Press, Jackson recalled his exploration of sixties counterculture. In the book, he talked openly about taking LSD and other drugs, which just about guaranteed that no NBA team considered him coaching material.

"I've never read the book," Krause once explained. "I didn't need to. I knew about Phil's character."

While putting together a staff that off-season, Krause set up Jackson to interview with Stan Albeck for the job of assistant coach. He showed up in Chicago with a full beard and wearing sandals and a straw hat with a large parrot feather in it.

"Stan and I had a very short interview," Jackson remembered.

Albeck later told Krause, "I don't want that guy under any circumstances."

Actually, Albeck wasn't much interested in Tex Winter's system either. Having run aground over coaching issues in his first tenure as the Bulls' GM, Krause wasn't about to have another blowup with his second opportunity. So he backed off and told Jackson he'd try him some other time.

Meanwhile, Krause had done some frantic last-minute maneuvering to draft Virginia Union's Charles Oakley, a bulky, little-known forward in the 1985 draft. As with many Krause moves, the pick was not a popular one in Chicago.

"Charles was a tough kid, and he didn't take anything from anyone," recalled former Bulls assistant Johnny Bach. "You could tell he was strong-willed as a person and he wanted to play.... He wanted to prove to people coming from a small school that he was worthy of his selection in the draft and he was committed to playing hard."

Oakley soon developed into just the power forward the Bulls needed, a protector of Jordan from the Bill Laimbeers of the world. Krause went looking for other pieces, what he called OKP, "our kind of people."

"Jerry took away a lot of things that this franchise didn't need," Phil Jackson would say later of Krause's early moves. "It didn't need certain types of people on the club. He had a certain idea of what type of person he wanted. He brought in character, or what he liked to think of as character. Good solid people. People who wanted to work hard."

The Needle

For all his ambition and insight, Krause quickly erred that first year back in Chicago in that he needlessly alienated Jordan, which would put their relationship on a negative footing for the next fifteen years. Among the early steps Krause took was the trading of Jordan's best friend on the team. "We traded Rod Higgins," Krause admitted later. "Michael was upset about that."

Krause later reacquired Higgins, only to trade him yet again. It was the kind of move that left observers wondering whether Krause took pride, perhaps even pleasure, in challenging Jordan. In his years of scouting, Krause had studied the game's all-time greats, just as he had put in hours scouting talent at America's traditionally black colleges. Krause was immensely proud of his background, and often expounded to Jordan on the game's greatest players, and on his own scouting credentials.

"I used to needle him," Krause recalled of his early conflict with Jordan. "I used to say, 'Someday you might be as good as Earl Monroe. You remind me of Earl and Elgin. You're a combination of Earl Monroe and Elgin Baylor, and you might be as good as both of them someday. Earl did it on the ground. You're doing it in the air. Elgin was the first one to do it in the air. You remind me of him.' And then every time after that, he'd say, 'That fuckin' Monroe.' Then, he'd say, 'Where'd you take Monroe? Second in the draft? Big fuckin' deal.' I think that whole thing with Michael stems from Earl Monroe."

Bulls employees who happened to witness these exchanges would cringe at Krause's insistence on challenging Jordan. "If you're gonna toss things out towards Michael, they better be true," Tim Hallam explained. "Because he never forgets and he never lets go."

Ultimately, the new GM's "needling" would ruin any chance he had at a cordial relationship with the star of the team he was managing. But Krause seemed driven by the disrespect he sensed in Jordan's response to him.

Jordan, meanwhile, pushed for the only thing he really trusted. He wanted the team to sign Buzz Peterson or to acquire Walter

Davis, and he seemed generally in favor of anything related to North Carolina, which left Krause rolling his eyes. After a while Jordan simply decided to avoid the new GM at all costs. Such were the gnarly twists in the plotline of Jordan's professional career. It hinged on a chemistry of two men chained together by providence, one badly in need of affection, the other doing everything possible to avoid giving it. The strangest part of their pairing was Krause's collection of insecurities and Jordan's absolute lack of them. Despite that, Krause would prove to be one of the strongest personalities who ever stepped into Jordan's path.

The acrimony between the two men sharpened as Jordan headed into his second season. Many of pro basketball's old hands thought that Krause seemed to be making the whole process unnecessarily difficult. "Michael was going to be the premier star in the NBA," Kevin Loughery recalled. "You had the man to build around. You knew you were going to get better every year by adding parts. You have to have a star in the NBA to have a good team. When you have a star, you have the opportunity to put the other pieces in. Not only was he a star, he could do so many things. He could handle three spots, the point, the off guard, the small forward. I guess if you had to put him down low, he could do that. He could rebound, he could pass. A star who could do so many things. He wasn't just one-dimensional like a lot of stars are. He made it easier to put a team together."

Among the new faces that Krause brought into training camp that year was George Gervin, the "Ice Man" who had starred for years for the San Antonio Spurs. He was one of the veterans who had participated in the All-Star freeze-out of Jordan, so the chemistry set the stage for some testy dynamics at training camp that fall. The team's young star didn't go out of his way to welcome Gervin, who knew if there was any bending to be done in the circumstances, he'd have to do it.

"He was a young guy on his way in," Gervin recalled of Jordan, then all of twenty-two. "He hadn't proven his greatness at that time. He had shown potential to be great. But he was a young guy in the league trying to make a name for himself like most young guys coming up."

True to his MO, Jordan soon challenged Gervin to a game of one-on-one. "We played," Gervin acknowledged, implying that he was no match for Jordan's boundless energy. "We shot around. I was a veteran on my way out, so he was messin' with the old Ice Man. He wasn't messin' with the Ice Man of old. You know what I'm sayin'? I knew that I was just there to contribute. I'd had my time in the life. I knew it was his turn, so I was just really playing out my last year in the NBA. He had his own style. Mike was a great athlete. He developed that jump shot later on in his career. I was a jump shooter and a scorer from the beginning. So we had different kinds of games. He jumped a lot. I glided a lot. I was like Fred Astaire. He was like a jumping jack."

The one-on-one broke the "Ice" between the two, but Jordan wasn't about to allow Gervin into his inner circle. "I didn't talk to him that much," Gervin explained, adding that he suspected Jordan still smarted over the All-Star incident. "I had nothing but respect for him back then because I saw the drive that he had. Inside hisself. Not on the floor. I'm talking about the drive that he had to try to win. You could tell that by the practices and stuff. He didn't let up. He had a hell of a drive in him, man. To succeed, man. And to win."

The older guard quickly saw the distinct line between Jordan's inner circle and the rest of the team. "He was close to quite a few guys, Charles Oakley, Rod Higgins. We really wasn't that close," Gervin recalled. "But that's just the way it was. You know, life is funny. The game is one thing, but the most important thing is building relationships. I think that was my greatest gift in my career is that I built some relationships with my teammates. I appreciated them and they knew it wasn't all about me."

The circumstances with the Bulls early in that second season revealed a challenge that Jordan would have to face eventually. His elite circle of friends set up an immediate division within any roster he played on. You were either in his circle or you weren't. The majority of his teammates, particularly in those early years, were kept at a cool arm's length, on the outside looking in. Jordan needed his cocoon to survive, but at the same time he would have to learn that no man was an island, Gervin observed. "You gotta work not to be on that island. You gotta work hard at it, man."

The Bulls opened the schedule in the late fall of 1985 with three straight wins, but in the third game, against the Golden State Warriors, Jordan suffered a broken navicular tarsal bone in his left foot, an injury that had altered or ended the careers of several NBA players. Predicting he would be back quickly, he sat out the next game with what was reported as an "ankle injury." It was the first game he had missed in his entire career, including high school, including even the broken wrist he suffered four weeks before his sophomore season opener at North Carolina.

"I feel like a fan," he told reporters the day after the injury at Golden State. "I can't do a thing. I've just got to watch them and cheer along."

Then came the diagnosis. "After that, the year was a complete disaster," Jerry Reinsdorf recalled. Jordan would miss the next sixty-four games. Around the league, veterans gave each other knowing looks. Jordan's relentless, all-out style had finally caught up with him. "He had it all the time," Gervin recalled, summing up the conventional wisdom. "That's why he probably got hurt, because he played so hard all the time."

The news of the broken foot fell like an avalanche on Nike, who had just invested millions in Jordan. "I mean the whole game was going to be over," Vaccaro recalled. "We realized that. Everything could have ended."

Jordan shared their fears. "I was a little bit scared," he explained later. "I didn't want to be bothered by anyone. I didn't want the phone to ring. I didn't want to watch TV. I didn't want to hear music. I just wanted plain darkness because this was something for me to deal with, and it was very painful. For the first time, I had to consider doing something else besides playing basketball, and it was very different."

Once the reality of his injury settled in, his first thought was to go back home, an idea that was met with immediate disapproval. "Michael wanted to go back to North Carolina and rehab there," recalled Mark Pfeil, the Bulls' trainer at the time. "We were able to get that across to Jerry Reinsdorf and Jerry Krause and set up a program for Michael in Carolina. He rehabbed, worked on his degree, and had some peace of mind. That probably made Michael ready to compete when he returned." Some observers, including several teammates, criticized Jordan for leaving the team while he was injured. Even though he had played in only three games, Jordan led the Eastern Conference in the fans' All-Star voting that winter.

"I was very frustrated, and at first I didn't know how to deal with the situation," Jordan recalled. "I walked away from it, went to North Carolina, worked on my degree and watched the team on TV. That's the best way I could deal with it."

While in Chapel Hill, he sat on Carolina's bench during games, which gave him the opportunity for the first time to sit back and observe the system that had molded him. As his foot began to feel better, he ventured into forbidden territory and began playing pickup ball, unknown to Reinsdorf or Krause. "I heard that much later, that after two weeks he was back on the court," Krause recalled. "I don't know if that's accurate but I heard it. He never said he played. We had a meeting three weeks later on the phone. 'How are you?' 'I'm much better.' 'The doctors still want you to rest. Come on in here in the next couple of weeks, we're going to look at you again.' This went on for two months."

"I knew he was playing down there because he told me," Sonny Vaccaro recalled. "I'm paraphrasing here, but he said, 'I'm going to go and see if this damn thing, this SOB, is okay. I'm going to see if I can do this. I need to be away from people and I know I'll be protected.'" That knowledge both reassured and further terrified the Nike staff that had bet on his career in a major way.

Without Jordan, Stan Albeck had to turn to Gervin as one of his main offensive options. Albeck had coached Gervin in San Antonio, so the Bulls switched to a set of plays to feature the Ice Man. "Stan tried the best he could under the circumstances," recalled Chicago radio reporter Cheryl Raye-Stout. "Without Michael that team had a lot of guys who didn't care. During the time-outs you had players like Sid Green who wouldn't even go in the huddles."

"It was hard for Stan," Sidney Green recalled in 1995. "Unfortunately, he had high expectations for the team and for Michael. Once

Michael went down, Stan had to change his whole game plan. He tried to build the whole team around George Gervin, but unfortunately George was on his last legs. But he still had the finger roll. Beyond George, we were all young.... You must also remember that that was the year Quintin Dailey had his problems, too." Dailey had fallen into a spiral of missed games and late appearances. After he missed a game in February, Krause suspended him. For the second time in eight weeks, Dailey entered a drug treatment facility.

"Quintin was late to another shootaround, and by then I knew he was messed up on coke," Krause said. "We were waiting around for him to show up for the game, and Stan said, 'I'm gonna play him if he shows up.'...I told him, 'The guy's done in a Bulls uniform.' I made the decision then to begin looking for another coach."

The team's lack of direction in Jordan's absence indicated just how much of a load he had been carrying. The Bulls record stood at 22–43 in March when he told management that he believed his injury was healed and he wanted to return. "I didn't want to watch my team go down the pits," he later explained. "I thought I was healthy enough to contribute something."

His plans caught Reinsdorf by surprise and sparked another harsh confrontation with Krause. The owner and GM had serious questions about the risk of Jordan's returning too soon.

"The thing that got Michael and me off on the wrong foot," Krause recalled, "was that he thought I said to him, 'You're our property, and you'll do what we want you to do.' I don't remember ever saying it that way. He just misinterpreted me. I was trying to keep him from playing because he had a bad foot and the doctors were saying, 'No, no, no.' And Reinsdorf was telling him about risk. He was a kid who wanted to play. And I couldn't blame him. But that's where it all started because we said, 'We're gonna hold you back.' We were all sitting in that room, and Stan wouldn't do a damn thing to help. Stan could have helped us explain the situation to Michael, but he was being selfish. He could have stood with us and the doctors who said Michael wasn't ready to play."

Krause recalled Jordan sitting there "with steam coming out his ears. He said, 'You're telling me I can't play?'"

The more they talked, the more Jordan's fury grew. "Here you are dealing with big businessmen who make millions, and my millions are like pennies to them," he later recalled. "All I wanted to do was play the game that I've played for a long, long time. But they didn't look at it that way. They looked at it as protecting their investment, to keep their millions and millions coming in. That's when I really felt used. That's the only time I really felt used as a professional athlete. I felt like a piece of property."

"I was scared to death," Krause said of the situation. "I didn't want to go down in history as the guy who put Michael Jordan back in too soon."

Jordan sensed that management wanted to keep losing to improve the team's position in the draft. "Losing games on purpose reflects what type of person you really are," he told the *Tribune*, a comment that would resonate years later when he became an NBA owner. "No one should ever try to lose to get something better. You should always try to make the best with what you have. If they really wanted to make the playoffs, I'd be in there whenever we had a chance to win a game."

"It was like a soap opera," Reinsdorf remembered in 1995. "We were too honest with Michael. We let him hear the report from the three doctors we consulted with over when he could come back. All three said the break had not healed enough. They said if he did play, there was about a 10 to 15 percent chance of ending his career. Michael was such a competitor. He just wanted to play. I thought he was entitled to hear what the doctors had to say. I never thought he'd risk his entire career. It just didn't make any sense to me. But Michael figured that the 10 to 15 percent risk meant the odds were 85 to 90 percent that he wouldn't get hurt. To me, it didn't fit any risk/reward ratio. Here the reward was to come back and play on a team that had already had a bad year. Why risk your whole career for that reward? Michael insisted that he knew his own body better than I did. So we reached a compromise, that he would play gradually, just seven minutes a half at first."

Jordan vented his anger by almost single-handedly driving the Bulls through a reversal of fortune.

"That's the way Mike was," Mark Pfeil explained. "If he didn't think something was gonna hurt him, he'd focus past it and play.

Sprains, groin pulls, muscle spasms, flu, Michael's first question always was, 'Is it gonna hurt me to play?' If I told him no, it was gone. He'd focus past it."

"They put a limitation on how many minutes Michael could play," Cheryl Raye-Stout remembered. "They literally ran a clock on how many minutes he could play. Stan would sit there and have to calculate the time. He was under duress the whole time with Michael's return. There was some skepticism that the minutes limitations were there to help them get a lottery pick. That's a question to which we'll never know the answer."

In one game, Albeck played Jordan longer than he was supposed to, Reinsdorf recalled. "I told Krause to tell him not to do that again. Stan told us what he thought of that. The next game was at Indiana, and with twenty-five or thirty seconds to go, the Bulls were down by a point. Just then Michael reached the seven-minute mark, and Stan pulled him from the game. He pulled him just to show us how ridiculous he thought the seven minutes were, how arbitrary it was."

The Bulls still won the game on a jumper by John Paxson, but Reinsdorf was furious. Albeck had made him look foolish.

"The one thing I could never understand," Pfeil said, "was how could Michael practice for two hours, yet he couldn't play but fourteen minutes?"

"Michael's minutes increased after it became obvious we could make the playoffs," Reinsdorf said. "Finally, Krause went down at halftime of a game late in the season and told the trainer to tell Stan to play Michael as many minutes as possible. I shouldn't have let him play at all that year. It was wrong."

God's Disguise

Jordan's return to full-time status helped the Bulls win six of their final thirteen games. They finished 30–52, just enough to sneak into the playoffs with a late-season win over Washington.

The eighth-seeded Bulls faced the top-seeded Boston Celtics in the first round. Led by team president Red Auerbach and coached by K. C. Jones, Boston would finish the year with a 40–1 home record. Larry Bird was in the process of winning his third straight MVP award, and the Celtics were moving through a period of four straight trips to the NBA finals, which would net them two championships. It was a great, great basketball team, with a frontcourt that included Bird, forward Kevin McHale, and centers Robert Parish and Bill Walton. They were all on a determined march to the franchise's sixteenth championship.

"It was a team," Bill Walton remembered, "that could win any type of game, had a complete roster, brilliant coach, phenomenal leadership in the front office with Red, spectacular fans, perfect home court advantage. And it had Larry Bird, who was the greatest player I ever played with. Larry Bird, who was able to ignite the home fans more so than any other player I ever saw. And as great as Larry Bird was as a player, he's an even better human being, a better leader. And as great as our visions and memories and dreams of Larry Bird are as a player, he was better than that. He was better because the game, the rules, the clock, the refs—it all put too many restraints on him because he was a creative artist. He was Michelangelo, he was Bob Dylan. He was the guy who saw things that nobody else did and then he was able to take that dream and that spark and turn it into action. There was nobody like Larry Bird."

Boston coach K. C. Jones had been perhaps the game's greatest ball pressure guard, winning championship after championship alongside Bill Russell. Jones's confidence was as supreme as his players' that April. He saw no need to make any special effort against the ragtag Chicago Bulls and their young star coming off the injured list.

"We really didn't have anything set up to double-team him," Kevin McHale recalled. "We didn't do anything. We just said let him score. And you remember the first game he went crazy."

Unburdened by double-teams, Jordan scored 49 points in forty-three minutes in Game 1, but Boston still squashed Chicago, 123–104.

"This one-on-one defense is not exactly working for the Celtics on Jordan," broadcaster Tommy Heinsohn said at halftime of that first game.

Sharing the assignment against Jordan for that series were Dennis Johnson and Danny Ainge, both excellent defenders, and substitutes Rick Carlisle and Jerry Sichting.

"After that first game we said we should probably double-team him or do some stuff," McHale recalled, "and K. C. Jones said, 'We'll think about it.' I mean they won thirty games. We won sixty-seven. There was no chance they were going to beat us."

Jordan had something else in mind three nights later before Game 2 in Boston Garden. "It was total silence in the locker room before the game," Sidney Green remembered. "Michael was extremely focused, and we knew he was intent on doing something big." The contest went to double overtime. In fifty-three minutes of playing time, Jordan took 41 shots and made 22 of them. The Celtics fouled him plenty, and he made 19 of 21 free throws. He also registered 6 assists, 5 rebounds, 3 steals, and 4 turnovers in the box score. His 63 points was the NBA's all-time single-game playoff record.

"That's God disguised as Michael Jordan," Bird said afterward. The comment would play for eternity in the Jordan highlight reel. For that single moment, he had frightened the cockiness out of the best team in basketball.

"In the first game he scored 49 and we won by 20," Walton recalled. "And we said, 'Ah, he'll never do that again.' So the next game he scores 63 points, fouls out the entire team, and if it wasn't for Larry Bird going crazy then we wouldn't have won in double overtime, 135–131."

Bird scored 36 points in fifty-six minutes of playing time that day, and it took scoring from Boston's entire roster just to counter Jordan's effort. McHale scored 27, Ainge 24, Johnson 15, Parish 13, and Walton 10.

"We really didn't scheme at all for him, to be truthful," McHale remembered. "We kind of just went out there and just said, 'Hey, well, you know we're just going to play our normal defense. If you score on us who cares?' No one assumed he'd get 60-some."

Walton recalled, "In the locker room after that second game, we said, 'This guy's pretty good. Why don't we just double-team him and let's see if Dave Corzine and the rest of the Bulls can do anything out there.'"

Facing double-teams and the sheer size of the Celtics, Jordan took just 18 shots in Game 3 in Chicago Stadium and made 8 of them. He finished with 19 points, 12 rebounds, and 9 assists as his team was swept, 122–104.

"We double-teamed him and got the ball out of his hands," McHale said. "We really schemed for him. People forget we swept that series. It was 3–0 and we went home."

The outcome of the series hardly seemed to matter. The entire NBA and its fan base were abuzz over Jordan's performance. Four years earlier, he had captured the attention of a nationwide audience with a dramatic shot to win a national championship. The performance against Bird and his Celtics carried the Jordan legend to new heights. Coaches from across the NBA were riveted, just as fans were, by what he had done against the very best team in basketball.

"It was marvelous," Sidney Green said. "I know Michael. He's the type of guy who loves for people to think that he can't do something. And that just added more fuel to his fire, to prove not only to himself but to everybody else that he could play injured and that he was ready to play."

More than anything, it was a message to the management of the Chicago Bulls. "That game," Reinsdorf admitted years later, "was when we began to realize just how great Michael could be."

It also marked an important moment for Jordan personally. "Up to that point, there was so many media guys saying he's good but he's not in the same class as Magic Johnson or Larry Bird," Jordan said, looking back years later. "I earned Larry Bird's respect—to me that showed me I was on the right track. Not the points that I scored, because at the end of the day we lost the game. It's a good highlight to watch, but not too much fun because I lost. That was the biggest compliment I had at that particular time."

Enter Collins

A few weeks after the season, Krause fired Stan Albeck, again angering the team's growing fan base. Reinsdorf felt that the coach had stood in the way when they wanted to hold Jordan back from his foot injury. Furthermore, Albeck had rejected the offensive advice of Tex Winter.

The choice of replacement came down to two men, broadcaster Doug Collins and, once again, Phil Jackson. Krause agonized a bit, then chose Collins, who had seen a lot of the league as a CBS broadcaster, though he had no coaching experience. "A TV guy? Really?" Reinsdorf had supposedly responded when Krause first posed the idea. But Collins had been a star player at Illinois State and was the top pick of the 1973 draft; he had also played a pivotal role on the ill-fated 1972 US Olympic team. Selected by the Philadelphia 76ers, Collins helped that club climb back from its disastrous 1973 season into championship contention by 1977. A three-time All-Star, Collins ultimately fell victim to the injuries that prematurely ended his career.

"It was very uncomfortable because Collins was a broadcaster and had traveled with the team before he was hired," recalled Cheryl Raye-Stout. "Stan Albeck would look over his shoulder, and there was Doug Collins. He served as a consultant briefly, and there was speculation that Collins was taking Stan's job."

"When I hired Doug, everybody laughed at me," Krause said. "A lot of people said, 'What the fuck are you doing hiring a TV guy?'"

"At the time, I was thirty-five," Collins would later recall, "and there had been nine coaches in ten years in Chicago. I was the kind of guy to roll up my sleeves and make something happen."

Jordan wasn't so sure about that in the beginning. In fact, he mistrusted Collins as another Krause invention. "When I first met Doug, I didn't think he knew what he was talking about," Jordan recalled. "I wondered when he first got the job. I mean, he was so young. But once I got to know him, I liked him a lot. He was bright, he was in control, and most of all, he was positive."

Not only did he bring this strength, but he added assistant coaches Johnny Bach and Gene Littles to the equation. Bach, in particular, would become a force within the team. Bach recalled of Collins, "I had coached him at the Olympics in 1972 and we had a good friendship and respect for each other. Doug called me and said, 'I'd like you to come here and join the staff.' It was a pleasure to go with Paul Douglas Collins. He was emotional and exciting, fired up. He really started this franchise, the Bulls, to winning again."

With the coaching hire completed, Krause turned again to the roster. He sent away Orlando Woolridge, Jawann Oldham, and Sidney Green and began stockpiling draft picks and cash. For the 1987 draft, he would have a store of first-round picks. But the team headed into the season with just one player on the roster who averaged double figures, and that player was coming off a major foot injury. At the time, the public had no idea just how motivated and angry Michael Jordan was. Krause had brought in a third-year guard from Portland named Steve Colter, and Jordan set upon him in training camp as if he were Krause himself. In games or at practice, it became increasingly obvious that the sensitive Colter couldn't play alongside Jordan. Like many point guards, Colter had trouble playing effectively without the ball in his hands. But Jordan had long had a habit, indulged by each of his coaches, where he would shoo the point guard off during the inbounds, take the pass, bring the ball up, and initiate the offense himself. In time it would become obvious that John Paxson, who didn't need the ball to be effective, was a better fit alongside Jordan. Krause would trade Colter before the season was half over and bring in the next in a long line of point guards who couldn't gain traction in Jordan's shadow.

Krause hired Jim Stack that year as his right-hand man. Stack had played at Northwestern, then in the pro leagues of Europe. He showed a knack for charting plays and an eye for the game, so in addition to assisting Krause, Stack also did advance scouting for the team. The Bulls front office and the team were already separating into two distinct worlds, but Stack's position allowed him to keep a foot in both of them. It was awkward negotiating the internal politics, Stack admitted, but when he wasn't on the road scouting, he was in practice with the team and going over his reports in team meetings. In addition to working for Krause, Stack bonded well with the coaches. Jordan, too. Because of those working relationships, Stack became part of the glue that held the organization together through more than a decade of conflict.

Stack had seen a lot of basketball around the world, but the most electrifying play he saw was right there in Bulls practices. "Michael was just a wrecking machine," he recalled, looking back in 2012. "We had more talented players at times playing alongside Michael, but they just couldn't withstand the immense prowess that he brought to the court. Poor Steve Colter. I thought he was one of the better guards when I got to the team, but Jerry ended up having to move him because he just wilted playing against Michael in practice."

Chapter 19

ATTACK!

THERE WAS SUBSTANTIAL public pressure heading into Doug Collins's first season for the Bulls to upgrade their roster with available scorers such as Eddie Johnson in Sacramento or a big man like Golden State's Joe Barry Carroll. Krause chose to wait, which led to fears among the fan base that the roster had been stripped of talent. There were preseason predictions that winning thirty games again might just be out of the Bulls' reach.

Some observers didn't think the Bulls could score enough to win, but those questions were answered on opening night against the Knicks in Madison Square Garden. New York featured a "Twin Towers" look with Patrick Ewing and Bill Cartwright, and used it to take a five-point lead midway through the fourth quarter. During a time-out, Jordan looked at Collins and said, "Coach, I'm not gonna let you lose your first game."

He scored the team's final 18 points to drive a 108–103 win. His 50 points set a record for points scored by an opponent in the Garden, which shattered the 44-point mark shared by Rick Barry and former Bull Quintin Dailey.

"I've never seen anything like Michael Jordan. Ever. Ever. Never," Collins said after hugging each of his players.

Afterward, as reporters listened in, Jordan told his father that the Knicks fans had goaded him into the big scoring night.

"So you were playing on the crowd, not even on the floor?" his father asked, teasing.

"I always play on the crowd," he replied.

"The excitement that came to the club from winning the opening game of the season, that was a turning point," Reinsdorf observed, looking back. "That was the year things started to build, and Michael was unbelievable." More specifically, it was the year that Jordan took over American basketball. His revolution ran both large and small. He entered the pro game in the age of "Daisy Duke" shorts, cut tight and short, and promptly created something better to his liking, baggy pants specially tailored 2 1/2 inches longer. Before too long, players would be taking the court in full-blown, knee-length pantaloons, easily his most enduring fashion statement.

His play became a style rage as well, with his now routine rock-a-baby dunks. Taking it all in was new assistant coach Johnny Bach. Like Tex Winter, Bach was in his sixties, a former military man, and a veteran coach, most recently head coach of the Golden State Warriors. Bach was more than eager to assist both Collins and Jordan but also like Winter, Bach was somewhat reticent about approaching Jordan at first.

"Assistant coaches, especially ones with some experience, sometimes you know when you should inject into a scene or when you should stay away from it," Bach recalled in 2012. "In those days, I watched him from a distance. His play was so good you couldn't believe it, the things he could do. I always thought the best thing was just to watch him and be of any assistance I could."

Bach's first duties under Collins were doing some advance scouting for the team and breaking down what he saw about opponents in team meetings. That was where he first made a connection with Jordan. In talking about the game, Bach had a knack for "using the right phrase," as he called it. "I used a lot of military terms because I had come from service with the Navy during the war." Jordan was immediately drawn to his language and his tales of World War II, where Bach had lost his twin brother, an aviator, in combat. "It just seemed to catch his attention," Bach recalled. But beyond his language, he had a sparkle in his eye, and dressed immaculately, something else that captured Jordan's fancy.

The older assistant coach talked often of Admiral William "Bull" Halsey, who took command of the naval war in the South Pacific, and used his words to send messages to an impressionable Jordan during games. "I would walk alongside Michael when a time-out was ending and say, 'For godsakes, Michael, attack, attack, attack. That's what Halsey said and that's what I'm telling you,'" Bach recalled. "I'd do that if I thought there was a time he wasn't attacking the basket. I didn't do it often. But he remembered it. That was sort of the beginning of the thing. As an assistant coach, you can't call a play for the guy, but I just thought I'd say, 'I haven't seen you out there doing the things that you can do.' The situation, as I saw it, was, why not stimulate him with something like, 'Hey, Michael, attack, attack, attack.' That's the little things I did, and our relationship was good that way." Jordan would begin referring to Bach as his personal coach, whose message became something of a mantra over the course of the season. It was all the encouragement the young star needed to create a new math for the game.

He would score better than 40 points on twenty-eight occasions that season. Six times, he ran up better than 50. In late November and early December, he scored more than 40 in nine straight games, six of them coming on a western road trip. Later, he would insist it was all out of necessity. "When I first came here, I had to be the igniter, to get the fire going," he recalled. "So a lot of my individual skills had to come out."

Jump

Word quickly spread among NBA circles that this version of Jordan was something new. In Phoenix, Walter Davis took note, recalled teammate Eddie Pinckney. "It was my understanding that Michael kind of idolized Walter a little bit," Pinckney recalled. "He was one of his favorite players. Walter at the time was a marquee player." As their first game with the Bulls approached, Pinckney noticed that Davis perked up and began preparing harder than he normally did.

"That was to me a little bit strange because Walter dominated his position during his time," Pinckney recalled. "He never really fretted about playing anyone. I didn't know it, but a huge contingent of players would go back to North Carolina and play during the summer."

Walter Davis, it seemed, did not want to give Jordan anything during the NBA season that could be used for trash talk during the summer sessions back in Chapel Hill. "I sort of knew what was coming," Pinckney said. "But Davis really knew what was coming. Michael put on a show. He actually put on a show. Those two were going at it. I mean, it wasn't about the way in which he scored. It was more about taking over the game. At some point or another you knew it was coming, these stretches like ten in a row or twelve in a row. And the way in which he did it was like these crazy assaults to the rim. He jumped from one side to the other and reversed. All that stuff, the wild assaults at the rim."

Most of all, Pinckney was struck by how Jordan had affected Davis. "He's a guy who was a really good player," Pinckney said, "and Jordan made him completely alter his approach to the game."

Nonetheless, the Bulls lost that game by two, despite Jordan's 43 points. Afterward, the team doctor lanced Jordan's swollen toe, Jerry Krause recalled. "Pus came out all over that thing. It was ugly. If you saw it you would want to throw up."

The doctor ordered Jordan back to Chicago to rest the toe for ten days, Krause remembered in a 2012 interview. "Now Michael gets on Doug Collins, and I leave, and fifteen minutes later Doug comes out in the hallway and says 'We've got to talk.' And he tells me what Michael says, that he wants to go to San Antonio the next night. He won't hurt himself and if it's bad he won't play, all the stuff you hear from a guy. Well, I was a little soft probably, too, so we let him go to San Antonio and if you look I think he got 52 that night."

Actually, it was another 43 points, another in that nine-game stretch of 40-point games for Jordan, on a bad toe. The Bulls would lose six of them, not quite as bad as it sounds seeing as eight of the nine games were on the road. Toward the end of the streak, Jordan scored 41 in Atlanta, but the Hawks' Dominique Wilkins answered with 57.

Jordan was getting the best of the league's best each game. As the Celtics had learned in the previous playoffs, he had become unguardable, at least by a single defender. In Jordan's first season, the Lakers had thrown Byron Scott and then Michael Cooper at him and held him down by denying him the ball. Those days were over, Cooper told one writer. "When people say I do a good job on Michael, or that so-and-so did the job, that's wrong. There's no way I stop him. I need the whole team. As soon as he touches the ball, he electrifies the intensity inside you. The alarm goes off because you don't know what he's going to do. He goes right, left, over you, around and under you. He twists, he turns. And you know he's going to get the shot off. You just don't know when and how. That's the most devastating thing psychologically to a defender."

The attacking that Bach urged upon him was so creative that *Sun-Times* sportswriter Rick Telander decided to ask about his leaping ability. "I've never had my vertical leap measured," Jordan replied, "but sometimes I think about how high I get up.... I always spread my legs when I jump high, like on my rock-a-baby, and it seems like I've opened a parachute, like, that slowly brings me back to the floor. I was really up against New York in our first game. On my last dunk I think I was close to eye level with the rim. Sometimes you just hit your wrists on the rim, but this time it was my elbows and everything. I almost over-dunked the whole rim."

He was as enthusiastic as any fan about his hang time. "I wish I could show you a film of a dunk I had in Milwaukee," Jordan told Telander. "It's in slow motion, and it looks like I'm taking off, like somebody put wings on me. I get chills when I see it. I think, when does 'jump' become 'flying'? I don't have the answer yet."

There was no better place to show off such skills than the Slam Dunk Contest at the All-Star Game weekend. The fans cast a record 1.41 million votes that season to send the player now called "His Airness" to the All-Star Game. "I think it's great the fans admire my style so much," he said in response. "I'm not going to do anything to disappoint them."

In those days, the Dunk Contest held a special appeal for the game's top athletes, emphasized by the fact that Jordan, less than a year after returning from a broken foot, entered the event, at Seattle's Kingdome, where he won with a series of slams that capitalized on his particular brand of flight. (Atlanta's Dominique Wilkins was injured.) This time there was no thought of freezing him out in the All-Star main event. Jordan's shadow now fell across the entire league. "Even at an All-Star Game, you couldn't take your eyes off of him," observed Mitch Lawrence, the veteran basketball writer for the *New York Daily News*. "Now you could watch Magic and Bird, don't get me wrong. But that was the thing about Michael Jordan. When you went to see him play, even in just a regular-season game, you had to watch him. There could be another superstar or two on the court. It didn't matter. Basically 95 percent of the time you're watching Michael Jordan. If he was getting a break, maybe you'd watch the other players, but mostly you were fixated. Now how many guys can you say that about?"

Jordan resumed his pace after the All-Star Weekend. In late February, he scored 58 against the Nets, breaking Chet Walker's old Bulls regular-season, single-game scoring record of 57. A few days later, despite a painful corn on his left foot, he blasted the Pistons for 61 in an overtime win before 30,281 screaming fans at the Pontiac Silverdome. Down the stretch, Jordan and Isiah Thomas and Adrian Dantley of the Pistons furiously swapped baskets.

"Isiah's play at that time pumped me to another level," Jordan would admit later. "He was making great shots and then I'd come down and make a great shot. It was great entertainment for the fans and great basketball." Of all his many huge games that season, the Pistons victory was by far his favorite. "Because we won," he explained. "And because I switched onto Adrian Dantley in the last few minutes, stole the ball three times, and held him without a basket. A victory for defense." Afterward the shell-shocked Pistons began working to come up with a scheme to prevent any such embarrassment in the future.

Jordan seemed to bound from one over-the-top performance to the next. "I don't know how he did it," teammate John Paxson said. "Every night someone else was standing in his face, and he never took a step back."

The *I* in *Win*

There was something in this unleashed hunger that gnawed at many people across the NBA. Among the few who dared to speak openly about it was Larry Bird, who told a reporter, "I don't like to watch the same guy take every shot. That's not what the game is all about."

Jordan thoroughly dominated the ball for Chicago that season, taking almost a third of his team's shots. It would be the first of Jordan's nine seasons leading the league in field goal attempts. The focus on one player at the expense of the team concept flew in the face of what Bulls assistant Tex Winter believed was important about the game. Despite Winter's misgivings, Doug Collins seemed wholly supportive of Jordan's volume scoring and was perhaps eager for even more, if it meant getting more wins. Originally shy about coaching Jordan, Winter began urging the third-year star toward a more fundamental approach to the game. Jordan immediately bristled.

"You know what he told me?" Jordan confided to writer Curry Kirkpatrick. "And when he said this, I knew one of us was over the hill. He told me, 'The highest percentage shot on the drive is to lay it up.' He asked me, 'Why do you go on trying those outrageous jumps and moves and dunks?' I couldn't believe it. I just stared at him and said, 'Hey, I don't plan this stuff. It just happens.'"

In his late sixties, Winter had more than four decades of first-rate coaching experience, as head coach at five colleges and the Houston Rockets. His specialty had been the development of the triple-post offense, which was by then viewed as antiquated. But where other people in basketball scoffed at Tex Winter as some sort of oddball, Krause had known him for years and deeply admired him and his offense, almost to the point of worship, and was irritated that neither Stan Albeck nor Collins followed Winter's offensive advice.

Winter's offense wasn't just Xs and Os, as he liked to point out, but a system, or philosophy, for playing the game, complete with an entire set of related fundamentals. The older assistant was focused on detail in a way that no other pro coach even considered. For example, he was agitated to no end that Jordan couldn't throw a basic chest pass to his liking. Albeck and Collins had resisted Winter's advice mainly because incorporating it would require them to give themselves over to his entire system, where he had each detail of the game spelled out. His system created an attack that offered immaculate floor spacing and a systematic breaking down of the defense. It allowed players to know where they were going to get their shots. Most important, it employed a two-guard front that allowed for floor balance. Winter's idea was that one player would always be able to get back on defense to prevent easy fast breaks by the opponent.

"Tex in his own way was a very obstinate, aggressive man," Johnny Bach recalled. "He believed in the triple post probably even before the gospel pages. That was his gospel. He wanted it installed. I don't know if Krause had told him, 'Yes, you can put your things in.' He not only had to convince Doug. He also had to convince Michael that this is an offense that is not only good for the team but one that Michael could operate in."

That would prove to be a tough sell, made tougher because Jordan saw Winter as one of Krause's guys and thus tainted, and a target for a little fun.

"Tex was like a grandpa to all of us," recalled trainer Mark Pfeil. "But the players would mock him. Michael used to tease him and stuff. Over everything. One time in practice, Michael sneaked up behind him and pulled Tex's shorts all the way down to his knees, and there was Tex's bare butt sticking out."

Winter never reported any of this to Krause, but the distance grew between him and Collins, the coach he was supposed to be mentoring. Winter believed he had been hired to teach, so he taught wherever possible, with the sort of frank, direct feedback that most players hadn't heard since middle school.

"When we step out on that floor at a practice session, I'm going to coach whoever shows up," Winter once said of his approach. "And I'm going to coach them the way I coach, whether it's Michael Jordan...or whoever it is. It doesn't make any difference. They know that. If I see Michael making a mistake, I'll correct him as

fast as I will anyone else. On the other hand, he's such a great athlete you have to handle him a little differently than you do the other
players. I don't think you can come down on him hard in a very
critical way, whereas some younger guy or some other guy you feel
you might be able to motivate by coming down on them pretty
tough."

Whereas Bach urged Jordan to attack, Winter spoke constantly
of the team approach. And his will could be every bit as strong as
Jordan's. Conflict simmered within the Chicago coaching staff,
exacerbated by Collins's determination to be his own man. "He
brought an enthusiasm that went beyond the normal," Bach said of
Collins in that first season. "He was fired up, especially in competition. Some coaches see very little out there. They're very good about
what they're teaching, and they don't see much more than that.
Indeed, Doug Collins has always been a coach that sees too much."
Collins could never seem to leave well enough alone and was always
adding new plays to his team's mix.

Given the conflict between his parents and the conflict among
his coaches, it was no wonder that Jordan seemed to be losing trust
in the authority figures around him. Criticism, however, always
seemed to get his attention. There was no question that the observations offered by Bird and Winter took Jordan by surprise and left
him a bit defensive. "I'm taking these raps as a challenge just to get
better and see that my team gets better," he said in one interview.
"But it's not as if I'm playing with a bunch of all-leaguers....Any-
body who thinks that is a damn fool."

In truth, Jordan's growing selfishness when it came to scoring
had begun generating resentment among his teammates. Some
years later, Jordan himself would come clean on the issue and
acknowledge his concentration on self rather than team. At the
time, his focus on his own game, his own abilities, seemed impenetrable. He heeded Bach's counsel, and persisted in the attack.

March brought another streak of five 40-plus games. In April, he
had an opportunity to become the only player since Wilt Chamberlain in 1962–63 to score better than 3,000 points in a season.
(Chamberlain had done it twice.) Jordan scored 53 against Indiana,
then 50 against Milwaukee, after which Bucks coach Don Nelson

took off his necktie and wrote "Great Season, Great Person" on it before giving it to Jordan. Nelson was another of the old-style, turn-loose-the-assassin coaches who would later trade subtle insults with Winter and Jackson across the competitive divide. The signed tie was his way of urging Jordan on, just like Bach.

The game's offensive monster rewarded his fans with his second 61-point performance of the season, this time against Atlanta in the Stadium. He finished the season with 3,041 points and a league-best 37.1 scoring average.

During the Atlanta onslaught, he scored an NBA-record 23 straight points. At the end of the game, he tossed up a half-court shot that fell just short, enough to leave purists like Winter shaking their heads even as fans across the league hooted in delight. As Jordan walked off the floor, Winter told him, "There's no *I* in *team*."

Jordan highlighted the moment in his 2008 Hall of Fame acceptance speech, recalling that he looked at Winter and replied, "Yeah, but there is in *win*."

The moment framed basketball's great debate, indeed the debate of American culture itself, about the individual versus the team or group. Only in retrospect would it become clearer for both Winter and Jordan that the philosophical confrontation they shared would have a profound effect on both of them, their later success, and how they both viewed the game.

Meanwhile, Jordan's "reward" for his season-long offensive display was being left off the first and second NBA all-defensive teams, which infuriated him. That season he had become the first player in NBA history to record more than 200 steals and 100 blocked shots. He had 236 steals and 125 blocks.

In the history of the league, Jerry West was the only scoring champion to ever make the all-defensive team. Jordan determined that he wanted to be recognized for having the "complete game." He had set Bulls records in six different single-season categories, all enough to drive Doug Collins's first team to a 40–42 record and another first-round playoff meeting with the Celtics. Bird and Boston, however, swept the series in three (while Jordan averaged 35.7 points), emphasizing Bird's and Winter's message that team strength could easily outshine a one-man show. Michael Jordan's Chicago

Bulls had lost nine playoff games and won just one in his first three seasons.

"He's a guy whose highlight films you most want to watch," Boston guard Danny Ainge said of Jordan. "But I don't know how much fun he'd be to play with."

Even so, it had been the kind of individual year that moved even his most determined critics to speak up. "Everybody always says it's me and Larry," Magic Johnson, whose Lakers defeated the Celtics for the league title that season, told reporters. "Really, it's Mike and everybody else." Jordan and Johnson had identified each other as the game's top players. Once Jordan's high school idol, Johnson now loomed as an unliked rival, and it wasn't just about winning. From the debate within his own team to his relationships with stars on other teams, Jordan faced substantial criticism.

"It's no secret around the league that, even with his four championship rings, Johnson harbors something that seems to be more than professional jealousy toward Jordan," Curry Kirkpatrick wrote in *Sports Illustrated*. "Commercially, at least, Magic should have been Michael seven years ago when he followed up winning the 1979 NCAA title for Michigan State with a tour de force sixth game in the 1980 NBA championship series, which the Lakers won over the Philadelphia 76ers."

It clearly still bothered Johnson and other veterans that Jordan's Nike deal and the promotional effort behind it gave him a status above even the league's most accomplished stars. Jordan, meanwhile, didn't hesitate to express his theory that Johnson had been behind Lakers owner Jerry Buss's push to trade James Worthy. "I don't hold anything against him," Jordan told Kirkpatrick. "I just think he doesn't like players who come from North Carolina."

It didn't help that Johnson and Isiah Thomas were making much of what was then their high-profile personal friendship. When Johnson sent an invitation to play in his coveted summer all-star charity game, Jordan tersely declined. It was obvious that the All-Star snubbing two years earlier still burned him.

The truth was, he faced a staggering array of commitments in the off-season. Jordan had laughed the first time David Falk ran the name "Air Jordan" past him. But in less than three years, he had become an unprecedented marketing force, with an estimated $165 million in sales of Nike shoes and merchandise alone. "First I thought it was a fad," Jordan would say, looking back on the response to his shoe line. "But it's far greater now than it used to be. The numbers are just outrageous."

Strangely, Phil Knight had begun to have second thoughts about his company's relationship with Jordan, which set up something of a drama that would unfold over the next year as talks continued about a new contract for Air Jordan. It was as if MJ had gotten too much power too quickly and it spooked Knight, Sonny Vaccaro explained. Such huge sales were difficult to sustain, and a slight dip had given the Nike chairman reason for pause. "Phil was ready to get rid of him," Vaccaro remembered. "Phil was ready to sign all the college teams and forget Michael. I said, 'You can't do that.'"

First of all, Rob Strasser had left the company and was now advising Jordan to push for his own product line. Knight rejected that idea and persisted in questioning the value of the company's relationship with Jordan until Vaccaro put together some numbers that made it clear that Nike couldn't gain anything near the Air Jordan sales in college markets.

Knight had a choice: to cut Jordan loose or to ride this surging, though sometimes frightening, tide. Ultimately Knight chose to stay the course with Jordan. Eventually, a fat new Nike contract would be signed, a deal that would open the door a few years later for the emergence of the Jordan Brand and create unimaginable wealth for an athlete.

"He got the big raise, then the Jordan Brand," Vaccaro said of Jordan's succeeding deals with the shoe manufacturer. "There's no question he bought in. I mean it was huge. Michael was in. That was a seminal deal in the history of deals. There's no question. And to Michael's credit and to Nike's credit, they created an empire."

"He was climbing so fast, and the product was so good," Johnny Bach remembered. "He tried on every new pair of shoes they were making. He was very proud of the product. He wanted to make sure he liked what he saw."

Jordan's image seemed to become one and the same with Nike, as he continued to both embrace and shrink from the metastasizing fame. As if the air time of the Nike TV ads hadn't been enough, CBS's *60 Minutes* had broadcast a ten-minute profile by Diane Sawyer that portrayed a playful, almost sweet Jordan, the kind of image-making you couldn't buy. David Falk was beside himself with glee. Backing up what his agent called *60 Minutes'* "commercial" was Jordan's first appearance as a cartoon character, in the popular syndicated comic strip *Shoe* by Pulitzer Prize winner Jeff MacNelly, who just happened to be a fellow Tar Heel. There seemed to be no connection that didn't work for Jordan. The first line of toys made in his image was scheduled to appear on shelves that Christmas.

Lacy Banks returned to the Bulls beat as a sportswriter for the *Chicago Sun-Times* in 1987 and was introduced to Jordan. His first impression of the star was that Jordan was atop a throne and quite taken with it, Banks recalled with a laugh years later. "Michael had come into possession of the world."

"It was like he was anointed," Sonny Vaccaro remembered. "I mean seriously, everything. I mean, even where he did something contrary to what was supposed to happen, it would come out all right."

Indeed, fans and opponents alike were beginning to grasp that the arc of Jordan's rise was broader and much, much higher than anyone had imagined. "In the age of TV sports," David Falk observed that summer of 1987, "if you were to create a media athlete and star for the nineties—spectacular talent, midsized, well-spoken, attractive, accessible, old-time values, wholesome, clean, natural, not too Goody Two-shoes, with a little bit of deviltry in him—you'd invent Michael. He's the first modern crossover in team sports. We think he transcends race, transcends basketball."

"Things were changing and Michael was in the middle of it," Sonny Vaccaro explained. "He was doing commercials for everybody, you know, and he became this entity."

McDonald's, Coca-Cola, Chevrolet, Wilson Sporting Goods, and a half dozen other companies used him to promote their products. The sums they paid him dwarfed his five-year, $4 million Bulls contract. Which meant that his schedule that summer was packed with everything from hosting TV shows to throwing out pitches at Major League Baseball games.

"It took getting used to, but now I enjoy all the off-court stuff,"

Jordan said during a quick promotional trip to Pittsburgh that summer. "It's like being back in school. I'm learning all the time. In college I never realized the opportunities available to a pro athlete. I've been given the chance to meet all kinds of people, to travel and expand my financial capabilities, to get ideas and learn about life, to create a world apart from basketball."

A big part of that world apart appeared more and more to include Juanita Vanoy. He had proposed on New Year's Eve, just as they were looking out across 1987 and wondering at all the bounty it seemed poised to bring. Indeed, he had purchased a new five-bedroom, five-thousand-square-foot home north of Chicago. As she helped him decorate it, they began to articulate the kind of life they might share together. The news of the engagement did not sit well with his parents, who remained caught in their own struggle for influence over his life.

The discreet activities that made James Jordan smile were the stuff of nightmares for Michael's mother and fiancée. "We live in a very tempting world," Sonny Vaccaro explained. "At that level, at Michael's level, it's unbelievable. He was good-looking, a young guy on top of the world. The stories are out there. But these things are just indigenous to fame and fortune. It's hard to be an idol."

Vaccaro traveled and worked with Jordan often enough to be surprised, even amazed, by his discretion. Even though he was young, Jordan was obviously wise enough not to put his friends and associates in awkward positions. He had his moments, but he was no rampant womanizer like Magic Johnson, who later claimed to have slept with as many as five hundred women a year at the height of his stardom.

To Vaccaro, the fact that Jordan was able to negotiate the tests of stardom further demonstrated the surprising scope of his talents and gifts. "When you talk about Michael, he obviously had that thing...that crossover appeal, whatever the hell it was," the older man said. "I use the word *charisma*, but it's like nobody can define what that really means. All the things we're talking about in his life, including the personal battle within his family, he overcame all that. There's something truly rare about that. There aren't too many human beings who can do that, in any walk of life."

PART VII

THE CYNIC

Chapter 20

THAT'S ENTERTAINMENT

His older sister had seen it in him as a child. His father and even Red Auerbach had identified it as his career was taking off. Jordan loved to entertain the crowd. His relationship with the audience was growing in ways that those around him struggled to fathom, including the university scholars who had begun to study him as a force in popular culture.

Yet even as he ceded his existence over to the public domain, there remained much that Jordan kept hidden. He did this willfully, out of his growing instinct for self-preservation and his insistence that parts of his life were no one else's business. Johnny Bach witnessed this with a sense of awe. An intense student of both the game and human nature, Bach was a grand philosopher, blessed with both charm and sincerity. Who knows where the narrative of Michael Jordan and the NBA might have gone had it not been for Bach and their conversations?

"If his eyes would light up and he was listening, I was fortunate that he listened," Bach said of their relationship and his opportunity to work with the game's greatest player.

Jordan fought to keep his self-indulgence private as well as the burdens he chose to bear beyond the game. "I thought in the early days, he was doing so much, it was unbelievable," Bach recalled. "He always visited with some person or child who had a last wish. He never turned anyone down. Every night he faced that, and I could never understand how he was strong enough to do it. Kids that were burned, brutalized, and dying by disease or something else. I can still remember he saw a kid who was brought in whose father had burned his face off him. They brought him in, and Michael talked to him in that old dressing room we had in Chicago Stadium before the game. He just talked to him. You couldn't imagine, a kid that was hideously burned. And Michael just talked to him. He put him on the bench, and during the game he would come over and ask, 'How'd you like that jump shot?' One of the officials came over and said, 'Michael, you can't have that kid on the bench. It's against league rules.' And Michael looked at him and said, 'He's on the bench.' He left our team time-outs to talk to the kid. I can remember John Paxson and I having tears in our eyes, looking at that scene, because the kid was so hideously burned. And here's Michael talking to him. So he had that greatness in him. It brought out scenes like that. That was repeated many times. He was a wonder man."

Jordan seemed to draw from the same vast emotional store that fueled his competitiveness, Bach recalled. "I felt that they abused it. He was asked for so many things by so many people that he had to have been wearied by all of these requests. But he always seemed to accommodate those that needed him the most. He went up in stature, not just as a player, but as an individual who could take that scene and make that child happy. I couldn't do it. I'll tell you that. I would have and did almost break down. He took pressures exceedingly well, whether it was the demand of the press, or the demand of the organization, or the demands of the game itself, basketball. He came out and did it more often than anyone else could do it. He had few poor nights. A poor night for him would be an all-star night for someone else. I admire him to this day. How he accommodated so many people I'll never know, never."

Jerry Krause, too, admired Jordan's innate ability with the less fortunate. The GM recalled that the only time the young star chafed at such duty was if someone tried to turn the moment into a public relations event. The things he did were to be kept quiet, strictly behind the scenes, Jordan ordered. "He did those kinds of things all the time," Tim Hallam remembered. "There was only one stipulation. He wasn't doing it for the publicity. He insisted on keeping things quiet. Absolutely no press."

Of course, the last thing Jordan seemed to need was a public relations effort. His performances on the floor assured that. And he privately complained that he already suffered enough from the perfection of his image. The audience had long displayed a weakness for sports stars and a strong desire to believe the very best about them, having elevated an array of figures to mythic status over what had come to be described as the "sports century." Little did anyone realize that this adulation of Jordan was just the beginning.

The boom in shoe sales mirrored the exploding business of the team itself. In Jordan's three seasons, the value of the franchise had more than tripled, and continued to grow with each tip-off. Jerry Reinsdorf was so pleased with these developments that he extended Doug Collins's year-old contract and made plans to give Jordan a new, extended deal.

Chicago's home attendance had grown by nearly 200,000 to 650,718, a jump of nearly a third over the previous year, when Jordan missed thirty-four home games. On the road, the Bulls also punched up the entire league's attendance by drawing an extra 276,996 fans, which generated another $3.71 million in revenue. The other owners recognized that the new golden goose was not Reinsdorf's alone. The increased popularity and cash flow boosted the confidence around the team. "We've reached a respect factor in this city," Collins told reporters. "We're no longer considered the Bad News Bulls."

Wooly Bully

All of these gains had been made, and the franchise had yet to hire Phil Jackson or to draft Scottie Pippen. Michael Jordan didn't know either of them—the two major relationships of his professional life—in the spring of 1987. Pippen would arrive via the 1987 draft, and Jackson would join the Bulls' employ that off-season as an assistant coach, charged with advanced scouting and other lower-ranked duties. Mostly, Krause wanted Jackson there so that he could pair him with Tex Winter for tutelage.

Somehow Krause talked Collins into hiring Jackson, who remained basketball's "odd duck," an intellectual sort who wore feathers in his hat and had the reputation for LSD usage revealed in his book. But this time pro basketball's resident hippie shaved and donned a tie for the interview, per Krause's instructions. Jordan had never heard of Jackson when he came to the team, and eyed him suspiciously as another Krause invention, but the initial impressions were strong enough to overcome the vibe.

It wasn't articulated that Jackson would be waiting in the wings as Collins's replacement, but such things were understood in the insular world of the NBA, and they generally made for tense palace intrigue. The NBA hadn't really made use of assistant coaches until the late sixties and early seventies because most franchises couldn't afford them or wouldn't pay for them. And why should Collins trust Krause, who had already fired two coaches in two years on the job? Still, the arrangement worked somewhat in Chicago because Jackson, for all his ego, was low-key and reserved.

The Bulls were a collection of strong personalities, with Jordan, Jackson, Collins, Bach, and Winter all somehow drawn together by this strange little man named Krause, and all kept on their toes by Jordan's growing frustration and cynicism. He had little faith in Krause's ability to find any sort of solutions for the team. And he remained quite angry over what he viewed as the GM's bungling of his return from foot injury. Yet Jordan had been raised to be respectful, both by his parents and by Dean Smith. He knew chain of command. He might take an occasional playful shot in a media interview, but when reporters asked him directly about the team's personnel, Jordan often deferred, saying personnel issues weren't his job.

Behind the scenes, though, he had plenty of doubt, and the 1987 draft would bring those doubts into focus, as Krause had worked to give the team two first-round picks. Pippen, taken with the fifth overall pick in a deal with the Seattle SuperSonics, was not an item of excessive internal debate.

The tenth pick, however, grew into an issue, with both Dean

Smith and Jordan exerting a certain pressure on Krause to select North Carolina's Joe Wolf or perhaps even Kenny Smith. Increasingly, GMs had grown leery of some Carolina players. Smith's system made it hard to judge their talents. Plus, the coach was persuasive, and he always wanted his players to be drafted as high as possible. An NBA GM could wind up in trouble if he let Smith cloud his thinking.

Krause was on edge that draft night about the tenth pick, but Reinsdorf told him to "go with his gut." So Krause selected Clemson's Horace Grant over Joe Wolf, which infuriated Dean Smith. The selection of a Clemson player over a Carolina player was galling to the coach because it could be used against him in recruiting.

"Dean Smith called me," Krause recalled, "and ripped my rear end, literally. 'How could you do that, you dumbbell?' Literally. And Michael said, 'What the hell? You took that dummy?!' And for years that's what he called Horace: Dummy. To his face. Dummy. Right to his face."

Krause had not consulted with Jordan about the pick, although he knew well what would have pleased him. "I talked to players, but I didn't talk to Michael because he wasn't old enough to understand at that point," Krause recalled. What was more unusual, the players he consulted with over personnel issues were on other teams. He often talked to Robert Parish of the Celtics and Brad Davis of the Mavericks. "Those relationships had built up over years," Krause later confided. "And they could tell me things because they had played against guys.

"Michael and I don't look at things alike," Krause explained in 1995. "Michael would have wanted me to have Buzz Peterson here the first couple of years, his college roommate. We used to kid about that all the time. Walter Davis was another one. He begged me to get Walter Davis. I wouldn't do it."

The situation fed into the growing animosity between the two men. A year earlier, Krause had picked Brad Sellers over Jordan's friend from Duke Johnny Dawkins. Now he bypassed a solid player from North Carolina. Years later, Krause would offer that Joe Wolf would probably have turned out just fine with the Bulls, that the North Carolina forward failed to develop mostly because he went to the lowly Los Angeles Clippers. Yet at the time, it was Jordan's experience that no one knew players better than Dean Smith and no stamp of approval was stronger than the Tar Heel logo. It was why he wore Carolina practice shorts under his Bulls uniform each game night, and under his street clothes each day. He believed deeply in all things Carolina. He had won a championship with Carolina, while the Bulls had been mostly a tinhorn operation, managed by the chaotic, insecure Krause, who had presented him with three coaches in less than three seasons.

Beyond all of that, Jordan just hated dealing with Krause, recalled the *Sun-Times*'s Lacy Banks. "Krause made it a lot more difficult than was necessary and that's why Michael hated him." By now, it was public knowledge that Jordan had nicknamed the team vice president "Crumbs," because everything he ate—and he ate a lot—supposedly looked good on him.

"Crumbs and I, we keep our distance," he told *Sports Illustrated* that off-season.

In time, Jordan would become less guarded about his disdain for the humorless GM. Over the coming seasons, when Krause came into the locker room, Jordan would sometimes lead his teammates in mooing or humming the theme music to *Green Acres*, antics that Krause mostly ignored or failed to recognize altogether.

When training camp started that fall, Jordan did what he always did: he turned the full force of his competitiveness on Krause's rookies and player acquisitions to see if they were strong enough mentally to compete. That was increasingly becoming a ritualistic test with Jordan. He had to see for himself, to confirm independently the work the GM was doing. Jordan's insistence and anger over personnel issues would settle into a theme that years later would haunt his own life as a basketball executive.

The truth was that a lot of NBA players simply weren't ready to compete alongside Michael Jordan, no matter what school they came from or who drafted them. Anyone who had made the roster was well aware of the mental gauntlet he required each teammate to run. It seemed obvious that he had little faith in those around him. "Michael initially thought he could just take over the game and always win it by himself," Bulls scout Jim Stack observed. "And he did that a lot, obviously, in the key time of the game to help us win. Until he really embraced his teammates and the idea that he could help us, I thought we were stuck for a while."

Much of his help the previous season had come from Charles Oakley, who had averaged 14.5 points and 13.7 rebounds, and John Paxson, who had 11.3 points while shooting almost 49 percent from the floor. "The thing you had to do with Michael Jordan is you had to gain his confidence as a player," Paxson explained. "You had to do something that gave him some trust in you as a player. He was hard on teammates as far as demanding you play hard, you execute. So there had to come some point where you did something on the floor to earn his trust. That was the hardest thing for new guys coming in, and some guys couldn't deal with it. Some guys could not play consistently enough or well enough, or they would not do the dirty work or little things. That's one of the reasons why Michael liked Charles Oakley, because Charles played hard. He did little things on the floor that Michael appreciated, but a lot of guys didn't understand that."

Pippen

The first time he met Pippen, Jordan looked at him and said, "Oh great, another country boy." It was an apparent reference to Pete Myers, Krause's sixth-round pick out of the University of Arkansas in 1986. Pippen came from the neighboring university, Central Arkansas.

"I'd never heard of him," Jordan said of Pippen. "He was from an NAIA school."

Pippen was from Hamburg, Arkansas, a former railroad town of about three thousand people that was also the home of *True Grit* author Charles Portis. Pippen was the baby of Preston and Ethel Pippen's twelve children. Preston Pippen worked in a textile mill, but his health failed during Scottie's high school years, perhaps limiting the opportunities for his youngest child. Pippen mostly sat the bench as a junior at Hamburg High, but he started at point guard as a six-one, 150-pound senior. For the second leg of his improbable basketball journey, his high school coach arranged for him to attend Central Arkansas as a team manager, a role Pippen had served in high school. "I was responsible for taking care of the equipment, jerseys, stuff like that," he once recalled. "I always enjoyed doing that, just being a regular manager."

His raw talent soon registered with basketball coach Don Dyer. "He wasn't recruited by anyone," Dyer once explained. "He was a walk-on, a six-one-and-a-half, 150-pound walk-on. His high school coach, Donald Wayne, played for me in college, and I took Pippen as a favor to him. I was prepared to help him through college. I was going to make him manager of the team and help him make it financially through college. When Scottie showed up for college, he had grown to six-three. I had had a couple of players leave school. I could see a little potential; he was like a young colt."

An NBA career had never even crossed Pippen's mind, not even in his dreamiest moment. But he had grown to six-five by the end of that freshman year and had established that he was one of the team's best players. "He had a point guard mentality," Dyer told the *Chicago Tribune* in explaining Pippen's evolution, "and we used him to bring the ball up the floor against the press. But I also played him at forward, center, all over the floor."

Scottie Pippen began to understand that things were different on the basketball floor. "I could be as good as I wanted to be. I developed confidence in my abilities." He blossomed into a two-time NAIA All-American. His senior year brought the kind of performance that got the attention of Marty Blake, the NBA's director of scouting. Pippen averaged 23.6 points, 10 rebounds, and 4.3 assists while shooting 59 percent from the floor and 58 percent from three-point range. Blake passed information about Pippen on to the Bulls and other teams. Pippen was invited to one of the NBA's tryout camps in Virginia, the Portsmouth Invitational, where Krause fell in love, as scouts are known to do. For one thing, now a full six-seven, Pippen had exceedingly long arms, which had long been a key for Krause in his evaluation of players.

"We watched him," Krause later recalled, "and I just got excited. I just got really shook up bad."

From there, Pippen was headed to the NBA's next camp, in

Hawaii. Krause notified Collins that they had a hot prospect. "When we told Doug Collins about Scottie, he was skeptical," Krause said. "So I put together a video of all the players in the Hawaii tournament and gave it to the coaches. I gave them names and rosters but no real information on the players. We let them see for themselves. After they came out of the video session, I asked if they had any questions, and the first thing out of their mouths was, 'Who the hell is Scottie Pippen?'"

From there, Krause worked a somewhat complicated deal with Seattle that netted Pippen for Chicago after the Sonics had selected him fifth overall in the 1987 draft. In return, Seattle got Olden Polynice, a center out of the University of Virginia. As a player from a small town and a small school who was suddenly thrust into the spotlight in Chicago, Pippen was understandably lost.

"He was a phenomenal talent but he was just so raw," Jim Stack recalled. "And Scottie, when we first drafted him, had those back issues. Because of that, he sat out a lot of training camp."

The back issues would be a huge factor in Pippen's career development, and in his relationship with the front office. But his fast friendship with the Bulls' other first-round pick, Horace Grant, helped him adjust that first year.

"The two of them came to Chicago the next day after the draft and went to a White Sox game," Cheryl Raye-Stout recalled. "They were sitting in the dugout with their Bulls caps on. They forged a friendship immediately.... And it translated onto the court because they felt really good about each other. They both had a lot of maturing to do. Scottie had it the most difficult coming from an NAIA school. Not being used to ever having media around, it was quite a shock for him."

The relationship between the two rookies became an infatuation of sorts. "Scottie is like my twin brother," explained Grant, who already had a twin brother, Harvey, also an NBA player. Pippen became his surrogate twin. The two shopped together, double-dated together, drove the same type of car, and lived near each other in suburban Northbrook. They even got married a week apart and served as each other's best man. It was the kind of relationship that cast an odd bent to the Bulls' already awkward chemistry. "Scottie called in one day and skipped practice because his cat died," recalled former trainer Mark Pfeil. "Horace called about fifteen minutes later and said he was with Scottie because of the grieving. Johnny Bach, our assistant coach, was absolutely furious. He got Horace on the phone and said, 'You get here. You oughta throw the cat in the garbage can.' Horace, when the team got together, wanted to have a moment of silence for Scottie's cat."

Such nonsense irritated Jordan. Krause recalled that practices soon became more entertaining than games in Chicago, with Jordan hunkering down and yelling at Pippen, "I'm gonna kick your ass!"

Early on, the goal of Jordan's harsh confrontations in practice was to toughen Pippen. Bach recalled that the young forward learned from the experience, although it didn't leave the two of them with a relationship noted for its warmth.

"When Scottie and Horace came in, Michael sensed the thing could be turned around," Mark Pfeil recalled. "But the thing that frustrated him was that they didn't have the same attitude. They were young enough to say, 'Hell, we get paid whether we win or lose.' And it was good enough for them just to get close."

Jordan cared only about finding some partners to help him compete. Collins took a similarly hard line, Bach explained. "Doug Collins had high demand on young players, and sometimes misunderstood them. High demand with a lot of emotional involvement with them. Doug brought them to a level of competing hard every night. He drove them. He emotionally got involved with them and got them to understand how important each game and practice was, and he drove them. Some people lead young players; he drove them."

Pippen continued to be troubled by his back that first season, which led some in the organization to suspect malingering, until he was finally diagnosed and underwent disk surgery during the 1988 off-season.

"My first year or two, I admit that I messed around a lot," Pippen once disclosed. "I partied, enjoyed my wealth, and didn't take basketball as seriously as I should have. I'm sure a lot of rookies did the same thing I did. You're not used to the limelight or being put in a great situation financially."

Even so, his talent presented great hope for the franchise, despite the fact that he weighed just 205 that first year. "Even though his body wasn't there, you could see signs," Jordan recalled. "As an open-court player, he was so much like Dr. J. He'd get the ball on the break with those long strides and next thing you know, he's at the basket. I think it took people by surprise to see how quickly he progressed and how his body responded to the style of play."

The Spat

Looking for some size and veteran leadership in the frontcourt, the team brought back thirty-eight-year-old Artis Gilmore to share center duties with Dave Corzine. Oakley was well established at power forward, and wanted to get the ball more. Collins didn't disagree with him, but it was hard to resist the Jordan option.

"We have to get to the point where Michael Jordan is not the sole source of energy on this team," Collins told reporters. "Both Michael and the Bulls know he can't survive long with the inhuman burdens we put on him. Of course, sometimes I'm not sure he's a mere human."

The optimistic plan was that Pippen and Grant would earn playing time, and that Jordan could merge his overpowering talents with the developing abilities of his teammates. "We have not proven anything yet," Collins told reporters. "Last year we were overachievers that played on emotion. Oakley's rebounding, Jordan's scoring, Paxson's steadiness, Corzine's toughness—all fell into place and allowed us to be average."

The season hadn't even started before trouble boiled up. In late October, Jordan accused Collins of cheating on the score of a scrimmage and walked out of practice. Headlines informed the city that the two weren't speaking. Jordan was fined, and Collins found himself under pressure to make the next move.

"Michael in the early days was both ambitious and strongwilled," Bach reflected. "Doug Collins also had a flash point. With that flashy personality and drive, I could see that at times it could rub a player the wrong way, especially someone like Michael Jordan."

"He has his pride; I have mine," Jordan told reporters. "We're two adults. In due time, words will be said. I'm not going to rush the situation."

"Doug knew he had to kiss and make up, and that's what he did," John Paxson recalled. "He had to calm his superstar. That was a little test he had. Had another player done that, you don't know what would have happened, because guys just don't walk out of practice. Just don't take off."

While the two soon patched up in public, the reality was that Jordan had little respect for his coach. Over the years, Collins would prove his stature in the game. "But at that time, he was immature," Sonny Vaccaro explained. "He just wasn't ready. It was obvious."

Jordan sometimes vented his frustration to Vaccaro about the coach. There were situations that led Krause to caution Collins about his behavior. There were suspicions that the GM was keeping track of the coach's indiscretions. They had clashed mightily that spring and off-season regarding player acquisitions. The blowup over practice only added to Collins's already substantial insecurities.

The coach was torn. He believed that Jordan dominated the ball too much for the team to win a championship. Jordan continued to force the point guards off the ball on the inbounds and take it himself, to control the offense. It meant that the coach could never get the Bulls into any sort of running game. The situation led Krause to believe that Collins was incapable of saying no to Jordan.

"It's got to be very difficult as a head coach to have a relationship with Michael and try to have that same type of relationship with other players," John Paxson observed almost a decade later. "You just can't do it. You have to give Michael leeway. On the floor you can't be as critical of him as you can with other players because of what he can do and what he means."

Impulsive and emotional, Collins revealed a tendency to blame his players for losses, sometimes in bitter, caustic terms that only alienated them. Teammates began encouraging Jordan to speak up about these issues, but he declined, pointing to the public furor that Magic Johnson stirred up in 1982 by taking on Lakers head coach Paul Westhead.

"As a head coach you're walking a fine line with Michael Jordan,"

Paxson said, looking back. "Not that he would ever do anything like that, but we all knew about the situation with Magic Johnson and Paul Westhead at the Lakers, when Westhead got fired after disagreeing with Magic. That's the power Michael could have wielded if he chose to. So Doug was walking a fine line. Early in Doug's career he handled it the best way he knew how."

The result was a rift in the Jordan-Collins relationship that Jordan worked hard to mask. Some thought the player and coach were reasonably close. They were not, Vaccaro said. "It was water and oil. I knew that." Jordan also took exception to Collins's antics during games, which contrasted sharply with the dignified calm that he so appreciated in Dean Smith. Many in the organization fed on Collins's zany energy. Jordan found it almost distasteful, but he kept that to himself because so many fans considered it an important part of the exciting young team.

"Doug was such an intense guy," recalled longtime Bulls equipment manager John Ligmanowski. "It was almost like he wanted to be in the game. He'd come downstairs soaked in sweat, totally drained after a game. It was fun because we were just really starting to get good. The team had come around."

Whatever his youthful shortcomings, Collins had the energy to drive the Bulls through the next stage of growth. "Doug was a great guy," Mark Pfeil explained. "He was interested in everything about people. He cared about them."

Cheryl Raye-Stout recalled that the media, particularly TV reporters, loved Collins. "He was very accessible to them. Doug was screaming and yelling and jumping and throwing....He definitely was demonstrative in his actions, and the guys who were key to this team were extremely young. Horace and Scottie, they hated him. He was growing up with them. He was new to the job. Here's a guy who came from the television booth. He was learning the process, too."

If Jordan felt any recrimination about the October incident with Collins, it was because he had begun—sometimes even more than his mother already did—to process things that happened to him in terms of his image, which had become the basis of his income. He acknowledged as much to Detroit reporter Johnette Howard in an interview several weeks later. "I felt bad that I did it that way," he said of walking out. "But I felt good that people perceived it the way it really was, that I'm just such a competitor."

This was becoming his go-to excuse for just about any behavior that might be interpreted as unseemly: it was because he was such a tremendous competitor. Blaming his own excessively competitive nature was a convenient out and, more importantly, the public seemed hungry to accept it. Even so, he had plenty of reason for concern about his image, he told Howard. "I'm put in a tough position with this team. It's hard for me to be a vocal leader with this team because everyone seems to view the Chicago Bulls as 'Michael Jordan's' or 'Jordan and company.' My name is always in the spotlight, and some people are naturally going to get jealous."

He worried that his treatment of his teammates in practice would be viewed as harsh. So he tried to keep things balanced, he explained. "If you show some tenderness and concern, people appreciate you more." He made a habit of trying to praise his teammates regularly in his media interviews.

Collins was popular in Chicago, and Jordan took pains after the practice incident to show him the proper respect. The coach had been rewarded with a contract extension, but some observers saw signs that the pressure was taking its toll on him. He had lost weight, wasn't eating well, and on many days looked drawn.

Jordan was also stressed, a situation, ironically, made worse by his financial success. The money and status continued to irritate players around the league. They had heard about his promotional contracts and saw his expensive suits and his gold necklaces. At the time, there were as many as twenty-four NBA players who made more than one million dollars a year while Jordan was locked into a contract that paid him about $830,000 for 1987–88. Sonny Vaccaro recalled that Magic Johnson never could understand how Jordan could have a shoe contract so much larger than any other star's. Vaccaro heard similar complaints from players all the time. He was now well known as Nike's money man, and it was his job to listen and to talk with the players in the game.

Lacy Banks heard it, too. The Sun-Times had assigned Banks to cover the Bulls that fall of 1987. Banks was also a Baptist minister and thus sometimes called "the Reverend" by those he worked with. He, too, was struck by Jordan's unusual relationship with wealth. "When I started covering Michael, he was still evolving," Banks remembered. "He hadn't even gotten a big contract yet. He had this principle that he signed his contract with Reinsdorf and he felt duty bound. If Reinsdorf wanted to break it and give him some money, he wouldn't turn it down. But he didn't feel it was his place to say, 'I think I'm worth more money now. I think you ought to pay me.'"

Jordan was making so much off the court, his basketball pay became a matter of pride. He didn't want to be seen as clamoring for more. The off-court income allowed him to say he didn't really play for the money. Others had said the same thing over the years, but Jordan was the first pro player who really didn't have to focus on his NBA salary.

Banks had covered Muhammad Ali for *Ebony* magazine and had gotten to know him, and he often contemplated just how misunderstood the boxer was. Ali had displayed tremendous courage in speaking out against the Vietnam War, well before that became commonplace, and he had paid dearly for his opposition to the war. This young basketball prince that Banks was now covering showed no such concern for social justice. Yet like most of the other people reporting on Jordan, Banks found that he admired the Bulls star. "I could see that he appreciated the fact there was a black guy covering the Bulls," Banks recalled in 2011. "We were very close the first few years."

The two would often sit together, playing cards and talking, on the commercial flights the team took in those early years. And so many times when Jordan didn't have his entourage on the road, Banks would be there to fetch orange juice and oatmeal cookies for Jordan after games—since the fans in the lobby made getting them himself an impossibility. They'd sit up until the wee hours, watching movies on SpectraVision or playing yet more cards. That's when Banks came to the conclusion that Jordan had a photographic memory. He could quote entire sections of movie scripts and could recall amazing details of the endless blur of games he played.

"I came to believe he was counting cards on me," Banks said of their titanic games of seven- and five-card stud and tonk. "He could call every bet, at least ninety percent of them. I was playing to try to win money. He was playing for relaxation and competition. In many ways, he fascinated me. Michael was a dream, and I had a nice, meaningful, enriching, enjoyable relationship with him."

He would be unfailingly polite with any woman who knocked on his hotel door late at night seeking affection. "That was before I realized he had a secret life going on," Banks explained. They were together so often in those early days that "people began calling me Michael's man," Banks explained. "That made me feel good and massaged my ego."

Especially with so many beautiful women wanting to meet Jordan. "You know Michael? Can you introduce me to him?" they would ask Banks, who always politely declined.

The sportswriter found Jordan amazingly patient not just with women but with the many strangers they encountered in airports and hotels. "He wouldn't brush people off," Banks said.

Jordan drew much of his approach from his parents. "They were quiet but sociable," Banks said. "There was a tremendous resemblance between his father and Michael, their facial expressions and speech patterns. Mrs. Jordan was a devout Christian. I never heard anything untoward about his mother or father, or his siblings."

The sportswriter spent time pondering how Jordan was misunderstood, not by the public as much as by his peers in the game. "When people begrudged him his success, they didn't understand," Banks recalled. "People thought he was being arrogant wearing the bling, and they begrudged him not so much for his talent but more for his marketing success. To have a multimillion-dollar contract with Nike was unheard of. What we all saw was that this guy is a marketing magnet and whoever had a piece of him was going to do well. The Bulls started drawing a capacity crowd, leading the league in attendance. Michael became king of the court."

It was a coronation that both opponents and certain people in the Bulls organization eyed with disdain.

Chapter 21

RULING JORDAN

THE BULLS OPENED the season in October 1987 with Brad Sellers, their first-round pick in 1986, at small forward, ancient Artis Gilmore at center, and Oakley at power forward. Jordan and John Paxson were the guards. Collins and management had agreed that Jordan needed to play fewer minutes and to share the responsibility with his teammates, but just the opposite occurred. Collins saw that Jordan wasn't going to allow the running game to happen. So he ran isolation plays for Jordan again and again, which consistently confounded the opposition.

For Jordan, 1988 would be a season of adjustment. His quickness to the basket was so great that teams had to force him to take jump shots and push him to give up the ball. The league had no rules against hand-checking and physical play in that era, so coaches started looking around for people strong enough to muscle him. Jordan worked on his outside shot, so as not to present a weakness that could be used against him. But he maintained that he was a much better shooter than people gave him credit for.

There was no team focused on Jordan quite like Detroit. The 1987 playoffs had been a watershed of sorts for the Pistons, who had battled for several years to unseat Bird's Celtics in the playoffs. They finally had what seemed like the edge in Game 5 of the 1987 Eastern Conference finals in Boston Garden with a 1-point lead over the Celtics and scant seconds to go. The Pistons were inbounding the ball along the sideline near their own basket, and Isiah Thomas wanted the ball from referee Jess Kersey. "Don't you want a time-out?" Kersey asked.

"Just gimme the fuckin' ball!" Thomas shouted over the noise.

So the referee gave Thomas the ball. He passed it in, then Bird stole it and hit streaking Celtics teammate Dennis Johnson for the go-ahead basket. Like that, Boston had a 1-point lead with a second left.

Kersey turned to a crushed Thomas.

"Now do you want a time-out?" the referee asked.

In the aftermath there was no good means to measure the depth of despair for Thomas and his teammates. They had also been deflated by Jordan scoring those 61 points to beat them in the Pontiac Silverdome. Detroit's coaches knew they would have to come up with a special effort to stop him in 1988. The Pistons were a team bent on breaking through. The Bulls and Jordan were clearly becoming a greater threat in the Central Division. Detroit coach Chuck Daly and his assistants began searching for a means to counter Jordan, and guard Joe Dumars was now at the center of their plans.

Dumars, in turn, was fairly obsessed with the challenge. "More than anybody else, that was the game I looked forward to," he said of playing the Bulls. "Chicago, I looked forward to that game, because he was so great that whatever greatness I had in me was going to have to be there that night."

Jordan and Dumars had much in common. "Southern, respect-ful," said Dumars in a 2012 interview. "These people, both fami-lies, taught the same thing. Respect people, carry yourself with some dignity, with some class and some character, and you stand on that. You don't waver."

Where Jordan idolized his great-grandfather Dawson, Dumars worshiped his father, Big Joe, who had served in General George Patton's army in World War II. Like Jordan, Dumars grew up play-ing on a court built by his old man, across the street from the larg-est liquor store in Natchitoches, Louisiana. The store had giant floodlights that used to shine on the Dumars's backyard, illuminat-ing the goal. Joe would often shoot alone until late at night when his father got home from his long workdays as a truck driver.

Dumars, too, was at first overlooked by basketball scouts. He wound up at McNeese State, a small liberal arts school in Lake Charles, Louisiana, in the midst of Cajun country. Also a starter from his freshman year, Dumars averaged 26.4 points his junior season, 1983–84, enough to finish sixth in the NCAA Division I scoring race. Like Jordan, Dumars broke a metatarsal bone in his foot, and like Jordan he took charge of his own rehab and began playing, contrary to medical advice. The same age as Jordan, Dumars stayed a year longer in college but followed Jordan's career intently, first at North Carolina, then as a rookie for the Bulls.

Jordan's foot injury meant that he was out much of Dumars's rookie season, so they had only a brief encounter that spring of 1986. "I was really interested to see how good this guy really is," Dumars recalled. "I think he had 33 points, and I remember this explosion, this athleticism, and you just go, 'Wow.' "

By the time they began competing head-to-head in the fall of '87, their similarities had lessened. After all, Jordan had blown up into a household name, and Dumars was still one of the best-kept secrets in the NBA. He played in the shadow of Isiah Thomas in the backcourt of the Pistons, and was known as an exceptional defender. He could score as much as his team needed and was a fine ball handler. Mostly, he went about his business quietly, which was remarkable considering the Pistons were the Bad Boys, a rough, profane club that had used a very physical style to push their way up the standings.

Dumars recalled that Isiah Thomas's focus on Chicago only added to the intensity they all felt. Thomas had grown up in the Windy City, on the hard streets of the West Side. "It was always about going back to Chicago," Dumars said of Thomas's mind-set before each game against the Bulls. "He was like, 'That's my hometown. I don't want to lose going back to Chicago.' And then having that kind of superstar in there in Michael, Isiah was focused."

Center James Edwards, who was a teammate of both Jordan and Thomas over his long career, said that for all their differences, the two men shared something essential: "They both were very driven to be the best they could be. Isiah was fired up everywhere, but of course he was fired up when he went home. It didn't take much to get him going. He was always on fire, no matter where we played."

With the hard feelings from the freeze-out at the 1985 All-Star Game fresh in Jordan's memory, the confrontations between the Bulls and Pistons always threatened to boil over. "Those games were intense, emotional," Dumars said. "It could be the middle of January, but it was always like the playoffs. Incredible intensity. Everybody was emotional in those games. Nobody wanted to lose. And we would sit there with tears in our eyes when we didn't win. I'm fortunate and blessed that I played in that kind of atmosphere."

In another subplot, Brendan Malone, Jordan's Five-Star coach, joined the Pistons staff. Off the court, Malone would spend time with Jordan and his parents at retreats hosted by Nike. By the time he went to work for the Pistons, Malone had spent a couple of years in the league scouting Jordan closely. "I'd go to the old Chicago Stadium and watch the games," he said. "And I knew the last eight minutes was Jordan Time. If he had 30 after the third quarter, I knew he was going to have 50. If he had 20 points after the third quarter, he was going to have 40. He took over in the last eight minutes of the game. What's so remarkable about Michael Jordan, and I've watched a lot of games, he never took a game off, he never took a possession off, he always played hard."

Especially against the Pistons. Both teams knew they were headed for a showdown in 1988. Chicago jumped out to a 10–3 start, which earned Collins coach-of-the-month honors for November and lifted Jordan's spirits. The feeling spread across the roster and breathed early life into what would come to be known as the Jordan swagger.

Ping-Pong

In the early days, he practiced that "swag" on Lacy Banks. Their game of choice was table tennis. Jordan had taken up the indoor game early in his Chicago days in a fit of competition with Rod Higgins. Banks was older and heavyset, and sweated profusely when they played. The competition had gotten going one day at the Deerfield Multiplex, where the Bulls practiced, when Banks mentioned that he was good at the game.

"You can't play Ping-Pong," Jordan told him.

They picked up the paddles to play, and Jordan said, "Let's make this interesting, twenty-five a game."

Banks won the first seven games and ran up some healthy winnings. He immediately noticed Jordan was reluctant to pay up, saying instead they'd keep playing and run a tab. "He never really paid me," Banks recalled. "Michael is a welsher. He bought a table and started practicing."

Soon they were playing before a varied audience at the Multiplex. Banks had also begun betting with Jordan when the team went on the road. On one occasion, the reporter lost a hundred dollars to the rich young star by cutting cards on the plane for twenty bucks a turn. Banks arrived back at the airport in Chicago and had to borrow his losses back from Jordan just to get his car out of the parking garage.

The sportswriter's plan was to dig out of debt with Ping-Pong one day after Bulls practice at the Multiplex. Things looked good for the reporter when he won the first six games, but typical of his scouting report, Jordan wanted to keep playing as a small crowd gathered.

Banks agreed, and like that, Jordan won two quick games and started talking. "Don't ever think you can dominate me," he said. "Never! I done figured you out, Lacy."

The more he won, the more he poured on the trash talk. "Chase that ball, Lacy. Run, run... Get it, Lacy! I got you now."

The very last time they played, Jordan won all seven games, Banks recalled. "He chalked me up as another conquest. I said, 'Let's play for fun.' He wouldn't do it."

"Michael Jordan and the Reverend were unlikely sparring partners, playing Ping-Pong at the old Multiplex, sometimes playing cards, arguing often," noted *Trib* basketball writer Sam Smith. "Jordan was famous, hedonistic, rich beyond belief. Banks was spiritual, middle-class, humble. And to the very end, the Reverend asked Jordan questions in news conferences that made MJ squirm."

"He had a gusto for living," Banks said in 2011 of the young Jordan. "He had this tremendous personality of energy, of humor, the energy of competition and the energy of daring. Certainly it was unlike any I had ever seen. When I was covering Ali—and I covered Ali before I covered Jordan—Ali was an oddity, a freak of nature as it were, a guy that big who could dance like a ballerina and could hit like a blacksmith. Even with covering a guy like Ali, I had never seen anybody with that inhuman amount of energy like Michael had."

It was taking every ounce of that energy to turn the Bulls around. A five-game losing streak in late December dipped them back toward .500, as their faith in Gilmore evaporated. The team released him before Christmas. January brought a colossal fistfight with the Pistons in Chicago Stadium and a rare win in the series for the Bulls. The melee erupted in the third quarter after Jordan grabbed an offensive rebound and faked Detroit's Rick Mahorn and Adrian Dantley on the putback. "Mahorn hooked Jordan around the neck and threw him to the ground," the Associated Press reported, "after which Jordan and teammate Charles Oakley went after Mahorn, with both benches clearing onto the floor."

Collins tried to intervene as Mahorn landed two rights to Oakley's face. Mahorn then turned on Collins, Bulls trainer Mark Pfeil recalled. "There was a tussle in front of our bench, and Doug Collins tried to grab Ricky Mahorn. Hell, Ricky threw Doug down twice. Threw him down on the floor. Doug jumped back up, and Ricky threw him over the scorer's table. Those were the things that always stood out in our minds. The Pistons were constantly doing those kinds of things. They just constantly beat and battered you."

"There is no doubt in my mind that both Mahorn and Dantley were attempting to injure me, not just prevent me from scoring, and that's what infuriated me," Jordan told reporters afterward. "But Detroit thinks they can intimidate us. And while Mahorn and Dantley had every right to prevent me from getting an easy 2 points, it did not give them the right to purposely try to injure me and knock me out of the game."

Oakley and Mahorn were ejected, but Chicago had stood up to the intimidation. "The Bulls always seemed a little intimidated by the Pistons, except for Michael," Pfeil said. "And he was always trying to get it across to the guys that this is the team we have to bridge ourselves over to get to the next level. Sometimes it took some yelling to get his point across. But against the Pistons, I think that's when Michael started stepping up as a leader. But in the backs of their minds, our guys were always thinking that something dirty would happen against the Pistons. Detroit would intimidate you every time they came in your building."

The Bulls zoomed off again from there on their way to a 50–32 record, the team's first fifty-win season in thirteen years. Jordan's mood improved, allowing for some bonding with his younger teammates. His expectations never made it easy, especially in practices, where he constantly raised the stakes. He had to push them, and at the same time find little ways to help bring them along. At the end of the day, however, he remained Air Jordan.

"I wouldn't say he was aloof or anything," Jim Stack recalled. "He just had his group of guys who had been in town since day one. Those guys just sort of followed him around like an entourage. He sort of insulated himself that way. It was interesting how he handled himself off the floor. He was still gregarious with his teammates. He just had those personal friends, and Michael was an extremely loyal guy. He had those guys with him all the time."

Even so, he still made time for his teammates. "It was in Phoenix in his hotel room," Lacy Banks said, recalling one such occasion, "and it was Mike Brown, Scottie Pippen, Charles Oakley, and Horace Grant. Michael had a suite and they were in there wrestling like kids and throwing each other over sofas. I was thinking, 'This is for members only.' This was Michael's inner circle and very few players were allowed to ascend into the inner circle, that sanctum of Michael's. They were saying things like kids would say, like, 'You can't beat me.' Corny stuff. They had the wrestler's stance and they would attack like sumo wrestlers. It was a test of strength, a rite of passage."

But a passage to what? Jordan still seemed committed to winning games by himself. Where they were headed and how they were going to get there was still vague. Chicago hosted the All-Star Game in February, which brought another milestone. Always meant to be a showcase for the league's talent, the event put Jordan front and center more than ever. He claimed his second Slam Dunk title in a narrow win over Atlanta's Dominique Wilkins, with a perfect score of 50 on his final dunk. Some observers, such as *New York Daily News* basketball writer Mitch Lawrence, smelled a little Chicago home cooking. "I remember sitting there saying to myself, 'There's just no way Dominique can win this. We're in Cook County where they steal elections,'" Lawrence recalled with a chuckle. "But I mean Jordan deserved it obviously and even Dominique admitted that, as great as he was that day. I still think Dominique had as good of a performance as you could have. The problem was the game was in Chicago, All-Star Saturday. By then I mean Michael had just grown in stature anyway."

Sports Illustrated photographer Walter Iooss had shot the 1987 dunk contest in Seattle and had come away disappointed with the images. He realized he needed different lighting and positioning to capture the faces of the competitors. He was in Chicago Stadium three hours before the start, and approached Jordan, asking if he could tell him how and where he was going to approach the goal during each dunk. "Sure," Jordan replied. "I can tell you which way I'm going."

He offered to put his finger on his knee before each dunk to indicate from which side he would approach the goal. Iooss was dubious that Jordan would remember to signal him, but sure enough Jordan cooperated. For the next-to-last dunk, Iooss positioned himself immediately under the basket stanchion and Jordan literally "fell into my arms," the photographer recalled years later.

On Jordan's final dunk, Iooss again stood under the basket as Jordan was set to take off from the far end of the floor. Jordan looked down the court at him and motioned with his fingers for Iooss to move slightly to the right. Jordan then took off, running the length of the floor to launch at the foul line for the perfect dunk, just as Iooss captured the iconic photo of Jordan flying, the ball poised to strike, his face pressed with a g-force of determination, and looming over his shoulders the Chicago Stadium scoreboard flashing with ads for Gatorade, Coca-Cola, and Winston cigarettes. The timing was indeed perfect.

The next night Jordan scored a record 40 points to earn the MVP honors in the All-Star Game, and the media noted that Isiah Thomas made a pronounced effort to get the ball to His Airness. Jordan's final points came on an alley-oop slam dunk from Thomas.

They paused afterward and pointed at each other, which proved to be little more than heavyweight contenders touching gloves before punching at the bell.

The Quiet War

Nothing made Jordan see red quite like Isiah Thomas walking onto the court before a tip-off. He emphasized that once again on national television early that April of 1988, by scoring 59 points in a 112–110 Bulls victory. His point totals against Detroit over the season had reverberated like a taunt—49, 47, 61, and 49—against a team that prided itself on its defense. "We made up our minds right then and there that Michael Jordan was not going to beat us by himself again," Chuck Daly said. "We had to commit to a total team concept to get it done."

The Pistons coaching staff determined to find a way to limit the Bulls' star during the fourth quarter. Detroit's strategy had always involved being physical. "Isiah and Laimbeer, they wanted me to let him drive," Joe Dumars recalled. "It was like, 'Let him drive.' As you know, it was a much more physical game back then, and they wanted to be physical and tough and nasty. And that's how they wanted to stop Michael."

"We were a very physical team with Isiah, Rick Mahorn, and Laimbeer," Brendan Malone agreed. "When Michael went to the basket and tried to score a layup, he was knocked down. They put him on the floor."

"He never gave an inch, no matter how battered he was," former Piston James Edwards recalled in 2012. "We used to put some wood on him, with Laimbeer and Mahorn out there. We used to punish him. He never faltered an inch. He kept going to the basket. He never stopped. He wasn't afraid of anything you did to him."

The Bad Boys of Detroit were known to stretch the rules, which only intensified Jordan's ire. In short time, he had come to hate the Pistons and their style of play. Yet, strangely, in his competitive relationship with Dumars, he took a different approach. "When he came on the court, we shook hands," Dumars recalled. "It was,

'Hey Mike, how's it goin'?' Never once in my fourteen years did he ever talk trash or anything with me. It was interesting because I would see him on television with other guys and there would be a whole lot of trash talking. I'm like, 'That's not the guy I play against.' Never once did he trash talk or say anything derogatory to me, ever. Not one time. I knew he could get tough with those guys on the other teams. I respected that about him, too. He knew this was just going to be a quiet war here with me."

Jordan always tested those guarding him, but Dumars remained expressionless.

Jordan also had to have a plan for playing Dumars. He knew that if the Detroit guard hit his first few shots, he could have a big offensive night. Whereas Jordan tended to hang back early, especially in big games, he took a different approach with Dumars and sought to be aggressive from the start, to keep him so busy defensively that he didn't have time to get his offensive game going.

Jordan let it be known that nobody in the league defended him better than Dumars, and the respect between the two men would eventually grow into friendship. "He's a down-to-earth guy, not that bad-boy image," Jordan once explained. "He loves competing. He's behind the scenes, not vocal. He didn't go out searching for stardom or notoriety. It found him."

The Detroit coaches, however, weren't much interested in friendship. They wanted to find a stronger defensive focus. To make sure there were no more outbursts against them, Chuck Daly and his assistant Ron Rothstein devised what would come to be hyped as the "Jordan Rules."

"They respected Michael and his greatness so much, Chuck and Ronnie and those guys, I think it was the ultimate challenge for any coach to try to come up with a game plan to try to slow this guy down," Dumars explained. "We were getting ready to play the Bulls one day in shootaround. One of my favorite coaches of all time, Ronnie Rothstein, our assistant coach, is about to show me what he wants. He said, 'Here's what Michael's doing, and here's what he's about to do.' He's showing me, and Chuck stops him and says, 'Hold on a minute. You ever guarded Michael? He does a pretty

Jordan battled Wake Forest's Anthony Teachey in both high school and college. (AP Images)

Going up against Houston's Clyde Drexler (*center*) in the 1982 NCAA tournament. (AP Images)

Hitting the winning shot against Georgetown in the 1982 NCAA championship game. (AP Images)

With (*left to right*) Matt Doherty, Sam Perkins, and Dean Smith in the fall of 1982. (AP Images)

Jordan, with Dean Smith, as he ponders leaving North Carolina in 1984. (AP Images)

Jordan came to consider Coach Dean Smith a "second father." (AP Images)

Playing against NBA players in an exhibition game for the 1984 U.S. Olympic team. (AP Images)

Jordan, shown here with Orlando Woolridge in Chicago in 1984, spent his career challenging teammates to one-on-on battles. (AP Images)

In his first
NBA game.
(AP Images)

Jordan's acrobatic
style created instant
danger in the NBA.
(AP Images)

Convalescing at UNC after he broke his foot during his second pro season. (AP Images)

Going for 63 against Boston in the 1986 playoffs. (Steve Lipofsky/ basketballphoto.com)

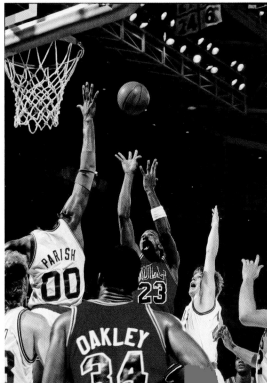

Flashing his
competitive anger.
(Steve Lipofsky/
basketballphoto.com)

Jordan and his early
Bulls in 1988.
(Steve Lipofsky/
basketballphoto.com)

Engaged in the "quiet war" with Detroit's Joe Dumars. (AP Images)

In the 1988 Slam Dunk Contest. (AP Images)

On the links
in 1988.
(AP Images)

With Bulls vice
president Jerry
Krause in 1988.
(AP Images)

With wife Juanita after the Bulls won the 1991 NBA title. (AP Images)

Bulls chairman Jerry Reinsdorf was confident that Jordan, though underpaid, would never ask for a raise. (AP Images)

On the medal stand with the Dream Team in 1992. (AP Images)

Jordan's image took a hit in 1993 after revelations of his gambling. (AP Images)

With his young family in 1993. (AP Images)

The Spirit was dedicated outside the United Center in November 1994. (AP Images)

Shown here with broadcaster Harry Caray, Jordan dreamed of playing pro baseball. (AP Images)

Wearing number 45 upon his return to the NBA in March 1995. (AP Images)

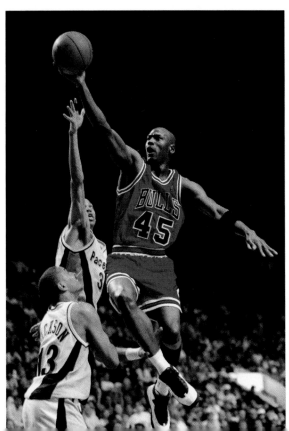

Jordan and Scottie Pippen embrace after winning the 1996 NBA title. (AP Images)

Pippen helps Jordan from the floor during the 1997 "flu game." (AP Images)

Even as a Wizard, he still worked the tongue. (AP Images)

Sitting courtside with Yvette Prieto at a Charlotte Bobcats game. (AP Images)

Jordan wept openly at his Hall of Fame induction in 2009. (AP Images)

good job of it. Let him tell us how he's going to guard him, how he's going to stop him, and we'll adjust to that.'"

· Like that, the Detroit staff had decided to build their plan on what Dumars thought. It was this ability to listen that made Daly a Hall of Fame coach. "They knew I was committed and passionate," Dumars said. "I didn't bring the frills. There wasn't a whole lot of smoke and mirrors to what I did. They knew I was dead serious when I stepped out on that court. And I tried to establish that from the first day."

The Pistons also used Dennis Rodman and Isiah Thomas on Jordan, Brendan Malone explained. "But Dumars was the primary defender. He had such quick feet and was so dedicated to playing defense."

The coaches and Dumars decided that no matter what, they would not double-team Jordan early in the game, even if he was scoring 20 points in the first quarter. "I didn't want him to see the double-teams early and figure them out," Dumars explained. "So I only wanted to double him in the fourth quarter."

The coaches and Dumars also decided that they did not want to force Jordan to pass the ball early because they did not want his teammates to get comfortable catching and shooting.

"We said, 'For the first three quarters, look, man, if he's rollin' that's fine, let's just stay in the game and keep it close,'" Dumars recalled. "Now all of a sudden in the fourth quarter, the ball swings and his teammates have to start making shots. So I didn't want any doubles until the fourth quarter."

The other primary element of the Jordan Rules called for Dumars to use his strength to force Jordan left toward the center of the floor when he had the ball. "I'm going to try and push him left every single time," Dumars explained.

"That's where the Jordan Rules came in," Malone recalled. "We took away all his trash, took away his drive by pushing him to the elbows, took away his baseline drive, and pushed him left. And when he got the ball down on the blocks in the post, we would come from the top and double-team him. That was the Jordan Rules. We did not want him to get to the baseline. On the wings we pushed him to the elbows. We pushed him on either wing to the elbow, and we would influence him to his left."

Anything less than the Jordan Rules would have meant defeat, James Edwards observed. "I mean if you didn't scheme against him, he could drop 50 on you at any time. You had to try to slow him down the best way you could. You had to at least double-team him and make him pass it. You had to make it as hard as you can. You had to use two guys. You couldn't guard him one-on-one. He was too good, too quick."

Asked about the Jordan Rules, Detroit's John Salley once quipped, "It's really two things. When Michael gets his hands on the ball, we all get down on our knees and pray. Secondly, we all go to church or synagogue before the game."

The Jordan Rules succeeded against Doug Collins's Bulls so well that they became textbook for guarding athletic scorers. In the seventeen regular-season and playoff games between the Bulls and the Pistons over two seasons, Jordan's average would fall by nearly 8 points to 28.3 per game. Most important, the Pistons would win fourteen of those games. The scheme helped Detroit break free in the Eastern Conference and win two NBA championships, but it also helped Chicago in the long run, by forcing Jordan and the Bulls to find an answer to Detroit's muscle. "I think that 'Jordan Rules' defense, as much as anything else, played a part in the making of Michael Jordan," Tex Winter said in 2004, looking back.

Each year the Bulls were getting better, Dumars said. "It was like driving and looking in your rearview mirror. We'd say, 'Man, they're gaining on us. They're coming.' You could see them coming. It wasn't long before that Ferrari went right by. Whoosh."

Most Valuable

Jordan again led the league in scoring in 1988, this time with a 35.0 average, and for the first time he was named the NBA's MVP. "It's a thrill," he said. The year before, he had been outpointed in the voting by Magic Johnson, who was on his way to leading the Lakers to back-to-back titles. For '88, Larry Bird finished second with sixteen first-place votes to Jordan's forty-seven. Jordan's 3.2 steals per game also led the league, and he was named Defensive Player of the Year and a member of the All-Defensive team, fulfilling another of his goals.

Krause, meanwhile, was named Executive of the Year, and Oakley again pulled down more rebounds than any player in the league, with 1,066. The biggest prize, though, was the Bulls' first playoff series win since 1981, a 3–2 defeat of the Cleveland Cavaliers. In the first two games of the series, Jordan scored 50 and 55 points. No one in NBA history, not even Wilt Chamberlain, had scored 50 points in back-to-back playoff games. In the decisive fifth game, Collins decided to move Pippen into the opening lineup for the first time. Pippen replaced the ineffective Brad Sellers and scored 24 points. Krause was overcome afterward. "This is a baby from Conway, Arkansas, upon whom we've put tremendous pressure," he told reporters.

"When I played against Scottie last summer, I could see he had the skills," Jordan said. "It was just a matter of, how do you get them out of him in a season? It took eighty-two games for him to do it, but he's done it. And I think it's going to help him for the rest of his career."

To celebrate, the Bulls donned T-shirts that said, "How do you like us now?"

"We're ready for the next round!" Jordan announced after the victory. At first, it seemed they were. They claimed the second game at the Pontiac Silverdome in their second-round series with the Pistons, and suddenly the Bulls had the home court advantage. But from there the Pistons zeroed in with their late-game defense on Jordan, and forced him to pass. They also resorted to their Bad Boy tactics. In Game 3, a 101–79 Pistons blowout in the Stadium, Jordan and Detroit center Bill Laimbeer scuffled. "I set a pick," Laimbeer said. "I guess he wasn't looking."

It was during this series that Los Angeles Clippers owner Donald Sterling phoned Jerry Reinsdorf and inquired about getting Jordan in a trade. Sterling badly needed the kind of player that would allow him to compete with the Lakers and Magic Johnson for the city's attention. He could offer Chicago a slew of draft picks, including two of the top six of the first round. A deal wasn't as far-fetched as it would seem in retrospect. Krause, who coveted draft picks like jewels, had begun to see that no matter how he built the team, Jordan would always get the credit for any winning. And Reinsdorf understood the criticism that the team could never win the NBA Finals with Jordan dominating the offense. The offer forced the Chicago front office to think about an alternative future without Jordan. With the right moves, it could be very attractive, Krause concluded. But Reinsdorf had already infuriated Chicago fans with his threats of moving the White Sox to Florida. Trading Jordan would have brought the wrath of the city down on his head. The owner knew he couldn't do it, and the Bulls passed.

Detroit took Game 4, and was in control in Game 5 when Jordan hit Isiah Thomas in the face with an elbow and briefly knocked him unconscious. Thomas was sent to the locker room but found the door locked. So he returned to the arena and later entered the game to provide enough edge to help the Pistons to advance, 4–1.

Teams had focused almost exclusively on stopping him, Jordan would say later, looking back. "And doing that exposed certain weaknesses on our team."

Yet he didn't see the solution coming.

Just before the 1988 draft, the Bulls traded Oakley to New York for center Bill Cartwright, a move that blindsided fans and players alike. Oakley was the team's primary muscle, not to mention Jordan's enforcer and closest friend on the roster. Cartwright, a seven-foot-one post-up center, had been plagued by foot injuries and was thought to be near the end of his career. The trade itself was bad enough, but the way it went down made it worse. Oakley was out on the town with Jordan, attending the Mike Tyson–Michael Spinks fight.

"Oak was in Atlantic City with Michael at a fight, and I couldn't find him to tell him about the trade," Krause recalled. "He found out about it because somebody ran up to him at the fight and told him. He told Michael, and Michael went bananas. 'How in the hell could Krause do this? He's screwing up the franchise.' Michael went nuts."

"We were in Atlantic City watching the fight," Jordan remembered. "I was pretty upset about the deal, and also to have to find out about it that way."

Jordan's wrath ignited the media and then the fans. Krause, who had taken great pride in drafting Oakley, was also deeply torn.

"Charles was strong and tough and mean," Johnny Bach recalled. "He was the hardest trade that we had to do because Jerry Krause not only loved him as a player, but I think he had a great affection for him as a person. And, to give him up and get Cartwright was almost against the grain. But the coaches really believed we couldn't win without Bill Cartwright, so we made the trade.

"It was traumatic for the team," Bach explained, "but I think it just took us the next step up. Our defense was anchored by a real professional. Bill was good in the locker room. He was good in practice, and he earned the respect of the team because he could play Patrick Ewing straight up. We didn't have to double Patrick Ewing. And that gave us a great deal of confidence. What made the trade so tough was that Michael looked at Oakley as a protector. Charles was ready to fly into any tangle. You hit Michael, you had to face Charles. But Bill, in his own way, toughened up the big guys we had and, in his own quiet way, Bill became very much of a terminator. Things stopped at the basket."

"It was a big gamble for this franchise, a huge gamble," Tex Winter observed later. "We were giving up a young guy for an old guy, but we felt like we needed to start with a good post-up center, particularly someone who could anchor our defense."

The deal also opened up playing time for a rapidly improving Horace Grant. "We needed a guy who could clog the middle, and we weren't going to win without one," Jerry Reinsdorf said. "I also knew that Horace Grant was coming on and thought that he'd be a better player than Oakley anyway."

Grant's superior quickness changed the defense. He and Pippen gave the Bulls two lightning forwards. With Grant on the floor, the Bulls could bring much more pressure to their defense. It would become a trademark. Bach took to calling Pippen and Grant "the Dobermans," the attack players in the Bulls' pressure, trapping defense. But at the time, the loss of Oakley soured Jordan's mood just when pressure was growing off the court as well.

Flight 23

As spring became summer, Juanita Vanoy had informed Jordan that she was pregnant, which further inflamed the ire of his parents, who suggested that she had allowed the conception to happen to secure her hold on their son. It was not a happy time, Sonny Vaccaro recalled.

Meanwhile, Jordan, in partnership with Nike, had opened a small chain of retail stores that were owned in part by his family. The Flight 23 by Jordan stores were to be run by James Jordan, Vaccaro explained. "They gave him something to make it look like he's making a dollar that he's not taking off his son. That was the general idea when it first happened. They said, 'OK, let's let James start a company. We'll have a store in Charlotte, and we'll have a store over here and over there.' "

The enterprise also provided the Jordan siblings a share in the ownership. Their brother's instant and overpowering wealth and fame had quickly trapped them in the impossibility of arranging some sort of normal life and employment. Ronnie, with his military service and his family, already had his life and career laid out, but the others found mostly complication at every turn. "You know how hard that must have been also," Vaccaro observed, "to be the brother or the sister of Michael Jordan, with the mother and the father having to maintain a semblance of balance where he's not just paying for everybody, which he basically ended up doing."

Sadly, the running of retail outlets only served to further exacerbate the family conflicts, particularly those between James and Deloris Jordan. Michael was engaged at every turn in his young life, from the immense challenge on the court to his many business dealings to his developing relationship with Juanita. Now he had to navigate a new level of intensity between his parents.

With the press and a large crowd attending the grand opening of the Flight 23 by Jordan store in Charlotte, his parents engaged in an ugly dispute in a back room of the retail space, his older sister recalled. "While we all were entangled in their conflicts to a certain extent, it was Michael who was pulled into them mainly and being affected by them the most. It was he who was having to endure the private battles and step out on the platform of the world and smile, even when his heart was breaking. He once told me that the worst thing about his success was what it had done to our parents."

While the public saw James Jordan as a nice, hardworking man, Nike quickly discovered that he was a nightmare running the small chain of stores. He was known to do some drinking, and he dealt with crises by ignoring them. He also ignored bills owed to suppliers, Vaccaro recalled. "He wasn't paying for the T-shirts and all that." Beyond that, there was increasing evidence that he was philandering, which further fired the conflict with Deloris. "James was a scoundrel and he created a lot of the problems," Vaccaro said. "It was horrible. He owed money and his kid was making zillions."

As a Nike representative, Vaccaro found himself in the middle of the conflict. "It was unbelievable," he said, explaining that he met separately with James Jordan and then his wife, in hopes of resolving the issues. Word of the problems had gotten to Phil Knight quickly, and the Nike chairman wanted them handled.

The Jordans came to a hotel in Beverly Hills where Vaccaro spoke to them separately. "I had a talk about the problem James was having," he explained. "I represented Nike, because Phil could never get next to these people. I had to go down and negotiate what James was doing and then I'd go to Deloris."

Jordan dearly loved and was loyal to both his parents, which made their conflict almost unbearable for him. "But he didn't take his father's side when it came to Nike," Vaccaro recalled. Jordan agreed with Phil Knight that Nike should buy out his parents' interests as soon as possible. Otherwise, the family was headed for a public relations nightmare due to James Jordan's mismanagement. The situation dragged out for three years while Jordan was engaged in his most intense battles with the Pistons.

At first, James Jordan resisted giving up his ownership, Vaccaro recalled. "He wanted to be separate, but you couldn't have a separate Flight 23 or whatever the hell he wanted to call it."

When it was finally made clear that Nike was going to take the stores back, James decided to take some of the proceeds from the sale and launch his own clothing company along with son Larry.

Not surprisingly, it wasn't long before that operation too was in trouble. That generated more conflict with Deloris Jordan and more headaches for their famous son.

"The public never saw the pain and the problem that existed," Sonny Vaccaro said. "I was in the middle of them when they were breaking away from Nike and James got involved in buying his own T-shirts. I was in the middle of all that."

"After the Flight 23 by Jordan catastrophe, he vowed that he would never have any business dealings with us," Jordan's older sister said of the experience.

"It was worse than you or others may think," Vaccaro agreed.

What made it worse, they all realized in retrospect, was that the conflict took away Jordan's family as a place where he could escape the pressures of fame, fortune, and competition. More and more, golf was becoming his means of escape. His other main discovery about his life was that even when he got away, his competitive urges and the adrenaline rushes they bred were still with him. He had long enjoyed small bets on all sorts of things, but especially golf. As the sanctuary of his personal life evaporated, he turned to golf for relief and to wagering to feed his craving for an adrenaline rush. And now that his life was larger, the bets became larger, too. What he didn't fully comprehend at the time was that he was putting on the line his own good name, which he guarded so tenaciously in every other aspect of his life. He continued to groom his public image, while keeping his golf gambling secret, documented only in the strange hieroglyphics of his scorecard. Soon it was hidden so well that often one of his own golf partners would have no idea of the lofty level of wagering Jordan was engaging in. The issue with his gambling, Jordan would soon discover, was not so much what it was, but what it was perceived to be.

Chapter 22

FLYING HIGH AND DRY

Jordan went to yet another "appreciation" event at Laney High during the 1988 off-season. During a break, he slipped outside for some fresh air. Dick Neher, his old Babe Ruth coach, snuck up behind him, grabbed him by the band of his trousers and underwear, and pulled up high and hard to deliver the kind of wedgie that only an ex-Marine could fathom. (It was perhaps Jordan's ultimate Hanes moment.) Stunned and instantly angered, Jordan whirled around, saw who it was, and told him, "Dick Neher, you're still the craziest white man I know." That was quite a statement, considering Jordan's relationship with Krause.

During that 1988 off-season, Krause had arranged for Tex Winter and Phil Jackson to coach the Bulls' summer league team and to use Winter's triangle offense. The franchise's main team had never used the triangle under Doug Collins, but the GM wanted Winter to teach Jackson the offense. The summer league team featured few of the players the franchise had under contract and focused instead on various free agents and rookies hoping to catch on with Chicago.

Doug Collins was well aware that the summer league team was using Winter's offense, and that Jackson was involved. But Collins didn't fully grasp that Krause would likely have supported any coach who actually listened to Winter. "Doug was very headstrong and confident, which you would expect," explained Jim Stack. "He had been a number one pick and had had a great NBA career. Doug really wanted to do things his way. At that young age, he sort of bucked against some ideas."

Besides, anyone could see that the Bulls were getting better, driving more exciting change for the franchise. For example, the supply of Bulls season tickets was exhausted by the fall of 1988. If you wanted to ride on the Jordan express, you had to get on the waiting list. His team coffers plump with revenue just four short years from the time that the Bulls seemed doomed, Jerry Reinsdorf rewarded his star with a contract extension that September, reported to be worth about $25 million over eight seasons. This new deal, too, would be outdated in record time.

They were all headed into a blizzard of cash. That season, the Bulls would lead the league in the sales of licensed merchandise and they would do so for the foreseeable future. "To put that in proper perspective," recalled longtime Bulls VP Steve Schanwald, "about 40 percent of all NBA licensed merchandise sold was Bulls-related." If only all that money could have bought Jerry Krause a little love, or at least respite from Jordan's ballooning frustrations.

The Conflict

As Jordan suspected, the early returns for his fourth NBA season proved troubling. The Pistons pushed them around on opening night in Chicago. Collins had Cartwright at center, Brad Sellers and Grant at forwards, and Jordan in the backcourt with Sam Vincent, who had come to Chicago from Seattle. Faced with glaring weaknesses there, Jordan again seemed to take it all on himself and broke out of the gate on his way to leading the league in scoring — and brashness too. He stole the ball during a November game and dunked on guard John Stockton, which prompted Jazz owner Larry Miller, who was sitting courtside, to snap at Jordan that he should pick on somebody his own size. Moments later, Jordan went to the hoop and dunked over six-eleven center Mel Turpin, then ran by Miller as he headed down the floor and asked the owner, "Is he big enough?"

The team, meanwhile, teetered along a mediocre path. Media critics had long pointed out that Larry Bird and Magic Johnson made their teammates better, while Jordan often seemed to be playing for himself. Assistant coach Phil Jackson had articulated a similar point one day about the need for Jordan to make his teammates better. Jackson said that it was something Knicks coach Red Holzman had emphasized to him years earlier. Collins thought Jackson had a good point, and ordered his assistant to go and inform Jordan of it immediately. Jackson took on the foolhardy mission, fully expecting an unwelcome response from the star. He was surprised, however, that Jordan listened with patience and seemed to appreciate the honesty, no matter how much the public discussion of it irritated him. Jordan's recollection of the moment had him rolling his eyes as the assistant coach walked away.

Jordan was beginning to grow as a team leader, although it wasn't a warm and fuzzy kind of leadership. It was mostly the pressure he put on his teammates to be good or be gone. Now, however, he was headed into the season fearing that Krause had just made a terrible trade for Cartwright that would make the team weaker and Jordan's job all the more difficult.

"At the beginning of the year it was frustrating and hard to accept," Jordan recalled. "Things were not going well, and it was getting to me. I had very high expectations, just like everyone, but there was a transition period we had to go through."

The coaches, however, had seen Cartwright's value, not only as a defender but as a leader. Jackson began calling Cartwright "Teach," and the name stuck. On the court, his teammates and opponents around the league knew Cartwright for his elbows. He held them high when he rebounded or boxed out.

"Michael really didn't know Bill Cartwright as a person," Krause recalled. "Michael made Bill prove himself. Michael did that with everybody. That was Michael's way. I knew what Bill was. Bill was gonna be fine with Michael. I told Bill, 'It's coming. He's gonna needle you. Michael's gonna drive you crazy.' Bill said, 'He ain't gonna do nothing to me.' "

It would prove complicated, former teammate John Paxson recalled. "Michael demanded nothing less than playing hard. If you missed shots when you were open, he didn't want to see that either. If Michael came off the screen and roll a couple of times and threw a quick pass to Bill Cartwright and he couldn't handle it, Michael wasn't going to go there again. That was kind of what happened early. If you do something and one of your teammates doesn't respond to it, you're going to think twice about going there. It's a natural thing. You always sensed with Michael that he was looking for perfection out of himself. There's a part of him that expected that of those around him, too."

If Jordan wasn't great almost every night, it was hard for the Bulls to win, so it only made sense that he wanted more out of his teammates. They all did. "I feel I'm very observant about the game," he said of his approach. "If things were going well, I didn't have to score too much. I could stay in the background and get everyone else involved."

It was imperative that his teammates be able to do their share, Paxson explained. "Michael challenged guys, and for some, their game didn't live up to that challenge. Brad Sellers, for example. It was tough for him to handle what Michael expected of him. Michael had a tendency to look at certain guys and say, 'You're capable of doing this. Why aren't you? I look at your physical skills. Why can't you?'"

Jordan made a connection with Paxson as a teammate, although the guard from Notre Dame was not physically or athletically imposing. Jordan often rated athleticism second to heart. He said he wanted teammates with the fearlessness to step up at crucial moments. Just as important, Paxson didn't need the ball in his hands, which removed one potential conflict. "I'm sure he looked at me many times and said, 'You're not capable of doing that on the floor,'" Paxson explained. "But I had an advantage with Michael in our basketball relationship. We spent a month overseas together when we were in college as part of an international team. I made a shot to win a game over in Yugoslavia, and I've got to believe that in the back of his mind, Michael remembered that about me as a player. He was able to trust me. At the same time, I don't remember Michael early on putting any pressure on Scottie Pippen or Horace. He knew that a lot of guys have to grow into the league. Michael was always more than fair with me. He was always positive with me and never said anything negative about me in the papers. That meant a lot to me. You can get battered down when the great player of the team says something critical of you personally. He didn't do that. I thought early on he was too reserved toward players at times. I'm sure he felt he was walking a fine line. 'Should I be critical? Should I just lay back and let these guys do their own thing?' I felt the more vocal he became as a leader, the better we were. Once he really started challenging guys, it made us better. We had to learn how to play with Michael as well as Michael had to learn to play with us."

The Point Guard

January found the Bulls struggling to stay above .500 and slipping into yet more conflict. Collins chafed at the assistants that Krause had hired for him. "I was upset because Doug basically wasn't listening to Tex," Krause explained, "and he wasn't listening to Phil Jackson. Doug did a great job for us for a couple of years. He took the heat off me from a public relations standpoint. Doug was great with the media. But he learned to coach on the fly, and he didn't listen to his assistants as much as he should have. Doug had a thing with Phil, too. As time went on, he was like Stan in that he got away from what we wanted to do."

Three weeks into the season, Juanita Vanoy had given birth to a boy, Jeffrey Michael, but Jordan's parents still opposed their son marrying the mother of his child. The birth of the baby was kept hush-hush throughout the season. Some writers knew about it but kept it out of their reports. Vanoy supposedly contemplated a paternity suit for about six months but ultimately decided to hold off. The tension was as thick in his personal life as it was in the locker room.

Finally, in late January, the team began a turnaround thanks to the improvement of Pippen and Grant, as Jordan began stepping up the pressure on them.

"I think Michael saw what kind of players Scottie and Horace could be," explained Will Perdue, a rookie backup center that season, "and he was very difficult on them at that time. He did it in a positive way, but at the same time he was challenging them to see if they would answer the challenge."

Complicating the chemistry was Jordan's continued exasperation with Cartwright, who was one of the few who stood up to the bullying and intimidation, Jim Stack remembered. Some would later describe the center's intense dislike of Jordan's tactics as something that approached hatred. "Bill felt that Michael chastised him unnecessarily at times," Stack said in a 2012 interview. "Bill was a guy with a lot of pride. He had built a lot of respect in the league." Stack didn't think the dislike reached the level of hatred on Cartright's part, but Perdue seemed certain that Jordan hated Cartwright. Perdue was pretty sure Jordan disliked him as well.

As for the enmity sent his way, Cartwright seemed to take it in stride. He had been the kind of player in New York who could average 20 points and 10 rebounds, Stack pointed out, adding that Jordan didn't seem to recognize the sacrifice Cartwright was obviously willing to make in becoming a role player in Chicago.

"Bill appreciated totally Michael's talent," Stack recalled. "But at the same time Bill wasn't just gonna accept his crap. Michael would test everybody. In practice, if Michael came to the hole, Bill was there to meet him. So many of the players before Bill Cartwright would totally acquiesce and defer to Michael. But Bill would take no shit…Michael could walk over just about anybody because he was so overwhelming with his talent. But Bill held his line. He said, 'This is my domain in here, and you stay out there.' And it had a galvanizing effect on the team. Bill was respected in the locker room for kind of standing up to Michael in a lot of ways, which was appreciated by everybody."

In March, Collins grew unhappy with the play of point guard Sam Vincent and benched him. The coach moved Jordan to the point, putting the ball in his hands even more than it already was. Craig Hodges, who had played for Winter at Long Beach State, was inserted into the starting lineup as the off guard. "It'll be interesting to see how Michael likes it," Collins said. Jordan responded by turning in seven straight triple-doubles (he would record fourteen triple-doubles between January and April), and the Bulls won six straight. Collins, it seemed, was positioning him to play the game the way Oscar Robertson had played it. Jordan took to checking his stats with the official scorekeeper during games, so that he would know just what he needed to ring up another triple-double. Soon, the league grew wise to what he was doing and ordered scorekeepers to stop providing in-game updates.

Then Hodges was lost for the rest of the regular season with an ankle injury, and the Bulls soon lost six in a row. The outspoken Winter had opposed Jordan's move to the point, and discord on the coaching staff mounted until Collins barred Winter from practice. "Tex was basically out of the picture at that time," Jackson recalled.

Krause wondered whether Collins might just wear the superstar out with all the extra duty. As an assistant coach, Jackson quietly observed that Jordan was being worked so hard that he was too tired down the stretch of some games. Jordan didn't particularly care for playing the point, but he had little trust in his teammates' ability to score.

And it was hard not to admire the work Jordan did as a "one" guard, where his ball handling allowed him to dance into spaces on the floor that opponents could never seem to reach in time. He would stop and start, hesitate and go, making every possession a workout on the defender's ankles. He learned quickly how to come off screens. Jordan was so elusive that help defenders had trouble just tracking him down for a double-team. He drew so much attention that Hodges, Pippen, and Paxson usually found themselves wide open for threes. Jordan worked the perimeter, too, and his jumper fell often that spring, which forced defenders to make themselves even more vulnerable and step out on him.

Chicago finished at 47–35 for fifth place in the conference, which earned the Jordanaires a first-round playoff matchup with the fourth-seeded Cavaliers, who had lost but four home games the entire season. Jordan had taken to listening to Anita Baker that spring, playing her song "Giving You the Best That I Got" before games for inspiration. He would need it. The Bulls had lost all six regular-season games against the Cavaliers, but that didn't stop Lacy Banks from boldly predicting a Chicago victory in the five-game playoff series. When other Chicago writers expressed doubt that the Bulls could survive, Jordan angrily challenged them and forecast a win in four games. Even casual observers could see that Cleveland had the size both inside and on the perimeter in Ron Harper and Craig Ehlo to slow Jordan down.

The Cavaliers held home court advantage, but Chicago moved to a surprising 2–1 series lead and had a chance to close it out in the Stadium in Game 4. Jordan scored 50 points but missed a late free throw, and Cleveland escaped in overtime to tie the series. He seemed devastated by the turn of events, but then tossed the self-doubt off quickly. Jackson recalled that when Jordan showed up the next day for the team flight to Cleveland, he virtually bounded down the aisle, telling his teammates to have no fear, they were going to win.

That enthusiasm burned right through Game 5 the following day. Jordan came out scoring and dishing, matching the Cavaliers bucket for bucket. Hodges and Paxson also stepped in to make a barrage of threes, and the game wound its way to a tight fourth quarter that produced six lead changes in the final three minutes. With six seconds to go, Jordan drove hard to his right at the top of the key. Ehlo reached across to stop him and was rewarded with a staggering blow to the face as Jordan scored to put Chicago up 99–98. Ehlo recovered to inbound the ball, then got it back and rolled in for a layup to give Cleveland a 100–99 lead with three seconds left.

During the time-out, Collins quickly drew up a play for center Dave Corzine to take the last shot, with the logic that it wouldn't be expected. Jordan reacted by angrily whacking the clipboard and telling his coach, "Just give me the fuckin' ball!" Collins quickly drew up a new look, with Brad Sellers inbounding. As he walked on the floor, Jordan whispered to teammate Craig Hodges that he was going to make the shot.

Cleveland coach Lenny Wilkens had planned to use forward Larry Nance's height to deny Jordan, but he slipped free, took the pass, and motored into the key for a jumper. Ehlo quickly picked him up and played textbook defense—on him every step until Jordan moved past him and rose up. Ehlo recovered, flying from the right, left arm outstretched to challenge the shot with an extended hand. But Jordan's elevation and hang time secured the moment. Ehlo had a hand in front of the ball, but his momentum carried him to the left as he fell away, and the form in red continued rising, reached his apex, then swished the game winner, 101–100, which ignited his famous fist-pumping celebration, replayed a trillion times over the ensuing years.

The moment was immediately dubbed "the shot." Krause's first thought while watching from the stands was that Brad Sellers had delivered a perfect inbounds pass that made the play possible. "That was the best pass I ever saw in basketball," he said in 2011. "He got that pass between three guys, really threaded the needle. I ran down on the floor and hugged Brad Sellers."

It was telling that in that moment, Krause had wanted to embrace his beleaguered draft pick. In 1986, Jordan had lobbied for the drafting of Duke's Johnny Dawkins, but Krause had taken Sellers instead, which became yet another bone of contention as Sellers struggled to fit in. It was certainly a fine pass, but perhaps nothing would better encapsulate the coming troubles. Krause and Jordan viewed the moment of euphoria from opposing perspectives. They were two willful, overbearing figures whose success was growing and spreading between them like a no-man's-land. As for Sellers, he would be gone from the Bulls after the season. Once a starter, he had averaged just 4 points and played just thirteen minutes per game over the playoffs.

Meanwhile, another piece of videotape from the game would also gain notoriety. The tape was a shot of the Bulls' bench after Jordan's 44 points delivered the victory, and it captured the beat writers sitting nearby, including Sam Smith and Bernie Lincicome of the *Tribune* and Lacy Banks of the *Sun-Times*.

"You see a shot of Doug Collins celebrating, and then Lacy's like jumping up and down and waving his fists over his head," recalled ESPN's J. A. Adande, who had worked with Banks at the *Sun-Times*. "There was a bit of Bulls fan in Lacy, you know, and it clearly came out in that moment, but he never let it cloud his journalistic duty."

Banks, the one journalist to challenge Jordan consistently, had been caught in a sudden, comical lapse of objectivity. He had something on the line, having predicted a Chicago win, but the moment spoke of an industry deeply conflicted by its adulation of Air Jordan. It would become increasingly difficult for the business of sports journalism to find any sort of restraint in an era where the moments—and the media profits—were becoming exceptional.

For Cleveland, meanwhile, the loss was devastating. Cavaliers center Brad Daugherty, Jordan's teammate from college, had seen it before. "I saw him go up," Daugherty said, "and I turned to box out, to look for the flight of the ball. I didn't see it, because Michael pumped, then brought it down. Then he went back up and hit the bottom of the net. I still don't know how he fit all of that into three seconds."

"We're going to New York, baby," an exuberant Jordan said afterward.

The energy from the win carried into the second round, where the Bulls went at it with coach Rick Pitino's Knicks, featuring Patrick Ewing, Charles Oakley, and Mark Jackson. With Jordan averaging 35 points despite playing with an aggravated groin injury, the Bulls took a surprising 3–2 edge into Game 6 in Chicago Stadium. Midway during the contest Scottie Pippen and New York's Kenny Walker were ejected for a brief flurry of punches. It was a major blow for Chicago, and it came just as Jordan was working his way through a 40-point, 10-assist effort. The Bulls seemed to have things in their grasp with a 111–107 lead with just six seconds left. But the Knicks' Trent Tucker hit a three-pointer, drew the foul, and completed a four-point play to tie it in a sequence that left Collins gasping on the sidelines, as if he couldn't get enough oxygen. MJ now found himself hoping that he could produce yet another miracle, a sequel to his act in Cleveland. This time, John Paxson put the ball in play, and once again Jordan motored into the lane, where he was fouled, knocked down actually, with a couple of seconds to go. He made both, the Knicks missed a good look at the buzzer, and Collins found enough breath for yet another fist-pumping, backslapping celebration at midcourt.

Bad Boys

Chicago was returning to the conference finals for the first time since 1975, when they lost to Golden State. This time they would face the Pistons, and once again the two teams' history was fresh and angry. In an April game, Isiah Thomas had slugged Bill Cartwright and had been suspended for two games. Thomas said privately that he would have preferred to play New York even though the Knicks had been very successful against the Pistons, and Chicago hadn't beaten Detroit all season. He was pushing his team hard to win its first NBA title, and he was concerned about the Bulls. Jordan was on an almost supernatural roll, having come up with brilliant performances to defeat Cleveland and New York.

For Game 1 of the Eastern Conference finals, Collins came out with Jordan playing Thomas. Jordan had gained some comfort at point guard, but this was the first time that Thomas had become his defensive assignment for long stretches. Jordan's height and leaping ability proved something of a distraction on the perimeter. Thomas's shots kept rimming out, which allowed Jordan to back off to let him shoot even more. If Thomas had been on target, Jordan would have been forced to come out farther and play him. Then Thomas could have driven by him, or had a clear path to push the ball inside to Detroit forward Mark Aguirre. But his misses from the perimeter left an impossible situation for the Pistons.

Thomas made just three of eighteen shots that afternoon. "Anytime that he would drive I was in anticipation of that," Jordan said afterward. "I wanted to make him shoot the outside shot, and he didn't hit that today. That's not to say I did an outstanding defensive job."

Detroit's other great jump shooter, "super sub" Vinnie Johnson, was cold, too. The Pistons fell behind by 24 in the second quarter, but they pushed and shoved their way back and retook the lead midway through the fourth period. They couldn't sustain it against Chicago's defense, however, and the Bulls took a 1–0 lead in the series, 94–88. The loss ended Detroit's twenty-five-game home-court winning streak and nine-game playoff winning streak. It also marked the first time in nine games that the Bulls had beaten the Pistons. The home-court advantage the Pistons had worked so hard for all year was gone in one afternoon.

"It's going to be hard to catch them on their heels like we caught them today," Jordan told reporters. "But we have a good chance to win the series."

In the Detroit locker room, the reporters were packed shoulder to shoulder as Thomas remained in the showers longer than usual. The longer he stayed, the larger grew the crowd of reporters waiting to interview him. Finally he emerged, worked through the throng, and sat, his back to the wall, facing a ring of cameras, lights, and microphones.

Just as the questions began flying, teammate Mark Aguirre parted the crowd and bent near to reach some lotion from a large dispenser. "Are we having grits tonight?" Aguirre asked, laughing, trying to break his friend's obvious depression.

Thomas gave a sickly smile and turned his attention to the microphones. One after another, in a calm measured tone, he answered all of the questions. The session went on for forty-five minutes, until the locker room was nearly empty, except for *New York Post* writer Peter Vecsey, who lingered, trying to extract something more from Thomas. *What really happened?*

Thomas finished tying his necktie and sighed heavily. His worst fears about Jordan seemed about to come true. The Detroit guard looked sick. "This is a strange game sometimes," he said.

He grabbed his gym bag and headed for the door. As he hit the hallway, Mike Ornstein, a friend from Los Angeles, stepped up and took the bag. "Let me carry this for you," Ornstein said and slapped Thomas on the back. They rode around aimlessly for several hours after that, Ornstein said later, and Thomas never said a word.

In the press room, columnist Shelby Strother of the *Detroit News* summed up the situation. "He just might die of natural causes," he said of Thomas.

However, there would be no need for any obituaries. Two nights later, Thomas scored 33 and Dumars 20 to carry the Pistons to a 100–91 win, evening the series at one all. The scene then shifted to ancient Chicago Stadium, where the Pistons came out strong on Aguirre's offense. They quieted the crowd, and with seven minutes left held a fourteen-point lead. But just as the fourth quarter seemed like Detroit's time again, Jordan surged, and the Bulls charged back to tie it at 97, leaving the Pistons with possession and twenty-eight seconds on the clock. Thomas worked the ball on the perimeter, and with ten seconds left, Laimbeer stuck out his knee to catch Jordan with an illegal screen. The call returned the ball to Chicago, and Jordan took control at the other end, putting down the shot to give Chicago a 99–97 win and a 2–1 lead in the series.

He had scored 46, the first time in the series that he had put together a solid offensive game. Knowing they couldn't allow that to happen again, the Pistons decided to make Jordan play point guard like a real point guard in Game 4. They double-teamed him and forced him to pass.

"When he puts his mind to it, you can't stop him," Thomas said of Jordan. "That's the whole key. We're hoping you can take his mind off of it."

As usual, Dumars had the primary responsibility with Jordan, but Vinnie Johnson and Thomas both took their turns, as did Rodman. Jordan shot five for fifteen in Game 4. As a team, the Bulls shot 39 percent from the floor. The Pistons shot 36 percent, but it didn't matter. Thomas scored 27, and the defense helped Detroit tie the series at two all with an 86–80 victory.

Afterward, Collins suggested to Jordan that he was taking too many shots and not hitting enough of them. Jordan responded with the sort of childishness that in another age would get a LeBron James excoriated by the press. In the Palace of Auburn Hills for Game 5, Jordan made his point by taking a mere eight shots from the floor. He made four of them for just 18 points, assuring another Detroit win, 94–85. It was the kind of job action that had driven Collins to privately tell Reinsdorf that the team simply could not win with Jordan. Yet the coach's critics again noted that he was the one feeding the monster by tolerating Jordan's every tantrum.

Mostly unaware of the petty drama playing out between the coach and star player, the Chicago crowd was loud for Game 6 in the Stadium. The noise surged early in the first period as Pippen suffered a concussion when he caught a Laimbeer elbow while crashing the boards for an offensive rebound. Pippen suffered no permanent damage, but left the game for the hospital, where he stayed overnight for observation. There was no foul called. Later in the contest, the Pistons center went to the line as the entire building thundered a deafening chant, "Laimbeer sucks! Laimbeer sucks!"

Thomas scored 33 points, as Chicago faltered despite Jordan's 32. Detroit prevailed again, 103–94, to end the series. As Jordan headed toward the bench in the final seconds, he paused to speak with Dumars. "He came by," the Pistons guard said later, "and shook my hand and said, 'Bring it back to the East.' I said, 'I don't miss you, Mike. See you next year.' There's always a fear that giving your most, giving your best, may not be enough with him."

Jordan was angry and frustrated, but he wasn't about to reveal his pain at the loss, Lacy Banks recalled. "He would say, 'Don't let folks know if you're hurting. Don't let other folks know your mind. You know as much about them as possible, but for them to know more about you is to give them an edge.' He hid his frustrations, he hid his sadness, his disappointment, his agony."

In the Chicago locker room, Collins railed against what he called Laimbeer's dirty play. Reporters immediately brought Collins's colorful comments to Laimbeer, who replied that he didn't even know Pippen had been injured until he ran to the other end of the court and looked back to see the trainers gathered around him.

As the media crowd thinned out, filmmaker Spike Lee, who had just begun the process of adapting his Mars Blackmon character to the Air Jordan commercials he was directing for Nike, was making his rounds through the locker room. He paused in front of Isiah Thomas's cubicle to take a few snapshots.

"Spike!" Thomas said. "How ya doin'? I saw you on TV this morning."

Lee offered a sickly smile and exchanged the weakest of handshakes. Jordan may have had a huge financial edge with his Nike endorsements, but Thomas and Detroit still owned the Bulls. The Pistons would go on to claim their first title with a sweep of the Lakers in the next round, and the Bulls would face yet another bout of recrimination, turmoil, and change.

They had suffered two straight setbacks to the Pistons, and a realization was slowly settling on the Bulls. "You couldn't play Detroit in an emotional way," John Paxson said in 1995, looking back. "You couldn't because that's the way they wanted you to play. They wanted to get you out of your game. We didn't have the big banging bodies to play that way, and when we got angry that played right into their hands. Unfortunately, that was Doug's emotional makeup.

"Our crowd would play into that whole thing, too," Paxson added. "And it never worked to our advantage. The Pistons were so antagonistic that it was just hard to maintain that control. It turned out to be a terrific rivalry for us, once we learned how to beat them. But for a while it looked like we were never going to get past them."

On July 6, 1989, Jerry Reinsdorf and Jerry Krause abruptly released Doug Collins, citing management's "philosophical differences" with the coach. It was a stunning move, firing a popular young coach just weeks after he had advanced the team to the conference finals for the first time in fourteen years. The jolting nature of the firing spawned a rash of rumors. The whisper campaign had it that Collins had become involved with a relative of one of the team's many owners. Krause acknowledged at the time that Collins had enjoyed an active social life—so active that Krause had to caution him to tone it down a time or two—but Krause said the rumors were patently untrue.

Krause said Collins was fired for two reasons: One, his intensity had grown too strong and was grinding up both the coach and the team, and two, he lacked an offensive philosophy.

Krause and Collins had clashed frequently over which players the Bulls should acquire, and at one point, the coach had reportedly gone behind the GM's back to Reinsdorf to try to get him fired. The only problem was that Reinsdorf was said to care little for Collins and had hired him only on Krause's recommendation. Collins's power play proved to be unwise.

"Doug didn't get along with Jerry Krause, and on a day-to-day basis, that began to grind on us," Mark Pfeil explained.

"Most of the local media weren't too surprised that Doug was fired," Cheryl Raye-Stout recalled. "There was a lot of anger by the fans. They didn't understand it. The Bulls had gone to Cleveland and won that series, and everybody thought, 'Gosh, Cleveland should have won.' The fans reacted bad, but there was so much tension. There was tension amongst the players; there was tension between Doug and management. It didn't seem like it was gonna be long-term."

"Doug was extremely popular with the media," Krause recalled several years later. "Everybody loved him except me. We were in the Eastern Finals against Detroit when I said to Jerry, 'I want to let Doug go.' Most owners would have said, 'Wait a minute. You brought him in here. He's your creation. He's just won fifty games and got us to the Eastern Finals.' Jerry didn't say that. He said, 'Why?' And I told him I didn't think we could win the world championship this way, and I thought this was a club that could win the world championship. That's the only reason we let Doug Collins go.

"No manager, no matter how strong he is, can fire the head coach without the owner's approval," Krause added. "When I first told Jerry, he said, 'Who do you want to coach the team?' I said, 'I don't want to make that decision until we decide that we're going to let Doug go. Let's decide Doug's merits first.' So we did that. After that, I said, 'I want to hire Phil Jackson.' I'd brought Phil on two years earlier as assistant coach. Jerry said, 'Fine.'"

"Doug's a very emotional guy," Jackson would later say. "He throws his heart into it, and from that standpoint he was very good for this basketball club. He was good at getting them directed to play with intensity and emotion. Then there came a level where they had to learn poise and control." That would be Jackson's assignment.

The team had gotten better each year under Collins's direction. Despite the ongoing conflicts, he did not see the move coming. "We brought Doug into the office," Krause said, "and I think Doug thought he was going to talk about a contract extension. He had his agent with him. I said, 'Doug, we're going to have to let you go.' The look on his face was shocking. We had our conversation with him, and I called Phil, who was fishing out in Montana. I told him, 'I just let Doug go.' He said, 'What?!' And I said, 'Doug's gone, and I want you to be the head coach. You need to get your ass in here on a flight today. Soon as you can. I got to talk to you.'"

In a prepared statement, Collins responded to his release: "When hired three years ago, I willingly accepted the challenge of leading the Bulls back to the type of team this city richly deserves. I'm proud of the fact that each year the team has taken another step towards an NBA championship, and played with intense pride and determination. Words will not describe the void I feel not being a part of Chicago Stadium and this great team."

The firing produced no great complaint from Jordan, Sonny Vaccaro recalled. "There was never a point where I got a phone call, or even a conversation, where Michael said, 'Well, Doug got screwed.' To him, it was like business as usual."

"Everybody liked Doug," John Paxson recalled. "The thing about it was, we had just come off of getting to the conference finals, of taking Detroit to six games. Our future was out there. The coach who had spent three years helping us do that was gone. That's where you give Jerry Reinsdorf and Jerry Krause credit. They truly believed that Doug had been good for that team to a certain point, but that there had to be a different type coach to get us to the next level."

"I think he's learned bitterly from experience," Johnny Bach said of Collins, looking back in 2012. "Doug handled that well. You could see his influence, if you want to go all the way back to Michael's third year in the league, from a young, fiery coach who sees so much and has passion. He was always after the officials and had a verbal strength, in that he was able to say what he saw. But the scene has to be good for you. In basketball you have to please a lot of people and you better win games. I think Doug had a lot to do with Michael growing. They were two people that were flaming, Michael with his game and ferocity, and Doug with his passion and with words. He could translate things in a torrid way."

Collins would later confide to friends that he thought Jackson had undermined him, although he never said so publicly. "That's how Phil came on the job," Lacy Banks observed. "He was the dagger that Krause used to stab Doug Collins in the back."

"Doug had a lot of plays," Jackson recalled in a 1994 interview. "There were forty or fifty plays we ran. We had a lot of options off of plays. We had five or six different offensive sets. You see that with a lot of teams. But that's not where I came from as a basketball coach, and that's not where Tex was philosophically. We believed in Tex's organized system." Krause later explained that he didn't know if his new hire would use Tex Winter's triangle offense. He was aware that Winter and Jackson had grown close while coaching the Bulls' summer league team, just as he had hoped.

"I brought Phil in and we talked philosophy," Krause said. "The first thing he said was, 'I've always been a defensive oriented guy, as a player with Red Holzman, and as a coach. That's what you want me for?' I said, 'Yeah.' He said, 'I'm going to turn the offense over to Tex, and I'm going to run the triple-post.'"

Chapter 23

THE DRIVE-BY WEDDING

For much of the 1988–89 NBA season, Jordan had been able to keep the media away from the story of his new son, until he invited *Sport Illustrated* writer Jack McCallum to a gathering at his home. There McCallum saw Juanita Vanoy hauling around a plump, healthy baby boy. The Bulls were playing at home that night, and McCallum recalled that he was approached by press officer Tim Hallam, who told him that Jordan didn't want anyone writing about the child. The request put McCallum on the spot. He had been allowed into Jordan's inner circle, but he was a journalist. He didn't want to break the news as the major story it was. Instead, McCallum mentioned it at the end of a piece he was writing that week.

Plenty of readers took notice, he recalled, as did Jordan, who was angry. Obviously the disclosing of the situation was not ideal for Jordan's immaculate image. But basketball's young star was proving quite human indeed, something that would become harder and harder to keep from his public.

Once the smoke of the 1989 playoffs had cleared, Jordan made his way through another summer of golfing and questionable living while trying to sort out the big issues of his life. In late August, he met Richard Esquinas, the part-owner, president, and general manager of the San Diego Sports Arena, at a fund-raiser there. They would begin a high-stakes golf relationship that helped feed Jordan's growing taste for golf and gambling—a relationship that later would blow up into scandal. For the time being, though, it was just another pot quietly simmering on the stove in his busy world.

Shortly after meeting Esquinas in San Diego, Jordan and a small entourage slipped over to Las Vegas, where Sonny Vaccaro introduced him to resort and casino magnate Steve Wynn. Vaccaro's brother worked for Wynn, who turned on the hospitality for Jordan and Juanita. While in town, the couple rode over to the Little White Wedding Chapel, famous for its drive-through matrimonial tunnel and its quickie celebrity weddings.

It had been an on-again, off-again betrothal since Jordan had first proposed at Nick's Fishmarket on New Year's Eve 1986. "He just wanted to get it over with," Sonny Vaccaro remembered. "There was nobody there."

Well, actually, Vaccaro and his wife, Pam, were there. And Fred Whitfield. But not many more.

"It was a well-timed decision to settle down and get married," Jordan said later. "It was like walking into another unknown situation. But I was ready to learn what marriage was all about. Every day you learn something. To live with another person for the rest of your life, that's something you have to work at. You're going to have some good times, some bad times. As a couple, as a unit, as a family, you gotta fight your way through it."

It had taken him a while to set aside his parents' concerns. He still relied on them heavily for advice and support. He hadn't wanted to displease them, but with his first child almost a year old, events had finally forced his hand. There was still no peace in the family over the move, Vaccaro said. "His parents didn't want him to be married in the first place. There were other problems when they got married. They didn't like his wife to begin with. But she's a great person. She got him through. I think if it had been a lesser person, if she wasn't as stable, wasn't as educated as she was, he would have been married three times. He'd have had problems with women, not that he didn't. But even more problems. Juanita should get much of the credit for making his life as stable as possible with all the demands that were on him."

Vanoy was "just a very classy lady," Vaccaro observed, not the type of woman who had to make things "all about herself." She was giving and patient, and their ability to converse seemed a key to Jordan's understanding himself and all that was happening to him, Vaccaro added, pointing out that celebrities like Jordan don't often encounter down-to-earth women like Vanoy. His marriage could be added high on the list of Jordan's immense good fortune. As his parents' relationship came apart before his eyes, Jordan now had a new stability that he could turn to. Juanita provided a refuge of home and family and sensibility.

Privacy had long been one of the most precious things in Jordan's life, Lacy Banks said of those days. "He and Juanita had a house in Highland Park off of Lake Cook Road. It was a large house, no mansion or anything. They would build the mansion later, 25,000 square feet. But Michael wasn't the kind of person to throw any soirees or anything like that. If he had any mass gatherings, he went to someone else for it like the golf course or some kind of party room or whatever. But Michael was not the kind of guy to throw any kind of parties with regularity."

One event that the couple made room for each year in their social calendar came on Halloween, when Jordan made arrangements to treat a large number of children from the community. He would make it a no-parents affair, where he could hand out treats to the children personally without the prying eyes of adults eager to gain information about his personal life. It was an activity that he had begun during his earliest seasons in the league and it would later expand, once he had built his mansion in Chicago's north suburbs.

"As he sensed his greatness and as his greatness increased and evolved, he became more aware of what he needed to do to maintain," Lacy Banks explained. "And he also became aware that he had the power to control the traffic in his life. If he didn't want you to be in there, and everybody wanted to be in there—because everybody wanted to be like Mike, be like him, to be with him— you weren't in there. Michael to a great degree was a very secretive person. Like a good gambler. And I can understand it. He couldn't open himself to any- and everybody."

Late in September, Jordan invited Esquinas to his resort home on Hilton Head Island (one of several Jordan properties) for a weekend of golf, gambling, and card games, a weekend he reserved before training camp each year to load up on fun before the long NBA season began. "If it was daylight at all, we were playing golf," Esquinas recalled. "If it was dark, we were playing cards."

Tonk was the hand of choice, the games played in quarters that "looked like something off a plantation," Esquinas said. The three Freds were there, as was Adolph Shiver, and one of the Freds got into it with Shiver, to the point that Jordan had to step in and separate them. It was not a pretty moment for the entourage.

On the final hole of the final day, Esquinas four-putted and lost a bet with Jordan. He promptly wrote a check for $6,500 to cover it.

"E-Man, I don't like to win that way," Jordan told him. Still, he accepted the check, and their intense little game edged up a notch.

The Game of Thrones

As an adolescent, Phil Jackson was said to have played lots of board games with his mother, who was often described as a spirited woman. She had played basketball herself, but that didn't seem to be nearly as important as the fact that she regularly matched wits with her youngest son in a Williston, North Dakota, household that had few modern conveniences, not even a television.

Young Phil lived much in his mind—reading, playing games, and quizzically observing the world—seemingly the natural development of a man who would employ so many mind games in his professional life. He certainly had plenty of challenges to contend with once he assumed head coaching duties for the Bulls. Tops on that list were the two bullies in the organization, Jerry Krause and Michael Jordan, and Jackson himself would come to be described as a bully by others who worked with him. Such figures are common in the world of competition, but the convergence of these three men in an unfolding power game led to great conflict, intrigue, and, ultimately, success for the Bulls.

What made their game most interesting was the fact that they each wielded decidedly different forms of power. Krause had the power of his intelligence, his drive, his vision, and his experience as a scout, which earned him the trust of Jerry Reinsdorf. Krause had behind him the power of the "organization," as he liked to call it.

Jordan had his own power, which has been documented here: his intelligence, his unsurpassed athletic ability, his drive and competitive nature, his work ethic, his charisma, and his great standing in the game. All of that combined to allow Jordan to make a lot of money for himself—and for Jerry Reinsdorf and his partners, as well as the NBA and its players.

Later, Jackson would develop his own great powers, but in those early months on the job, he had his own experience, his ability to relate to players, his very different perspective, his intelligence, his competitive nature, his cunning, and his great powers of observation. It was no small point that he owed everything to Krause, his kingmaker. No one else had had the slightest interest in Jackson, except the New York Knicks, who had taken notice of him as an assistant coach with the Bulls.

Sam Smith once quipped that one of the immediately noticeable things about Krause was that he spent too much time going on and on about his successes. The GM reveled in the role of talent scout, finding young, talented people and helping them advance. For example, he talked often about his bright young assistant, Karen Stack, and her brother Jim, whom he also hired and then promoted. He liked to find hidden talent and watch it work. Being a kingmaker, however, gave him a sense of superiority, which in turn left him feeling free to be brusque and difficult with the people he brought along.

"Jerry has a real gruff side," Jim Stack admitted. "Jerry's a very stubborn guy and a very prideful guy, too."

As an assistant, Jackson had watched Krause's overbearing manner in dealing with Doug Collins and wanted to avoid challenging Krause unnecessarily. When Krause was a young scout and executive working for the Bulls in the 1970s, he had been treated harshly, often ridiculed, by coach Dick Motta, another driven sort who had never played college or even high school basketball. Motta had a knack for motivating his players by humiliating them, but he seemed to reserve a certain scorn for Krause, former Bulls GM Pat Williams recalled.

"Krause and Motta are obsessed people, but in totally different ways," observed Bob Logan, who covered the Bulls for the *Trib* in the 1970s. "They couldn't stand each other, so it was interesting to watch 'em go at each other."

Motta started winning in Chicago, and he was soon offered a job by another team. Krause desperately wanted the Bulls to let Motta go, but the popular coach stayed on and continued tormenting Krause until he drove the chubby young scout out of the organization. That perhaps explained in part Krause's eagerness to dismiss Doug Collins in 1989 right after the team had played its way into the conference finals. That was the last possible opportunity for Krause to get rid of a coach he did not get along with. In another year, if Collins guided the Bulls to the league championship series, it would have been impossible for Krause to remove him. Having reached his position of power, the GM was not about to be undone by a puppy of a coach. Jackson saw that and went out of his way to keep Krause happy.

For his part, Krause had made a new young king, an eager and willing protégé in Jackson. Obviously, it wasn't just his dislike of Collins and his self-preservation that motivated Krause. The GM still had deep respect for Tex Winter and his offensive system. He likewise had long been struck with Jackson. He had a vision that the two men working together could do something special.

In his first position as head coach, Jackson's primary power was his quiet self-confidence. Everybody around him felt it, most importantly Jordan. "If you're gonna coach a player like Michael Jordan, you better have some shit with you," Tim Hallam once observed. "And Phil had some shit with him."

"Phil Jackson, with his approach, probably he and Michael had the best accord," Johnny Bach explained. "They both had reached that stage in their lives where they both knew who they each were."

Collins had many strengths, but his insecurity played out in a difficult way. On a certain level, he wanted to be loved by his players, particularly Jordan, which simply wasn't possible. Jackson, on the other hand, showed little interest in that. "The most important thing is that he has never sought their love," Bach said of Jackson, looking back. "There are many coaches who want to be loved, who have to be loved and go down in flames as a result of it. Pro athletes just aren't going to do that. They aren't going to give you that love if you seek it."

Jackson had a subdued, mirthful view of the game. He enjoyed sitting back and watching players struggle against its impossibilities. As an assistant, he presented something of a mysterious figure. That mystery would only grow when he became head coach—and would become key to the firm grasp he held over his team.

On the Bulls staff, Tex Winter had spent the most time with him. The older coach had first been impressed by the detail and perceptiveness of the scouting reports that Jackson produced. Later, when they coached in summer league together, Winter was stunned by Jackson's seemingly total recall of events in games, even games long in the past. He had a perfect memory, Winter decided.

One of Jackson's first tasks as head coach was to settle the roster. He established a pecking order, Bach recalled. "Phil would explain hierarchy to his team. How many coaches could do that? He'd put that long arm of his way up in the air when he told them. Phil would say, 'Here's what hierarchy is.' He put his hand way up in the air to say, 'That's where Michael is, up there, way up there.' Then he'd come down the ladder, and he'd point to some guy and say, 'This is where you are, way down the ladder.'"

It sounds like a simple thing to do. Everyone on the team knew Jordan was the top dog, but most coaches try to preserve the lie that things are equal when they're not. Jackson got that out of the way from the very start, which left just about everyone involved with an appreciation for his honesty and directness, especially the one who mattered most.

"Michael enjoyed the way Phil coached, he really did," Bach recalled. "And it was different." It would take years for the public to understand just how different.

Jackson's eccentricity was somewhat unsettling for his players. His unique coaching style derived in part from a deeply psychological approach to the game. Both his mother and father were fundamentalist preachers, and he had lived as a child near an Indian reservation. At a young age, he came to love all things Native American, to the point that he checked out every book he could find in the local libraries about Indian culture. In college, he had been fascinated by William James's book *The Varieties of Religious Experience*. As a New York Knick, he had been transformed into a bicycle-riding, dope-smoking hippie. In addition to his Native American philosophies and interests in Zen Buddhism, Jackson soon revealed a way of sitting back and looking at himself and the team. He sought to teach each of his players to achieve his own perspective. Through it all, he exuded the sense that he knew what he was talking about. And of course there were his basketball credentials: championship experience with the Knicks, and his championship team in the CBA.

"People forget he was in the CBA, and being in the CBA was worth thirty years of coaching, because you drove the cars," explained Bach. "You served as a trainer and psychologist, because you had mostly the failures and nuts who couldn't make it in the NBA because they were disrespectful of the game, of their coaches, of their teams. So here you have the have-nots, and he put them together and won a championship.

"You could see Phil had a knack of looking at his teams, not impassionately," Bach added. "He doesn't tip you off to where he is emotionally. He saw a lot, didn't rush in for answers, had a quiet confidence underneath it all. He had played for some fine coaches in Bill Fitch and Red Holzman."

Fitch had coached Jackson at the University of North Dakota and Holzman had guided him with the Knicks. "You're talking about two very different guys," Bach said. "One, Fitch, emotional, tough, and outspoken. The other guy, Holzman, quiet but had learned this business. I played against him as a player. Crafty, a backcourt player. He played for Nat Holman with that fast-passing, moving offense. Red Holzman was one of Nat Holman's beloved players. I think Phil with his unusual background absorbed a lot from them both. He came from North Dakota. His father and mother were tent preachers. He'd been in ROTC."

Jackson soft-pedaled his eccentricities at first. It would take time for him to get his players to accept meditation and mindfulness and his other unique practices. In time, Jordan would take great benefit from Jackson's Zen approach and the mindfulness sessions he provided the team, no matter how unusual they seemed, though he often kept a playful distance in those early years.

"Michael would always have some pithy or irreverent statement to make when Phil tried these things," Bach recalled. "It was nothing disrespectful. Phil is very able to handle relationships like that. I kind of enjoyed Michael's irreverence. It wasn't harmful, wasn't nasty. Michael's humor added that little spark in the coach-player relationship. It was exciting. We would all ask, 'What did Michael say?'"

Some of Jackson's more bizarre practices would be revealed only later, when he coached the Los Angeles Lakers. Chief among them was the drum. In what had to be a first at any level of basketball, Jackson beat a tom-tom on game days. He explained that the ritual had a routine purpose in the lives of the Native Americans, and he wanted the same for his players. The drum was his means of calling them together, to get their hearts pounding for competition.

"I guess the drum is basically for gathering in terms of Indian customs," explained Derek Fisher, who would later play for Jackson in Los Angeles. "They would hit the drum so that people would come together. Whether it was time to eat or time to meet or whatever. He just does that on game days when it's time for us to go in and watch film. It's different. But that's part of who he is, his life experiences. He chooses to share that with his teams."

Jackson evoked the Native American mysticism of the white buffalo (a symbol of rare and special knowledge) and took to burning sage in the locker room in Chicago. "That's done to drive away the evil spirits," Fisher said of the sage. "I think everybody kind of knew that he enjoyed doing different things. And he kind of touched on the things that he would like to do when he first talked to us."

When he first appeared beating the tom-tom and chanting, many players fought to suppress snickers. It was unlike anything they'd seen from other coaches. Perhaps more than anything, it suggested just how confident and persuasive he was, to be able to build acceptance for such practices among his teams. Bach was right: Jackson didn't seek their love, just their acceptance of his unusual approach to the team as an odd cult of sorts.

When he started out in Chicago, Jackson didn't beat the drum as often or as insistently as he did later in Los Angeles. Still, his approach underpinned his desire to share a great intuitive feel for the game with his players. From that shared intuition, Jackson would develop a deep and abiding love for his team. There were Bulls employees who came to dislike him, but even they later talked of Jackson's obvious love for his team, and they admired him for it.

Jackson first had to find a way to protect the team from the destructive potential of its star's megawatt existence. Jordan was twenty-six in 1989 and already awash in fame and fortune. In the rapid-rise nature of American pop culture, he had become something of an instant icon. The circumstances threatened to swamp them all.

First, there was Jordan's growing selfishness, something the star himself would later acknowledge. "I thought of myself first, the team second," he later admitted. "I always wanted my team to be successful, but I wanted to be the main cause."

"I was nervous when I took over the Bulls," Jackson remembered, "but it wasn't the kind of nervousness where you lose sleep at night. I wanted to do well. I was anxious about having a good relationship with Michael. I was anxious about selling him on the direction in which I was going."

Jordan, too, had long been aware of the importance in pro basketball of the relationship between a team's coach and its star player. If a coach couldn't gain the respect of the star, or lost that respect, then the coach would lose the team. It all hinged on that player-coach relationship.

"You knew what Michael was going to give you every single night as a player," Jackson said. "He was gonna get those thirty points; he was gonna give you a chance to win. The challenge was, how to get the other guys feeling a part of it, like they had a role, a vital part. It was just his team, his way."

The next issue was Jordan's stature. As Lacy Banks had said, he was a mesmerizing young prince. "He had such hero worship in the United States among basketball fans that living with him had become an impossibility," Jackson explained.

Since his first days as an assistant coach, he had studied Jordan, and not just on the court. In fact, the coach had always toyed with the Zen fantasy of what it would be like to encounter the young Buddha. Now he knew. "I had roomed on the same floor of hotels as he did," Jackson recalled in 1995. "Michael always had a suite because of who he was, and the coaches got suites, too, because we needed the space for team meetings and staff meetings. Michael basically had to have someone stay in his room with him. I'd hear murmuring in the hallway, and there'd be six or eight of the hotel staff, cleaning ladies, busboys, getting autographs and standing in the hallway with flowers. It was incredible, and he was constantly bothered." To save Jordan from his situation, and to better establish the team identity, Jackson decided to deconstruct some of the world that had built up around the star. The coach knew that would require dealing with the sensitive issue of family and friends.

Jim Stack had become friendly with all of the major figures in Jordan's inner circle, from his father to Adolph Shiver to George Koehler to the Freds. "They just loved Michael," Stack said, "and Michael just took care of them. Adolph was there all the time. Adolph was a very friendly guy and always around but not overbearing in any sense. He just enjoyed the lifestyle and what Michael laid out for him. He was a real confidant for Michael, socially and away from the court. I don't know how they were getting by in terms of employment, but it seemed to me that Michael just sort of took care of him all those years. Michael enjoyed the consistency of seeing them all the time. I think it had a settling effect as to what he did off the court."

Shiver had begun to generate income by hosting parties for NBA players at the All-Star Game each year, a business that expanded steadily with his Jordan connection. Howard White, Sonny Vaccaro, and eventually Fred Whitfield were all employed by Nike. Koehler, Gus Lett, and a variety of others were there in security or service capacities.

"Traveling in airports, he needed an entourage to get through," Jackson acknowledged. "He had brought people along on the road with him. His father would come. His friends would come on the road. He had just a life that sometimes alienated him from his teammates. It became a challenge to make him part of the team again and still not lose his special status because he didn't have the necessary privacy."

Even so, Jackson decided there would be limits. "So I knew," he recalled, "that we had to make exceptions to the basic rules that we had: 'Okay, so your father and your brothers and your friends can't ride on the team bus. Let's keep that a team thing. Yeah, they can meet you on the road, but they can't fly on the team plane. There has to be some of the team stuff that is ours, that is the sacred part of what we try to do as a basketball club.'"

That was another thing that set the agenda and would eventually leave the team's PR assistants rolling their eyes. Jackson threw around the word *sacred* like the son of "tent preachers" that he was. Jackson had that sanctimoniousness that great coaches like John Wooden always seemed to have. It made losing to them so hard for other coaches to stomach.

The Scrum

There were further complications, in that Jordan's circle was beginning to include media figures, including broadcasters Quinn Buckner and Ahmad Rashad. A former NFL receiver, Rashad worked for both NBC Sports as a sideline reporter and the NBA's entertainment division as host of *Inside the NBA*. Rashad was a picture of the changing face of media. He brought a certain charm and stylish sophistication, a departure from the gritty old days of lumpy guys with notebooks and microphones and drab clothes. The media was changing, just as MJ and the league were changing.

Rashad's relationship with Jordan proved to be spun gold for Rashad, as it was for Jordan himself, who was always on the lookout for media interpreters that he could trust. "It was good for Ahmad, because he was a football guy," explained Matt Guokas, who later worked at NBC with Rashad. "Now all of a sudden he was put into a sport that he knew only as a fan. He really didn't know it like he knew football. Then he's asked to be a sideline guy and come up with little stories and that kind of thing and to develop relationships with players. It's not the easiest thing in the world except that

Ahmad is and was a personable guy. He got along with everybody. He developed that relationship with Michael. Once again it was through the Nike thing. I used to go on those Nike trips when I was coaching and Ahmad would always be there and somewhat involved, as a guest of Michael or whatever. And every time that Michael went to New York they would get together and go out. And every time that we went to Chicago, Ahmad would go out with him or to his house or wherever. They just had that close relationship. And Ahmad did not abuse it. He did not break any confidences."

Jordan became known for such alliances. In his first seasons, he became friendly with Mark Vancil, a *Sun-Times* reporter who later turned freelancer and produced several elegant and informative picture books with Jordan, and with Michael Wilbon, a Chicago native who wrote sports for the *Washington Post*.

Bulls press officer Tim Hallam had been around long enough to witness most of this change, and noticed that a certain unseemliness still lingered. Hallam was fond of calling that tight circle of media around Jordan each night the "pig fuck." After every game, two dozen or so sportswriters and camera crews would crowd around the star, pressing their questions, squeezing in ever closer to catch every word. Hallam got it that Jordan craved the spotlight, but could never figure out why he insisted on the "pig fuck" in the steamy locker room after every game. Jordan had taken to showering in private quarters and dressing in what had become a seemingly endless supply of immaculate, perfectly tailored suits. He'd return to his locker looking as if he'd walked right out of the pages of *GQ*, and then he'd take position among the reporters as they'd push in around him. The klieg lights of their cameras would bounce a dazzling white on his familiar onyx pate, broken only by the tiniest rivulets of sweat as he held forth on the game he had just played.

As the crowd grew with each succeeding season, Hallam reasoned that it would have been much easier to hold a postgame news conference in an interview room with the star standing at a podium, but Jordan wanted to meet the crowd in the steamy, strangely primal locker room. Why would he want to take those fine suits into that crowd, Hallam wondered. But intimacy was the

382 | MICHAEL JORDAN

very essence of the pig fuck. Jordan knew that some detached, sterile news conference would never do. He wanted to be at the center of that huddle of reporters as much as they wanted to crowd in around him. Meanwhile, his teammates were left each night to eye the mass with a mix of awe and disdain. Occasionally, they would garner some attention, but Jordan had come to live in the scrum. The stories and reports filed by the media radiated that closeness. The media referred to him as Michael, as if each of them knew him well and had shared a personal audience. As a result, millions of people the world over came to know him on that first-name basis. Michael.

Fans soon came to treasure that relationship, as if they too had special access to him, special insight into what he thought and felt. Yes, Babe Ruth and others had inhabited their own eras, but rarely had a mere athlete managed to convey so completely the experience to his fans. With Jordan, it went beyond kinship. It was decidedly personal. His talent and accomplishments—his absolute superiority—became theirs. They knew him. They could predict his successes, then gloat about them afterward. He was more reliable than any other soul in their lives. Most important, it was beyond race. If only Dawson Jordan could have been there to see it.

"He became more than a basketball player," longtime NBA reporter David Aldridge observed. "No black athlete had ever had that happen before. Nobody had had that happen before. As great as Ali was, and Ali was obviously viewed as more than a boxer, he sort of took this anti-commercial position. On everything Jordan was the first black athlete, not just to cross over, but I mean, to become an icon of popular culture."

Even the idolized white athletes from earlier eras, commercialized figures such as Mickey Mantle, had not had the opportunity to achieve such a status in the culture, Aldridge reasoned. "Nobody had done that before. His importance, in that regard, I think has always been somewhat underplayed. You know, it's no small thing that middle-aged, white, conservative males felt okay with their teenaged white sons or their teenaged white daughters having Jordan posters up in their rooms. That was not nothing. That's a big deal."

* * *

Aldridge would later move to ESPN and Turner Broadcasting, but during the 1989–90 season he was still a *Post* reporter following the Washington Bullets and was just beginning to get comfortable talking to Jordan in those last months when the star was still easily accessible to reporters in the Bulls locker room. He encountered Jordan, who was affable and eager to engage the media that fall. Only later would it become clear that Jordan had a hidden agenda: he hoped to gather information about his opponents around the league. "In that old Chicago Stadium locker room, his was the first locker when you came in, on the right, and he'd be sitting there and, you know, would talk," Aldridge remembered. "He was a different guy back then. He really picked your brain about the team you were covering. What's going on with this guy or that guy, or why are they doing this? He seemed genuinely interested in different teams around the league. He was very receptive and liked talking to reporters back then. He seemed to enjoy the kind of give and take that you have. I remember thinking, 'Gosh, for a guy who has got as much attention on him as this guy, he's as close to normal as you could possibly expect.'

"You could talk to him," Aldridge explained. "You could talk to a lot of the people that he was close to. Even then, he was close to Fred and Adolph and all those guys. I didn't think of them as, just kind of like, hangers-on. Howard White was pretty established at Nike, and I knew that Fred Whitfield was a very smart guy, financially. I never did think of those guys as sycophants. You know, I always thought, 'This guy did this for him and this guy did this for him.' And that's how it rolls."

Of all the changes that Jackson sought to make, limiting the media availability to the team was perhaps the easiest. With the league having added five new expansion teams, Jackson wanted to keep the increasing numbers of fans and reporters at bay. They encroached on what the coach saw as the team's essential space. Jackson provided some protection for Jordan just as his fame was about to surge yet again, while raising the profile of the entire league.

"I got a curtain for our practice facility, so that practice became our time together," the coach explained. "It was just the twelve of us and the coaches, not the reporters and the television cameras. It wasn't going to be a show for the public anymore. It became who are we as a group, as people....Michael had to break down some of his exterior. You know that when you become that famous person you have to develop a shell around you to hide behind. Michael had to become one of the guys in that regard. He had to involve his teammates, and he was able to do that. He was able to bring it out and let his hair down at the same time. Over his years in pro basketball, Michael had learned to mark out his own territory. He had his own stall at every arena where he might find the most privacy, or he might find a territory in the trainer's room. He had two stalls in the old Chicago Stadium. That was his spot because there were twenty-five reporters around him every night. We continued the protocol of all that, but we also made efforts to create space for him within the team. If we hadn't done that, the rest of the world was going to overrun us, if we hadn't done things the right way. So we said, 'Let's not all suffer because of his fame. Let's give ourselves space and exclude the crowd.' I guess I created a safe zone, a safe space for Michael. That's what I tried to do."

Jackson made his subtlest move of all in defining the small group of players and coaches as "the team," apart from the rest of the organization, particularly "management." In so doing, the coach was drawing a tight circle, a boundary, for keeping Jerry Krause separate from the team. Although he made no definitive steps to enforce this boundary, Jackson established it all the same. First, it made sense to separate Jordan from Krause, since the GM always seemed to set the star off with one comment or another. Besides, Jackson could see that Jordan naturally liked keeping the circle around him tight. Such shrewd moves went a long way toward helping Jackson establish a comfort zone in his relationship with his star. The coach made an effort in those early years to accommodate his overbearing and aggressive boss while working to shield Jordan from him as often as possible. It wasn't so much that Jordan needed protection as it was that the team didn't need the turmoil.

"Phil, he really separated players and management," Jim Stack recalled. "He kept the players in a circle and management was outside the circle. As time went on, there was some stuff that Jerry could have diffused and handled better. Jerry probably would tell you that himself." Stack operated in both worlds, because he worked with Krause yet also scouted for the coaching staff. In time, it became more difficult to cross over between the two, he recalled. The barriers became more pronounced, as did the conflict, as Krause pushed against the boundaries that Jackson tried to establish. But in his first years as coach, Jackson was concerned with finding a balance that allowed them all to get along and prosper.

Jackson got help from Winter and Bach, and new assistant Jim Cleamons, easily the best coaching staff in basketball. For all their experience, they marveled that first season as Jackson took control of the team and built strong, open relationships with the players, especially Jordan. Like Winter before him, Jackson, as an assistant coach, had been a bit wary of Jordan. But the two men soon found themselves enjoying the give-and-take of their individual meetings. Jackson confirmed his belief that Jordan was extremely bright, able to discuss things and to challenge him in conversation and debate. Jackson was eager to engage his players and, more than anything, to put them in position to win.

"I think Phil came in with the basis of some very sound philosophy," Tex Winter recalled, looking back several years later. "I mean the philosophy of life. He recognizes that there are a whole lot of things more important than basketball. He doesn't take himself too seriously. We all take basketball pretty seriously at times. Even then, he's inclined to relax. I'm amazed at times in the course of the game how he sits back and lets things happen. He likes people to be able to solve their own problems, and so he gives his players the reins. On the other hand, when he sees they're out of control, then he starts to pull them in a little bit. I think this is his strength, the way he handles the players and his motivation, his personal relationship with the players. That's borne out by the fact that they'll accept his coaching, they'll accept the criticism, even though sometimes it's pretty severe with certain players. They accept that because it's who he is, because he's Phil."

In a few short months, the coaching climate around the team

had improved. Many challenges remained, but the mind-set had shifted. "It was a magical combination of a team that needed its coaches and coaches who needed the players," Bach said in 2012. "And no one was in the way. There was no ego, no need for someone to have more fame than the rest. They were ideal situations. As I look back on it, the best days of my life."

Chapter 24

THE TRANSITION

Dᴇꜰᴇɴꜱᴇ ᴅᴏᴍɪɴᴀᴛᴇᴅ Pʜɪʟ Jackson's first training camp as coach of the Bulls. He had been a baseline-to-baseline player for the Knicks, and he wanted the same for his Bulls. "See the ball," Red Holzman used to tell his New York teams in terms of pressure defense. Jackson certainly wanted them to have vision, but it was first and foremost a matter of conditioning. To play defense for Jackson, you had to be able to reach those higher gears and stay there.

"When Phil came in, our first training camp was as difficult a camp as I'd ever had," Paxson recalled. "It was defensive-oriented. Everything we did was, start from the defensive end and work to the offensive end. Phil basically made us into a pressure-type team. Defensively, he knew that was how we would win."

"We were gonna play full-court pressure defense," Jackson said. "We were gonna throw our hearts into it."

That required a competitive focus, and Jackson figured to build that by turning Jordan and Pippen loose on each other. They had been pitted against each other in Pippen's rookie year, but now Jackson made a priority and a habit of it.

"Phil took over," Johnny Bach recalled, "and I think he found the right mix for Michael and Scottie and the younger players. And what it was, was heavy competition, so that Michael each day had in front of him Scottie Pippen. A lot of times Phil would put Scottie with the best team and put Michael with the irregulars. The competition was fierce. Phil would seek to do this very quietly, not overtly. It would be a game to ten baskets, and the losers would have to do some silly thing like running a set of sprints or something. If it was only one game and Michael lost it, he might say, 'Hey, Phil, we're going another ten.' We'd go ten more baskets. It was probably exactly what Phil wanted, but he was always like, 'Well, let's see....I don't know if we can....Okay, if you want to throw it up, let's go.'"

"The competitive angle was good," Bach said in another interview, in 2004, his eyes sparkling at the memory. "Scottie learned at the hand of the king. I always said of Scottie, 'Here's the pretender to the throne, and of Michael, here's the king sitting there.' I think Scottie had to learn that way. Come every day, and play every day hard. And find that game that he did, of being on top of the floor, bringing the ball up the floor, and being just a physical tormenter on defense with those extended arms. He had like Michael a little bit of that joyous smile. He enjoyed what was going on."

The effort brought immediate returns, Bach recalled. "Pippen got better. Now, he had to play Michael every day. That would give you a headache. Practices were very intense in those days."

And not just for the team's two stars. Rookie guard B. J. Armstrong from Iowa was pitched against veteran John Paxson. The competition triggered a dislike between the two that added to the intensity of practices.

"That was one of Phil's dictums," Bach explained. "He wanted competition between them."

Whatever improvement the Bulls made under Jackson would hinge on the maturing of Pippen and Grant, the two young players with the most potential to give the defense its bite. As the schedule opened there was a sense that they had grown. "He's on the cusp of greatness," Bach said that fall of Pippen. "He's starting to do the kinds of things only Michael does."

"It's just a matter of working hard," Pippen said. "I've worked to improve my defense and shooting off the dribble. I know I'm a better spot-up shooter, but I'm trying to pull up off the dribble when the lane is blocked."

In addition to Armstrong, Krause had brought in two other rookies, all three in the first round, including center/forward Stacey King and forward Jeff Sanders. That August, Krause had re-signed free agent guard Craig Hodges, and picked up an old standby in a trade with Phoenix, forward Ed Nealy, who became a favorite of both Jackson and Jordan with his earthbound brawn and willingness to hustle.

The team developed some confidence as they moved through the preseason undefeated in eight games. Yet everyone knew the Bulls still had to get comfortable with Winter's strange new offense. And then there was the matter of Cartwright, who was something of a loner on the team. Jordan still openly resented the big center, who seemed to have trouble catching the ball in traffic. The triangle meant he was going to have the ball more than ever.

Time to Read

On opening night, Jordan scored 54 in Chicago Stadium in a duel with Cleveland's Ron Harper, who finished with 36. The Bulls won in overtime but lost the next night to Boston. Three nights later, they beat the Pistons by 3 in the Stadium as Jordan scored 40. It was obvious the Bulls were doing different things on offense, but their early efforts were almost hard to recognize as the triangle.

After a West Coast road trip, they finished November with an eight and six record, and it became clearer that Jackson's decision to use Winter's pet system was a major gamble. Winter had spent years developing his triple-post offense, an old college system that involved all five players sharing the ball and moving. Winter had used it successfully everywhere he coached in college, where he had enough practice time to teach it. But in his one NBA head coaching job with the Houston Rockets in the 1970s, he had gotten fired after star Elvin Hayes refused to learn the system. By the 1990s, the triangle remained totally foreign to most pro players. With their heavy schedules, professional teams simply didn't have the necessary practice time. But Jackson was determined to have an offense that featured ball movement, and he certainly had the backing of management. Winter, however, knew better than anyone that the switch would require nothing short of a revolution.

For years the pro game had worked on isolation plays and one-on-one setups, while the triple-post, or triangle, used very little in the way of set plays. Instead the players learned to react to situations and to allow their ball movement to create weaknesses in defenses. Doing that meant that the players virtually had to relearn the game, from Winter's own peculiar interpretation of the fundamentals to the way they approached the floor. No longer were they merely running through rote plays. They now had to learn to stop and read and react to the defense. It was as if each position was played like a quarterback, particularly for the guards and wings.

The offense focused on the post with a wing on each side, positioned high and extended out from the foul line to create spacing. More important, it was a two-guard front, which meant that the guards aligned together, spaced apart at the top of the floor. One of them would initiate the first pass, then "fill the corner," or take position in either corner of the half-court, which would require a defender to move with him. This immediately created an unbalanced floor and gave the remaining four players, especially Jordan, room to work. Understandably, the man filling the corner had to be a reliable three-point shooter, which made Paxson and Hodges ideal.

The offense did not feature a traditional penetrating point guard. Winter wanted the defense penetrated mostly with the pass. The rule of thumb was that it often took two years or more to gain true comfort in Winter's system.

For that reason, the coaches agreed to modify the triangle to a one-guard front that first season. They were going to ease the team into it. Even so, only Winter fully understood the offense, which meant that Jackson turned over huge amounts of the practice to him. Soon enough, Winter was virtually organizing and running entire sessions, which was remarkable power ceded to an assistant coach. Suddenly, he went from the elderly advisor nobody paid attention to, to the man running the show.

"There were a lot of competitive people put together in that offense, which Tex alone could run," Bach recalled. "And Phil was the ideal coach, who could step away and say, 'Players have to find their tempo. The players have to improve. They have to handle a lot of situations. I'm not here to settle every single thing.' Phil was able to do it. He was really great."

The key test was Jordan, a player who was already a master at reading the floor. The triangle required that the most highly skilled players, the guards, share the ball with the less skilled, the post players. That would lead to some turnovers, Jordan saw immediately.

He chafed at what he came to call the "equal opportunity" offense.

"It took some time," Paxson recalled. "Michael was out there playing with these guys, and unless he had a great deal of respect for them as players, I think he figured, 'Why should I pass them the ball when I have the ability to score myself or do the job myself? I'd rather rely on myself to succeed or fail than some of these other guys.'"

"The more he learned about it, the more he saw how steadfastly Tex believed in it," Bach said of Jordan. "And Phil was the head coach and he was saying how things were going to be. It was like a gold mine. You got players in the system, seeing it, and prospering."

But that took much selling by Jackson, and months with the team under Winter's instruction. At first, the primary selling points for the triangle were that it brought floor balance and it gave Jordan room to work. Both were obvious. The floor balance alone made the Bulls a better defensive team right away, because the offense always left a guard at the top of the key ready to "get back" on defense. The coaches knew they could win some games on this ability to defend in transition.

"Whatever offense you teach, you must be able to defend after the shot is taken," Bach offered. "You have a duty to know where to go. Tex's offense gave you the balance and the ability."

The transition was not easy. Some observers, such as Chicago *Tribune* reporter Sam Smith, sensed an atmosphere bordering on mutiny over Jackson's first two seasons as Jordan's frustration built. Jackson worked against this by playing the good cop to Tex Winter's bad cop.

"I've always been very much impressed with Michael as well as everyone else has been," Tex Winter said, looking back. "I've never been a hero worshiper. I saw his strong points, but I also saw some weaknesses. I felt like there was a lot of things that we could do as a coaching staff to blend Michael in with the team a little bit better. I thought he was a great player, but I did not feel that we wanted to go with him exclusively. We wanted to try and get him to involve his teammates more. Until he was convinced that that was what he wanted to do, I don't think we had the chance to have the program that we had later down the line."

Different types of players reacted to the offense differently. For guards and wings, there was much to learn. Post players had less of a challenge, but running the triangle required a change in the instinctive way that most pros had learned to play.

"For me it was great," recalled John Paxson. "A system offense is made for someone who doesn't have the athletic skills that a lot of guys in the league have. It played to my strengths. But it tightened the reins on guys like Michael and Scottie from the standpoint that we stopped coming down and isolating them on the side. There were subtleties involved, teamwork involved. But that was the job of Phil to sell us on the fact we could win playing that way."

It helped tremendously that Jordan had played in a system at North Carolina, Winter explained, looking back. But it also may have added to his skepticism.

"Everything was geared toward the middle, toward the post play," Jordan recalled. "We were totally changing our outlook...and I disagreed with that to a certain extent. I felt that was putting too much pressure on the people inside."

Jackson brought Jordan into his office and said, "The ball is like a spotlight. And when it's in your hands, the spotlight is on you. And you've gotta share that spotlight with some of your teammates by having them do things with the basketball, too."

"I know that," Jordan replied. "It's just that when it comes down to getting the job done, a lot of times they don't want to take the initiative. Sometimes it's up to me to take it, and sometimes that's a tough balance."

Making these changes would require much patience. The operative phrase became that Jordan was "going to have to learn to trust his teammates."

"There were times when Michael knew he was going to get 40 points," Jackson said. "He was just hot those nights. He was going to go on his own, and he would just take over a ball game. We had to understand that that was just part of his magnitude, that was something he could do that nobody else in this game could do. And it was going to be okay. Those weren't always the easiest nights for us to win as a team. But they were certainly spectacular nights for him as a showman and a scorer."

The process tested Jackson's brand-new relationship with Jordan. Yet it also provided the opportunity for that relationship to deepen. It wasn't just his teammates that Jordan was learning to trust. It was his coaches as well.

"A lot of times," Jackson explained, "my convincing story to Michael was, 'We want you to get your 30-some points, and we want you to do whatever is necessary. It's great for us if you get 12 or 14 points by halftime, and you have 18 points at the end of the third quarter. Then get your 14 or 18 points in the fourth quarter. That's great. If it works out that way, that's exactly what it'll be.' Who could argue with that? We'd tell him, 'Just play your cards. Make them play everybody during the course of the game and then finish it out for us.'"

Later, Winter would look back and marvel at Jackson's determination to stick with the offense and his persuasiveness with Jordan. They didn't know it at the time, but they were embarking on the most remarkable era in pro basketball history, rooted in the great discipline Jordan and his teammates began developing that first year.

"Phil was definitely set on what we were going to do and he wouldn't waver," Winter recalled. "Even though the triple-post offense evolved through my many, many years of coaching, Phil was sold on it even more than I was at times. There's times when I would say. 'We should get away from this. Let Michael have more one-on-one opportunities.' And Phil was persistent in not doing so. It's to his credit that we stayed to his basic philosophy of basketball."

Their philosophy, their system, made Jackson's Bulls unlike any other team in the NBA.

As Christmas presents that first year as head coach, Jackson began the practice of giving his players books. He gave Jordan a copy of Toni Morrison's *Song of Solomon,* the allegorical story of a man searching for gold. The team's transition unfolded in fits and starts that December. Jackson's Bulls would find bursts of momentum and go on winning streaks. First came a five-game run right before the holidays, then another five heading into the New Year. The offense continued to struggle, but the defense came alive. Across the league, other coaches began talking about it—and fearing it.

By January the offense had come together enough for the Pistons to take notice after beating the Bulls by 10 in Detroit. Even though they had won, Joe Dumars recalled spotting a new challenge. "I went back to Isiah after the game and I said, 'We've got a problem.' He said, 'What? What are you talking about?' I said, 'This is going to cause some problems. Where he is on the court with the angles and stuff. That now causes major problems for me.' Before when he just had the ball out front and he was going one-on-one, he was facing everybody and you could see where he was. And I knew where the help was, but when he caught that ball in the post in the triangle and guys started cutting, I didn't know where help was going to come from then. So I knew the very first game they ran the triangle, we had a problem, and we won the game. But he was flashing from the weak side, he was in the post. He was in new spots where we had never had to double him like that before. When we did double, he just threw it in and waited and then everybody cut. With the triangle, you throw it in, guys cut baseline. I knew this was going to be a problem."

"We saw immediately that it was going to be harder to double-team Jordan with the Bulls using the triangle," Brendan Malone recalled.

For the first time in his four seasons in the NBA, Dumars recalled taking note of that older gent on the Bulls' bench. It was Tex Winter. The triangle guy. Across the league, opponents began making the same discovery.

"Tex's offense emulated the offense I had played in with New

York," Jackson explained. "The ball dropped into the post a lot. You ran cuts. You did things off the ball. People were cutting and passing and moving the basketball. And it took the focus away from Michael, who had the ball in his hands a lot, who had been a great scorer. That had made the defenses all turn and face him. Suddenly he was on the back side of the defenses, and Michael saw the value in having an offense like that. He'd been in an offense like that at North Carolina. It didn't happen all at once. He started to see that over a period of time, as the concepts built up."

The offense showed promise, but Jordan wasn't yet convinced the team itself was ready to win a championship. He began calling for changes in the roster in advance of the 1990 trade deadline in February. The fans also complained that the Bulls' front office needed to make a move right away.

Once again, Jordan called for the acquisition of Walter Davis. "What turned the tide was when Michael told us we needed to go out and get Walter Davis," Jim Stack remembered. "It was like do or die that year, that '89–'90 season. Michael said we wouldn't be able to win the way we were constituted."

Krause sent Stack out on the road for about ten days scouting Davis, to see if he could help the Bulls. "Walter Davis was, I felt, basically done defensively," Stack recalled. "The way Phil was coaching, Davis was not going to be able to guard the guys like Mark Aguirre, Xavier McDaniel, Larry Nance. Indiana had Chuck Person. There were a lot of gifted, physically strong small forwards in the Eastern Conference. He physically was not going to be able to guard the guys we needed to guard. So we didn't make a move at the trade deadline."

The Calm

In February, the Bulls began to falter again, and during a West Coast road trip things reached a low point with four straight losses. Even worse, Cartwright missed several games as he struggled with sore knees. The All-Star break in Miami quieted some of the noise. Pippen joined Jordan on the Eastern squad for the first time, and

Hodges won the three-point shootout by making nineteen straight shots.

Jordan and Dumars hadn't known each other personally until that All-Star Weekend, when Jordan phoned to invite Dumars and his wife, Debbie, up to the Jordans' room for dinner and conversation. The couples hit it off that evening, and the two men advanced their friendship. "Our wives talk all the time," Jordan said later that year of the budding relationship. "We had the opportunity to play with him at the All-Star Game and see him on the social side. I'd always admired his athletic ability and basketball talent, and a good friendship has been built. There's a mutual respect because of the talents we have to put against each other when we play.... But we can't get too close now because we have to compete against one another. It's hard to compete against a good friend. To compete against a good friend, you tend to get a little bit relaxed and joke around a little bit too much when you should be serious. But that won't happen because we both are focused on what we have to do for our respective teams."

The Bulls resumed their pursuit for chemistry after the All-Star Game and continued to search out a feel for the offense. In late March they launched into a nine-game winning streak that was ignited by Jordan's all-time best scoring performance, 69 points in an overtime win against Cleveland. He also took in a career-high 18 rebounds that night. He made 23 of 37 field goal attempts from the floor and 21 of 23 free throws. He also had 6 assists, 4 steals, and just 2 turnovers in fifty minutes of playing time. As stupendous as it was, Jordan's outburst hardly fit the ideal of Winter's ball-sharing offense.

Like nearly everything else, Jackson used it as a teachable moment, Johnny Bach recalled. "Michael had a huge night of scoring. I know Phil used that. It was presented the way Phil could present things. It was, 'You're this good, but you're going to have to make a couple of our other players better.'"

Jordan might not have heard the message from any other coach, but there was something in Jackson's approach that began to get through. It began with his remarkable patience and apparent serenity, evidenced first by his ability to sit calmly during games and watch the action. Bach marveled at the difference between Collins and Jackson. "This guy would be worn out. Sweat was pouring off of him, veins were bulging," he said of Collins. "Doug had given every ounce of his energy. Phil on the other hand had this ability to sit there through the evening. He could walk off afterward and nod to people. He might have reached that same fever pitch as Collins had during the game. Phil had reached that pitch internally, but he never showed it externally."

Bach especially admired Jackson in the heat of games. "Phil was at his best in that cauldron," he said. "Like the psychologist that he is, he's going to find a very different approach to solving problems. He will not get in your face and say, 'Let's get this settled now.'"

Both Bach and Winter would find themselves pushing him to call time-outs during stretches when the team was obviously struggling. "Phil would just look at me," Bach remembered. Both Winter and Bach decided they would request a time-out twice, and if Jackson didn't respond they would stop pushing. "He has this strength, this resolve," Bach said, "to endure whatever the results are."

Jordan had quickly come to identify with Jackson's calm. In that respect, Jackson reminded him of Dean Smith. Rick Fox, who also played for Smith and later for Jackson, agreed that the two were much the same in their on-court demeanor, except for the profanity that decorated Jackson's speech.

Jackson rarely raised his voice in dealing with his team after games. He was often consoling after losses, focusing on their effort. He would later sit with Winter for hours, studying videotape of each game and planning practices and adjustments.

"He is a hands-on manager, but with a different approach in every way," Bach explained. "It's deeply psychological. It's from the heart, except that he's able to separate it from his emotions. He's sort of a mystery to the players because he is not predictable. He doesn't overreact, or sometimes even react at all. Yet he has a firm hand. The great strength of Phil is that he is always very aware of what is happening. He could see things on the bench, or in the locker room, but he never moved too quickly to fix things. He would only do that after he had thought about it. Then he would do just what was needed to calm the situation and the problem."

Because he didn't have to make play calls constantly, the triangle also contributed to Jackson's calm. "You see coaches running up and down the sidelines all the time making a play call, which to me, especially in playoff series, plays into your hand," Paxson observed. "If you scout well, you know how to defend against those set plays. Phil sold us, then made us believe the more subtle you are on your offense, the more successful you're going to be. You can do some damage if you're reading the other team's defense and reacting rather than worrying about calling some play that the coach wants from the sideline."

Detroit Once Again

The win streaks propelled them to a 55–27 finish, good for second place in the Central Division behind the sixty-win Pistons, the defending world champions (who defeated the lakers for the 1989 title). Almost every night, Jordan had led them in scoring, but Pippen had emerged as a threatening defender who could also run the offense like a point guard. Few teams had a means of matching up with him, particularly when they also had to worry about Jordan. Once again Jordan harvested another batch of honors: All-NBA, All-Defense, and his fourth consecutive scoring title. Plus he led the league in steals.

The Bulls lost to Detroit in the last game of the regular season, their third straight defeat at the hands of the Pistons, which sent Jackson's team into the playoffs with Jordan harboring hard feelings about some of his teammates' inability to contribute to the cause. Pippen was playing well, and Jordan's feelings softened in the first round as Chicago dumped Milwaukee three games to one. In the next round, against Philadelphia and Charles Barkley, Jordan was nothing short of overwhelming. He averaged 43 points, 7.4 assists, and 6.6 rebounds as the Bulls advanced in five games, despite the fact that Pippen's seventy-year-old father died during the series, and he missed a game to fly home to Arkansas for the funeral.

"I never played four consecutive games like I did against Philly," Jordan would say later.

For the third straight year, the Bulls' season would be defined by a bruising battle with the Pistons, once again in the conference finals. In essence, it was the big exam for Jackson's new style of play.

Recalling the playoffs the year before, when Bill Laimbeer knocked him out of Game 6 with an elbow to the head, Pippen said, "There were times a few years before the flagrant foul rules, when guys would have a breakaway and [the Pistons] would cut their legs out from under them. Anything to win a game. That's not the way the game is supposed to be played. I remember once when Michael had a breakaway, and Laimbeer took him out. There was no way he could have blocked the shot. When you were out there playing them, that was always in the back of your mind, to kind of watch yourself."

As Jordan predicted, his developing friendship with Dumars did nothing to dull the competition between their two teams. The Pistons continued to flaunt their much-ballyhooed "Jordan Rules," which were really just simple common sense: Force Jordan to give up the ball. Gang up on him as much as possible, knock him to the floor. And make things really ugly. The matchup always seemed to inspire the worst sort of paranoia among the Bulls—both players and coaches—who seethed over videotapes the Detroit coaching staff had sent to the league offices suggesting that Jordan was benefitting from too many unwarranted foul calls. Earlier in the playoffs, Detroit's John Salley had pointed out for reporters that the Pistons were a team and the Bulls were a one-man show. "There's not one guy who sets the tone on our team," Salley remarked with a smile. "That's what makes us a team. If one guy did everything, we wouldn't be a team. We'd be the Chicago Bulls."

Indeed, Jordan's own teammates were quite aware of the difficulty of playing alongside their leader. As former teammate Dave Corzine had once pointed out, if anything went wrong for the team, it was never Jordan's fault. Somebody else always took the blame. Despite the best efforts of the coach to install the ball-sharing triangle, Jordan still dominated the club, to the point that Craig Hodges and others referred to him as "The General."

True to form, the Pistons slammed Jordan around in Game 1 of the 1990 conference finals. Detroit hit only 33 of 78 from the floor, and one of those was an Isiah Thomas lob pass to John Salley that inadvertently went in the basket. As always, the Pistons' hell-for-leather defense saved them. "It was more like a rugby match," Phil Jackson said glumly.

The key effort for Detroit was 27 points and plenty of defense from Dumars. He slowed Jordan to 34 points. The rest of the Chicago starters scored a total of 31, which was enough for a blueprint Bad Boys win, 86–77, and a confirmation of Salley's snide remark.

Jordan got banged up after flying high into the lane in the first quarter. A group of Pistons led by Dennis Rodman laid him down on the floor, bruising his hip. "I think I had my legs cut out from under me," he said afterward. "And if so, I don't know who did it. I think it's the type of injury that could linger."

It did linger, at least into the next battle. The Pistons snatched a 43–26 lead in the middle of the second quarter of Game 2, while Jordan opened stiffly. Chicago trailed 53–38 at the half, when Jordan entered the locker room, kicked a chair, and stormed at his teammates, "We're playing like a bunch of pussies."

Chastised, they returned to the floor in the second half with much more energy. And Jordan finally warmed enough to put the Bulls back in front, 67–66, at the 8:24 mark of the third period. But it was short-lived. Dumars finished with 31 points on 12 of 19 from the floor, giving the Pistons a 2–0 series lead with a 102–93 win. Meanwhile, Jordan made just 5 of 16 shots to finish with 20 points. Immediately afterward, he ripped into the Bulls for their uninspired performance and left the locker room without speaking to reporters. He would later suggest that his criticism was directed at himself as much as his teammates.

The writers gathered around Dumars in the Detroit locker room and asked him how he had stopped Jordan. The Pistons guard paused and looked up at the ceiling, as if searching for help. You don't stop Jordan, he explained. The obvious answer was that for the first two games, he had gone at Jordan offensively, and lit him up. At least that's what Jordan's irritated teammates pointed out privately. But at a practice following the first two losses, Jordan grew infuriated when he thought Pippen and Grant were goofing around and failing to take the situation seriously.

For much of his tenure in Chicago, Johnny Bach had painstakingly edited and produced the scouting videotapes of opponents that the coaches showed before each playoff game. The assistant coach often spliced in war movie clips to illustrate basketball points, but Jackson himself wanted to take over the job from Bach that first season. He illustrated the videotapes during the Pistons series with clips from *The Wizard of Oz*. He took a clip of Dumars zipping past Jordan on a drive, then spliced in a shot of the scarecrow. After another mistake, Jackson showed a shot of the cowardly lion, and after another, the tin woodsman, all to the amusement of the players, until John Paxson pointed out that the coach was basically insinuating his players had no heart, no courage, and no brains.

Fortunately, this negative tenor eased in Game 3 in Chicago Stadium. Jordan defended better, scored 47, and got enough help from his teammates for a 107–102 win. Isiah Thomas had broken out of a 5-for-21 shooting slump to score 36, but the Bulls won the rebounding battle, 46–36, and second shots gave them the edge, and a victory.

At one point in Game 4, the Bulls held a 19-point lead, but Dumars scored 24 points and again led the Pistons' charge. Twice the lead was cut to three, but the Bulls made 18 of 22 free throws to maintain their edge. While the Pistons outrebounded the Bulls 52 to 37, they couldn't sink baskets, hitting only 29 of 78 attempts. On a bad ankle, Detroit's Dennis Rodman had 20 points and 20 rebounds, but Jordan delivered bigger, with 42 points, and Chicago's other four starters finished in double figures in a 108–101 Bulls win.

Suddenly the Bad Boys, who liked to keep the pressure on the opponent, found themselves facing a must-win situation at home.

Both James Edwards and Bill Laimbeer shook off their slumps for Game 5 and helped the Pistons take a 3–2 series lead with a 97–83 win as Dumars held Jordan to 22 points. Sick with fever and a cold, the Detroit guard had played 38 minutes. "With Jordan, there's nothing you can do but work, hope, and pray, and Joe did all three,"

Chuck Daly said. Dumars played the series with the sort of heart for which Jordan would later be lionized, but his performance would become almost forgotten in sports history.

Jordan's message seemed to have gotten through to his teammates, however. The Pistons returned to Chicago, held Jordan to 29 points, and still lost Game 6 in a blowout. The Bulls forced the Pistons into 25 percent shooting in the third period and expanded a three-point edge into an 80–63 lead to open the fourth. Detroit lost 109–91. And like that, the Bulls had forced a seventh game.

"We are more driven than ever to win this thing," Jordan declared.

Game 7, however, quickly turned disastrous for Chicago. Paxson was nursing a badly sprained ankle, and Pippen developed a migraine headache just before tip-off. "Scottie had had migraines before," trainer Mark Pfeil explained. "He actually came to me before the game and said he couldn't see. I said, 'Can you play?' He started to tell me no, and Michael jumped in and said, 'Hell, yes, he can play. Start him. Let him play blind.'

"Horace Grant kind of backed up a little bit in the game, too," Pfeil added. "It was more a matter of maturity than wimping out. It took a certain period of time before they would stand up and say, 'Damn it, I've been pushed in the wall enough.' Scottie played with the headache, and as the game went on he got better."

The Bulls, however, did not. The second period was particularly awful, and Chicago never recovered. The Pistons advanced with a blowout, 93–74.

"My worst moment as a Bull was trying to finish out the seventh game that we lost to the Pistons in the Palace," Jackson recalled. "There was Scottie Pippen with a migraine on the bench, and John Paxson had sprained his ankle in the game before. I had to sit there and grit my teeth and go through a half in which we were struggling to get in the ball game. We had just gone through a second period that was an embarrassment to the organization. It was my most difficult moment as a coach."

Furious with his teammates, Jordan cursed them yet again at halftime, then sobbed in the back of the team bus afterward. "I was crying and steaming," he recalled. "I was saying, 'Hey, I'm out here busting my butt and nobody else is doing the same thing. These guys are kicking our butt, taking our heart, taking our pride.' I made up my mind right then and there it would never happen again. That was the summer that I first started lifting weights. If I was going to take some of this beating, I was also going to start dishing out some of it. I got tired of them dominating me physically."

With each Chicago loss in the playoffs, critics had grown more convinced that the Bulls were flawed as a one-man team. "They kept running into Detroit and it didn't look like they had any idea of how to beat Detroit," recalled journalist David Aldridge. Some observers pointed out that it had taken Wilt Chamberlain, Jerry West, and Oscar Robertson years to lead teams to the NBA title, and perhaps Jordan fell into the category with those players. Others wondered if he weren't headed for the same anguish as Elgin Baylor, Nate Thurmond, Pete Maravich, and Dave Bing, all great players who never played on a championship team.

Jordan was infuriated by such speculation and the criticism. He was literally nauseated by the losses each year to Detroit.

Losing to Isiah Thomas was very difficult. In some ways, however, the burden of the loss fell on Pippen. Everyone, from the media to his own teammates, had interpreted the headache as a sign of faintheartedness. Lost in the perspective was the fact that the third-year forward had recently buried his father.

"I'm flying back from the migraine game," recalled Cheryl Raye-Stout, "and who should be sitting across from me but Juanita Jordan. And she says, 'What happened to Scottie?' I said, 'He had a headache.' She goes, 'He had a headache?!' And she just shook her head."

After his biggest games, Jordan liked to save his shoes and store them for posterity. After the Game 7 loss, he wanted no mementos. "The last time they lost to the Pistons, we were all checking out of the hotel room and Scottie was in there with him," recalled Lacy Banks, who often claimed Jordan's game shoes as a donation to auction off for the local heart association. "He said, 'I don't want any of this stinky stuff. Here, Lacy, take these ol' stinky shoes. I don't want to see them anymore.'"

Mostly Joe Dumars would remember the pain on his face at the end of Game 7. "I saw it in his eyes," Dumars said. "He came and shook hands and quietly said, 'Congratulations, good luck.' I remember seeing the hurt and disappointment in his face. I saw a deep hurt."

It was going to take far more than Phil Jackson's burning sage to purify Jordan and his Bulls. Jordan wasn't sure what would be needed, but he knew that it was he who would have to force the agenda.

"With Phil we lost again," Mark Pfeil recalled. "After that, Michael said, 'Hey, now we've gotta go over the top, and I'm gonna take us there. If you don't want to be on the boat, get off.'"

Chapter 25

THE GOD OF BASKETBALL

İт was тне odor of piss that somehow still played on Sonny Vaccaro's mind years later.

They were in a godforsaken bathroom on a US Army base in Germany in late August 1990. Michael Jordan was about to play against himself in basketball for about two thousand troops packed into a tiny gym. He had not wanted to make a trip, which took him away from golf and from Juanita, now five months pregnant with son Marcus (who would be born on Christmas eve). But here he was in Europe, thanks to Vaccaro's moxie and guile, which had begun to wear dangerously thin with Nike chairman Phil Knight.

The world was on edge as the Gulf War had just gotten under way, but Jordan had his own reasons not to pack up and head to Europe for ten days that summer. The Game 7 loss to the Pistons in May had cast a certain mind-set over the entire Bulls roster and brought surprising focus to the off-season. The anger had sparked a constructive optimism among his teammates, and Jordan wanted to be able to seize that moment.

This Nike trip proposed by Vaccaro was scheduled to occur right before training camp opened, so he'd have to rush back to Chicago. The last thing Jordan wanted to do was jam up his schedule with any sort of public silliness. Playing in an exhibition game for US troops held a certain appeal, although he preferred to keep such events very low-key. Mostly, he thought he could get in a visit with older brother Ronnie, and that made the trip worthwhile.

An even more questionable item on the itinerary was Jordan's commitment to play for both sides in an all-star game that opened the Spanish league season. It made absolutely no sense to interject Jordan into the Spanish league's big moment, except for the chance to broadcast America's brightest star in action to much of the Spanish-speaking world.

The whole thing felt strange. Plus, wartime travel presented huge security issues. Only after Vaccaro commandeered a Nike corporate jet and made detailed security plans at each stop did Jordan warm to the idea.

"It was a public relations tour," Vaccaro explained. "It was the first one Nike ever did like this. It was huge. Michael did the first of anything we ever did and I went with him."

This junket would become the prototype tour for a generation of American pro basketball stars promoting shoes over the ensuing two decades. But at the time, there was another, darker reason for the hastily planned escape. That summer Nike had gotten embroiled in an ugly public relations spat with Jesse Jackson's Operation PUSH. Rev. Tyrone Crider, one of Jackson's young lieutenants, had taken over as PUSH executive director and targeted the shoe industry's lack of involvement in the African American community. Crider's complaint with Nike was that the Oregon company had no black board members, no black vice presidents, and a scarcity of black department heads. Nike had deals with other black endorsers beyond Jordan, and Crider acknowledged as much. But the PUSH leader said that he was taking on Nike because in a few short years it had become the industry leader.

The company and PUSH had begun discussions that summer, but they ended abruptly when PUSH demanded to see Nike's books and Nike countered with its own demand to peek inside PUSH's finances. Crider responded by ordering a boycott of Nike products by African Americans. "Don't buy Nike. Don't wear Nike," he said in announcing the campaign on August 12. Some observers suggested that Crider had miscalculated in taking on Nike, that PUSH would surely lose. Still, the company wanted no showdown with

PUSH and made offers to rectify any shortage of African Americans in its power structure. This effort would eventually boost Jordan's own position with the company and help provide impetus for the creation of the Jordan Brand. But in the interim, the star was in danger of being drawn into a nasty dispute, with headlines in major papers across the country. The last thing Nike wanted was to see Air Jordan on TV, being hit with questions about the conflict.

On August 15, Jordan released a statement saying that all of corporate America needed to provide opportunities but that PUSH's targeting of Nike was out of bounds. "It is unfair to single out Nike just because they are on top," his statement read.

After releasing his comments, he departed quickly for Europe. Just as Sonny Vaccaro had once come up with an idea to put Jordan in the spotlight, he had now come up with something that would take him out of it. Nike would make changes, and Crider would leave PUSH after the boycott fizzled out in early 1991 when it became clear that African American buyers were reluctant to stop buying the shoes.

Still, the incident served notice to Jordan that such highly charged issues could and would create headaches regarding his business interests. The 1990s would bring allegations by human rights organizations that Nike was employing hundreds of sweatshops worldwide in the manufacturing of its products, an issue that would quickly ensnare Jordan in his growing roles with the company.

Jordan had also found himself caught in another huge issue that summer of 1990 when he was asked, through his mother, to endorse the campaign of Harvey Gantt, an African American Democrat who was trying to pry the hardline conservative Jesse Helms out of his US Senate seat representing North Carolina. It was a close, racially charged campaign, made famous by Helms's "Hands" political ad that showed a white man losing his job to a minority because of unfair racial quotas. The ad, written by Republican strategist Alex Castellanos, played on white resentment. When asked to get involved in the campaign, Jordan had famously told Gantt's people that he couldn't because "Republicans buy shoes, too."

Politics had not been the path to prosperity for his grandfather Edward Peoples, nor for generations of black North Carolinians, and it wasn't a priority for Deloris Jordan or her son in 1990. The response angered many and yet pleased many others. Lacy Banks and others in Chicago shook their heads. It was not, Banks would note years later, the kind of answer that Muhammad Ali would have chosen. The refusal to help Gantt, who lost the race, incensed social activist and former NFL star Jim Brown, who said of Jordan, "He's more interested in his image for shoe deals than he is in helping his own people."

At the other end of the spectrum were people like Kenny Gattison, who had played against Jordan since high school. He said that the comment made possible Jordan's full crossover as a product endorser, because he stayed free of political controversy. "That's what made him an icon," Gattison offered, "because he never uttered a word and never gave people a reason to bash him."

Looking back in 2008, Michael Wilbon observed in his *Washington Post* column, "It seemed to officially usher in a period in which athletes made a conscious choice of commerce over politics. Neutrality offended fewer people. African American athletes, with Jordan leading the way, appealed commercially for the first time to the mainstream." (Jordan would contribute to Gantt's second unsuccessful run at Helms and later gave money to Democrat presidential contender Bill Bradley. Jordan even threw a very public fundraiser for Barack Obama during the 2012 presidential campaign.)

Still, the 1990 election brought a watershed moment in Jordan's public image. ESPN's J. A. Adande recalled the comment as a demarcation for many of his friends in their worship of His Airness. "I had friends that wanted absolutely nothing to do with Michael Jordan because of that," Adande said, "because they thought he was derelict in his social duties. They couldn't get over that. They couldn't enjoy Jordan the player because they really didn't have any respect for Jordan the person." Adande himself couldn't fathom why Jordan wouldn't want to take on a known racist. Pushed on the issue by *GQ* magazine several years later, Jordan explained that at age twenty-seven, he was focused on building his basketball career, not on politics.

"I later understood that, but when I was younger I agreed with Jim Brown," longtime NBA journalist David Aldridge recalled. "I was like, 'Come on, Michael! You can take a stand on this. You're Michael Jordan! What're they gonna do to you?'...I was horrified. Literally, I was like, 'C'mon Michael! You can't be that venal! Or that crass! It can't always be about you! It's gotta be about something bigger than you, because our whole life as black people, it's always been about something bigger than us. That's why you do the things that you do, because there's people who were ahead of you that made it possible for you to do that.' I thought, 'How could Michael Jordan not take a stand on this, or how could he not support Harvey Gantt?' I agreed with a lot of the people that took him to task for that."

The longtime NBA reporter said the moment was a pivot point. Endorsing Gantt might well have sent Jordan off in another direction, in which he could have been appreciated as someone who stood up for social justice, instead of standing up for self-interest.

"I remember him saying one time, 'I'm not a politician,'" Lacy Banks recalled in 2011. "Mike had a weakness in that. He never really aggressively identified with the mainstream causes."

Given his discomfort over such public confrontations, it made sense that Jordan decided to get away with Sonny Vaccaro to Europe that August, just as things were heating up.

"With Michael, it was always that trust thing," Vaccaro explained. "He listened. I was the guy he listened to. He didn't want to go. The Gulf War had just started. It was a perilous time. I asked him to go. I made Nike give me a private plane. We took a private plane so we had security. We went to private airports; we had the guys in uniforms. The guns were there. What a trip it was. We went to Paris. We went to Germany. We went to Spain."

Which was how they ended up in the funky old bathroom on the Army base in Germany. With no marketing woes to worry about, Germany would prove to be the emotional part of the journey, with the troops gathered and still so many unknowns about the conflict. Plus his brother Ronnie would be there.

"Michael judged the dunk contest and played on an Army-based team," Vaccaro recalled. "It was all Nike-related sponsors. He played against himself for the soldiers in Germany. He played in the game in a small gym, maybe two thousand soldiers are there.

The game plan was he was going to play five or ten minutes for team A, then he'd play five or ten minutes for team B. Then we'd sneak out the back door to the limo 'cause the crowds were all there and the media and you couldn't get in this little gym."

Jordan and Vaccaro sought refuge in the gym's ancient restroom. There was a bench and old-style open urinals, a long metal trough that stank, hardly the kind of accommodations that were anticipated when Vaccaro sold the idea of a grand European marketing junket. Jordan never said a word about the conditions.

"I closed the door right before the start of the game," Vaccaro recalled. "We're in there just the two of us. I go to the bathroom, and he's bouncing the ball. I had closed the door and then someone comes and says it's time to start the game. I said, 'Let's go Michael.' He said, 'No, leave me alone for another minute.'" Vaccaro studied Jordan a moment before realizing what was happening.

"That sucker was getting ready to play this game. Why am I saying this? He was bouncing the ball getting ready for the game. That's who he is. He was going to play his best no matter what the hell the atmosphere or the circumstances were. He was in a pissy old urinal in goddamned Germany and he's getting ready to play the game like it's UNC against Georgetown in the Superdome. That shows you the mentality he's carried throughout his whole life."

Jordan tore into that first half, driving his team to a lead. In this game, his opponents were Americans, and it was easier to read them on the floor. He still took those early moments to gauge what he faced, but from there he attacked in fierce Jordan fashion, producing steals in head-spinning numbers, slashing to the rim, toying with three-pointers, and when the action slowed, posting up just to test the people around him.

"On the court he's a bastard," Sonny Vaccaro remembered thinking.

Jordan may not have known what to do with the politics of protest, but he certainly had no equivocation about competing. The situation was "love of the game" personified. Instead of playing limited minutes each half, Jordan consumed the entire game. "He plays for team A the first half for twenty minutes," Vaccaro recalled. "Then halftime, he changes his jersey and plays for team B."

The halftime score, if Vaccaro remembered correctly, "was 40 to 25 for Michael's team. Now he changes his jersey and he plays for the other team."

The players he had just humbled now became his teammates, just as if he was back in a Bulls practice where Doug Collins had decided to do a switcheroo. So Jordan began searching through his new roster, trying to find out who would stand up and who wouldn't.

"You can guess the story," Vaccaro said. "End of the game it was like 82 to 80. Michael beat himself. He played all forty minutes of the game with the soldiers."

The real marketing segment of the trip came in Barcelona, where preparations for the 1992 Olympics were under way. Jordan made highly publicized visits to the offices of Nike, to the Olympic staff, even to Associated Club Basketball, the Spanish league offices. "They wanted Michael to go to Barcelona and he actually put a shovel in the ground for the new stadium they were building for the 1992 Olympics," Vaccaro explained. "He did one press conference in Madrid and another in Barcelona. He was the jury in a slam dunk contest at the Spanish all-star game put on by Nike for young people."

And once again he played himself, this time with the Spanish pros. Jordan took a little longer to read his European opponents, trying to sense their different game. It helped that he had the Olympic experience from 1984. He floated a few jumpers, got his bearings, and then went to work, all to the delight of the packed arena in Barcelona.

The Spanish crowds cheered Jordan's every move, leaving fans and media alike to declare that the "god of the basketball" had descended into their presence. Jordan's grand reception would help drive something akin to a coronation in Barcelona two years later.

"It promoted Nike on a grand scale," Vaccaro said of his brainchild. "Now Michael was an icon."

The trip marked a subtler but perhaps larger personal transformation for Jordan, beginning with the fact that he had listened, Vaccaro explained. So much of what had been done before had rested on Deloris Jordan's guidance. But Vaccaro saw the first real emergence of the business and marketing force that Jordan was becoming. He was leaving behind the mind-set of a petulant young prince and was taking ownership of the brand, doing what was necessary to make it grow. He was applying his work ethic and competitive spirit and maturity to something beyond basketball. Not that Jordan hadn't always tended to his responsibilities, but now it was as if the adolescent who had vowed to never have a job had finally gotten one.

Slam Dunk

During a whirlwind spin through the City of Light, taking in the Seine and Champs-Élysées and the Arc de Triomphe, Jordan had so much fun he told a friend that seeing the sights got him to thinking about co-owning a team in Europe and playing there after he retired from the NBA.

The change was obvious, Vaccaro said. "For much of my time with him, during those first years in the NBA, he still was a young kid feeling his oats, partying, girlfriends, and all that stuff before he and Juanita got married. I was part of that whole thing. I saw it. Now he's maturing. He now knows what he has. He was assuming responsibility with his empire off the court with Nike. He was becoming a part owner now."

His next contract would acknowledge what Phil Knight already begrudgingly knew, that the power of Michael Jordan had evolved into a full equity partnership with Nike. And PUSH had been there to guide the process along. "His next contract would be the Jordan Brand," Vaccaro said.

Dee Brown got a taste of the new Jordan when the Celtics' rookie guard won the Slam Dunk Contest at the 1991 NBA All-Star Game in Charlotte. The only problem was, he felt a lot like the old Jordan. The NBA had tried to persuade him to enter the contest in his native Carolina, but Jordan had declined, figuring he had nothing to gain and much to lose.

But when he arrived in Charlotte, his competitive juices started flowing as he watched Brown win the Slam Dunk Contest with a soaring, blindfolded slam. What really mattered were the shoes on Brown's feet, Reebok's trendy Pumps. Not long after the contest ended that Friday night, Brown found himself in a back tunnel waiting for another event to start. And suddenly, there was Jordan.

"It was weird," Brown recalled. "I was a rookie and I had just won a contest maybe two hours before. It was just me and Michael and security. And I'm sitting there, so he comes up to me and says, 'Good job, young fella. You did a really good job.' Then he kind of said, 'You know I got to go at you more now.'" Brown was taken aback by the comment and more than a little intimidated. "Why?" he asked. "Michael goes, 'You know you've started a shoe war.' I go, 'What does that mean?' I'm oblivious. This is Michael Jordan. I'm twenty-one years old, just won a dunk contest. I didn't comprehend what he said. He could have told me that my face is falling off, I would have been like, 'Thank you.'"

Later, Brown began to wonder, how did Jordan even know where he was? Had the star made a point to seek him out to put him on notice? The more he thought about it, the more he realized that Jordan had done just that.

"I started figuring it out," Brown said. "You hear all the stories about Michael and how competitive he is. He already had it in his mind that what I did with that pump-up shoe, that what it was going to be was a competition between his shoe and that shoe. Forget about basketball, it went to the competition of 'Now I got to kick your butt in something else. I know you can't guard me. I'm the best player in the world. But just because you did that little Reebok thing, now I got to step my game up on the shoe business.'"

In a few short months, Jordan had stepped into a new identity that very few were aware of at the time. He was the player as shoe executive. As Vaccaro pointed out, Jordan was becoming far more accomplished in this business role than the public realized or understood.

"The Reebok Pump kind of blew up a little bit for a time there," Brown said with a laugh in a 2012 interview, adding that soon enough, however, the issue was settled decisively. "Obviously Michael stepped the shoe game up. That tells you what kind of competition it turned out to be. Everybody is wearing Jordans now."

The Wages of Change

The twenty-seven-year-old man with the unquenchable appetites and boundless energy finally returned Phil Jackson's phone calls early that fall of 1990 as training camp was set to open. The coach had been calling through much of the off-season, but Jordan had been off, into everything, it seemed. At one point that summer, he had found time to play in a charity golf tournament in Philadelphia, with Charles Barkley as his caddie. The two hit it off immediately. Chuck was immensely talented, and his sense of humor made it so much easier for Jordan to deal with all the bullshit that was now piling up around him. Somehow Barkley always kept him chuckling. Soon enough he had stitched into his life a running phone conversation with Sir Charles. Jordan had thought he could talk some shit, but Barkley? Jordan had to laugh when the Alabama fat boy told him he would be taking the league scoring title away from him for the upcoming season.

When Jordan got back to Chicago and the Bulls that fall, he was sporting a diamond stud in his ear, to go with his shaved head. It was a risky move for a guy to whom image was everything. Before long, the alpha-male "Jordan look," could be seen everywhere, in men of all races and colors.

Jordan and agent David Falk were also engaged in serious conversations about his move beyond basketball. They had begun to see "the four corners of the basketball court as a limitation, rather than a platform," Falk would later explain. Just that season, some business partners were set to release a line of evening wear for men, "23 Night for Michael Jordan," in partnership with After Six, the formal wear brand. "We've never had such excitement," Marilyn Spiegel, a vice president of marketing for After Six, told *People* magazine. "Michael is the nineties man."

Jordan stood six-six, weighed 195 pounds, with a forty-five-inch chest and a thirty-three-inch waist, what would prove to be the perfect clotheshorse of a model. Evening wear would simply be the next in a stream of products over the decade — clothing, fragrance, jewelry, underwear, and so on — that would define what came to be known as the "metrosexual" male.

"I became very fashion-conscious when I was young," Jordan told *People*, recalling his experience taking home economics at Laney High. "I picked up on different styles, and I would always want them, but I couldn't afford them." Now, of course, he could afford it all, but had come to a point in his career that he no longer took great joy from the game that made it all possible. He hardly bothered watching NBA games when he was off. This was one of the themes in a book being developed behind the scenes by *Chicago Tribune* beat writer Sam Smith. Slated to be published in the fall of 1991, the book was based on information provided to Smith by unidentified sources in and around the team. It would reveal a monumentally selfish Jordan who had grown cynical, angry, bitter, and untrusting in his six NBA seasons.

This was the situation that Phil Jackson faced as he sat down with Jordan for their first preseason powwow. Jackson recognized that he had come to a crossroads in just his second season coaching the team. He wanted to discuss how "Michael and his Jordanaires," as they were called, would approach the upcoming schedule.

Jordan had hoped the coach was going to tell him they were abandoning the triangle offense, but that was hardly the case. The coach not only expected the team to adhere to the system more closely, but he also informed Jordan that it would be better for the team if its star wasn't so focused on winning another scoring title. Perhaps Charles Barkley had been reading Jackson's mind.

There was no pleasant end to the meeting, just as there would be no pleasant beginning to the season. As early as 1989, when the Bulls decided to put Pippen's mug on the upcoming season schedule, Jordan had come to believe there was a "de-Michaelization" going on within the franchise, a determined effort to step out of the shadow he cast. He had heard inside reports of a Krause comment that if the team had Hakeem Olajuwon in his place, the Bulls would have won two titles already. He perceived a growing belief in the front office that he was not the kind of player who could anchor a championship team. In retrospect, it might seem ludicrous that he believed he wasn't being promoted. His face was all over the pro game. But those around him had long learned that reality and Jordan's competitive mind often inhabited parallel universes. More than ever, when he wanted to stoke the fire, he simply conjured up something in his mind to produce the heat. The people around him often had trouble separating the real from the imagined.

What was undeniably real was the success of the Pistons' physical defense. Jordan knew that other coaches would soon take a similar approach, and he intended to prove them all wrong. "Everyone's going to make me take the outside shot," he said, derisively.

Also coming into clarity was the evolving relationship between the league and television. NBC had outbid CBS for the NBA's broadcast deal, putting millions of new dollars into players' pockets. Jordan's own contract, renegotiated just two years earlier, was already obsolete, leaving him as only the seventh highest paid player in the league. Even worse, Pippen's renegotiated contract had him earning about $760,000 that year, when many of his lesser teammates were making more than a million. Pippen thought it a good idea to hide out in a Memphis hotel room rather than report for training camp that season, until his agent convinced him that such a path would be disastrous.

The financial issues would cause tremendous discord within the Chicago franchise over the coming decade as it became clear to players and their agents just how tough a businessman Reinsdorf was. The owner prized the art of the deal above everything, and had long ago made up his mind to avoid the bad player contracts that paralyzed so many teams. He had a strict policy of avoiding renegotiating deals at all costs, and while he might have done so for Jordan, Reinsdorf knew that his star would not ask for a raise, which meant that he could take his time evaluating the situation.

The team chairman's approach to "winning the deals" with his players and their agents involved a timeworn tactic of the lowball. It was Krause's job to make extremely low offers that infuriated players and their agents, then Reinsdorf would step in with a better offer. But the owner knew what used-car dealers knew: if you start with a lowball, you usually wind up getting the other side to give up too much in the deal. While effective, that approach meant that

Jordan wasn't the only player on the roster who despised Krause. An array of the Bulls and their agents held the GM in special contempt.

Over the summer of 1990, Krause had drafted a Croatian teen sensation named Toni Kukoc but still had to convince him to play for the Bulls at some point. At the time, European players were largely ineffective in the far more physical NBA. Krause's excitement over Kukoc only drove Jordan's sense of "de-Michaelization" as the team began trying to come up with endorsements and side deals to lure Kukoc, who was under contract to a European team.

When Jordan and Pippen learned that Krause was working to squirrel away two million dollars of salary cap space to cover the costs of bringing Kukoc to America, that only inflamed them further.

It was hardly the ideal time for Jackson to reveal that the team would again use the "equal opportunity" offense and to suggest that Jordan's scoring and minutes played should drop for the good of the team. But like that, the die had been cast: it would be Jackson's wits versus Jordan's will. Of course both would have plenty of the opposite measure. Jordan truly liked Jackson and wanted to cooperate, but only within limits.

After six seasons in the league with a variety of coaches and teammates, Jordan believed mostly in himself. In Mike he trusted. All others were open to question. That was the condition under which they would all have to proceed in the fall of 1990.

PART VIII

SOMETHING GAINED

Chapter 26

TRIANGULAR

O NE OF JORDAN'S simple escapes when he managed to land for a few days in Chicago was the couch at his mother-in-law's house on the South Side, where he could zone out on TV and load up on Dorothy Vanoy's old-fashioned mac and cheese. Juanita was six months pregnant, with an active two-year-old underfoot; she, too, sought the sanctuary of her mother's home. It was as good a place as any for Jordan to keep track of Krause's off-season maneuverings to upgrade the roster.

The Bulls had had money to spend that off-season to fix several serious issues with the roster. Jackson liked big guards, big perimeter defenders, to work his pressure defense. Plus Bach had pointed out that they needed a tough, veteran guard who could stand up to Jordan and tell him to go to hell when he started pushing too hard and taking over the offense. Danny Ainge fit that bill and was available in Sacramento, but the Kings were controlled mostly by former Bulls coach Dick Motta, who was not about to make any deals that would help his old nemesis Jerry Krause.

Once again, the focus turned to Walter Davis, who was now a free agent with Denver. Jordan agreed to renegotiate part of his contract to help the Bulls around salary cap issues, but only if they would use the money to sign Davis. The deal seemed to have momentum, until Davis's wife made it known she wanted to remain in Denver. Jordan was stunned.

So Krause decided to acquire New Jersey's Dennis Hopson, a former Big Ten player of the year and a high first-round draft pick, for guard depth. For defensive help at small forward, they added Cliff Levingston, a free agent out of Atlanta. Krause also signed undrafted free agent forward Scott Williams out of North Carolina. Jordan was elated to finally have a fellow Tar Heel on the roster and took Williams under his wing. Two of the team's first-round draft picks from 1989, B. J. Armstrong and Stacey King, had matured a bit and were considered ready to provide more help.

Most important was yet more development from Pippen, who made the transition from being a wing into a point guard role, Jackson said. "He became a guy who now had the ball as much as Michael. He became a dominant force."

Pippen arrived in training camp with three years of experience battling Jordan in practice. The transformation in his competitive attitude could now be measured in his desire to score. He, too, wanted to be like Mike. More specifically, he wanted more money out of the team; to get it in this stats-driven business, he realized that he had to score. The only problem was that his new hunger would throw yet another monkey wrench into Jackson's plans for using the triangle.

The Bulls encountered turbulence just out of the gate with a loss to Philly in which Sir Charles outscored His Airness, 37 to 34. The smack-talking gabfest was on between the two then. The Bulls went on to make it three straight losses to begin the season, then plodded to a 5–6 record over the first three weeks, which didn't fit at all with anyone's expectations. It was in the ninth game, in Seattle, that Jordan and mouthy rookie Gary Payton started trading trash talk in advance of the game. Jordan scored 33 and the Bulls won handily, but he played just twenty-seven minutes, which increased his anxiety about Jackson's efforts to prevent him from winning the scoring title.

Release

The mediocre start had prompted at least one phone call from Reinsdorf to Jackson to check in, but only the closest watchers saw any signs of perspiration out of the coach. It wasn't the phone call that troubled Jackson nearly as much as the routine sight of Jordan and Pippen ignoring Winter's offense and instead attacking the defense one-on-one. Jordan's conspirator and early instigator in these departures was Johnny Bach, who whispered his opinion. "Johnny would say, 'Fuck the triangle. Just take the ball and score. Get everyone else to clear out,'" Jordan recalled.

Jackson would tolerate Bach's insubordination only so long, but it played an important role in the evolution of the team's style of play.

"He had to be released from the offense sometimes," Bach explained in a 2012 interview, adding that he believed his input was needed. Bach believed in Winter's offense, but he also saw that the team's star needed to make his own adjustment to it. Jordan was a master at reading defenses, so picking up the triangle was a charm for him. And while there was no shortage of drama, something else was happening. Jordan, who had once readily given himself over to Dean Smith's offense, was exploring ways he could use the triangle to his advantage. It was fascinating to watch Jordan's intelligence at work in that situation, Bach recalled, almost like a brilliant actor bringing his own masterful interpretation to a great script, while rewriting entire scenes and dialogue. "The player has to be aware of how he fits into things," Bach explained, looking back. "Michael knew the triple post backward and forward. He could play any position in it."

By and large, the triangle offense provided a format that allowed Jordan to relate to his less talented teammates. The structure of the triangle demanded that the ball be passed to the open man. Once Jordan began complying with that, once he trusted enough to do that, the tension began to ease. A system quickly evolved in which Jordan would play within the triangle for three quarters, and then—depending on the pace and rhythm of the game—would break out of the offense in the fourth quarter to go on scoring binges. These fourth quarters each night produced their own tension, with Tex Winter anxious that Jordan was trying to do too much by himself. Some nights when he did just that, the team would stumble. But far more often, the result would be mesmerizing.

Jordan's life off the court during the season had fallen into a familiar pattern. He'd either stay in his room for marathon card games with his tight circle, or he'd slip off to a nearby golf course to zip through a round or two. He'd often manage this in the afternoons, after practice, while his teammates were napping.

As the season progressed, the team found enough balance to allow for the integration of Horace Grant (12.8 points, 8.4 rebounds) and Paxson (8.7 points while shooting .548 from the floor). A key problem was the bench's inability to hold leads. Armstrong, Hodges, Perdue, King, Levingston, Williams, and Hopson all worked hard to execute the offense, but it remained Jordan's scoring that made things work. He would get irritated by the bench's struggles, but it ultimately meant more time on the floor for him and more scoring opportunities.

More importantly, it was the defense that carried them along after the shaky start. Bach's presence served to energize, but the assistant coach would suggest that his contribution was merely window dressing next to the commitment and effort Jackson put into making defense a large part of his team's identity. "I had a little part in the defense," he explained, "but it took Phil to manifest it and make it clear to the team."

This clarity resulted in the first signs that they might be a very good team. In December, the Bulls' defense held the Cleveland Cavaliers to just 5 points in one quarter at Chicago Stadium, where crowds presented an atmosphere as intimidating as the defense. The Bulls lost to Boston in Chicago the third game of the season. They wouldn't lose at home again until Houston stopped them March 25, a run of thirty straight home wins.

The defense essentially bought time for the offense to come along. When it did, the role players, such as Paxson, began to prosper. "John Paxson was one of the people who made all of the difference in the world, because of his attitude," the coach recalled, looking back in 1995. "He was going to play full-court pressure and be a facilitator in this offense."

They finished February with an 11–1 record, which included a road win in the Palace of Auburn Hills just before All-Star Weekend. Isiah Thomas was sidelined, but the victory sparked the Bulls toward the first signs of belief. "Just winning a game in their building gave us confidence because we'd had such a tough time beating them," Paxson recalled. "Phil had sold us on playing our game, not being retaliatory against the Pistons. That's what really helped us along."

The outcome charged Jordan with optimism and yet more confidence, if that was possible. "When we went in there and beat them right before the All-Star break, that's when I knew we could beat them in the playoffs," he recalled. "We had been on the road for something like two weeks, and it just came together. I could feel it then."

The seven-foot-one Cartwright had been key to the Bulls' new maturity in dealing with the physical Pistons. Cartwright could be as stubborn as Jordan, which also helped the team learn to face up to Detroit. "One of the things that got to us," Jackson explained, "was that Detroit used to have a way of bringing up the level of animosity in a game. At some level, you were gonna have to contest them physically if you were gonna stay in the game with them. If you didn't want to stay in the game with them, fine. They'd go ahead and beat you. But if you wanted to compete, you'd have to do something physically to play at their level. Bill stood up to the Pistons. Bill's statement was, 'This isn't the way we want to play. This isn't the way I want to play. But if it is the way we have to play to take care of these guys, I'm not afraid to do it. I'm gonna show these Detroit guys this is not acceptable. We won't accept you doing this to us.' You can't imagine how much that relieved guys like Scottie Pippen and Horace Grant, guys who were being besieged constantly and challenged constantly by more physical guys like Dennis Rodman and Rick Mahorn."

March brought a nine-game winning streak that helped them gain the all-important home-court advantage for the playoffs. They closed the schedule with another four-game win streak, including another win over the Pistons that brought Chicago's record to 61–21.

Determined to prove his point and still fulfill Jackson's wishes, Jordan managed to again lead the league in scoring at 31.5 points per game (to go with 6 rebounds and 5 assists per outing). Pippen had found a higher plateau for his game as well. He played 3,014 minutes that season, and averaged nearly 18 points, 7 rebounds, and 6 assists.

As the playoffs got under way, Jordan was named the league's MVP for the second time.

They opened against the Knicks and won the first game by a record 41 points, then went on to sweep them, 3–0. Next Charles Barkley and the 76ers fell, four games to one. During a two-day break in the playoff series with Philadelphia, Jordan and writer Mark Vancil motored over to an Atlantic City casino. They dragged back to the team hotel about six thirty the next morning, and Jordan still made the Bulls' practice at ten a.m., which was no great surprise to anyone who knew him. The media took note of it, and later it would be cited as the first tremor in his rolling quake of troubles.

Basketball brought him back to a reality of sorts. The Bulls dispensed with the Sixers, setting up the only rematch that Jordan wanted: the Bad Boys in the Eastern Conference championship series. Detroit was an injured and fractured team in May 1991. Chuck Daly had been named the coach for the upcoming 1992 US Olympic team, and Isiah Thomas returned from injury that April perhaps sensing that he wasn't in Daly's plans for the roster. He began publicly criticizing his coach, hinting that his Olympic responsibilities had taken his attention off the Pistons. Daly sought to quiet his star, but Thomas persisted in his pointed remarks. Privately, Daly was said to be furious at the suggestion he wasn't doing his job. "All I've done is one meeting and look at some films," he told reporters.

Jordan and his teammates clearly smelled blood. The Pistons managed to make a strong rush early in Game 1. "We were beating them in the first game," recalled Brendan Malone. "That's the quietest I had ever heard Chicago Stadium. And then off the bench came Cliff Levingston, Will Perdue, and Craig Hodges. Levingston and Perdue went to work on the glass, and Hodges was red-hot in that series."

With that spark, the Bulls went on to take the first three games with an attitude. They were executing their triangle offense better, and that gave them the edge, Malone recalled. "They had gotten better with more time in the offense. It was difficult to double-team Michael and leave someone wide open." Ultimately, Winter's offense had created some operating room for Jordan and produced open shooters around him. After the series, the Pistons would be left to answer criticism that they had focused too much on Jordan and left his teammates with good, clean shots.

"You have to put the majority of your focus on him," Dumars said, looking back at the season. "It's hard to go on the floor and not focus on that guy because he can dominate so much of what happens. It's hard to walk on the floor and not think about what he's going to do."

On the eve of Game 4 in Detroit, the atmosphere around the series turned harsh when Jordan unleashed his pent-up anger in a press conference. "The people I know are going to be happy they're not the reigning champs anymore," he said of the Pistons. "We'll get back to the image of a clean game. People want to push this kind of basketball out. When Boston was champion, they played true basketball. Detroit won. You can't take that away from them. But it wasn't clean basketball. It wasn't the kind of basketball you want to endorse. We're not going to try to lower ourselves to that kind of play. I may talk some trash, but we're playing hard, clean basketball. They've tried to provoke us and we've kept our poise."

Jordan then concluded boldly, "I think we can sweep this team."

The Pistons, particularly Thomas, were enraged by his tone and comments. "No, we're not going to get swept," Thomas vowed.

Dumars made no such claims, but he was taken aback by Jordan's antipathy. "It surprised me," the Detroit guard confided later. "I was disappointed that he started bad-mouthing what our championships had meant to us."

Brendan Malone, however, had seen the end coming for Detroit's physical style earlier in the playoffs when NBA commissioner David Stern said he was shocked by what he saw as hard fouls and "thuggery" starting to become the approach of other teams as well. "That type of basketball ended," Malone said. "I think it stopped when David Stern went to the playoffs that year and saw players get into a fight right in front of him. He decided he was going to clamp down on the physical play in the NBA."

Officials then hit the Pistons with a flurry of flagrant foul calls early in their series with the Bulls, Malone said. "One was on Joe Dumars, who was physical but who wasn't considered over the top.

And I knew then the league had made a decision that you couldn't play that way anymore."

As he had forecast, Jordan exerted his will the next day, and Chicago swept Detroit. At the end of the game, Thomas and the Pistons stalked off the floor without shaking hands or congratulating the Bulls. Daly had asked them not to do it. The snub angered television viewers and Chicago fans and perhaps cost Isiah Thomas an opportunity to be on the Olympic team.

"It was incredibly satisfying, the fact that they had to walk by our bench," John Paxson recalled on the twentieth anniversary of the victory. "You could still see Isiah was kind of ducking down, shoulders kind of slouched, trying not to be seen....But it did kind of validate what we believed in—that we played the right way. They were really good, but their time had come and gone, and it was our turn now."

Rather than join Thomas in the protest, Dumars stopped to congratulate his foe. He too was upset with Jordan's comments, but he remembered the pain in Jordan's face at the end of each of the previous seasons. "That look is the reason I stopped and shook his hand when they beat us," Dumars recalled in 2012. "I was not going to walk past the guy and not shake his hand. I shook Phil's hand and Michael's hand and a few of the other guys. I figured if that guy can shake my hand with that kind of hurt and disappointment he had in his face, there's no way I'm going to walk off this court and not shake his hand."

Thomas and the rest of the Pistons had been enraged by what they saw as Jordan's disrespect, Malone recalled. "That was also Phil Jackson and Tex Winter," the Detroit assistant said. "It was an attitude that their way was the only way to play basketball. I thought that was insulting. There are all kinds of ways to play basketball. They had that attitude. But it was just their time to win. Horace Grant and Scottie Pippen had matured and were ready to play. Pippen really came of age and so did Horace Grant, and Michael finally had some help to win a championship."

Dumars attributed some of the incident to the fact that Thomas was simply a poor loser. The Detroit star had also reacted poorly four years earlier after a loss to the Celtics.

"Isiah has never said to me, 'I hate Michael Jordan,'" Dumars explained in 2012. "He has said to me, 'I hate losing.' Regardless of who it was, Isiah would have hated losing that series. That's what I make of the situation."

The snub was a slap in the face, a final insult for the Bulls, and it ensured that their hard feelings against Detroit would endure. "I have nothing but contempt and disgust for the Pistons organization," Jerry Reinsdorf said, looking back four years later. "Ultimately, David Stern felt the pressure and made rules changes to outlaw their style of play. It wasn't basketball. It was thuggerism, hoodlumism.... That's one of the things that made us so popular. We were the white knights; we were the good guys. We beat the Bad Boys, 4–0, and they sulked off the court the way they did. I remember saying at the time that this was a triumph of good over evil. They were hated because they had used that style to vanquish first the Celtics and then the Lakers, who had been the NBA's most popular teams for years."

The vanquishing of the Bad Boys had been such a hurdle for Jordan and his Bulls that even though they still faced the league championship series, they couldn't help but pause for celebration, memorably kicked off by Jerry Krause. "He comes in the front of the plane and he's celebrating," Jackson recalls. "He's dancing, and the guys are going, 'Go, Jerry! Go, Jerry!'" The days of mooing had been put on hold, but the players still had no idea what to make of their most unusual GM. "He's dancing," Jackson recalled with a grin, "or whatever he's doing, and when he stops, they all collapse in hilarity, this laughter, and you couldn't tell whether it was with him or at him. It was one of those nebulous moments. It was wild."

Magic Time

In the recent past, the Bulls had pondered acquiring both Danny Ainge and Buck Williams, but both of those players wound up in Portland with Clyde Drexler. The Trail Blazers had ruled the 1991 regular season in the Western Conference with a 63–19 finish, but the long-dominant Lakers led by Magic Johnson found a way to prevail in the conference finals and ousted Portland, 4–2.

Suddenly, Chicago was hosting the opening of a dream of a championship series for basketball fans, Michael versus Magic, the Bulls versus the Lakers, and ticket manager Joe O'Neil found himself in a nightmare situation. It had never been easy finding enough home game tickets for Jordan while avoiding making his teammates angry. As the Bulls began moving farther into the playoffs and playing bigger games, the ticket challenge grew, particularly in terms of meeting Jordan's demands.

"I kind of knew the number he was looking at," O'Neil recalled. "I always told him, 'Don't surprise me. Don't tell me you need twenty tickets at the last minute,' which he did all the time."

One of the biggest issues was finessing Jordan's requests while keeping Pippen and Grant happy, O'Neil explained. "I remember going into the locker room telling Scottie and Horace and the guys, 'You get four extra tickets for the game. Don't ask me for any more. There are no more tickets. That's it. Four tickets for everybody.' Then I'd hand Michael a packet of like forty."

The issue grew so large that O'Neil told Jordan to hide his tickets from his teammates. Finally, the ticket manager began meeting Jordan surreptitiously, in a hockey locker room in Chicago Stadium, to give him the tickets.

Ticket demand got out of control once it became clear that the Bulls would be hosting the Lakers in Game 1. "We were about four days out from the Finals starting and I was overwhelmed," O'Neil remembered of that first year. "I didn't have enough tickets. Michael needed this, and everybody needed this. I remember going home, getting home about seven that night and walking in to my wife and saying, 'Susan, I don't think I can do this. I'm overwhelmed. The whole world is coming after me. It's Michael versus Magic. I don't have enough tickets. I don't think I can do this anymore.' My wife said to me, 'I have an idea. Why don't you take out the garbage?' So I walked out and took out the garbage. I'm pulling it out to the street, and the light goes on across the street and the guy runs out, hands me a credit card and says, 'I hate to do this to you, Joe, but can you get me two?' I go back in the house and tell my wife, 'I got an order for two taking out the garbage.'"

This wasn't the first time a matchup of Michael and Magic created an instant and controversial demand. In 1990, promoters planned to stage a one-on-one game between Johnson and Jordan for pay-per-view television. Jordan, who had spent his life challenging people to one-on-one, found the idea immediately fetching. But the NBA nixed the event—which would have paid big money to the participants—after Isiah Thomas, who was then the president of the players' association, objected. Jordan lashed out at Thomas's intervention, charging that the Detroit guard was jealous because no one would pay to see him play.

Johnson said he would love to play the game, but he declined to get involved in the scrap between the two. "That's their thing," he said.

Johnson did, however, have some fun speculating over the outcome. Actor Jack Nicholson, the Lakers' superfan, said that if he were a betting man, he'd put his money on Jordan, the premier individual player in the game, as opposed to Johnson, who was considered pro basketball's consummate team player.

Johnson, though, refused to concede any speculation. "I've been playing one-on-one all my life," he said. "That's how I made my lunch money." Asked his best one-on-one move, Johnson said, "I didn't have a best move. My best move was just to win, and that's it. I did what I had to do to win."

Basketball fans were disappointed that the one-on-one match wasn't held. "A lot of people wanted to see it," Johnson said at the time. "Michael is really disappointed. His people are disappointed. We're all disappointed. It was something we were all looking forward to."

That summer of 1990, Jordan had agreed to play in Magic's charity all-star game, but tried to consume too many golf holes the day of the event and arrived late. Rather than start the event without the star of the league, Johnson had decided to delay it to give Jordan time to be there for tip-off, which reportedly infuriated Isiah Thomas. Apparently Jordan was delighted that he had inconvenienced his nemesis.

With the championship series, Magic Mike of Laney High was

finally coming face to face with his hero. Johnson, having led the Lakers to five NBA titles, was seen as the ultimate purveyor of the team game, while Jordan was the one-man show who couldn't seem to keep from referring to his teammates as his "supporting cast," no matter how many times he was reminded not to do so. As if that wasn't trip enough down memory lane, Jordan also faced his two college teammates James Worthy and Sam Perkins. Worthy had a badly sprained ankle, which greatly reduced his mobility. Some insiders figured that Worthy's injury would cost the Lakers the series. His loss would be a tremendous blow to Los Angeles. Others, such as former Lakers coach Pat Riley, who was broadcasting the series for NBC, projected that the Lakers would still use their experience to win.

Jordan and his Bulls played nervously out of the gate but still managed a two-point lead at halftime in the first game. The second half, however, became a matter of the Lakers' post game, run through Perkins, Vlade Divac, and Worthy, versus Chicago's jump shooting. It came down to jump shots at the end. Perkins hit an unlikely three-pointer while Jordan missed an eighteen-footer at the buzzer to give Los Angeles Game 1, 93–91.

Jordan scored 36 with 12 assists, 8 rebounds, and 3 steals on 14 of 24 shooting from the floor, but even this magnificent performance left some of his teammates quietly fuming about his shot selection and one-on-one play. Although his team had just lost the home-court advantage, Jackson actually seemed relieved after the game. He had seen that Los Angeles struggled any time Johnson was out of the game. Jackson figured that would prove too great a burden for a player at the end of his career, and he was right.

There was another development that Jackson hadn't foreseen. He had begun the series with the six-six Jordan defending the six-nine Johnson. And in Game 2, that effort brought Jordan two early fouls. His teammates, particularly Grant and Cartwright in the post, had already gotten off to strong starts. Jordan's time on the bench did two things: it gave them more opportunities, and it meant that the taller Pippen would move over to cover Johnson.

At the time there was an assumption that the twenty-five-year-old would struggle to handle basketball's wiliest veteran, the master point guard of his time. Just the opposite happened. The long-armed Pippen immediately limited Johnson, and suddenly the momentum shifted. With Jordan and Pippen taking turns guarding him, the Lakers big guard shot just 4 of 13 from the floor. Pippen, meanwhile, contributed 20 points with 10 assists and 5 rebounds as the Bulls won Game 2 in a swarm.

"We started to see that we were wearing him down from a physical standpoint," Pippen happily recalled, "especially myself being able to go up and harass him and trying to get him out of their offense. He wasn't as effective as he had been in the past against some teams, being able to post up and take advantage of situations. I saw the frustration there."

"Some of it was to rest Michael," recalled Johnny Bach. "We didn't want him on Magic all the time. Scottie went in, and suddenly we realized that he was so long and so big that Magic could not throw those over-the-top passes. We called them halo passes, right over the top of the head. He would throw the ball right past littler guys. But now Scottie was in front of him. He was really a little taller than the six-seven he said he was. Scottie had long arms and big hands. And Magic was starting to fade. He was getting older. Youth doesn't wait for the aged."

Jordan had opened the game in a generous mood, sending no-look passes to Cartwright and Grant for easy baskets. From that beginning, the Bulls shot better than 73 percent from the floor to drive a blowout, 107–86. Jordan made 15 of 18 from the floor to finish with 33, plus 13 assists, 7 rebounds, 2 steals, and a block. Jordan scored thirteen straight field goals through the heart of the second half, a streak capped by perhaps his most memorable attempt with a little under eight minutes left in the game. He took a pass at the top of the key and attacked the basket head on through traffic. He rose in the lane with the ball outstretched high in his right hand to dunk until he encountered a defender, then switched to his left at the last instant and reached around the left side of the goal to flip in a bank shot that left the building buzzing, Phil Jackson smiling and shaking his head, and broadcaster Marv Albert raving. This one would be labeled "the move" to sit in tandem with "the shot" from 1989 against Cleveland.

Even with his grand performance, Jordan was outshot by Paxson, who went 8 for 8 from the floor. "Does Paxson ever miss?" Perkins asked afterward.

Perhaps the thorniest issue was Jordan's taunting of the Lakers' bench as the blowout unfolded, pumping his arms or appearing to give the dice a shake and a roll after he made baskets, especially "the move." Los Angeles would file a complaint about him with league offices, and even his teammates attempted to restrain him.

Despite the loss, the Lakers had gotten a split in Chicago Stadium and were headed home for three straight games in the Great Western Forum. They had a huge advantage in experience over the Bulls, and just about all of the experts figured that would be the difference.

The first order of business for the Bulls before Game 3 was a videotape Jackson had prepared showing Johnson sagging off Paxson to play a zone and create havoc for the Chicago offense. Jordan had to recognize this and give up the ball to the open shooter, the coach emphasized, a message he would repeat after each of the next two games. Even though Jordan averaged better than 11 assists during the 1991 championship series, the issue hung over the team.

Having Pippen defend Johnson in Game 3 backfired on Chicago in the second half as the Lakers moved to a 13-point lead when center Vlade Divac found it easier to score over the shorter Jordan. The Bulls narrowed the lead to a half dozen at the end of the third, and trouble caught up with the Lakers from there. Johnson continued to weary from the heavy minutes he had to play, and Worthy's ankle finally became the factor the Lakers coaches had feared it would. Jordan hit a jumper with 3.4 seconds left to send Game 3 into overtime. There, the Bulls ran off 8 straight points for a 104-96 win and a 2-1 lead in the series. In Game 4, the Bulls harried Los Angeles into shooting 37 percent from the floor. They managed a total of 30 points over the second and third quarters. Perkins, in particular, found the going difficult in the low post while shooting one of fifteen from the floor. Cartwright led an interior defense that delivered a 97–82 win. Jordan turned in yet another stellar night in his first championship series, with 28 points, 13 assists, 5 rebounds, and 2 blocks.

"I can't believe this is happening," Magic Johnson told reporters.

"It's no surprise the way they've been defending," Laker coach Mike Dunleavy said of the Bulls. "They are very athletic and very smart."

Suddenly, the Bulls were on the verge of the improbable, but they'd have to be patient. "We went up 3–1 and had a long wait, from Sunday to Wednesday, for Game 5," recalled Bulls equipment manager John Ligmanowski. "Those three days took forever. Before we had even won it, Michael would get on the bus and say, 'Hey, how does it feel, world champs?' He knew. That was a pretty good feeling. We just couldn't wait to get it over with."

The eve of Game 5 brought a meal of crow for Jordan. He publicly acknowledged what Cartwright had done for the team. "He has given us an edge in the middle," he said. "He has been solid for us.... This guy has turned out to be one of the most important factors for this ball club, and he has surprised many who are standing here and who play with him."

Later told of Jordan's comments, Cartwright brushed them off. "That stuff really isn't important to me," he said. "I've always figured what goes around comes around. What's really important to me is winning a championship."

Every Bulls starter had taken at least 10 shots in Game 4, a testament perhaps to Jordan's trust and proof that Jackson had a will of his own. He had rarely confronted Jordan directly in his time coaching the team. When he wanted Jordan to do something, he would often tell the team it was time to do it. When he had criticism for Jordan, it was instead directed at the team. It was a means of communication that the coach and star player would settle into over the course of their years together. They both obviously knew what was going on and found the practice acceptable. The other players on the team would sometimes complain about it quietly. But they too accepted it as a quirk of the circumstances.

As Game 5 twisted toward its conclusion, this dynamic produced a moment of lore, one that Jordan's teammates—and even future teammates—would come to treasure. With a championship hanging in the balance, with John Paxson open and Jordan ignoring him while continuing to attack mostly one-on-one, Jackson asked impatiently during a late time-out, "MJ, who's open?"

Perhaps stunned by Jackson's sudden directness, Jordan said nothing.

So Jackson asked again. "Who's open?"

The story has been passed along by the many Jordan teammates who supposedly suffered his demands and indifference over the years.

"It's one of my favorite stories," Steve Kerr, who filled Paxson's role on subsequent Bulls' teams, said in a 2012 interview. "Michael's having a rough second half, they're double-teaming him, and he's forcing some shots. And Phil calls a time-out with, like, minutes left in the game. And he's looking right at Michael and he goes, 'Michael, who's open?' And Michael won't look up. He goes, 'Michael, who's open?' Finally, Michael looks up at him and goes, 'Pax!' And Phil goes, 'Well, throw him the fuckin' ball!'"

Paxson would make five long buckets in the final four minutes as time and again, Jordan penetrated, drew the defense, then kicked it out. Paxson would finish with 20 and Pippen 32 as the Bulls closed out the championship with a 108–101 win in Game 5. The moment was met by a numbed silence from the Forum crowd, recalled Bulls broadcaster Jim Durham in 2011. "The one thing I'll remember is the Bulls dancing off the floor and everybody else just sitting there watching it."

On the floor in the quiet aftermath, Laker superfan Jack Nicholson hugged Jackson, and Magic Johnson sought out Jordan to offer his congratulations. The two had become closer during the series after Johnson approached Jordan and told him that they needed to forget their differences. The event was the true beginning of their friendship, Jordan would say later. "I saw tears in his eyes," Johnson said of their conversation after the final buzzer. "I told him, 'You proved everyone wrong. You're a winner as well as a great individual basketball player.'"

The tears became a tide as Jordan made his way through the bedlam of the locker room to inhabit the moment he'd sought for seven years. "I never lost hope," he said as his wife and father sat nearby. "I'm so happy for my family and this team and this franchise. It's something I've worked seven years for, and I thank God for the talent and the opportunity that I've had."

"That scene with Michael crying, with his dad and with his arms around him," Jim Durham recalled. "Finally he had won, and he had won doing it his way."

Once the tears started, Jordan couldn't seem to hold them back. "I've never been this emotional publicly," he said. "When I came here, we started from scratch. I vowed we'd make the playoffs every year, and each year we got closer. I always had faith I'd get this ring one day."

Delivering the final game had come down to Paxson hitting the open shots, Jordan said of the moment that Jackson had forced upon him. "That's why I've always wanted him on my team and why I wanted him to stay on my team."

"It was done and over, and it was dramatic, like a blitzkrieg," Jackson recalled. "Afterward, there was a lot of joy. There was Michael holding the trophy and weeping.... It was special."

Later, the Bulls took the party to their quarters at the Ritz Carlton in Marina del Rey. "I remember going up to Michael's room," John Ligmanowski said. "He told me to order like a dozen bottles of Dom Pérignon and enough hors d'oeuvres for forty people. We're at the Ritz Carlton, and I call down to the concierge. I said, 'Yeah, send up a dozen bottles of Dom and hors d'oeuvres for forty people.' So they were like, 'Wait a second.' They didn't want to send it up because they knew it wasn't Michael on the phone. So I handed the phone to him. He grabbed the phone and said, 'Send it up!'"

The Bulls returned to Chicago and celebrated their championship in Grant Park before a crowd estimated at between 500,000 and a million fans. "We started from the bottom," Jordan told the sea of happy faces, "and it was hard working our way to the top. But we did it."

Behind the scenes, winning it all seemed to ease the conflict between Jordan and Krause. "We wound up winning that first championship," Jim Stack remembered, "and Michael never said anything again publicly about whether we needed to make this trade or that move. There was a begrudging respect that Michael finally gave Jerry, but Jerry really had to go out of his way to earn it.

In those early years Michael was really relentless on Jerry in terms of his basketball acumen."

In the wake of the championship Jordan eased Krause out of his crosshairs, Stack recalled. "The hatred subsided there for a while."

Chapter 27

THE GAMBLE

After taking his team to the Promised Land, Jordan abruptly veered into the wilderness, even as Gatorade was preparing to release its tour de force ad with that overpowering refrain: "I wanna be like Mike." Time would reveal that the limitations to what he could achieve in basketball were largely self-imposed. While he had just claimed his first pro championship and thus had begun to refute criticism about his ability to be a team player, Jordan had already embarked on a path in his off-court life that threatened the good name he had built so carefully.

That summer, Jordan and Richard Esquinas, the part owner of the San Diego Sports Arena, engaged in a series of high-stakes golf matches and began keeping a running tab of their wins and losses. "We were always very flexible in payments," Esquinas would recall later. The gambling hit a new level that September in Pinehurst, North Carolina, when Esquinas lost $98,000 to Jordan in a day of golf. He wanted Jordan to take a double-or-nothing bet, and to emphasize that, he wrote Jordan two checks for $98,000 each. What he didn't tell Jordan was that he wasn't sure he had the funds to cover either. He wouldn't have to, as it turned out. Jordan accepted the bet, and the two gamblers went at each other later that month over an adrenaline-fed, ten-day spree at the Aviara Golf Club in San Diego. Jordan not only lost the $98,000, but ended up down an additional $626,000. Jordan, too, wanted a double or nothing. Esquinas, who was on a hot streak, said he pleaded with Jordan not to go double or nothing but finally agreed to it.

"Once again, he went into a long story about his wealth," Esquinas would later recall. "He could handle $1.2 million, he said, should he happen to lose. 'Let's play for it,' he said. 'E-Man, I can't believe you won't give me this game.' I was trying to get him to comprehend the magnitude of losing at such a level, to defer this insistence that we engage once again. Not only did he want to continue this chase, he was demanding it. 'I do not want this game,' I said, 'but I must be honest with you. You lose and you pay. That's the only way I'll give you a shot. And, if I beat you, that's it. No more of this double or nothing.' "

Jordan promptly lost, bringing his total debt to what Esquinas claimed was $1.252 million. He seemed a bit shaken after the loss but returned home to Wilmington for the grand honor of having a stretch of Interstate 40 near his Gordon Road boyhood home named after him. Dean Smith was there, his plaid sports jacket contrasting with Jordan's sleekly cut tan suit with a dapper silk pocket hanky. The tears streamed down his face in the Indian summer heat at the ribbon-cutting ceremony. Juanita gently wiped them away after he returned to his seat, but perhaps the most tender moment had come before the ceremony started, when James Jordan, dressed in his own dapper light blue suit and sporting a "Be Like Mike" button on his left lapel, stepped onto the platform to shake his son's hand. Still seated, Jordan looked up at his father with a broad, beatific grin and patted his shoulder.

That same week, Jordan had been named to the 1992 US Olympic basketball team. The announcement came after a negotiation in which Jordan was adamant that he would not play on the team if the roster included Isiah Thomas. After his intense and sometimes unpleasant experience on the 1984 Olympic team, Jordan had been reluctant to get involved in what would come to be called the Dream Team. Jack McCallum of *Sports Illustrated* reported that the selection committee decided not to invite Thomas because of questions about how he might affect the team's chemistry. The story suggested that neither Chuck Daly nor Detroit GM Jack McCloskey, who was on the selection committee, had put up much of a case for including Thomas. More than anything, the story damaged the

Pistons' hopes of recovering from their disastrous loss to Chicago in the playoffs. Their chemistry had taken a severe hit.

Meanwhile, Esquinas had begun phoning Jordan to inquire about payment for their wager. Esquinas would reveal three years later that Jordan replied with a laugh, "Rich, I just might as well shoot you as to give you a check for $1.2 million."

The comment left Esquinas more than a bit fearful and prompted him to contemplate the great value Jordan held for various interested parties. "I feared that I'd be perceived as a threat to Jordan, and the things that come with those fears," he said. "I played it off," Esquinas would reveal later. "But he was definitely drawing the line that he wasn't going to pay the full amount. What he was saying was, 'I'm not paying the full amount.' And right there, I knew I had trouble collecting."

The Book of Revelations

Although the golf losses remained out of public light, Sam Smith's book *The Jordan Rules* would land as another bombshell in his life that fall and immediately set the entire organization on edge. It was an intensely negative portrait of Jordan, but also of frumpy Krause and his substantial hubris. Phil Jackson would later note that the book had accomplished something truly rare: it gave Jordan and Krause something they agreed on.

"Sam Smith made some money on that book," the GM would say several years later. "I hope he chokes on every dollar."

The book, however, was truly revelatory about the hard edges of Jordan's competitiveness. Always hugely sensitive, he was angered and deeply hurt by the depiction. The public, meanwhile, soaked it up, delighted by this figure with a diamond-hard will who drove everyone around him to an odd amalgam of misery and greatness. Rather than damage Jordan's image, it spurred yet more worship. The impact of *The Jordan Rules* contributed to Jordan's sense of being besieged, and to the fabric of what Jackson called "the pack."

"*The Jordan Rules* was very divisive to the team," the coach recalled.

Horace Grant served as one of the sources, which angered Jordan. "I knew people were going to start taking shots at me," Jordan told Mark Vancil. "You get to a point where people are going to get tired of seeing you on a pedestal, all clean and polished. They say, 'Let's see if there's any dirt around this person.' But I never expected it to come from inside. Sam tried to make it seem like he was a friend of the family for eight months. But the family talked about all this hatred they have for me. I mean, if they had so much hatred for me, how could they play with me? ... I don't know how we won if there was so much hatred among all of us. It looked like we all got along so well."

The same resentment surfaced just weeks later when Jordan decided not to join the team in the traditional Rose Garden ceremony with President George Bush. Instead, he headed off on a golf trip with a group of pals that included childhood friend David Bridgers. The White House fuss spurred yet more discord between Grant and Jordan.

"I think it was a situation where Horace felt demeaned, felt that he was made light of, and he wanted to be a person of importance," Phil Jackson observed. "There were some things about Horace that bothered Michael. Basically, Horace says whatever comes into his mind in front of the press. One of the situations that was exacerbating to Michael came after our first championship when Horace and his wife and Michael and his wife went to New York. They went to dinner and to see a play. While they were out, Michael basically told Horace that he wasn't going to see President Bush. Michael said, 'It's not obligatory. It's on my time, and I have other things to do.' Horace at the time had no problem with it. He knew about this in a private situation and said nothing. Yet when the press came into the picture later, after the story became public, and asked Horace if it bothered him, he made a big issue of it. Basically, the press had put the words in his mouth, and he felt it was a good time to make this kind of statement."

"No way am I going," Jordan told reporters when asked about the traditional visit. "No one asked me if the date was convenient. It's OK if the other guys go, but the White House is just like any other house. It's just cleaner."

Just days before the White House event, Jordan had made something of an awkward appearance on *Saturday Night Live*, along with Jesse Jackson and the rap group Public Enemy. Jordan didn't want to do it, but Sonny Vaccaro talked him into it and even went to New York to sit in NBC's green room with him.

Phil Knight had recently fired Vaccaro from Nike, but he moved on to successes with other athletic shoe companies. "When Phil let me go, Michael called me. One of the first calls I got," Vaccaro recalled. "He said, 'What can I do? You want me to call Phil?' And I said, 'No, it's done.'"

Like Rob Strasser and others who had moved on from Nike, Vaccaro had pushed for Jordan to demand his own brand in the wake of the overwhelming success of the Air Jordan shoe. "I was so much involved in making sure that Michael asked for that," Vaccaro said. "I mean, that was my last will and testament to Michael. I told him, 'You've got to get a piece of this company.' I mean, that's what it was." One of Vaccaro's last chores for Nike and Jordan was cleaning up the final details of the mess with the Flight 23 stores and James Jordan. "Michael was frustrated with not being able to just close it down," Vaccaro recalled. "It got to the point where he stood up and said that James had to close it down. If money could stop it, it had to be stopped."

That same busy month NBC aired *A Comedy Salute to Michael Jordan*, a Comic Relief prime-time special to raise funds for homeless children. Tickets to the event, which was taped at the Chicago Theater in July, ran as much as $400, and thousands filled the streets outside, hoping to catch a glimpse of Jordan. He and Juanita sat in a box in the audience, obviously embarrassed as an array of stars worked their way through skits about him.

Emcee Billy Crystal kicked off the event by poking fun at the vast number of products endorsed by Jordan. "I have Michael Jordan everything," he said. "I even have Michael Jordan contact lenses. They make everybody else look shorter and slower."

To repay NBC for all its effort in producing the fund-raiser, Vaccaro finally got Jordan to agree to do *Saturday Night Live*. "That was the biggest thing in the world to do," Vaccaro said, "and he was a little bit nervous about doing it. He almost didn't do it."

Sports Illustrated's Jack McCallum was there in the green room, too, observing a Jordan both entertained by the *SNL* cast and put upon for autographs. The producers had wanted to do a skit about an effort by Jordan to keep Isiah Thomas off the Olympic team, but he refused. His opening segment in hosting *SNL* was roundly flat and unfunny, and Jordan certainly rued the decision afterward.

It was in the wake of these events that Jordan's first real troubles surfaced. In December, police surveillance of a Charlotte man, a convicted cocaine dealer named James "Slim" Bouler, turned up a $57,000 check that Jordan had written to him. Bouler was later charged with money laundering after a tax-evasion investigation. Both Bouler and Jordan told authorities that the money was a loan, but Jordan was soon caught up in Bouler's troubles and would later be served with a subpoena to testify in the case against him.

Then in February 1992, a bail bondsman, Eddie Dow, was murdered during a robbery at his home. Thieves took $20,000 in cash from a metal briefcase on the premises but left three checks worth $108,000 written by Jordan. The lawyer handling Dow's estate confirmed that the checks were for gambling debts owed by Jordan to a North Carolina contractor named Dean Chapman and two other men. Press reports revealed that Jordan often hosted small gatherings for golfing and gambling at his Hilton Head Island residence, where Jordan had lost the money. Dow had been to at least three such gatherings, according to his attorney. Jordan was also known to host Mike's Time, a gathering for golf and high-stakes poker before training camp each season.

The reports prompted NBA commissioner David Stern to issue a reprimand to Jordan. The league soon launched the first of two "investigations" into Jordan's activities, although they were limited in scope. Neither Jerry Krause nor Sonny Vaccaro was approached about an interview. Krause said in 2012 that the Bulls were as surprised as anyone else when Jordan's issues came to light, but they never made any attempt to learn more about his off-court activities. That was surprising, considering that Krause worked in the Los Angeles Lakers' front office in the late 1970s. The Lakers, according to former GM Pete Newell, employed off-duty LAPD vice officers to keep track of players' activities. Phil Jackson would later accuse Krause, aka "The Sleuth," of spying on the off-court activities of Bulls players, which Krause also denied.

"I have complete confidence in him as a person," Krause said of Jordan. Nike took a similar approach. "In his private life, he should be able to do what every other person can do. He's not the president or the pope," replied Dusty Kidd, a Nike spokesman, when queried by reporters.

"He had problems," Sonny Vaccaro recalled in 2012. "He's the only guy that could have survived the gambling stuff. You know that, don't you?"

Twenty years later, Krause offered his take on the matter, too. "I didn't know that there were gambling issues," he said. "I knew he played cards on the airplane. You'd hear the guys yelling at one another. I didn't know what the stakes were. Later on I found out that they were very high. But all the great old-timers in the NBA used to gamble. I was used to that. I was used to guys playing cards. That's the way of the NBA. As for Michael, it was just his way of living. So what? He had the money. He was never nonprofessional. That sucker showed up every night and he was ready to play. I saw him do tons of charitable things, good deeds. And tons of asinine things, too. He is who he is."

Dominion

One by one the icons who had stood so long in front of Jordan fell by the wayside. Isiah Thomas and his Pistons crumbled, then melted away like the Wicked Witch of the West. For Larry Bird, it was the indignity of age, the back troubles, the ball short at the rim, the dismissals in the early rounds of the playoffs. But the biggest icon fell on November 7, 1991, while Jordan was at practice. Lon Rosen, Magic Johnson's agent, phoned Bulls PR man Tim Hallam that morning.

Rosen delivered to Jordan the same bad news that a small circle of the NBA elite had gotten. Magic Johnson would announce his retirement immediately that afternoon in Los Angeles because he had recently tested positive for HIV, the virus that causes AIDS.

Stunned, Jordan gathered himself, then asked about his childhood hero, "Is he gonna die?"

It was the question on the minds of millions as that strange and curious NBA season opened. And many high-profile players quietly went on their own to get tested, because so many of them had partied in the same LA playground where Johnson had explored excess. Jordan himself was not free of these rumors, including one in which he was said to have wagered large sums with teammates over which Hollywood starlets he would bed during the team's West Coast road swings. He was likewise rumored to have collected on at least one such bet, although how he supposedly confirmed his success was left unclear.

As for basketball, the Bulls opened the season 1–2, and it looked as though they might be in for another transition, marked by more internal struggles and frustration. No team had repeated as NBA champions since the days of Boston's Bill Russell dynasty until Pat Riley drove his Lakers to a second straight title in 1988. But the pressure of that push had destroyed his relationships with his players. Riley was soon gone and Magic Johnson thoroughly depleted. Jackson was aware of the risks of pushing such an agenda. A host of side issues were already driving his desire to have his players explore meditation and the Zen mentality. For whatever reason, they soon showed extraordinary focus.

"The one great thing about this group of guys," Jackson would say, looking back, "was that they never let the external stuff bother the team's play on the floor."

Krause set the roster with a November trade, sending disgruntled Dennis Hopson to Sacramento for reserve guard Bobby Hansen. After those two early losses, they quickly gained clarity and rode on the wings of a new, emerging force, Scottie Pippen. In 1992, Jordan was far and away the best player in the league, Jim Stack observed, "but Scottie had caught up to the point that their games were 1 and 1A."

In looking back on the development four years later, Tex Winter pointed out that Pippen, like Magic Johnson, had grown into that special type of player who "made his teammates much better...I think more so than Michael. It's my personal opinion that there

are times — not always, certainly — but there's times when Michael
detracts from his teammates. You're not gonna find that much in
Pippen. He's totally unselfish. Michael should be selfish because
he's such a great scorer. Michael is uninhibited, and Michael is
gonna look to score most of the time when he's in a position where
he thinks he can, whereas Scottie on many occasions will pass up
that opportunity just to get his teammates involved."

Jordan obviously was basketball's great force, but it was Pippen
who learned to channel that force in ways that few other players
could.

As he had displayed in the championship series, Pippen had
developed into a defensive presence that, in turn, made the Bulls a
great defensive team. There would be much focus on the triangle
offense as the team got better and better at executing it that season,
but their defense gave opponents reason for pause.

"Their defense is so terrific already," plainspoken Utah coach
Jerry Sloan said after studying the Bulls, "that when they decide to
step it up a notch, they can annihilate you. If you panic in that situation, you're in trouble, and most teams panic."

Jackson himself would come to call it "cracking the case," that
moment in the game when his team would rise to another level.
Feeding their opponents' panic, they raced out to a 37–5 record,
including a fourteen-game winning streak in November and December, the longest in the franchise's history. In January they ripped
off another thirteen straight, then slipped late in the month and
into February, going only 11–8.

"We had a phenomenal start to the season," recalled Chip Schaefer, who had been hired as the Bulls' new trainer. "We had a 37–5
record. But then we headed west and lost four of six games before
the All-Star break. Michael got ejected in Utah when he head-
bumped Tommie Wood, the official. We were in a triple-overtime
game, and Wood called a foul on Michael in the third overtime. It
was an accidental head butt. Michael was vehement in his argument, and they bumped heads. Wood ejected him from the game,
and we wound up losing with Jeff Malone's free throws."

Jordan also fouled out of a game that season. He would not foul
out of another game for the rest of his years with the Bulls, despite

being an aggressor in Jackson's pressure defense. In 930 regular-season games in Chicago, he would foul out just ten times. He would foul out just three times in another 179 playoff games with the Bulls. Since the days of Wilt Chamberlain, the NBA had been a league that did not like to lose its stars to disqualification.

"It was a galling loss," Bulls VP Steve Schanwald remembered of Jordan's ejection in Utah. "Prior to the call, the game was one of the greatest ever. If not for that call, it likely would have been the NBA's first quadruple overtime game ever."

"Then Michael had to sit out the next game, which was the game in Phoenix," Chip Schaefer recalled. "So he just flew on to the All-Star Game in Orlando."

Pippen and Jackson joined him there a day later. Even though he had retired in November, Magic Johnson was allowed to return for the All-Star Game, where he owned the weekend and was named MVP.

That spring, in the wake of the revelations about his golf and gambling binges, Jordan addressed the strange arc of his life in an interview with the *Tribune*'s Melissa Isaacson. "It's just one of those things that happened," he said of his sudden fame. "And it shocked everybody. It's a hell of a burden and it's just one of those things that I stumbled into. Then you see people counting on you so much that you start to try to constantly maintain it, and that's when the pressure starts to mount. Suddenly, everything you do, you have to stop and think, 'How is this going to be perceived?'"

He had been contrite at first. The public still did not yet know about Richard Esquinas. Jordan's connections with the cast of unsavory characters captured in the police reports and hearing transcripts had been quite enough. "At some point in my life, I probably would have to face it," he told Isaacson. "Very few people go through their lifetimes without scars. And I went through a six- or seven-year period without them. Now I have a couple of scars and I've got to mend them and keep moving on. The scars won't go away, but you know you're going to be a better person because of them."

That might have been true if he had found some other outlet. His was a cycle of high-level competition, interspersed with golf, marathon poker games, and hanging out with his entourage. Also in there he managed to fit in time with his family.

"I tell my wife that I have a split personality," he said. "I lead two lives. Because in some ways, I'm projected to be a thirty-eight-, thirty-nine-year-old mature person who has experienced life to the fullest and now he's more or less settled down and focused on very conservative things. But the other side of me is a twenty-nine-year-old who never really got the chance to experience his success with friends and maybe do some of the crazy things that twenty-seven-, twenty-eight-, twenty-nine-year-old people will do. And sometimes I have those urges to do those things, but it can only be done in the privacy of the very small group of people who really know you as that twenty-nine-year-old person."

Isaacson asked if Jordan could just live as his alter ego. If he had, it would have likely been a short life, and Jordan acknowledged as much, just as he acknowledged that he felt ill at ease with a life beyond basketball, one in which he attempted to endorse political candidates or stand up as a role model. Jordan offered that he simply wasn't experienced enough to do those things well.

"Everything seemed to snowball for the good," he said of his wealth and success off the court. "From a financial situation, it's worth it. But away from that, it has been a burden to a certain extent. It caused extra pressure, but at the same time, it earned the respect and admiration of a lot of people. Everyone likes to be respected and admired."

In March, Richard Esquinas came to town to watch a Bulls victory over the Cavaliers in the Stadium, a night when Jordan scored 44. The next night, Esquinas joined Michael and Juanita and the Chicago Bears' Richard Dent and his wife at the Jordan home for dinner. Jordan and Esquinas had been dickering over the golf debt for months. They had played intermittently over the season, and Jordan now owed just under a million. Eventually, the topic came up that night. He and Jordan retreated to the kitchen, where their tone turned heated. Jordan asked him to back off because the revelations of his other golf gambling had turned up the pressure on him.

"You have to give me some space," Esquinas recalled Jordan

telling him. "You have to give me some time. I've got these other things to deal with."

The Bulls closed out the schedule that spring with a blistering 19–2 run to finish 67–15, the franchise's best record. "We just coasted the rest of that season through one winning streak after another," Bulls trainer Chip Schaefer recalled. "The team was almost bored with success and could turn it on and off whenever they wanted to."

With the structure of the triangle offense taking the ball out of his hands a bit more, Jordan's average had dipped to 30.1 points per game, but it was still enough to claim his sixth straight scoring crown and to win his third league MVP award. He and Pippen were named to the All-Defense first team, and Pippen earned All-NBA second team honors.

"We really had an outrageous year," Jackson said. "We won sixty-seven games, and basically I felt like I had to pull back on the reins, or they would have tried to win seventy or seventy-five."

The postseason, however, brought a changed atmosphere, featuring a showdown with Pat Riley's New York Knicks, a team that had reprised Detroit's Bad Boys tactics. "We had injuries, and we had to face New York," Jackson recalled. "And teams were coming at us with a lot of vim and vigor. We lost seven games in our championship run. It wasn't as easy this second time. There had been a challenge to our character as a team."

In the first round of the playoffs, the Bulls faced the Miami Heat, a 1989 expansion team making its first postseason appearance. Chicago quickly claimed the first two games in the best-of-five series, then headed to Miami for Game 3. "In Miami's first home playoff game ever, it was clacker night," recalled Bulls broadcaster Tom Dore. "What they said was, any time Michael gets the ball or shoots a free throw, go nuts with those clackers. Make all kinds of noise. Well, it worked in the first quarter. The Heat had a big lead. And in fact, we were wondering, 'Can the Bulls come back from this?' And Michael stopped by the broadcast table and looked at Johnny Kerr and me and said, 'Here we come.' That's all he said. Boy did he ever. He went absolutely berserk, scored 56 points and the Bulls won, swept the series."

The trial by fire came early that year, in the second round of the Eastern playoffs. The Knicks muscled their way to a win in Game 1 in Chicago Stadium. B. J. Armstrong helped even the series at 1–1 by hitting big shots in the fourth quarter of Game 2. In Game 3 in New York, Jordan finally broke free of the cloying defense for his first dunks of the series. Powered by Xavier McDaniel, New York fought back to even it with a win in Game 4. In critical Game 5, Jordan took control by going to the basket. The Knicks kept fouling him, and he kept making the free throws, 15 in all, to finish with 37 points as the Bulls won, 96–88.

"Michael is Michael," Riley said afterward. "His game is to take it to the basket and challenge the defense. When you play against a guy like him, he tells you how much he wants to win by how hard he takes the ball to the basket."

The Knicks managed to tie it again with a Game 6 win in New York, but the Bulls were primed for Game 7 in the Stadium and walked to the win, 110–81.

They resumed their struggle in the conference finals against the Cavaliers, who managed to tie the series at two games apiece, but the Bulls had just enough to escape Cleveland, 4–2. Jordan had carried his team to a second straight appearance in the league championship series, this time against the Portland Trail Blazers, the team that had bypassed him in the 1984 draft in favor of Kentucky big man Sam Bowie. Whether that decision qualified as one of the greatest sports blunders of all time had been debated in Oregon over the years every time Jordan burned Nike's hometown team for big points. Bowie, who had missed two years of his career at Kentucky with a slow-to-heal broken leg, would admit in 2012 that he lied to Portland team physicians during a 1984 physical to evaluate his leg. He said he told them he had no leg pain when in fact he did. The irony is that it was Jordan, not Bowie, who first went out with serious injury, although Bowie would never reach his potential. In another irony, it was the Blazers who made it to the league championship series a year before a Jordan-led team reached it. (Portland lost the 1990 title to Detroit.)

The Blazers of 1992 featured Clyde Drexler, Danny Ainge, Cliff Robinson, Terry Porter, and Buck Williams. Fans savored the opportunity to see the match-up with Drexler, who had an athleticism that matched Jordan's. Veteran observers sensed that Jordan, with his long memory, might try to make a statement as the series was set to open, but none of them could have imagined his outburst in Game 1 in Chicago Stadium. He scored an NBA Finals record 35 points in the first half, including a record 6 three-pointers, enough to bury the Blazers, 122–89. He finished with 39 points after making 16 of 27 field goal attempts, including the 6 three-pointers, all highlighted by his trademark shrug.

"The only way you can stop Michael," said Cliff Robinson, "is to take him off the court."

"I was in a zone," said Jordan, who had focused on extra hours of practice shooting long range before Game 1. "My threes felt like free throws. I didn't know what I was doing, but they were going in."

In Game 2, Drexler fouled out with about four minutes left. But the Blazers rallied with a 15–5 run to tie the game, then managed to win, 115–104, on the strength of Danny Ainge's 9 points in overtime. The Blazers had their split with the series headed to Portland for three games. But the Bulls' defense and a solid team effort— Pippen and Grant scored 18 each to go with Jordan's 26 in Game 3—ended thoughts of an upset, although this time Jordan missed all four of his three-point attempts.

The Blazers struggled to stay close through most of Game 4, then moved in front with just over three minutes left and won it, 93–88, on a final surge to even the series at 2–2. Jordan had made just 11 of 26 field goal attempts in Game 4, and it was clear that the critical Game 5 would be a test of endurance, with both teams having played more than a hundred games on the season. Jordan came out aggressively, attacking the basket repeatedly, drawing fouls, and pushing the Bulls to an early lead. Chicago's coaches had surprised Portland by spreading the floor with their offense, which allowed Jordan open shots off of numerous backdoor cuts. He made 16 of 19 free throws to finish with 46 points, enough to give the Bulls a huge 119–106 win and a 3–2 lead. The Blazers had pulled close, but Jordan's scoring kept them at bay over the final minutes. His clenched fist and defiant grimace afterward served as yet another reminder to Portland of what had been missed in the 1984 draft.

The Bulls fell into a deep hole in Game 6 back in Chicago, down 17 points late in the third quarter. Then Jackson pulled his regulars and played Bobby Hansen, B. J. Armstrong, Stacey King, and Scott Williams with Pippen. Hansen stole the ball and hit a shot, and the rally was on with Jordan on the bench leading the cheers.

With about eight minutes to go, Jackson sent him back in, and the Bulls powered their way to their second title, 97–93, bringing the Stadium to an unprecedented eruption, the first pro championship won in Chicago by a Chicago team since the 1961 Bears won the NFL title at Soldier Field.

"The final against Portland was a dramatic night for us and all Chicago fans," Jackson recalled. "We came from 17 down at the end of the third quarter to win the championship. What followed was an incredible celebration." The Bulls retreated to the locker room to engage in the usual ritual, spewing their champagne, wearing their new hats backward. Meanwhile, their fans remained upstairs in the Stadium, thundering on in celebration. "The team had gone down to the dressing room to be presented with the Larry O'Brien trophy by David Stern and Bob Costas," remembered Bulls vice president Steve Schanwald. "Jerry Reinsdorf and Jerry Krause and Phil Jackson and Michael and Scottie stood on a temporary stage and accepted the trophy. But we didn't have instant replay capability, so the fans were not able to share in that moment. Up in the Stadium, we were playing Gary Glitter on the loudspeaker, and the crowd was just reveling in the championship.... I went down and asked Jerry Reinsdorf if we could bring the team back up. He said, 'It's all right with me, but ask Phil.'"

Jackson put two fingers in his mouth and whistled. Everything got quiet. "Grab that trophy," he said. "We're going back up to celebrate with our fans!"

Jordan grabbed the trophy, and the team followed him back upstairs. As they came through the tunnel, the game operations crew blasted "Eye in the Sky" by the Alan Parsons Project, the Bulls' intro music.

"All of a sudden the crowd just exploded," Schanwald recalled. "It was a 10,000–goose bump experience. All of a sudden some of the players, Scottie and Horace, and Hansen, those guys got up on the table so that everybody could see them in the crowd. Then Michael came up and joined them with the trophy, and they started dancing."

Jordan held up two fingers for the crowd, then flashed three, and the roar was deafening. Jackson enjoyed the scene for a time, then retreated back downstairs to reflect quietly alone. "Things had been up and down," he said later, "but we had had this one goal together, and despite our differences, we had focused on that one goal. I told the guys, 'A back-to-back championship is the mark of a great team.' We had passed the demarcation point. Winning that second title set us apart."

A few days later in Grant Park, Pippen again told hundreds of thousands of people that Chicago was going for a three-peat. The crowd cheered in response, but before Jordan could contemplate another title run, there was another little matter he had to deal with.

Chapter 28

ALL THAT GLITTERS

THE SMART PLAY might have been for Pippen and Jordan to decline their invitations to play for the United States in the 1992 Olympic Games in Barcelona. Krause hoped for as much. He wanted the Bulls' superstars to rest over the summer. They both agreed to play, however, and Jordan soon found himself enmeshed in the Dream Team, the first US Olympic team to include the best of American professional basketball. The group in red, white, and blue would be feted across the globe like mythical superheroes. Perhaps it was good for basketball, but it says much that their most competitive moment in terms of the game itself would come in an intra-squad scrimmage. They made chumps of everybody else and did a great deal of showboating in the process, reducing the supposedly hallowed Olympic contests to pointless, mismatched affairs. Jordan knew all of this heading in and wasn't shy about saying it.

"When you look at the talent and the teams we're supposed to play against, it's a massacre," he had said months before the event. "It should never be close. We taught them the game of basketball. We've got people who have the ability and the height. We're talking about the greatest players that play the game now and the team is the best team that's ever been put together. Who's going to beat us? The Japanese? The Chinese? They can't match up to the athleticism we're going to have on this team. Not to mention the mental advantage we're going to have here with Magic, or whoever's gonna play the point. You have Stockton, Barkley, me, Robinson, Bird... come on. These are the people that the Europeans look up to, so how can they beat us? If any game is even close, it will be a moral victory for Europe."

Blowouts had been a regular feature of previous Olympic basketball games, even when the United States relied solely on amateur players. Now, American professionals were lining up to be paid between $600,000 and $800,000 each for their much-hyped appearances. Surely, if the "Olympians" weren't already narcissists heading into the event, they would emerge with egos larger than many of the countries they faced. The US Olympic committee discreetly approached each player about donating his salary back to the cause. Jordan readily complied. Some others, who weren't raking in his Nike cash, hesitated, then gave all or part of it back. And the casinos in Monaco, where the team made a promotional visit on the eve of the Olympic Games, certainly took a share, too.

Jordan used the team's training camp in La Jolla, California, to resume his golf challenge with Richard Esquinas. Playing between and around practices, he was able to reduce his gambling debt to $902,000. Esquinas would later tell the *Los Angeles Times* that Jordan's Olympic teammates were aware that he was wagering. "But everybody knew not to come near the question of how much," Esquinas said.

Jordan made most of his gains on the last day that they played, June 25, at La Jolla Country Club.

Esquinas joined Jordan one evening for a card game in Magic Johnson's Torrey Pines hotel suite, a hundred bucks a hand, with pots that got up to as much as four thousand. Clyde Drexler and Pippen were among the crew, as were several collegians from the scrimmage team, including Bobby Hurley, Chris Webber, and Eric Montross. None of the collegians had the bank to join in the game, which made them the targets of Jordan's and Johnson's jibes. Esquinas recalled that every time Jordan put money in the kitty, Johnson would needle him about his "tennis shoe" cash. They may have become friends, but Johnson, it seemed, would never be able to get over Jordan's Nike deal, the gift that kept on giving.

Soon enough some girls showed up to distract the card players, and the evening would prove to be one in a run of party nights for the Dream Teamers. Esquinas's days with Jordan, however, had come to an end. They would continue to wrangle over the golfing losses, with various estimates suggesting that Jordan paid somewhere between $200,000 and $300,000, some of it in a series of $50,000 checks written by Juanita Jordan. Esquinas would bide his time, plotting a way to bring the matter to Jordan's attention one final time.

The Olympics afforded the NBA's top stars their first real opportunity to spend time together and to get to know each other better. The group quickly learned of Jordan's indifference to rest. Throughout the experience, he would stay up long hours, smoking cigars, playing cards, hanging out, anything to avoid rest, leaving Charles Barkley and others shaking their heads in wonder.

"It was," said Chuck Daly, the team's coach, "like Elvis and the Beatles put together. Traveling with the Dream Team was like traveling with twelve rock stars. That's all I can compare it to."

The Americans played fourteen games on their way to winning the gold, and their smallest margin of victory was 32 points. The subtext for the gathering was the continuing rivalry of Michael and Magic. Despite his HIV-positive status, Johnson had made the roster, yet another highlight in the emotional sequence of events that marked the protracted end to his playing career. He seemed intent on asserting his continued dominance as the game's best, never mind that his Lakers had lost convincingly in 1991. He and Jordan traded barbs over who was tops, then settled it during an intrasquad scrimmage when the team stopped over in Monaco before heading to Barcelona. It was closed to the press, but the competition featured one team led by Johnson and the other by Jordan, detailed in Jack McCallum's book, *Dream Team,* celebrating the event—and its excesses—twenty years later. Johnson's "Blue" team, featuring Charles Barkley, Chris Mullin, David Robinson, and Christian Laettner, jumped out to a big lead, with Jordan and Johnson jawing away at each other. Jordan's team, with Scottie Pippen, Karl Malone, Patrick Ewing, and Larry Bird, managed to storm back to win over a furious Johnson, who grew angrier afterward as Jordan serenaded him with the song from his Gatorade ad: "Sometimes I dream...if I could be like Mike."

"It was the most fun I ever had on a basketball court," Jordan would say later.

Magic Mike had conquered the hero of his youth for a final time.

The affair had turned heated, but in the end, even Johnson, the natural-born leader of the assemblage, had to acknowledge that his time had passed. And Jordan had asserted once again that he was the king of the NBA hill.

Team USA claimed the gold with a 117–85 win over Croatia on August 8, 1992. "They knew they were playing the best in the world," Daly said afterward, in part as justification for the mismatches. "They'll go home and for the rest of their lives be able to tell their kids, 'I played against Michael Jordan and Magic Johnson and Larry Bird.' And the more they play against our best players, the more confident they're going to get."

The lone sticking point for Jordan had been Reebok's sponsorship of the team, which forced him to wear the logo of his business competitor, a matter he addressed by draping an American flag over the Reebok insignia during the ring ceremony. It was something neither demanded nor contrived by Nike, Sonny Vaccaro said, but Jordan's solution delighted company officials and demonstrated the depth of his legendary loyalty.

One day not long afterward, Jordan and Pippen sat on the Bulls team bus talking about their Olympic teammates and the games. "Just imagine," Pippen told Jordan, "how good Clyde Drexler would be if he worked on fundamentals with Tex Winter."

Like so many NBA players, Drexler was operating mostly off his great store of talent, absent any serious attention to the important details of the game. Jordan had been surprised to learn how lazy many of his Olympic teammates were about practice, how they were deceiving themselves about what the game required.

One of their highlights had been their determination to shut down Croatian star Toni Kukoc, Krause's "find" who was scheduled to join the Bulls for the 1993–94 NBA season. Kukoc was befuddled and embarrassed by the way they defended him during their competition. It was the same treatment that Jordan had leveled on every acquisition or rookie that Krause had brought to the team, but in the midst of Olympic play some thought it seemed strangely out of place, none more so than Krause himself.

At home, awaiting Jordan, was his subpoena to testify in Slim Bouler's criminal trial in North Carolina. He would be asked to explain why Bouler, a convicted cocaine dealer, was in possession of a $57,000 check from His Airness. Jordan had first told authorities the money was a business loan, but under oath on the stand, he confessed it was for poker and gambling losses from one of the weekends at his Hilton Head home. He was not asked about the other three checks found in the briefcase of Eddie Dow, the bail bondsman who had been murdered during a robbery in February.

Jordan had publicly acknowledged his lie in an interview with a Chicago newspaper several days before the trial began, saying he was "embarrassed to say it, at first, but the truth's got to come out."

On the stand, he explained that he lost the money playing $1,000 Nassau with Bouler and others at Hilton Head, although Jordan denied that he had been the victim of hustlers. "It was just bad golf in a three-day period," he said. David Stern called Jordan to New York to discuss his activities and the company he had been keeping. Later, at a press conference, Jordan suggested that the men tied to him through the checks weren't actually friends but mere acquaintances who had boasted of their activities with him. The paper trail was real, however, and growing.

As the season was set to open, the NBA issued a reprimand of Jordan for gambling on golf and keeping unsavory company, which left him somewhat contrite during training camp. He told reporters he wouldn't quit gambling but he would lower the stakes. "Winning is great, but when you lose that amount and get all the abuse I got, it ain't worth it any longer," he said. "I think people can accept my losing forty or fifty dollars. It's easy to relate to. A twenty-dollar Nassau is something I should stick with."

Twenty-dollar Nassaus involved betting a limit of twenty on the front nine, twenty on the back nine, and twenty on the total score for eighteen holes, making for a bet that would not exceed sixty dollars total.

The season ahead brought a welcome diversion from his time on the witness stand. He and the Bulls would try to win a third straight title, something that had not been done in almost thirty years, since Bill Russell and his merry Celtics won eight straight championships in a period when the NBA had only eight to ten teams.

The Jordan Rules had captured him reflecting on his impending retirement and gave fans a glimpse of Jordan talking of stepping away from the pressure sometime in the next five years. He couldn't quite see the road ahead yet, and anyhow, he had a championship to win. But in that moment, no one had any idea how hard the coming year would be.

The Phoenix

Phil Jackson's mind seemed to work in snapshots. One was a Jordan dunk over Miami's Rony Seikaly in the first round of the 1992 playoffs, memorable as a throwback to Jordan's brush-high-against-the-rafters sort of stuff from his earlier days. "That was just an awesome slam over Seikaly that was one of those kind where he had to power over the top of everybody and look down at the basket," Jackson recalled as the 1992–93 NBA season was set to open.

It brought back memories for Jackson of a time before Jordan ruled the world. Things had changed that much for them all over a matter of just twelve months. They had gone from people who couldn't win it all to dominators. "He used to do it for photo opportunities," the coach said of Jordan's dunking, as if he were talking about some entirely different creature. "He did it for the entertainment value. He did it for the in-your-face effect. Now it's more or less a high-percentage shot. He has enough posters floating around."

With the transformation Jordan had undergone, the dunk against Miami now seemed like one of his final unrestrained moments. It wasn't just that Jackson had changed Jordan's thinking about his approach to the game. It was also the effect of his off-court activities and the stress that Jordan had heaped on himself, atop all that others had piled upon him. "It bothered me last year in the playoffs and at the end of last season," Jackson observed, still trying to process the team's run to two championships. "I could see that he was running dry. It got a little bit old and basketball usually doesn't get old for him many games out of the season. But it felt as if it did, particularly when there were so many things happening on the outside and he became the focal point of everyone's perception of the athlete, what happens when things go wrong, the White House, *The Jordan Rules*. A multitude of things that happened off the court affected him."

The coach addressed the issues in a talk with his star, telling him that his love for the game, his ability to find intrigue and freshness in it, had to be renewed for the Bulls to survive the grind of trying to win a third straight championship. A host of mileposts lay in their immediate path, among them Jordan's thirtieth birthday just weeks down the road. He had to find a measure of joy in returning to the court, Jackson said.

The *Trib*'s Melissa Isaacson visited the issue with Jordan on the brink of the season. "It has to be fun," he told her. "I have to enjoy myself."

That had become easier with the recent birth of his third child, Jasmine, a bright-eyed baby girl. His sons were a pair of grinning bear cubs, into everything and reminding Jordan of the good ol' days with his brother Larry.

His main hope was that all of the off-court headaches were behind him now, that all he would have to consider this season would be his family and the game. That proved to be wishful thinking. Sam Smith's revelatory book had set the agenda for the end of his career, an agenda that was now being hastened by the off-court issues.

Jackson took some comfort in the fact that Jordan still had three years left on his contract, which might allow him to see beyond the current headaches.

Asked by Isaacson how he would know he had reached the end of his playing days, Jordan replied, "When guys I used to go past start going past me.... I want to always stay ahead of my competition, to always have the upper hand."

His game would have to continue to evolve, but one thing remained steady: he wanted to hear no talk of reduced playing time.

The entertainer in him remained very much alive. "I still have the desire to create," he said that November. "That's part of me. Always will be."

Yet he was well aware that the way teams had begun to defend him would limit the acrobatics of his previous seasons. Since the Bulls had moved to the triangle, he had spent considerable time developing his post-up moves because the offense continued to offer him interesting ways to work closer to the basket, behind the defense, where it became harder to double-team him. The process of watching him adapt the offense to his own game fascinated Tex Winter. Jordan obviously understood how it reconfigured the floor. He could read where the opportunity lay like no other player who had come before him, which even allowed Winter to see his beloved triangle in new and different ways.

Jordan also understood instinctively that the changes would require a re-education for his fans and the basketball public. He had seen the public's misreading of the end of Julius Erving's career and wanted to avoid that for himself. "When Dr. J retired, everyone said 'Yeah, he should get out of the game, he's old,'" Jordan explained. "But Dr. J was still a good player. It was just that people, from years of playing against him, knew some of his tendencies and tried to push him into situations where he couldn't be as creative as he used to be. He was taking what the defense was giving him."

Encouraged by his coach, Jordan was already preparing a similar adjustment, which would be aided by an offensive system that rephrased the new tactics presented by the defense as gifts. Jackson believed it was no longer a matter of how high he jumped. The opponents' new defensive tactics actually worked in Jordan's favor by forcing him to a more sustainable approach.

"My game is less spectacular because I'm taking more outside shots," he acknowledged. "People saw...my creativity a little better because I was going to the hole more and creating more and dunking on people more and more. It's tough to get in there now because everyone's clogging the paint. Most of my inside play now is strictly from post-ups. When I'm on the perimeter, either the double-team is started or they back up and give me the jump shot."

Jumpers were always a function of the confidence of the moment, not just for Jordan but for anyone playing the game. The triangle provided him an important option if he got backed into that corner. Instead of shooting jumpers or trying to knife through the defense to attack the basket, he could now slip into the low post and feel confident that the offense would deliver him the ball at just the right moment.

"It's just an adjustment to the way people play me," he explained, "and it's not really because of my physical deficiency or deterioration. It's more the way teams are playing me."

Watching Jordan find those post-up moments in the previous playoffs had made Jackson confident that his star would continue in adjusting his game, sustaining his success. Jordan cautioned that he wasn't going to engage in wild experimentation, just subtle adjustment. And he did offer this promise to his many fans: there would still be dunks. "My game is such that creativity is always going to be a part of it," he told Isaacson. "But it just happens. It's not something I plan. It was something I was taught very early in my career. To go out and try to please the crowd, you never really play the game you want to play."

Despite all that, the 1992–93 season still opened with a quick, unforeseen flare-up when Horace Grant took umbrage at Jackson's allowing Jordan and Pippen to sit out portions of training camp. The coach was concerned that they recover from their busy summers. Grant complained to reporters about "double standards" and "preferential treatment." Later in the season, he would accuse Pippen of arrogance. Ultimately, this sniping would cause a rift between the two friends, but both agreed that they weren't as close as they had been. It was the sort of divisiveness that Jackson loathed. To go with it, the Bulls encountered a rash of physical ailments. Cartwright, thirty-five, and Paxson, thirty-two, had off-season surgery on their creaky knees, and Pippen would be troubled by a bad ankle for most of the year. For Jordan, the pains were first his arch, then his wrist, and always the ever-present tendinitis in his knees.

B. J. Armstrong, who had struggled with the Bulls' triple-post offense, finally was comfortable enough to replace Paxson in the starting lineup. The coaches had decided that the twenty-one-year-old Armstrong was simply better equipped to play in the Bulls' pressure defense, and that would make the difference in the play-offs. Plus, he would lead the league in three-point shooting, hitting better than 45 percent.

For the regular season, however, Jackson planned to back off from the pressure defense, hoping to conserve his players' energy and health. The move irritated Jordan, who felt that without their defense, games became harder to win. The change also revealed another issue for the veteran club: boredom. The slowed pace worked against them until at one point during the season Jordan called an on-court huddle and told his teammates to resume the pressure. Later, he debated Jackson's strategy with reporters. "Maybe we gamble and we lose our legs," he said. "I still don't think we get conservative now. When we slow down, things get too deliberate."

If nothing else, the issue demonstrated the mental interplay between the coach and star player. Sometimes it resembled a board game in which Jordan was perfectly capable of holding his own.

In the end, these issues merely added entertainment value. Their only real opponent was what Jordan called "monotony," that loss of joy that had concerned Jackson at the start of the season. December would bring the coach's two hundredth win. He had reached the mark faster than any coach in league history. Concerned as he was about his off-kilter team, he took little sense of achievement from the milestone.

"Guys were hurt," Jackson explained. "Pippen with his ankle, Jordan with his plantar fascia. All of those things prevented us from getting a rhythm. We weren't in great condition. So when practices were done hard and precise, we ended up suffering in our game effort."

Rather than miss games, Jordan had to sit out his favorite time with the team. "I have always liked practice," he said, "and I hate to miss it. It's like taking a math class. When you miss that one day, you feel like you missed a lot. You take extra work to make up for that one day. I've always been a practice player. I believe in it."

His loss of being able to experience joy in practice was the first major sign, he would say later. Practice was where he had played some of his best basketball. The things he did there were the prelude to his performances in games. He had always approached it with tremendous anticipation and enthusiasm. It had never been something to just get through, or to sit out.

"I knew it was time for me to get out," he would say later, looking back.

"They were tired," recalled Bulls trainer Chip Schaefer. "No question. Michael and Scottie were tired in the fall of '92. That was just a tough long year and really a tough year for Michael. It seemed like one thing after another. The press was picking on him, things just happening all year long. As soon as one thing would let up, it seemed like another came into play. There was one book or one incident constantly. It got to be not about basketball but personal things that really shouldn't have been part of it at all. You could just see it starting to wear on him a little bit. In some private moments, he expressed that. It was really evident that he was getting tired, tired physically, tired mentally of the whole thing."

The situation left Jackson digging in his bag of mental tricks to keep things fresh and to keep his team motivated. "Phil played a lot of mind games," Jordan recalled. "He waged psychological warfare to make you realize the things you have to do to be a winner."

Some rewards along the way helped out. On January 8, Jordan scored his twenty thousandth career point, a total he had reached in just 620 games. The only man to do it faster was Chamberlain, who reached the milestone in 499 games. "It looks like I fell short of Wilt again, which is a privilege," Jordan said. "I won't evaluate this until I'm away from the game. I'm happy about it, but we still have a long season to go. I'm sure as I get older, I'll cherish it more."

No matter how hard Jackson worked, the team always returned to the same issues. In a telling span of games that same month with Orlando, Magic coach Matt Guokas instructed his roster, which included rookie center Shaquille O'Neal, to keep their attention on Jordan. "Every time he had the ball at the free throw line extended and below, we would double-team him with the next closest guy," Guokas recalled. "Then we made sure we would rotate to John Paxson because we were concerned about his shooting. We were leaving a lot of things open. And Michael just carved us up."

He found open teammates, and everyone reveled in the victory. Left unguarded for stretches, Pippen and Grant had big nights and the Bulls won easily. Two games later, the teams met again in Chicago Stadium, and this time, Guokas elected to let Jordan roam while they worked to keep his teammates covered. Orlando was missing starters Nick Anderson and Dennis Scott that night.

"I said, 'There's no way we double-team him,'" Guokas recalled. He tabbed role player Anthony Bowie to take Jordan on defense. "I said, 'I don't care what he gets, but no dunks, no layups. Make sure you're back on defense. Give him all the jumpers he wants.' Which was the way everybody played Michael earlier in his career. So we go out and we're dropping off of him, playing about eight to ten feet off, taking away his drive. But it's one of those nights where he's hitting his jumper."

Jordan took shot after open shot, a career-high 49 attempts, 7 more than all of his teammates combined, and they began to look disgusted while the Magic kept it close. "We're still in the game," Guokas recalled. "And their guys are not."

The contest went to overtime, and Jordan finished with 64, his second-highest game. The Magic, though, came away with the win, confirming for Guokas that the best strategy was still to try to make Jordan a one-man team.

In March, Washington Bullets rookie LaBradford Smith scored 37 against him in Chicago, and afterward Jordan claimed Smith had told him "Nice game, Mike." Jordan was supposedly furious at the comment. In the postgame show, he talked of being embarrassed and how it wouldn't happen the next night, when the two teams were scheduled to meet again in Washington. He later said he would get all 37 points back by halftime, and spent much of the time talking about his retribution and psyching himself up. Although he seldom came onto the floor early for pregame shooting, he was out there the next night, working himself into a groove. He started the game 8 of 8 and would go on to post 36 by the half. He finished with 47, but it would be years before he admitted that he made the whole thing up. Smith had never said anything to him. He had falsified the entire affair as a means of driving himself to play at a higher level. The question was, how much longer could he play mind games with himself?

For each of the previous four seasons, his team had played more than one hundred games, and his knees had begun to feel every one of them. A week later in Houston, he sat tiredly in the locker room before the game and recognized that he was losing his legendary focus. His teammates, consumed with their own issues, were much the same, and Jordan realized this was exactly why teams failed to repeat as champions.

Jackson had sensed earlier in the season that his team was headed to the point where the players thought more about the future than they did the game in front of them. "My biggest lesson about being successful is that you don't change," Jordan would explain later. "The people around you change. When we became successful as an organization, a lot of people around this organization started to change. A lot of people can't deal with being successful."

First, he said, they become focused on their own interests, on what they don't have. "That's not a fun mentality to have," he added.

He then began telling his teammates he was done. They'd have a couple of beers after a game, and he would talk about it. No one believed him. But he began telling others, too, like his father, the people in his entourage, Dean Smith, and other confidants. His teammates considered it merely bellyaching. Jordan decided that if he was nearing the finish, he wanted to close it out in the right fashion.

Would he and his teammates be able to outrun these bad thoughts long enough to win another title? Dean Smith had always wanted to come see Jordan play in Chicago, and he showed up at one of the final regular-season games that spring. They visited before the game, and Jordan told his old mentor that he was thinking about moving on from the game. Jordan went out and played self-consciously that night, mindful that Smith would reserve his greatest scrutiny for his defensive play. In Carolina practices, the coach awarded points for defense, not offense. Any time that he knew Smith was watching him on TV, Jordan tried to make sure he focused on defense. He would laugh to himself, thinking that he was almost a decade out of school and still Smith had that power over him. On this night late in the season, he played poorly on offense and put all of his energy into defense.

With two final losses, to Charlotte and New York, the Bulls finished with fifty-seven wins, their fourth straight fifty-win season, good for another divisional championship, but they had lost home-court advantage for the playoffs to the Knicks. Individually, Jordan would claim a seventh straight scoring crown (30.3 points per game), tying him with Wilt Chamberlain. He would be named All-NBA first team again, and both he and Pippen would make the All-Defense first team.

"It's a funny thing to look at the history of the NBA and the way teams kind of rise and fall," trainer Chip Schaefer noted. "For all intents and purposes, it looked like it was going to be New York's year. They paid their dues. The Knicks absolutely destroyed us, beat us by 37 points in late November that year. They played like it was Game 7 in the playoffs. We went in kind of yawning. No big deal. Michael sprained his foot early in the game, and they just crushed us. We still won fifty-seven games that year, but we just kind of foundered."

For two years, the Knicks had seen their championship hopes end in seven-game playoff battles with the Bulls. They figured they needed the home-court advantage to advance out of Jordan's shadow. New York coach Pat Riley drove his team to sixty wins and gained that edge. The Bulls, meanwhile, seemed almost distracted heading into the playoffs. But they quickly picked up the pace, sweeping three from Atlanta in the first round, then devastating the Cleveland Cavaliers again by winning four straight. Jordan capped the series with a last-second game winner in Cleveland that closed the chapter on his domination of the Cavaliers.

"Once the playoffs rolled around," Schaefer recalled, "Michael managed to turn it on again. But we faced New York again. We didn't have home court so there really wasn't much reason to be optimistic about it."

Jordan hated the Knicks. "They play like the Pistons," he said testily. Moreover, Jackson and Riley still disliked each other from their playing days. In Game 1 in Madison Square Garden, the

Knicks knocked Jordan into a 10-for-27 shooting night and won, 98–90. "I told the team I let them down," Jordan said, but the same thing happened in Game 2. He missed 20 of 32 shots, and New York seized a two-game lead, 96–91. Afterward, the smugness in the city was tangible—and for good reason. "Now the Bulls are down two games and have to beat the Knicks four games out of five games if they are going to have a chance at three titles in a row," wrote *New York Daily News* columnist Mike Lupica.

The outcome was further weighted in the aftermath with a *New York Times* report that Jordan had been seen at an Atlantic City casino in the wee hours before Game 2, suggesting that perhaps he wasn't properly rested for competition. Jackson and Krause quickly came to his defense. "There is no problem with Michael Jordan," Krause told reporters. "He cares about winning and is one of the great winners of all time."

"We don't need a curfew," Jackson added. "These are adults.... You have to have other things in your life or the pressure becomes too great."

Jordan himself was unrepentant, but his father stepped up and explained to reporters that he had encouraged his son to go to Atlantic City. Privately, however, many around the team were staggered by the father's poor judgment. Jordan already faced scrutiny and an NBA investigation over the Slim Bouler case, and James Jordan thought it might be a good idea for his son to go gamble in Atlantic City in the midst of a playoff series?

With this issue hovering over the team, the series moved to Chicago. "The Bulls came back for practice at the Berto Center," recalled veteran Chicago radio reporter Cheryl Raye-Stout. "I've never seen as much media gathered for an event. Michael stepped out of the training room, and I said, 'Michael, would you just go over the chain of events for us? Would you tell us what happened and where this story is coming from?' He did, and then a television newsperson from a local Chicago station started grilling him as though he were an alderman being convicted of a crime. Chuck Goudie from Channel 7 was saying things like, 'Do you do this before every game? Do you have a gambling problem?' He kept hammering and hammering away, and eventually Michael just shut up and walked away."

Jordan ceased speaking with the media, and his teammates followed suit, which would lead to fines from the NBA for violating media policy.

James Jordan had hovered around for years, smiling pleasantly, joking with those in and around the team, continually encouraging his son. Now, with the tension high and his son seething, he picked a rainy Sunday to talk to the media outside the team's practice facility. "I don't mind speaking for Michael," he said. "He's my child. You do whatever you can for your child."

He had told Michael privately that he believed he had no more challenges on the court, that it was the off-court issues that were driving him away from the game, and now James began his talk with the reporters first by almost pleading, but then his voice lost any softness. "He knows he's in the fishbowl, under the microscope," the father said, adding that there should be some time in Jordan's life where that was not the case. "You just have to say, 'Hey, this guy's human.' I mean, what is enough? That's the big question right now, what is enough? Pretty soon, when you keep tipping the bucket up, there's not going to be anything in there after a while. You're going to pour it all out. And that's what we should start realizing as fans."

Trying to offer insight about his son, James Jordan told reporters, "My son doesn't have a gambling problem. He has a competition problem."

The immediate competition problem was the Knicks. Jordan was sure his Bulls would win. The hole was deep, it seemed, but they had found the bottom. With Pippen taking charge, Chicago won big in Game 3 in the Stadium, 103–83.

"The moment I knew we were going to win that series was after Game 3," Chip Schaefer recalled. "After we'd beat them pretty soundly and brought the series back to 2–1, Patrick Ewing made a comment that, 'We don't have to win here in Chicago.' As soon as I heard him say that, I knew we were going to win the series. If you have that attitude, you may lose a game and lose your edge. You can't assume you're going to win all of your home games. As soon as he said that, it told me he was counting on winning all their home games, which wasn't going to happen. It was Scottie who got us that series. He always seemed to have a knack when Michael might have been having a tough time, to step up and do what needed to be done."

Jordan did his part, too, by turning his anger into a searing focus, first with 54 points to drive Chicago to a win in Game 4, 105–95. Then, it was Jordan's triple-double (29 points, 10 rebounds, and 14 assists) that dominated the statistics column in Game 5, when Chicago took the series lead, 3–2. But it was Pippen's successive blocks of putback attempts by New York's Charles Smith late in Game 5 in New York that closed off the Knicks' hopes. Then, when the Bulls completed their comeback in Game 6 in Chicago, it was Pippen again doing the final damage, a corner jumper and a trey, in a 96–88 victory.

The road had been rocky, but the Bulls were returning to their third straight NBA Finals, where Jordan would face his old caddy Charles Barkley, both of them at the top of the game for that instant. After several frustrating years in Philadelphia, Barkley had been traded to Phoenix before the 1992–93 season, and like that he had been reborn, earning league MVP honors and leading the Suns to sixty-two wins and a trip to the Finals after a serious playoffs bout with the Houston Rockets.

"It was a great Finals, when you look back on it, from an entertainment standpoint, competitive standpoint," recalled Matt Guokas, who had coached Barkley in Philadelphia. "I think Charles, in his mind, felt recognized as a guy who was on the same plane with Michael Jordan."

With the championship meeting, the personal competition between the two friends would now fall under the view of the larger audience. "Any time we'd get in a close game with the Bulls, Charles would want to guard Michael the last two or three minutes down the stretch," Guokas recalled. "He had the guts, he had the stones. And Charles was not afraid to fail, either. He knew that there was a possibility that Michael could make him look bad. But he was almost the equal of an athlete that Michael was."

Barkley was always annoyed by Jordan's seemingly constant residence in a hotel room somewhere. "Sir Charles" loved to get out and carouse, to interact with the public, which was where he'd always found trouble in his Philadelphia days. But in Phoenix, the array of golf courses in the Valley of the Sun had meant that he had no trouble attracting Jordan for some fun.

The title bout between them was certainly hard fought, but it left a bitter aftertaste, with suggestions from the Bulls camp that Jordan had intentionally "played" Barkley for several years, softening him up with lavish gifts, so that he could dominate him on the court. Barkley himself would later be left to wonder, despite three years of friendship. Jordan had been displeased with Barkley's practice habits with the Dream Team in Barcelona, and would later admit that he drew a competitive edge from that. Pippen, meanwhile, was not a Sir Charles fan and would later publicly berate him for "kissing Michael's ass," an accusation that left Barkley bristling. Yet it would remain largely an unanswered question. Had Jordan hoodwinked Barkley just when he was close to the main prize? Afterward, Jordan offered that the main difference between them was experience. He knew what to expect from the series in terms of pressure, but Barkley really didn't. You had to be ready for that kind of burden, Jordan said.

For the TV audience, Barkley and Jordan were squared off in a pop culture war. Nike commercial versus Nike commercial. In his ads, Jordan pondered, "What if I were just a basketball player?" while Barkley in his spot declared, "I am not a role model," playing on his controversial public image. Some critics saw him as another highly paid but irresponsible performer. Others understood that Barkley's statement was a reminder that pro athletes were merely media images and that the real responsibility for instilling values in young people belonged in the home. Barkley explained as much, but that did little to deter his critics, who focused on the tabloid gossip, highlighted by supposed sightings of him with Madonna at a Phoenix restaurant. There was Jordan's gambling, and Sir Charles was always Sir Charles.

The irony in 1993 was that Barkley had shown no forethought, no hesitation in trashing his own public image during his early NBA seasons, while the more circumspect Jordan had proceeded cautiously, always saying and doing the correct corporate things while persistently building Chicago into a winner. At times, when

Barkley's occasional bar fights or misguided public statements made headlines, Jordan had publicly come to his defense, the primary message being that Charles may tend to run his mouth before thinking, but he is an honest, genuine person and a tough competitor. Now, however, Jordan had arrived in Phoenix with his own pack of tabloid hounds sniffing out the trail of scandal.

Fortunately, the basketball was good enough to eclipse the other story lines. When the series opened in the brand-new America West Arena, the Bulls had plenty of confidence. They had always done well against Barkley's Philadelphia teams. Pippen's and Grant's defense would shackle the burly forward again, and B. J. Armstrong had the quickness to stay with Phoenix point guard Kevin Johnson.

As if willed by a media strategist's perfect timing, Jordan's shadow life again surfaced on the eve of the championship series. No sooner had the Atlantic City casino jaunt fallen out of the news than Richard Esquinas stepped forward with a self-published book, *Michael & Me: Our Gambling Addiction... My Cry for Help!* In the book Esquinas went into great detail about his high-stakes golf wagering with Jordan.

In a taped interview on NBC at halftime of Game 1 of the Finals, Jordan admitted that he had lost substantial sums to Esquinas but nowhere near the figure claimed. Esquinas, meanwhile, presented copies of his tax returns and copies of Jordan's checks. He had apparently paid off approximately $300,000 of the debt before turning to a Chicago lawyer to keep Esquinas at bay.

"Gamblers don't belong in sports," wrote columnist Dave Kindred in *Sporting News*. "They are vulnerable to extortion. They are vulnerable to temptations to bet on what they know best, their game. These vulnerabilities undermine the public's confidence that the games are honest. But Jordan doesn't seem to care. It's as if he lives his life by the gospel decreed in his shoe shill's pitch: Just do it."

At no time was Jordan alleged to have bet on any NBA games, his defenders pointed out. If that was the case, it was the only thing Jordan didn't bet on, *Newsweek* suggested. "At practice he'll wager on trick shots or play Horse for cash. On the Chicago Bulls' plane, he runs games of twenty-one or tonk, a sort of gin rummy. On the road, he hosts all-night poker games in his hotel room. Three years ago the team began using its own charter plane to protect the players' privacy—but also, it seems now, to keep away the embarrassing view of the hundreds of dollars spread across airport-lounge tables, the stakes in Jordan's card games."

Questions about whether these distractions would hinder the Bulls were quickly put aside when Chicago claimed the first game, 100–92. Jordan scored 31 and Pippen 27, while the Bulls' defense harassed Barkley into shooting just 9 for 25.

Perhaps the Suns had merely blinked in their first time in the championship spotlight, but they sank deeper into trouble in Game 2. Barkley and Jordan each scored 42 points, but Jordan's accompanied a near triple-double with his 12 rebounds and 9 assists, plus 2 steals, all in forty minutes of playing time. He also made 18 of his 36 shots from the field and both of his three-point attempts, helping the Bulls to a 111–108 win.

The Chicago defense also clamped down on Kevin Johnson and wing Dan Majerle to take the 2–0 series lead. Part of the win can be attributed to a defensive scheme drawn up by Johnny Bach for Armstrong to counter Kevin Johnson, who grew frustrated and sat out much of the fourth quarter. Suddenly Phoenix faced three games in Chicago and the prospects of a sweep. But somehow the Suns managed to scratch out a 129–121, triple-overtime win in Game 3. "I thought it was never going to end," Jackson said afterward.

Jordan responded with 55 points for a 111–105 win in Game 4 to give the Bulls a 3–1 series lead. Phoenix allowed him time and again to glide inside for handsome little dunks and bank shots. In forty-six minutes of playing time, he had made 21 of 37 from the floor, to go with 13 made free throws, 8 rebounds, and 4 assists. Phoenix pulled to within two at the end, but Armstrong's pressure and a key late steal closed it out. Jordan's point total tied Golden State's Rick Barry for second place on the all-time NBA Finals single-game list. The record was held by Elgin Baylor, who scored 61 in a game against Boston in 1962.

Up three games to one with Game 5 on their home floor, the

Bulls stood on the verge of their third straight. However, they strangely teetered there. Jordan swore to his teammates that he wouldn't accompany them back to Phoenix if they failed to deliver the championship in the Stadium. To back that up, he scored 41 points in forty-four minutes on 16 of 29 shooting from the field, with 7 rebounds, 7 assists, and 2 blocks. Regardless, Chicago stumbled, and the Suns busied themselves with defense. Jordan's easy baskets disappeared as Phoenix congregated in the lane.

With Johnson scoring 25 and Barkley 24, the Suns got the win they needed, 108–98, to return the series to Arizona. Chicago's previous championships had been marked by riotous celebration that rocked the city, so before Game 5, many merchants had boarded up their stores. "We did the city a favor," Barkley said as he left town. "You can take all those boards down now. We're going to Phoenix."

Jordan was furious over the loss and angry with his teammates, who were grappling with their own disappointment. Behind the scenes, his wife and older sister pleaded with him to arrange for his jet to take the family to Game 6. He finally relented, perhaps figuring that the cost of the trip would stoke his focus on the task at hand.

The Jordan family remained riddled with division, with James and Deloris still fighting over proceeds and royalties from the sale of the Flight 23 stores. Sis described the circumstances as miserable as her parents sought to pull their children into the conflict, especially Michael. Sis sat back and looked at her brother in that moment with "no longer enough hours in his days, or enough hands to handle the many tasks that had been set before him." She recalled, "I watched from afar as Michael juggled life on and off the court...riding the waves of mega success and bringing his teammates as well as his family along for the ride."

"Michael seems to sense what a team needs," recalled Bulls broadcaster Tom Dore. "They had just lost. But Michael walked on the plane going to Phoenix and said, 'Hello, World Champs.' He's got a foot-long cigar, and he's celebrating already because he knows the series is over. He knew, going to Phoenix, that they were going to win. It wasn't a question with him, and I think that's what the team had. They just had this arrogance. They weren't mean about it. They just felt like they were going to win."

That moxie seemed to drive Chicago through the first three quarters of Game 6 as the Bulls' phalanx of guards—Jordan, Armstrong, Paxson, and seldom-used reserve Trent Tucker—fired in 9 three-pointers over the first three periods to stake Chicago to an 87–79 lead.

There, once again on the brink of the title, the Bulls turned cold. They missed 9 shots and had 2 turnovers their first 11 possessions of the fourth quarter. The Suns closed within a point, then surged to take a 98–94 lead with ninety seconds left. After a miss, Jordan pulled down a defensive rebound and wound his way through traffic to the other end for a short bank shot. It was 98–96 with 38 seconds to go. The shooting by Suns wing Dan Majerle had helped Phoenix back into the series, but on their next-to-last possession he delivered an air ball, which brought the Bulls one more chance, with 14.1 seconds to go. After a time-out, Jordan inbounded the ball to Armstrong, then got it back and passed ahead to Pippen. The play was drawn up to go back to Chicago's sure thing. But Pippen saw that Jordan was covered, so he motored into the lane, where he was greeted by Suns center Mark West. Alone on the near baseline was Grant, who had scored a single point in the game, and who had had a stick-back opportunity moments earlier and had almost thrown the ball over the backboard. Pippen whipped him the ball. With the game on the line, Grant passed up the shot to send the ball out to Paxson, all alone in three-point land to the left of the key.

"I knew it was in as soon as Pax shot it," Jordan said.

The three-pointer, along with Grant's block of Kevin Johnson's last shot, ended the suspense and brought the Bulls their third championship.

During the Finals, Jordan had averaged 41 points per game, breaking the championship series record of 40.8 points per game set by Rick Barry in 1967.

The party was restrained back in his suite after the game. Jordan was shirtless, in gym shorts. George Koehler was there, opening bottles of very expensive champagne. Quinn Buckner, too. But the quiet celebration was more about family. Sis and her mother sat with Michael on one couch. James sat facing them on another with Roz. They relaxed and smiled, and Michael even pounced on his younger sister for a brief wrestling bout. It would be the last time they were all together.

As his personal misery had mounted, there was little question among Jordan's close associates that he had grown weary of the grind and the lack of privacy. In his public comments, he had made oblique references to retirement. He might have done it earlier if he hadn't feared losing his product endorsement fees and Nike sales, writer Sam Smith had noted in *The Jordan Rules*. His off-court troubles had only increased the public perception that he might leave the game after this third title.

Reporters converged upon him afterward in the media sessions to ask if indeed he planned to retire. "No," he assured them. "My love for this game is strong."

PART IX

FAR AND AWAY

Chapter 29

THE LEXUS

HE HAD MADE winning seem too easy. Only Phil Jackson and the Bulls' tight inner circle understood what a grind the three straight championships had been—that Jordan had been able to succeed with huge doses of will, mental strength, and even fear.

That tightly wound ball of purpose drifted in limbo that summer of 1993 as he neared a vortex of trouble and pain. Leading him there was James Jordan, whose world was likewise collapsing around him. He faced a paternity suit by a Chicago woman. The businesses he had started with Larry after the Flight 23 fiasco were now failing, as authorities moved in to collect unpaid taxes and suppliers began removing items from store shelves over unpaid bills. He was engaged in a furious battle with Deloris; joint bank accounts were closed, thus destroying the final shred of credit for his business. Payroll was unmade, and each phone call from his secretary seemed to bring yet more troubles. According to his older daughter, her father wearily complained to his children that his wife was trying to ruin him in the eyes of his children.

On July 22, 1993, James and Deloris Jordan each left their home in a Charlotte suburb and headed off in different directions. Mrs. Jordan caught a flight to Chicago to visit her son, and Mr. Jordan got into his cranberry-colored Lexus and headed across the state to Pender County to bury an old friend. The Lexus, a gift from his son, was an item of pride for James Jordan. The vanity license plate read UNC0023. The next day he was scheduled to fly to Chicago to enjoy a celebrity baseball game his son was hosting. Afterward his wife and son were scheduled to take an extended vacation in California.

Mr. Jordan's fifty-seventh birthday had come and gone by the time his older daughter took a phone call from his secretary on August 2. She told Sis that she was alarmed. While James Jordan usually checked in every day, the secretary had not heard from him in almost two weeks. It was then that the daughter learned of the dire circumstances of her father's business. Payroll checks had bounced, causing employees to walk off the job. The secretary also told the daughter that Mr. Jordan had missed his flight to Chicago on July 23.

For years, James Jordan had traveled for days at a time, trying to keep pace with his son's busy schedule. "He would go off alone a lot," his son explained later, "sometimes if he and my mother had a disagreement, or just to be on his own. He enjoyed retirement so much and doing whatever he wanted to do whenever he wanted to do it. So it wasn't peculiar."

Sis then phoned her mother, who had just returned home after nearly two weeks on the road, and relayed the secretary's concerns. Deloris Jordan noted that the house appeared just as she had left it, and that it appeared no one had slept in the beds. But she sought to allay her daughter's concerns, saying that wherever James Jordan was, she was sure that was where he wanted to be.

Growing Concern

On August 4, Sis again phoned her father's business and discovered that he still had not checked in. Two days later, she learned that her mother and Larry had visited the business and that Deloris Jordan had paid the outstanding bills. To the daughter, the payment seemed a sign that perhaps her parents were beginning to get past their conflicts. That weekend Sis phoned her mother, who said she suspected that Mr. Jordan was in Hilton Head, where he was thinking of moving.

Several days later, a neighbor phoned and told Sis to turn on the television. James Jordan's Lexus had been found stripped and vandalized. It was upon hearing this same news that Michael realized something was dreadfully wrong.

"He treasured that car," Jordan said later.

Police had found the Lexus on August 5 near a wooded area off a main road in Fayetteville, North Carolina. The back window was smashed out, and the car had been stripped of its stereo speakers, tires, and vanity plates. Authorities had tracked the vehicle through a Lexus dealership and then contacted the Jordan family. Authorities searched the area around the vehicle but found nothing. They were able to determine that Mr. Jordan had attended the funeral July 22, then visited with a female friend that evening before leaving to make the three-and-a-half-hour drive home to Charlotte.

"It is not unusual for Mr. Jordan not to let someone know where he's at for a couple of days, but certainly not for twenty-plus days," Captain Art Binder of the Cumberland County Sheriff's Department told reporters.

Upon receiving the news, Michael left for North Carolina. Authorities soon connected the car to a badly decomposed body that had been found August 3 in a swampy creek near McColl, South Carolina. The local medical examiner later acknowledged that the remains had been placed in a body bag and left in the bed of his pickup truck for most of the day. South Carolina authorities eventually conducted an autopsy, took photographs, and determined that the victim had died of a single .38-caliber gunshot wound to the chest. On August 7, a part-time coroner had collected the jawbones and hands from the unidentified corpse and ordered the remains cremated.

"It was my decision as to what I had to do," the coroner, Tim Brown, told reporters after it was confirmed that the victim was Michael Jordan's father. "I had a body that was decomposing and there was no means of refrigeration."

Stunned by the notification, the Jordan family began making hurried arrangements for a funeral that weekend at the Rockfish AME Church in Teachey. Meanwhile, authorities quickly tracked calls made from a cell phone in the Lexus to two eighteen-year-olds from Lumberton, North Carolina. On the same day as the Jordan family held the service in Teachey, authorities arrested Larry Martin Demery and Daniel Andre Green and charged them with first-degree murder, conspiracy to commit armed robbery, and armed robbery. Green had been paroled two months earlier after serving less than two years for a conviction in Robeson County for assault with a deadly weapon with intent to kill and armed robbery, according to Robeson County sheriff Hubert Stone.

James Jordan, according to investigators, had become a victim of circumstance when he stopped his car in a well-lighted place alongside Interstate 95 near Lumberton in the early morning hours of July 23. The teenagers were armed and had reportedly talked of robbing someone that night as they waited at a nearby exit, when Jordan apparently pulled off the road to rest, said Captain Art Binder.

The two shot and killed Jordan and discovered who he was only when they looked in his wallet, Binder said. "Once they realized that it was Michael Jordan's father, they wanted to make sure they tried to cover their tracks the best way they could. It took them a while before they decided South Carolina would be the place they would put the body."

They drove thirty miles to a remote area just across the South Carolina border, where they dumped James Jordan into the swampy creek. They kept the Lexus three more days, took videos of themselves boasting about the event, then left the car on a dirt road on the outskirts of Fayetteville, about sixty miles from where they dumped the body.

"As this matter unfolds, you will find that what happened to Mr. Jordan was the kind of random violence that all the public are concerned and afraid of," said Jim Coman, director of the North Carolina Bureau of Investigation. "It could have been any one of us."

The Speculation

The circumstances immediately created an outbreak of conspiracy theories. Why was there a rushed cremation? Why wasn't James Jordan reported missing? How could he have been gone for weeks without his family suspecting anything? Did the murder involve Michael's gambling? How could his fifty-seventh birthday have passed with no one in his family even noticing that he was missing? The mystery deepened after Deloris Jordan told authorities that her husband had last spoken with her on July 26, and a local convenience store clerk reported that she had seen someone who looked like James Jordan with the two teens in her store several days after the reported crime date. Investigators later concluded that both were mistaken.

The family, meanwhile, faced an emotional ceremony that Sunday, August 15. The church was packed, with many more outside as Jordan walked slowly to the pulpit to address two hundred mourners, including B. J. Armstrong, Ahmad Rashad, and David Falk. "I've always wondered how it felt to stand behind one of these," he said with a slight smile.

Jordan spoke softly, in a voice that cracked with emotion, of his father's qualities. He thanked both his parents and talked of the efforts they had made to provide for their children's upbringing and education and to encourage them to set goals to live by.

"Don't dwell on his death, but celebrate the life he lived," Jordan said of his father.

He then held his mother tightly, smiling and whispering in her ear as he escorted her out of the church to the graveyard. James Jordan was remembered by many in the community as the industrious young man eager to show that he knew how to get things done.

"He would keep you laughing all the time," James Jordan's seventy-one-year-old second cousin, Rev. Andre Carr of nearby Rocky Point, told the *Tribune*. "It seemed like he always had something funny to say. There was something about his spirit, his sense of humor that he was a friend of everybody. You'd meet him and it was like you knew him all your life. He was the type of father who liked everything to be uplifting. He was such a happy guy."

The following Thursday, Jordan released a statement through Falk's office. "The many kind words and thoughtful prayers have lifted our spirits through difficult times," he said. "I also want to express my appreciation to the local, state, and federal law enforcement officers for their efforts. I am trying to deal with the overwhelming feelings of loss and grief in a way that would make my dad proud. I simply cannot comprehend how others could intentionally pour salt in my open wound, insinuating that faults and mistakes in my life are in some way connected to my father's death." He targeted "unsubstantiated reports" as particularly galling for his family.

Jordan had been scheduled to play in the Rose Elder Invitational Golf Tournament that Friday at Lansdowne Resort in Leesburg, Virginia. The following Tuesday he also faced a decision about whether to attend his own Michael Jordan/Ronald McDonald Children's Charities Celebrity Golf Classic, at Seven Bridges Golf Club in Woodridge, Virginia. He ultimately decided to make a low-key appearance at both events, even as speculation over his father's death continued to occupy the airwaves.

"That's what killed us about Norm Van Lier here in Chicago," Phil Jackson recalled of the former Bulls guard turned broadcaster. "He was broadcasting theories about Michael's father's death and gambling and the NBA and all this stuff. Michael had to go talk to Van Lier and say, 'Norm. Cool this stuff about gambling and the NBA and the grand scheme and all this other stuff about my father's death. There's no conspiracy going on here.' That's the paranoia that builds in people's minds and sometimes drives you crazy."

From their earliest days together, Jackson had shown a strong intuitive sense of how to support and sustain Jordan. The coach had become Jordan's companion and guide. And Jordan did the same for Jackson, as their ideas and separate visions had invigorated one another. But basketball had no place in Jordan's thoughts as he struggled with his father's death over the ensuing weeks.

As training camp neared that fall, David Falk informed Jerry Reinsdorf that Jordan was prepared to retire. James Jordan's death wasn't mentioned as a reason, but the owner knew that the trauma of the loss was driving the decision. There would be immediate speculation that Jordan was retiring in protest over a contract that left him woefully underpaid. But Reinsdorf refuted that: "Michael said to me, 'This is not about money. I don't want to play basketball anymore. I want to be retired.'"

"What do you want to do?" Reinsdorf asked Jordan.

"I want to play baseball," Jordan told him.

The owner recalled that he asked Jordan if he had spoken with Jackson, and Jordan replied that he was hesitant to do that. "Knowing Phil, the psychology major, he was going to try to get in my head and see where I stood," Jordan recalled.

Jordan, though, knew what he wanted. While Jackson certainly knew how to push his buttons, the coach was careful to tread softly when they met. He pointed out that Jordan possessed a great gift from God and that leaving the game would deny millions of fans the benefit of that gift. Jackson said he should think over his decision. But Jordan was firm. "No, this is it," he said.

Jordan had a question of his own for Jackson. He wanted to know how the coach would get him through another eighty-two-game regular season, because he had absolutely no motivation, saw no challenge in it. Jackson had no good answer. Jordan didn't want to end his career on a down note, with declining skills and facing excessive criticism, the way Julius Erving had finished.

So Jackson changed course one final time and asked Jordan if he had thought about a sabbatical. But that wouldn't do. Jordan wanted no lingering, no loose ends. Jackson realized it then, and told Jordan he was on his side. Then the coach told him that he loved him and began weeping. Although he had braced himself for a difficult encounter, Jordan was caught off guard by the emotion, especially when he informed his teammates and coaches. Toni Kukoc, who had just come to the United States to play with the Bulls, had gotten particularly emotional, which struck Jordan in return. His other teammates seemed similarly affected. He realized then that people could spend years working together and not know the depth of their feelings for each other.

Johnny Bach recalled Jordan informing the coaching staff: "He said, 'I'm gonna retire, guys.' I couldn't believe it. We wished him luck. It was a shattering day."

On October 6, 1993, Jordan publicly announced his retirement from the Bulls. "I would've made the same decision with my father around," he said during the announcement.

"Five years down the road," he said, "if the urge comes back, if the Bulls will have me, if David Stern lets me back in the league, I may come back." The comment would spark yet more intrigue and speculation that Jordan, during his discussions with David Stern, had been told to retire, perhaps even forced out.

Dave Kindred again weighed in: "Was there a trade-off? 'Hey, MJ, you 'retire,' we drop the 'investigation.' Was Jordan advised/ ordered by NBA commissioner David Stern to go away—go play baseball or something—and let the gambling stories die?'"

Sports Illustrated also noted the speculation that Jordan was leaving to avoid the NBA's latest investigation of his wagering and that Jordan didn't mention his gambling in the news conference.

Falk and Stern both said emphatically there was no link between Jordan's gambling and his retirement, with Stern adding that for anyone to even suggest that was "scurrilous and disgusting."

Stern told reporters that the league's latest investigation of Jordan was now closed, emphasizing that he was certain Jordan had never bet on NBA games and was not suffering from gambling addiction.

Much later, in a 2005 interview with Ed Bradley on *60 Minutes,* Jordan appeared to finally acknowledge the problem. "Yeah, I've gotten myself into situations where I would not walk away and I've pushed the envelope," Jordan told Bradley. "Is that compulsive? Yeah, it depends on how you look at it. If you're willing to jeopardize your livelihood and your family, then yeah."

As Sonny Vaccaro observed, Jordan was so big, so important to the NBA, he was the only player who could have survived the gambling mess. A lesser player would have been suspended, Vaccaro said, adding that the NBA chose to deal with it by shutting the books on its inquiry.

It seemed highly unlikely that David Stern would have forced Jordan from the league. Jordan, however, would later express anger with Stern for not doing more to take on the conspiracy theorists who tied James Jordan's death to his son's gambling debts, even though nothing in any investigation pointed to that possibility.

The move to retire came so swiftly that he had no time to notify his mother, who was in Africa. "I was in Kenya with Michael's mom and a group of school kids," recalled Bulls vice president Steve Schanwald. "It had been so peaceful out there. We were on safari in a remote portion of Kenya, living in tents. No newspapers, no radio, no TV, no nothing. I told the people that the world could be coming to an end, and we wouldn't know. Two days later we flew back to Nairobi, back to civilization for the first time in about ten days. I got off the plane and got on the bus that was going to take us to have lunch. The bus driver was reading a newspaper, a tabloid called the *Daily Nation*, Kenya's national newspaper. On the back page, there was a picture of Michael, and the headline said, 'Michael Jordan Retires.' I thought it was somebody's idea of a bad joke. But two days earlier, Michael had announced his retirement. Apparently, Michael's mom didn't know. I went up to her and thanked her for lending us her son for nine great years. She said, 'What are you talking about?' I said, 'Mrs. Jordan, your son retired two days ago.' She said, 'He did? I don't believe it!' So I went and got the newspaper and showed her. That was how we found out about Michael retiring.

"That night at dinner I bought some champagne for everybody and we toasted Michael on his great career. But by the time I got back to Chicago, the festive mood was gone. People were definitely depressed. It happened with such suddenness, it was so out of the blue, that it kind of took the wind out of people's sails."

Perhaps the greatest emptiness was felt by the NBA's leadership, who now had to replace the greatest attraction in basketball history. Ironically, there were also reports that Stern had asked Jordan not to retire, but neither man discussed the moment in detail. That question would linger forever, another knot in the great mass of Jordan's resentment.

Chapter 30

THE DIAMOND DREAM

Steve Kerr arrived in Chicago not long before the Bulls opened their training camp in 1993. A free agent guard with slow feet, a shock of blond hair, and a deadly shot, he brought a mix of eagerness and concern to the task of making the roster. He'd heard all the stories circulating around the NBA about how difficult it was to be Jordan's teammate. But within a week of signing his contract, Kerr saw the Jordan factor mysteriously disappear.

Instead, his only MJ connection over the coming weeks would be a glimpse of Jordan when he slipped in to observe the practices of the team he had just deserted. The void Jordan left was profound. He had long hinted at his departure; now, soon after the announcement, he was back, as if to ascertain exactly what his absence looked like, in hopes that the finality of it might actually help him find his way. By his own admission, the newfound family time that he could now embrace did nothing to ease his mental state. He was still grieving—something his public and the media had failed to recognize—and trying to formulate a direction for his new life.

"He came every once in a while," Kerr remembered. "He would just come in and watch practice. I think he just wanted to see the guys and stuff. So we saw him a few times. He came to some games that year, sat in a suite at the United Center." Even this silent specter on the sidelines at practice seemed intimidating, a reminder of how the team was about to evolve.

"I think it really sort of became Phil's team at that point," Kerr observed. "Even though I wasn't there before that, I'm sure Phil was dominant and his presence was felt before that, but it really became Phil's team after Michael retired because it had to be. He was the dominant presence. The characters, the egos we had on the team...we had some great players. But, you know, Scottie was never a guy who was going to seize control of a team from a leadership standpoint. He was everybody's favorite teammate, but one of the reasons for that was he was vulnerable. And Phil was not vulnerable."

Some observers had underestimated Jackson, suggesting that his success was a function of Jordan's ability, but they had failed to grasp just how dominant a personality the coach presented. That became essential on a team whose best player was beset by insecurity and was battling management over his pay. A few years earlier, Pippen had insisted on a long-term contract that quickly became obsolete as the league's salaries grew. Although the team did agree to return money that he had deferred, Reinsdorf was not going to renegotiate.

"I think Scottie was vulnerable because he was human," Kerr explained. "It's the reason everybody loved him. You know, he signed that long contract. He was clearly underpaid. It was tough for him to live with that. He felt like he wasn't appreciated. All the feelings that are associated with almost every human being, that was Scottie, and that's why we all really appreciated him, because we felt we were more like him, even though we weren't physically. We were all more like him emotionally than like Michael. Michael didn't even seem human, he was so confident and so strong."

Jordan would quickly begin to appear considerably less superhuman. He had been lost since his father's murder in August, and each succeeding account of the details served to intensify his grief, as he would acknowledge later. Yet he was also drawn to it, pausing whatever he was doing whenever another story about his father and the subsequent arrests popped up on television.

Jordan had rarely projected frailty or weakness, but now he was privately in search of relief. Word began to circulate that fall that, with Reinsdorf's blessing, he had been showing up at the White

Sox training facilities at Comiskey Park to take batting practice on the sly. In typical Jordan fashion, he was there five days a week, sorting out a game he hadn't played in more than a decade, with the help of White Sox players Frank Thomas, Mike Huff, Dan Pasqua, and Julio Franco. He had his sights set on returning to the game his father had loved dearly and had continued to talk about, even as Jordan had come to rule basketball.

"It was really his father's dream that he play baseball," Phil Jackson observed months later. "His father wanted to play pro ball and did play semi-pro. When his father passed away, I think Michael was kind of living out his father's dream. That's one of the things I thought when I heard it. 'Jeez, this guy wants to go play baseball in the major leagues?' But then I realized basketball players are always fantasizing that they could play baseball."

The Sox

Jordan revealed his plans to *Chicago Tribune* columnist Bob Greene, with whom he had worked on the book *Hang Time*. They were driving past Comiskey Park one day when Jordan indicated that might be a place he would soon be working. The ride itself was revelatory to the columnist because of the often manic behavior of people they encountered all over the city—grown men stopping their cars in traffic and jumping out, or rapping on his Corvette window to get Jordan to sign a piece of paper. Greene was amazed to see that Jordan had more or less come to accept these sometimes alarming intrusions as part of his daily routine. No wonder he spent so much time in hotel rooms with the door double-bolted, the columnist thought.

But by now the star was used to offering up just about every shred of his privacy to the hungry god of his public being. He had made a trip to California, where he was riding bicycles along the beach with a friend when they encountered a pickup game in a park. Jordan wanted to join them, and when his friend approached the players they thought he was kidding until they saw His Airness in the flesh standing nearby. He then jumped in and regained a bit of that old joy with the game. But a huge crowd gathered in an amazingly short time, and he had to leave before it turned crazier. Jordan told Greene he was thinking about using the scene for a new commercial, and the columnist couldn't tell if he was joking.

Greene kept the baseball news to himself, but others in Jordan's circle were beginning to process the idea. Sonny Vaccaro, now working for one of Nike's competitors, remembered Jordan calling him about the decision. "He said here's what I'm thinking of doing and he convinced me. He told me he was going to do it. I never heard anybody suggest he do it. He said, 'I'm going to try the baseball.' He always thought he was a baseball player. He said that's how he was going to deal with it.... And it was easy for him to do because he relished that challenge."

Vaccaro was struck that with Jordan's decision to play baseball, the issue of his gambling would just go away for the NBA. "It wasn't easy for Michael, but he realized he'd made some poor decisions, and he apologized to the people affected and he moved on," David Falk later said, giving the conspiracy theorists a new morsel on which to feed. "It took a lot of guts to retire when he did. It took a lot of guts to go play baseball and run the risk of failure after being incredibly successful at something else. But Michael is fearless."

Jordan phoned Bob Greene in January to break the story officially. He had continued working at the Comiskey training facility for weeks with the plan of going to spring training with the White Sox in Sarasota, Florida. This was not a "fantasy baseball" scenario, Jordan told Greene. This was to be the real deal. There would be plenty of doubters, but he had always been driven by those betting against him. For many, the question became: Was it a penance, or a pilgrimage? Or both?

He arrived in Sarasota just days before his thirty-first birthday, along with Greene, who was working on another book. The first day was telling. There were the White Sox in T-shirts and shorts, ready for calisthenics, and at his locker was Jordan, fully dressed in his game uniform, number 45, like a youngster waiting for Little League to start.

"All of a sudden I felt like a kid again," he had said earlier, of the anticipation. The only difference was the legendary approach, which would prompt White Sox hitting coach Walt Hriniak to describe him as "one hardworking motherfucker." And when you told him something, he listened, Hriniak would marvel.

Not that either of those things would make it easy to turn him into a big league player. He hadn't played organized baseball since he quit the Laney High School team in March 1981. But in his determination to learn to hit big league pitching, Jordan came early and stayed late each day at spring training. Still, the futility was obvious almost from the start.

Much of it had to do with the sheer size of his legend. Anticipating his big moment, thousands of fans had descended upon Sarasota. Team officials had erected barriers around Ed Smith Stadium just to handle the crowds. Spring training had always been a sleepy affair, but now there were extra security and PR people everywhere and escorts to and from the team bus. And the press was out in force.

Crowds of people pressed against the chain-link fences, all of them wanting autographs, which Jordan dutifully tried to oblige, another problem in that it again contrasted with his teammates' habit. Players had refused to sign for years, citing their union agreements, which had long left Reinsdorf shaking his head in disgust. But here was Jordan obliging crowds of autograph hunters and conducting press conferences, threatening to widen the gulf with his new teammates, some of whom treated him coolly from the start.

Jordan's escape from all this was the house he had rented in a nearby gated community. There, he could sit on the back deck at night, gazing up at the stars with awe and wonder, perhaps as Dawson Jordan had done a century earlier. He sensed his father's presence with him everywhere he went, whenever some little detail of the game struck a chord of memory of James Jordan pitching the ball to him in the backyard.

Jordan would tell himself, "We're doing this together, you and I, Pops."

He longed for the friendly encouragement that James had brought him every day of his basketball life. Although he would never show it or relent from the task, soon enough the challenge began to wear on him, as it did on his thousands of fans, who had come to Florida looking for the magnificent athlete who had thrilled them in hoops, only to find an awkward, hesitant figure, so clearly out of place.

After years as the alpha male in basketball, as Phil Jackson liked to call him, here he was just hoping to make the team. He found himself looking at the manager's lineup each day, something he hadn't had to do since that fateful day at Laney. His new teammates did have to concede at least one thing: the dude was not afraid to look bad. He laid it all out there, trying to beat it down to first base to turn his dinky grounders into hits. He came close several times but rolled hitless through his first ten at bats. He was too tall, some said, and presented too big a strike zone. Even he agreed. "Look at these arms," he said, comparing his long limbs with those of his teammates.

Among the many media who came to witness the spectacle was Steve Wulf of *Sports Illustrated,* who filed a derisive account that his editors made into the infamous cover that declared: "Bag It, Michael! Jordan and the White Sox Are Embarrassing Baseball." "He had better tie his Air Jordans real tight if I pitch to him," Seattle Mariner fireballer Randy Johnson told Wulf. "I'd like to see how much air time he'd get on one of my inside pitches." Not everyone commenting in the piece was as brazen, and some sought to be quoted anonymously. George Brett, a former third baseman who had moved into the front office of the Kansas City Royals, was frank: "I know a lot of players don't want to see him make it, because it will be a slap in the face to them."

Bob Greene would later note that this was the same magazine that had used Jordan's image on its cover dozens of times to increase newsstand sales, and in TV ads promising readers all sorts of Jordan-related goodies if they would subscribe. Deeply wounded, Jordan vowed never again to speak to a representative of the magazine, and he never did, despite all that would come after.

As always, such humiliation only stoked his fire. "I'm really trying to learn this game," he told those around him.

A half-dozen games into the preseason schedule, he finally reached base on a fielder's choice. His fielding was becoming slightly less of an adventure as well. In his first night game, played against the Twins, he made a nice play in the sixth inning in right field, then later hit the ball down the third base line for a single. Right behind him, Dann Howitt knocked a home run, and like that, Michael Jordan had scored a run, and was later mobbed by his teammates in the clubhouse.

But there was no way he was going to be among the twenty-five who made the big league roster that season. A week before spring training broke, he was assigned to the Birmingham Barons, in Alabama, in the Double-A Southern League, a "prospects league" mostly for young talent. He spent the final week in Florida working with the other minor leaguers, a thirty-one-year-old hopeful among pimply teenagers.

Sweet Home, Chicago

On April 7, Jordan returned to Chicago to play in the Windy City Classic, a big league exhibition game between the White Sox and Cubs at Wrigley. At first, Sox manager Gene Lamont wasn't going to start him, but 35,000 fans showed up to see him play. To their roaring delight, Jordan walked out in the first inning, his shades artfully resting over the bill on his cap. He went two for five, with two RBIs in a game that was called a 4–4 tie after ten innings. His able play in right field and his work at the plate drew standing ovations, so rare for baseball, from the happy crowd.

"What a day for Michael Jordan," declared Cubs broadcaster Harry Caray. Before the contest, Caray had interviewed Jordan, who made no effort to contain his broad, boyish smile. Jordan was doing just what every kid dreamed of doing, Caray acknowledged. But, he wanted to know, would he be upset if he made all of this effort only to discover he couldn't hit big league pitching?

No, Jordan replied, that "would simply be a credit to the game of baseball." He was there to see if he could do it and to have fun trying, he explained.

His associates would later remark that it was easily the happiest day of his baseball life, if not the happiest ever. The game, broadcast on superstation WGN, served notice to viewers nationwide that perhaps this Jordan baseball thing wasn't so silly after all.

The next day he arrived in Birmingham to find the place aswarm with thousands of fans. They had come from all over the country, a great Jordan tide that would continue to wash over minor league baseball in the coming weeks, setting attendance records and stripping the souvenir booths of every available item.

J. A. Adande traveled to Birmingham to do a story about the phenomenon for the *Washington Post*. "I remember going down there and just sitting there and looking at him out in the outfield and it just seemed surreal," he recalled. "This is Michael Jordan and he's sitting here in this ballpark, a minor league ballpark, in Birmingham, Alabama. How is this possible?"

Bob Greene, too, was struck by the spectacle of thousands of people sitting for hours one night in a downpour during a rain delay, just for the hope of seeing him play. Jordan had been profoundly embarrassed during spring training at the spontaneous outbreak of fans chanting, "I want to be like Mike." That kind of fervor was unheard of in major league spring training, but this was the minors, the backwater of baseball, and still they came and ogled and chanted.

He rewarded them with seven strikeouts in his first nine at bats on the opening weekend of the season in Birmingham. He connected twice, one a pop fly, the other a ground out.

The press corps, with many familiar faces from his basketball days, was startled by the absence of that old sparkle of supreme confidence in his eyes.

"It's been embarrassing, it's been frustrating—it can make you mad," he told longtime hoops writer Ira Berkow of the *New York Times*. "I don't remember the last time I had all those feelings at once. And I've been working too hard at this to make myself look like a fool. For the last nine years, I lived in a situation where I had the world at my feet. Now I'm just another minor leaguer in the clubhouse here trying to make it to the major leagues."

He explained that the seed was planted way back in 1990, before he had hoisted a championship trophy. "It began as my father's idea," he said. "We had seen Bo Jackson and Deion Sanders try two sports, and my father had said that he felt I could have made it in baseball, too. He said, 'You've got the skills.' He thought I had proved everything I could in basketball, and that I might want to give baseball a shot. I told him, 'No, I haven't done everything. I haven't won a championship.' Then I won it, and we talked about baseball on occasion, and then we won two more championships. And then he was killed."

He didn't hesitate to speak of his father's presence with him as he went about the business of realizing that dream. "I talk to him more in the subconscious than actual words," he said that first weekend, talking as he sat in front of his new locker in the Barons' spacious clubhouse. " 'Keep doing what you're doing,' he'd tell me. 'Keep trying to make it happen. You can't be afraid to fail. Don't give a damn about the media.' Then he'd say something funny—or recall something about when I was a boy, when we'd be in the back- yard playing catch together like we did all the time."

The Bus

Word quickly got out that Jordan was buying an expensive new bus so that he could travel the back roads of the South in luxury with his new teammates. It wasn't true. He didn't even rent the bus, as he had offered. The Barons' regular bus supplier had simply decided to provide the team with a deluxe bus, complete with reclining chairs and a lounge in the back to help ease the boredom of those long stretches between Nashville and Raleigh and Green- ville and Orlando.

Jordan explained that the nicer bus gave him room to stretch out, but he admitted there was another reason. "I don't want to have a bus break down at one o'clock at night in the South," he said. "You don't know who's going to be following you. I don't want to be caught in a predicament like that. I think about what happened to my dad."

Those same thoughts had prompted him to purchase two fire- arms, which he kept in his suburban Chicago home. Always aware of his surroundings, he had become even more watchful in the wake of his father's murder.

There was talk of him bonding with all the minor leaguers around him, and he did play dominos in a back area of the clubhouse for light cash, which gave his teammates the opportunity to peer into his wallet fat with bills. But often he kept to himself, sitting alone during the long bus rides.

That was the same emotional barrier that had existed on every team he had ever played on since he was six years old. Back in Chicago, he had confided to Johnny Bach the alienation he felt for years as a kid in baseball, as the only black on a team of whites. Those earliest experiences in baseball had also shaped him. Much of Phil Jackson's work as a coach had focused on breaking down the barriers between Jordan and the rest of the team.

This spin through the minor leagues brought back those early moments with his dad, as well as the old alienation. So the distance between Jordan and his minor-league teammates wasn't surprising. He wasn't rude or ugly or arrogant, not in baseball. But he did keep to himself and his entourage, which had shrunk to just George Koehler. Juanita would visit and bring the kids on some weekends. But most of the time it was Jordan, Koehler, and his grief. Jack McCallum had pushed Jordan to talk about the experience in 2011, which prompted a somewhat testy reply. "It was baseball," he said. "The Barons. There were a lot of lonely nights out there, just me and George, on the road talking. And I'd think about my father, and how he loved baseball and how we always talked about it. And I knew he was up there watching me, and that made him happy. And that made me happy, too."

Having grown up in North Carolina, Jordan found Alabama no great culture shock. He settled into a rented house in Birmingham with a basketball goal that allowed him to engage the neighborhood kids. He found the area's best golf courses and rib joints and pool halls. Soon enough, a relaxed Jordan produced a twelve-game hitting streak that pushed his average up over .300. But then he struggled through a prolonged slump as the season stretched into the dog days of summer.

"He is attempting to compete with hitters who have seen

350,000 fastballs in their baseball lives and 204,000 breaking balls," Rangers pitching instructor Tom House would say of Jordan that season. "Baseball is a function of repetition. If Michael had pursued baseball out of high school, I don't doubt he would have wound up making as much money in baseball as in basketball. But he's not exactly tearing up Double-A, and that's light years from the big leagues."

When Jordan had announced his retirement the previous October, Lacy Banks had written a column the next day predicting that he would one day return to basketball. With his batting average sinking, Banks came to Birmingham for three days to push him on the issue. But Jordan denied it.

"I still don't buy it," Banks wrote in the *Sun-Times*. "And his recent batting slump is our ally."

Sitting at his locker, Jordan laughed when Banks asked him about a "glorious return" to the NBA.

"You make it sound like some kind of religious event or something," Jordan snickered.

"Jordan was very adamant that his basketball days were behind him," recalled J. A. Adande, who had worked with Banks at the *Sun-Times*. "And Lacy goes back and asks him, 'Is there even a teeny-weeny chance?' And Michael said something like, 'There's always a chance, but right now it's real teeny and real weeny.'"

Even with that dismal slump, Barons manager Terry Francona could see that Jordan was making dramatic improvement. At his lowest point, he had stayed after a game one night to ask what the manager really thought about his future in the game. Jordan would admit later that the talk had come just as he had begun to entertain thoughts of giving up. He didn't want to go on as a joke and, worse, to take the place of a younger prospect who had a better chance. But Francona pointed out that progress was typically slow in baseball development and that he was starting to see substantial gains for Jordan. The effort had been extraordinary and unfathomable to people who knew baseball.

Over the last month of the season, he batted .260, which lifted his average to a measly .202. In 436 at bats, he had managed 88 hits, including seventeen doubles and a triple. He had stolen 30 bases and scored 46 runs. Such steady improvement earned him a promotion. He was assigned to the Scottsdale Scorpions of the Arizona Fall League. It seemed to represent a victory, although few beyond Terry Francona and some White Sox executives saw it that way.

For Jordan himself, it represented a murky window to his future. His once magnificent confidence was now in tatters all around him, yet he remained cautiously steadfast. He was driven by emotions that few if any understood. He had arrived at this point in his life so completely wrapped in silent fury that even he failed to recognize it. This blinding yet unarticulated rage would play out in incongruous ways over the coming years, until the central question of his life became: Would he ever be rid of it?

Chapter 31

COME AGAIN

As LONG, TALL Michael Jordan busied himself trying to match the rhythm of his swing to the rhythm of the pitcher, he was also keeping an eye on the world he had left behind. He had kept up with the adventures of the Bulls and was amused by the NBA's feeble attempts to replace him as the marketing engine for the game. He was particularly curious to follow Pippen's breakout year that spring of 1994. No longer under Jordan's shadow, his old sidekick had shown surprising growth as a premier player. He had been named the MVP of the All-Star Game in February and on the season had averaged 22.0 points, 8.7 rebounds, 5.6 assists, and 2.9 steals per game as the Bulls posted fifty-five wins that year, just two fewer than the previous season with Jordan.

At first glance, the team appeared to be doing quite well, but behind the scenes Pippen's anger simmered. The Bulls made their way through the Eastern Conference playoffs to a showdown with the Knicks that saw Chicago fall behind two games to none. Game 3 was suddenly critical, and the Bulls had built a lead, only to watch it dwindle in the fourth period. With just 1.8 seconds left, New York's Patrick Ewing scored inside to tie the game at 102. On the bench during the ensuing time-out, Phil Jackson drew up a play that called for Pippen to inbound the ball to Toni Kukoc for a final shot. Pippen cursed the coach and sat on the bench, fuming and refusing to go back in. Andrea Kremer, an ESPN reporter with a camera crew just feet away, witnessed the entire scene, including the anger and shock of Pippen's teammates. Bill Cartwright, in particular, was both stunned and furious.

Nonplussed, Jackson directed Pete Myers to inbound the ball. Kukoc caught it and swished a twenty-two-footer as time expired for a dramatic victory, the fourth such game he had won that season with a last-second shot. Any celebration, however, was overshadowed by the outrage over Pippen's actions. It was explained to the media that Pippen had felt disrespected, that with the year he had had, he felt the final shot should have been his. Hardly mentioned was Pippen's simmering envy of the European player, who in his first year already had a salary to rival his own. After the game, Jackson told reporters: "As far as the last play goes, Scottie Pippen was not involved in the play. He asked out of the play. That is all I'm going to say about it."

"Phil and I kind of exchanged some words," Pippen told reporters in the locker room afterward. "That was pretty much it. It wasn't Phil taking me out of the game, we pretty much exchanged words and I took a seat. I think it was frustration. We really blew this game as much as we possibly could. We were able to pull off the win. Toni made another outstanding shot and it was a well-called play by Phil."

Jordan, in Birmingham, was transfixed. "Poor Scottie," he told reporters, little realizing at the time how much the incident would come to affect his own career. "I kept telling him it's not easy being me. Now he knows." Jordan felt sorry for Pippen, and he knew that the incident was going to cause his friend much trouble.

"I apologized to the team and to Phil Jackson," Pippen told reporters several days later. "I don't think I have to apologize to anyone else."

The Bulls ultimately lost the series to the Knicks in seven games.

"It was a devastating thing," Steve Kerr said at the time. "Scottie never could have judged the magnitude of his actions. I felt so badly for him." Krause was infuriated by the incident. Pippen had already spent much of the season engaged in a nasty public argument with the GM over his contract. "I don't think you can call me a quitter," Pippen said in defending himself. "I think you can look at it and say I made a stupid mistake. That's pretty much it. I haven't been a quitter. I think I go out and approach the game as hard as anyone. I play smart, I play hard, and I play as a team player."

Although Pippen was considered one of the best in the league, Krause began efforts to trade him but had trouble finding a deal that would net a player of comparable value. Finally Krause put together a trade with Seattle that would have brought power forward Shawn Kemp plus a draft pick, which would allow Krause to select Eddie Jones, a bright young guard out of Temple. But at the last minute, Seattle's owner backed out of the trade, and the subsequent series of news stories revealed Krause's plans. Pippen, who was already unhappy over his contract, was further enraged that the team planned to trade him.

The lingering hard feelings set the tone for a tumultuous off-season. Horace Grant, who was a free agent, became engaged in a similarly messy feud with Jerry Reinsdorf and soon left the team to sign with the Orlando Magic. In the acrid atmosphere, Cartwright announced his retirement, only to resurface on the SuperSonics. John Paxson also decided to retire.

Jackson watched the breakup of his very good team while involved in testy negotiations of his own with Krause for a new contract. The coach had already executed the off-season's most questionable move when he abruptly fired Johnny Bach just days after the playoffs ended. The dismissal came at a terrible time in the older assistant coach's life, just weeks before his seventieth birthday. The irony, Bach recalled, was that the coaching staff had probably never worked better together than during the 1994 season. "At the end of that year I had every reason to think my contract would be renewed," Bach recalled. "The first person that told me was Phil. He said, 'We're not gonna renew the contract.' I was stunned. Before I could say much in defense, he said, 'It's really best for you that you do leave. The organization has made up its mind.' I was disappointed. Shocked is a better way of saying it. I didn't quarrel. I just couldn't believe it. I went to see Krause and he said the same thing. I just got up and left. I had a lot of crisis in my life at that time. I was in the divorce courts ending a long-term marriage. I had to move. I thought everything was collapsing around me that summer. Then I had a heart attack. It was all a shock, and it took some time to believe and trust people again."

The mysterious dismissal smacked of retaliation. Bach had apparently fallen into Jackson's disfavor because he had at times encouraged Jordan to follow his own instincts and ignore the triangle offense. Some in the organization felt that Bach's relationship with Jordan threatened Jackson's control of the team, even though Bach was also a strong supporter of Jackson's. There was clearly something about Bach that annoyed Jackson. "We were very different people," Bach acknowledged.

At the time and in accounts several months later, Jackson portrayed Bach's firing as a result of Krause's anger over *The Jordan Rules*.

"It was Jerry Krause's relationship with Johnny Bach that created a very uncomfortable situation," Jackson said of the firing several months later. "It made this have to happen eventually. It had gone all wrong. It was bad for the staff to have this kind of thing because we had to work together. Jerry basically blamed Johnny Bach for a lot of the things in *The Jordan Rules*. And there's no doubt that Johnny did provide that information. Jerry felt that Johnny talked too much. And Johnny, in retrospect, felt that animosity that Jerry gave back to him, the lack of respect, so Johnny refused to pay allegiance to Jerry just because he was the boss.

"It had gone on for too long a period of time," Jackson said. "I could have kept them apart, at bay from one another, I suppose for a while longer. But I didn't like the fact that it wasn't good teamwork. That was my staff and my area. I agreed to do it. I felt it was a good opportunity because Johnny had an opportunity to get another job in the league quickly. It worked out fine for Johnny, although I would just as soon have not put him through the disappointment, or have to go through the situation myself."

It would be several years before events revealed that Jackson was seeking to cover up his own role in the book. Sam Smith eventually disclosed to Reinsdorf that Jackson, not Bach, was among the sources for the book. Reinsdorf violated Smith's confidence to reveal Jackson's role in the book to Krause. The revelation instantly infuriated the GM, who alleged that Jackson had deceived him into believing that Bach was the anonymous source for most of the inside detail. Smith later independently confirmed these events and Jackson's role in his book. "Phil and the players had much more of a role than Johnny Bach," Smith said.

"Phil lied to me," Krause said when asked about the matter. "Phil actually got Johnny fired."

"It was Phil's idea to fire Bach," Jerry Reinsdorf alleged as well. "Phil told me that the bad relationship between Krause and Bach had made things impossible. It was Phil's idea. Nobody told him to do it."

Once he recovered from the heart attack, Bach was eventually hired by the Charlotte Hornets. It was several years before he learned the alleged reason for his firing, that he had supposedly provided the inside information to Smith. Bach said he went back and read the book three or four times looking for damaging information he might have provided. His quotes, though, were on the record and hardly scandalous.

"I didn't see a single quote in that book that was out of order," he said. "Sam is obviously a good investigative reporter. There was a portrait in there that Michael did not like, based on whoever gave it to Sam." The book "was quite an accurate portrayal," Bach said. "I don't think Sam painted someone as he wasn't."

Krause said he was distraught that he had been deceived into firing an innocent man. By the time the lie was uncovered several years later, Bach was working in Detroit as an assistant coach. One night when the Pistons were in Chicago to play the Bulls, Pistons executive Rick Sund told Bach that Krause would like a word with him. Bach had mixed feelings but agreed to the meeting, and was more than a bit surprised. "When Jerry spoke to me he was emotional, and so was I. I always thought the organization had made that move, not Phil. I thought it was a huge concession on Jerry's part to come up to me. I thought he meant it," Bach said of Krause's apology. "And I accepted that."

Bach would later address the issue with Jackson, but what was said would remain between the two of them, Bach said. "I'd rather leave it be. Certainly he knew how I felt. I always thought we had a relationship that was strong enough. We had sat there on the bench together for five years. As an assistant coach you don't always know about these things that are going on. It was always foolish, kind of an indictment that I could never defend myself. Now the whole thing is not important. Once it was."

The incident, however, revealed an intriguing element of Jackson's strategy with Jordan. Why had he risked the job he had coveted or that key relationship with the game's brightest star by providing a reporter with information about his boss or about Jordan? One longtime Bulls employee who worked with Jackson on a daily basis figured the coach did it to gain more control over his team. After all, the book had served to further alienate Krause from the players, thus securing Jackson's role as their leader, the team employee said. "It was, 'Let's get down on Michael. Let's whip this guy and keep him in line for my purposes.' It was his way of getting on Michael's side by alienating him from the media," the Bulls employee suggested. "That was why Phil always used it's the Us-Against-the-Media approach, the Us-Against-the-Organization approach, because if he did that, then he could be the leader of the pack."

For years, the coach did not address the allegations by Reinsdorf and Krause, although in a 2012 interview Jackson pointed out that The Jordan Rules had been immensely important in the evolution of the Bulls because it brought Jordan down to a level that was closer to his teammates. Certainly, Jackson was within his rights as a coach to want to speak with one voice to his players, but he had resorted to an extreme subterfuge to exert control. "Phil is the master of mind games," Jordan had said of the coach on several occasions.

Jordan was dismayed at the news of his favorite coach's dismissal, although he had no idea what had really happened. On numerous occasions in the future, he would make a point of involving Bach in his life. Yet Jordan also reflected on the special relationship he had shared with Jackson, the long talks they had, the debates and exchanges — not just about basketball, but about life in general.

"We talked about so many different things," Jordan said of those sessions. "We used to get into philosophies more than anything."

It was obvious that both he and Jackson enjoyed the talks immensely. "We used to challenge each other," Jordan said. "I think I would learn from him, and he used to learn a little bit from a player's perspective at that time. He had played years back, but I was giving him a thought process for a new era. It was a lot of give and take. Much more listening from me. Not disagreements but more or less concepts, with him saying, 'Think about this and think about that.' "

The implicit running theme, ironically, had been greater trust. Jordan would recall that his trust in Jackson grew over time. As he won Jordan over and the Bulls began claiming championships, the coach found new ways to motivate the superstar and to maintain offensive balance between Jordan and his teammates. From there, Jackson pulled together an array of influences to shape Jordan's mental approach to performing under intense pressure. Obviously those lessons had aided Jordan not just in basketball but in his baseball life as well.

The Stadium Again

That September, Jordan came to Chicago to play in the Scottie Pippen All-Star Classic, a benefit game for Jesse Jackson's Operation PUSH. At first, he was hesitant to accept the invitation, perhaps because of hard feelings left over from the boycott four years earlier. However, the event would afford him one final chance to play in Chicago Stadium, which was scheduled for demolition in the coming months to make way for the $150 million United Center, just across Madison from the Stadium. The lure of the Stadium proved too strong, and Jordan showed up to find a packed house eager to reclaim him. His team, dressed in white, took on Pippen's crew in red, and the two old teammates went at each other with surprising fierceness. Jordan didn't want anyone thinking that he'd "lost this or lost that." He found his old fire and took 46 shots for the game, making 24 of them, for 52 points. His group won, 187–150, in an evening that may have set a record for standing ovations. When it was over, he embraced Pippen near the scorer's table, waved to the crowd, and walked to center court, where he hitched up his shorts and bent over on all fours to kiss the floor, a final, emotional farewell to the platform of his rise to greatness.

"I was kissing the Stadium good-bye and kissing good-bye to my years of playing there," he told reporters afterward. "But I was not kissing basketball good-bye. I'll always love basketball, and I'll always play it. I just won't play organized ball."

Indeed, he played quite a bit of pickup ball that fall in Scottsdale, where he went to play in the Arizona Fall League. Terry Francona had noticed that in Jordan's final month in Birmingham he had begun driving the ball much harder when he hit it. His bat speed had improved, and he was starting to gain a base in his spindly lower body. Indeed, he hit a respectable .255 at Scottsdale, in a league of the game's top young prospects.

Bob Greene went to Arizona with Jordan and noted the lonely, windswept nature of the experience, the chilly games before mostly empty bleachers. Later that fall, Deloris Jordan phoned her son and detected something in his voice that told her she needed to visit him. A few days later, George Koehler picked her up at the airport and took her to the stadium for his game. The crowds were relatively sparse in Arizona, compared with Birmingham, but Greene watched Jordan step out of the dugout that evening and stand there, searching the crowd until he found her. Then his eyes lit up and he smiled broadly, a rare sight during his months of grief.

Later that fall, he returned to Chicago for "A Salute to Michael," a ceremony to retire his number 23 jersey in the Bulls' brand-new arena. In conjunction, the team planned to unveil a bronze statue of His Airness in action, called *The Spirit,* outside the new building. The statue was a burden to Jordan. He had seen a model of it and had somehow agreed to it, but his elevated public image had already made his life a nightmare. He was a real person, he confided to Greene, not a statue, and its presence outside the United Center only served to further wall him in. It was an immediate hit, however, attracting countless tourists from around the country and around the world.

Jordan's better sense warned him to avoid the ceremony, and it proved to be even worse than he had imagined, packaged as it was into a nationally broadcast program for TNT. After a series of staged segments and awkward skits, Reinsdorf and Krause were introduced, and the crowd of 21,000, still quite angry over the team's summer of discontent, booed lustily.

"C'mon, now," Jordan chastised the fans. "Both Jerrys are good guys."

It wasn't as if "the two Jerrys" hadn't heard it before. At virtually every rally or celebration of the Bulls' three straight championship seasons from 1991 to 1993, Krause had been the target of merciless booing from Chicago crowds. Trainer Chip Schaefer, sitting nearby, could see Krause's wife, Thelma, break down in tears during the booing. The GM had long ago inured himself to the anger of fans, but the sight of his wife in tears, being consoled by Dean Smith, made him furious.

"Dean came up to her later on and said that it was nice of Michael to mention my name," Krause recalled. "Thel looked at him and said, 'Too late! Bullshit, that's too damn late! He could have done a lot more much earlier.' Dean was pretty pissed....I was really proud of my wife. She said that to a couple of people that night. She told Dean Smith off. She told several people off that night. She was pissed. She sat there with tears in her eyes after that happened."

Like his wife, Krause resented Jordan's refusal to ever speak up in his defense. "Michael could have done a bunch of things through the years," Krause said later, "but he didn't."

"Jerry's never been able to project a good personal image," Phil Jackson observed at the time, "and that's been the thing that's destroyed his public persona as far as the audience goes here in Chicago. They see him as someone like the mayor. The mayor always gets booed in public. Jerry represents that kind of guy. He has to do a lot of the dirty jobs....He'd done that to the point where he's sort of made himself an unlikeable character."

Nevertheless, Krause had endured. "All general managers make mistakes," Reinsdorf said. "Jerry's incredibly loyal, but the main thing is that he gets results. He gets results because he works very hard, and he has a good eye for talent."

"Poor Jerry's been kicked around from pillar to post by everybody, including me," longtime Chicago sportswriter Bob Logan said at the time. "But he got what he wanted in life. He's running the franchise. He's got three championship rings. Yet I don't think he's ever spent a day where he's completely satisfied. There's always something else he wants, or something that doesn't quite work out."

Not long before Jordan's tribute, Krause had admitted that he looked forward to having a team that won a championship without Jordan on the roster. "Jerry and I have talked about it," Krause said frankly. "Hell yeah, we want to win after Michael because there is a certain vindication in it and there is a certain personal thing in it. Yeah, I mean I have an ego. I don't think that it is huge, but it ain't small. And I think I'm good at what I do, and for one time I want the world to say that I won, and it wasn't because of Michael." Unfortunately, he had missed his chance in the failed 1994 playoffs.

Even on this night of retirement celebration, Phil Jackson sensed that the desire to play again was stirring within Jordan. Some NBA owners had mentioned quietly to Reinsdorf that maybe the league itself should offer him a major compensation package to lure him back to basketball. Afterward, a reporter asked Jordan if he could be lured back to basketball with a $100 million contract offer. "If I played for the money," he said testily, "it would be $300 million."

If he played for money, he certainly wouldn't have been in baseball, where his light stipend was supported by his estimated $30 million in endorsement income that year. Major League Baseball had been paralyzed by a strike in August, and it dragged on through the holidays that year and right into February. The minor leagues were not affected, so Jordan reported to spring training a week early only to realize that the fight between owners and players over money wasn't going to end anytime soon. Then, he had a misunderstanding with White Sox management over dressing room and parking arrangements. But what really drove him away was the growing sense that he would be used as a draw for spring training. He had absolutely no appetite to be a replacement player or, worse, a scab. Finally, he packed up his father's dream for good and headed home. He notified Reinsdorf in a phone call.

"I think you're quitting baseball for the wrong reasons," Reinsdorf said.

"No," Jordan said. "I've made up my mind."

"What do you want to do?" the owner asked.

"I don't know," Jordan replied.

"He had hit .260 in the Arizona Fall League," Reinsdorf confided later. "I thought he was really making progress. But the strike had made it all but impossible for him to play for the White Sox in '95."

On March 10, he announced his retirement from baseball, saying that his minor league experience had allowed him to rediscover the work ethic that had made him a great basketball player. "I met thousands of new fans," he said, "and I learned that minor league players are really the foundation of baseball. They often play in obscurity and with little recognition, but they deserve the respect of the fans and everyone associated with the game."

Jordan hadn't failed baseball, Phil Jackson noted. "Baseball failed him."

Berto Center Days

At first Jordan tried to enter Bulls practices discreetly, but that wasn't likely to work out, especially with the team plodding through a drab landscape. The first warning was almost imperceptible. A cell phone call to an old friend perhaps. Or maybe a puff of smoke outside Jackson's office. Whatever it was, the signal somehow got transmitted to all the right people that March. MJ was thinking about coming back? He's just gonna come to practice in his gear and see how things go?

So began the year the world truly lost its mind over Chicago basketball.

"There were rumors for weeks about his coming back," recalled Chip Schaefer. "I was having dinner with Larry Krystkowiak and Luc Longley and Steve Kerr, guys who hadn't played with Michael before. These guys were so excited about the prospects of playing with him, like kids almost in how they felt about it. I remember sitting there and listening to those guys and thinking, 'Boy, you have no idea how hard it is playing with him.'"

It had been a weird year even before Jordan got there, Steve Kerr recalled. The Bulls had been good without Jordan the previous season, but the '95 roster was considerably weaker. The dissension and controversy had finally caught up with them. "I felt like what happened was, the first year he was gone, his presence was still felt and the team still had a swagger," Kerr explained. "We had Cartwright and Paxson and Horace Grant, all these guys who were clearly still champions and felt that way and it carried over even with Michael gone. But, by the next year, it had started to wear off. We missed Cartwright and Paxson and Grant. We missed their leadership. So, all of a sudden we were depleted physically and leadership-wise. And reality kind of set in. We just sort of faded and lost our edge and our energy. We were struggling."

Jordan had been in and out of their practices earlier that season, but there hadn't been any bonding whatsoever with the team, Kerr said. "He came to practice some, occasionally, but he was really unapproachable for those of us who didn't play with him, just because of who he was and his presence. He's kind of an intimidating guy, as you know, especially if you don't know him. You just don't wander over to Michael Jordan and say, 'Hey, what's up?' He was like this looming presence. None of us knew him very well."

Within days, he was in gear and in practice, with enough energy to drive a storm surge. But it still wasn't clear if he had decided to return. The first leak came on local sports talk radio, and the madness was on. The next ten days would bring the greatest tease in the history of sport. Was Michael Jordan returning to basketball? A village of satellite trucks and media representatives from the major networks and national publications converged on the practice facilities at the Berto Center in anticipation of some kind of announcement. Yet large screens covered the picture windows of the practice facility. The media could hear the shouts, the squeaking of sneakers on the gym floor. They were told that Jordan was practicing with the team but that he hadn't yet made up his mind, that the details were being worked out. Meanwhile, in practice sessions he wore the yellow vest of the second team and ran point guard against the regulars.

Jordan versus Pippen. Just like old times.

"Just to be able to play with him is fun," said center Will Perdue, who had played on all three championship teams with Jordan. "Just to be able to watch him."

In truth, the situation wouldn't have gotten so crazy, the hype so large, if it hadn't dragged on for those ten teasing days. But Reinsdorf wanted him to wait. And Jordan himself wavered that week, pausing, trying to figure out if he was returning to basketball out of disappointment over the baseball strike, or if he was coming back because he loved the game. While he waited, the fans came in droves to the Berto Center as if drawn by a great magnet. The crowd spilled over into the parking lot of a hotel next door, eager to catch a glimpse of His Airness as he left practice each day. But he remained silent, which kept the twenty-four-hour cable news shows fed and lines buzzing on sports radio talk shows across the continent.

After about a week, the collective impatience began to mushroom, with some callers on Chicago's sports radio talk shows claiming that Jordan was toying with the public, which might have been true. David Falk, who noticed everything, savored the conditions. His client was generating the kind of coverage that couldn't be bought. *USA Today* reported that the stock value of those companies that employed Jordan as a spokesman had zoomed up $2 billion on the various stock exchanges in recent days, leading to further suggestion that Jordan was engaged in some kind of financial manipulation.

By that Thursday, March 16, Jackson signaled that it had all gotten to be too much. He told Jordan not to attend practice that day because the media crowd at the Berto Center had grown too large. That afternoon, the coach told the assembled media that Jordan and Reinsdorf were engaged in discussions and that a decision was probably three or four days away. Even with the monster distraction that he was, Jordan had shown that he could boost the team with just a little practice time. That Friday night, the Bulls capped a three-game winning streak and raised their record three notches above .500 by defeating the Milwaukee Bucks in the United Center. There'd been speculation that Jordan might make a sudden appearance in uniform for that game, but only his security advisers showed up to evaluate the arena.

Then, abruptly the next morning, Chicago radio stations reported that the deal was done, that Jordan would make his announcement that day, and that he would play Sunday in a nationally televised game against Indiana. Down on LaSalle Street, the managers at Michael Jordan's Restaurant heard the news and decided to restock the gift shop yet again. The restaurant's business had been slow in February, but the hint of Jordan's return had crowds packing the place virtually every night in March. Fans kept a vigil at the Jordan statue outside the United Center, which had quickly become something of a shrine. Over at the Berto Center, a crowd of fans and reporters milled about, with some fans leaning from the balconies of the Residence Inn next door, all waiting for the official word.

Suddenly, practice was over, and like that, Jordan's Corvette appeared on the roadway, with the fans cheering wildly as he gunned the engine and sped off. Next came Pippen in a Range Rover, pausing long enough to flash a giant smile through the vehicle's darkly tinted windows. Moments later, NBC's Peter Vecsey did a stand-up report outside with the fans rooting in the background. He told the broadcast audience that Jordan was returning, that he would play against Indiana on Sunday and would probably pull his old number 23 jersey out of retirement. Excitement coursed through the city. Chicago, quipped one radio sportscaster, was in a state of "Jorgasm."

The star of stars had broken his silence with a two-word press release, issued through Falk. It read, "I'm back."

That Sunday Jordan violated NBA rules and flew down to Indianapolis on his private jet. The plane landed, and he sat alone inside it on the runway. He was about to play his first NBA game since his father's passing, and he wanted to let his mind roll back over some very personal memories. Then he rode downtown with an armada of limousines carrying his security force of twenty. He would need them to negotiate the crowds that had gathered around Market Square Arena, where security workers had erected yet more barricades.

Waiting for the game to start, Pacers coach Larry Brown took in the atmosphere and quipped that it seemed like "Elvis and the Beatles are back."

Finally, shortly after noon, he emerged with his teammates from the visitors' locker room and stood before a crowd gathered in the hallway. He chomped his gum, looked around with a serious frown, and made ready to resume the career that had been interrupted by an eighteen-month "retirement."

At last, the maddening foreplay was coming to an end, and the basketball public could celebrate the return of its pharaoh. All the high priests of hoop were there. "NBC brought in the big guns for that one," recalled Matt Guokas, who had ascended to the role of color analyst. "They even flew in Bob Costas to host the pregame show."

If Jordan had decided to stage his own Super Bowl, it couldn't have seemed like a bigger deal. Surrounded on all sides by cameras, the Bulls made their way out into the arena, opening yet another chapter in the saga of Air Jordan, but there was something not right with the picture. He was wearing jersey number 45, his minor league and junior high number, instead of the familiar 23 that he had made so famous. He had decided to keep number 23 retired because it was the last number his father saw him wear, Jordan later explained. Champion, the sportswear manufacturer that held the NBA license for jerseys, immediately added an extra shift and began producing more than 200,000 number 45 jerseys for sale around the world.

The crowd hardly seemed to care that he looked somewhat stiff and rusty against Indiana that afternoon. He made just 7 of 28 shots, but his defensive intensity helped the Bulls take the division-leading Pacers to overtime before losing. Afterward, he broke his silence to address the hoopla of the preceding ten days.

"I'm human," he said. "I wasn't expecting this. It's a little embarrassing."

His return had been delayed while he sought assurances that the Bulls would keep Pippen and Armstrong—assurances that Reinsdorf declined to make. Jordan said he had also taken his time evaluating his own motives, making sure his love of the game was genuine. That, he said, was the reason he returned, not financial considerations. He pointed out that the league had a moratorium on renegotiating contracts while it worked out a new labor agreement with the National Basketball Players Association, so he was forced to play for the $3.9 million salary he had left behind in 1993. (Although not required to, the Bulls had paid his full salary for 1993–94, and they would cover the full amount for 1994–95, although Jordan played only a portion of the season.) His return, he said, was based solely on his love for basketball.

"I wanted to instill some positives back into this game," he said of his return, indicating his displeasure at some of the NBA's highly paid young players. "There's been a lot of negatives lately, young guys not taking care of their part of the responsibility, as far as the love of the game. I think you should love this game, not take advantage of it...be positive people and act like gentlemen, act like professionals."

From there, the Michael Jordan Comeback Revue headed to Boston Garden, where three nights later, he scored 27 points by shooting 9 of 17 from the floor. This time the Bulls won. Next up, he treated his followers to a last-second shot for a win against Atlanta, setting up the big show at Madison Square Garden.

Knicks coach Pat Riley had become alarmed when he saw that Jordan was already starting to get his rhythm back against the Hawks. Riley, one of pro basketball's most knowledgeable figures, knew when a storm was headed his way. Jordan and Falk sensed it coming, too. Jordan had wanted some games to warm up before facing Riley's rough crew, with six-five John Starks, who had defended him well in the past. The Chosen One's return to Gotham would draw the largest regular-season audience in the history of cable network TNT's NBA coverage, and the city itself bristled with excitement. "Bulls Over Broadway" flashed a huge marquee near the Garden. All anyone could talk about was the "history." Nothing lit up Jordan's eyes like New York's grand venue, dating from his rookie season. The Garden had been the site of statement after statement, the loudest of which came in his return from foot injury in 1986, when he set the building record for points scored by an opponent, with 50.

This night had the same feel, with his aura thick in the atmosphere.

"I came out here to score," he said afterward, as if he needed to explain himself.

Everybody had seen that in those first New York minutes. His jump shot started falling in the opening quarter, as Starks backed off just enough to prevent his drive. He allowed Jordan to get into what he liked to call his rhythm, that flow he sought in everything he did, from batting to golf to basketball to table tennis with Lacy Banks. From there, he seized the Knicks by the throat, and even Spike Lee and the courtside homers were secretly delighted. His scoring line was 49 by the end of the third quarter, and he went on to break his own Garden record. In the process he branded the moment on his board of legendary feats: his "double nickel" game, as he finished with 55.

With all that, it was the ending that blew Manhattan's minds. The Knicks kept close, but Jordan had the ball and the game in his hands in the closing seconds as he surveyed the floor and drew what seemed like the entire defense. There, all alone under the basket was his new teammate, Bill Wennington, ready to make the winning dunk.

Afterward, Riley looked as if he'd been gnawing the leg of the scorer's table the entire forty-eight minutes. "He's the only one in the history of this game that's had the impact that he's had," he conceded.

In the interview room, Jordan presented Starks with one last bit of trash. "I think he forgot how to play me," he said, unable to resist another temptation to score.

The performance, more than any other single thing, created the impression that somehow, magically, he was ready to pick up where he had left off, that he was ready to simply waltz right into a fourth championship. Perhaps no one fell harder under this sway than Jordan and his coaches and teammates. The record itself buttressed their belief. With Jordan in the lineup, the Bulls rolled through the last weeks of the spring, going 13–4, built on two six-game winning streaks that sent the atmosphere in the United Center soaring. Brand-new when the season opened, the "UC" as it would quickly come to be called in Windy City jargon, seemed awkward and foreign to Jordan, who had once vowed never to play there. He relented, of course, but didn't like it and quipped that he'd like to "blow it up." That spring, Chicago Stadium sat across the street, with a huge hole in its side from the demolition in progress. On game nights, the lights were on inside the old "sandstone sarcophagus," as if the ghosts of contests past were waiting, like the rest of Chicago, for good friend Michael and his crowd. Jordan, however, was struggling through bouts of very ordinary play, accompanied by tension behind the scenes.

"It's a weird thing to play sixty-five games without someone," Steve Kerr said, looking back in 2012, "and then that person, who just happens to be the most dominant figure in the sport, just shows up, you know, and plays. It was an adjustment period for sure. And we were all giddy. We were all so excited because we knew we had a chance to win again."

In their time alone with him, however, the team was adjusting to a new undercurrent of contempt. Kerr was stunned at the way Jordan seized control of the entire team's mental state, for better or worse. "We had no idea," Kerr said. "He was so intense...and condescending in many ways. None of us felt comfortable. On a daily basis, he would just dominate practice, not physically, but emotionally and in an intimidating fashion. He was going to make us compete, whether we wanted to or not, you know. There's certain days where it's like, you're an NBA player and you're exhausted. Every team goes through this. There's just days and you're gonna go and get your shots up, but you just need your rest. And Michael doesn't need rest....He doesn't sleep, even today, he doesn't need rest. And other guys do, and so on those days when people were tired, he would ridicule us and cajole us and...you know, just yell at us. It was tough. It was hard to deal with."

To the basketball public, it had all the appeal of a storybook ending. The Bulls finished in fifth place in the Eastern Conference and had no home-court advantage in the playoffs. Still, they managed to oust the Charlotte Hornets in four games in the first round. Johnny Bach had been hired by the Hornets and sat on their bench, watching the series wistfully. Jordan greeted his old coach warmly.

"I would have loved to be there," Bach said years later, looking back. "But it was not to be."

Jordan had readily accepted Jackson's account that Krause had necessitated Bach's firing. That and the conflicts with Pippen had served to halt any thawing in his relationship with the GM brought about by the first three titles.

Chicago's next opponent was the Magic. Horace Grant had joined Shaquille O'Neal in the Magic frontcourt, with Anfernee Hardaway, Dennis Scott, and Nick Anderson providing Orlando with athleticism and shooting to go with their power in the post. They had whipped the Bulls in the United Center shortly after Jordan's return. This one would be a decidedly personal series, with Grant eager to give Reinsdorf, Krause, Jackson, and Jordan a good look at what they had, in his mind, always seemed to disrespect.

The Bulls played their way to a 91–90 lead in Game 1 in Orlando but lost on Jordan's two late-game turnovers, one a steal by Anderson when all Jordan basically had to do was dribble out the clock, a flashback to his final game in high school. "Number 45 is not number 23," Anderson said afterward, adding that Jordan didn't seem as explosive as he had been before he left for baseball.

"We agonized a little bit for him this year when he went through the postseason drama," Jackson said later. "But knowing Michael so well, I put my arm around him after that first game against Orlando when he lost the ball and said, 'As many times as we won behind you, I never expected to see this happen. Let's use it for our tool. Let's use it to build a positive. You're our guy, and don't ever forget that.' You never think you'll have to go to Michael and talk about something like that."

Jordan refused to speak with the press afterward. He showed up for the next game wearing his old 23, an unannounced jersey change that drew the Bulls a $25,000 fine from the league. The NBA also enforced its policy that required Jordan to begin addressing the media again.

"I didn't take that in a harsh way," Jordan would say of Anderson's comment a few days later when finally forced to talk. "I set such a high standard two years ago, and in twenty games I haven't lived up to that. And that's what I'm going to be judged on. I have to live up to my own expectations."

The Bulls won Game 2 to even the series and take away home-court advantage. They fully expected to take control back in the United Center for Game 3. Jordan scored 40, but he took 31 shots and seemed to forget at times that the Bulls had a team offense. Orlando took the critical game, but Jordan trimmed back his shot selection in the fourth game, which allowed Chicago to even the series. Asked about his future, as the reporters and camera crews packed ten-deep around him, he replied, "Everyone has an opinion about Michael Jordan except Michael Jordan. I came back for this season and next season, and from that point on, we have to evaluate it."

From there, he missed shots, made miscues, and watched Grant's play shift the series. Jackson had decided to double-team O'Neal while leaving Grant unguarded, figuring that if Grant made shots, they would only be two-pointers. It backfired. Grant answered Jackson's strategy by scoring early and often, which emphasized a Chicago weakness at power forward. The Magic closed out the series, 4–2, on the Bulls' home floor, and Orlando's young players hoisted Grant to their shoulders and carried him off in celebration.

In the hallway outside, the Bulls coaching staff seemed numb with disbelief. Nick Anderson was right, Tex Winter confided. "Michael isn't the same player."

"He's aged like everybody else has aged," Jackson agreed later. "But he's still Michael Jordan."

Jackson predicted that Jordan would regain his touch and shoot better than 50 percent for the next season. "You can bet your bottom dollar on that," the coach said. "Will he break through all the defenses that people bring at him, the double-teams and triple-teams? No. But he'll probably start knowing where to pass the ball better. Michael lost perspective of where the passing would have to come from a lot of times."

Jordan had needed the team-building of a full eighty-two-game schedule, Jackson said, looking back some weeks later. "He saw and heard the criticism that went on in the postseason. There was a lot of the blame game going on in Chicago, a lot of people whining and gnashing teeth. Michael's going to use that for his strength."

It was a profoundly humbling moment for Jordan, Steve Kerr recalled in 2012. "He gets the ball stolen from him at half-court by Nick Anderson. We had the game won. We lose that series. He had some phenomenal games and some very poor games, so I always thought it was the failure of the playoffs that drove him. But, I think baseball had to figure in there, too, because his last title was in '93, so he goes two full years without feeling like he's on top of the world."

Failing his team had bruised his outsized pride. For years he had taken the Bulls' fortunes on his shoulders and lifted them with brilliant performances in front of millions of adoring witnesses. Now it was his fall that was on display.

Chapter 32

TRAINING CAMP

Mᴵᴄʜᴀᴇʟ Jᴏʀᴅᴀɴ's ᴍᴜᴄʜ-ʜᴇʀᴀʟᴅᴇᴅ return had served to reveal mostly what he didn't know. He hadn't really known vulnerability, at least not on a basketball court. "The game taught me a lesson in the disappointing series I had last year," he would admit that fall. "It pushed me back into the gym to learn the game all over again."

Fans and media naturally shifted the blame elsewhere, onto Chicago's offense. In the days following the loss, the sports talk shows in the city buzzed over the possibility that the triangle no longer worked for the Bulls. Even Tex Winter himself harbored doubts and badly wanted to know Jordan's thoughts on the issue.

"With his impulsiveness," Jackson recalled, "Tex said, 'Phil, I'd like you to ask him, does he think we need to change the offense? Can we play this triple-post offense? Is it something we should plan on using next year? I want you to ask him just for me.' So I did, and Michael said, 'The triple-post offense is the backbone of this team. It's our system, something that everybody can hang their hat on, so that they know where to go and how to operate.'"

"By that time, Michael had won three championships playing the triangle, so he had complete trust, in the offense and in Phil," Steve Kerr explained. "You know, Phil would tell us in practice repeatedly, he'd say, 'I don't run the triangle for Michael or Scottie. Those guys will score, no matter what offense we run. I run this for the rest of you guys.' He would say that in front of Michael, and I think that was smart, because everyone knows, in some ways, that offense was restricting Michael's abilities. If the goal was to try to get him 40 points, we could have just run plays for him and cleared out for him and he could have gotten 40 points. But we weren't going to win that way, and Michael knew that already."

Far more than the offense, the team's future still hinged on a nagging question about Jordan himself: What if he up and quit again? It seemed pretty clear to some observers that his time as the game's dominant player had passed. There was even speculation among some Bulls staff members that he might retire again rather than deal with the hassles of NBA life. This speculation intensified over the summer as Jordan became involved in the battle over a collective bargaining agreement between the NBA and its players. He had never shown the slightest interest in league labor issues, and had determined never to seek to renegotiate his contract with the Bulls. Yet, here he was, at the urging of David Falk, taking a leadership role in a renegade effort to decertify the players' union and force the league into giving its players a better deal with more freedom to negotiate. The issue was eventually resolved, but it left the impression of a new Jordan, more aggressive in off-court issues.

Despite the public anxiety over his and the team's future, the Bulls coaching staff remained quietly upbeat about their prospects. They saw that Orlando's talented young team would be the main contender in the Eastern Conference, and if the Bulls hoped to win another championship they would have to match up with the Magic. Chicago needed to find a power forward, to strengthen their post play, and to find bigger guards to counter Orlando's trio of Anfernee Hardaway, Nick Anderson, and Brian Shaw.

Krause's first move was to leave fan favorite B. J. Armstrong unprotected in the upcoming expansion draft. A bigger guard to replace Armstrong was already on the roster—former All-Star Ron Harper, whom Krause had signed in 1994 to help fill the void created by Jordan's retirement. A series of knee injuries had precipitated a decline in Harper's athleticism since his days as a young superstar with the Cleveland Cavaliers. He had been frustrated with the triangle offense, but Jackson persuaded him that if he improved his conditioning, he would be a factor for the coming season.

Likewise, Jordan needed to retool both his mind-set and his workouts, in order to replace what Reinsdorf called his "baseball body" with a leaner basketball body. Jordan was scheduled to spend the summer months in Hollywood making the animated Bugs Bunny film *Space Jam* with Warner Bros. Surprisingly, the Bulls' coaches weren't worried about their main player spreading himself too thin in this new age of vulnerability.

"We didn't worry about Michael," Winter said. "We figured Michael could take care of himself."

For the most part, his "gym" would be a temporary floor in the Hollywood studio he occupied while making his film. There, Jordan could work on his game yet be within reach of the film crew when he was needed to shoot a scene. For years, Krause had encouraged Jordan to make a greater effort at weight lifting, but Dean Smith had never been a fan of bulking up his players, an influence that had resonated with Jordan.

The more Krause talked about weight lifting, it seemed the more Jordan scoured the landscape for open tee times. But Orlando had gotten his attention. Krause had long wanted Jordan to work with team weight lifting director Al Vermeil, the brother of former Philadelphia Eagles coach Dick Vermeil, but Jordan eyed suspiciously anything suggested by the GM. Instead, he turned to Tim Grover, Juanita Jordan's personal trainer. Jordan, Harper, and Pippen worked out every morning with Grover, referring to this group as the "breakfast club." In time, the Bulls would come to be considered one of the best-conditioned teams in the history of the game. And Grover would soon be in top demand as the guru who guided the rebuilding of MJ's body.

"I've never seen anybody work harder than Michael Jordan," Grover said that fall. "He fulfilled his normal summer obligations—shooting commercials, making some personal appearances—and he shot a movie. But his conditioning program always remained his primary objective."

For Jordan, the torturous off-season program was just the

beginning of a yearlong effort to regain his earlier dominance in the NBA. As he neared his thirty-third birthday, he tried to prepare himself to face not only the game's talented young players but the specter of his own youth.

"I'm the kind of person who thrives on challenges," Jordan explained at the time, "and I took pride in people saying I was the best player in the game. But when I left the game I fell down in the ratings. Down, I feel, below people like Shaquille O'Neal, Hakeem Olajuwon, Scottie Pippen, David Robinson, and Charles Barkley. That's why I committed myself to going through a whole training camp, playing every exhibition game, and playing every regular-season game. At my age, I have to work harder. I can't afford to cut corners. So this time I plan to go into the playoffs with a whole season of conditioning under my belt."

He needed to keep playing that summer, even as he spent long days on the film lot. Jordan arranged to set up a court and invited an array of NBA players to join him for pickup games between takes on the set. He had great fun with the summer competition. But by the time he wrapped the film, packed up, and headed back to Chicago for training camp, his focus was sheathed in an inexplicable fury. It would be woe unto anyone who stepped in his way.

The Anger

The first time Jim Stack suggested the idea Jerry Krause ignored him. He knew Jordan and Pippen would go nuts if they brought Dennis Rodman anywhere near the Bulls. And Jerry Reinsdorf? They all hated the Pistons, the thug-assed Bad Boys.

But Stack was pretty sure it would work.

"Jim Stack came to me early in the summer and asked me to look at Rodman," Krause said. "When I put him off, he finally pleaded with me. He talked me into finding out if all the bad things we had heard were true. Without Jim's persistence, we wouldn't have looked behind all the rumors to see what the truth was."

The deeper they investigated Rodman, the more Krause became intrigued. Friends, enemies, former coaches, former teammates—

the Bulls contacted a wide variety of people about Rodman. Chuck Daly told them he would come to play and play hard. Krause still hesitated.

"Everybody in the league was scared to death of Dennis," said Brendan Malone, the former Detroit assistant.

Reinsdorf was likewise cautious: Take it slow. A guy like that could wreck everything in a matter of days.

Rodman himself couldn't believe it when he was first contacted. But Krause realized about halfway through their conversations that he liked the guy. Satisfied, Krause sent Rodman to speak with Jackson, who spent hours trying to read his attitude. Clearly, Rodman wanted to join the Bulls to play with Jordan. He even allowed the team to talk to a psychiatrist he had been seeing. The staff figured Pippen and Jordan would be a very tough sell, but the two of them thought it over. "If he's ready and willing to play, it will be great for our team," Pippen said. "But if he's going to be a negative to us, I don't think we need that. We could be taking a huge step backwards."

Once Jordan and Pippen agreed, Krause traded longtime backup center Will Perdue to San Antonio for Rodman in early October, just days before training camp opened.

And like that, Dennis "The Worm" Rodman, the NBA's thirty-four-year-old adolescent, became a Chicago Bull. He was looking for a two- or three-year deal in the neighborhood of $15 million. "I'll put five million in the bank, live off the interest, and party my ass off," he told reporters, which, as time would reveal, is exactly what he did.

In recent seasons, the Bulls had come to rely on a trio of centers, Will Perdue, Bill Wennington, and Luc Longley. Perdue could block shots, Wennington had a feathery offensive touch, and Longley, at seven-two and 290 pounds, had the huge body to go against giant forces like Shaquille O'Neal. None of the three Chicago centers constituted a complete force on his own, but collectively they formed what the press had taken to calling a "three-headed monster," a patchwork solution assembled by the coaches. Perdue would be traded, and Rodman would be the power forward that helped out the surviving two-headed monster at center.

For help in handling Rodman, the team signed his teammate

from San Antonio Jack Haley, and then brought in another former Bad Boy, James Edwards, to help out with the center chores. Later they would add yet another former Piston big man, John Salley, all as part of their Rodman plan. The Bulls coaches figured that with Jordan back full-time and committed to winning a championship, with Pippen, Longley, and Kukoc maturing, with Harper refurbishing his game, and with Rodman in town, they had just about all of the major pieces in place. The Bulls had long hated the Bad Boys, but now they were set to deploy a slew of them.

The only problem would be making it work. Rodman arrived in Chicago with his hair dyed Bulls red with a black Bull in the crown and his nails done in a layered Bulls motif. "I understand that they're a little leery and a little cautious of having someone like me in here," he said. "They wonder how I will respond to the team. I guess they'll find out in training camp and during the preseason. I think Michael knows he can pretty much count on me doing a good job. I hope Scottie feels the same way."

The wild saga of Jordan's return had finally calmed in Chicago, but now the city found itself engaged in the next media whipsaw, the introduction of "The Worm." Who could have foreseen that the Bulls' fan base would fall so instantly and completely in love with the tattooed man? He arrived in town on the verge of bankruptcy and soon had a fistful of endorsement contracts and cash to throw around. Throughout its history, the city of broad shoulders had seen a steady parade of gangsters and curious madams, crooked politicians and honorable shysters, but Rodman was easily one of the most colorful customers Rush Street had ever known. As Jackson would soon note, his new forward was a clown of the first order. After all, who could fail to notice a guy who showed up for a press conference in a wedding dress?

If it hadn't been for his grand entrance, fans might have realized that a bizarre, almost hellish training camp was unfolding that fall. It would take years for the truth to leak out about what really happened in those long, foreboding days at the Berto Center. When it was over, the Bulls rolled out of the station like a trainload of parolees, as frightened as they were frightening.

"I got a glimpse of it right away," Steve Kerr recalled in 2012.

"Camp was insane, how competitive and intense it was. Michael was coming off the comeback when he hadn't played that well in the playoffs, at least as far as his standards were concerned. He was out to prove a point and get his game back in order. So every practice was like a war."

If Dennis Rodman had any thought about acting up, he ditched it immediately—Jordan was that intimidating. In fact, Rodman didn't even speak to his new teammates, preferring instead to work in a silence that would grow stranger with each passing day. "It was a tough training camp because everybody was guarded," Jack Haley would explain later in the season. "Again, you're Michael Jordan. You're Scottie Pippen. Why would you have to go over to Dennis? Michael Jordan made $50 million last year. Why would he have to go over and basically kiss up to some guy to get him to talk? They came over and shook his hand and welcomed him to the team, and this and that. But other than that, it was a slow process."

"I think everybody was skeptical of what might happen," recalled John Paxson, who had been hired as an assistant coach. "But we were also optimistic as to what could happen. The optimism stemmed from Phil's personality. We felt that if there was anyone around the league who could get along with Dennis and get Dennis to respect him as a coach it would be Phil."

Central to the uneasiness about team chemistry was the relationship between Rodman and Pippen. "No, I have not had a conversation with Dennis," Pippen acknowledged early in the year. "I've never had a conversation with Dennis in my life, so I don't think it's anything new now."

It was a blessing, in retrospect, that the Rodman sideshow served to obscure what was really happening in training camp. Jordan was even more difficult than he had been the previous spring. He was far more strident in his relationships with his teammates upon his return from retirement. "When he came back after the murder, he was a different animal," Lacy Banks explained. The team, after all, had been rebuilt while Jordan was away from the game. There was little question that he found himself working with a group who had no real idea how to win a championship.

"A lot of these guys have come from programs who have never

experienced the stages of being a champion," Jordan explained in acknowledging his rough approach with new teammates. "I'm just speeding up the process."

Another factor had been that summer's lockout. At Falk's bidding, Jordan had led the failed effort to decertify the union, with Steve Kerr on the other side of the issue. Reinsdorf had opposed Jordan "being out front" on the issue, but he did it anyway. "We had an underlying edge from the lockout," Kerr recalled, "and I was the Bulls' player rep and Michael was one of David Falk's guys and they weren't happy at all with the union leadership, so there was kind of an undercurrent of that. Every drill, every practice was so intense."

Kerr sensed an extra level of irritation, perhaps even dislike, from Jordan. It did not seem racial in any way, he recalled with a laugh. "He never used race in any comment. He was above that. He didn't discriminate. He just pretty much destroyed all of us. But, I think it was calculated, for sure. He tested every guy. You may not have known it at the time, but he was testing you and you had to stand up to him."

Kerr's time to stand up came on the third day of training camp. "This is what I remember," he recalled in 2012. "We had a scrimmage and the starters were beating up on us. We were the red team and they were getting away with fouling. Michael was just being incredibly physical. And Phil had left to go up to his office. He had to go tend to a phone call or something, and so Phil's absence definitely led to a situation where it was a little out of control. Michael was talking all kinds of shit. It really is kind of a blur as to what he was saying, but I got really fed up, you know, because I felt like they were fouling every time and Michael was fouling. The assistant coaches are reffing and they don't want to call a foul on Michael. He's talking, and I start talking back.

"I'm not sure anyone had done that before," he said with a laugh.

Kerr got the ball, and Jordan again fouled him. "He was guarding me and I think I used my off arm and threw an elbow or something, to get him off of me, and he kept talking. Then I'm yapping and the next play, I'm running through the lane and he gives me a forearm shiver in the middle of the lane and I give him one back.

And he basically came after me. As Jud Buechler says, 'It was like a velociraptor.' I was like the kid in *Jurassic Park* who got attacked by the velociraptor. I had no chance. It was just mayhem. We were screaming at each other, and our teammates, thank God, they all ran in and pulled us apart. But I ended up with a black eye. Apparently, I got punched. I don't even remember getting hit."

It was the first and only fistfight in Kerr's life. "We were barking at each other, and it got out of hand," recalled Kerr, the son of a career diplomat. He was just letting us know how they were kicking our ass. I knew they were kicking our ass. He didn't have to tell me about it. Why wouldn't that piss me off? It's natural. Other guys were pissed off, too. He just happened to be guarding me at the time."

Jackson saw the incident as a serious and immediate threat to the team's chemistry. "Michael stormed out of practice," Kerr said, "and Phil came down and came over to talk to me. He said, 'You and Michael have to patch things up. You gotta talk to him and you gotta patch it up.' I got home and there was a message on my phone, on my answering machine, from Michael, and he apologized. And it was weird, it was like from that day forward, our relationship was great. Like, you know, a few days after that, where it was a little weird just because of what had happened, but clearly he accepted me from that point on."

With that one incident, Jordan had assumed complete control of the team. Where before he had used his anger and mental intimidation to push the group, he now added the implied threat of violence. He had created an atmosphere that for the next three seasons would allow him to drive the Bulls at the pace he set. He wasn't alone in this effort. He formed a partnership with Jackson, the team's other dominant personality, to create a fiercely disciplined group.

It was why Jackson referred to Jordan as the alpha male. Jackson sought to temper and direct Jordan's fierceness with Zen teachings, mindfulness, meditation, and other practices. "He didn't articulate much on a personal level," Kerr said of Jordan's approach. "He articulated plenty on a basketball level. I mean, he had his opinions. In the film sessions, he would talk all the time, and Phil would some-times ask him to talk, so he exerted his influence on us through the game, but not so much on a personal level."

This unprecedented approach was at its most extreme in that first training camp after Jordan's return, but the dynamic contin-ued for three very successful, very turbulent seasons, Kerr said.

"He knows he intimidates people," Jackson would say that fall. "I had to pull him in last year when he first came back. He was com-fortable playing with Will Perdue...he was tough on Longley. He would throw passes that, at times, I don't think anybody could catch, then glare at him and give him that look. And I let him know that Luc wasn't Will Perdue, and it was all right if he tested him out to see what his mettle was, but I wanted him to play with him because he had a big body, he wasn't afraid, he'd throw it around, and if we were going to get by Orlando, we were going to have to have somebody to stand up to Shaquille O'Neal."

Jackson, who had always made an effort to keep the team's hier-archy clear, now had Jordan as his enforcer. They had help from Tex Winter, who also had a harsh way of going after players if they slacked off.

The Zen

Jackson had brought in George Mumford, a psychologist and mind-fulness expert who taught the players to meditate and do together-ness exercises. Mumford also counseled individual players to help them grasp the team dynamic, which consisted in part of Jordan bullying them and Jackson using his influence to keep everybody on board. What was remarkable was to see Jordan come to embrace Jackson's softer efforts with the team, Kerr pointed out. "That was the key to the whole thing. If Michael hadn't trusted Phil, it never would have worked for any of us. But Michael had such great respect for Phil that he embraced those methods."

It often felt incongruous that Jackson would use thirty minutes of precious practice time to have his players sit on the floor and meditate in the dark—only to face Jordan's wrath as soon as the drills started. As Kerr said, Jackson told them that he didn't run the triangle offense for Jordan, but for the rest of the players. The meditation seemed to fit a similar, but converse, pattern. The coach didn't really have meditation so much for the rest of the players. He had it in hopes that it might prevent Jordan from chewing up one promising teammate after another.

In short time, Jordan gained a level of trust with Mumford and told the psychologist that if he'd met him earlier in his career he might not have spent his life a prisoner in his hotel room.

Pippen also helped enforce the hierarchy. He could flash his anger, but was an understanding and compassionate leader. He had graduated from MJ's school of hard knocks, and by the fall of 1995, Pippen and Jordan acted as partners at the heart of the team, Kerr observed. "By the time I got there, they had a great relationship. You know, they had their breakfast club where Harper and Pippen would go over to Michael's house and lift weights in the morning. They would go lift weights and then show up to practice together. Those three were really tight. And it was the perfect role for Scottie, as we all know, not having to be the man, but being able to dominate in his own way."

Jordan was still the alpha male, but his pairing with Pippen had created a two-man unit in which the sum was far greater than the individual parts. "They were a perfect combination, at both ends," Kerr explained. "They were both so versatile defensively, they could just switch and cause so much havoc. And then offensively, Scottie really preferred to pass and Michael preferred to score. By the end, I think, one of our last championships, Michael basically pulled him under his arm and announced to the crowd that it wouldn't have been possible without Scottie. So, in the end, it was an incredible relationship."

It was in this atmosphere that Dennis Rodman was injected, into Chicago's most unusual team chemistry. Everyone on the inside was eager to see how he would fit into a new hierarchy and identity that fall. "They hardly ever spoke," Kerr said of Rodman and Jordan. "There was just this respect, this underlying respect that you felt. It was really easy to feel it, because Michael never picked on

Dennis. Never. And Dennis was like subservient to Michael in an emotional way, not in a physical way. He never did anything for Michael that he didn't do for the rest of us, but there was just this understanding that Michael is the 'greatest' and I'm below him, and so I'm not going to mess with him, and vice versa. It was really interesting."

The primary target of Jordan's fury would remain the team's foreign-born stars, Luc Longley from Australia and Toni Kukoc from Croatia. By all accounts, including Jordan's, his treatment of them was harsh, and it lasted over his final three seasons in Chicago. "Those guys were so talented, particularly Toni, who was incredibly gifted," Kerr said. "And Luc was a huge piece, literally and figuratively. I mean we needed him to man the paint and anchor the defense and rebound and you had to light a fire under Luc to get the best out of him. So, I think there was a reason that Michael and Phil and Tex and Scottie all stayed on those guys. It was because they needed it. They needed the kick in the pants. I think Toni was just so laid back. I'm very laid back on the surface, but you can get to me. And I have a button that can be pushed, especially when I was playing.... I could get so angry, like I did that day, that I could snap. I never saw Toni snap, though. I never saw Luc snap, and so it was like they were just fair game for Michael."

Tex Winter had seen every sort of team dynamic but was transfixed by the evolution of Jordan after his return. "It's another way he has of challenging himself," the older coach theorized, pointing out that if Jordan was so hard on his teammates, it allowed him little room for personal letdowns.

Kerr agreed. "If you look at his past, it's filled with moments of sort of created challenges for himself to raise his level. The thing that amazes me is that the standards he has set are so unbelievably high that it's almost unfair that he has to maintain them. It's incredible. Every arena that we go into all season long, he's expected to get 40 points. He loves it. That's the amazing thing about him. The combination of incredible talent, work ethic, basketball skills, and competitiveness. It's just an unbelievable combination."

Looking back two years later, Jordan would acknowledge that he had sometimes come down so hard that he had run people off.

"You have a better understanding for me as a leader if you have the same motivation, the same understanding for what we're trying to achieve, and what it takes to get there," he explained. "Now, if you and I don't get along, certainly you won't understand the dedication it takes to win. So if I run 'em off, I don't run 'em off with the intention of running 'em off. I run 'em off with the intention of having them understand what it takes to be a champion, what it takes to dedicate yourself to winning. I'm not hard every single day. I mean there are days where you have to relax and let the tension flow or ease. But for the most part, when you have to focus, you have to focus. As a leader, that's what I have to do.

"And I'm not by myself," he emphasized, echoing Kerr. "Pip does the same, and Phil does the same. But I do it more consistently, I guess, because I've been here the longest. I feel obligated to make sure that we maintain the same type of expectations, the same level."

Jordan knew intimidation well, having taken a beating from the Pistons. And it would have to be taught to others. He had made that decision in 1990, when he had laid his heart on the line and realized afterward that his teammates hadn't done the same. He would not find himself in battle again with faint hearts around him, he decided. "That's going through the fucking stages of being on a losing team to a championship team," he said in retrospect, his eyes narrow as he frowned. Jordan had grabbed the team by the throat to elevate its emotional level. Just the realization of that had staggered Steve Kerr. So this is what it is, he said to himself.

Jordan readily acknowledged that his status in pro basketball allowed him to do things that perhaps no other player—probably no coach, even—could get away with. "You don't want to do it in a way that they misinterpret the relationship," he said. "It's nothing personal. I love all my teammates. I would do anything. I would extend myself to make sure they're successful. But they have to do the same. They have to have a better understanding of what it takes."

The fact that Jordan occasionally chased some would-be teammates off "may be a good thing," Kerr said. "You've got to kind of weed out the people who can't really help out. And Michael has a way of finding those guys, finding weaknesses...

"Obviously we all have weaknesses," Kerr added and laughed. "Except for Michael. And what he does, he forces us to fight and be competitive, to fight through those weaknesses and not accept them, to work on them, and to improve ourselves." Make no mistake, though, Kerr said, what Jordan did was pure challenge. "There was not a whole lot of encouragement."

"I suspect that Larry Bird was the same way," said trainer Chip Schaefer, "and I know from observing countless Lakers practices during my time at Loyola Marymount that Magic Johnson was a bitch at practice. You drop one of his passes, you miss a layup, you miss an assignment on defense—man, if eyes could kill, that's the way it was."

It would take time for this harsher Jordan to gain focus in the public mind. Bruce Levine, a reporter for a Chicago sports radio station, had gotten to know Jordan well over the years. Slowly, Levine saw what James Jordan's death had meant for the star. "Up until then, he was the most unaffected superstar, because he wouldn't allow things to get to him," Levine explained at the time. "He would still sit in the locker room before the game and stretch out with us and talk for a half hour or forty minutes about everything but basketball. He would stretch out on the floor, and we would just sit for forty-five minutes and talk about everything. We'd have fun. He'd ask questions. He's very inquisitive, a guy who wanted to learn about things. He was still learning about life and educating himself. But once the situation occurred with his father and the way the media portrayed that funeral, he never had the same feeling for the media again. He distrusts most media, even people like myself who are peripherally friends with him. It just changed. He became hardened by it to a certain extent. He's still very gracious with his time, but the fun kind of went out of it for him and for us."

What made Jordan's harshness so difficult to read was that it often came wrapped in the mirth of his trash talk. "Michael has made up his mind that he's going to enjoy his time of playing basketball," Tex Winter observed. "I think he made his mind up a long time ago. He enjoys playing, and he wants to keep it fun and loose. And that's what he attempts to do. His methods sometimes in my mind are questionable. But if that's what it takes for him to enjoy himself and to challenge himself, then so be it."

It remained Jackson's job to integrate this new, harsher version of Jordan into the roster. Since Jordan's return, the coach had continued to remind him that the team was only as strong as its weakest link, which had precipitated the fiery training camp. The coach's bag of tricks included the mind game, the deceit, the motivational hide-and-seek, and, when necessary, the rare frank assessment, or even confrontation. As their time together went on, the nature of Jackson's effort became more political, more soothing and understanding. The respect he showed Jordan presented an obvious double standard, however.

"Phil would make references to things with Michael as 'We need to do this,'" backup center Bill Wennington observed one day after a game. "Whenever there was a problem with Michael in a meeting, it was like 'We need to do this.' If it was me, it was like, 'Bill, you have to go box out.' When it was a Michael thing, it was a 'we' thing. For us, it was, 'Steve, you need to take that shot.' Michael would maybe miss a box out, and it was like, 'Well, *we* need to box out now.' Just little things like that. But if you understand the reason for it, and the reason that the team was good, it's all part of it."

Jordan had long accused Jackson of playing mind games, but he played them as well, only far more harshly. "That's what it is, mental," Jordan said. "You gotta force them to think. This team is not a physical team. We don't have physical advantages. We have mental advantages."

"They were vicious," Kerr said of Jordan's particular brand of mind games. "But the good thing was, we had to deal with them in practice. But we knew that our opponents had to deal with them every game."

Muggsy Bogues could confirm that. At a key point during the '95 playoff series between the Bulls and Charlotte Hornets, Jordan backed off of the five-foot-three Bogues and told him, "Shoot it, you fucking midget." Bogues missed the shot, lost his confidence, and later reportedly told Johnny Bach that the play started his career down the path to ruination.

Friend or foe, Jordan knew how to get through to those around him on a deeply psychological level. Chicago sports broadcaster Jim Rose gained rare insight to this once when he played in a charity basketball game with Jordan against several other NBA stars. Rose had covered the team and knew of Jordan's competitive demands, so the broadcaster spent weeks practicing for the game. But during the game he blew a layup, which sparked Jordan's fury.

"You're not black enough," Jordan supposedly barked at Rose, deeply offending the broadcaster, so much so that Rose immediately fired the ball at Jordan. Jordan later apologized. But the incident revealed how intuitive he was in knowing which buttons to push to get through emotionally to his teammates. "He did it all in good fun," Rose said. "Michael doesn't like to lose at all. I missed the layup. I got mad and threw the ball at him and stormed off the court. Michael doesn't have a mean bone in his body. He's a wonderful person, but there are some times when his competitiveness takes over."

Jim Stack often found himself marveling at the gap between the Jordan that the public adored and the often ugly, domineering figure of Chicago practices. "Nike helped create that image for him," Stack observed, adding that there was substantial truth to what the public saw. "Michael was raised well. James and Deloris did a hell of a job. But when he was in his competitive mode, he could flip the switch and keep it there. Off the court, he was one of the most engaging, charismatic figures of all time. I put him up there with Muhammad Ali in that category. He was engaging and respectful and knew the right things to say. But when you flipped that competitive switch with him, he'd rip your heart out."

PART X

FURY

Chapter 33

THE CARNIVAL

Having been chastised and assaulted and terrorized, the Bulls emerged from training camp turbocharged, and Dennis Rodman, with his multihued head bobbing up and down, was much more than a hood ornament. His energy and enthusiasm alone made the team instantly better. The way he collected offensive rebounds in bunches almost made shooting percentages irrelevant. His teammates seemed assured that if they happened to miss a shot, the crazy, fist-pumping Worm would come up with the ball for another shot. He drove the point home with 10 rebounds in the first preseason game.

"Once he gets a little more familiar with everybody out on the floor and there's more continuity, he's going to start to shine," Jordan cautiously predicted. Jackson saw much the same.

"The very first preseason game of the year," Jack Haley recalled, "Dennis goes in the game, Dennis throws the ball up in the stands and gets a delay-of-game foul and yells at the official, gets a technical foul. The first thing I do is I look down the bench at Phil Jackson to watch his reaction. Phil Jackson chuckles, leans over to Jimmy Cleamons, our assistant coach, and says, 'God, he reminds me of me.'"

The United Center crowds became infatuated with his pogo-stick approach to the game, and were rewarded at the end of each contest with Rodman hurling his sweat-soaked jersey to the fans, after which he would prance bare-chested to the locker room. Female fans responded in kind. Whenever he would venture into bars across the city women seemed compelled to lift their shirts and show him their breasts. The season seemed destined to take Chicagoland to new and different places.

Until that time, Rodman had acted as if there were no limits, but Jordan's presence instantly provided them. The media went on and on about how Phil Jackson would handle Rodman, but Jackson could relax because Jordan provided all the presence that any coach would ever need.

Lacy Banks loved to make predictions, some of which had forced him to eat crow over the years. During the preseason that fall, he predicted the Bulls would win 70. As if on cue, Jordan went for 42 points against the Charlotte Hornets in an opening-night win at the United Center, setting in motion an epic momentum.

Unfortunately, the opening game would also feature an ugly confrontation between Juanita Jordan and her husband's family as they shared a skybox. Juanita was entertaining her family and friends in one part of the skybox, while the Jordans gathered and enjoyed each other's company in a way that apparently offended Juanita. Sis recalled their surprise when her brother's wife angrily lashed out at them at the end of the evening. There must be some mistake, Deloris Jordan and her children thought. But the next morning, Michael made an angry phone call to his mother and cursed her out. He expressed resentment that the family had encroached on his peace of mind.

While the exact nature of the conflict was unclear—it appeared to be as much a matter of accumulated conflict as anything—the episode would mark a period of Jordan's estrangement from his mother and siblings. At one point, he changed the locks on the offices of the James R. Jordan Foundation to bar her access. Further tension built behind the scenes as his brother Larry began developing a plan for a Jordan cologne. While aware of his brother's activities, Michael had begun working with established perfume industry intermediaries through his agents to develop his own line. Michael eventually informed his brother of his plans, but only after Larry had spent substantial time and money developing the idea. The older brother was crushed by the news, and Deloris Jordan grew furious with her famous son. Michael offered his brother a role in the cologne product, but that apparently did little to ease the hard feelings in the family that had been building since James Jordan's death. Clearly, however, Michael Jordan had learned his lesson from the Flight 23 stores fiasco. He did not want to be in business with family.

Private dramas like these, along with the murder trials of the two men charged with James Jordan's killing, formed much of the backdrop of the magical 1995–96 NBA season. The trial, motions, and deliberations ran for months, concluding in March with the convictions and life sentences for the two killers. For the most part, the sports media respected Jordan's desire not to speak about the proceedings, so the harsh circumstances of the case played out for months on the news pages, juxtaposed against the ongoing celebration of the Bulls' spectacular season.

In his tirade with his mother, Jordan had vented months of anger and frustration. From an early age, Jordan had always loved his family. But it would become increasingly clear that the young men who killed his father stole precious things from Jordan himself in the process. The families of murder victims are deeply, profoundly changed by the experience and often find it difficult to identify with anyone, even family members, in the aftermath. Jordan's father had been gone two years, an important period in the grieving process, but much conflict remained.

Steve Kerr's own father, an educator at the American University of Beirut, had been assassinated by terrorists when Kerr was a freshman at the University of Arizona. Jordan knew that the two of them shared something that no one else on the team had faced, yet never once in their years together did they discuss this. Jordan was leading the most public of lives while walking one of the most difficult private paths that any person could take.

"Even from his teammates, he kept it very close," Kerr said. "I would say in five years of playing with Michael, we probably shared just a handful of meals together, and I'm not talking about team meals or meals on the plane. I mean, like, going out at night with the team and having dinner. Michael would stay in his suite every night. He was a prisoner of his own life. Once or twice a year we'd end up at the same restaurant, at the same table with five, six of our teammates, but I never had just a breakfast, just the two of us, or lunch, just the two of us. It just never happened, because of the world that he lived in. Every single other teammate I shared very quiet moments, where you could discuss things...intimate things. But I never, ever even had a chance to bring anything like that up with Michael. Because, even though he was the leader of the team, the dominant presence on the team, he was always a little bit apart from the rest of us, too."

There was little time to process the situation with the most extraordinary of seasons upon them. One relief available on a Jackson-Jordan team was that the hierarchy quickly fell in place. At center, Longley seemed eager to face the challenge of being a starter, and Wennington was comfortable in his role as a backup. And thirty-nine-year-old James Edwards, the former Piston, gave them further depth at the post.

"It was kind of weird going there after all those battles we had with those guys," recalled Edwards, who was also curious to see how Jordan received Rodman. "But Michael seemed to have a lot of respect for Dennis. As long as he did what he was supposed to do on the court, that was all that Michael was concerned about."

Krause had also brought in guard Randy Brown to work with Kerr as backcourt reserves. Coming off the bench were Jud Buechler, Dickey Simpkins, and first-round draft pick Jason Caffey out of the University of Alabama. The other factor in the mixture was Toni Kukoc's reluctance to play the sixth man, or third forward. He wanted to start, but his role in the lineup had gone to Rodman.

Yet no sooner had Rodman started to settle in with the Bulls than a calf muscle injury sidelined him for a month. Even so, they rolled out to five straight wins, the best start in team history. If the early success did anything to make the Bulls complacent, the Orlando Magic snapped them back to attention in the sixth game, just as the Bulls were breaking in their new black with red pin-stripe road uniforms. Orlando guard Penny Hardaway outplayed Jordan, giving the Magic a key home victory. The Bulls responded with two quick wins back in Chicago before scorching through a western road trip winning six of seven games. The trip opened in Dallas, where Chicago needed overtime and 36 from Jordan (including 6 of the Bulls' final 14 points) to win, 108–102.

"This is a very aggressive basketball club and very confident," Jackson said afterward. "I think people are surprised who we are, or are surprised how we are playing, or they're not comfortable with our big guard rotation. It is giving us some easy offensive opportunities so we are getting going early."

They finished the western road swing in early December with Jordan scoring 37 in a win over the Los Angeles Clippers. "I feel I'm pretty much all the way back now as a player," he said, reflecting on the first month of the season. "My skills are there. So is my confidence. Now it's just a matter of me going out and playing the way I'm capable every night."

In his years before baseball, Jordan had shot a stellar .516 from the floor, but the numbers dipped to just .441 during his seventeen-game run over the spring of 1995. Now, he was up to .493. His scoring, too, was headed back up to a 30-point average from the nine-year low of 26.9 in 1995. Lacy Banks put together a comparison showing that if Jordan played through the 1998 season, he would rest third on the all-time scoring list with almost 29,000 points, behind only Wilt Chamberlain and Kareem Abdul-Jabbar, the all-time leader with 38,397.

Banks asked him about going for the all-time record.

"Forget Jabbar," Jordan replied. "No way do I plan to play anywhere close to twenty years."

"He's right where I knew he'd be about now," Ron Harper told reporters. "And that's leading the league in scoring and pulling away from the pack. He's removing every shadow of a doubt that he's the greatest player of all time."

"Age-wise, I think I'm old," Jordan said on the issue. "But skill-wise, I think I'm still capable of playing the type of basketball I know I can play.... The question people end up asking me the most is, how do I compare the two players, the one before baseball and the one after. Quite frankly, I think they are the same. It's just a matter of putting out the stats to show that they are the same. And I think by the end of the year hopefully, you will see that it's basically the same player with two years in between. Right now, I'm still being compared to Michael Jordan, and according to some people, I'm even failing to live up to Michael Jordan. But I have the best chance of being him because I *am* him. In the meantime, I'm improving and evolving."

Next

The season also saw a wave of talented young players come into the league. None of them figured they needed to study Jordan on tape, LA shooting guard Brent Barry recalled, because they'd all spent their lives watching him on TV. But catching him in person was a different experience.

Eddie Jones joined the Lakers that fall out of Temple. "When I saw Michael walk onto the court, it just excited me," he recalled. "I knew he was gonna go after me. I knew whatever player he faced he was definitely gonna attack.... When Michael went against somebody that was known as a defender, that ignited him. He just wanted to go out and take you out in the first quarter. That's just his competitiveness. He lived for that. He wanted to show you that, 'Hey, all these people are saying that you're a defender. I want to show you how well you defend.'"

Jerry Stackhouse, a rookie out of North Carolina, learned that same lesson after boasting that he could hold his own against Jordan, based on their summer showdowns back in Chapel Hill. "Nobody can stop me in this league, not even Michael Jordan," he told a reporter for a story in the morning papers in Philadelphia. That night, Jordan talked his way through 48 points and allowed Stackhouse a mere 9.

"It was just very clinical," said Julius Erving, who was watching from the stands.

Later that season, Jordan would score 53 against the league's hottest young star, Grant Hill, who was coached by Doug Collins. Collins immediately understood the difference between the two. "Grant is more inclined to want people to like him and to make people happy," Jordan's former coach observed. "Michael will cut your throat out."

Chicago turned in a 12–2 record in November and 13–1 for December to begin 1996 with an astounding 25–3 record, and was in the midst of an eighteen-game winning streak after having run through a twelve-game streak earlier. With each victory, speculation grew as to whether Chicago could win seventy games, breaking the all-time record for wins in a season, set by the 1972 Los Angeles Lakers with a 69–13 finish. Jerry West, the Lakers' vice president for basketball operations, who was a star guard on that '72 club, said that only injuries could keep them from winning seventy.

"I look at the Celtics back in '86 back when they had Bill Walton and Kevin McHale coming off the bench," Jordan said, in trying to compare his team with others he had known. "Those guys were tough to deal with. Those guys played together for a long time. We're starting to learn how to play together, but those guys were together for a period of time. They knew arms, legs, and fingers and everything about each other. We're just learning fingers."

It was pointed out to Jordan that most great NBA teams had a dominant low-post defender, someone to stop other teams in the paint. "We don't have that kind of animal," he admitted. "But I think Pippen compensates for that. I don't think any of those teams, other than maybe the '86 Boston Celtics, had a small forward that was as versatile on offense and defense as Scottie Pippen is."

Meanwhile, Tex Winter had begun worrying that Rodman's focus on another rebounding title was tearing at the team fabric. Beyond that, Winter wondered whether Rodman really had a handle on his emotions. But with each game, each road trip, the former Piston seemed to find ways to relate better to his new teammates. "Dennis was different," Kerr remembered with a laugh. "Dennis wanted to be close to us, he just didn't always know how. He was just so shy. What ending up happening...the white guys ended up bonding with Dennis because of his love of Pearl Jam and the Smashing Pumpkins. We'd go to concerts with him...and in the end, Dennis felt a lot more comfortable around the white guys than he did around the black guys. We definitely felt comfortable around him and would go out with him, once in a while, have a big night out, have a ton of fun. That was our way of bonding with him."

Rodman bonded with Jordan and Pippen on the court, as the Bulls evolved into a defensive force. What Rodman lacked in height he made up for in strength as he lifted weights around the clock. It was hard for opponents to muscle him out of the post, which helped shore up Chicago inside—if other teams even managed to get inside. Bringing the ball up-floor, the first thing opposing guards often encountered was Jordan at the top of the defense, bent low, his gaze fixed, telling them, "Come on, I'll give you a jump shot. Shoot it! Oh, you don't want it?" As the season wore on it became clear that many teams wanted absolutely nothing to do with Chicago.

During their big start, the Bulls had toyed with opponents through the first two or three quarters before flexing their might and finishing strong. When they rolled through January at 14–0, Jackson began talking openly of resting players just to lose a few games and slow things down. He seemed worried that his team would get so drunk with winning during the regular season that their energy might be spent by the playoffs. "You can actually take them out of their rhythm by resting guys in a different rotation off the bench," he explained. "I have considered that."

Jordan wanted no part of it. His focus was unbreakable. Fascinated by his play, Julius Erving sat down with him for a televised interview and asked about the shift in his approach as he aged. "Mentally, in the knowledge of basketball, I'm better," Jordan replied. "Physically, I may not have the same speed or quickness. But the mental can override the physical. I can't jump from the free throw line like I used to."

"You seem to operate in a zone that seems to be reserved only for you," Erving told him. "What's it like when you're there, Mike?"

"It's like every move, every step, every decision you make, it's the right decision," Jordan replied.

Jordan was "in the moment," as George Mumford described it. Every player could fall into a zone on occasion, but he now seemed to reside there. He had transformed his approach into a collection of post-up moves and midrange jumpers that opponents struggled to defend. He became a post weapon, much like a great center who could attack consistently. He did this despite tendinitis in his knees that required ice before games, and sometimes forced him to sit out practices.

In mid-February, he scored 44 against the Pacers, to go with Pippen's 40. Matt Guokas, doing color analysis for the game, pointed out that Elgin Baylor and Jerry West, two of the game's greatest scorers, had done that once or twice. More and more, Pippen and Jordan were becoming the perfect tandem. As Jordan went baseline repeatedly in just about every game that season, Guokas pointed out, "It's one of the Jordan Rules. You don't ever give Michael baseline."

The Bulls juggernaut pushed through February at 11–3. And although March was interrupted by Rodman head-butting an official and getting suspended for six games, the Bulls still finished the month at 12–2. The seventy-win season that Lacy Banks had predicted was beginning to seem possible.

"What amazes me most about our team," said Jack Haley, "is that we probably have the league's greatest player ever in Michael Jordan, we have the league's greatest rebounder in Dennis Rodman, and we have what is probably this year's MVP in Scottie Pippen, and what amazes me most is the work ethic and leadership that these three guys bring to the floor night in and night out. With all of the accolades, with all of the money, with all of the championships, everything that they have, what motivates them besides winning another championship? How many months away is that? And these guys are focused now."

Rodman marked his anticipation of the big event by showing up as a blond, highlighted by a swirling red streak. Then, headed into the team's historic week, he opted for a flamingo-pink shade. They earned win number seventy in Milwaukee on Tuesday, April 16, and closed the regular season with a road win in Washington for a 72–10 finish.

The Miami Heat fell in the first round of the playoffs in three quick games. Next came a grunting rematch with the Knicks, who managed an overtime win at home about which Jordan was nonchalant. He scored 35 in Game 5 in Chicago to finish them off, 4–1. After one late bucket, he backed down the floor and waved bye-bye to Knicks fan Spike Lee, sitting courtside with a towel wrapped around his shoulders. "I've always been known as a player who could finish off a team," Jordan said afterward.

To prepare the team for Orlando, Jackson spliced shots of *Pulp Fiction*, the story of two hired assassins, into the scouting tapes of the Magic. His players got the clear message. Rodman held Horace Grant scoreless for twenty-eight minutes of Game 1, until the Orlando forward injured his shoulder in the third quarter and was lost for the year. The meeting of the two best teams in the league ended 121–83, a 38-point humiliation for Orlando.

Commissioner David Stern had presented Jordan with the league MVP trophy before the game. "You still set the standard for greatness, determination, and leadership," he told him.

They were behind by 18 at halftime in Game 2 when Jackson walked into the locker room and told his team they had the Magic just where they wanted them. Indeed, the Bulls had toyed with opponents all season. They won going away as the once-powerful Magic headed into a slide. "Guys like Michael and Scottie, when there's blood in the water, they can smell it," Kerr told a reporter afterward. "They're ready for the kill."

The strangest sight of the conference finals was Rodman defending the massive Shaquille O'Neal straight up, loading the big center on his thigh and hoisting him off the block. Sitting courtside, working as a scout, Brendan Malone marveled at what Rodman had brought to the Bulls and how Jordan had adapted his game.

Orlando fell in four straight, an exclamation mark on Jordan's response to his failures a year earlier. "He's the baddest dude to ever lace up a pair of sneakers," Orlando's Nick Anderson said of Jordan after he scored 45 points in Game 4 to complete the sweep. Dr. Jack Ramsay, the former coach turned analyst, pointed out that the Bulls star had done it by immersing himself within the team.

Seattle

The Bulls fidgeted through a nine-day layoff waiting for Seattle to advance in the West. The 1996 NBA Finals opened on June 5 with the Bulls listed as ten-to-one favorites to defeat the Sonics, who had won an impressive sixty-four games during the regular season. The only anxiety that Jordan felt was the approach of Father's Day. He was mindful that the last time he was in the championship series, three years earlier, his family—including his father—had celebrated the title in his Phoenix hotel room. As this next milestone approached, the family now showed signs of fracture, although his mother still made an effort to support him. On the eve of the series, Princess Di visited Chicago for a medical fund-raiser at the Field Museum of Natural History. Deloris Jordan, a serious Diana fan, was confounded by the conflicting events. She wanted to attend the candlelit evening of dinner and dancing, so she slipped into an evening gown and attended the dinner with the princess, then changed clothes and dashed across town to watch her son. "I know Michael expects me to be there," she explained.

The NBA had credentialed approximately 1,600 journalists from around the globe to cover the event. The whole world would be watching, as was usually the case for Jordan's performances, particularly now that his new sidekick, Rodman, had yet another hairdo, with various red, green, and blue hieroglyphics and symbols scrambled on his skull. Reporters asked Jordan if he could still take flight and launch the dunks that made him famous, now that his game consisted largely of post-ups and jumpers. "Can I still take off? I don't know," he said. "I haven't been able to try it because defenses don't guard me one-on-one anymore. But honestly, I probably can't do it.... I like not knowing whether I can do it because that way, I still think I can. As long as I believe I can do something, that's all that matters."

Seattle coach George Karl had hired Brendan Malone to scout the Bulls during the playoffs in hopes that he could help them employ the infamous Jordan Rules for the series. As the Finals were set to open, Malone and Chuck Daly encountered Jordan in a hallway in the arena. "Michael came walking by me," Malone recalled in a 2011 interview. "He was upset because I had come with the knowledge of how to try and defend him."

"You're not going to beat me," he told Malone sharply.

"He was ticked off," Malone recalled. "Chuck looked at me and said, 'You've got him upset.'"

"You have to try to match their intensity," Malone told reporters at the time. "Forget Xs and Os. They are going to try and cut your heart out right away, right from the first quarter."

He was both right and wrong. Jordan would certainly attack, but the outcome was also about matchups. George Karl had six-ten Detlef Schrempf cover Jordan to open the series, with the idea that as soon as he dropped into the post, guard Hersey Hawkins would immediately double-team. It was a huge mistake. Jordan scored 28 points, and there was plenty of balance, as Pippen scored 21, Kukoc 18, Harper 15, and Longley 14. Karl later shifted Gary Payton, the NBA's defensive player of the year, to cover Jordan, but it was too late. In the fourth quarter, the Bulls' defense forced 7 turnovers, and Kukoc came alive with 10 points in what had become a typical Chicago finish. They took the advantage, 107–90.

Chicago shot 39 percent in Game 2, but that just meant more rebounds for Rodman. He finished with 20 boards, including a record-tying 11 offensive rebounds. Jordan struggled, but willed in 29 points. And the defense forced another 20 Sonics turnovers, including a batch during a three-minute stretch of the third period when Chicago pushed the margin from 66–64 to 76–65.

Jordan had grown furious with Kukoc for passing up shots. "Are you scared?" he taunted Kukoc. "If you are, then sit down. If you're out here to shoot, then shoot."

Kukoc hit two treys, and Jordan rewarded him moments later with a pass for a slam, and the Bulls took the second game, 92–88. With Harper's knee hurting, Jackson and Winter figured they were in for a fight with the next three games in Seattle's KeyArena. But the Sonics were strangely subdued for Game 3. With Kukoc starting for Harper, the Bulls were vulnerable defensively, but they forced the issue on offense from the opening tip. With Jordan scoring 12 points, the Bulls leaped to a 34–12 lead by the end of the first quarter. By halftime, the lead had stretched to 62–38. Jordan finished with 36, but the big surprise was 19 from Longley, who had struggled in Game 2. Asked what had turned the big center's game around, Jackson replied, "Verbal bashing by everybody on the club. I don't think anybody's ever been attacked by as many people as

Luc after Friday's game. Tex gave him an earful, and Michael did, too. I tried the last few days to build his confidence back up."

Chicago sat poised for a sweep, what would have been a 15–1 run through the playoffs, the most successful postseason record in NBA history. The next two days of practice took on the air of a coronation, with the media hustling to find comparisons between the Bulls and pro basketball's great teams from the past. ESPN analyst Jack Ramsay said the Bulls just might be the greatest defensive team of all time. "The best defenders in the game are Pippen and Jordan," he said. "They're just so tough. In each playoff series, they take away one more thing from the opponent, and then you're left standing out there naked, without a stitch of clothes. It's embarrassing."

The key to the Bulls' drive was Jordan, Ramsay added. "He is such a fierce competitor that he brings everybody beyond their individual levels. I watched Steve Kerr, who had the reputation of being a no-defense guy, a good spot-up shooter. Now you watch him, he's out there playing defense, challenging everybody that he plays, he's right in their face. He may get beaten, but he's not going to back down from the chore. He now puts the ball on the floor and creates his own shot. That's something he never did before. Michael's influence on all those players is tremendous."

It was before Game 4 that George Karl, who had also played for Dean Smith at Carolina, realized he hadn't done enough to rattle Jordan. So he arranged for Tassie Dempsey, who had cooked for Tar Heels basketball players for thirty years, to fly to Seattle to cheer on the Sonics. Jordan was shocked to see her that Thursday before the game and asked her, "Mama D, what are you doing here?"

"I came to cheer for George," she replied.

Karl's wife told a disbelieving Jordan, "Michael, Mama D's our good luck symbol."

The always-superstitious Jordan told her, "Then you're going home, Mama D. If you're bringing them luck, you've got to go home."

Gary Payton proved to be a bigger problem for MJ than Mama D. Payton had spent much of the series guarding Pippen, but Karl saw that he was effective on Jordan in parts of Game 3, so he switched

Payton over to cover more of Jordan in Game 4. Ron Harper was struggling with painful tendinitis, which meant that Jordan spent more time covering Payton. Chicago suddenly lacked the vital ball pressure that was so key to its defense. Without Harper, Jordan and Pippen couldn't roam to create havoc. The Sonics settled the outcome with a second-quarter blitz from which Chicago never recovered. Frustrated by Payton's defense, Jordan furiously berated both his teammates and the officials. Midway through the fourth quarter, Jordan was called for a double dribble. He flashed his anger again and stomped his foot, obviously rattled. He left the game minutes later, having hit just 6 of 19, and barked furiously from the bench in the closing minutes, with Pippen laughing, squeezing his shoulder. Payton had done the job, and Seattle fans were left to wonder what might have changed if Payton had spent more time on Jordan earlier in the series.

Harper sat again in Game 5. Given a second chance to close out the series, the Bulls struggled, fell behind, then closed the gap, only to fall a second time, 89–78. The series, miraculously, was returning to Chicago. THE JOY OF SIX, the Seattle newspapers declared the next day in a headline.

Jordan was livid about the failure to close it out. Backup center James Edwards had taken to dropping by Jordan's room during the playoffs to have a postgame cigar with Ahmad Rashad and Jordan, who always had an attaché case filled with the finest smokes. There was usually something interesting going on there, Edwards recalled. But when he stopped in after Game 5, he was startled at Jordan's fury. "I had never seen him that upset before. He kept saying, 'We should have won today. It should be over.' I told him we would get it when we got home. He didn't want to hear that at all. He kept saying it should be over."

He was ending the year just as he had opened it, with his harshest emotions on display. He had wanted to end the series as soon as possible, to unburden himself of the immense pressure he had shouldered since deciding to return. The championship showdown had not been his best performance. He had shot 41.5 percent from the field and would average 27.3 points for the series, well below the 36 points he was averaging during the playoffs. But there was another reason for his anger and disappointment: he had wanted to end it before Father's Day. "He's always on my mind," he said.

That Sunday was Game 6, Father's Day. He felt the rush of emotion and chose to dedicate the game to his father's memory. The United Center crowd thundered at every turn that afternoon, with prolonged applause during introductions. The sound waves seemed to compress, then explode, when announcer Ray Clay got to, "From North Carolina...." Taking all this in, the Sonics stood courtside, chomping their gum and setting their jaws. The audience exploded again moments after the tip-off when Pippen went to the hoop with an underhand scoop to open the scoring. With Harper back, the Bulls' pressure returned, and they picked the Sonics clean time and again. Harper would play thirty-eight minutes; every time he paused, an assistant trainer would coat his knee with a spray anesthetic. Inspired by his presence, Pippen pushed the Bulls out of the gate in the first period with 7 points and 2 steals, giving Chicago a 16–12 lead. To settle the matter, the Bulls produced a 19–9 run in the third period, capped by Pippen dishing on the break to Rodman, who flipped in a little reverse shot, then thrust his fists skyward, bringing yet another outburst from the building, which got louder yet when he made the free throw for a 62–47 lead. Jackson had left Jordan on the bench for a long stretch at the end of the third so that he would be fresh for the kill in the fourth. But with Jordan an emotional wreck and facing double-teams, at least some of the momentum would come from Kukoc, who canned a three from the corner to push it to 70–58. Kerr followed with another three with 2:44 to go, and the entire building seemed to be dancing to "Whoomp! (There It Is)." Pippen's final trey on a kick-out from Jordan came at fifty-seven seconds; moments later, for the last possession of this very historic season, Jordan dribbled near midcourt, then relinquished it to Pippen for one last, delirious air ball.

Jordan broke loose from Jackson's embrace to join a mad scrum for the game ball. He tumbled briefly to the floor with Randy Brown. Then he was gone, the game ball clutched behind his head, disappearing into the locker room, trying to escape the NBC cameras, searching for haven in the trainer's room, weeping there on the floor in joy and pain over his memories on Father's Day.

"I'm sorry I was away for eighteen months," he said after being named Finals MVP. "I'm happy I'm back, and I'm happy to bring a championship back to Chicago."

The players then jumped up on the courtside press table for a victory jig to acknowledge the fans, just as they had in 1992, the last time they had won in Chicago. With them was Rodman, already shirtless.

"I think we can consider ourselves the greatest team of all time," Pippen said with satisfaction.

"This is the nineties, but they play with a learned mentality from an earlier time," George Karl said. "This is an old-time package. I don't know about the Bird era or the Magic era. They were great teams, but this Bulls team has that same basic mentality. I like their heart and I like their philosophy."

In the euphoria of a championship moment, athletes and coaches tend to favor restraint. Why promise another championship and bring on the debilitating pressure? Why not bask in the accomplishment, especially if you've just delivered arguably the greatest season in the history of the game? But that had never been Jordan's way.

"Five is the next number," he said with the same sort of smile that had once so disarmed Sonny Vaccaro.

Chapter 34

THE RECKONING

Having fought his way back to the top, Jordan's time now came around to free agency and the opportunity to rectify the great discrepancy between his salary and those of other top players in the league. With the Bulls, contract negotiations often left tempers flaring and people taking offense. Wealth and fame didn't make any of them immune to getting their feelings hurt. Just the opposite, actually: the bigger the ego, the deeper the bruise.

"The summertime is when all that stuff erupts with Michael," Steve Kerr observed at the time. "We win the championship, and he goes to the podium and makes his plea for another crack at it." That infuriated management, Kerr said. "Then it goes on all summer."

Reinsdorf and Jordan had always enjoyed what appeared to be a strong relationship. As player salaries skyrocketed in the 1990s, Jordan was said to be understandably bothered that his contract paid him in the range of $4 million annually, while a dozen or more lesser players in the league earned twice that. At the same time, he was far too proud to ask for a renegotiation. His answer was to live up to the deal he had signed in the highest fashion. Yet when he abruptly retired in the fall of 1993, there were the inevitable insinuations that he did so in part because of his contract.

The Bulls continued to pay Jordan in his retirement, which, according to one of Reinsdorf's associates, was a gesture of loyalty from Reinsdorf to Jordan. More cynical observers pointed out that by continuing to pay Jordan, the team also kept his salary slot open under the league's labyrinthine salary cap rules. If nothing else, the circumstances suggested the difficulty of fostering personal relationships amid the conflicts of business. Even kind gestures could be interpreted as ploys.

In one sense, Reinsdorf and Jordan were partners in a lucrative sports-entertainment venture. The problem was that as a player, Jordan was barred from having any real equity position in the relationship. As a result, Reinsdorf was management, and Jordan was labor. The labor costs were fixed, while the profit percentages were soaring for those with a piece of the action.

Jordan, of course, was making his tens of millions off the court. Still, his relatively meager player contract created an inequity. And when he returned to the game in 1995, he returned under his old contract, which meant that the Bulls' payroll itself remained well under $30 million, and the team could continue raking in tens of millions in profit. That, of course, was in addition to the tremendous growth in equity that Jordan's brilliant play and the flurry of championships had created for the team's owners. Reinsdorf's group had purchased the club during Jordan's rookie season for about $15 million, then watched its value grow to better than thirty times that over the ensuing decade.

There was a strong sense that Jordan was "owed," felt not just by Jordan and his representatives but by virtually anyone who had anything to do with the NBA. Jordan's play and leadership through the historic 1995–1996 season solidified that notion. With the close of the campaign, his long-term contract finally expired. And then the real trouble started.

Just days after the championship celebration, the star's representatives and Reinsdorf began discussing his new contract. In a 1998 interview, Jordan recalled his approach: "What I instructed my representative was, 'Don't go in and give a price. I've been with this team for a long time. Everyone knows what this market value may be, or could be. If he's true to his word and honest in terms of our relationship, listen to what he says before we offer what our opinions may be.' Falk's instruction was to go in and listen, never to negotiate. Because it shouldn't have come to a negotiation. We didn't think of it as a negotiation. We felt it was an opportunity for the Bulls to give me what they felt my value had been to the organization."

Jordan, however, was also well aware of Reinsdorf's reluctance to let go of money. The star believed a drawn-out negotiation would only demean what he had accomplished for the Bulls. So Jordan and his advisors entertained offers from the New York Knickerbockers. Would Jordan have given up the Bulls for the Knicks?

"Yes," he said.

In fact, the Knicks had put together a few million in base salary for Jordan to be augmented by a megamillion personal services contract with one of the Knicks' affiliated companies. When he learned of the deal, Reinsdorf was reportedly so infuriated that he demanded an opinion from the league's front office on the legality of the move as a way around the salary cap. The Bulls chairman supposedly threatened a lawsuit to block the Knicks, but a highly placed person at the NBA counseled Reinsdorf about the futility and possible backlash of filing suit against his popular star and the Knicks.

David Falk wanted a substantial one-year contract to reflect Jordan's contribution to the Bulls and the game. But Reinsdorf offered nothing specific, so Jordan stepped into the proceedings.

"As I know it, no numbers were ever talked about until I was into the game," Jordan recalled. "No one wanted to put the numbers out on the table. Everyone was jockeying to see who was gonna put the first number out, which we were not gonna do. We had a number in our heads, but we really felt like it was the Bulls' place to tell us what our net worth was. And to do it from an honest state, not influenced by David, not influenced by me. Just what they felt I'd meant to the organization."

Finally exasperated at Reinsdorf's reluctance to make an offer, Jordan was pulled into a conference phone call with his agent and Reinsdorf. At the time, he was playing golf. But he told Reinsdorf that if the team wanted to re-sign him it would be a one-year deal for better than $30 million. And that Reinsdorf had one hour to agree.

"At the time they were negotiating I was in Tahoe for a celebrity golf tournament," Jordan explained. "And we had some conversations with New York. And we were gonna meet with them right after we met with Reinsdorf, and I think that was within an hour's time. David wanted the Bulls to make their offer and discuss it before we go down and have a conversation with New York. But [Reinsdorf] knew he had a window in terms of the conversation with New York."

Krause would later describe Jordan's approach to the timing of the negotiations as "cold."

Although he would never admit it or discuss it publicly, Reinsdorf was wounded. He had assumed he had a personal relationship with Jordan. After all, hadn't he extended the opportunity to Michael to begin a pro baseball career with the White Sox? Hadn't he always made the effort to make clear his respect for his star player? Reinsdorf later told close associates that he began to think Jordan had faked their friendship to take advantage of him. After the hurt came Reinsdorf's anger. But he realized he had no choice. He had to accept the terms.

Even Reinsdorf had trouble arguing with the amount Jordan had asked for. In fact, the star could have pushed for far more and enjoyed the support of public opinion. But in agreeing to the deal, Reinsdorf made a comment to Jordan that would further damage their relationship. Reinsdorf said he would live to regret giving Jordan the $30 million.

"Michael is bitter at Jerry," a Bulls employee later explained, "because when Jerry agreed to pay him the $30 million, Jerry told Michael that he would regret it. Michael stood in the training room one day the next fall and told all his teammates, 'You know what really pissed me off? Jerry said, You know what, Michael? I'm gonna live to regret this.'

"Michael said, 'What the fuck? You could say, You deserve this. You're the greatest player ever, you're an asset to the city of Chicago and the organization. And I'm happy to pay you $30 million. You could say that, but even if you don't feel that way and you're going to regret it, why are you telling me that?' Luc was standing there and said, 'Really? Jerry told you he was going to regret it?' Michael said, 'He told me that. I couldn't believe my owner told me that.'

"That creates tremendous bitterness," the team employee said.

"I said I *might* live to regret it," Reinsdorf clarified.

Jordan recalled: "Actually, he said, 'Somewhere down the road, I know I'm gonna regret this.' It demeaned what was happening. It took away from the meaning of things. The gratitude seemed less because of that statement. I felt it was inappropriate to say that."

The team chairman had reportedly made a similar comment to John Paxson a few seasons earlier, when Paxson had finally won a decent raise after several seasons with a contract that paid him relatively little. Upon signing the deal, Reinsdorf had told the hard-working Paxson, "I can't believe I'm paying you this kind of money." Although Paxson, who would later become president of the Bulls, never discussed the comment, sources with the team confirmed that he was angered and insulted. Both Jordan's and Paxson's negotiations revealed that management's mentality was that Reinsdorf had to "win" every contract negotiation with every player. That attitude erased any good feelings between players and management, a former player said. And it usually resulted in bitterness from Krause or Reinsdorf whenever they "lost," the player said.

"He's loyal, he's honest," Phil Jackson said of Reinsdorf. "He's truthful. His word means something. But there's something about going in and trying to get the best every time. Winning the deal. When it comes to money, to win the deal.

"He has actually said those things, according to people I've been close to," Jackson said of Reinsdorf's comments, "and those things really hurt. Because most everybody really likes Jerry Reinsdorf.

"But," Jackson added with a laugh, "Jerry is Jerry. Jerry is...Jerry doesn't spend money freely, even with himself. He wants value for money. Who doesn't? The salaries that have happened in the past ten years have been real difficult for owners to swallow. Large money. It's an amazing amount of money."

The Worship

Rookie Ray Allen stood nervously in the hallway of the United Center, waiting to catch a glimpse of the Chosen One, much like a young Brahman hiding in an olive grove waiting to catch sight of the Buddha. A first-round draft pick of the Milwaukee Bucks, Allen had spent countless hours studying videotape of Jordan, one favorite sequence in particular. "It's the one that he beat a Starks and Oakley double-team and took it baseline for a jam on Ewing," he confided. Allen had watched it again and again, transfixed.

Concern crept over him as the moment approached. It was only a preseason game. What if Jordan chose to sit it out? But suddenly he was there, in his crisp home whites, striding toward the arena. Allen's heart did a little tip drill at the sight, his eyes widened, and he gathered himself to challenge his hero, remembering every little detail so that he could tell his home boys what it had been like. Mostly Allen was nervous because he wanted to play well.

"Just being introduced to Mike for the first time, just the game time prep for it, thinking about it, then finally seeing him," Allen said afterward, his voice trailing off wistfully.

Allen had enjoyed a fine sophomore year at the University of Connecticut not quite two years before and had thought about turning pro then. It was the era before rookie salary caps, and the industry had begun scouring colleges for "the next Michael Jordan," a fool's errand, and an expensive one. Allen's own teammate at Connecticut, Donyell Marshall, had gotten a guaranteed $40 million deal to leave early (and turned out to be a bust). Allen decided to stay in school another year, to remove any deficiency from his game before testing Jordan.

After a good junior year, he had made his move, and now Allen found himself face-to-face with the master, trying to appear nonchalant as he lightly brushed fists with Jordan. He allowed himself only the quickest glance into the killer eyes, to see the amused glint, the twinkle of that ultimate confidence, the Air up there.

The ball went up and Allen was off to a memorable first quarter. "I didn't want to be passive when I played him," he confided afterward. "I didn't want him to think I wasn't ready for the challenge."

Allen knew Jordan would ease into the affair and that he needed to be aggressive against him right away. He demonstrated that he could get his shot and scored over Jordan in a variety of ways. A trey, a pull-up jumper, a drive down the lane for a slam. The "Hallelujah Chorus" was playing in his head, but his game face showed nothing. He scored 9 points in the quarter and had Jordan scrambling to cover him, even talking a bit of trash, trying to get inside his head.

After it was over, Allen stood in the Bucks' locker room with a dazed expression, as if he had just inhabited a dream. "Mike is Mike, unbelievable," he said, his tone now shifted by the experience, trying to sound more like a veteran.

"Ray Allen's gonna be a good player," Jordan appraised. "I like the way he came out at the beginning of the game."

Another wave of talent had come into the league with the 1996 draft, drawn by the environment of instant wealth Jordan had created for them. Joining Allen would be the teenager in Los Angeles, Kobe Bryant, and Allen Iverson in Philadelphia, among others. The 1996 off-season had brought a massive reshuffling of veteran players as well. With nearly two hundred free agents on the market, teams offered up more than a billion dollars in contracts to select stars, virtually all of that money made possible by Jordan's presence in the sport. None of these moves was more dramatic than Shaquille O'Neal's jump to the Los Angeles Lakers from Orlando for a $123 million contract.

The Bulls played a preseason game at the Thomas & Mack Center in Las Vegas that season, an odd choice given Jordan's gambling history and Rodman's own struggles (he had made nineteen different junkets to the craps tables there in recent months alone and had lost mountains of cash, Jack Haley revealed). Yet Rodman's freak-show look fit perfectly with the grotesque backdrop of the Vegas strip. In this culture of concocted celebrity, Jordan's rebounder was the ultimate concoction. He had married himself that summer in a publicity stunt in New York for his new book, *Bad as I Wanna Be.*

NBA preseason games were notoriously unenthusiastic road shows, exhibitions that the league staged in strategic global locations — Mexico, London, Japan — or in out-of-the-way arenas near a star player's hometown or college. In the old days the Bulls set up games in Chapel Hill. This trip, however, offered a memorable look at Jordan at the height of his power, before the coming acrimony managed to drag him down and out of the game. He was clearly a man in full.

The Bulls had actually opened their preseason a night earlier in Albuquerque in the first of a pair of games against Seattle, a rematch of the championship series. Afterward, they hurried out of Albuquerque on their private—and lavishly accoutered—jet and arrived in Las Vegas shortly after midnight. Steve Wynn, the chairman of Mirage Resorts, provided both Rodman and Jordan with complimentary four-thousand-square-foot villas for their stay. The rest of the Bulls, meanwhile, were assigned rooms in the hotel. Jackson cancelled the team's morning shootaround, allowing Jordan to take in as many golf holes as possible.

The Saturday night game between the Bulls and the SuperSonics featured a battle between Jordan and Craig Ehlo that involved so much pushing and shoving that Jordan even took a quick swing at Ehlo that was missed, or ignored, by the officials. Jordan laughed about it afterward. "I've played against Ehlo so many times," he said. "He can get away with it sometimes. I can get away with it sometimes. That's the beauty of the game of basketball. I have so much respect for him and so much competition in competing against him that it's always fun to go against him and see who can get away with the dirt first. That's what it is."

The premiere of *Space Jam*, Jordan's animated film with Bugs Bunny, was also in the mix. "I think it's gonna do fine," he said. "But I'm very nervous about it. This is a whole new arena for me, but it's just been a lot of money invested in me, and hopefully I did my part. I tried to do it the best I could, and if it's good…great. I may do it again. If it's not, certainly I'll know where I stand in that career. I'll stick to the thirty-second commercials." The film would eventually rake in $400 million, a towering success, prompting David Falk to urge Jordan to do another, but by then he had changed his mind and would turn down all offers over the ensuing years.

As he left the locker room that night, a boy with a brand-new basketball and a black indelible marker stepped out of the shadows, too cowed to speak.

Jordan furrowed his face and looked at the boy. "Do I get paid for this?" he asked as he reached for the ball and marker. "Normally I get seven digits."

Somehow the boy managed to speak.

"I...I got five dollars," he offered hopefully.

Jordan smiled. "No problem," he replied, trying to make it clear that he was just joking.

The marker, though, was nearly out of ink, and when Jordan stroked his signature across the face of the ball, it barely took. Jordan frowned.

"Man," he said, "you gave me this cheap pen."

Panic and disbelief spread across the boy's face. He jammed his hand in his pocket to bring out a raft of pens for another try.

"I thought you were reaching for some money," Jordan said, laughing.

He could be excused for thinking that the young fan was digging for cash. For years now he had been on the receiving end of an immense transfer of wealth. In the 1995–96 season alone, it was estimated that he had raked in better than $40 million in off-court endorsement income. For 1996–97, the numbers would surge again, with the introduction of his new cologne line (it sold 1.5 million bottles the first two months on the market) and his role in *Space Jam,* which set ticket sales records on its opening weekend. He had come to earn that sobriquet Spike Lee had bestowed upon him in their Nike commercials: he was Money indeed. People from around the world now paid to see him, to be near him, to wear his shoes or his jersey, to drink his Gatorade and gobble his French fries at McDonald's, to buy his Hanes briefs, to whack his golf balls, to read his books, and to enshrine his trading cards.

Jordan's personal take was a fraction of the treasure he created for the NBA (not to mention what he did for the University of North Carolina Tar Heel brand). His entry into the league in 1984 triggered a ballooning of the NBA's annual revenues tenfold, from under $150 million that year to an astounding $2 billion or more per season by the mid-1990s.

Despite appearances, Phil Jackson could be forgiven for the anxiety he felt that preseason. Behind the scenes, the internal conflict between his players and management, and between Jackson himself and management, had already started to heat up. "It will be a very different year," the coach said that Saturday night in Las Vegas. "I just don't know what to anticipate. I try not to anticipate. Just let it happen. Our whole scenario, our whole buildup of this ball club, is that we alone can destroy our opportunities."

Off and Running Again

Jordan had grown accustomed to Jackson's efforts to soothe him just enough to make it all workable. The coach never tried to bank Jordan's great flame; he needed only to adjust the heat enough to get them to another confetti moment. Jordan now saw the practicality in it all, from Tex Winter's offense to George Mumford's meditation and mindfulness exercises. He could now sit on the floor in the dark at practice and think good thoughts as well as anyone.

"He's our guru," Michael Jordan quipped when asked about the coach's quirkiness. "He's got that yen, that Zen stuff, working in our favor."

James Edwards watched with keen interest the dynamic between Jackson and Jordan. It was a perfect marriage between a player and a coach, he decided. "Phil knew what Mike was thinking and Mike knew what Phil was thinking. That's how close they were."

They all understood when Jackson talked of the spiritual connection to the game. Jordan credited the approach Jackson outlined in his book *Sacred Hoops* with showing him how to relate to less-talented teammates. "I think Phil really has given me a chance to be patient and taught me how to understand the supporting cast of teammates and give them a chance to improve," he said. Jackson never was able, however, to train Jordan to stop calling his teammates his "supporting cast," a reminder that the Bulls' organization was not a perfect world. The imperfection was evidenced by a growing funk hanging over the club for much of the 1996–97 season.

The early part of the schedule was populated with more handsome win streaks and more fat games from Jordan. He had lost eight pounds in the off-season, down to 209 from 217, to help ease the tendinitis that had often slowed him the previous year. The sleeker Jordan and his teammates opened the season with twelve straight wins, highlighted by Jordan's 50 points in a 106–100 win in Miami, with Jordan smiling and jawing with Heat coach Pat Riley much of the way. The Bulls had just flown in from a game in Vancouver to find the Miami players talking in the local papers about how the Bulls had disrespected them in sweeping their play-off series.

During the game, Riley had jokingly called Michael a rat after one dazzling play. "He's such a competitor," Jordan said of Riley afterward, smiling. "I am too. You know you're at the tail end of your career. You better enjoy yourself these last few moments of stardom or success or whatever it is. That drives me more than anything.

"My motivation is for a perfect run," he added.

He celebrated Thanksgiving by scoring 195 points in five games. In December, he scored 30 against the young Lakers, to go with Pippen's 35 and Kukoc's 31, just to show he could spread the wealth around. From there until mid-February he dropped by for performances on all his old friends: 45 on the Cavs, 51 on the Knicks, 45 on Gary Payton and Seattle, 47 on Denver.

New York coach Jeff Van Gundy, who coached two of Jordan's best friends, Oakley and Ewing, had called him a con man, which prompted a season-high 51 on the Knicks. "His way is to befriend them, soften them up, try to make them feel he cares about them," Van Gundy had said. "Then he goes out there and tries to destroy them. The first step as a player is to realize that and don't go for it."

"I was prepared to do whatever it took to win," Jordan said afterward. He had reached the 50-point mark for the thirty-sixth time in his career. "There were times where things were going so well, everything seemed to be in slow motion. I didn't rush. I just relaxed and played."

"It was probably a tactical mistake by the coach of the Knicks to attack Michael in the press. I thought he went out and played with a vendetta, a score to settle," Jackson said.

Jordan finished the night with yet another fadeaway, a twenty-footer, to close out the win, then yelled at Van Gundy.

"Some choice words," Jordan said. "I guess I didn't make any friends out there tonight."

Van Gundy's words were poorly chosen, he added. "I think they were more geared to motivating his players. But I don't think, on the court, they have befriended me. I don't go on the court expecting to make friends. But when I leave the court, I don't take what happened on the court away with me. We're only playing a game. I don't view it as a war away from the game. If he feels like I take advantage of my friends, that's fine."

Such moments propelled the Bulls. They had again consumed the schedule in great gulps and finished with a 69–13 record, tied for the second-most wins all time. Jordan had averaged 29.6 points and won another scoring title, his ninth. He had been named to the All-Star team for the eleventh time and recorded there in Cleveland the first triple-double in All-Star Game history. The 1997 All-Star Game marked the league's fiftieth anniversary, and he and Pippen were honored with inclusion on the list of the game's fifty greatest players. He had scored his 25,000th career point in San Antonio in November. By April he had moved past Oscar Robertson for fifth on the all-time scoring list.

Together

As the playoffs neared, Jackson again called for his team to develop true "togetherness." This time around, he spliced into the scouting videos clips from *What about Bob?* The movie starred Bill Murray as a mental patient who tried to move in with his selfish and unlikeable psychiatrist. Obviously, the psychiatrist was Krause. "Every time he used game clips, he'd put in pieces of the movie," said Bulls center Bill Wennington. "Basically we saw the whole movie. He was implying that we got to come together, that we got to use baby steps to move along and start playing well..."

Jackson also included clips of old Three Stooges movies.

"Tex Winter likes to sing a song when we get together for our morning sessions," Bill Wennington explained. "He likes to sing, 'It's time we get together. Together. Together. It's time we get together. Together again.' That song is played once in the Three

Stooges when Moe swallows a harmonica, and they're playing him on a harmonica. They're playing that song."

The togetherness theme also hung over the heads of Jordan, Jackson, and Rodman, all on one-year contracts. Would they be back with the Bulls for another season? The Chicago press was rampant with speculation, and the uncertainty tugged at the team's peace of mind and motivated them, too.

Perhaps most significantly, the "togetherness" theme was a subtle reminder to Jordan not to crush his teammates with anger and criticism. Jordan, Pippen, and Harper were solid as a core. Rodman, of course, was an entity to himself. So was Kukoc, who was somewhat isolated by cultural differences. Simpkins, Caffey, and Brown shared some off-court time, and then there was the Arizona contingent of Buechler and Kerr, joined at times by Longley, the Australian, and Wennington, the Canadian.

The Washington Bullets fell in Game 1 of the first playoff round but charged out to a lead in Game 2, as all of Jackson's talk about togetherness dissipated into the United Center haze. Washington took the halftime lead, 65–58, despite Jordan's 26 points. He greeted Jackson and his teammates in the locker room with a face full of anger. "Michael was pretty upset at the half, and Phil wasn't real thrilled either," Kerr acknowledged. "But there weren't many adjustments other than attitude adjustments. Michael just raised his voice a little bit and said we had to play better."

Jordan and their defensive traps propelled the Bulls on a 16–2 run in the third that pushed the crowd out of a slumber. The defense was a group effort, but on offense Jordan worked almost alone, jabbing jumper after jumper. During time-outs, he sat motionless, a towel draped over his shoulders, head bowed, trying to conserve energy. With five minutes left in the game, he drove and scored, pushing Chicago up by three. Moments later, he got the ball back, motored into the lane, and flexed a pump fake that sent the entire defense flying. As they settled back to earth, he then stuck a jumper. He finished the next possession with an impossible falling-down shot from the right baseline that pushed the lead to 7 and his point total for the evening to 49.

When the Bullets cut it to 103–100 with about a minute to go, Jordan answered with another jumper and a bank shot, the latter coming with thirty-four seconds left and driving the lead to 107–102. He then wrapped up a 55-point night (the eighth time in his career that he had scored better than 50 in a playoff game) with two free throws that provided Chicago with a 109–104 win and a 2–0 series lead.

The thirty-four-year-old Jordan's conditioning alone was astounding, Longley said afterward, in that it allowed him to score and play intense defense for more than forty-four minutes. "These are the games where he demonstrates who he really is," the center added. "Those performances you definitely marvel at. What I marvel at is how many of them you see a year. Perhaps he only had three or four 50-point games this year, but the 30- and 40-point games he has almost every night. The fact that at his age he can come out physically and do things he does every night, that's what really makes me marvel."

Washington was moved aside with the next victory, and the Bulls turned their attention to humbling the Atlanta Hawks, four games to one. Despite the team's momentum, the coaching staff worried that Jordan had been pressing on offense, as if he felt he had to carry the entire load. "Michael has not shot well," Winter confided. "He has not shot well the whole series. The fact that he's gonna take 25 or 27 shots, and he's not shooting well, then that puts quite a burden on your offense. If he's not shooting any better percentage shots than that, then he shouldn't be taking so many of them. Phil's told him not to force things, not to try to do too much, to move the ball. And Michael knows that. Michael's a smart player. But he's so competitive, and he's got so much confidence in himself that it's hard for him to restrain. I've never been associated with a player who has any less inhibitions than he does. That's one of the reasons he's a great player. He has no conscience."

Atlanta fell away in Game 5, although three minutes into the contest, Jordan drew a technical for wagging his finger after dunking on Dikembe Mutombo, who was himself known for finger wagging. The win sent Chicago to a seventh appearance in the Eastern Conference finals in nine seasons. It was assumed that the Knicks would be their opponents, but Riley's Heat showed up instead, which was fine with Jackson, who had told his players, after an upset loss to Miami late in the 1996 season, "Never lose to that guy."

Chicago jumped out to a three-game lead, which seemed to Jordan like a good time to play forty-five holes of golf in Miami. Bulls photographer Bill Smith followed him to the course and stepped up to catch a shot of him in a cart. "Out of my way, Bill Smith," Jordan said as he gunned the cart and sent the photographer hopping away with a laugh.

Jordan paid for his fun the next day, making just 2 of his first 22 shots in Game 4. Eddie Pinckney, then playing for the Heat, remembered the ending well.

"It was my last year as a professional player, and the Bulls were about to eliminate us," recalled Pinckney. "They had reserved a special restaurant to celebrate after the game. Pat Riley got wind of this and told us players he was really upset. We go out and we're winning the game by a lot, maybe 15 or 20 points, and Phil Jackson takes everybody out. The game's pretty much over. Well, [Heat guard] Voshon Lenard decides he's going to start talking to Michael Jordan. How we're going to go up to Chicago and kick their ass. Jordan comes back in the game and starts scoring and scoring, and he's yelling at the top of his lungs, 'You guys are not going to win another fucking game!' He's screaming at the top of his lungs, 'You fuckers are not winning another one!' He was pissed."

Finding themselves down 21 points with the clock ticking down, the Bulls watched Jordan launch into his attack mode. He spurred Chicago on a 22–5 run that pulled them within four, 61–57, at the end of the third. The Heat surged right back at the beginning of the fourth, pushing their margin back to 72–60. Jordan then scored 18 straight points for Chicago, a display that trimmed the Miami lead to just one with only 2:19 to go. The ending, however, came down to the Heat making a final 6 free throws, good enough for a Miami win.

"That's one of my favorite Michael games of all time," Steve Kerr said, looking back in 2012. "Because if you look at the stats from that game, he's 2 for 22 going into the fourth quarter, and there were air balls involved. It was clearly related to all the holes of golf he and Ahmad Rashad had played the day before. But the fourth quarter, he went nuts. He's yelling at the Heat bench, but it was the greatest display of confidence I've ever seen in my life...bar none. I mean, how do you go from 2 for 22, in a playoff game against a great defensive team, in the first three quarters, when you're missing all those shots? He wasn't shaking his head, he was just going about his business and something finally clicked and he went with it."

Those who witnessed the spectacle were not likely to forget it. Jordan had scored 20 of Chicago's 23 points in the fourth quarter. "When he started making them, they just came, came, came, came, came," said Tim Hardaway. "He's a scorer; he's the man."

Asked about his miserable first half, Jordan glowered, "We're not concerned," he said.

"We go back to Chicago now and we could not get the ball up the court," Pinckney recalled with a laugh. Jordan opened Game 5 with 15 in the first quarter, good enough for a 33–19 Bulls lead, leaving little doubt as to the outcome.

"They are the greatest team since the Celtics won eleven in thirteen years," Riley told reporters afterward. "I don't think anybody's going to win again until Michael retires. Sometimes you can build a great team, and you'll never win a championship because you had the misfortune of being born the same time that Jordan went through his run."

Houston and Utah were battling in the Western Conference finals, and Jordan admitted he'd like to take on the Rockets. Olajuwon had been drafted ahead of him back in 1984 and had led his team to two titles while Jordan was away playing baseball. The cherry on top of that tempting sundae was Charles Barkley, now a Rockets forward. On the other hand, Utah could also get him motivated. Jazz forward Karl "The Mailman" Malone was set to be named the league MVP, even though Jordan had won his ninth scoring title with a 29.6 average. Jordan had been named to the All-NBA first team and, along with Pippen, the All-Defense team. Malone had finished second in the scoring race and was named to the All-NBA first team for the ninth time. His selection appeared to be based on the entirety of his career, an approach occasionally taken in other MVP selections. Jordan's fans, however, would long complain that he had been robbed of yet another MVP. Pat Riley didn't think it mattered who won the West. "I think Chicago's going to win it against anybody," he said.

Utah's John Stockton settled the issue in Game 6 of the Western conference finals with a last-second shot that sent the Jazz to the league championship series for the first time in their three decades of existence. Stockton, Malone, and company forced the issue in Game 1 of the championship series at the United Center. With less than a minute left, it was 82–81 Utah, when Jordan stepped to the line for 2 free throws and his fans chanting "MVP!" He hit the first to tie it, then missed the second, quieting the crowd. Next it was Malone's turn to shoot 2 when Pippen whispered in his ear, "The Mailman doesn't deliver on Sunday." He missed both in the noise, and the Bulls controlled the rebound with 7.5 seconds left. Amazingly, Utah decided not to double-team Jordan on the last shot. When it swished, twenty-one thousand fans leaped out of their seats in exultation. Jordan had finished with 31 points on 13 of 27 shooting.

Game 2 was a blowout, driven by Jordan's 38 points, 13 rebounds, and 9 assists. He would have registered a triple-double if Pippen hadn't blown a late layup, costing him the tenth assist.

The Jazz won Game 3 back home in Salt Lake City even though Pippen tied an NBA Finals record with 7 treys. Unknown to the fans and media, Game 4 would hinge on a critical error by Chicago's staff, in what was to be the Bulls' biggest disappointment of the season. Their offense sputtered, but their defense was spectacular for 45 minutes. In short, they played well enough to win. With 2:38 to go in the game, they had willed their way to a 71–66 lead and seemed set to control the series 3–1. But that's when John Stockton took over, and the Bulls uncharacteristically stumbled. It would later be learned that a Bulls team assistant had mistakenly replaced the players' Gatorade with GatorLode, a heavy drink used for building carbs. "It was like eating baked potatoes," explained trainer Chip Schaeffer. Chicago's players complained of stomach cramps and Jordan even asked to sit for a time, something he never did at a key moment.

Stockton cut into the late lead with a twenty-five-foot three-pointer.

Jordan, who had returned to the game despite the stomach distress, came right back with a trey, and when Utah's Jeff Hornacek missed a runner, the Bulls had a chance to close it out. Instead, Stockton timed a steal from Jordan at the top of the key and drove the length of the court. In a move that awed Utah coach Jerry Sloan, Jordan recovered, raced downcourt, and managed to block the shot, only to get whistled for a body foul.

From there, the Jazz worked to a 74–73 lead. With seventeen seconds left, Chicago fouled Malone, setting up repeat circumstances from Game 1. His first shot knocked around the rim before falling in, smoothing the way for the second and a 76–73 lead. With no time-outs, the Bulls were left with only a rushed three-point miss by Jordan, which Utah punctuated with a breakaway slam for the 78–73 final, the second-lowest-scoring game in league championship history. The series was deadlocked at 2–2.

Flu

Jordan had seen his shooting plummet to 40 percent after having shot 51 percent in the first two games. What came next was the great "flu game." Years after the event, the story lingered that Jordan had indulged in late-night cigar smoking, card playing, and drinking, supposedly at a chateau in the Utah mountains, on the eve of Game 5. The official word the next day was that he had been hit with a "viral illness."

"I was doing the game," recalled former NBC color man Matt Guokas, who was working with Marv Albert. "Marv was so good as a play-by-play guy. He had the sense of drama. On that particular game, I was thinking to myself, 'What's the big deal? Michael plays great all the time.' But Marv had a sense of the moment in making it supreme for the fans watching it. The other thing was, there were conspiracy theories of what was really wrong with Michael. We just took it at face value that he had the flu and just went ahead and played. But according to the stories and rumors, he was supposedly at Robert Redford's chalet up in the mountains playing poker all night and partying too hard."

ESPN's Jalen Rose would be caught articulating a similar claim in an Internet video clip in 2012. Whether it was a real virus or the "Milwaukee flu" will forever be caught up in the Jordan mystery. Certainly he was known for sleeping little and playing much in and around his basketball life. Regardless of what made Jordan sick, his play was the genuine thing. As Game 5 approached, the anxiety was hanging over the Bulls like the thunderstorms that rolled up Utah's cottonwood canyons. The first shock hit his teammates at the morning shootaround. He was too sick to attend? Jordan miss a key practice? Never.

"It's kinda scary," said Bulls reserve forward Jason Caffey, sitting wide-eyed in the locker room before the game. "You don't know what's going on when it's like this." In the darkness of the training room a few feet away, Jordan lay quite still. Yet it was a circumstance that veteran Jordan observers had seen before, dating back to high school days.

"Michael's sick?" one reporter asked. " He'll score 40."

Despite Jordan's well-known flair for the dramatic, this performance was no act. "I've played a lot of seasons with Michael, and I've never seen him so sick," Pippen said afterward. "I didn't know if he would even put his uniform on. He's the greatest and definitely the MVP in my mind."

He appeared to operate on adrenaline for a time. He scored Chicago's first 4 points, then faltered weakly while Utah rushed out to a 16-point lead early in the second quarter, 34–18. Jordan, though, fixed his focus on the rim and started taking the ball inside. He contributed 6 points on a 19–6 run that pulled the Bulls to within three, at 42–39.

The Bulls caught a break when Malone was forced to sit with an early third foul. Jordan's inside work also produced 8 free throws in the second quarter and helped give Chicago its first lead, 45–44. Malone found more foul trouble in the third period as the pace slowed, but Utah forged a 5-point lead to start the fourth and quickly expanded it to 8.

By then, Jordan had fought off the weakness and found his zone. He scored 15 points down the stretch to pressure the Jazz, possession after possession. The Bulls were down by one when he went to the free throw line with forty-six seconds to go. He hit the first and snatched up the loose ball when he missed the second. Moments later he hit a three on a pass from Pippen, and the Bulls had ridden their championship experience to a 3–2 series lead. Jordan stood under the Utah basket punching his fists into the air triumphantly as the game ended.

"As far as big wins, I think this is as big a win as we've had in a playoff situation like this, especially getting down in the first half and having fought back," Phil Jackson said.

"I almost played myself into passing out," Jordan said. "I came in and I was dehydrated, and it was all to win a basketball game. I gave a lot of effort and I'm just glad we won because it would have been devastating if we had lost. I was really tired, very weak at half-time. I told Phil to use me in spurts, but somehow I found the energy to stay strong and I wanted it really bad."

He finished with 38, after hitting 13 for 27 from the field with 7 rebounds, 5 assists, 3 steals, and a block. "He hadn't gotten out of bed all day, standing up was literally a nauseating experience, and he had dizzy spells and so forth," Jackson said. "We were worried about his amount of minutes, but he said, 'Let me play,' and he played forty-four minutes. That's an amazing effort in itself."

Pippen's defensive play and fine floor game also made the victory possible. He contributed 17 points, 10 rebounds, and 5 assists. "Michael was great, this we all know," said Charles Barkley, who was sitting courtside in the Delta Center. "But I thought one of the keys to the game was the second quarter. Utah had a chance to blow the Bulls out and didn't. One of the reasons the Jazz didn't was because Scottie made some big plays during Chicago's run."

The series finally returned to Chicago, where Jordan finished the season's business with another perfect Hollywood ending. The Jazz took the lead early and valiantly held it until the Bulls pressure took over down the stretch. Jordan contributed 39 points and two hours of defense, all capped off with a sweet little assist to Steve Kerr, who was still kicking himself for missing a three that could have sent Game 4 into overtime. "Steve's been fighting with himself because of Game 4," Jordan explained afterward. "He kept his head in the pillow for hours because he let the team down, because everyone knows he's probably one of the best shooters in the game, and he had the opportunity to pick us up and give us a lift, and he was very disappointed.

"When Phil drew up the play at the end, which everybody in the gym, everybody on TV knew was coming to me," Jordan continued, "I looked at Steve and said, 'This is your chance, because I know Stockton is going to come over and help. And I'm going to come to you.' And he said, 'Give me the ball.'" That's something John Paxson would have said, Jordan pointed out. Kerr drilled it, the building exploded in delirium, and Chicago had its fifth.

"Tonight Steve Kerr earned his wings from my perspective," Jordan said, "because I had faith in him, and I passed him the ball, and he knocked down the shot. I'm glad he redeemed himself, because if he'd have missed that shot, I don't think he could have slept all summer long. I'm very happy for Steve Kerr."

"I made that shot, at the end, when he passed me the ball," Kerr recalled, laughing as he looked back. "And I'll always remember, he got interviewed after the game and he said, 'Well, Steve Kerr earned his stripes.' And I remember thinking, 'I haven't earned my stripes yet?! Wait, we won the title last year. I made some shots. I've done some good things for this team.' I didn't realize it. 'I haven't earned my stripes yet?'"

Such was life in the supporting cast.

Much of the rest of the roster had struggled, but Scottie Pippen had played off Jordan masterfully. Jordan was the obvious MVP, but Pippen had been there throughout. Jordan said he would keep the MVP trophy but give Pippen the car that accompanied the award.

"I'm going to make sure he gets the car," Jordan said, "because he's like a little brother to me. He goes through the pain, and we work out every day. He's joining me, working out every day to stay healthy and get out here and provide for the organization and the city so that we can be healthy and continue to be champions."

As he talked, Jordan grew bolder and called for Jerry Reinsdorf to keep the team together for the opportunity to defend the title for the coming season. To the public, it seemed like the obvious gesture. But to those in the know, it spelled more trouble.

Chapter 35

FIRING UP THE BUS

Even as he led the Bulls to their fifth championship, Jordan began seeding his team's undoing by verbally abusing Jerry Krause on the team bus. Ever since he returned to the game, Jordan had displayed a new anger and aggressiveness with the GM. He was upset with what he felt was Krause's unwarranted treatment of Pippen, and had been led to believe that Krause was responsible for the firing of his favorite coach, Johnny Bach. Even though Jackson tried to dissuade Krause from riding the bus and being around the team, the GM always looked for some way to be a part of the group. However, his presence on the bus left him open to be the butt of Jordan's jokes, which grew sharper during the championship series in Utah. Was it Jordan's anger? Was it his bullying nature gone out of control? Whatever the answer, the confrontations on the team bus in 1997 set in motion a new round of conflict.

"It was unfortunate the way it went down," Jim Stack said. "It didn't need to be like that."

Perhaps not surprisingly, alcohol was a factor. In the first half hour after a road win, Jordan and various teammates would often down five or six beers and fire up cigars—nothing unusual in professional basketball. Jordan certainly wasn't inebriated when he started baiting Krause. But he was buzzed enough to turn loose his wicked sense of humor.

For years, Jordan had sat at the back of the bus after games, zinging teammates and anybody in range with his laser-like sarcasm. He had his favorite regular targets. He would tease Kukoc for his showing in the 1992 Olympics, or for his defense. Equipment manager John Ligmanowski presented an easy target because of his weight. He recalled trying to come back at Jordan, but it was hard to do. Jordan also used humor to police the roster, Ligmanowski said. "If he doesn't feel somebody's doing their job, or sucking it up to go play, he'll say something. He'll get a dig in and let them know how he feels."

Asked about his back-of-the-bus barbs, Jordan said, "I don't take things too seriously. I take them serious enough. I'm able to laugh at myself before I laugh at anybody else. And that's important. I can laugh at myself. But then I can be hard."

He was particularly hard on Krause during the playoffs in Utah. At least some of it could be attributed to Krause's constant needling of Jordan over the years in a misguided attempt at bonding.

"Jerry Krause! Jerry Krause!" Jordan yelled from the back of the bus one day. "Hey, Jerry Krause, let's go fishing. It's BYOP—Bring Your Own Pole. Don't worry. If we don't catch anything, you can just eat the bait yourself."

The players in the back of the bus exploded in laughter, while team staff up front bit their lips. Krause was the team's vice president and general manager, not to mention their boss. Jackson, who was never the target of Jordan's barbs, seemed somewhat amused.

"Those guys would get a few beers in 'em back there, and then they'd start in on him," one Bulls staff member said.

"Phil sometimes sits there and says nothing," said another Bulls employee. "You're Phil Jackson and your boss is being hammered by one of the players. At least say something. Phil does not stick up for him in any of those situations. It's just like school kids, like school kids ganging up on somebody."

"I don't know in retrospect what Phil could have done," Chip Schaefer said. "It's not like he would have turned and said, 'That's enough, Michael.'"

With the team winning and on its way to a championship, Krause endured the abuse in silence. Occasionally when the barrage got especially heavy, the GM would turn to whoever was sitting nearby and say, "The mouth from North Carolina is at it again."

"Maybe it's a defense mechanism as far as Jerry is concerned," Tex Winter said of Krause's silence. "But it doesn't seem to bother him that much. I think he's got a pretty thick skin."

"Brad Sellers, now he was a good draft pick," Jordan would yell from the back.

That day, as the team rode back to its quarters in nearby Park City, Chip Schaefer recalled, "We were reduced to like twenty-five miles per hour in these buses because we'd have to climb up over this big summit to get to Park City. It just sort of created this situation where it went on and on."

"Hey, Jerry Krause, this bus went faster yesterday without your fat ass on it!" Jordan yelled, followed by the team's laugh track.

"Krause doesn't have much to go back at Michael with. He calls him Baldy or something silly like that," a Bulls employee observed. "When those guys are having their beers and they're back there smoking their cigars and they're buzzed over a victory, if Jerry said anything back to them he'd just be feeding the fire. They would just come back with something worse. That's the way they are."

"They'll have a couple of beers after a game," Schaefer said. "I don't think anybody is abusive about it. They drink their Gatorade and GatorLode, and they like beer, too. Teasing is a cruel thing. It's cruel when it's done on a playground with six-year-olds and ten-year-olds and fifteen-year-olds, and it's cruel with adults, too. Have I heard comments before and cracked a smile? Probably. But I've also heard comments before and wished in my heart that he would just be quiet and leave him alone."

"That was always very uncomfortable," Steve Kerr recalled. "I remember Jud Buechler one time saying, 'Can you imagine James Worthy treating Jerry West this way?'"

Known for testing everybody on the team, Jordan had other targets besides Krause. "I remember one time, on a different trip," Kerr recalled, "Michael started yapping from the back of the bus and Krause was up at the front. And Ron Harper kind of joined in, and then Michael quickly dismissed him, like, 'No, no, you're not allowed to do this. I'm only allowed to do this.'"

Although players getting on each other has long been a fact of life with sports teams, it was obvious to Kerr that Jordan didn't like the idea of a team rebellion. "He just wanted to torment Krause. He tested everybody, but that wasn't a test. That was genuine. And I'm not sure where it came from. It was embarrassing. And I'm not really sure why he felt compelled to do it, but he did it."

These were moments of complete humiliation, Kerr recalled, adding that he'd never been in another situation where one man did that to another, especially someone supposed to be his supervisor.

Luc Longley admitted that while Jordan's barbs made the players laugh, the moment could also be uncomfortable, especially if you were the butt of Jordan's jokes. "They're a little bit tense at times. But for the most part, they're pretty funny," Longley said. "He's in a position where he can crack on people fairly securely. But people crack back at him, and he handles that just as well. It's usually not a mean thing."

"I think there's always been a tension there," Bill Wennington said. "For whatever reason, Michael just always gets on Jerry. Whenever Jerry's around he's gonna get on him, especially if it's a team function where all the players are around. Michael's gonna get on him. And the bus is a closed area, so there's nowhere for anyone to go. So you just gotta sit there."

"He's very smart," Chip Schaefer said of Jordan. "The worst thing you can do is try to come back at him. If you don't, it'll fizzle out. Like if he starts making fun of you, you don't turn back around and say, 'Who you talking to, Baldy?' Then you've elevated it to his level. You're better off just laughing it off and hoping it will move on to somebody else maybe."

"Michael's ability puts him in a position where he feels he can go out there and do that," Wennington explained. "As far as what he does with the team, he's a great basketball player and he's our team leader. And team leaders can zing anyone. It's a totem pole, and he's high man on the totem pole right now, so everyone under him's gotta take it. What you gotta do—at least what I do—is just take your lumps. If you start to zing him back, no one's gonna side with me. They're all gonna side with him, 'cause no one wants him zinging them. So it'll be twelve against one. So you just take your two minutes of lumps...

"He'll ride anyone," Wennington added. "They'll get in the mood, and they'll just start picking on someone, and that's it. But you gotta be careful 'cause every now and then, he'll zing someone and you laugh a little too loud, and he'll turn around and look at you like, 'Let's go for you!'"

Not surprisingly, Jordan's jabs were a lot easier to take after a win. "He's cracking on people all the time," Kerr said at the time. "Those are fun moments. Those are moments that really last in the memory. He said some incredibly funny things. I think what makes them kind of special is that it's just us on the bus. It's just the team. They're kind of intimate moments because they're right after an emotional game, one way or another. The guys get going on the back of the bus, and it's very entertaining."

"Michael is a very funny comedian," Ron Harper said. "He keeps everybody loose. When it's very tense, when there are tight ballgames, he keeps you very, very loose. He has an ability to say things that you don't expect. He scores from the back of the bus a lot. He gets on Jerry Krause a lot."

Asked if Krause took the ribbing well, Harper laughed ruefully. "He don't have a choice, does he?"

"I think Jerry has the ability to maybe recognize Michael for what he is," Tex Winter said. "He knows that Michael has the personality that likes to challenge people and belittle people and berate people. I think he just accepts that. He really doesn't have much choice, as great a basketball player as Michael is. And Jerry's the first to tell you that. Everybody recognizes how valuable Michael is to this ball club." At the same time, Winter believed that the situation added to Krause's frustrations in dealing with the team. Did Jordan cross the line with Krause? "I guess maybe that there isn't even a line because he crosses it so often," Winter said, adding that the situation was simply a byproduct of the mingling of "the personalities, their egos."

Another Bulls employee with insight into the relationship said that Krause would never believe it, but Jackson had actually asked Jordan to ease up on the general manager. According to one witness, Jordan replied that he knew he shouldn't go so hard but admitted, "Sometimes I just can't help myself."

"I think they've visited about it," Winter agreed. "Phil has talked to Michael about trying to accept authority a little bit more as it's handed down from Jerry. I think Phil has helped a little bit in that regard. But on the other hand, sometimes I feel like he doesn't help as much as he maybe should, to be honest with you." Winter said that he told Jackson he needed to do more to ease the situation.

"He seemed to let a lot more things hang out, Michael did at that time," Jackson said of Jordan's return to the Bulls. "More honest with his feelings, more outspoken. He would speak about things that he hadn't before. But there's always been that thing. Jerry will tell you, 'I'm the one person who told him he couldn't play, and Michael's gonna hold that against me for the rest of his life.'"

"I express myself more vocally now than I would have ten years ago," Jordan said when asked about the incident after the playoffs.

In the moments after the 1997 Finals, one team employee watched Jordan embrace Krause. "He grabbed him and he hugged him," the employee said. "It wasn't a quick embrace because it was the right thing to do at the moment. It was a hug, a heartfelt hug. And Michael hugged Krause's wife, Thelma. She was just smiling. It was almost like family."

In the ensuing summer of confrontations and negotiations, there would be no more heartfelt hugs. In fact, it was pretty clear that the hugs were gone forever.

The Last Time

As always, the basketball court was one place where everything became lucid and clear for Michael Jordan. All the edges there were sharp and clean, walled in by the crowd noise and the fortress of his concentration on the task, especially in that final season. If every decision he made wasn't perfect, it was close. He had reached a level of play that staggered the people who had watched him most closely over the years.

Isiah Thomas, Doug Collins, and Bob Costas were broadcasting a game together that season when they concluded that they should simply stop talking about Jordan on the floor because everything he did was so good and correct and precise that nothing else could be said. It was quite possible that no one ever did anything better than Michael Jordan played basketball late in his career.

His team was now in its seventh year using Tex Winter's triangle offense. That brought order to the floor, but it was Jordan's role in the offense that often sparked it to life. He could take a single step and move an entire defense. There was no one who knew Winter's offense better than he did, perhaps not even Winter himself. Jordan always had a special kinesthetic sense, an ability to read the floor. The offensive system refined that sense by bringing order to the context. Jordan saw its limitations and figured out how to behave within them until he saw a better option.

Jordan didn't need the offense and often chose to go off on his own, but there were thousands of possessions where he used it to perfection. He worked constantly in the post, and the triangle made it difficult for teams to double-team him. So many times all he had to do was turn toward the baseline, away from the double-team, to find an open shot. He could get his shot any time he wanted simply by dribbling to places that no one else seemed to be able to go—or even to think to go. But the offense, when he used it, produced shots for him in bunches. And he was simply a splendid shot maker.

"I coached him for three years," Doug Collins said, "and to see the way this man still plays the game is incredible."

Even his opponents seemed eager to see what he was going to do next. At age thirty-five, he was in perfect condition, and for a time that season people began to consider the possibility that he might somehow be getting younger. The nine pounds he had lost certainly made him seem younger. Most other players lost the battle for youth, but he had found a plane where age seemed almost irrelevant.

"The guy has an engine that never quits and never dies," Isiah Thomas marveled.

The beauty of Jordan on the floor stood in harsh contrast with the ugly conflict with the GM. After the hazing Jordan delivered on the bus in Utah, the conflict seemed to consume Krause. He would protest that none of it bothered him, but everything he did said otherwise. The abuse of Krause was one of a host of exchanges that had soured relations among Bulls players, coaches, and management. Then they had won the title, and Jordan had stepped to the podium during the celebration and called for Reinsdorf to bring Jackson and the players back for another run. The moment had offended Reinsdorf because Jordan had used the occasion to force his hand, rather than allowing the team chairman the opportunity to graciously make an offer.

Jordan, however, knew that he had the emotion of the moment, that it would be the best time to make his play. He wasn't going to sit back and let the issue be settled in the Bulls' boardroom. But his public appeal for Reinsdorf to bring them back for another year set a pattern for the turbulent 1997–98 season, in which Jordan and Jackson would take their side of the issue to the public and Reinsdorf would fume in private.

As far as a new deal for Jordan, the negotiations were relatively uncomplicated. He signed another one-year contract for more than $30 million. Jackson, on the other hand, argued bitterly with Krause over the value of a coach. Krause did not want to acknowledge that the salary for coaches was changing. Finally, in July 1997, Krause announced a one-year, $6 million deal for Jackson, but he emphasized that this would be Jackson's last year with the team, no matter what—even if the Bulls went 82–0.

"It was pretty obvious that Jerry mismanaged that press release and kind of let his own feelings out," Jackson said later.

"I certainly didn't mean to say it with glee," Krause acknowledged. "Sometimes I don't do it right."

The GM did not identify exactly what had led to Jackson's scheduled departure, but the relationship between the coach and general manager had obviously crumbled. "This is it," Krause simply said. "Phil and I know it. We all know it." Krause had set himself in opposition to the immensely popular Jackson. Things only got worse when training camp opened and Jordan announced that he would retire if Jackson was not retained.

Suddenly, Jerry Krause had taken on two of the most popular people on the planet.

The proclamation was senseless and it resonated throughout the season, with the public growing more fearful and irritated every day, bringing an intense heat down on Reinsdorf. The media and fans again began referring to them as "the two Jerrys," the scoundrels who wanted to break up the Bulls. Krause wore the mantle as if born to it.

The spark that set the entire house aflame came on media day, usually reserved for players and coaches to answer questions from reporters about the upcoming season. Krause, as he sometimes did, chose to engage the media as well. In response to a question, he made the remark that players don't win championships, organizations do. He would later insist that he had used the phrase "players alone" don't win championships.

That may have been true, but subtle details often get lost when animosities degenerate into a slugfest. The GM should have known, after better than a decade of working with Jordan, that seemingly harmless things could set him off. In one sentence, Krause had become the LaBradford Smith of 1998.

The reporters later told Phil Jackson what Krause had said. "He would say that," the coach said testily.

Krause had stirred the pot, but the real issue was Pippen. Jerry Reinsdorf's refusal to pay him what he felt he deserved would endure as the one inexplicable facet of the team's great tangle of conflict. "It was unfortunate," Jim Stack said, looking back in 2012. "I think Scottie's contract was the biggest issue, the fact that we weren't gonna be willing to pay him what he was going to be able deservedly to earn. We were in a tough situation. Scottie had yet to get a superstar contract. His deal was up in the summer of '98. Scottie clearly wanted a multiyear deal. We just weren't in a position to do that."

Simply put, Reinsdorf and his partners, who had made hundreds of millions off the Bulls in a short time, didn't want to pay Pippen what other players of his caliber were earning, which was about $15 million a year. They had been paying him less than $3 million per year, far below his value. Pippen was key to Jordan's success, but Reinsdorf wanted to trade him for cheaper assets. That would allow Reinsdorf to win the deal, but it was hardly the way to treat the best basketball team in history. The going price for Pippen's services was forecast to run in the neighborhood of $45 million over three seasons. Reinsdorf was already paying Jordan better than $30 million per season and was determined to keep the team payroll, the largest in NBA history at that point, in line. Conversations with Krause and Reinsdorf kept turning to how they were going to pivot away from the Jordan era. They were so busy leaving it, they failed to comprehend what they had while they had it.

This was obvious to Pippen, who was already prone to pouting. He had been injured and was supposed to have surgery right after the 1997 season ended. Instead, angry that the team wanted to dump him, he waited until late in the summer to have the surgery, which meant that he would be sidelined for weeks at the start of the season. Always a subtle reader of the team, Sam Smith detected that Jordan was also angry with Pippen. If so, it was obscured by his growing anger with Krause and Reinsdorf.

Jackson knew that Krause's bumbling move would provide perfect cover for Reinsdorf. It led the public to believe that the conflict was about Jordan and/or Jackson versus Krause, when it was really about Reinsdorf not wanting to pay Pippen. Jordan had not made himself available to the press on media day, but the next day, after the team's first day of practice, he addressed Krause's opening day comments. "I'm very consistent with what I've always said," Jordan told reporters. "That's what I mean. If Phil's not going to be here, I'm certainly not going to be here."

What if Jackson goes to another team next season, a reporter asked. Would Jordan follow?

"No," he said. "Totally. I would quit. I wouldn't say quit, I'd retire."

When asked whether Krause's comments would affect the team on the court, Jordan replied, "Not unless Jerry plays. And he doesn't play."

Pippen's delayed surgery put immense pressure on Jordan. For the previous two years, Jordan's performance on the court had kept the team together. As long as the Bulls won championships, he believed, Reinsdorf would not allow Krause to break up the team. But with Pippen out, Jordan now had to carry that burden by himself. In some ways, it was similar to the burden he carried as a Little Leaguer. When he played well, his parents were happier. It was perhaps a variation of one of the major themes of his life.

Pure Naked Mind

The Bulls struggled to be mediocre that fall, going 6–5 in November. They earned a seventh victory when Jordan scored 49 points, which allowed them to survive the Clippers in double overtime. Although injured, Pippen still traveled with the team, and two games later, in Seattle, he was inebriated as the team boarded a bus at the airport. On the bus, he attacked Krause verbally. There was immediate speculation that Krause, who already disliked Pippen, would use the incident as a reason to deal him before the league trading deadline in February.

The mindfulness training provided by Jackson and George Mumford was aimed at teaching Jordan to be in the moment. He decided that if this season was going to be his last, he wanted to stay focused and enjoy it. By the week before Christmas his play had helped the team improve its record to 14–9. The Lakers came to Chicago that week, which provided him a better look at teenager Kobe Bryant, whom the media had cast as yet another "next Michael Jordan." For years, the media had heralded a succession of young players touted as the next dominating superstar, until the role itself took on a name: "Heir Jordan." In the early 1990s, Southern Cal's Harold Miner had the sad misfortune of being labeled "Baby Jordan" and believing it. Ron Harper had even done his turn as the guy next in line, until he suffered a major knee injury. He recovered but was no longer the high flyer he had been. Grant Hill, too, labored under the hype as a Detroit Piston rookie in 1994, although time revealed he was a player more along the lines of Pippen. Jerry Stackhouse followed Hill into this mire of embarrassment in 1996, and in December 1997, it was Kobe Bryant's turn.

Jordan seemed to take great pains to issue a proper lesson to these pretenders to his throne. Yet Bryant seemed so similar to Jordan in key ways that he impressed even the reigning king. And like Ray Allen, Bryant had been studying videotape of Jordan for years, so much so that he was beginning to take substantial heat as a Jordan wannabe. Bryant, however, showed that night in Chicago that he could walk the walk, particularly when it came to doing a decent imitation of Jordan's offensive moves.

"He's got a lot of 'em," Jordan himself admitted.

Lakers guard Nick Van Exel liked to joke that it could all be attributed to the Jordan highlight videotape that he lent to Bryant in the fall of 1996, just days after Bryant joined the team as an eighteen-year-old rookie out of Lower Merion High School in Philadelphia. That night it was clear that Bryant had spent plenty of time studying the tape, because he had just about all of Jordan's moves down pat, even the famous post-up gyrations where Jordan would twitch and fake his opponents into madness.

How would Bryant do matched up against Jordan? At the least, the question temporarily distracted the Bulls from their anxiety over Krause, Pippen, Jordan, and Jackson. His Airness drove the Bulls to a big lead in the first quarter that night, providing ample time in the second half for a Jordan-Bryant showdown.

"Michael loves this stuff," Ron Harper said of the meeting between the two. "[Bryant] is a very young player who someday may take his throne, but I don't think Michael's ready to give up his throne yet. He came out to show everybody that he's Air Jordan still."

Jordan scored 36, and Bryant produced a career-high 33. It was a night for highlight clips with both players dancing in the post, draining jumpers from the perimeter, and weaving their way to handsome dunks. "I had that same type of vibrancy when I was young," Jordan told reporters afterward. "It's exciting to match wits against physical skills, knowing that I've been around the game long enough that if I have to guard a Kobe Bryant... I can still hold my own."

Jordan did attempt to show restraint, despite the urge to settle the one-on-one matchup. "It was a challenge because of the hype," Jordan said. "But it's also a challenge not to get caught up in the hype, not to make it a one-on-one competition between me and Kobe. I felt a couple of times that it felt like that, but I had to refrain from that, especially when he scored on me. I felt a natural tendency to want to go back down to the other end and score on him."

Of the generation that had grown up worshiping His Airness, Bryant appeared to be one of the best imitators, although their games were far from identical. "Defensively, I just have to get used to playing against a player who has skills similar to mine," Jordan explained. "I try to pick a weakness and exploit it."

As they were going at each other in the fourth period, Bryant stopped the Chicago star to ask a question. "He asked me about my post-up move, in terms of, 'Do you keep your legs wide? Or do you keep your legs tight?'" Jordan said. "It was kind of shocking. I felt like an old guy when he asked me that. I told him on the offensive end you always try to feel and see where the defensive player is. In the post-up on my turnaround jump shot, I always use my legs to feel where the defense is playing so I can react to the defense."

Jordan added that Bryant's biggest challenge would be "harnessing what he knows and utilizing what he's got and implementing it on the floor. That's tough. That's experience. That's things that Larry Bird and Magic Johnson all taught me. There's no doubt that he has the skills to take over a basketball game."

Bryant, the son of former NBA player Joe "Jellybean" Bryant, was eager to impress. "Michael loves challenges," he said. "He loves to answer the bell. But at the same time, my father always taught me growing up that you never back down to no man, no matter how great of a basketball player he is. If he's fired up, you get fired up. You go out there, and you go skill for skill and you go blow for blow."

When he saw Bryant's leaping ability, Jordan admitted to being a bit awed by the talent on display: "I asked Scottie Pippen, 'Did we used to jump like that? I don't remember that.' He said, 'I think we did, but it's so long ago I can't remember it.' I felt like I was in the same shoes of some of the other players I've faced," Jordan explained. "He certainly showed signs that he can be a force whenever he's in the game. He has a lot of different looks. As an offensive player, you want to give a lot of different looks, so that the defense is always guessing."

"He's a very smart competitor," Bryant said of Jordan. "I could tell that he thinks the game, whether it's the tactical things or little strategies he employs on the court. I'm checking him out and analyzing him, so that I can do the same thing. But he's just better at it, because he's been doing it a while. He's very smart, very technical. You just don't naturally acquire that…" Bryant paused at the thought. "When you have the talent to go along with that," he said, "that's what you call the whole package."

Despite the issues swirling around his team, Jordan continued his climb up the record books. In a December 9 win over New York, he passed Moses Malone (27,409 points) to take over third place on the NBA's list of all-time scorers, having passed Elvin Hayes (27,313) just two weeks earlier. His impact was marked in other ways as well. A game against Phoenix on December 15 marked the five-hundredth consecutive sellout for the Bulls, the longest such streak in the league, and the foremost sign of Jordan's value to the game.

Everywhere he went, people asked if he was really going to quit if the Bulls didn't bring back Jackson. "I'm just taking it game by game," he said time and again. "Whatever happens, happens. Nobody knows what it's going to be."

He took on Ray Allen and Milwaukee January 2 and scored 44, shooting 15 of 22 from the floor. He burned the Knicks for 44 in the Garden a week later, but he was always burning the Knicks. He turned in six 40-point games in three weeks, including dumping 45 points on Houston and his buddy Charles Barkley. "If he beats you, he lets you know," Barkley said of his trash talk. "And he stomps you when you're down."

Having seen that side of Jordan for three years, both Toni Kukoc and Luc Longley were asked that spring to reflect on their difficulties as Jordan's whipping boys. His criticism could be tough, Longley admitted. "But he does let up. He's gotten better about it as he's gotten to know me. He understands what different guys can tolerate, respond to. It was heavier early on. But he knows me better now, knows what I can and can't do. I don't get tired of it at all. It's part of the dynamic of this team."

Kukoc, though, said he wouldn't mind at all if Jordan decided to put a sock in his mouth. "Sometimes, those things you can take hard right away," the Croatian forward said. "They might not always be pleasant and good to hear." When Jordan turned harsh, Kukoc said, he'd wait to calm down, then go tell him that it was too much. And Jordan was always willing to listen. "He has no problem talking about things, discussing things," Kukoc said. "I wouldn't give it back to him. I'm not that kind of person that can go kind of hard. I'm gonna wait five or ten minutes and try to talk to him about things." Both teammates acknowledged, however, that Jordan presented a singleness of purpose that was hard to dent.

He continued to search for emotional ploys to help him produce 40-point games. As he aged, the younger players seemed to do the trick. That spring he reserved 40-point games for Gary Payton in Seattle and Michael Finley in Dallas. The week of his thirty-fifth birthday in February, he again took on Bryant in the All-Star Game in New York and again won the duel.

The trading deadline passed in February without Krause dealing Pippen, who had returned from injury, as the Bulls marched ahead to claim their last prize. They encountered appreciative crowds throughout the spring. It didn't matter where they played, the buildings all sparkled for Jordan as a zillion flash cameras snapped final photographs of Air Jordan in action. He had long ago learned to ignore camera flashes during his free throws, but there was a new urgency to it now. He had played a role in founding the age of basketball as entertainment, and tens of thousands of fans paid homage to him each game night. Hundreds more, sometimes thousands, gathered outside the arenas. Outside his hotels. In the streets, hoping to catch a glimpse as Jordan and his teammates exited their bus. Countless others sent him tributes, filling a succession of storage rooms with cards and letters and flowers and gifts and requests. Even at the age when the athletic skills of most players begin to show dramatic erosion, he was once again leading the league in scoring, averaging better than 28 points a game, and although he had come to rely on his excellent jump shot in recent seasons, Jordan could still display the leaping ability and confounding body control that amazed spectators and drove television ratings. He'd shown that he was still capable of taking over virtually any game, an ability that few, if any, of his younger opponents would ever come close to displaying.

"Can Michael play any better?" longtime Bulls photographer Bill Smith asked one night before a game. "Is this 1987? How can he walk away? I have a hard time accepting it."

"We've been through this a thousand times, and nobody can really figure out what the plan is," said Steve Kerr, acknowledging that management's moves had left him and his teammates stumped. "In Chicago, everywhere we go, people are asking us, 'How can they possibly think about breaking this team up?' And frankly, we don't have any answers for that."

In February, while the team was in Utah, Krause made headlines by reiterating to *Chicago Tribune* columnist Fred Mitchell that this was definitely Jackson's last season with the team, bringing the controversy back to the surface. It was a gigantic mistake, said the *Trib*'s Terry Armour. "When we were in Utah, that's when Krause said, 'We'd love to have Michael back, but if Michael wants Phil back, it's just not gonna happen.' On that road trip, every stop we went to, somebody in a different city said, 'Hey, Michael, is this your last year?' He'd say, 'Oh yeah, it could be. If Phil's not coming back, I'm not coming back. So I'm treating it like it's my last one.' I think Krause just got fed up with reading it and said, 'Okay, I'm gonna strike now and I'm gonna say, 'You know we want Michael back, but he's not coming back under Phil.'"

"I think Krause just wants control," Pippen said. "He wants to win a title without Michael. And he wants to win one without Phil. And me. Just to be able to say he's great at what he does."

"Why," Jordan asked, "would you change a coach who has won five championships when he has the respect of his players and certainly the understanding of his players to where they go out and play hard each and every day? Why? I think it's more or less a personality conflict, and that has a lot to do with it. It certainly can't be because of [Jackson's] job and what he's done with the players and the respect he's won from the players. His success as a coach is certainly impeccable. I don't think that can be questioned. I think it's more personal than anything."

After Jordan blasted management at a global media gathering at the All-Star Weekend in New York, Reinsdorf wisely called for a moratorium on publicly discussing the issue. It was the best move he could make, short of trying to explain the tangled conflicts.

"All talk about retirements, replacements, or rosters changes are premature," the chairman said in a statement released by the team.

"This management brought this coach and these players back this season to try to win a sixth NBA championship. With half the season and the playoffs still ahead, that should be everyone's total focus. That's my focus. Period."

The fight degenerated into an ugly exchange of low blows. Jackson let it be known that one of the issues involved Jordan's routine of going to the bathroom right before games. Krause always seemed to visit the restroom at the same time, which angered the star, who saw it as a violation of his privacy. Then it was leaked that Jackson had pulled a boneheaded move that year, buying underwear for a girlfriend that he mislabeled in shipping. The package was returned to his office, where an assistant, thinking it was for Jackson's wife, forwarded it to their house. The ensuing blowup meant that Jackson spent the season living out of a Chicago hotel room.

Jackson's players rallied round him in the crisis, which led Krause to suggest that the coach was using the situation to his advantage. "Phil is a player's coach very definitely," Tex Winter agreed. "It's very obvious that the players love him. Anytime that you can get a superstar like Michael Jordan going to bat for the head coach the way he has, even to the extent to say that he's not going to play anymore unless he plays for Phil, you're not gonna find that very often. That's a wonderful relationship. It's an indication of how Phil has cultivated that relationship."

"Jerry wants to be the most powerful person in the organization, and it's hard for him to allow Michael just to be Michael," Jackson said. "Michael doesn't want power. He wants to be one of the players. But he wants a person who's not gonna boss him around or shove him around or squeeze him into corners and do those types of things. That's what it's all about."

As the playoffs neared, Jackson seemed to feel a tinge of guilt that his conflict with Krause would contribute to Jordan's career ending prematurely. "The only downside of this whole thing, in my mind's eye," the coach said, "is the fact that if Michael Jordan's not ready to retire, we're taking one of the greatest players, or heroes, that we've had in our society and limiting what he can do. We're deprived of seeing someone extremely special go out the way he wants to go out, in the style he wants to go out, because we've never seen someone of his age with the superstar status that he's had. I don't know of another sports hero in our history who has been able to play at this level at this age. Michael has just destroyed the concepts of what we think of as normal, of what a man his age should be able to do.

"So that's the only downside in this whole thing," Jackson concluded. "Jerry Reinsdorf and I have a good relationship. Jerry Krause and I understand each other. We may not have as close a relationship as we used to, but we understand each other. I know he's got a direction he wants to follow, and he knows I've got some things on my agenda."

Jordan's teammates marveled that he was able to continue performing at a championship level with the future of his career in doubt. "Michael is such a professional, such a player first, that he puts it in the background," Steve Kerr said. "Michael doesn't mess around. He plays." Yet Jordan's public relations skills rivaled his athletic abilities, and he used them to counter Krause's efforts to fire Jackson. "He's obviously a PR machine with all of his endorsements," Kerr said of Jordan. "His image is obviously very important to him. And I think, in one regard, that means that he doesn't want to look like the guy who's trying to take over the organization.... He's very savvy."

"There's more bullshit flying around this team than a dairy in a tornado," said Luc Longley. "There's always something going on. Dennis is always doing his thing, or something's going on. Michael's retiring, or Jerry's making noise. We've had more controversy or circumstance around this team in the last three years, so we've had a lot of practice at putting things out of our minds."

When it came time to play the season's last game in Madison Square Garden in March, Jordan put on a pair of his early Air Jordans and didn't let the fact that they were too small stop him from scoring 42 on Jeff Van Gundy's team. Then he did it again for good measure, scoring 44 points on the Knicks in Chicago the last day of the season.

Interviewed before that last game, Magic Johnson said of Jordan, "I thought I was the most competitive person I ever knew, until I met Michael."

Jordan had taken Krause's pronouncement from media day and kept it right there in front of him. "Players don't win championships...." Or, as Tim Hallam, who had worked with him for years, described it, "That's a strong-willed motherfucker right there."

Sixth Sense

Ultimately, the only hope the Bulls had to keep the team together was to win again. Anyone who saw Jordan play down the stretch that spring knew that he stood a good chance of forcing the agenda one more time. As things worked out, it would come down to Utah again, although the Indiana Pacers, now coached by Larry Bird and led by Reggie Miller, almost derailed the reunion. In the Western Conference, the Utah Jazz had hummed along, just ahead of Chicago in the race for home-court advantage if the teams made it to the championship series. Utah stumbled first, with a key road loss in Minnesota, and Chicago claimed the best record in the league. The Bulls, however, also faltered. They lost in Cleveland, then defeated Orlando and became the first team in the league to win sixty games. But then the Pacers came to the United Center and challenged the Bulls physically, and won handily, 114–105. In the aftermath, the Bulls lost again, this time on the road in Detroit, and finished the season at 62–20. That left them tied with Utah, except that the Jazz had won both games against Chicago during the regular season.

Reggie Miller fired the Pacers as they pushed the Bulls through a grinding seven-game series in the Eastern Conference finals that spring. Chicago prevailed only by virtue of home-court advantage. After defeating Indiana on Sunday, May 31, the Bulls practiced in Chicago on Monday, then jetted to Utah for a rematch with the Jazz for the league championship.

Utah coach Jerry Sloan continued to operate by his dictum: "It's a simple game if you go out and lay your heart on the line every night." John Stockton and Karl Malone epitomized that ethos. The guard and power forward had long been a pick-and-roll machine. Stockton would become the league's all-time assist leader, and

Malone would become just the third player to score better than 30,000 points. The Jazz always put up a nasty fight, battling every way possible, and there were always plenty of accusations that Stockton was a dirty player, but Jordan admired them both. To prove it, he longed to beat them again. But it was never about mental devices when he faced the Jazz. Just buckle your chinstrap and see who's best.

In Game 1, the two teams clawed their way to overtime, but in the extra period Stockton victimized Kerr on a late shot in the lane to give the Jazz a 1–0 lead in the series. As was their trademark, Jackson and his staff made their adjustments for Game 2, which involved spreading their triangle offense and opening the floor up for easy baskets by their cutters. In the first half, the triangle had never worked better.

"Tonight it really shined bright for us," Jud Buechler said. "It's an offense designed for everyone to touch the ball, to pass and cut. And the guys did that tonight, instead of going to Michael every time and posting up. Early on everyone got involved, and that really helped out for later in the game."

"The first half was beautiful," Winter agreed. "We followed through with our principles a lot better. Got a lot of cutting to the basket. And Michael gave up the ball. He was looking to feed cutters." But the old coach let his frustration show. "The second half we abandoned it, aborted it," he said. "We tried to go way too much one-on-one. Michael especially forced a lot of things." If the Bulls had stuck with their scheme they might have won by a dozen, the coach figured. But Jordan had delivered a win against Indiana in Game 7 by going to the basket and drawing fouls. He attempted to do the same in Game 2 against Utah, but the officials weren't giving him the calls. Instead, Jordan wound up on his back while the Jazz scooped up the ball and headed for easy transition baskets. Suddenly a 7-point Chicago edge had turned into an 86–85 Utah lead with less than two minutes to go.

"I don't know what it is," Winter said afterward, shaking his head. "Michael, he's got so damn much confidence."

Jordan pushed the Bulls back ahead, 88–86, with a layup with 47.9 seconds left. But moments later, with the game on the line and the score tied at 88, Kerr got open for a transition three. "I missed the shot and the ball went right to me," said Kerr. "Lucky bounce. As soon as I got the ball, I saw Michael underneath and just flipped it to him."

Jordan finished, was fouled, and made the ensuing free throw to send the Bulls to a 93–88 win, the victory they needed to wrest away home-court advantage.

Back in Chicago, after a practice, Winter admitted that where he once held out hope that the team might remain intact he now saw that as the remotest of possibilities. "I don't think it's necessarily a shame to break it up," he said. "It's too bad that has to be, but you have to have changes. And it could be well timed." He didn't sound convinced, but it was Krause's main talking point. Winter had figured the Bulls would struggle to win the title in '97, yet here they were a year later, in solid position again to rule the league. If the team returned, it would likely be too far past its prime to meet expectations in 1999, the coach reasoned. Jordan continued to surprise, but Rodman seemed to be wearing down, and getting stranger. Pippen had back troubles, and some observers worried that he was checking out mentally. But Jackson had always been a man to renew his teams. Keeping the key parties together would take some therapy. But only Reinsdorf could heal the relationship between Jackson and Krause, Winter said. As it would turn out, the team chairman made an attempt late in the process, but by then it just wasn't possible.

"Perhaps we could have enjoyed it more if we could have appreciated it," Jackson said.

During the playoffs, the coach confided that despite the hard feelings, he and Krause would always be bonded by their mutual success with the Bulls. But Jackson said there was almost no chance of his return. He said he had tried to make it clear to Reinsdorf in 1997 that it was virtually impossible for him and Krause to keep working together. The implication was that the team chairman had faced a choice, the coach or the general manager, and had sided with Krause. But the coach was seldom one to close off options.

"If it comes down to a chance of Michael playing and not playing, then my responsibility would be to him and to the continuation of his career, and I would have to consider it," he said. "I have to be a person that is loyal to the people who have been loyal to me. I feel that conviction. The only thing that would take me basically out of the mix would be my own personal well being, my own personal physical and emotional health in dealing with this."

Pippen, Harper, and Jordan made their best argument by overpowering Utah's guards in Game 3 in the largest rout in NBA history. The performance reiterated how absolutely dominant the Bulls could be as a team and Pippen could be as an individual defender. The Chicago bench closed out the proceedings for a 96–54 victory. The margin was so great that a cross-country flight that had radioed in for a game update for a Utah fan had to call back a second time to confirm the score. Utah coach Jerry Sloan expressed surprise when he was handed a box score. "This is actually the score?" the Utah coach said. "I thought it was 196. It sure seemed like they scored 196."

With that one game, Jordan and his Bulls had made their case against Krause's plans to rebuild. They weren't too old, and Pippen was too special a player to toss away in a trade. "I almost feel sorry for them," Jackson said privately in discussing how Krause and Reinsdorf's agenda had been shattered and how they might come to be viewed by Chicago sports fans.

It would be Rodman's free throw shooting, usually an adventure, that settled Game 4. He hit four in the closing seconds to go with his 14 rebounds to seal an 86–82 Chicago win and a seemingly insurmountable 3–1 lead in the series.

As it turned out, Game 5 became a case of celebrating too early, as the Bulls basked in their impending victory. To be fair, it was also Stockton and Malone making a case of their own for an 83–81 Utah win. Even Jordan admitted getting caught up in the anticipation. "I really didn't have a tee time," he told reporters, "because I anticipated drinking so much champagne that I wouldn't be able to get up." He was 9 for 26 from the floor and Pippen 2 for 16.

It was Kukoc's 30 points on 11-of-13 shooting that gave them a chance to win it at the end, despite Malone's 39 points. The Bulls got the ball back with 1.1 seconds to go, and during the ensuing time-out, Jordan sat on the bench taking in the situation, "inhabiting the moment," as Jackson and George Mumford had taught him to do.

A few moments later, Jordan missed a falling-out-of-bounds shot, but that didn't prevent his treasuring the moment. "I'm pretty sure people were hoping I would make that shot. Except people from Utah," he said. "For 1.1 seconds, everyone was holding their breath, which was kind of cute. No one knew what was going to happen. Me, you, no one who was watching the game. And that was the cute part about it. And I love those moments. Great players thrive on that in some respects because they have an opportunity to decide happiness and sadness. That's what you live for. That's the fun part about it."

With the series back in Utah, the Jazz had the same plan for Game 6 as for every contest: lay it on the line. They charged out early and seized control. Pippen, meanwhile, pulled up with horrendous back spasms and wound up back in the locker room, where a massage therapist literally pounded on his back trying to drive the spasms out. One team employee reported Krause standing in a corner of the room, almost transfixed, watching Pippen absorb the blows, eager to get back in the game to help Jordan.

"I just tried to gut it out," Pippen said. "I felt my presence on the floor would mean more than just sitting in the locker room. I knew I was going to come back in the second half, but I just didn't know how much I was going to be able to give."

Pippen found a way to provide enough help to Jordan, who had fallen into another of his unstoppable trances. He would score 45, including the final jumper at the top of the key.

After the final shot, he stood there for all to see, poised, arm draped in a follow-through, perfect.

Later he wouldn't want to give up the moment. Who could blame him? His bucket gave Chicago the win, 87–86.

"Things start to move very slowly and you start to see the court very well," he said, explaining the last play. "You start reading what the defense is trying to do. And I saw that. I saw the moment."

Stockton got one final shot, but Ron Harper hustled to help him miss.

Jordan and his coach then met on the court for one long, final embrace. They would never be so close again.

Jordan slept deeply and peacefully on the plane ride home with everybody else wondering where things were headed next. Jackson's answer was to decline Reinsdorf's offer to stay with the team, choosing instead to ride off on his motorcycle. The players and coaches closed out their experience with a private, emotion-filled team dinner in the days after the championship game. They all expressed their love and regard for one another, and the tears flowed.

Jackson later told the *Sun-Times*'s Rick Telander that he might have stayed on. "I did feel it was time to take some time off," he said. "What would have changed things is if management had said, 'Stay on until Michael is finished, until he retires.' But they never suggested that."

During the spring of 1996, he and his attorney, Todd Musburger, had suggested a five-year coaching proposal, but Reinsdorf turned them down, Jackson said. Next, the coach had suggested a two-year agreement at about $3 million per season. Again, Reinsdorf declined.

"We probably could have stayed intact one more year at least and made another run at a title," Jim Stack said in 2012. "But the timing of the contracts, and then there were a lot of hurt feelings with the way Phil had sort of positioned the team against management. At the time, Phil was saying publicly that if Sylvester Stallone could make ten million a film, he couldn't imagine how much would Michael be worth for eighty-two games a year. He really said some things that probably weren't the most appropriate things to say publicly.

"I think Jerry Reinsdorf in particular had had enough," Stack added. "The way they were taking care of Phil financially, I guess that didn't sit that well with Jerry Reinsdorf. And all of those years that Jerry Krause had to deal with being outside the circle."

Reinsdorf seemed to be betting that Krause could rebuild the team fast enough to keep the fans interested. He admitted that they almost broke up the team by trading Pippen in 1997. "We considered giving up a shot at the sixth title to begin rebuilding, and we would have given it up if we could have made the right deal," Reinsdorf said. "The reason we considered breaking the team up is that we wanted to minimize the period of time between winning the last championship and getting back into contention with the next team." In other words, he hoped to minimize the time between the Jordan era and the next act on the United Center stage.

"We now have very little to trade, very little to work with in rebuilding," Reinsdorf said later and added, "Michael couldn't care less about what happens [to the team] after he leaves.

"There's never been a power struggle," the team chairman said. "Phil never asked for Krause to be removed. It never happened. Phil never told me he thought we were a house divided. He said it was difficult to work with Jerry Krause but not impossible. Phil never ever said that. He did express the fact that it was very strained. I asked him, 'Has anything changed? Do you want to coach another season?' He said, 'No.'"

Reinsdorf said that he returned to Chicago and asked one more time. "Wednesday night after the title we had our office celebration, I sat down with Phil and told him, 'If you've changed your mind, we want you back.'" The offer was unconditional, and it stood regardless of whether Jordan returned, Reinsdorf said. "Phil said, 'That's very generous.' I told him, 'Generosity has nothing to do with it. You've earned it.' He took a deep breath and said, 'No, I have to step back.'"

Reinsdorf also said that he had assured Jordan that if he wanted to play, his one-year contract (in excess of $36 million) would still be there.

Although Tex Winter had long worried that Jordan's fame was overshadowing the game, the star addressed that in the aftermath: "I think the game itself is a lot bigger than Michael Jordan. I've been given an opportunity by people before me. To name a few, Kareem Abdul-Jabbar, Dr. J, Elgin Baylor, Jerry West. These guys played the game way before Michael Jordan was born. Michael Jordan came on the heels of all that activity and with Mr. Stern and what he has done for the league, gave me an opportunity to play the game of basketball and I played it to the best of my ability. I tried to enhance the game itself. I tried to be the best basketball player I could be."

In looking back, Steve Kerr recalled his favorite memory of Jordan and his final Bulls team. It involved a typical Phil Jackson assignment for his players as the 1998 regular season came to a close.

"Phil had this great moment," Kerr explained. "It was the last day of the regular season and he told us, 'Tomorrow, at practice, I want everybody to write down a few words about this experience you've had with this team. It can be anything, you can write a poem. You can just write a letter to your teammates. You can take some lyrics from a song that are meaningful. Whatever. But bring something tomorrow.' Half the guys brought stuff, about half the guys forgot. I forgot. But Michael brought something and it was a poem that he wrote about the team."

It was the ultimate triumph of Jackson's effort over the years. Jordan, the game's angry man and all-time badass, had written a poem. "It was shocking," Kerr recalled. "What happened was, every guy ended up saying something, whether they read something or said something. Phil told me later that June, his wife, had told him about this and suggested the idea. And so what he did was after each guy spoke, whoever had written something down had to crumple up the paper and put it into a big coffee can. It was like a Folgers can. Then when everybody was done, he lit a match and he lit the contents on fire in the coffee can. The lights were out and there was this glow in the room. And it was like, 'All those memories that you guys just talked about, those are ours and nobody else is gonna see.' He didn't say that, but it was the metaphor. This is ours and they're gone and they'll forever live within us and nobody else will ever see 'em."

Phil Jackson burned Michael's poem?!

"I know, that thing would be worth millions right now, right?" Kerr said, laughing at the memory. "Michael's poem was, what does this mean to you? What does this experience mean to you and where have you been and where are you going? It was so cool. In a legacy of powerful moments that Phil, you know, left with us, that was by far the most powerful one. I'll never forget it. I was crying. A lot of guys were shedding tears."

It had been such a long, hard, exhilarating ride being Jordan's teammate, moments of supreme triumph interspersed with one sort of shell shock or another every single day.

"It wasn't just Michael," Kerr said. "It was the experience. We all knew that we were living through this era that was so special and we were so lucky to be a part of it. There were so many players and athletes and people who would have killed to have been a part of that. We were so lucky to have been a part of it, to go through this run, and it was ending. And we knew how special it was. And that was Phil's genius was that he... that's how he bonded our team. He made us communicate and he brought us together in so many different ways. And, it wasn't going to happen without Phil, because Michael wasn't going to make it happen himself, because he was above the rest of us. He was better than the rest of us and he wasn't a guy, like Scottie, who was human enough to have those emotions and frailties that you could relate to. So, we couldn't relate to Michael, but Phil brought us together with the different things that he did."

Jackson had brought Jordan full circle, the Michael Jordan who had been that insecure adolescent, who went from being a star Little Leaguer to not even getting in the game the next season because he was too skinny for Babe Ruth ball, Michael Jordan who sat the bench, the lone black kid, always among the white teams, Michael Jordan whose father had given the impression of rejecting him, the driven Michael Jordan who had proved to his father again and again and again, night after NBA night, how valuable he was, in every way imaginable.

"That's what made him a badass," Kerr concluded, laughing, "was that he wasn't just a talent. It was the understanding of it all, the work ethic, the game itself, the strategy involved. He got it all. He understood all of it."

That, of course, only served to heighten the sorrow by season's end, the six championships notwithstanding. All that he had been through—his father's death, the humiliation of baseball, the infuriation of the trial, the alienation from his mother, his bitter negotiations with Reinsdorf, the silly battles with Krause, his frustration with Pippen—it had all passed. And there he stood, resplendent in basketball perfection, with no place to go.

PART XI

THE AFTERLIFE

Chapter 36

LIMBO

In the minds of so many, Jordan should have simply inhabited that final perfect tableau against Utah for the rest of his known life: standing there with the clock drained down, his right arm and wrist hanging like a question mark in follow-through, the ball floating toward the goal, the sea of faces in the backdrop caught in suspense. Air Jordan, unconquered and unbowed till the end.

There could be no better capstone, a career launched by one world-famous last-second shot, then after two dreamlike decades, to close it all out with another peak moment. Other famous athletes were known for their big moments, but no one had ever had so many of them, no one had made them seem so routine.

Then to have his career all come down to that grand finale in Utah?

Seemingly everyone's inclination, including Jerry Reinsdorf's, was to leave it alone. "Don't do another thing," they told him time and again over the ensuing months. "You've achieved perfection. How can you possibly improve on that?"

But that wasn't possible.

Just a couple of days after the NBA Finals had ended so gloriously in Salt Lake City, never mind the grind of driving his Chicago Bulls to three straight titles, he was pressing to get on the links.

Jordan had spent hours playing a video game version of what was then his all-time favorite course, the Fazio designs at Barton Creek near Austin, Texas, with its stunning cliff-lined fairways, abundant waterfalls, and limestone caves. Now that another long NBA season was over, he planned to treat himself to the real course.

And this is where Keith Lundquist came into the picture. Jordan was coming to Austin that Monday to play a couple of afternoon rounds at Barton Creek. A couple of days earlier, he had phoned to see if Lundquist, a Texas golf pro, could hook him up to play Great Hills that Monday as a tune-up.

Great Hills was closed on Mondays, which would be a perfect time to accommodate Jordan and his party. So the club pro told Jordan he'd have things ready for him. He assumed that the star, now all of thirty-five, would welcome a leisurely pace to unwind from the NBA grind.

But that Monday, Lundquist's phone rang at an absurdly early hour. Jordan was on the line, explaining that his private jet was landing and he was heading to the course. Lundquist blinked awake and looked again at the clock. Then he jumped out of bed and hustled to meet Jordan at the pro shop.

Lundquist arrived at Great Hills to find an expectant MJ on the practice tee, furiously driving balls into the darkness. Lundquist had been a pro for a while, but he had never seen anybody doing that.

When they shook hands, the pro felt his paw disappear into Jordan's huge mitt. It was true, he realized. MJ was decidedly larger than life.

As light broke across the sky, Jordan and his foursome, which included former NFL receiver Roy Green, were off. His Airness was determined to get in as many holes as possible before appearing at a noon charity event.

Lundquist went along to usher Jordan over the course. "I told him where to hit the ball, the yardages, and the tendencies of the greens," Lundquist recalled of that day. "He didn't play particularly well on the front nine. It was just a few days after the championship finals in the NBA. He was smoking cigars and enjoying himself. The foursome had a little action out there but nothing heavy. He hit the ball exceedingly well, way beyond what I thought he could do. He can hit it. There's no question about that."

By the time he reached Great Hills' challenging back nine Jordan was clearly getting it together, Lundquist said. "He showed great touch around the greens. His hands were enormous, and he had enlarged grips for his clubs. His hand-eye coordination was really good. It's obvious that his athletic skill goes all the way across the board."

By the back nine, club members had also discovered that Michael Jordan was on the closed course. An impromptu gallery of sixty or seventy quickly gathered. It was a development that greeted him nearly everywhere he played. Orlando attorney Mark NeJame once recalled gazing out the window onto the golf course outside his home one morning to see a cart tearing down the fairway. "A minute later, I saw at least fifteen carts racing each other down the course," he recalled. "It was MJ in the first cart and fifteen members in hot pursuit trying to catch a glimpse of him."

Jordan was personable and obviously accustomed to being followed around, Lundquist said. "He made a point during the round of coming over and chatting with me. He was using these Wilsons. I told him, 'You could find better clubs.'"

Jordan agreed. "They pay the bills," he said, referring to his endorsement deal with the manufacturer.

Richard Esquinas once observed that Jordan played golf like he played basketball, always forcing the tempo and trying to find an advantage in it. That certainly seemed to be the case that day in Texas. Consuming hole after hole, the foursome clipped along at a strong pace, enough to tire anyone, thought Lundquist, who then tagged along to the charity event in the noon sun, where an animated Jordan engaged easily with the throng of children and adults. That afternoon, Jordan knocked off another huge helping of golf holes on the handsome Fazio courses at Barton Creek. He finished just in time to ride to San Marcos for a charity basketball game in the evening.

"He played every minute of the game that night," Lundquist said. "He had to have been on the court at least two hours. I'd never seen anything like it."

Afterward Jordan repaired to one of Austin's fine restaurants, where he stayed well into the early morning, first carving up a steak, then smoking cigars and sipping expensive wine until it was time to run to the airport and jet away as dawn was again breaking in the Texas sky.

Jordan departed, leaving Lundquist to contemplate the otherworldly appetite that he had just encountered.

Perhaps retirement would work well for Jordan. He had the bank account, the private jet, and the immense curiosity and energy to stalk the known world in search of the perfect golf round. It sure sounded ideal to observers such as Lundquist, except for one thing: Could it possibly be enough?

Jilted

Jordan would later admit to feeling jilted by Jackson's decision to leave the Bulls behind. A man of his word, Jordan had vowed to retire if Jackson wasn't his coach. It was hard to measure the impact of his split with Jackson, explained a close associate of both men. "When you manipulate somebody, you get what you want. But when that person finds you out, finds out he has been manipulated, that leads to alienation. That will affect the relationship, no matter how strong it once appeared. That's the consequence of manipulation."

Jordan later gained clarity on Jackson in the wake of the final championship, on the firing of Johnny Bach and other things, but mostly it was the sense that Jackson had walked away from him. Jordan had managed to overturn Krause's edict that Jackson was through, yet the coach had left them all standing there, jilted.

Krause then moved swiftly to deal Scottie Pippen to Houston. Pippen would collect his riches as a result of the trade, but the fracture with Jackson and the rupture of the team only drove his sense of alienation. Jordan, who trusted few people to begin with, now trusted even fewer. One close associate who had been a part of the tight circle that Jackson built with the team ran into Jordan later that year and immediately sensed that any warm feelings that had been created were now gone. "We talked," the associate said, "but it left part of me feeling that he didn't trust me anymore, not in the same way at least. It was like we were cool, but now we weren't cool anymore."

If the trust that was the Bulls was gone, did that mean the experience was a mirage?

With Pippen traded and Jackson gone, it became a foregone conclusion that Jordan would retire. But that move was delayed by a labor dispute between the NBA owners and players. It was an easy time for Jordan to lose himself as the NBA owners locked out the players over the 1998 off-season while they argued over a new collective bargaining agreement, one necessitated by his own huge contract. The owners simply didn't want to be paying Jordan-size money to lesser players. The situation bought him more time to play around, ostensibly as he deliberated his future.

During one of these lost weekends, he accidentally sliced a tendon in his hand with a cigar cutter, which required surgery and threw his future into further doubt.

Meanwhile, his relationships with his mother and siblings were likewise in the various stages of suspension. Sis continued to struggle with her emotions concerning her father. Shortly after his death in 1993, she had begun writing her book, only to abandon the project in 1995. She remained a persistent critic of her rich and famous younger brother, especially over his gambling substantial sums while she and other members of the family struggled financially. It wasn't that he didn't help them; for instance, he bought a tractor-trailer rig for his uncle, Gene Jordan, which allowed him to work as a trucker well into his seventies. Sis estimated that her brother had given her a total of about $100,000 over the years. She didn't expect him to take on her or her children as a responsibility, but she and others had become embittered by the revelations of the large sums he wagered. Her criticism apparently had a price. She noted that each of his family members received a brand-new vehicle from their brother's Nissan dealership except for her. She was given the keys to a used car. She pointed to that slight as evidence that he used his wealth to control them.

By 1997, Sis and Michael had stopped speaking to each other. He had given everyone in his immediate family expensive jewelry pieces commemorating each of his NBA championships, but in 1998, he did not give her the championship jewelry. In 1999, after his retirement, he reacted angrily upon learning that she was back working on her book. She said that he remarked that the book would be her attempt to sponge off of his reputation by making exaggerated claims. Her reply was that she was simply not one of the numerous yes-men in his life, telling him what he wanted to hear, that she had known him and loved him long before he became famous, that unlike other relatives who offered the same criticisms in private, she was not afraid to speak out.

Later that year, golfer Payne Stewart died in a plane crash, not long after winning the US Open, leading Sis to think about how much time her brother spent zipping around the globe in his private jet. She phoned and left a message that she was concerned about him and wanted to know if he was OK. He sent a message through his mother that he was fine. He didn't speak to her personally, she later suggested, because "Michael has a tendency to run from things he does not want to face, and his wealth affords him the opportunity to do that in many ways."

While Jordan remained in touch with his mother, they were not nearly as close as they once were, friends and acquaintances noted. In the fall of 1996, they had made an emotional appearance together at the University of North Carolina to announce a $1 million gift to create a Jordan Institute for Families in the school of social work. If people wondered where Jordan got his legendary energy and drive, they needed to look no further than Deloris Jordan, who would continue to write and travel the globe to talk about family issues well into her seventies. A good portion of his charisma also came from his mother, Jim Stack observed. "She's a wonderful lady, very cordial. He had components of all those things in his personality." The UNC Jordan Institute fit with her great positive energy and message, perhaps as a way for her to deal with issues that she had struggled with as a young mother.

Later, word would circulate around Chapel Hill that the school was having difficulty collecting the gift. Was it his legendary stinginess, or was it a sign of the growing gulf between the star and a mother who had become one of his harshest critics? Or was it both?

In time, the gift would be made, and the institute would offer an array of programs for the school of social work, an important element in the Jordan family legacy.

The summer of 1999 marked the sixth anniversary of James's death. Of the immediate family, Michael had been closest to his father, who had been his seemingly constant companion and advisor, his most ardent admirer. James had always been the one at his side, keeping things moving in a positive direction, offering constant encouragement in the face of the mountainous pressures Jordan encountered with the increasing complexity of his life. It seemed clear that for the remainder of his existence Jordan would be caught between the two angels of his nature: his mother in one ear, encouraging a selfless public life lived at the foot of the cross, and his father in the other, telling him to take his fun where he could find it, because he had surely earned it.

Mother and son had endured their battles in the wake of James's death, Sis reported, to the point that Michael had changed the locks on the foundation offices to deny her access there for a time. He had even attempted to limit her use of his name in her activities, according to his older sister. Yet Jordan continued to pay his mother a monthly stipend in addition to other financial support. And while they would get past their conflicts to some degree, the relationship appeared to have sustained some damage.

His father was gone, but it seemed that in many ways, the elder Jordan's influence loomed even larger than it had when he was alive. For some, the primary evidence of that was the lifestyle Jordan pursued away from the public eye. Others, however, saw that simply as a well-deserved release from his caged life in hotel rooms.

Either way, Sis claimed to have seen it all coming. Like others in the family, she had supported the pretense that he was still the loving, caring, gentle younger brother she had known. "With the birth of his bigger-than-life image, he has become imprisoned by his public status and hardened by the strain of success," she would write. "Eventually the pressures of being 'always on display' and the pressure to live up to the public's expectations lessened his ability to relax, even with family." He had become a "walking and talking conglomerate," she alleged.

In all fairness, his defenders said, that corporate existence was the essence of his long-term success. His emergence as a business figure was a large part of what distinguished him from the crowd of former athletes reduced to trying to wring a few dollars from their earlier glory.

In 1999, Jordan was facing the challenge of trying to construct a second act. According to one study, as many as 90 percent of retired NBA players were broke within a few years of the end of their playing days. Many of them were ripped off by agents and money managers. Others were victims of an educational system that taught them little or nothing about managing wealth. Most of them fell victim to "the life," a pricey style of living that proved impossible to sustain after their playing days were over.

In contrast, Jordan's role as a partner with Nike, and his other endorsements and investments, brought him new millions each year. His wealth was routinely estimated at as much as $500 million, and he was often described as the first billion-dollar athlete. He had achieved long-term success despite the vagaries of a life in professional basketball, much as his grandfather Peoples had prospered despite the impossibilities of sharecropping. Better yet, Jordan's feats remained fresh in the memories of so many of his contemporaries. For years, interviewers had asked Jordan about his most memorable performances, and his reply had often been the standard: "I'll wait until my run is over before I evaluate what I accomplished."

The response was understandable, though his public displays of emotion had long suggested that he reveled in those accomplishments. Passion was his signature. He had celebrated with memorable outbursts that riveted the attention of the global audience.

As with the others who had helped create the cultural icon who became MJ, Sonny Vaccaro often marveled at the breadth of Jordan's reach and popularity. "Prior to Michael no one had ever been marketed the way we marketed him," Vaccaro said. "And no one ever put as much emphasis on an individual athlete to sell a product."

By 1999, Jordan stood alone at that pinnacle of a sports-hero mythologizing culture. How deep was his global penetration? The

Financial Review would express great surprise in December 1999 upon learning that as early as 1992, a survey of Chinese schoolchildren had named Jordan one of the two greatest figures of the twentieth century, along with Zhou Enlai, the longtime Chinese premier. This was a good five years before the making of *Space Jam*, and well before Jordan's legend had gained its most serious momentum, with his first "retirement," the public fervor of his comeback, and the winning of his final three championships in storybook fashion.

"The nomination of Jordan seems bizarre," the *Financial Review* noted, "except that black sporting and athletic achievement provides some of the defining images of the twentieth century."

"How big is Michael Jordan?" *Newsweek* magazine had asked in 1993. "We all know he is a living god to tens of millions of American kids, the most media-genic sports figure in history, a one-man conglomerate who can move goods and services the way a few words from a Federal Reserve chairman can move financial markets."

His return in 1995 had driven his profile even higher. Four years later, 800 reporters converged on Chicago's United Center to cover his second retirement news conference, fully aware that an era was ending. "Michael is one of the most important athletes, obviously. But even beyond that, he's one of the most important cultural figures in the history of the US," Todd Boyd, a University of Southern California professor specializing in sports and culture, said at the time. "I don't think that's in question. When you talk about an athlete who clearly dominated his sport but also transcended the sport in terms of his success as a brand, his ability to market products, just what Michael Jordan came to stand for after a while was perhaps the biggest transition anybody's been able to make from the basketball court to the highest realm of American popular culture."

At the height of his popularity, the public often expressed surprise at any hint of irregular behavior by Jordan. But the greater surprise, as Sonny Vaccaro had suggested, was that there wasn't more of it to hint at. How could he not have been corrupted? Vaccaro asked. "It would have been humanly impossible. How could you not? Remember he had the Mars Blackmon commercials he was doing in the early nineties with Spike Lee. They were immensely popular. Then he went on to do a film and commercials with Bugs Bunny and Looney Tunes. He won all those championships and became the greatest athlete in the world."

So, indeed, Jordan's older sister was correct in assessing that the profound experience had changed him, Vaccaro added. "It's been another Michael since we created the commercialism.... He became another Michael. That took on a life of its own at such a young age. I don't know how you turn back from that."

His admirers made the case that considering other victims of boundless success, such as Elvis or Michael Jackson, Jordan had done quite well in holding his ground against the many destructive options available to the lost and lonely inhabitants of such fame. This would remain true, even in the many storms that lay ahead in his second act as a basketball executive and team owner. Where before, his larger-than-life performance on the court always helped obscure his imperfections, his life as an executive offered no such cover. In fact, Jordan soon learned that it would only expose and amplify the negatives.

Reinsdorf's Loyalty

The NBA lockout finally ended in December with a target of starting play in January 1999, which allowed Jordan to announce his retirement to an assembly of worldwide media gathered at the United Center on January 13. Still, he declined to make his decision any more certain than 99.99 percent certain. Never say never, he said.

"Mentally, I'm exhausted. I don't feel I have a challenge. Physically, I feel great," Jordan said in explaining the move. "This is a perfect time for me to walk away from the game."

Some noted he didn't sound all that convincing. "I think the league is going to carry on, although we've had our troubles over the last six months," he said, referring to the league's struggles over the new collective bargaining agreement that caused it to miss nearly half of the 1998–99 season. "I think that is a reality check for all of us. It is a business, yet it is still fun. It is still a game. And the game will continue on."

But it would have to do so without him.

"I'm just going to enjoy life and do things I've never done before," he explained. In short, he said, his newfound freedom would be consumed by his wife and three young children, his love for golf, and his many commercial endorsements.

"I see Michael doing a lot more carpooling," Juanita Jordan told the crowd of reporters when asked for her vision of Jordan's future.

"Unfortunately," Jordan continued, "my mother, my family, brothers and sisters, could not be here. But as you see me, you see them. My father, my mother, and certainly my brothers and sisters. They are here, through me, and they, along with myself, say thank you for taking me in and showing me the respect and gratitude you have shown me over the years I have been here. I will be in Chicago for the rest of my life. My wife won't allow me to move nowhere else. I will be in Chicago and I will support Chicago teams."

One reporter asked if Jordan might consider using his many talents to save the world. Jordan avowed that he was no savior. Indeed he had failed to save the championship team that he had desperately sought to keep together. Yet Jordan made scant mention of the dispute at his retirement press conference other than to point out that Bulls management had their work cut out for them.

"We set high standards around here," he said with a hint of a smile.

"I want to say thank you to the two gentlemen here, Mr. Stern and Mr. Reinsdorf, for presenting me with the opportunity to play the game of basketball and certainly giving me the opportunity to come to Chicago, meet my beautiful wife, and build a family here," he said. "And my family in North Carolina and a lot of my friends who have come up to support this day, support me, and who have always supported me once I stepped foot on the basketball court and even when I didn't play on the basketball court. I want to say thanks to both of those gentlemen and all the fans of Chicago for allowing me to come here and they have adopted me as one of theirs.... We are hopefully going to be known as a championship city and I hope it continues on even when Michael Jordan is not in uniform. I will support the Chicago Bulls."

He and Juanita had talked at his press conference of his slipping into a quiet existence and finally being a regular dad. He truly loved his children, had from the very start, so it seemed possible—until he actually tried to do it. The world's golf courses were waiting for him, his Jump 23 jet just sitting there, beckoning him to go anywhere he damn well pleased, to play cards all night en route, puffing cigars and joking with his pals. He continued to consume holes in what seemed like great gulps, virtual orgies of golfing and gambling, now tempered only slightly after his troubles in the early nineties. He would later be accused of pulling pal Tiger Woods into this strange and exclusive orbit, to the point that when Woods encountered his very public issues with sexual addiction, one of the golfer's representatives complained that running around with Jordan in his bacchanalian pursuits led to Woods's downfall.

Even though Jordan had walked away from basketball, his competitiveness raged on, to the point that he truly craved action, always looking for the next buzz, playing rounds into the evening darkness with however much on the line he needed to make him feel that certain edge. Was it the adrenaline that addicted him, or was it the sense of escape from his life in the public eye where he was paid so well to be so perfect? Likely it was both and much more, including the fact that, given his inability to show himself in public, his golfing schedule kept him together with his friends. After two decades, he knew little else but a cycle of hanging out with the entourage, taking just enough meetings to sustain his business life, shooting commercials, all mixed with enough landings in Chicago to hold his family life together.

Or so he thought.

Whatever the root of it all, the days of his impromptu celebration in Austin in June 1998 had turned into weeks, then months, then a full-blown lifestyle. As Lacy Banks pointed out, Jordan had assumed the air of royalty, a status happily bestowed upon him by an adoring public. His insistence on the big expectations that came with such an existence hadn't gone away with his retirement. Through all the golf and unchecked fun, he soon decided that he wanted a place for himself in the game, to put into effect the values he had so clearly established as a player. He would teach the next generation important things about the game, he explained to reporters.

His first thought was that he would assume an important position with the Bulls, as a part owner with a role in management. To some, it seemed almost ludicrous that he would have such an expectation in the wake of the raging conflicts of his final seasons in Chicago. Jordan's anger alone was enough to make a tough guy like Jerry Reinsdorf blanch. Yet his Nike experience suggested a precedent. He had endured no small differences of opinion with Phil Knight over the years, but his presence and involvement with the shoe company had brought vast growth and wealth to Nike. Accordingly, he was rewarded richly with unprecedented power and influence over its direction.

Clearly, his efforts and energy had driven a similar growth for the Bulls. But if Jerry Reinsdorf ever considered a similar reward for Jordan, there is no record of it. It would have seemed logical to keep the immensely popular hero involved with the franchise, and it might have paved the way for Jordan to make yet another comeback in Chicago.

Bringing Jordan into Bulls management would have meant altering or lessening Krause's role, if not his outright termination, considering the hard feelings between the two men. In 1999, those feelings were fresh in the minds of both Krause and Reinsdorf. They had had their faces rubbed in the circumstances again and again by the Chicago media over the 1997–98 season. Jordan was always right, and it seemed as if they were always wrong.

"We used to have a saying," Krause recalled in 2012. "We said we could line up all the media at State and Madison streets, and Michael could have pissed on each one of them, pissed right in their faces, and they would all say, 'Oh, the nectar of the gods!' That's how much he had the media in Chicago. He had complete control."

The bitterness between the parties meant that letting Jordan join the Bulls as a minority owner was never a real consideration, regardless of how much money he had made for the stockholders.

"Jerry never talked to me about it," Krause said in 2012 of

Reinsdorf's response to Jordan's interest. "It was never mentioned." Krause did recall the topic being raised by some in the media. "I kind of laughed it off because I know Michael," Krause said. "He's proven what kind of management skills he has."

Krause also knew Reinsdorf quite well. "Jerry is a very stubborn human being," he explained, adding that loyalty was a huge factor for Reinsdorf. The team chairman's loyalty was reserved foremost for Bulls stockholders, Krause explained. Although Jordan's efforts had made the stockholders quite wealthy, his role in management would be an entirely different matter, Krause said. "That could have been a bad fiduciary responsibility. I think Michael thought he would have it. Michael thought he was going to get everything. He didn't know what the job was. He had no idea."

Krause also indicated that hard feelings over Jordan's final two contracts also remained a factor. "We had contract things with Michael that were not fun, that were bitter." Some of those feelings stemmed from the way Falk treated Reinsdorf in those negotiations, Krause said. Krause hastened to add that he and Reinsdorf respected Falk, in part because he was so tough in negotiations. Such respect did little to soften the hard feelings for Jordan.

Jim Stack, who would later leave the Bulls to become an executive with the Minnesota Timberwolves, said that the question of Jordan remaining in Chicago was made more difficult by all of the years he had pushed for the team to acquire North Carolina players. "The other component of that is that Jerry Reinsdorf really trusted and believed in what we were doing as management," Stack said of the team's administration under Krause. "Jerry Reinsdorf had had a taste of what Michael was pushing on us with the Walter Davis thing and some other things he wanted to do. I don't think Michael would have been satisfied with coming to the Bulls in some figure-head position. He would have wanted to be hands-on making the decisions. That would have been difficult. Even if Jerry Reinsdorf had wanted to bring Michael back, I don't think it would have been in a position that Michael would have been satisfied with or accepted."

Stack, who had worked closely with both Jordan and Krause, shuddered at the thought of them in the same front office. "There was no way those guys could have worked hand in hand," he said. Jordan shouldn't have been surprised by his rejection from Reinsdorf, observed reporter David Aldridge, who had long covered the NBA. "I never got the sense that Reinsdorf ever thought of Michael as an executive. I mean, you can tell when somebody's being prepared to move into the front office. It doesn't take much to figure that out. I never had the feeling that they were prepping Michael for that role. Never."

Perhaps a case could have been made that Jordan's continued association with the franchise would have been in the stockholders' best interests. He was, in fact, the league's one proven attraction, what Jerry West liked to call "a license to print money." Jordan's value was not only in the tremendous growth in the team's revenue and value during the Jordan era, but also in the city of Chicago itself, especially the flourishing of the blighted neighborhoods around Chicago Stadium that had been transformed into a vibrant economic community, with the bars, restaurants, and other businesses that appeared with the opening of the United Center, "the building that Michael built." Would Reinsdorf allow his anger to get in the way of doing what was in the best interests of the team's stockholders and the city?

As for the idea that Reinsdorf "owed" Jordan anything in the wake of the team's overwhelming success, Krause said simply, "We paid Michael a lot of money to play basketball." Jordan's final contract, which paid him $33 million per year, confirmed that assertion, except that the career earnings rankings for NBA players, released in 2012, offer a different view. On the list of the all-time NBA moneymakers, Jordan ranked eighty-seventh, just behind David Lee. Jordan's career earnings as an NBA player were a relatively modest $90 million. The list reveals that Jordan's success made it possible for the generation of stars that followed him— Kevin Garnett, Kobe Bryant, and Shaquille O'Neal—to approach $300 million in earnings. Jordan had often pointed out that his success was built on the generation who came before him, who earned a relative pittance. He said it stood to reason that he would earn less than those who followed.

Yet Jordan also ranked far behind even his contemporaries. Patrick

Ewing led the group of players from Jordan's era, with $119 million in earnings. Scottie Pippen raked in $109 million, much of which he earned after leaving the Bulls. Hakeem Olajuwon earned $107 million, with Gary Payton, Reggie Miller, and Karl Malone all earning more than $100 million.

The record reflects that the Bulls extended no great largesse to Jordan in recognition of the wealth he brought the team's shareholders. Lakers owner Jerry Buss, for example, paid $14 million to Magic Johnson upon his retirement, in part to express gratitude for leading the team to five NBA championships and helping to greatly increase the franchise's worth.

Buss and Johnson, however, had what has been described as something akin to a father-son relationship, whereas the once strong Reinsdorf-Jordan relationship had suffered tremendously with the feud over Pippen and Jackson, to the point that Reinsdorf promptly spurned Jordan once he retired from playing.

Jordan's income shortfall can also be explained by his attitude. He claimed always to be playing "for the love of the game." Even later, when he returned to playing, he would do so for a minimal amount. He took great pride in earning his substantial wealth—more than a billion dollars by some estimates—"off the court."

Jerry Reinsdorf almost certainly denied his partners yet more riches by declining to hire Jordan. Yet the team chairman was like most everyone else. He had had enough of the conflict and allowed Jordan to ride off into the sunset. "In the end Michael felt like there was still more gas left in the tank," Jim Stack said. "But it ended with him having to walk away without a choice, which was really hard for him."

Krause did request one final meeting with Jordan late in his career. The occasion had led Krause to think of his first meeting with Jordan fourteen years earlier, in the spring of 1985. After that came the foot injury, and from there the two men watched their differences multiply. "The animosity and all that really started to come into play then," Sonny Vaccaro recalled. "And it carried on until it really got to be an ugly thing."

"My job was not to be Michael's ass kisser," Krause offered.

Krause still felt the need for some sort of reconciliation or closure and hoped perhaps a meeting might help clear the air, so he asked him to come to his office at the Berto Center. He began by confessing that all of the years he had needled Jordan by telling him that Earl "The Pearl" Monroe was better, he was not being truthful.

"You were better than him early in your career," Krause said, "but I couldn't tell you that."

"I knew it," Jordan replied, as if he had at last been supplied with a "gotcha" moment.

"He was like, OK," Krause recalled of the moment. "It was very brief. Michael and I are never going to break bread. He remembers everyone who ever didn't think he was going to be great. He remembers every negative story that's ever been written about him."

He would certainly remember Jerry Krause, even after he had landed elsewhere.

Chapter 37

THE WIZARD

AT FIRST JORDAN seemed headed to Milwaukee to become part owner of the Bucks. But Bucks owner Herb Kohl backed out of the deal at the last moment. As it turned out, Jordan's new domain would be Washington, DC, where he connected with Ted Leonsis, the America Online magnate who had become a part owner of the Washington Wizards, once the infamous Washington Bullets. Jordan had looked in Charlotte, at the Hornets, but owner George Shinn was in the process of infuriating the fans in the basketball-crazy state, who deserted the franchise in droves. The Hornets would pack up and flee to New Orleans, leaving behind a city feeling thoroughly betrayed by the NBA experience.

Chicago Sun-Times columnist Jay Mariotti maintained that Phil Jackson, who coached the Lakers to the NBA title in 2000, wanted Jordan to join that team. The money was supposedly minimal, but it would have been an opportunity to be a part of a Lakers team that was poised to win more titles. Jordan supposedly declined, ostensibly because Washington was offering a piece of the team with the understanding that in time Jordan would become the majority owner.

Washington, as opposed to Los Angeles, was a city that had to be reminded that there even was an NBA experience. The Wizards/Bullets had established a well-crusted mediocrity that stretched back over two decades. The fact that Jordan connected with Abe

Pollin's team, with such a struggling franchise, came as a surprise to many. During the NBA lockout just months earlier, Jordan and the Washington owner had engaged in a bitter exchange witnessed by several players, among them Reggie Miller, who would later credit Jordan with helping the players turn the tide in the negotiations to get a better deal with the league's owners.

"In '98–99, we were having a meeting in New York and all the players were supposed to be there," Miller recalled. "Michael Jordan supposedly had just retired. When we all got there, there was Michael Jordan getting ready to face off with some of the owners and the commissioner and he almost got into a shouting argument with the late, great Abe Pollin. Michael Jordan was going at Commissioner Stern and Pollin, talking about if you keep writing these bad checks to these bad players, maybe you need to give up ownership of your team."

Pollin had complained about the difficulties of running a team.

"Then sell your team," Jordan brashly told Pollin.

"Neither you, Michael, nor anyone else, is going to tell me when to sell my team," Pollin shot back.

It seemed unlikely that the two would be able to work together. Jordan, however, was too valuable a connection for a team like Washington to turn down. It was easy to imagine His Airness bringing some luster back to the idea of professional basketball in the nation's capital. "The buzz was incredible," David Aldridge said of the announcement that Jordan would join the Wizards as a minority owner and basketball executive. "I remember like it was yesterday. The headline was above the fold, in the *Washington Post*. This was the newspaper that took down Richard Nixon. The headline above the fold was JORDAN COMING TO WASHINGTON. So it was big, huge."

By the fall of 1999, when Leonsis began making the move to pull Jordan into ownership/management with the Wizards, the hard feelings had seemingly melted. Pollin was ebullient in his public statements about the game's greatest player joining his team. The negotiated partnership between Pollin and Jordan was a merging of the old NBA with the new. Pollin, who owned a construction company, was in his early forties when he bought the old

Baltimore Bullets in 1964. One of Pollin's earliest employees was a portly young scout named Jerry Krause. They would remain friends and confidants for decades. Pollin would also grow close with a young lawyer working for the NBA named David Stern, who in 1984 would become the league's commissioner.

Pollin was mostly connected to the old-line NBA, especially Detroit Pistons owner Bill Davidson, Aldridge recalled. "I think he had a great affinity for the older owners in the league, who maybe had an appreciation for what it was like to meet a payroll back when you weren't sure how you were going to do it. And he certainly felt like a mentor for Stern. I know he had a good relationship with Jerry Krause and I know they talked a lot about a lot of different things."

That high regard for Krause, however, wasn't necessarily shared by the people who worked for Pollin, Aldridge recalled with a laugh during a 2012 interview. "There's a lot of people in the Bullets organization who think Jerry may have overstated his role in drafting Earl Monroe, that sort of thing. When you had asked people about Jerry in the Bullets organization, there would be some eye-rolling and, 'Oh, yeah, that's the guy that discovered Earl Monroe.'"

Krause, however, remained a big part of Pollin's "talk" network of owners and GMs around the league. Pollin and Krause were known to share opinions and a view of their respective teams in their discussions. It later became clear that the Washington owner had a certain view of Jordan long before he joined the Wizards franchise.

It appeared that the good news for both Pollin and Jordan was that they shared a similar trait: they were extremely loyal to old friends. Considering that in 2000 Pollin was entering his fifth decade owning the team, he had a lot of such friends, many of whom were on his Wizards payroll. Although his franchise had become one of the league's sorriest operations, the first decade of Pollin's ownership, in Baltimore, had culminated in Monroe's leading the team to the 1971 NBA championship series, where they were promptly swept by the Knicks. Even with that success, ticket sales remained dismal in Baltimore, which pushed Pollin to follow through on his original plan to move the team to Washington. In

1973, he built the Capital Centre in the Maryland suburbs as the home for the Bullets and the pro hockey team he founded, the Capitals.

The seventies would be the high-water mark for the Bullets. With K. C. Jones as coach, they dominated the 1975 regular season only to be swept in the league championship series by the Golden State Warriors, a huge upset. Pollin soon turned to old Krause nemesis Dick Motta as coach, and the Bullets returned to the championship series in 1978 with young center Wes Unseld and star Elvin Hayes. There, they won the franchise's only championship, beating the Seattle SuperSonics in seven games. For 1979, the two teams again returned to the NBA Finals, where Seattle claimed the championship, but the glory years would end there.

The owner had lost both an infant son and a teenage daughter to heart disease. That, perhaps, helps explain the close relationships he formed with Unseld, his center from the glory years, who would remain a Bullets fixture as a coach and executive, and Susan O'Malley, the daughter of a business partner and political ally, who became a longtime team executive in charge of marketing and public relations.

Among Pollin's values, Aldridge observed, was the answer to the question, "How do you treat the people you work with?" Pollin treated his people extremely well, although his loyalty over time had worked "to the detriment of the organization," Aldridge said. "I started covering the Bullets in 1988, and by 2008, if you went to a game, I'd say, maybe 60–70 percent of the employees were still there. You go, 'What's going on here?' You certainly aren't rewarding these people for success because the Bullets were a bad franchise. Maybe the Clippers were worse, but that's not saying much."

Another owner might have at least decided to change leadership to shake up the culture of the team. Not Pollin, Aldridge said. "You looked at it and asked, 'Why are you keeping all of these people?' Abe, he was an incredibly loyal guy. He wouldn't fire Wes Unseld, even though Wes's record, if you looked at it, was not sterling. I mean, you're talking about seven or eight years as the coach and then GM."

In the best season that Aldridge covered the team, they finished

40–42, he recalled with a laugh. "That was the zenith of my years covering the Bullets. It was horrible. They were as bad as you could be for a long time. Were there a lot of reasons for that? Sure. And many of those reasons were not anybody's fault, but the bottom line is the bottom line. The NBA is a results-oriented business, right? You knew that Abe was incredibly loyal. He was incredibly loyal to Susan O'Malley for a long time. He was incredibly loyal to Wes for a long time. Even the PR people never, never changed, until they left of their own volition. I don't remember him firing anybody. Abe was loyal. And he expected loyalty in return, but I think, more important than that, he expected a certain amount of respect."

Pollin had done much to earn respect in the Washington community. He gave substantial sums for relief for the city's indigent population. His building of the MCI Center in downtown Washington in 1997 brought a dramatic and sorely needed surge of financing to revive the nation's capital. Yet with basketball, he and his teams had largely been chumps. At least that was how they were seen around the NBA at the turn of the century. The owner believed Jordan's involvement would help alter that image.

There was no question that at thirty-seven, Jordan was an elder statesman of the game, but by the time he began his romance with the Wizards in 2000, he still lacked management experience. He had been a high-energy basketball player whose sole method of assessing player potential was through personal confrontation on the court. While he had unprecedented experience playing the game and leading his teams, he had never assembled any sort of roster or even done coaching at any level.

Even so, Abe Pollin was desperate to upgrade his team and generate some buzz, which put Jordan in a strong negotiating position. Pollin agreed to certain concessions, but it was Jordan's pushing for those concessions that apparently created the first hardening of feelings in the relationship even before it got off the ground. First was the issue of time. Jordan wanted only a part-time involvement, to allow room for his other business interests, including his obligations to shoot TV commercials. The schedule also cleared plenty of free time for his golfing and other interests. Contractually, he wanted an obligation of attending no more than about a half dozen games each season. He also wanted no heavy role in publicizing or marketing Wizards games. That proved difficult for the long-suffering team staff to swallow, especially given Jordan's magnetism.

"It was a worldwide story," David Aldridge explained. "I'm just talking about the impact of Jordan coming to Washington, in any capacity. As an executive, or as a player. It was just enormous. He would get standing ovations just when they would show a picture of him sitting in the owners' box, there would be standing ovations. And it was like, 'Wow!' And he was like cringing, he didn't want to do that, so he would go hide in his office, where they couldn't see him."

These conditions immediately chafed at the team's long-term staff, particularly Pollin's favorites. To aid in his executive duties, Jordan brought in old, trusted friends Rod Higgins, who had experience as a coach and executive with Golden State, and Fred Whitfield, who had worked for both Nike and David Falk. He also hired Curtis Polk, who had worked for years with Falk. The Wizards were loaded with bloated contracts for aging players, and Jordan's people set about the work of ridding the franchise of those destructive deals. It was a textbook approach to rebuilding a franchise, but any real accomplishments would soon be lost in the acrimony that was to follow.

Jordan also brought in his old friend Johnny Bach, now in his late seventies, to assist the coach he had yet to hire. He tried to lure John Paxson to Washington from Reinsdorf's staff in Chicago, but Paxson declined. He also tried to hire Mike Jarvis to coach. "Jarvis wanted too much money," Aldridge explained. Leonard Hamilton finally agreed to become his coach, and the die was cast. There were smiles aplenty at the beginning, but Jordan and Pollin were clearly eyeing each other. Jordan observers wondered how his demanding nature and the attendant anger would play in the nation's capital. As it turned out, there was conflict aplenty.

Jordan had spent years under the guidance of Phil Jackson, who had a knack for creating tension within an organization by nurturing an us-versus-them mentality between the team and management. Jackson had used that to great effect with the Bulls, until it became toxic, and he would do the same with the Lakers. The hard feelings in Chicago existed between Jackson and a substantial amount of the team's staff. During the 1994 playoffs in New York, Jackson won praise for lightening his team's mood by having them skip practice one day and load on a bus for a visit to the Staten Island Ferry. What wasn't known was that a block from the team's hotel, Jackson told the bus driver to stop and ordered the only woman on the bus, a veteran publicity assistant, to get off. The woman was humiliated by the move and soon left the team's employment. It was one of several moves that led some staff members to resent Jackson.

"Phil was very good at that," Krause offered. "He wasn't the only coach to create that us-versus-them atmosphere between the team and the staff. A lot of NBA coaches do that to some degree. But Phil was good at it."

Perhaps Jordan didn't intentionally set out to create such an atmosphere in Washington as the manager of basketball operations, but that was what he had known in Chicago. Soon enough Pollin and his staff felt a divide and took umbrage.

"He wrote the checks," David Aldridge said of the Washington owner. "You've got to have a certain amount of deference. People may think he's past his prime and he doesn't know what he's talking about, all those things, but he still owns the team. I tell you what happened, there was an atmosphere where, when Michael came in and he brought all of his people in—he brought Higgins and he brought Fred in and Curtis Polk and all those people— there was this sense of, 'Okay, step aside. The real movers and shakers are taking over now. You just stay over there and be quiet and we'll throw you a bone every once in a while.'

"I remember," Aldridge said, "that it didn't take very long before you started hearing things from people in the organization. You know, 'Hey, Abe wants to have lunch with Michael.' He hadn't had lunch with him in two months or four weeks or whatever it was. And so, you would hear these things and you would go, 'Wow! This is something he needs to keep an eye on.' I think Michael's people pushed the other people to the side."

Susan O'Malley had gone to work for the Bullets and moved up through the ranks to become a team vice president. She had always been aggressive in terms of marketing the Bullets and then the Wizards. But because the team wasn't good, she and the staff had settled into a pattern of marketing tickets not on the notion of seeing the Wizards play but by promoting the marquee players and teams that would come into town.

"That is what they did," Aldridge said of the Wizards' marketing staff. "They marketed the other team. 'Come see the other team play because our team is not very good.'...When Michael resisted that, it caused some angst."

Jordan took the old hard-line approach, similar to that of longtime Boston Celtics boss Red Auerbach, who believed that the strength of the team and how well it played should sell the tickets.

"Susan wanted to utilize Michael in ways that he did not like," Aldridge observed. "He said, 'I don't want to be a show pony. I don't want to come out and shake people's hands.' And that was a problem."

After so many years in the spotlight, Jordan had also arranged to have tougher public relations practices that restricted journalists' access to him. That, in turn, meant there would be no sense of intimacy with the media in Washington similar to the sway he once held with the media in Chicago.

He wanted to do less, not more, publicity and promotional work in his new capacity. His routine denials of O'Malley's requests for his time began to erode the relationship as well. All it took was a few TV shots of Jordan exiting an arena parking lot in his car with Illinois license plates to emphasize a dramatic shift in the Jordan approach. Known as a relentless worker during his playing days, Jordan was now an absentee figure.

Aldridge and his fellow sports journalists tried to figure it out. "You know, Tony Kornheiser and Michael Wilbon and I would have these debates all the time. Kornheiser said, 'He's got to be out front. He's got to be a man of the people and hang out.' I tended to agree with Wilbon, who used to say, 'They've got TV sets in Chicago. It doesn't matter where he is, as long as he's doing his work.'"

In sports, it only matters if you lose, and Leonard Hamilton's teams not only lost, they descended into open conflict, right on the bench. Hamilton would prove many times over that he was an excellent college coach, but even Johnny Bach couldn't protect him from clashing with pro players. The nadir came in the middle of a game one night when Hamilton called for arena security to remove one of his players, Tyrone Nesby, from the bench after they got into a heated disagreement.

"Michael had his opinions on what he wanted to put together," Johnny Bach recalled. "He never got really going because he had a college coach who had never coached in the pros. Things didn't work out well."

Looking for a way to get the thing headed in the right direction, it occurred to Jordan one day that spring that the best way to help the organization might be to play, to come back and teach these young players about respecting the game and playing hard. That was how he had lifted the Bulls up from their misery. By playing. Yes, he was younger then, but he reasoned that now he knew so much more. Yes, he had gotten fat as an executive, and his knees were in terrible shape. But he could begin working with old friend Tim Grover, who now had an exclusive training facility in Chicago, where Jordan himself was an investor. Grover would get him back in shape.

Johnny Bach thought it was a terrible idea and immediately began trying to talk him out of it. "For the good of the franchise, he was trying to please Abe and play," Bach recalled. "He knew we wouldn't win in a big way."

That was the thing that stunned David Aldridge. Jordan, who had always cared about winning, was going to put his reputation on the line, knowing full well that the team couldn't win, not in the way that the public would expect. But he was willing to do that anyway, to get the franchise turned around. It was like baseball all over again; he was headed into something that was doomed from the start.

"I wanted him not to play," Bach said. "I told him he had nothing to prove anymore in life. I saw the struggle he had with it. To try to play the type of game he'd always had. It didn't come as easily. Fatigue would set in in practice. He had to work on the bicycle to get the tone he wanted in his legs. He struggled to make sure he could play. I thought he was taking on more than he could do. I've watched guys come back to the game, I've watched fighters come back to the game. I had seen DiMaggio struggling in center field. I had seen Joe Louis hammered out of the ring. There are very few people like Rocky Marciano. He won them all and he walked away. That's what you have to do. I was hoping Michael would do the same thing. What more could he win? My whole hope was that he would perform well there in Washington. And he did. He averaged 22 points a game, and he filled the arena."

Pollin was delighted at the news that Jordan was considering a return. He would bring tens of millions in revenue to the team and, better yet, Jordan would have to sign away his minority ownership in the team, since NBA rules did not allow a player to hold ownership shares while competing.

The original plan, in Jordan's mind, was that when he was done playing he would take the minority shares back and complete a deal to buy majority ownership of the team. Jordan did not call Falk in to negotiate the deal. There could be no deal, no assurances. He would have to trust Abe Pollin to hold his shares, then return them to him when he was done as a player. Jordan, who was slow to trust after his experience in Chicago, agreed to trust Abe Pollin. He was the guy who never fired anyone, who kept all of his old associates around.

The Wizards completed another dismal season that year and later won the number one overall pick in the NBA draft lottery. Jerry Krause remembered flying home from the lottery, with Fred Whitfield and Rod Higgins on the same plane, some rows behind him. He was pretty sure they were laughing at him behind his back. "I remember thinking, 'They'll fuck it up,'" Krause recalled.

The league had not yet instituted rules that allowed players to be drafted only after they had played at least one year of college, so the field that year was filled with big teenagers. The Wizards took a six-eleven high school senior out of Georgia named Kwame Brown, who had been named the MVP of the McDonald's All-American Game. The Bulls had two high-number draft picks, and Krause picked hulking Eddy Curry and Tyson Chandler. Jerry West, selecting for the Memphis Grizzlies, took Spaniard Pau Gasol.

"He was the best player coming out of that high school class by far," Marques Johnson, the former UCLA great and basketball broadcaster, said of Kwame Brown. "I watched that game—17 points, 7 rebounds, 4 or 5 blocked shots in that McDonald's All-American Game."

"I knew all three of those kids, Eddy Curry and Chandler, too," recalled Sonny Vaccaro, who still spent considerable time evaluating high school stars. "Michael asked me about it, and I thought Kwame was the best one." At the very least, Jordan's staff figured that Brown would bring energy, rebounding, and athleticism to the Wizards' post game.

Jordan had also recruited Charles Barkley to begin training with him with the idea that they would return to the game together. Barkley agreed, which in retrospect probably should have been a sign for Jordan. There was no way that Barkley, an outstanding TV commentator who had gotten far fatter than Jordan after his playing career ended, could get back in good-enough shape to step on an NBA floor. The two of them evoked visions of Mick Jagger and Keith Richards attempting a comeback in short pants, smoking and joking in the layup line. But the Rolling Stones they were not.

While he was getting the old gang together, Jordan figured he'd include another golden oldie on the bill.

"All of sudden Doug was there," Bach said. "I didn't know he was coming."

Doug Collins had traveled a good road since getting fired from the Bulls. He had done an interesting but unsatisfying job coaching the Pistons, then returned to TV to resume his role as arguably the best NBA game analyst and color man in the business. Now, the man who could never say no to Jordan was coming to Washington just when Jordan needed someone to tell him no.

Jordan declined to announce that he was returning, although he threw himself into the task of training with Grover in Chicago that summer. Even Collins didn't know for sure what he was going to do. But the basketball public recognized the circumstances. There was Jordan, doing the drama queen thing one more time, a rumor about a return, a city dying for both relief and a new identity, and old guys with calculators rapidly figuring out how much they could make if he laced up those $200 sneakers one more time.

The atmosphere at Grover's facility, Hoops the Gym, took on an electricity that summer, although it was mostly low wattage, nothing like '94 or '95 when Jordan was bouncing between baseball and basketball. There were no satellite trucks this time, only *Sun-Times* columnist Jay Mariotti hanging outside the gym in what was mostly a one-reporter vigil. Jordan walked gingerly past him on aching knees each day. They exchanged something close to pleasantries, but Mariotti could never extract a confirmation.

Jordan reached into his old bag of tricks to ramp up the atmosphere in the gym, plenty of trash talk and the promise of embarrassment if you weren't ready to play hard. A number of friends and NBA stars joined in the games, ostensibly to help out, but they were also there to measure their games against his declining powers. Jordan was looking to confirm that he still had it, and what he saw and felt there gave him confidence.

One day Jordan, who had spent weeks hard at work getting back into shape, broke two ribs in a collision with Ron Artest. The injury set his conditioning back four weeks. Another man might have seen that as the sign to stop. Indeed, Barkley had already given up the fantasy. Jordan, however, was set to announce his return in September, only to delay it when the terrorist attack of 9/11 staggered the country. He waited respectfully for several days, then announced his return and the donation of his entire million-dollar salary for the season to the victims.

"Obviously, when I left the game, I left something on the floor," Jordan told reporters in announcing his comeback. "You guys may not be able to understand that. After we won the last title, I didn't sit down, ready to quit the game. I didn't want to go through the whole rebuilding process at that time. If Phil had stayed there and the team had stayed intact, I would have still been playing."

"I am returning as a player to the game I love," he had said in a prepared release. "I am especially excited about the Washington Wizards, and I'm convinced we have the foundation on which to build a playoff-contention team."

On the first day of October, he showed up for his press conference wearing black Air Jordan sweats, including a black hat with "JORDAN" stitched in red across the front. That same day the NBA released a $140 replica of his Wizards jersey for sale.

Former Georgetown coach John Thompson was among a list of basketball figures who were immediately skeptical. "I'm worried for Michael—I'm happy, but I will say I definitely did not want to see him come back. I think the expectations are going to be so unrealistic based on the standard that he set," he said. "Plus, all that stuff about him jumping from the foul line is over. His game is going to be on the floor now. We're going to start calling him Floor Jordan."

"If I fall, I fall," Jordan, a can of Gatorade placed strategically by his side for the cameras, told reporters. "You get up and move on. If I try to teach my kids anything, it's to have a vision and try....If I do it, it's great. If I don't, I can live with myself."

There was a generation of young, athletic players eager to take advantage of him in his advancing years, he admitted. "My head is on a block," he said. "The young dogs are going to chase me around. Well, I'm not going to bark too far away from them either. I'm not running from nobody. If anything, it'll be a great challenge." Mostly, he wanted to avoid the sense of regret that had invaded his life since being forced to desert his game in Chicago. "There's an itch that still needs to be scratched here," he said. "And I want to make sure it doesn't bother me the rest of my life."

The token salary raised eyebrows. It meant that Jordan was making a $30 million gift to a team he no longer owned. Ready to greet his comeback were yet more authors doing books, especially *Washington Post* reporter Michael Leahy, who was also writing about Jordan for the newspaper. Where Bob Greene had enjoyed Jordan's friendship and access while writing *Rebound*, his book about the baseball days and Jordan's return to Chicago, Leahy and Jordan were soon engaged in a contentious association.

Leahy pictured a Jordan too egotistical and adrenaline-addicted to take proper care of his knees and conditioning. The broken ribs had set Jordan's work back considerably. He limped through training camp, which he staged down in Wilmington, a nice treat for the old hometown. During exhibition season in late October, Leahy's running account of the comeback tracked Jordan up at Connecticut's Mohegan Sun casino the night before a game. Jordan, down $500,000 at the gambling tables, stayed till the sun came up and he had won his money back, plus about $600,000 more, all the while unaware that Leahy was providing a running play-by-play of the event for readers back in DC.

Jordan and his staff had filled the Wizards roster mostly with journeymen players. Shooting guard Richard "Rip" Hamilton was the bright young talent in a mostly bare stable. He and Jordan would eventually clash, while Doug Collins struggled with a growing sense that he was letting Jordan down.

Even so, Pollin's fancy new building, now called the Verizon Center, was packed every night with Washingtonians who had long ignored the Wizards. Now they came out in droves to see MJ try to turn it around.

Meanwhile, Leahy discovered the roster shell-shocked at what it meant to be Jordan's teammate. The initial thought was that Kwame Brown might turn out to be an athletic young frontcourt player just as Horace Grant had been for Chicago. Asked during exhibition season if he had indeed drafted "a Doberman" like the one Johnny Bach had coached back in Chicago, Jordan frowned.

"He's got a lot to learn," he said of Brown.

Brown was a lighthearted kid from a troubled family when he stepped into camp with Jordan. He had smallish hands for a post player and almost no clue of how to please his new boss. Looking back years later, Brown would recall being so green at the time that he didn't even know basic basketball terms, what it meant to set a pick or a screen. Jordan was there with a helping of his usual fire. Someone leaked to Leahy that Jordan had screamed at the new kid and called him a "faggot" in front of the team. It didn't play well in the *Post* that week, nor later in Leahy's book, *When Nothing Else Matters*.

Krause, meanwhile, was working the phones, digging for information from his sources on the Wizards staff. "Kwame was an outstanding prospect," Krause remembered. "I heard that Michael got on his ass so hard that he ruined that kid. His father was in jail. His mother was going to jail. He had all kinds of family problems. He was not the kind of kid you scream at. According to the people I knew on that club, Michael wrecked him."

Jordan's competitive approach was jarring to Pollin's longtime staff members, to say the least. In phone conversations, they commiserated with Krause, who had his own stories about dealing with Jordan. "The whole staff hated him," Krause recalled. "I knew a whole lot of that staff. They would tell me, 'Jerry, he's garbage.' Wes Unseld hated his guts. Unseld was a Pollin guy."

Brown would go on to play more than a dozen years in the league, a solid role player, never a star. "MJ didn't do all that like people think," Brown said in a 2011 interview, looking back on his tumultuous rookie camp. "It was really more the veterans and Doug's coaching," Brown said of his disappointing rookie season. "It wasn't really yelling. It was more trying to coach me. There was a lot of things I didn't know. I remember the terminology I didn't know coming out of high school, things they were trying to teach me, things like blind picks, things I just didn't know. If you draft a young guy out of high school you've gotta take time and understand that they don't know the NBA terminology. You've gotta have guys there to develop young players."

Jordan's staff plucked veteran guard Ty Lue as a free agent from the Lakers roster because he brought them speed and quickness at point guard. Lue developed an immediate rapport with Jordan, but they both knew Lue was going to have to slow things down a touch to accommodate an older star with bad knees.

"The pressure was on him because he wanted to win so much," recalled Lue. "He came back at the age of thirty-eight and put his legacy on the line and everything. I thought it was great. All you had to do with MJ was just play hard. If you played hard and gave it everything you had every night, he had no problem with you. Now if you came down, you lay down, and you weren't playing hard, then anybody would have a problem with you if you do that. If you step on the basketball court, you should give it everything you got and that's all he wanted."

Watching from afar were his former teammates. Now playing with the Portland Trailblazers, Pippen watched the games and box scores and talked on the phone regularly with Jordan. "I think he understands now since he's gotten away from it, what he had in Chicago is no longer there," Pippen confided one night early in the season. "It's no longer there and will never be there. He's not in that environment of good players and good coaches and teammates and people who understand him and understand how to play the game."

Jordan had little of that around him now, Pippen said. The time away had given them all time to think about what they had experienced in Chicago. Tex Winter had not only provided them with the all-important structure of the triangle offense, he had done unprecedented things, Pippen explained. "He is so attentive to the fundamentals and the details of the game. And he never wavers from that. Most NBA coaches, frankly, they get away from the fundamentals and the footwork and chest passes and shooting. They don't want to take time with it. Tex is the opposite of that. He always said basketball is a game of habits."

It was hilarious to see Winter and Jordan going at it on many days, Pippen recalled. "Very comical. You had Tex loving to share a lot of his knowledge and Michael giving him a lot of shit. He'd say, 'That ain't gonna work in today's game. Maybe in the forties and fifties, but not today's game.' But he knew. Tex and Michael really had a great relationship, though."

Jordan knew the value of Winter's approach, Pippen said. That's why the team's two stars had been so willing to work at Winter's fundamentals in practice each day. In fact, that determination to get better at the fundamentals would be their true legacy, Pippen predicted. "We accepted anything that would take us to the next level. We had a very positive mental attitude about what we had to do in practice, the fundamental things Tex wanted us to do, to make us better. We saw the things we could accomplish if we played hard, if we trained hard."

Beyond the fundamentals, it was Pippen's experience of going against Jordan in practice that made him a great player. "I think it came from adjusting to him," he said. "I learned how to pick my places when I could be in control and be dominant. Learning that helped me when I was on the court without Michael."

Likewise, the Bulls experience aided Jordan in coping with diminished athleticism as an older player, Pippen observed. "He can't get to the hoop the way that he did even three or four years ago. But no one can really say that he's lost a lot, because he can do so many other things. And the knowledge he has of the game is just so great. I don't think he'll have a problem scoring big points. He can still score. Winning will be the problem now."

Watching Jordan had invariably led Pippen to wonder what might have happened had the Bulls not been broken up. "I think we could have been pretty competitive if we had stayed together," he said. "We would have had something there with our knowledge and experience. We would have still been very competitive."

In fact, it seemed quite possible that the Chicago Bulls might have won at least one more, if not two or three championships, if they had all treated one another just a little better. As it was, the Bulls without Jordan were struggling mightily. Saying Charles Oakley was always one of his favorites, Krause had brought the forward back to the team. Pippen said Oakley was unhappy to be back with the Bulls. "I talked to him yesterday," Pippen said. "He told them, 'If you all didn't care about MJ and Scottie, I know you don't care about me.' "

As for the young Wizards, Pippen advised them to focus on learning from Jordan in practice. Steve Kerr agreed with that assessment. "It's not a question of how he's gonna play. You know Michael's gonna get his numbers. He may not be on *SportsCenter* as often with the windmill dunks. The big question is, can he handle the losing? Can that team turn the corner? That's gonna drive him nuts. He's gotta teach them how to play, but I don't know if he's gonna be able to teach them. I think his competitive drive is gonna take over, and it has taken over. People don't realize how difficult it is to play alongside Michael. You have to do all of your learning in practice because, in game situations, that's where he tends to take over. And he wants them to play at his level.

"It's very tough," Kerr added. "It's a matter of Michael and them getting to know one another, getting an understanding. It's difficult for them to have an understanding of what's a good shot. Do I defer to him? Do I just go on and play? It's very difficult for them to know."

Indeed, Jordan would have problems with several of the players the Wizards were paying to play basketball. "You know," Ty Lue said, "guys wasn't playing hard every night. And you know when you got a guy like that who's been competitive his whole life, a guy who will come back and play at the age of thirty-eight and come in here every morning early working on his game, last one to leave each day, playing through knee pain and knee injuries, you got a problem if you don't play hard for a guy like that.

"He was playing through his knees," Lue explained. "His knees were messed up. He wasn't used to the back-to-back games and had been off for a while. It was definitely tough on him. He never missed a practice, never missed games, he played through injury. I think that's what hurt him the most. Like I'm out here giving you everything I have and some guys are not playing as hard as they could be."

The one thing that surprised them all was Jordan's patience.

Brent Barry, a guard with San Antonio at the time, had long studied Jordan. He was intrigued by the differences he saw in this third and final segment of his career. Still hard-nosed, Jordan had made himself into a teacher, Barry recalled. "The difference was just methodical. Just much more patient with possessions where he could basically dictate to the defense what it is that he wanted them to do in order for him to make plays. The plays that he was making at that time were not plays for him to score. It was plays to set up guys. It was plays to show some of the younger players in Washington, 'Hey you can do this and when you have the ball, you can impact what's going on in a certain possession by moving it, by moving yourself.'

"He did so much more coaching later on in his career while he was on the floor to help out Doug and to help the young guys," Barry explained. "His game just became more of a practice every night for those guys to watch, how effective you can be if you learn to do things fundamentally."

Slowly at first, then with gathering speed, things began to improve for the Wizards. Then, right before New Year's, Jordan abruptly showed the first indication of a dramatic turnaround. He hit the wall and scored a career-low 6 points in a loss to the Indiana Pacers. The total ended his record 866-game streak of games scoring 10 points or more. He answered immediately in the next game, against the Charlotte Hornets in Washington, by scoring 24 in the fourth quarter and finishing with 51, just six weeks before his thirty-ninth birthday.

"He kind of went back in time tonight," Charlotte forward P. J. Brown told reporters afterward.

He had made 21 of 38 shots from the field, and 9 of 10 free throws, with 7 rebounds and 4 assists in thirty-eight minutes of playing time. He could have broken Earl Monroe's Wizards franchise record of 56, but the game was a blowout and Collins sat him for the final three minutes.

"You think the guy's got a little pride?" Collins said. "He had a tough night in Indiana, and I think he was going to come back and show who he is.... I've seen this guy do some unbelievable things, but at age thirty-eight to do this tonight is incredible."

He had made fadeaway after fadeaway and even a dunk. "It's been a long time since someone said that I was hanging in the air," Jordan said. "I felt real good in the first half. My rhythm, my timing was perfect, and I had the defense guessing. It was one of those nights."

The last time he had scored 50 in a game was in the spring of 1997, when he rang up 55 in the playoffs against Washington.

The next game, he just missed turning in another big performance. "It was just incredible," David Aldridge recalled. "He almost got 50, back-to-back nights. I saw both of those games. And he was pissed after the second game. It was so funny."

New Jersey forward Kenyon Martin came into the second game telling the press that he wanted to cover Jordan. "I remember Kenyon Martin saying, 'I want him. I want to guard him,'" Aldridge recalled. "And Michael schooled him. You know, he had nothing. He's doing this on guile and smarts and just knowing the game. He's got no physical ability left...and he's got no hope, and he almost scores fifty! It was unbelievable."

Aldridge recalled that on press row he leaned over to Jay Mariotti and said, "Are you watching the same game I'm watching? Do you know how incredible this is, that this guy is doing this here?"

Jordan began to build the confidence among his teammates, to the point that he had them believing they could make shots many of them had never made before. Beginning in December and running through the All-Star Game, the Wizards rang up a 21–9 record. That would be the high mark for Michael Jordan's Wizards, however. His knees became a factor, and the team really didn't have the players to sustain the momentum. Resentment had been brewing since training camp with some players, partly over Jordan's imperial bearing, and partly over the fact that he was an owner, not on paper but in reality, who had handpicked his old coach to run the team. Beyond that, there was a growing yet largely unarticulated conflict with Rip Hamilton, the team's best young scorer.

That January, in the midst of it all, Juanita Jordan filed for divorce in Chicago, and soon a reporter from the *Sun-Times* showed up in the Wizards' locker room to question Jordan about the split. Interview sessions with Jordan, dating back to Chicago, had always focused on basketball issues. Now, it was incongruous, painful for some, to witness the confrontation, which came after a win over the Los Angeles Clippers. The reporter asked if his divorce was inevitable. "None of your business," Jordan shot back. A Washington publication offered a detailed account of his attempts that same night after the game to make a play for a woman in a Washington nightspot, with help from members of his entourage, including Tim Grover.

He was named an All-Star that February, but his appearance is mostly remembered for a missed dunk. On April 2, he scored his career low, 2 points, in a 113–93 loss to the Lakers. Two days later, the team announced he would miss the rest of the season due to knee troubles. The Wizards finished out of the playoff race, with a losing record.

"The first year was tough," Johnny Bach recalled. "The second year was tougher. It was much harder to keep that tone and maintain those minutes on the floor. And still teams were playing with that kind of dedication in trying to stop Michael. The game is a physical one. I think he had done far more than anyone else. Because he had been so good before, his scoring 22 points a game wasn't satisfactory to him or to the public."

The Wizards traded Rip Hamilton to Detroit for Jerry Stackhouse in the off-season, and Jordan made ready to compete again in the fall of 2002. "That last season was just...wow! I mean, it was bad as you can imagine," David Aldridge recalled. "And I think, again, it reinforced among some people the notion he's been a terrible executive. And he did pick the roster."

The plan for the second year was for Jordan to play reduced minutes while serving as the sixth man for the team. "All during that preseason he said the same thing over and over," Aldridge recalled. "He was going to be the sixth man. He was going to let Stackhouse be the guy. And he would come in and clean up with the second-team guys, and I remember thinking, 'That makes a lot of sense!' In fact, I picked him to be the sixth man of the year, just based on that. Because, I thought, a reduced Michael Jordan, going up against bench guys, is going to score 16 to 17 a game. It made all the sense in the world. And then, like, two weeks into the season, it ended. I don't know if it was his ego or if he just didn't think Stackhouse was good enough. He just put himself back in the starting lineup."

The move brought complaints that Doug Collins once again couldn't stand up to the team owner wearing the uniform. "I defended Doug," Aldridge said, "in print and on TV, saying the very thing, 'You put your coach in an impossible position by just deciding you're going to start again.' I never will understand why he did that, because it made so much sense for him to come off the bench. It really made a lot of sense. It would have reduced his minutes, reduced the wear on his knees, if he's playing twenty-four minutes a game instead of thirty-seven. I think it would have worked. But he just could not sit there and watch."

Jordan's conflict with the recently traded Hamilton came to the fore when the Wizards met Detroit that next season. "When he traded him to Detroit, Rip was kind of mad about that," Ty Lue recalled. "We're playing Detroit in a game, and Rip is going extra hard. He's talking trash at MJ, and MJ'd be like, 'It wasn't personal, Rip. I'm just trying to play.' Rip was still talking stuff, so MJ said, 'Listen, Rip, how are you going to talk trash to me when you're wearing my shoes? Like you have Jordan Brands on your feet. So how are you going to talk trash?' We all laughed at that. It was just business. I think he liked Rip. I thought he just tried to get a more aggressive scorer in Jerry Stackhouse, a guy who could put it on the floor, who could create his own shot, draw a double-team, and just put the team in the best position to win. That's what I thought he was trying to do. Wasn't anything personal."

For his former teammates and coaches, a bigger event was his first game against Pippen, early that December. "It will be hotly contested, believe me," Tex Winter offered. Although each scored 14, the game wasn't close. Pippen's Trailblazers won 98–79. "I know Pip, and I know he wanted to come out and play well," Jordan told reporters. "Believe me, I wanted to come out and play well too. His horses were ready, and my mules were sick. I have to take some razzing for the time being."

Jordan continued to struggle with his knees, with the physical challenges of the game. On December 15, he once again scored just 2 points in a game. However, he rounded back into form, and that February returned to the All-Star Game, where he was a surprise starter. He scored 20 to eclipse Kareem Abdul-Jabbar as the leading scorer in All-Star Game history. But it was a torturous evening in many ways. He missed his first 7 shots, had 4 shots blocked, and missed a dunk. He scored a late bucket to give the Eastern Conference a lead, only to have the game tied by Kobe Bryant. In two overtime periods, Jordan missed 3 shots, and the East fell, 155–145.

The season became the kind of farewell tour that Jordan had once vowed he would never do. When the Wizards visited Los Angeles for his final game against the Lakers, Kobe Bryant offered a parting gift. "Kobe just wound up destroying him in the first quarter, like 40 points in the first half of that game," J. A. Adande recalled. "That was like the true end and the passing of the torch. I mean it had to be humbling for him. I mean there was nothing he could do about it."

The previous season, when Bryant had run through a streak of 40-point games, Jordan had remarked that he and Bryant seemed to share a trait: they both had sought to distance themselves from their contemporaries. For Jordan, that had largely been to achieve more than the immensely talented Clyde Drexler. Clearly, however, Jordan remained Bryant's top mark.

As the Wizards came down the stretch that season, Jordan's

relationships with several of his teammates deteriorated. In Chicago, Phil Jackson had developed strategies, like the mindfulness sessions with George Mumford, to help Jordan relate to less-talented teammates. Heavy on group dynamics, Jackson's entire approach was aimed at playing to the strengths of each player while moderating their weaknesses. In Washington, there was no Phil Jackson, no George Mumford, no offense from Tex Winter, and, almost just as important, no Pippen. Jordan didn't have any of the outlets of the past, and he seemed to have very little trust in the key players around him. "Whatever trust he once had, he no longer had," said an associate. "That was a very lonely place to be."

It was about to get worse. About three weeks before the season ended, Jerry Krause learned of the trouble that was coming. "I called Abe Pollin," he recalled in 2012. "He told me, 'I'm gonna fuck that friend of yours. He thinks he's fucking me. You watch. He doesn't know.' Abe was a tough son of a bitch himself."

Shortly after that, basketball writer Mike Wise of the *New York Times* got a phone call from a source, who told him the shocking news that Pollin was going to cut Jordan loose at the end of the season. Wise began doing interviews and soon learned that Jordan had few friends among the staff and players beyond his own hand-picked managers, that he had overplayed his hand with Pollin.

"I knew there were problems," David Aldridge recalled. "That's why I thought one of the first things Michael was going to do was go to Abe and say, 'Look, we may have messed up here. Here's what we're going to do. You're the owner. We understand that. We're not going to do anything you don't want to do. I apologize if my people were rude to your people, if they were condescending to your people. It won't happen again.' He never had a chance to have that meeting."

The *New York Times* ran Wise's story about Jordan's troubles, forecasting that Pollin was going to dump him. Ty Lue remembered being surprised at the tone of it. "How could he be trashed like that?" Lue said. "You have a guy who comes back at the age of forty, still averages 20 points a game, still shoots a high percentage from the field. I mean, I thought he was great. But, it wasn't going to be the same old Michael there, which we knew, but his will to win, his passion for the game, it was all the same."

Brent Barry recalled reading the story and being outraged by the attitudes of some of the players expressed there. "You know what, though?" Barry said. "That's not his cross to bear. When a player like that takes the time to talk, teach, express what it is that you need to do in order to achieve your maximum potential, it's up to them to do it. Because let's face it, that is your job. Now if Michael had never taken the time to do that, that would have been another story."

"I thought they could work together," Aldridge said of Jordan and Pollin, "that they'd figure a way to work together, at some point, but not after that. Obviously, there were a lot of people that were airing their grievances when that *Times* story came out. That was kind of like the shot across the bow that this is way more serious than you guys know."

The story seemed so far-fetched that neither Jordan nor David Falk seemed to believe it could be true — a grave miscalculation. "I think he could have survived all of that if he had shown more deference to Abe Pollin," Aldridge said of Jordan. "I think that was the beginning of the end, the lack of deference. This was a *New York Times* story. It was clear, once that story came out, that this was the way it was going to go, because you don't put something out in the *New York Times* unless you plan on doing something, right? So, even though I could not get it independently confirmed, it was obvious that it was placed there by someone who had an agenda. I think whoever was responsible for getting that story to the paper was very smart, because I think most of the local media were viewed as sympathetic to Michael and weren't going to be willing to carry that line of attack."

A veteran basketball writer, Wise had never been enamored of the version of Jordan he saw in Washington. He was struck by how lost in his own world Jordan seemed, like an Elvis figure, someone who had lost touch with reality. Jordan and his associates were the picture of arrogance in Washington, Wise said, looking back in 2012.

Johnny Bach had a different view. Yes, Jordan may have been detached, withdrawn at times while trying to play, but Bach saw Jordan as being eager to please Pollin, willing to put his reputation aside to help the team even though he knew it had no chance to win. For the second year in a row, the team finished 37–45 and out of the playoffs. Jordan's last night in a Washington uniform had provided a sweet scene, with emotional Wizards fans showering him with warmth and love. The season—indeed, the entire experience—had been a tremendous disappointment to Jordan, but he smiled broadly and genuinely seemed to enjoy the fans' attention that final evening.

Despite the *Times* story, Jordan walked into his meeting with Pollin after the season fully expecting to be rewarded for all he had done. After all, the franchise had been in miserable financial shape when he got there. Jordan and his people had rid the team of several disastrous player contracts and cleared up the financial situation, allowing the team to acquire younger players. He had played two years for a minimal salary, which he had given to charity. All the while, the team had enjoyed sellout after sellout every night he played, an unprecedented attendance record that helped the franchise erase its losses and rake in an estimated $30 to $40 million in profits.

Pollin's message was short and harsh that day. He presented Jordan with a severance payment, reportedly worth several million by various estimates. Jordan apparently left the money on the table and exited the meeting swiftly.

Abe Pollin, the man who never fired anybody, had fired Michael Jordan. Many in pro basketball were stunned at the turn of events. Jordan was viewed by many as a national treasure, as the game's most important figure, the man who had brought billions in profits to the NBA.

"That was savage," said Pat Williams, who had been an NBA executive for four decades and knew both men. "You suddenly had these two camps that were absolutely split. It was an organization heading in two different directions. It rocked Michael."

"That ended up very badly," recalled Johnny Bach. "Suddenly he was out. All of his guys, we were all out of a job. I don't understand it either, whatever was said between people. Michael is the kind of person, he lives up to his word. And if you give him your word, you better live up to it. They had agreed. There were things you couldn't put in writing."

Even the players on the roster were taken aback.

"That is hard to take," Ty Lue offered. "I mean when a guy comes back and plays and makes up all the money you lost in the last five years in two years of playing...he makes it up in two years and then you repay him like that? It was a sad day."

Even Washington, the city of dirty tricks, seemed staggered by the turn of events. "Now," Aldridge explained, "there's a great debate in Washington over this: Did Abe willingly use Michael until he could no longer use him and just cast him aside? I think a lot of people believed that, you know. I think a lot of people believed that. It was no secret what Michael expected to happen. It wasn't like it was a surprise. He thinks he's going to go back to being an executive. He was pretty open about that the whole time he was playing. I mean, it wasn't like he just sprung it on somebody, like three weeks before he decided to retire."

Aldridge said he leaned toward believing that Pollin never planned to live up to his agreement to bring Jordan back.

"I tend to agree," he said, "that Abe was never going to sell the team to Michael, was never going to give Michael more than 50 percent of the team. I never believed that."

Jordan had a final night on the town after being fired that day, an event much documented in Internet accounts that portrayed him as something of a lost soul.

"He went away," David Aldridge recalled. "He went away....I didn't see him for a very long time after that."

Chapter 38

CAROLINA

THE CHARLOTTE BOBCATS certainly didn't feel like a step forward, at least not for a long time. But Jordan resurfaced there in 2004. Robert Johnson, the publishing magnate, had been granted the expansion franchise to replace the Hornets, who had left town for New Orleans in one of the league's most bitter chapters. The Hornets had been one of the league's leading small-market teams, with the brand-new Charlotte Coliseum in 1989 soon packed to the rafters each night with adoring fans cheering stars like Alonzo Mourning, Larry Johnson, and Muggsy Bogues. But within a decade owner George Shinn was agitating for yet another new arena with skyboxes that could increase revenues and make the team more competitive. The scene had gotten progressively uglier during the protracted fight over funding for an arena. At one point, Shinn was charged with sexual assault, a public relations nightmare that seemed to be the last gasp for the Hornets. Fans turned away, so Shinn packed up the team and abandoned the city, now left with nothing but distaste for pro basketball.

In the wake of all that, the Bobcats expansion franchise had opened for business in a beautiful new downtown arena for the 2004–5 season, but fans responded tepidly. As the first African American to assume majority ownership of a major sports franchise, Johnson had great interest in striking a deal with Jordan to come in as a minority owner in charge of basketball operations.

Jordan had patched his marriage back together, but this job would require him to spend more time on site. The new post would prove to be far from ideal for restarting a family life.

Billiards

Daniel Mock was working as a bartender in late 2004 at the Men's Club of Charlotte, an upscale topless bar on the south side of the city. As a child, Mock had worshiped Jordan, with posters on his wall and every jersey possible in his collection. He had even gotten Jordan's autograph at a celebrity golf tournament, and had treasured the memory of following his hero around the course. So he was stunned one night a decade later to see Jordan, Robert Johnson, Charles Oakley, and Dallas Mavericks owner Mark Cuban come into the Men's Club to be seated in the small, private bar area where he worked. It was a large club spread across two floors, with four bars, three stages, and sixty topless dancers going nonstop every night.

"They came in the Men's Club, and I was in awe of it," Mock recalled with a laugh. "I freaked out, and all the waitresses were making fun of me. When they first came in, they sat down, and I got their order, and I had a bunch of girls dancing for them."

Two tables were pulled together so the men could eat dinner among the company of the dancers, who came in shifts to perform privately and sit at the table with Cuban, Jordan, and Johnson. Oakley went over and sat at the small bar that Mock supervised a few feet away. They soon struck up a conversation in which Mock informed him that Jordan was "just the idol of my lifetime."

"Really," Oakley said. "I'll get him over here."

Mock panicked, as if he were about to be introduced to the prettiest girl in school.

"No, don't do that," he said.

Between songs, each of the topless dancers would go sit on the men's laps. The club had a line of dancers rotating in and out at Jordan's table six at a time. They would dance for five minutes or so, then sit with the men.

Finally, Mock went over to speak to Jordan. "I said, 'Mr. Jordan, how is everything tonight?' They were smoking huge cigars. 'I just want you to know I got your autograph when I was eleven in Lake Tahoe. You were the idol of my youth.'"

"You still got that autograph, kid?" Jordan asked.

Mock explained that he had it locked away for safekeeping.

"Well, you better hold on to it," Jordan said with a laugh.

The group had champagne and dinner. It was the kind of place where they could pick their lobsters out of a tank and watch their steaks being prepared. After they ate—their tab was well over $1,000 by then—Jordan got up to play pool at a nearby table with three of the dancers. He walked by just as Oakley was explaining to Mock that they were playing golf early the next morning at Firethorne Country Club. Mock, an avid golfer, had worked at the club.

"Jordan said, 'Yeah, Firethorne's tough,'" Mock recalled. "I told him I used to work there."

"Really?" Jordan said, suddenly stopping and looking at Mock. "Tell me about it."

The bartender then launched into an extended description of the lay of the course, and offered advice on which clubs to use on which holes, where to use a 3-wood, where not to. "He sat there like five minutes, just staring at me, like he was recording everything," Mock said. "Then he played pool. He played doubles, him and this little Chinese chick against these two tall blondes, Pamela Anderson types. They're playing topless. He's got a huge cigar in his hand, and he played one-handed. And every time he'd go to hit, he'd be standing there with this huge cigar in his mouth. He'd have one hand behind his back, kind of resting the cue on the table. And every time he'd go to hit, one of the girls would get down on the table and hang her tits on the table.

"I was sitting there with Oakley," Mock recalled with a laugh, "and he'd go, 'Oh, just another night for Mike.' That's how it was all night."

Johnson left early, but Cuban, Jordan, and Oakley stayed until well past the two a.m. closing time. Mock was astounded to learn that they had a five o'clock tee time.

Mock got up the next morning to phone a pro at the club, one of his old friends, who informed him that the staff had wanted Jordan to tee off at six thirty in the morning. "He said that was too late," the bartender recalled. "He got them to let him go off at 5:45 in the morning, right as the sun was coming up. I told him, 'They were up till three.' He said, 'Come on, two hours' sleep?'"

The pro asked him how he knew they were up so late. Mock told him they had been at the Men's Club. "He said, 'No way,'" Mock remembered with a laugh. "He said, 'We've got a bunch of members who wanted to go out behind them. So Jordan bought out four tee times, so they wouldn't have anybody around them.' So they bought out four tee times after being at the club till the wee hours and spending God knows how much. I think the girl said the bill was about eighteen hundred. I'm pretty sure Cuban paid for the whole thing."

The pro reported that Jordan, Oakley, and Cuban whisked around the course and were done by nine thirty. The appetite, it seemed, still raged on.

From there, Jordan settled in as an executive for the Bobcats, a period punctuated by his continued travels about the globe, golfing and gambling and partying. It seemed no great surprise that he soon faced divorce once again, after seventeen years of marriage to Juanita. The divorce was finalized in December 2006 and estimated by *Forbes* to have cost Jordan $150 million, said to be one of the largest settlements in history.

In a few short years, his once seemingly untouchable image had taken a huge hit, with the madding crowd routinely having a field day on the Internet, taking him to task for his missteps. More miscalculations followed, with Charlotte's drafting of Adam Morrison as the third overall pick in 2006. Morrison would prove to be a huge disappointment and another blow to the Jordan mystique. As the criticism mounted, some Jordan observers wondered why he had never once spoken with Krause about the substantial challenge of being an NBA personnel executive. Others knew that Jordan would never have taken that route. He was viewed as being walled off by his fame, limited in discussing matters beyond his tight inner circle.

Quietly, however, Jordan had done the next best thing, or perhaps even better than speaking with Krause. Jim Stack had moved on from the Bulls to become an executive with the Minnesota Timberwolves. He and Jordan talked frequently about player issues.

"We had a lot of dialogue between 2004 and 2008," Stack recalled, adding that like any other executive Jordan routinely sought opinions from a variety of figures in and around the game.

They had talked extensively about the drafting of Adam Morrison, Stack said. "Adam was a very gifted offensive player. He later proved to have limitations with his diabetes. He was kind of a frail kid to begin with, then the NBA schedule took a toll on him. I had talked with MJ about it. We spoke candidly. At that point in the draft, there wasn't a clear-cut guy to take. It was just a bad draft."

Being an executive requires both great effort and good fortune, Stack explained. "You do all that work and get in position, hope to have a little luck, and the right player is available to you." Still the job seemed to take Jordan out of his game, throwing off his timing somehow. People who saw Jordan scouting players at NBA draft camps were struck by what seemed to be his damaged confidence. Although as congenial as ever, Jordan seemed unsure of himself in the wake of his difficult experiences. His weary countenance reminded acquaintances of just how much Jordan had been through since the end of his glory days. In fact, sometimes his body language seemed as out of place as it had in the foreign world of baseball over a decade earlier.

Bryant

During the NBA's predraft camp in 2008, he sat alone, high in the end zone seats of the Disney sports complex in Orlando, watching the college hopefuls and free agents run through drills and games on the floor below. He seemed distracted enough that when a reporter asked for an interview, Jordan agreed, as if glad to be relieved from watching lesser players seemingly running in sand. The interviewer's questions eventually got around to Kobe Bryant.

Phil Jackson had won three championships earlier in the decade in Los Angeles, and that spring the Lakers had again come alive, led by Kobe Bryant. Jordan had watched with interest as Bryant filled his old role in the triangle offense, working for Jackson and Winter. The Lakers guard had spent years trying to Be Like Mike, from his shaved head as a teen to the aped Jordan mannerisms, although Bryant went out of his way to deny that he was a copycat. He was, it seemed, the best of a generation of Jordan wannabes, of the legion of players who sought to inherit the mantle. Bryant was the one, perhaps, who actually could.

Jordan himself had long been an interested observer of Bryant's pageant, as had Jackson and his staff. Comparisons of the two players routinely generated heated debates on the Internet. Frankly, Jordan didn't see what all the fuss was about. After all, human behavior is mimetic. Humans copied and aped one another, like every rock band that for decades had sought to be the Beatles or the Rolling Stones, who themselves had derived so much from the great American bluesmen of previous generations.

Obviously his play had created a path for Bryant, Jordan observed that day. "But how many people lighted the path for me? That's the evolution of basketball. There's no way I could have played the way I played if I didn't watch David Thompson and guys prior to me. There's no way Kobe could have played the way he's played without watching me play. So, you know, that's the evolution of basketball. You cannot change that."

In conversation, it quickly became obvious that Jordan respected Bryant, without any hint of condescension. He respected any player who did the work, who had the mental toughness. Bryant passed both those tests, he said. "So he's not one that's so different than me, but he is different than me. People just have to understand that, and realize that you may see a lot of similarities, but he's definitely different."

Even if you set aside Bryant's obvious debt to Jordan, what made the comparison so interesting for Jordan was the fact that Bryant played in the same triangle offense that he did, with the same coaching architects, Jackson and Winter. It was a system that created room for a superstar to operate, Jordan said. "The triangle's a great offense to get people to get spacing, to get in the right position. But, then you've got talented people like Kobe who can play it and involve everybody and make everybody that much better."

Winter had begun developing his system years before, based on six principles of team play. But when he started coaching Jordan in 1985 he realized that you needed a seventh principle—that an extremely talented player can trump all other principles.

You have to adjust everything for a great player, Winter had long conceded.

"Tex is absolutely right," Jordan said that day, smiling, remembering his many moments in Bulls practice with Winter fussing about one issue or another. "And Kobe's going through the same process."

That fans resented Bryant's own journey through the system was silly, Jordan observed. "Kobe does everything, when you talk about greatness or success. Success is very similar, no matter what. It's nothing you're going to say of anyone previous of you because you've got to have similar characteristics to achieve it."

It wasn't so much about copying a style as it was about pursuing a proven formula for success, Jordan said. "And success is in store for him. He's done the work to do that, to achieve that."

Jordan indicated that he had been able to relive some of his own career by watching Bryant. The two had shared phone conversations about things that only they could understand. Told during the 2008 championship series that Jordan had said flattering things about him, Bryant's ears perked up immediately, almost like a kid hungry for an autograph. "MJ was talking about me?" he asked. "That's my man." It was obvious that Bryant drew support and confidence from the relationship.

A few years earlier, the Lakers' coaching staff had concluded that Bryant and Jordan were much alike, almost eerily so, when it came to the alpha male qualities of their competitive natures. The two were ruthless when it came to winning, everyone agreed. And their skills were similar, although Jordan's hands were larger. The major difference between the two came with college experience. Jordan had played in a basketball system at North Carolina, thus he was better prepared to accept Winter's triangle, the team concept. Bryant had come into the league directly from high school with stars in his eyes.

"I tend to think how very much they're alike," Winter observed. "They both display tremendous reaction, quickness and jumping ability. Both have a good shooting touch. Some people say Kobe is a better shooter, but Michael really developed as a shooter as he went along. I don't know if Kobe is a better shooter than Michael was at his best." Jackson too acknowledged the similarities but allowed that there was only one Jordan.

Observers liked to point out that Jordan played on a Bulls team with no great center, but Winter always countered that Jordan was a great post-up player and, indeed, was the premier post weapon of his time. Bryant himself came into the NBA with great post skills, but there was never room for him to play in the post with Shaquille O'Neal occupying the lane during their years together with the Lakers.

Winter doubted that Jordan would have been a good fit playing with O'Neal.

In a lot of ways, Bryant was Jordan's equal as a post player, Winter said, except for one critical element. Jordan was much stronger, the coach said. "Michael had a knack for holding his ground a little better than Kobe."

Like Jordan, Bryant found much of his success playing small forward, instead of guard, which allowed him to work "behind the defense," as Winter had often explained it. Even with all of Bryant's offensive success, Winter said that the Lakers needed to keep the ball moving, that Bryant's teammates still deferred to him too much, just as they did with Jordan.

Another difference, according to Winter, was their leadership style. Jordan admitted to harsh, sometimes cruel, treatment of his teammates to get them ready to perform under pressure, whereas Bryant took a kinder, gentler approach.

Then there was the incomparable Pippen. You could not overestimate the contribution of Pippen, Winter often said.

Springfield and Beyond

Jordan met supermodel Yvette Prieto during this period, and his life began to change. The Bobcats struggled mightily, were supposedly losing tens of millions a season, while Internet sites such as

TMZ became a Greek chorus for His Airness. It seemed that controversy and criticism lurked behind each moment. He was voted into the Hall of Fame in 2009, the first year he was eligible, and that would become his next cross to bear.

George Mumford once remarked that you had to see what people did, not what they said, to evaluate them. As the induction neared that August, it was Johnny Bach whom Jordan chose to accompany him, not Phil Jackson. The longtime assistant coach, now in his eighties, had fallen on hard times with a divorce settlement that took away his NBA pension. Jordan paid to have his old "attack" coach at the event in high style. He also asked two Bulls employees from his first days with the team—ticket manager Joe O'Neil and PR man Tim Hallam—to fly with Jordan, Prieto, and a small group that included George Koehler on his jet to the event in Springfield, Massachusetts.

"It was quite a thrill, to be honest with you," O'Neil said of the experience. "I started with the Bulls many years ago. Michael must have been a freshman or sophomore in high school when I started here. Timmy Hallam and I were a couple of the first people Michael met in Chicago. It was a very different time then. He wasn't the mega superstar. Now, I don't know who is the most recognizable person on the planet, but he's got to be right up there. To sit on that plane with Michael and his girlfriend going to the Hall of Fame, I can't tell you what it meant. We sat and just laughed and told stories about the early years, sneaking out to play golf, doing this and doing that. Michael didn't forget people. He brought Johnny Bach out for the Hall of Fame. I think that Michael's closest friends in a lot of ways are not celebrities. He's got buddies that he hangs around with and golfs with and hangs out with. Of course he's got a million celebrity friends. But the people he hangs around with day in and day out are just regular guys and I think he enjoys that."

They spent the flight talking about his first year in the league, the Bulls' crazy roster, their trash can golf matches in the office, about waiting for lines of children coming and going before the Bulls could get on the practice floor at Angel Guardian Gym. They laughed and reminisced, and O'Neil noticed that the closer they got to Springfield, the more nervous Jordan seemed to become.

"As much of the limelight and glamour as Michael has had, I think that sometimes when the spotlight is on him, a shyness comes out," O'Neil observed in a 2012 interview. "I think he was a little bit uncomfortable with the whole thing because it was such a big thing with Michael Jordan going into the Hall of Fame. I think in some ways he looked forward to it just as in some ways he looked forward to it being over, too. George was on the plane with us. Even to this day, George and I will say, 'Can you believe where we are and where we came from?'"

As for his speech, O'Neil noticed that Jordan didn't have anything prepared. "He didn't really have it written that much," his old friend recalled. "He wasn't really sure what he was going to say. He was nervous going out there."

Jordan had asked his former idol, David Thompson, to present him and stand there with him in his moment before the assembled basketball elite, who had shelled out big dollars to be there for basketball's crowning moment, to see Michael in the ultimate spotlight. It was then, in the emotion of the moment, that Jordan chose to unburden himself and reveal his competitive heart, to address all the things, real or imagined, that had driven him over the course of his life. Even for longtime Jordan observers, who felt they knew him well, it was surprising, and even disappointing. To much of the public, it was nothing short of shocking as he revisited his anger over being denied a place on the varsity as a high school sophomore, over Dean Smith keeping him off the cover of *Sports Illustrated* as a college freshman, over his exchange with Tex Winter involving the *I* in *win*, over his dislike of Jerry Krause, even over a dispute with Pat Riley about a hotel room in Hawaii. He seemed to insult as many people as he thanked that day with his frank approach.

Phil Jackson watched the event on TV in a crowded sports bar, where he saw the surprised reactions among the patrons. Jackson, though, immediately understood that Jordan was merely trying to explain his great competitive nature, the only problem being that just about all of the things that had spurred Jordan on in his life were hugely negative and hard for people to comprehend. It all translated into something of a disaster.

662 | MICHAEL JORDAN

"Michael Jordan's Hall of Fame talk was the Exxon Valdez of speeches," wrote Rick Reilly in *Sports Illustrated*. "It was, by turns, rude, vindictive, and flammable. And that was just when he was trying to be funny. It was tactless, egotistical, and unbecoming. When it was done, nobody wanted to be like Mike."

No one was more stunned—and then more elated—than Jerry Krause. "I sat there," Krause recalled in 2012. "I was a little, shall we say, surprised. But again, that's Michael. I was surprised that he'd done it on that stage. I was very shocked that he nailed Dean. Me? You could expect it. Dean? That was hard. Dean must have sat there thinking, 'What?' Dean must have been shocked. We lived with it long enough to win six championships, and you understand who it's coming from."

Krause contrasted it with Dennis Rodman's highly emotional self-admonishment upon his own induction two years later. "Dennis could behave terribly," Krause said. "But Dennis is good-hearted. He did things to harm himself. But Dennis would never hurt another human being, except himself. Michael? Michael doesn't care if he hurts people. He's not all there at times. I'm not saying he's nuts. I've seen so many times where he was incredibly gracious. I would assume it would be a psychiatrist's delight to take him and break him down. That would be very interesting. He's one of the smartest basketball players I ever worked with, but that Hall of Fame thing, that speech, helped me make people realize how stupid he is. I had umpteen people come up to me after that speech and say, 'I didn't realize Michael was such an asshole.'"

Jackson was an excellent psychologist who brought out the best in Jordan, Krause said. "We had a very good basketball team with high-strung egos. He took those egos and put them in the right place. He understood the players and how to get them to work together."

The other key was Winter, Krause said. "Tex was tougher on Michael than anyone in terms of perfection. Michael didn't like the triangle. He said, 'What's that motherfucking thing gonna do for us?' It took a good year for him to accept it, but then he realized how he could work in the post because of the offense."

As the former GM talked (he had been eased out by Reinsdorf in

2003) about the Hall of Fame speech, he began to relax and talked about what a great, great competitor Jordan was, how not one single time in all their years together had Jordan shirked from the hardest tasks and the heaviest burdens. Krause said that he had a library filled with videotape of every one of Jordan's magnificent performances, and yet the experience had been so bitter that he had never viewed even one of them. He reiterated, "He is what he is. Michael and I will never break bread together."

So much of the harshness was driven by the narcissism of the age of constant media and worship, Krause said. "If Michael had played in the days of Elgin and Oscar and those guys, you wouldn't have had that. If you put Oscar and Elgin in today's atmosphere, the same thing would have happened to them. Bill Russell would have been making thirty million a year, too."

As Jordan had said so many times, however, his timing was his own. In the spotlight, he had been as he always was, defiant and unbowed. As Sonny Vaccaro observed, "It was like he was anointed. I mean seriously, everything. I mean, even where he did something contrary to what was supposed to happen, it would come out all right."

He moved on from Springfield, even as sports columnists at newspapers large and small, sports talk radio hosts, Internet sites, and TV commentators all roundly criticized the speech. Mostly, they scratched their heads, perplexed and angry that they had been denied a moment of joyful celebration with a hero long admired by generations.

"I think his heart is in the right place, I really do," said David Aldridge.

But the public had wanted something more satisfying from the man who had changed everything.

The Owner

He turned then to the task of completing his purchase of the Bobcats. For the first time in history, a former player would be the majority owner of an NBA team. David Stern and Jordan had never been close, but now Stern worked behind the scenes to make the transition happen, and once it happened, he continued to help in the adjustment. Somehow overlooked in the process was the closest thing the public would get to an answer about an enduring mystery. Jack McCallum had sought to answer the question that so many had asked: Was Jordan forced from the game in 1993? There was nothing to the conspiracy theories about his gambling, Jordan said again and again in interviews in 2011 and 2012, and he had long resented that Stern hadn't stepped up and said more to make the matter clear at the time. The commissioner knew of his great anger, but as McCallum pointed out, Stern was in an awkward position. If he said too much or protested too much, that would only feed the conspiracy buffs. Jordan took the commissioner's approach as indifference.

Whatever was said between the two men was left with them, and neither discussed it or offered any further details. The evidence at most was circumstantial, but strong, it seemed. If Jordan had indeed been forced from the game, the commissioner obviously had welcomed him back as a player. But he would never have seen fit to agree to Jordan as an owner. After all, Jordan had hardly repented his ways. (In 2007, NFL player Adam "Pacman" Jones joined Jordan at a high-stakes craps table in Las Vegas. All night, Jordan insisted that no one else touch the dice—only he was allowed to roll the bones. In a 2014 interview, Jones recalled that he won a million dollars that night while Jordan lost five million.) "I don't know that there ever really was a gambling issue," Krause said. If there had been, it seemed highly unlikely that Stern would have worked so hard to make Jordan's ownership a reality. Short of anything to the contrary, that stood as the best evidence that Jordan's departure for Birmingham was just what the record showed: his grief and sorrow come to bear in a desire to feel close to his father in baseball.

As for the Bobcats, they had laid off dozens of staff in 2009. Now that Jordan was the majority owner, the team began refilling those positions and tackling a host of business issues. The arena had never earned any naming rights, and they promptly sold those to Time Warner Cable. One by one, the staff lined up all the best things to do to improve the franchise. In meetings they soon discovered that Jordan was a great listener—something his mother, and then Dean Smith, had learned years earlier. He began meetings with season ticket holders, usually at the most difficult times, such as after embarrassing losses (and there were many of those).

At first, he was greeted with good fortune as an owner. He had hired Hall of Fame and fellow University of North Carolina alum Larry Brown as his coach. Jordan assumed the reins of the franchise in early 2010 and watched the Bobcats make the playoffs for the first time in its short history that spring, but then he had to peel off some of the team's best players in a difficult cost-cutting move during the off-season. Observers noted that the loss of point guard Raymond Felton and center Tyson Chandler contributed to the Bobcats' struggles in 2011. Which in turn meant that Jordan soon came to a bitter parting of the ways with Brown, who later went on *The Dan Patrick Show* and complained that people around Jordan "don't have a clue," that they are all "yes-men" who made him "sick" when he worked there, and that Jordan planted "spies" to check on the coaches.

To replace Brown, Jordan brought veteran coach Paul Silas out of retirement as his coach, but the team struggled and sank that spring. It was then that Jordan began to put on his gear and visit practice to test his players. "He's very knowledgeable about the game," Silas observed at the time. "He's been there, he's won championships, so he understands what it takes. A tough guy, he's very respectful of the players, a players' guy. But he's also equally firm. He just wants everybody to carry the threat."

Old friend Rod Higgins, the team's top basketball executive, needed a center before that season and considered Kwame Brown, then a free agent. Brown represented an embarrassing chapter from Jordan's Washington episode, and Higgins thought he'd best seek the owner's approval before signing Brown, who had in his decade in the league established a record as a journeyman center who could defend and rebound.

"If you think he can help us win, sign him," Jordan said.

Now, he found himself in practice once again facing Brown.

"Our relationship is the same," Brown said that spring when

asked about Jordan. "MJ's MJ. It's never been what everybody thought it was. It's a boss-player relationship. And that's how it is. It's not always going to be peaches and cream when you're not performing. But also as a person MJ is a great guy. He's a great owner to play for, and that's why I came here to play for him."

Asked about a forty-eight-year-old Jordan in practice, Brown said, "He definitely went hard. He's a little older now.... He can still get his shots off, though. He's still holding his own. I don't know about up and down, but half-court he's still good."

As for the infamous trash talk?

"That's what he does," Brown said, laughing now. "I mean, he's MJ. Would we talk trash back to him? No, no, no. But what other team has an owner that comes into practice and can actually still play? He comes into practice, the level of play and the competition picks up. He's talking noise, he's joking. It's good for him to be around because everybody wants to play hard...."

"You better play hard," he said with another laugh.

As the Bobcats struggled that spring, Jordan continued to take immense heat as an executive. But he had agreed to bring on board Rich Cho, one of the league's most talented young personnel evaluators, to run the basketball operations. It was a huge concession by Jordan, observers said. Trusting had never been easy for him, but it had finally become essential, many said.

"There's definitely a method to the madness," Jim Stack said of Jordan. "Michael is very, very, very bright. Very shrewd. Very knowledgeable. Nothing he does is by happenstance. He's very calculating. Very measured. I think he ultimately has a lot of clairvoyance with where he is going, but sometimes it doesn't work out the way it needs to. You clearly learn along the way. He's a quick study. When something happens, he'll make the necessary adjustments. But as an owner or a manager, it's not a part-time gig. You gotta be there nonstop. Being that he's Michael Jordan, the icon, it's tough for him to be on the spot like he needs to be 24/7, in order to do justice to what he needs to be doing there. He's realized his life is not conducive to that role. He's agreed to step back a bit on being the final decision maker. His stubbornness as a youth might have kept him insisting that he was going to figure it out and do it on his terms.

But he's matured and understands he has to step back and not be on the front lines. I see that as a huge level of maturity in him as a person and a human being. He never would have done that back in the day. Never. His way was to go harder and stronger, and figure out a way to get it done, just like he did in getting past Detroit, in those challenges he had before he finally broke through."

Jordan soon found that all the concessions had only guaranteed him more trouble than he ever imagined. He and his staff watched a brief revival of the team's fortunes that spring of 2011 before deciding to pull the trigger on a trade of the team's veteran leader and All-Star, Gerald Wallace, to Portland for draft picks and an odd assortment of role players. It was a move designed to rebuild the team, to take losses in order to gain younger players for the future, but instead the deal sent the Bobcats reeling into a losing streak. And Wallace, a family man and strong community figure in Charlotte, later told the media that he felt "betrayed" by Jordan. It's a fair guess that some of the players in the Bobcats' locker room felt the same way. Jordan clearly understood this. As a player, he had sat in locker rooms feeling confused and betrayed as Chicago Bulls management traded away his best friends and competitive brothers in moves aimed at building the franchise's future. Now it was Jordan's turn to be the bad guy. In the days after the trade, he offered the community little more than stony silence, which led some observers to conclude that Jordan was insensitive and uncaring about the harshness of the deal. In fact, the move was unpleasant for Jordan. A smart-ass might have pointed out to Jordan that the Wallace trade was the kind of deal that Krause would have had the brass to make.

For a time, Jordan employed his old friend Charles Oakley as a Bobcats assistant coach.

"He's a good guy," Oakley said of Jordan one night after another loss, adding that the modern NBA players were spoiled crybabies who didn't understand what it meant to buckle down, to toughen up and work.

Jordan smiled at a bystander and quipped that if Oakley could just get 10 rebounds a night, then he himself could come back to the game and score big time. "If he can get 10, I can get 20," Jordan said gamely.

If only that had been the case. Jordan knew well that he faced a long, narrow path to success with a small-market NBA team, a troubled road where respect was won one step at a time.

The next day he was up early and about the town, leading his players in public service projects for the local schools, where he had ponied up hundreds of thousands of dollars to keep middle school sports programs from being lost to budget cuts.

That summer, the league embarked on yet another player lockout, this one angrier in many ways than all the others. There had been a time when Jordan had entered the fray on the side of the players in their battle with the owners. Now, however, he was a majority partner with minority partners who had been hit hard by the team's millions upon millions in losses. He entered the labor fray aggressively on the side of the owners. It was what he was supposed to do. He had a fiduciary responsibility to his partners to help strike the toughest, best deal available. To the public, however, he was still Air Jordan and now widely castigated as a traitor to the cause. He was the one majority black owner among the many faces of older white men.

It was a low, low time.

But the lockout ended that winter, and as bad as the times seemed in 2011, they would sit in his rearview as a shimmering oasis by the time he had absorbed the shellacking of 2012, when a young Charlotte team, stripped of its veteran leadership and talent, faced an unprecedented slaughter, one that would leave Jordan lampooned time and again as the Greatest Loser in the history of the sport.

The Loser

One bright spot emerged in that disaster of a season on a night that the Pistons visited Charlotte. Jordan was speaking with a writer when he learned that Joe Dumars, Detroit's top basketball executive, had come down for the game. "Joe's here?" Jordan said, his eyes wide. He turned immediately and walked down the hall to the Pistons' locker room just as Dumars was emerging. He threw his arm around the shoulder of his old nemesis, who faced his own headaches in Detroit, and they walked arm in arm down the hallway. Jordan wanted him to meet Prieto, his fiancé, who seemed to have brought happiness and a sense of calm to basketball's disappointed man.

By the time his forty-ninth birthday neared in February, print, Internet, and broadcast media had begun calling him the worst owner ever. The final touch of irony was that his team would close the season on a twenty-three-game losing streak for number 23. Many nights he had seemed like a lion caged in the building as the team collapsed. They finished the strike-shortened season at 7–59, a .106 winning percentage, the worst record ever posted in an NBA season. The previous record had been held by the 1973 Philadelphia 76ers at 9–73 (.110). With Rich Cho helping guide the strategy, Jordan's club had traded away big contract stars and opted to go with an even younger, less-experienced roster that would net the team a high draft pick.

Jordan insisted that he and his staff had a vision for the team, and while they didn't expect the team to be so bad, they were sticking to their plans. At the end of the regular season, he removed Paul Silas as coach, a decision Silas said he agreed with, and moved him into a front office position.

The prize in the draft lottery that year was Anthony Davis, the star of Kentucky's national championship team, but even with the price of a terrible record, Jordan's luck deserted him. New Orleans won the top pick in the lottery, and the Bobcats, picking second, took Michael Kidd-Gilchrist, another impressive young wing off of Kentucky's team.

Jordan's late tenure in Charlotte had been marked by rumors that he was throwing his hands up and selling the team, rumors that he vigorously denied. A generation of players who had come of age with him continued to look at him as their role model. Players like Eddie Pinckney and Anthony Teachey and many who had competed with and against him held out great hopes that he would turn things around. Others quietly said that if he couldn't do a better job he should just sell the team.

Before he died in 2012, Lacy Banks expressed his disappointment in how Jordan's life after basketball had turned out. Banks cited his experience covering Muhammad Ali and said that Jordan should find some means of giving back to humanity, of trying to be the lion that Ali had been. Unprompted, many others expressed the same desire. Sonny Vaccaro said it was time for Jordan to find some great thing to put his energies into, besides his own hedonism. He would be well served to follow his mother's lead, Vaccaro offered.

Jordan was too self-focused to do such a thing, Jerry Krause said. "He thinks the world owes him."

Yet it seemed that his time in Charlotte was being overlooked just as his time in Birmingham with the Barons had gone unappreciated. Later, following a documentary film on his baseball days, a variety of observers came forward to say that they hadn't realized what a great thing he was doing by persisting in baseball, making himself into a player. Likewise, his efforts in Charlotte were critical to the region's economic health and had begun to show signs of generating real growth, despite all of the frustration and challenges. That seemed to be indicated when President Barack Obama chose the Time Warner Cable Arena in Charlotte as the site of the 2012 Democratic National Convention, the place where he would accept the nomination to run for his second term.

The overwhelming negativity of the 2012 season, however, produced yet a new round of rumors that Jordan was going to sell in the face of great losses and great disappointment. He rushed to counter them by stating publicly that he was invested in Charlotte for the long run, no matter how long it took to rebuild an NBA presence in the region.

He faced a coaching hire that summer, and there were reports he was considering either the tough old pro Jerry Sloan, now in his seventies, or a bright young face, Brian Shaw, who had been a player and an assistant with Phil Jackson on the Lakers. Jordan, however, went for a surprise choice, the virtually unknown Mike Dunlap, a coach with a reputation for tough practices and heavy conditioning. It was in practice that Jordan had made his stand as a player, and practice where he hoped to dig out of his hole as an owner.

His young team ran out to a surprising start that fall of 2012, winning more games in a few weeks than the previous team had won in an entire season, but inexperience soon caught up with them and they fell into an eighteen-game losing streak, although they continued to play so hard during the losing that hope somehow glowed through the grinding experience. In the midst of such challenge, some close observers noted that Jordan seemed happier now that he and Prieto were engaged. There were fewer golfing junkets, and he seemed more focused on the task at hand. The two would be married in 2013 in the wake of a huge media celebration of Jordan's fiftieth birthday. Despite all the good feelings, the Bobcats again stumbled that spring. In the off-season, Jordan decided to change coaches yet again. He hired Lakers assistant coach Steve Clifford and watched as the Bobcats, still one of the youngest teams in the league, showed substantial improvement that fall. Over the summer, Jordan had procured the rights to the Hornets name. New Orleans would become the Pelicans, and for the 2014–15 season Jordan would preside over the Hornets back in Charlotte. Meanwhile, he spent much of the year attempting to sell his 56,000-square-foot mansion in Highland Park, north of Chicago, first for $29 million on the open market, then at auction for a reported $18 million, before dropping to a substantially lower asking price.

Toward the end of 2013, it was announced that the new Mrs. Jordan was expecting. (She would give birth to identical twin girls named Victoria and Ysabel in February 2014, just days before Michael's fifty-first birthday, leading ESPN and other media outlets to joke that the father had just gotten "a new pair of Jordans.") Slowly but persistently, he had built a new momentum in his life. He began working out more earnestly and making an effort to lose dozens of pounds, amid persistent rumors that he planned to return to the game to play briefly. It was something he had long hinted that he might do — come back at age fifty to compete again. Mostly it served as proof that his karma twisted on, taking his life from one indelible fantasy to another.

If what Jordan was encountering in Charlotte was a power play, then it was proving to be like any other, won only after a long, hard road and much suffering. During the dark nights in Birmingham, he had visited often with his departed father, so it wasn't much of a leap to figure that on his bleakest nights in Charlotte, Jordan again likely sat alone in the darkness of his arena reviewing all that had unfolded with James Jordan, telling the old man of his dashed expectations and embarrassments.

It's also not hard to imagine on those nights that Jordan's thoughts veered toward fantasy, or at least visualization, settling on the best thing that he could ever hope to find as an owner. There, shimmering for him in the distance, is a grand season, a deep play-off run at another championship. In Jordan's vision, it's probably not hard to imagine that all of his family is there in spirit, even Dawson Jordan, there with Clementine, his sweetheart, on his arm. Medward and dear old Miss Bell, too. All the Jordans, in fact, and the Peoples. They're all there. Deloris and Sis and Larry and Roz and all their cousins and kin, aglow with pregame expectations.

In the midst of this final fantasy, the buzzer sounds. It's almost time for the tip-off, but the arena is suddenly astir. Michael is nowhere to be seen.

He's in his office in the bowels of the arena, sitting and talking with James as he has his entire life. The son's eyes are bright and wide and starting to fill to the point that he's fighting to see his old man through the blur. He's suddenly struck to ask the enduring question, "What do you think of me now, Pops? How about all of this? Do I still have to go back on in the house?"

One can also imagine Jordan pausing then, realizing what his closest friends and his many fans understood long ago, that he doesn't have to ask anymore. His long-raging debate can be put away forever now. The answer is right there in front of him, in front of all of us. Something he can clearly see.

ACKNOWLEDGMENTS

I've often pointed out that there have been so many books written about Michael Jordan that he has his own genre.

So why the need for another one?

Well, my answer is the same that most authors give: This one provides lots of new information.

No, really. This book does provide much new information on Jordan. Just as important, it provides a new context for our consideration of the life of Michael Jordan. We know a lot about him, but the new context changes much about how we view what we already knew.

A new book also doesn't mean that the old ones are obsolete. To the contrary, any number of the previous books written about Jordan remain immensely valuable and were essential to me in putting together this mosaic of his life—a mosaic that has been a huge challenge considering how intensely the Jordan family guards its privacy and secrets. Who can really blame them given the nature of fame in the media-driven postmodern age?

To that end, the little-known book by his sister Deloris, *In My Family's Shadow,* which was published privately in 2001, goes a long way in opening a window to the difficulties the Jordans have faced over the years.

Jordan's own work with the writer Mark Vancil was also important in providing me access to his thoughts, as has been the work of certain journalists: Melissa Isaacson, Lacy Banks, Rick Telander, Jack McCallum, and Sam Smith, among numerous others.

Smith's *The Jordan Rules* is the text that first pulled back the drapes for a look at Jordan's complex personality.

Rebound by Bob Greene is another fascinating volume, although it's often overlooked within the literature of MJ for Greene's better-known *Hang Time*.

Although he never got to interview Jordan, David Halberstam offers an important view of the cultural context in which Jordan worked in *Playing for Keeps*. Some of my own books provide a similar background, including *Blood on the Horns*, the story of the Bulls' divisive 1998 season; *Mind Games; And Now, Your Chicago Bulls;* and several other works about Jordan and the NBA.

I want to acknowledge the work of all the dozens of writers who covered basketball and Jordan's career before me: Mitch Albom, Terry Armour, Lacy Banks, Greg Stoda, Chuck Carree, Mike McGraw, Terry Boers, Mike Wise, Clifton Brown, Dave Anderson, Phil Berger, Frank Deford, Bryan Burwell, David Dupree, Scott Ostler, Ira Berkow, Shelby Strother, Charlie Vincent, Mitch Chortkoff, Robert Falkoff, Bill Gleason, Bill Hall, Scott Howard-Cooper, Mike Imrem, Melissa Isaacson, John Jackson, Paul Ladewski, Bernie Lincicome, Bob Logan, Jay Mariotti, Kent McDill, Corky Meinecke, Mike Mulligan, Skip Myslenski, Glenn Rogers, Steve Rosenbloom, Eddie Sefko, Gene Seymour, Sam Smith, Ray Sons, Paul Sullivan, Mark Vancil, Bob Verdi, Bob Ryan, Roy S. Johnson, Tony Kornheiser, Dave Kindred, Pat Putnam, Sandy Padwe, Jack McCallum, Sam McManis, Doug Cress, Mike Littwin, John Papanek, Leonard Koppett, George Vecsey, Alex Wolff, Bruce Newman, Jackie MacMullan, Steve Bulpett, Peter May, Mike Fine, Will McDonough, Ailene Voisin, Drew Sharp, Terry Foster, Steve Addy, Dean Howe, and many, many others whose front-line work greatly aided this book.

As much as it was the literature, it was the people who helped me provide this in-depth account of Jordan's life.

Among the many I've interviewed, certain figures stand out for their major contributions to my understanding of Michael Jordan. They include Maurice Eugene Jordan, William Henry Jordan, George Gervin, Ray Allen, Rod Higgins, James Worthy, Patrick Ewing, Joe Dumars, Bill Billingsley, Michael Taylor, George Mumford, Tex Winter, Johnny Bach, Steve Kerr, Sonny Vaccaro, Jerry Krause, Billy Packer, Kenny Gattison, Tim Hallam, Jim Stack, Joe O'Neil, Dick Neher, David Aldridge, Lacy Banks, Ed Pinckney,

J. A. Adande, Kevin McHale, Bill Walton, David Mann, James Edwards, Ralph Sampson, Terry Holland, Don Sublett, Howard Garfinkel, Matt Guokas, Chuck Carree, Tom Konchalski, Brendan Malone, Brick Oettinger, Fred Whitfield, Charles Oakley, Kwame Brown, Daniel Mock, Brent Barry, Mike Wise, Eddie Jones, Jeff Davis, Ken Roberts, Walter Bannerman, Dick Weiss, Magic Johnson, Art Chansky, Scottie Pippen, and Michael Jordan himself, as well as many others who talked freely about their experiences.

None of this would have been possible without my wife, Karen; my daughters, Jenna and Morgan; and my son-in-law Mike Hollowell—all of whom, in addition to giving support, also freely contributed their time to transcribe the many interview tapes for this project.

I am deeply indebted to Dan Smith and Mike Ashley for reading portions of the manuscript and offering assurances, as well as to Doug Doughty, who offered advice on interview subjects, and to the staffs at the libraries of Pender, Duplin, and New Hanover counties. Also vital were the special collections and, in particular, the Southern Folklife Collection at UNC's Wilson Library, plus Adam Ryan's Jordan video collection.

For their friendship and encouragement, I am indebted to my son, Henry Lazenby, and son-in-law Jon Thumas, as well as good friends and colleagues Ran Henry, Lindy Davis, Steve Cox, David and Deloris Craig, Ric and Emmy Moore, Mudcat Saunders, Neal Turnage, Andy Mager, Scott and Sue McCoy, Pat and Sue Flynn, Billy and Kathleen Driver, Tonia and Jake Lucas, Beth Macy, Michael Hudson, Jorge Ribeiro, Bryan and Becky Tinsley, Gary Burns, and so many others.

As always, my agent, Matthew Carnicelli, was essential to the project, as were key staff members at Little, Brown, including Michael Pietsch, Ben Allen, Malin von Euler-Hogan, and Peg Anderson. A very special debt is owed to editor John Parsley for the mountain of work and dedication he plowed into this book.

Finally, a special thanks to my siblings, Jeanie and Hampton, and our late parents, William Lowry Lazenby and Virginia Hampton Lazenby, who taught me to love reading and basketball from a young age.

NOTES AND SOURCES

Interviews

I would like to thank the following for granting interviews for this book and for other projects of mine over the years that provided insight for this work. They include, in no particular order: Art Chansky, Ralph Sampson, Jerry Krause, George Mumford, Michael Jordan, James Worthy, Tex Winter, Ty Lue, Mike Wise, Jay Mariotti, Daniel Mock, Lindy Davis, Kwame Brown, Shaun Livingston, Rick Bonnell, Steve Kerr, Brent Barry, David Mann, William Henry Jordan, Maurice Eugene Jordan, Raphael Carlton, Dick Neher, Howard Garfinkel, Walter Bannerman, Joe Dumars, James Edwards, David Aldridge, Doug Collins, Kenny Gattison, Dee Brown, Chris Pika, Scottie Pippen, Jimmy Bain, Charles West, Sonny Vaccaro, Matt Guokas, Tim Hallam, Joe O'Neil, Jim Stack, Rod Higgins, Doc Rivers, Charles Oakley, Lacy Banks, George Gervin, Bill Walton, Kevin McHale, Mitch Lawrence, Chuck Carree, Jeff Davis, Pat Williams, Mike Taylor, Mary Faison, Bobby Jordan, William Billingsley, Ken Roberts, Johnny Bach, Marques Johnson, Jerry Sloan, Brick Oettinger, Anthony Teachey, Terry Holland, Bill Thacker, Tom Konchalski, Brendan Malone, Billy Packer, Ed Pinckney, Patrick Ewing, Ric Moore, Clarence Gaines, Jr., Fred Whitfield, Dick Weiss, Chip Schaefer, Phil Jackson, John McLendon, Clarence "Big House" Gaines, Doug Doughty, Alex Rivera, Dean Smith, Tom McMillen, John Thompson, Jonathan Kovler, Donald Sublett, Rod Thorn, Bill Blair, Irwin Mandel, Mark Pfeil, Kevin Loughery, Steve Schanwald, Jerry Reinsdorf, Bill Gleason, Cheryl Raye-Stout, Sidney Green, Jess Kersey, Bruce Levine, Tom Smithburg, John Paxson, John Ligmanowski, Will Perdue, Bob Logan, Isiah Thomas, Chuck Daly, Bill Laimbeer, Mike Ornstein, Shelby Strother, Tom Dore, Gary Vitti, Eddie Jones, Bill Wennington, Ron Harper, Nick Van Exel, Kobe Bryant, Bill Smith, Terry Armour, Jud Buechler, Luc Longley, Jason Caffey, Dennis Rodman, Keith Lundquist, Jack Haley, Dr. Jack Ramsay, Ray Allen, Jim Cleamons, Jerry West, Magic Johnson, and Dr. Jerry Buss.

Magazines, Newspapers, and Websites

Extensive use was made of publications and websites, including the *Chicago Defender*, the *Chicago Tribune*, the *Chicago Sun-Times*, the *Daily Southtown*, the *Detroit News*, the *Detroit Free Press*, the *Daily Herald*, *ESPN The Magazine*, *Hoop* magazine, the *Houston Post*, the *Houston Chronicle*, *Inside Sports*, *Sport* magazine, the *Los Angeles Times*, *The National*, the *New York Daily News*, the *New York Times*, the *New York Post*, the *Charlotte Observer*, the *Wilmington Journal*, the *Wilmington Star-News*, the *Greensboro News and Record*, the *Durham Sun*, the

Winston-Salem Journal, the *Roanoke Times, USA Today, The Oregonian,* the *Philadelphia Inquirer,* the *San Antonio Express-News, Sports Illustrated, Lindy's Pro Basketball Annual, Basketball Times,* the *Boston Globe, The Sporting News, Street & Smith's Pro Basketball Yearbook,* the *Washington Post,* ESPN.com, *Keeping It Heel* (blog), *Bullets Forever* (blog), *The Basketball Jones* (blog), *Deadspin* (blog), *Hoops-Hype* (blog), *The Golf Nut Society* (blog), NBA.com, and Bulls.com, among others.

Demographic Research

Four thousand Pender County, North Carolina, death certificates, 1910–1930.

Census records in Pender County, North Carolina, for Jordan, Hand, Burns, Keilon, Peoples families, 1890, 1900, 1910, 1920, 1930.

Pender County marriage records for Dawson Jordan, Clementine Burns, and Ethel Lane.

Death and birth records for Charlotte Hand, Isac Keilon, Clementine Burns Jordan, Dawson Jordan, William Edward Jordan, James Jordan, Rosabell Hand Jordan, and Inez Peoples.

Selective service records for Dawson Jordan and Edward Peoples.

Duplin County and New Hanover County real estate records for Jordan family.

North Carolina Department of Agriculture Report, 1922, UNC Collection.

Books

Beckett, Dr. James, publisher. *The Definitive Word on Michael Jordan: As Told by His Friends and Foes.* Dallas: Beckett Publications, 1988.

Bloodworth, Mattie. *History of Pender County, North Carolina.* Richmond: Dietz Printing Company, 1947.

Bondy, Filip. *Tip-off: How the 1984 NBA Draft Changed Basketball Forever.* Cambridge, MA: Da Capo, 2007.

Boyd, Todd. *Young, Black, Rich, and Famous: The Rise of the NBA, the Hip Hop Invasion, and the Transformation of American Culture.* New York: Doubleday, 2003.

Carden, Bruce, and Bob Condor, eds. *Bulls Da Champs.* Chicago: Tribune Publishing, 1992.

Chansky, Art. *Light Blue Reign: How a City Slicker, a Quiet Kansan, and a Mountain Man Built College Basketball's Longest-Lasting Dynasty.* New York: Thomas Dunne, 2010.

Chansky, Art, Eddie Fogler, and Dean Smith. *March to the Top.* Chapel Hill, NC: Four Corners, 1982.

Conser, Walter H. *A Coat of Many Colors: Religion and Society along the Cape Fear River of North Carolina.* Lexington: University of Kentucky Press, 2006.

Esquinas, Richard, and Dave Distel. *Michael & Me: Our Gambling Addiction — My Cry for Help!* San Diego: Athletic Guidance Center Publishing, 1993.

Featherston, Alwyn. *Tobacco Road: Duke, Carolina, NC State, Wake Forest, and the History of the Most Intense Backyard Rivalries in Sports.* Guilford, CT: Lyons Press, 2006.

George, Nelson. *Elevating the Game: The History and Aesthetics of Black Men in Basketball.* New York: Simon & Schuster, 1993. Print.

Gergen, Joe. *The Final Four: An Illustrated History of College Basketball's Showcase Event.* St. Louis: Sporting News, 1987.

Godwin, John L. *Black Wilmington and the North Carolina Way: Portrait of a Community in the Era of Civil Rights Protest.* Lanham, MD: University Press of America, 2000.

Greene, Bob. *Rebound: The Odyssey of Michael Jordan.* New York: Viking, 1995.

Halberstam, David. *Playing for Keeps: Michael Jordan and the World He Made.* New York: Random House, 1999.

Hirsch, Arnold R. *Making the Second Ghetto: Race and Housing in Chicago, 1940–1960.* Chicago: University of Chicago Press, 1998.

Isaacson, Melissa. *Transition Game: An Inside Look at Life with the Chicago Bulls.* Champaign, IL: Sagamore Publishing, 1994.

Jackson, Phil, and Charley Rosen. *More Than a Game.* New York: Seven Stories, 2001.

Jackson, Phil, and Hugh Delehanty. *Eleven Rings: The Soul of Success.* New York: Penguin Press, 2013.

———. *Sacred Hoops: Spiritual Lessons of a Hardwood Warrior.* New York: Hyperion, 1995.

Jordan, Deloris. *In My Family's Shadow.* Elkins Park, PA: Jordan Signature Publishing, 2001.

Jordan, Deloris, and Gregg Lewis. *Family First: Winning the Parenting Game.* San Francisco: HarperSanFrancisco, 1996.

Jordan, Michael, and Mark Vancil. *For the Love of the Game: My Story.* New York: Crown, 1998.

Jordan, Michael, and Pat Williams. *Quotable Michael Jordan: Words of Wit, Wisdom, and Inspiration by and about Michael Jordan, Basketball's Greatest Superstar.* Hendersonville, TN: Towlehouse Publishing, 2004.

Kirk, J. Allen. *A Statement of Facts Concerning the Bloody Riot in Wilmington, NC, of Interest to Every Citizen of the United States.* Wilmington, NC: n.p., 1898.

LaFeber, Walter. *Michael Jordan and the New Global Capitalism.* Expanded edition. New York: W. W. Norton, 2002.

Lefler, Hugh Talmage. *North Carolina History Told by Contemporaries.* Fourth ed. Chapel Hill: University of North Carolina Press, 1965.

McCallum, Jack. *Dream Team: How Michael, Magic, Larry, Charles, and the Greatest Team of All Time Conquered the World and Changed the Game of Basketball Forever.* New York: Ballantine, 2012.

Mobley, Joe A. *The Way We Lived in North Carolina.* Chapel Hill: University of North Carolina Press, 2003.

Naughton, Jim. *Taking to the Air: The Rise of Michael Jordan.* New York. Little, Brown, 1992.

Parker, Bobby. *Michael Jordan: Before the Legend.* Wilmington, NC: Wilmington Star-News, 1999.

Powell, William Stevens. *North Carolina: A History.* Chapel Hill: University of North Carolina Press, 1988.

———. *North Carolina through Four Centuries.* Chapel Hill: University of North Carolina Press, 1989.

Prather, H. Leon. *We Have Taken a City: The Wilmington Racial Massacre and Coup of 1898.* Southport, NC: Dram Tree, 2006.

Randall, Stephen, ed. *The Playboy Interviews: They Played the Game.* Milwaukie, OR: M Press, 2006.

Smith, Dean, John Kilgo, and Sally Jenkins. *A Coach's Life: My Forty Years in College Basketball.* New York: Random House, 1999.

Smith, John L. *Running Scared: The Life and Treacherous Times of Las Vegas Casino King Steve Wynn.* New York: Barricade, 1995.

Smith, Sam. *The Jordan Rules.* New York: Simon and Schuster, 1992.

Strasser, J. B., and Laurie Becklund. *Swoosh: The Unauthorized Story of Nike and the Men Who Played There.* New York: HarperBusiness, 1993.

Telander, Rick. *In the Year of the Bull: Zen, Air, and the Pursuit of Sacred and Profane Hoops.* New York: Simon & Schuster, 1996.

Walker, J. Samuel. *ACC Basketball: The Story of the Rivalries, Traditions, and Scandals of the First Two Decades of the Atlantic Coast Conference.* Chapel Hill: University of North Carolina Press, 2011.

Williams, Roy, and Tim Crothers. *Hard Work: A Life on and off the Court.* Chapel Hill, NC: Algonquin, 2009.

Newspaper, Magazine, and Online Articles

Adderton, Donald V. "Parenting Doesn't Stop after Superstardom." *Wilmington Morning Star.* July 19, 1996.

Almond, Elliott. "Two Accused of Random Killing of James Jordan." *Los Angeles Times.* August 16, 1993.

Aschburner, Steve. "Jordan's Sick Performance in '97 Elevated His Reputation." NBA.com. June 11, 2012. http://origin.nba.com/2012/news/features/steve_aschburner/06/11/jordans-sick-game/index.html.

Badenhausen, Kurt. "The Business of Michael Jordan Is Booming." *Forbes.* September 22, 2011.

———. "Michael Jordan Hosts $3 Million Obama Fundraiser in New York." Forbes.com, August 22, 2012. http://www.forbes.com/sites/kurtbadenhausen/2012/08/22/michael-jordan-hosts-3-million-obama-fundraiser-in-new-york/.

Barbour, Brian. "IC Looks at Michael Jordan's Recruitment." *Tar Heel Blog.* November 7, 2011. http://www.tarheelblog.com/2011/11/ic-looks-at-michael-jordans-recruitment/.

Bear, Aaron. "Twenty Years Later, Jordan's Shot Still the Stuff of Legend." Associated Press. April 2, 2002. Available online at http://journaltimes.com/sports/twenty-years-later-jordan-s-shot-still-the-stuff-of/article_65cf03c1-0334-5a94-8782-410379224cf0.html.

Berkow, Ira. "Sports of The Times; Air Jordan and Just Plain Folks." *New York Times.* June 15, 1991.

Biro, Liz. "Did Michael Jordan Work at Whitey's?" *Port City Foodies* (blog), StarNews Online. December 11, 2010. http://foodies.blogs.starnewsonline.com/18422/did-michael-jordan-work-at-whiteys/.

Bowker, Paul D. "Cherish Mike's Memory." *Wilmington Morning Star.* January 12, 1999.

———. "A Perfect Time…to Walk Away." *Wilmington Morning Star.* January 14, 1999.

Bradley, Mark. "Jordan Joins Top Echelon of Stars." *Wilmington Morning Star.* December 23, 1989.

Carree, Chuck. "6-run Sixth Lifts 'Cats over Bucs." *Wilmington Star-News*. April 2, 1980.

———. "Bucs Jolt Vikes from League Lead." *Wilmington Star-News*. April 26, 1980.

———. "Chicago Bulls' Jordan Goes to Camp." *Wilmington Morning Star*. June 16, 1987.

———. "Cougars Nip Laney, 43–38." *Wilmington Morning Star*. February 6, 1980.

———. "Jordan Brothers Dump Kinston." *Wilmington Star-News*. January 30, 1980.

———. "Jordan Scores 39 as Tar Heels Subdue Tech." *Wilmington Star-News*. January 30, 1983.

———. "Jordan's Special Day Follows Early Taste of Fame." *Wilmington Star-News*. May 16, 1982.

———. "Laney Drubs 'Cats, 63–49." *Wilmington Star-News*. February 9, 1980.

———. "Laney Squeezes Cards." *Wilmington Morning Star*. February 13, 1980.

———. "Laney's Jordan: Versatile Prep Standout." *Wilmington Star-News*. April 27, 1980.

———. "Wilmington Preps Prepare for Baseball Season Debuts." *Wilmington Star-News*. February 24, 1980.

Charlotte Business Journal. "Nike's Larry Miller Talks Michael Jordan, NBA." Morning edition. July 24, 2012.

Chicago Tribune. "MJ in 1981." McDonald's Corp. photo handout from April 11, 1981. Chicagotribune.com. Accessed January 16, 2013. http://www.chicago tribune.com/sports/basketball/bulls/michaeljordan/chi-p2-mj -wmtn20090903161659,0,5614999.photo.

Clary, Mike. "Efforts Intensify in Jordan Homicide Case: Investigation—FBI Partly Focusing on James Jordan's Business Interests in South Carolina." *Los Angeles Times*. August 15, 1993.

CNNSI.com. "Jordan's Journey—Timeline." Jordan's Journey website. August 22, 2001. http://sportsillustrated.cnn.com/basketball/nba/features/jordan/news/ 2001/08/22/jordan_timeline/.

Coates, Ta-Nehisi. "Michael Jordan's Greatest Shot." TheAtlantic.com. June 7, 2011. http://www.theatlantic.com/entertainment/archive/2011/06/michael -jordans-greatest-shot/240034/.

Crowley, Michael. "Muhammad Ali Was a Rebel. Michael Jordan Is a Brand Name." *Nieman Reports* 52, no. 3 (Fall 1999): 41–43.

Deeks, Mark. "All-Star Memories: Michael Jordan's Last Hurrah." *The Basketball Jones* (blog), TheScore.com. February 26, 2012. http://blogs.thescore.com/ tbj/2012/02/26/all-star-memories-michael-jordans-last-hurrah/.

Delios, Hugh, and George de Lama. "Golf Partners Confirm Sketches of Jordan's Gambling Mania." *Chicago Tribune*. June 6, 1993.

Didinger, Ray. "Jordan Recalled with Pride by Local Folks." Knight Ridder / *Tribune* News Service. May 12, 1991.

ESPN The Magazine. "Sonny Vaccaro Is the Godfather of Basketball's Summer Culture." N.d.

Featherston, Al. "Jordan's Arrival." *Inside Carolina Magazine*. January 2011.

Fennell, Bettie. "Basketball Flows in Her Blood." *Wilmington Morning Star.* November 28, 1993.

Fluck, Adam. "Scottie Pippen and the 1991–92 Chicago Bulls." Bulls.com. June 23, 2012. http://www.nba.com/bulls/history/scottie-pippen-and-1991-92 -chicago-bulls.html.

———. "Tex Winter and the Pursuit of Perfection." Bulls.com. August 12, 2011. http://www.nba.com/bulls/history/winter_pippenpaxson_110812.html.

Freeman, Eric. "Michael Jordan Will Present Nike's Phil Knight at the Basketball Hall of Fame." *Ball Don't Lie* (blog), *Yahoo! Sports.* August 29, 2012. http:// sports.yahoo.com/blogs/nba-ball-dont-lie/michael-jordan-present-nike-phil -knight-basketball-hall-153529349--nba.html.

Ginnetti, Tony. "Trailblazing *Sun-Times* Sportswriter Lacy J. Banks Dies." *Chicago Sun-Times.* March 21, 2012.

Granderson, LZ. "The Political Michael Jordan." ESPN.com, August 14, 2012. http://espn.go.com/nba/story/_/id/8264956/michael-jordan-obama-fund raiser-22-years-harvey-gantt.

Grant, Cathy. "Confusion Keeps Things Jumping for Non-aerial Jordans." *Wilmington Morning Star.* November 18, 1985.

———. "Jordan Returns Hometown's Love." *Wilmington Morning Star.* June 20, 1987.

Gross, Jane. "Jordan Makes People Wonder: Is He the New Dr. J?" *New York Times.* October 21, 1984.

Halberstam, David. "A Hero for the Wired World." *Sports Illustrated.* December 23, 1991.

Hamm, Matt. "Happy Birthday Michael Jordan." *Keeping It Heel* (blog). February 17, 2012. http://keepingitheel.com/2012/02/17/happy-birthday-michael-jordan/.

Hendrickson, Brian. "Wagging His Way to Greatness." *Wilmington Morning Star.* January 14, 1999.

———. "Way Back When Scrawny Kid Loved to Play." *Wilmington Morning Star.* January 24, 1999.

Hersch, Hank. "Passing the Test." *Sports Illustrated.* May 25, 1992.

———. "Sitting Bulls They Weren't." *Sports Illustrated.* May 22, 1989.

Hirschberg, Lynn. "The Big Man Can Deal." *New York Times.* November 17, 1996.

Hoffer, Richard. "Sitting Bull." *Sports Illustrated.* May 27, 1996.

Hooks, Jerry. "Jordan to Skip Last UNC Season." *Wilmington Star-News.* May 6, 1984.

———. "Jordan Unanimous All-ACC." *Wilmington Morning Star.* March 6, 1984.

The Hoop Doctors (blog). "Basketball History: A Letter from Duke's Coach K to Michael Jordan." November 17, 2011. http://thehoopdoctors.com/ online2/2011/11/basketball-history-a-letter-from-dukes-coach-k-to-michael -jordan-pic/.

Howard, Johnette. "Father's Day." *Sports Illustrated.* December 30, 1996.

Howell, Margaret S. "Family Priorities: Kids & Sports." *Cape Fear Tidewater,* 1984.

Johnson, K. C. "An Extraordinary Father-Son Relationship, Tinged by Tragedy." *Chicago Tribune.* September 10, 2009.

———. "Krause Reflects on a Life of Scouting." *Chicago Tribune.* July 7, 2012.

Joyner, James. "Michael Jordan's Big Brother." *Outside the Beltway* (blog). May 15, 2006. http://www.outsidethebeltway.com/csm_james_jordan_usa_retired/.

Kerby, Trey. "More Stories of Michael Jordan Being Michael Jordan." *The Basketball Jones* (blog), TheScore.com. September 29, 2011. http://blogs.thescore.com/tbj/2011/09/29/more-stories-of-michael-jordan-being-michael-jordan/.

Kirkpatrick, Curry. "Hooray for the Red, White, Black and Blue!" *Sports Illustrated*. July 23, 1984.

———. "In an Orbit All His Own." *Sports Illustrated*. November 9, 1987.

———. "It Was Trial by Fire." *Sports Illustrated*. April 30, 1984.

———. "The Old Soft Shoe." *Sports Illustrated*. November 25, 1992.

———. "A Towering Twosome." *Sports Illustrated*. November 18, 1983.

Kornheiser, Tony. "They've Got the Hang of It." *Sports Illustrated*. October 29, 1984.

Kurkjian, Tim. "Reading the Signs." *Sports Illustrated*. February 28, 1994.

Laird, Sam. "The Bay Citizen; Shoe Marketer Who Enriched N.C.A.A. Takes on His Creation." *New York Times*. March 13, 2011.

Lake, Thomas. "Did This Man Really Cut Michael Jordan?" *Sports Illustrated*. January 16, 2012.

———. "A Letter to Michael Jordan: Shame on You for Refusing to Help Pop." SI.com. August 14, 2012. http://sportsillustrated.cnn.com/2012/writers/thomas_lake/08/13/letter-to-michael-jordan/.

Layden, Tim. "March 14, 1981: When the NCAA Tournament Became Madness." *Sports Illustrated*. March 14, 2012.

Lewis, Michael. "Jordan Legacy Stays Strong in Chapel Hill." *Wilmington Star-News*. January 1999.

———. "Words from the Web about MJ." *Wilmington Morning Star*. January 13, 1999.

Littwin, Mike. "Jordan Hasn't Been Spoiled by Fame." *Los Angeles Times*. March 1984.

Los Angeles Times. "NBA Roundup: Jordan Fights Pistons with Points; Bulls Win." January 17, 1988.

Mandell, Nina. "Michael Jordan, NBA Legend, Engaged to Yvette Prieto." *New York Daily News*. December 29, 2011.

McCallum, Jack. "Air Jordan, Air Bulls." *Sports Illustrated*. May 16, 1988.

———. "The Bad Boys Get Better." *Sports Illustrated*. June 5, 1989.

———. "Bang-up Battle in the East." *Sports Illustrated*. June 4, 1990.

———. "The Creature Was Too Much for the Giant." *Sports Illustrated*. January 18, 1982.

———. "The Everywhere Man Alone on the Mountaintop." *Sports Illustrated*. December 23, 1991.

———. "Eye of the Storm." *Sports Illustrated*. June 15, 1993.

———. "For Whom the Bulls Toil." *Sports Illustrated*. December 11, 1991.

———. "Friends and Foes Together." *Sports Illustrated*. May 31, 1993.

———. "Helping Hands." *Sports Illustrated*. December 17, 1990.

———. "His Highness." *Sports Illustrated*. June 17, 1991.

———. "The Lips Were Zipped." *Sports Illustrated*. June 7, 1993.

———. "Lords of the Rings." *Sports Illustrated*. September 18, 1991.

———. "Mission Impossible." *Sports Illustrated*. November 6, 1989.

————. "On the Edge." *Sports Illustrated*. June 15, 1992.

————. "The Power and the Glory." *Sports Illustrated*. November 9, 1992.

————. "Psycho Series." *Sports Illustrated*. June 1, 1992.

————. "The Quiz Kid." *Sports Illustrated*. November 6, 1989.

————. "Reaching for Greatness." *Sports Illustrated*. June 22, 1992.

————. "Show of Shows." *Sports Illustrated*. June 10, 1991.

————. "Un-fath-om-able." *Sports Illustrated*. May 15, 1989.

————. "A World of Their Own." *Sports Illustrated*. September 30, 1991.

McGee, Ryan. "So Unlike Mike." ESPN.com. September 4, 2012. http://espn.go.com/nba/story/_/id/8336863/michael-jordan-ultimate-nba-failure-owner-charlotte-bobcats-espn-magazine.

McGrath, Dan. "Blemish on Jordan's Career: Gambling Jordan Gambled with His Image." *Chicago Tribune*. September 10, 2009.

McGraw, Mike. "Miller Thinks Jordan Helped Solve '99 Lockout." *All Bull* (blog), DailyHerald.com. October 12, 2011. http://blogs.dailyherald.com/node/6392.

McIver, Wanda. "Port City People: Profiling Michael Jordan." *Wilmington Journal*. November 27, 1980.

Morrissey, Rick. "Chapter 8: Birmingham." Chicagotribune.com. September 10, 2009. http://www.chicagotribune.com/sports/basketball/bulls/michaeljordan/chi-michael-jordan-chicago-bulls-chapter-8,0,4130420,full.story.

Mr. Tarheel (blog). "UNC Basketball Article—1982 Championship." N.d. Accessed November 7, 2013. http://www.mrtarheel.com/bballart1.html.

Neff, Craig. "Leaping Lizards, It's Almost Iguana." *Sports Illustrated*. November 17, 1986.

Nelson, John. "Stars Find Instant Riches Also Bring Problems." *Wilmington Morning Star*. February 22, 1987.

Newman, Bruce. "Time Waits for No One." *Sports Illustrated*. November 8, 1993.

Ozanian, Mike. "Michael Jordan Seeking Equity for Charlotte Bobcats?" *Forbes*. April 27, 2011.

Podmolik, Mary Ellen. "Michael Jordan Lists Suburban Mansion for $29 Million." *Chicago Tribune*. February 29, 2012.

Powell, R. J. "Bucs End Skid, Top Warriors." *Wilmington Star-News*. January 12, 1980.

————. "Bucs' Rally Sinks Bearcats." *Wilmington Morning Star*. December 28, 1979.

————. "Laney Ousts Vikings; Jordan Paces Victory." *Wilmington Morning Star*. February 19, 1980.

————. "Laney's Pair Trims Vikes, Evans, 76–64." *Wilmington Star-News*. January 26, 1980.

————. "Southern Wayne Turns Back Bucs." *Wilmington Star-News*. January 24, 1980.

Prada, Mike. "Michael Jordan Week: Remembering the Best Moments of His Wizards' Tenure." *Bullets Forever* (blog). August 28, 2012. http://www.bulletsforever.com/2012/8/28/3267404/michael-jordan-week-washington-wizards-moments.

————. "Michael Jordan Week: Remembering the Worst Moments of His Washington Tenure." *Bullets Forever* (blog). September 1, 2012. http://www.bulletsforever.com/2012/9/1/3284906/michael-jordan-week-washington-wizards-memories-worst.

————. "Michael Jordan Week: Why His Tenure in Washington Was Complicated." *Bullets Forever* (blog). August 27, 2012. http://www.bulletsforever .com/2012/8/27/3266075/michael-jordan-week-washington-wizards.

Pruitt, Thomas. "Michael Jordan Week: A Statistical Retrospective." *Bullets Forever* (blog). August 29, 2012. http://www.bulletsforever.com/2012/8/29/3274878/ michael-jordan-week-a-statistical-retrospective.

Reid, Cherner. "Larry Brown: Michael Jordan Needs People to Challenge Him." *USA Today.* April 21, 2012.

Rivenbark, Celia. "Jordan Casts Lasting Shadow over Boyhood Home." *Wilmington Morning Star.* February 28, 1995.

Roberts, Lee. "Early Cut Only Inspired Jordan." *Wilmington Morning Star.* February 24, 1991.

Rushin, Steve. "A Lot of Hot Air?" *Sports Illustrated.* January 17, 1994.

Sacks, Glenn. "Jordan Vs. Jordan: In Defense of Michael Jordan." Glennsacks.com. N.d. Accessed November 7, 2013. http://www.glennsacks.com/jordan_vs _jordan.htm.

Sanders, Deborah M. "Jordan to Be Honored." *Wilmington Journal.* August 23, 1984.

Scheitrum, Kevin. "Stripes Before Stars: The Story of the 1983 U.S. Pan-American Games Team." NBA.com. Accessed November 7, 2013. http://www.nba.com/ dleague/news/stripes_before_stars_1983_panam_2011_10_25.html.

Seal, Mark. "The Temptation of Tiger Woods," parts I and II. *Vanity Fair,* May 2010, June 2010.

Shanken, Marvin R. "One-on-One with Michael Jordan." *Cigar Aficionado,* July/ August 2005.

Smith, Sam. "Michael Jordan and Joe Dumars Are Close, It Turns Out…" *Chicago Tribune.* May 23, 1990.

————. "Michael Jordan Hall of Fame—Introduction." Bulls.com. August 21, 2009. http://www.nba.com/bulls/news/jordanhof_intro_090821.html.

————. "Michael Jordan's 63 Points in 1986 NBA Playoffs May Have Been Greatest Game Ever Played." Bulls.com. April 20, 2011. http://www.nba.com/ bulls/history/michael-jordans-63-points-1986-nba-playoffs-may-have-been -greatest-game-ever-played.html.

The Star Online. "Grant Rates Playing with MJ and Pippen as Career High." July 16, 2012. http://www.thestar.com.my/Story.aspx?file=%2F2012%2F7%2F16 %2Fsports%2F11669573.

Stoda, Greg. "Dismal Fourth Quarter Cost 'Cats Shot at Tourney Title." *Wilmington-Star News.* December 29, 1979.

————. "Jordan, Heels Aim at Indiana." *Wilmington Star-News.* March 21, 1984.

————. "Laney Subdues Vikings, 75–65." *Wilmington Star-News.* December 15, 1979.

Strasser, J. B., and Laurie Becklund. "Flying High with Air Jordan—Nike: Company's Products Line Takes Off, but Reebok Becomes No. 1. Sonny Vaccaro Is Told that He Is Quitting." *Los Angeles Times.* February 18, 1992.

Sudo, Chuck. "The *Chicagoist* Flashback: Michael Jordan's Final Shot as a Bull." *Chicagoist* (blog). June 14, 2012. http://chicagoist.com/2012/06/14/the_chi cagoist_flashback_michael_jo.php.

Sunday Star-News. "Michael Jordan: Wilmington Junior Wants Second National Title." February 19, 1984.

Swift, E. M. "Farewell, My Lovely." *Sports Illustrated.* February 19, 1990.

———. "The $40 Million Man." *Sports Illustrated.* June 10, 1996.

———. "Reach Out and Touch Someone." *Sports Illustrated.* August 5, 1991.

———. "Sink, Blast You!" *Sports Illustrated.* August 14, 1989.

Taylor, Phil. "Gored by the Bulls." *Sports Illustrated.* June 3, 1996.

———. "A Happy Turn to a Horror Story." *Sports Illustrated.* June 21, 1993.

———. "Is Jordan Enough?" *Sports Illustrated.* May 8, 1995.

———. "The NBA's Long, Cold Summer." *Sports Illustrated.* October 18, 1993.

———. "Resurrection." *Sports Illustrated.* March 27, 1995.

———. "Slammed!" *Sports Illustrated.* June 17, 1996.

———. "Three for Three." *Sports Illustrated.* June 28, 1993.

———. "Toy Story." *Sports Illustrated.* January 29, 1996.

———. "Wanna Be Like Mike…" *Sports Illustrated.* September 4, 1995.

———. "What Goes Up…" *Sports Illustrated.* March 20, 1995.

Telander, Rick. "Ready…Set…Levitate!" *Sports Illustrated.* November 17, 1986.

———. "The Sleuth." *Sports Illustrated.* March 15, 1993.

———. "The Wrong People for the Job." *Sports Illustrated.* December 23, 1991.

Thomas, Al. "Michael Jordan: Hero of the Hardwood." *Cape Fear Tidewater,* 1984.

———. "Worthy's Advice Aids Freshman Jordan." *Wilmington Star-News.* January 12, 1984.

Verducci, Tom. "Keeping His Guard Up." *Sports Illustrated.* December 12, 1994.

Weir, Tom. "Michael Jordan Fires Back at Larry Brown's Criticisms." *USA Today.* April 25, 2012.

Wetzel, Dan. "For Nike, Jordan Delivered the Goods and More." *Yahoo! Sports.* September 8, 2009. http://sports.yahoo.com/news/nike-jordan-delivered -goods-more-060300645--nba.html.

Whisnant, Scott. "Jordan Was Focusing on Family, Says Local Friend." *Wilmington Morning Star.* August 14, 1993.

Whisnant, Scott, and Celia Rivenbark. "Michael Jordan Eulogizes His Father." *Wilmington Morning Star.* August 16, 1993.

Whitacre, Jake. "Michael Jordan Week: Examining His Personnel Decisions with the Washington Wizards." *Bullets Forever* (blog). August 30, 2012. http:// www.bulletsforever.com/2012/8/30/3260528/michael-jordan-executive -washington-wizards-examining.

Whitaker, Lang. "The Dream Will Never Die: An Oral History of the Dream Team." *GQ,* July 2012.

White, Gina. "Michael Jordan's Parents Possess the Same Modesty as Does Their Famous Son." *Wilmington Journal.* N.d.

Wilbon, Michael. "Remembering a Pioneer, Role Model." ESPNChicago.com. http:// espn.go.com/chicago/nba/story/_/id/7723614/michael-wilbon-remembers -impact-lacy-j-banks-had-career.

Wilmington Journal. "Interview with James and Delores Jordan." April 15, 1982.

———. "Jordan's Shot Most Memorable in 1982." December 29, 1982.

———. "Michael Jordan: The Man." November 18, 1983.

Wilmington Morning Star. "As Jordan Goes Forward, Former Coaches Look Back." January 24, 1994.

————. "Bucs Take Cage Debut." December 1, 1979.

————. "Bulls in Business, Without Jordan." January 12, 1999.

————. "Co-defendant Tells about Robberies." January 25, 1996.

————. "Coroner Defends Actions." August 23, 1993.

————. "DA: Green Killed for Greed." February 28, 1996.

————. "Defense Attacks Victim's Character as Trial Opens." January 4, 1996.

————. "High-Flying Michael Jordan Has North Carolina Cruising Toward Another ACC Title." February 19, 1984.

————. "In James Jordan's Search for a Place to Rest, He Lost His Life." August 16, 1993.

————. "James Jordan Mourned by Friends in Wilmington." August 14, 1993.

————. "Jordan Chides Media for Linking Gambling, Death." August 20, 1993.

————. "Jordan Hits 42 in Laney Victory." February 15, 1980.

————. "Jordan Is ACC Player of Year." March 14, 1984.

————. "Jordan Named All-American." March 20, 1983.

————. "Jordan Paces Bucs past Kinston." December 19, 1979.

————. "Jordan, Perkins Spark Tar Heels." January 5, 1982.

————. "Jordan Recalls Days at Laney." December 6, 1985.

————. "Jordan Recalls Early Roots." July 9, 1985.

————. "Jordan's $43.9 Million Tops Athletes' Incomes." December 4, 1995.

————. "Journal Interviews Michael Jordan." March 29, 1984.

————. "Laney: Bucs Face Rebuilding Task." December 2, 1979.

————. "Laney Falls to Goldsboro." May 16, 1980.

————. "Memories of Michael." December 26, 1983.

————. "Witness Describes Jordan's Last Moments." January 26, 1996.

Wilmington Star-News. "Bucs Fall to Cards." April 5, 1980.

————. "Bucs Rip Bears for Fifth Win in Six Games." December 22, 1979.

————. "Bucs Rout Cards." May 14, 1980.

————. "Bucs Trim Saints, 9–2." March 16, 1980.

————. "County Girls', Boys' Basketball." March 13, 1980.

————. "Goldsboro Rips Laney." January 3, 1980.

————. "Jordan, Bucs Nip Kinston for Fourth." April 30, 1980.

————. "Jordan, Smith Win." April 27, 1980.

————. "Jordan Wants Four Titles." March 16, 1983.

————. "Laney Defeats Kinston." April 29, 1980.

————. "Laney Erupts over Cougs, 8–2." May 7, 1980.

————. "Laney Succumbs, 67–54." February 2, 1980.

————. "New Bern Edges Bucs, 4–3." May 3, 1980.

————. "Remembering Mike." N.d.

————. "Saints March over Laney." April 2, 1980.

————. "Saints Nip Laney Bucs, 40–35 in OT." February 21, 1980.

————. "Saints Trounce Laney." December 12, 1979.

Wise, Mike. "Amid Much Speculation, Insiders Say Decision Set." *Wilmington Morning Star.* N.d.

Wolff, Alexander. "Getting Right to the Point." *Sports Illustrated.* January 23, 1984.

————. "In the Driver's Seat." *Sports Illustrated.* December 10, 1984.

————. "1 North Carolina." *Sports Illustrated.* November 28, 1983.

Wulf, Steve. "Err Jordan." *Sports Illustrated.* March 14, 1984.

Multimedia

"Jordan Love Letter Sparks Anger." ABCNews.com video. Posted July 5, 2011. http://abcnews.go.com/US/video/michael-jordan-love-letter-sparks-anger-13998684.

"Jordan's First College Game—N. Carolina vs. Kansas. 1981." YouTube video, 9:20, from original television broadcast, November 28, 1981. Posted July 14, 2007. http://www.youtube.com/watch?v=0If76KJR0Xs.

"Kobe Bryant 42 Points at Half vs Jordan (55 Total) 2002-03." YouTube video, 10:00, from original Fox Sports Net broadcast, March 28, 2003. Posted January 19, 2008. http://www.youtube.com/watch?v=u-2Hd-Ly2CQ.

"Michael Jordan: 1983 Pan American Games (USA-Brazil)." YouTube video, 6:35, from original television broadcast, August 29, 1983. Posted May 25, 2009. http://www.youtube.com/watch?v=zFZakGAvf1c.

"Michael Jordan 1988: 59pts Vs. Detroit Pistons on CBS." YouTube video, 6:22, from original television broadcast, April 3, 1988. Posted August 7, 2006. http://www.youtube.com/watch?v=_7S76yjxSWE.

"Michael Jordan 39 Pts vs. Georgia Tech—College Career High—1983." YouTube video, 9:17, from original television broadcast, January 29, 1983. Posted March 14, 2011. http://www.youtube.com/watch?v=X5HwFGO0U8I.

"Michael Jordan: 61 Pts vs Detroit Pistons (1987.03.04)." YouTube video, 9:22, from original television broadcast, March 4, 1987. Posted December 31, 2008. http://www.youtube.com/watch?v=MEfnu6Kla5Y.

"Michael Jordan Interview 1986 (Back from Injury)." YouTube video, 2:59, from original television broadcast, April 20, 1986. Posted January 29, 2009. http://www.youtube.com/watch?v=KhgDmNZvqgk.

"Michael Jordan (Interview after Madison Square Garden Debut) November 11, 1984." YouTube video, 4:33, from original television broadcast, November 11, 1984. Posted October 7, 2010. http://www.youtube.com/watch?v=Vlvi00DBoko.

"Michael Jordan Interview with Rosie." YouTube video, from original *Rosie O'Donnell Show* broadcast, n.d. Posted August 13, 2009. http://www.youtube.com/watch?v=oXi_7wPd8LQ.

"Michael Jordan (Maryland vs North Carolina) February 19, 1984." YouTube video, 3:50, from original television broadcast, February 19, 1984. Posted October 4, 2010. http://www.youtube.com/watch?v=MtW678Tk2dY.

"Michael Jordan Rock the Cradle vs Maryland and Len Bias (1984)." YouTube video, 0:48, from original television broadcast, January 12, 1984. Posted November 11, 2010. http://www.youtube.com/watch?v=udvQko1EQWs.

"Michael Jordan Top Rookie Plays Part 3." YouTube video, 4:09, compilation of television broadcast clips, n.d. Posted September 19, 2010. http://www.youtube.com/watch?v=KN1FoxDM9CQ.

"Michael Jordan (USA vs NBA Stars) 1984." YouTube video, 11:39, from original television broadcast, July 9, 1984. Posted September 9, 2012. http://www.youtube.com/watch?v=a4qy1klDae4.

"NBA Slam Dunk Contest—Michael Jordan Vs Dominique Wilkins." YouTube video, 4:40, from original television broadcast, February 6, 1988. Posted February 20, 2007. http://www.youtube.com/watch?v=wqPRdzrjWpU.

"North Carolina at Maryland, 1984 (Jordan—Len Bias)." YouTube video, 10:55, from original television broadcast, January 12, 1984. Posted July 12, 2007. http://www.youtube.com/watch?v=y4u4MdSGSD0.

"Phil Jackson Comparing Two of the Greatest Shooting Guards of All Time!" YouTube video, 1:26, from original television broadcast, n.d. Posted August 12, 2012. http://www.youtube.com/watch?v=yhpmciL7480.

"Rare Interview with Michael Jordan's Dad." YouTube video, 1:11, from original television broadcast, n.d. Posted August 11, 2008. http://www.youtube.com/watch?v=itzEYiV36vA.

"Set Goals, Dream Big; By Deloris Jordan." YouTube video, 0:45, from filmed speech by Deloris Jordan, n.d. Posted February 13, 2012. http://www.youtube.com/watch?v=QEDratfvJHs.

"UNC Freshman Michael Jordan vs Kentucky." YouTube video, 3:05, from original television broadcast, December 11, 1981. Posted March 11, 2009. http://www.youtube.com/watch?v=NIq7ma7c6UE.

Vaccaro, Sonny, interview by Lowell Bergman. "Interview: Sonny Vaccaro." *Frontline.* November 18, 2011. Transcript available at http://www.pbs.org/wgbh/pages/frontline/money-and-march-madness/interviews/sonny-vaccaro.html.

INDEX

ABOUT THE AUTHOR

ROLAND LAZENBY is the author of the critically acclaimed bestseller *Jerry West: The Life and Legend of a Basketball Icon,* among numerous other books. He has spent the past three decades interviewing NBA players, coaches, staff members, and other figures while writing about the league. He can be found on Twitter @lazenby. He lives in Virginia.